SUPPLY CHAIN MANAGEMENT

SUPPLY CHAIN MANAGEMENT

John T. Mentzer
editor

SAGE Publications
International Educational and Professional Publisher
Thousand Oaks ■ London ■ New Delhi

For information:

Sage Publications, Inc.
2455 Teller Road
Thousand Oaks, California 91320
E-mail: order@sagepub.com

Sage Publications Ltd.
6 Bonhill Street
London EC2A 4PU
United Kingdom

Sage Publications India Pvt. Ltd.
M-32 Market
Greater Kailash I
New Delhi 110 048 India

Printed in the United States of America

Library of Congress Cataloging-in-Publication Data

Mentzer, John T.
　　Supply chain management / by John T. Mentzer.
　　　　p.　cm.
　　Includes bibliographical references and index.
　　ISBN 0-7619-2111-7 (cloth: alk. paper)
　　1. Business logistics.　2. Industrial procurement—Management.
　3. Materials management.　4. Physical distribution of goods.　I. Title.
　　HD39.5.M445　2000
　　658.7—dc21　　　　　　　　　　　　　　00-010197

02　03　04　05　06　07　7　6　5　4　3　2

Acquiring Editor:	Marquita Flemming
Editorial Assistant:	MaryAnn Vail
Production Editor:	Diane S. Foster
Editorial Assistant:	Victoria Cheng
Typesetter/Designer:	Barbara Burkholder
Indexer:	Molly Hall
Cover Designer:	Michelle Lee

Contents

Acknowledgments

This book is the work of many people besides the authors, and they all deserve recognition. First, the many scholars who went before us and thought and wrote about supply chain management provided invaluable insights to this book. In fact, the original idea for writing this book came from a recognition that so much was being written on the subject that it was time for an all-encompassing definition of "supply chain management." To these supply chain scholars, we are most grateful.

Special thanks go to Dr. John Kent of Southwest Missouri State University and the students in his Fall 1999 Supply Chain Management class (Tiffany Blackwell, Heather Erwin, Wendy Farthing, Sam Hollon, Jim Lambert, Alessandro Lequio, Karen Mende, Alex Norton, Calvan Teh, Apichat Traihattakan, Warawuth Werakul, Teri A. Whitmore, Poh Onn Yap, and Patricia Yap) for so thoroughly reviewing an early draft of this book. They caused considerable rethinking and rewriting to meet the needs of students in supply chain management.

The supply chain executives who agreed to be interviewed for this book provided insights necessary to write it, and we thank them for their input and considerable effort. We are indebted to Paul Burke (CVS Drugstores), Joe Casaroll (General Motors), Susan Dickerson (Federal Express), Norm Ellis (Qualcomm), Frank Hathaway (then with Avery-Dennison), Joe Jernigan (CVS Drugstores), Mike Kash (General Motors), Nick LaHowchic (The Limited), Tom McHugh (CVS Drugstores), Paul Mooney (Exel Logistics), Brian Newton (Exel Logistics), Ron North (Avery-Dennison), Larry Rhoton (Eastman Chemical Company), Sonny Rogers (Lockheed Martin), Joel Sutherland (J. B. Hunt Logistics), Barbara Thompson (Phillips Electronics), Rich Thompson (Ernst & Young), Bill Turner (Coca-Cola), and Teresa Wulff (Federal Express).

We received invaluable assistance from the academic reviewers (Dr. Carol
C. Bienstock, University of Memphis; Dr. John Kent, Southwest Missouri State
University; and Dr. Lisa Williams, University of Arkansas) and practitioner
reviewers (Barry Dale, president of ShipChem.com; Herb Johnson, executive
vice president of Premier, Inc.; Richard Ramage, vice president supply chain of
Nestlé USA; and Mike West, CEO of HomePoint.com) who read the near-final
draft of this book and "held our feet to the fire" on readability, content, and
accuracy.

We hope this book brings clarity and comprehensive insight to the phenomenon of supply chains and to their management. For students, we hope the book
aids in understanding the scope and specifics. For practitioners, we hope the
book provides insights into the nuances of managing supply chains. For
researchers, we hope this book generates additional questions, the answers to
which will continue to enrich our understanding and ability to manage supply
chains.

1

What Is Supply Chain Management?

JOHN T. MENTZER   SOONHONG MIN

WILLIAM DEWITT   NANCY W. NIX

JAMES S. KEEBLER   CARLO D. SMITH

ZACH G. ZACHARIA

Executive Summary

In this chapter, we provide an overview of the concepts that are relevant to supply chain management, introduce a model of supply chain management, and provide an overview of the organization of this book. In short, we provide an initial answer to the question, What is supply chain management (SCM)? Specifically, in this chapter, we

- Review, categorize, and synthesize various definitions of SCM and "supply chain"
- Examine the insight of supply chain managers from 20 different companies whom we interviewed in an effort to understand the alternative uses of the term "supply chain management"
- Identify the antecedents and consequences of SCM and propose the boundaries of SCM in terms of business functions and organizations
- Present a conceptual model and definition of SCM
- Provide a unifying definition and framework to establish a consistent means to conceptualize SCM

- Use the definition and framework to guide the remaining chapters of this book, each of which offers insights regarding the status of research and practice in a particular aspect of SCM and suggests a direction for future investigation
- Present a series of managerial and research implications

Throughout, we provide the insights of the supply chain managers we interviewed. Finally, we discuss the conclusions from this chapter and the layout of the book. From these discussions, we conclude the following:

- A **supply chain** is defined as *a set of three or more companies directly linked by one or more of the upstream and downstream flows of products, services, finances, and information from a source to a customer.*
- A **basic supply chain** consists of *a company, an immediate supplier, and an immediate customer directly linked by one or more of the upstream and downstream flows of products, services, finances, and information.*
- An **extended supply chain** includes *suppliers of the immediate supplier and customers of the immediate customer, all linked by one or more of the upstream and downstream flows of products, services, finances, and information.*
- An **ultimate supply chain** includes *all the companies involved in all the upstream and downstream flows of products, services, finances, and information from the initial supplier to the ultimate customer.*
- A **supply chain orientation** is *the recognition by a company of the systemic, strategic implications of the activities and processes involved in managing the various flows in a supply chain.*
- **Supply chain management** is the *implementation of a supply chain orientation across suppliers and customers.*
- **Supply chain management** is *the systemic, strategic coordination of the traditional business functions within a particular company and across businesses within the supply chain, for the purposes of improving the long-term performance of the individual companies and the supply chain as a whole.*

Without such a clear understanding of SCM and its related concepts, we cannot expect wide application of SCM in practice or research.

Introduction

Management is on the verge of a major breakthrough in understanding how industrial company success depends on the interactions between the flows of information, materials, money, manpower, and capital equipment. The way these five flow systems interlock to amplify one another and to cause change and fluctuation will form the basis for anticipating the effects of decisions, policies, organizational forms, and investment choices. (Forrester, 1958, p. 37)

More than 40 years ago, Forrester (1958) introduced a theory of management that recognized the integrated nature of organizational relationships in distribution channels. Because organizations are so intertwined, he argued that system dynamics can influence the performance of functions such as research, engineering, sales, and promotion. He illustrated this using a computer simulation of order information flow and its influence on production and distribution performance for each channel member, as well as the entire channel system. More recent replications of this phenomenon include the "Beer Game" simulation and research covering the "Bullwhip Effect" (Lee, Padmanabhan, & Whang, 1997b).

Discussing the shape of the future, Forrester (1958) proposed that after a period of research and development involving basic analytic techniques "there will come general recognition of the advantage enjoyed by the pioneering management who have been the first to improve their understanding of the interrelationships between separate company functions and between the company and its markets, its industry, and the national economy" (p. 52). Forrester identified key management issues and illustrated the dynamics of factors associated with what we call today supply chain management (SCM).

The term supply chain management has risen to prominence over the past 10 years (Cooper, Ellram, Gardner, & Hanks, 1997). La Londe (1997) identified positions at 43 different companies that carry "supply chain" in their titles. SCM has become such a "hot topic" that it is difficult to pick up a periodical on manufacturing, distribution, marketing, customer management, or transportation without seeing an article about SCM or SCM-related topics (Ross, 1998).

The reasons for the popularity of the concept are manifold; however, several specific drivers can be traced to trends in global sourcing, an emphasis on time- and quality-based competition, and their respective contributions to greater environmental uncertainty.

- Corporations have turned increasingly to global sources for their supplies. This globalization of supply management has forced companies to look for more effective ways to coordinate the flow of materials into and out of the company.
- Companies and distribution channels compete more today on the basis of time and quality. Having a defect-free product to the customer faster and more reliably than the competition is no longer seen as a competitive advantage but simply a requirement to be in the market. Customers demand products consistently deliv-

ered faster, exactly on time, and with no damage. Each of these necessitates closer coordination with suppliers and distributors.

- This global orientation and increased performance-based competition combined with rapidly changing technology and economic conditions all contribute to marketplace uncertainty. This uncertainty requires greater flexibility on the part of individual companies and distribution channels, which in turn demands more flexibility in channel relationships.

All these factors have made the concept of SCM more important to companies and, as a result, more often written about in the business press.

Despite the popularity of the term supply chain management, there remains considerable confusion as to its meaning. Some authors define SCM in operational terms involving the flow of materials and products (Tyndall, Gopal, Partsch, & Kamauff, 1998), others view it as a management philosophy (Ellram & Cooper, 1990), and still others view it in terms of a management process (La Londe, 1997).

With so many different views of the concept, it seems reasonable that managers and researchers have become suspicious of whether SCM actually exists and, if so, whether the term is, or should be, used differently in different situations. In fact, some have questioned the existence and benefits of the phenomenon. For example, Bechtel and Jayaram (1997) ask, "Is the concept of SCM important in today's business environment or is it simply a fad destined to die with other short-lived buzzwords?"

Such skepticism suggests a need to examine the phenomena of SCM more closely in order to clearly define the term and concept, to identify those factors that contribute to effective SCM, and to suggest how the adoption of an SCM approach can affect business strategy and corporate performance. The goal of this book is to address each of these areas as a means to help managers and researchers more effectively investigate, understand, communicate, and accomplish SCM.

Our purpose in this chapter is to examine the existing management research and the insight of supply chain managers from 20 different companies whom we interviewed in an effort to understand the alternative uses of the term "supply chain management." A unifying definition and framework are offered to establish a consistent means to conceptualize SCM. The definition and framework are used to guide the remaining chapters of this book, each of which offers insights regarding the status of research and practice in a particular aspect of SCM and suggests a direction for future investigation.

In this chapter, we review, categorize, and synthesize various definitions of SCM and "supply chain." We identify the antecedents and consequences of SCM, and we propose the boundaries of SCM in terms of business functions and organizations. We then present a conceptual model and definition of SCM. The model is accompanied by a series of managerial and research implications.

Throughout, we provide the insights of the supply chain managers we interviewed. Finally, we discuss the conclusions from this chapter and the layout of this book.

What Is Supply Chain Management?

Ross (1998) noted that discussions of SCM are often shrouded in complex jargon that has clouded management's understanding of the concept, limiting its effectiveness for practical application. This section is, thus, dedicated to reviewing, classifying, and synthesizing some of the widely used definitions of "supply chain" and "supply chain management" in both academia and practice. The goal of this discussion is the development of one, comprehensive definition upon which managers and future researchers can build.

Defining the Supply Chain

The definition of "supply chain" seems to be common across authors (Cooper & Ellram, 1993; La Londe & Masters, 1994; Lambert, Stock, & Ellram, 1998). La Londe and Masters (1994) proposed that a supply chain is a set of firms that pass materials forward. Normally, several independent firms are involved in manufacturing a product and placing it in the hands of the end user in a supply chain—raw material and component producers, product assemblers, wholesalers, and retailer merchants are all members of a supply chain (La Londe & Masters, 1994). By the same token, Lambert, Stock, and Ellram (1998) define a supply chain as the alignment of firms that brings products or services to market.

Christopher (1992a) defines a supply chain as the network of organizations that are involved, through upstream and downstream linkages, in the different processes and activities that produce value in the form of products and services in the hands of the ultimate consumer. In other words, a supply chain consists of multiple firms, both upstream (i.e., supply) and downstream (i.e., distribution).

Given these definitions, for the purposes of this book, a **supply chain** is defined as *a set of three or more companies directly linked by one or more of the upstream and downstream flows of products, services, finances, and information from a source to a customer.*

As one third-party logistics company executive we interviewed put it,

> A lot of people are talking about supply chains today, but there are so many definitions that often people within the firm are on different pages with what they are talking about, and our customers are totally confused. When people are working with different definitions of a supply chain, it can make

it very difficult for firms to work together toward the concept of supply
chain management.

Therefore, we have distinguished between various types of supply chains.To be
more precise, we will distinguish between a "basic supply chain," an "extended
supply chain," an "ultimate supply chain," and a "partnership." A **basic supply
chain** consists of *a company, an immediate supplier, and an immediate customer directly linked by one or more of the upstream and downstream flows of
products, services, finances, and information.* An **extended supply chain**
includes *suppliers of the immediate supplier and customers of the immediate
customer, all linked by one or more of the upstream and downstream flows of
products, services, finances, and information.* An **ultimate supply chain**
includes *all the companies involved in all the upstream and downstream flows
of products, services, finances, and information from the initial supplier to the
ultimate customer.*

Although the supply chain concept considers the multiple links that guide
the flow and transformation of raw materials to finished goods and the ultimate
consumer (Cooper & Ellram, 1993; Houlihan, 1988; Stevens, 1989), most articles only explore dyadic relationships in the channel (Cooper & Ellram, 1993),
generally for reasons of research parsimony. Although these studies offer
important insights into aspects of supply chain management, we maintain that
cooperative relationships between two companies are distinct from supply
chains, because this type of relationship does not involve any one company in
simultaneous upstream and downstream relationships. Such dyadic relationships are defined here as **partnerships** or **alliances**.

All these types of channel structures are represented graphically in Figure
1.1. Notice that the two-way arrows indicate that more than just products flow
through supply chains and partnerships—products, services, information, and
finances, at a minimum, flow through such linkages. Notice, also, that Figure
1.1d illustrates the complexity that ultimate supply chains can reach. In this
example, a third-party financial provider may be providing financing, assuming some of the risk, and offering financial advice; a third-party logistics (3PL)
provider is performing the logistics activities between two of the companies;
and a market research firm is providing information about the ultimate customer to a company well back up the supply chain. This very briefly illustrates
some of the many functions that complex supply chains can and do perform.

Although we address this point in greater depth later in this chapter, it is
important to realize that implicit within these definitions is the fact that supply
chains exist whether they are managed or not. If none of the organizations in
the examples in Figures 1.1b, 1.1c, or 1.1d actively implements any of the
concepts discussed in this book to manage the supply chain, the supply
chain—as a phenomenon of business—still exists. Thus, we draw a definite
demarcation between **supply chains** as phenomena that exist in business and

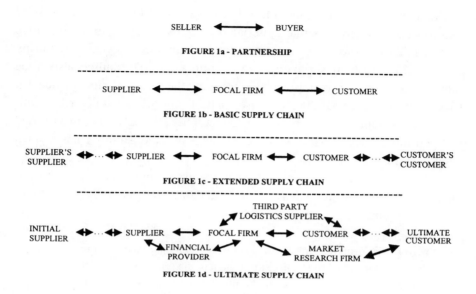

Figure 1.1. Types of Channel Relationships

the **management of those supply chains**. The former is simply something that exists in distribution channels, while the latter takes overt management efforts by the organizations within the supply chain. As one of our interviewed executives said,

> Supply chains are something that exist out there, whatever name you give it, it just exists, what you do with it is what's important.

Given the potential for countless alternative supply chain configurations, it is important to note that any one organization can be part of numerous supply chains. Wal-Mart, for example, can be part of the supply chain for candy, for clothing, for hardware, and for many other products. This multiple supply chain phenomenon begins to explain the network nature that many supply chains possess. For example, AT&T might find Motorola to be a customer in one supply chain, a partner in another, a supplier in a third, and a competitor in still a fourth supply chain. Note also that within our definition of supply chain, the final consumer is considered a member of the supply chain. This point is important because it recognizes that retailers such as Wal-Mart can be part of the upstream and downstream flows that constitute a supply chain.

Definitions of Supply Chain Management

Monczka, Trent, and Handfield (1998) argue that the structure of SCM requires traditionally separate materials functions to report to an executive responsible for coordinating the entire materials process, as well as requiring joint relationships with suppliers across multiple tiers. The authors also argue that a strategic, proactive approach to managing the supply chain is critical for survival beyond the year 2000 because the best supply chain will have a competitive advantage. By the same token, Christopher (1992a) argues that the real competition is not company against company, but rather supply chain against supply chain.

La Londe and Masters (1994, p. 38) compared a supply chain strategy to alliances and partnering strategies and suggested that they generally involve elements including

> two or more firms in a supply chain entering into a long-term agreement; . . . the development of trust and commitment to the relationship; . . . the integration of logistics activities involving the sharing of demand and sales data; . . . [and] the potential for a shift in the locus of control of the logistics process.

Stevens (1989, p. 3) stated that

> the objective of managing the supply chain is to synchronize the requirements of the customer with the flow of materials from suppliers in order to effect a balance between what are often seen as conflicting goals of high customer service, low inventory management, and low unit cost.

Monczka and colleagues (1998, p. 78) stated that SCM is a concept

> whose primary objective is to integrate and manage the sourcing, flow, and control of materials using a total systems perspective across multiple functions and multiple tiers of suppliers.

Houlihan (1988, p. 13) defined four differences between supply chain management and classical materials and manufacturing control, including

> (1) The supply chain is viewed as a single process. Responsibility for the various segments in the chain is not fragmented and relegated to functional areas such as manufacturing, purchasing, distribution, and sales. (2) Supply chain management calls for and in the end depends on strategic decision making. "Supply" is a shared objective of practically every function in the chain and is of particular strategic significance because of its impact on overall costs and market share. (3) Supply chain management

calls for a different perspective on inventories which are used as a balancing mechanism of last, not first, resort. (4) A new approach to systems is required—integration rather than interfacing.

Jones and Riley (1985, p. 19) state that

supply chain management deals with the total flow of materials from suppliers through end users.

Referring to Stevens (1989), Houlihan (1985, 1988), and Jones and Riley (1985), Ellram and Cooper (1990, p. 2) define supply chain management broadly as

an integrative philosophy to manage the total flow of a distribution channel from supplier to the ultimate user.

As illustrated above, the definitions of SCM differ across authors. They can, however, be classified into three categories: a management philosophy, implementation of a management philosophy, and a set of management processes. The alternative definitions and the categories they represent suggest that the term "supply chain management" presents a source of confusion for those involved in researching the phenomena as well as those attempting to establish a supply chain approach to management. Research and practice would be improved if a single definition were adopted.

SCM as a Management Philosophy

As a philosophy, SCM takes a systems approach to viewing the channel as a single entity, rather than as a set of fragmented parts, each performing its own function (Ellram & Cooper, 1990; Houlihan, 1985). In other words, the philosophy of supply chain management extends the concept of partnerships into a multifirm effort to manage the total flow of goods from the supplier to the ultimate customer (Ellram, 1990; Jones & Riley, 1985). Thus, SCM is a set of beliefs that each firm in the supply chain directly and indirectly affects the performance of all the other supply chain members, as well as ultimate, overall channel performance (e.g., Cooper, Ellram, et al., 1997).

SCM as a philosophy of channel management seeks synchronization and convergence of intrafirm and interfirm operational and strategic capabilities into a unified, compelling marketplace force (Ross, 1998). SCM as an integrative philosophy directs supply chain members to focus on developing innovative solutions to create unique, individualized sources of customer service value. Langley and Holcomb (1992) suggest that the objective of SCM should be the synchronization of all channel activities to create customer value. Thus,

SCM philosophy suggests the boundaries of SCM include not only logistics but also all other functions within a firm and within a supply chain to create customer value and satisfaction. In this context, understanding the customer's values and requirements is essential (Tyndall et al., 1998). In other words, SCM philosophy drives supply chain members to have a customer orientation. As one executive we interviewed put it,

> The purpose of supply chain management is to improve customer value and satisfaction—that is really why we are doing this.

Based upon the literature review, it is proposed that SCM as a management philosophy has the following characteristics:

1. A systems approach to viewing the channel as a whole, and to managing the total flow of goods inventory from the supplier to the ultimate customer,
2. A strategic orientation toward cooperative efforts to synchronize and converge intrafirm and interfirm operational and strategic capabilities into a unified whole, and
3. A customer focus to create unique and individualized sources of customer value, leading to customer satisfaction.

SCM as a Set of Activities to Implement a Management Philosophy

In adopting a supply chain management philosophy, firms must establish management practices that permit them to act or behave consistently with the philosophy. Previous research has suggested various activities necessary to implement an SCM philosophy successfully (see Table 1.1).

Bowersox and Closs (1996) argued that to be fully effective in today's competitive environment, firms must expand their **integrated behavior** to incorporate customers and suppliers. This extension of integrated behaviors, through external integration, is referred to by Bowersox and Closs as supply chain management. In this context, the philosophy of SCM turns into the implementation of supply chain management: a set of activities that carries out the philosophy. This set of activities is a coordinated effort called supply chain management between the supply chain partners, such as suppliers, carriers, and manufacturers, to respond dynamically to the needs of the end customer (Greene, 1991).

Several authors (e.g., Cooper & Ellram, 1993; Cooper, Ellram, et al., 1997; Cooper, Lambert, & Pagh, 1997; Ellram & Cooper, 1990; Novack, Langley, & Rinehart, 1995) have suggested key actions and behaviors that represent the implementation of an SCM philosophy. First of all, **mutually sharing information** among channel members is required, especially for planning and monitoring processes (e.g., Ellram & Cooper, 1990; Novack et al., 1995; Cooper, Ellram, et al., 1997; Cooper, Lambert, & Pagh 1997). Cooper, Lambert, and Pagh (1997) emphasized frequent information updating among the supply

Table 1.1 Supply Chain Management Activities

1. Integrated behavior
2. Mutually sharing information
3. Mutually sharing channel risks and rewards
4. Cooperation
5. The same goal and the same focus of serving customers
6. Integration of processes
7. Partners to build and maintain long-term relationships

chain members for effective supply chain management. The Global Logistics Research Team at Michigan State University (1995) defined information sharing as the willingness to make strategic and tactical data available to other members of the supply chain. In this book, it is proposed that open sharing of information such as inventory levels, forecasts, sales promotion strategies, and marketing strategies reduces the uncertainty between supply partners and results in enhanced performance.

Effective SCM also requires **mutually sharing channel risks and rewards** that yield a competitive advantage (Ellram & Cooper, 1990). Risk and reward sharing should happen over the long term (Cooper, Ellram, et al., 1997). Risk and reward sharing is important for long-term focus and cooperation among the supply chain members (Cooper, Lambert, et al., 1997). Risk and reward sharing is no easy problem to solve. As one executive we interviewed said,

> The sharing of rewards is a very, very difficult equation to solve. Everyone is right there conceptually, but the minute you move one dollar from one organization to another, unless you can show where another dollar is coming back . . . it becomes a morass.

Third, **cooperation** among the channel members is required for effective SCM (Ellram & Cooper, 1990). Cooperation refers to similar or complementary coordinated activities performed by firms in a business relationship to produce superior mutual outcomes or singular outcomes that are mutually expected over time (Anderson & Narus, 1990). According to Cooper, Ellram, et al. (1997), cooperation is not limited to the needs of the current transaction and happens at several management levels (e.g., both top and operational managers), involving cross-functional coordination across the channel members. As one executive interviewed put it,

> The most difficult part of moving to supply chain management is getting the people to walk cooperatively towards a shared objective as opposed to their individual parochial objectives.

Joint action in close relationships refers to carrying out the focal activities in a cooperative or coordinated way (Heide & John, 1990). Cooperation starts with joint planning and ends with joint control activities to evaluate performance of the supply chain members as well as the supply chain as a whole (e.g., Cooper, Lambert, et al., 1997; Novack et al., 1995; Spekman, 1988). Joint planning and evaluation involve ongoing processes over multiple years (Cooper, Ellram, et al., 1997). In addition to planning and control, cooperation is needed to reduce supply chain inventories and pursue supply chainwide cost efficiencies (Cooper, Ellram, et al., 1997; Dowst, 1988). Furthermore, supply chain members should work together on new product development and product portfolio decisions (Cooper, Lambert, et al., 1997; Drozdowski, 1986). Finally, design of quality control and delivery systems is also a joint action (Treleven, 1987).

La Londe and Masters (1994) proposed that a supply chain succeeds if all the members of the supply chain have *the same goal and the same focus of serving customers*. Establishing the same goal and the same focus among supply chain members is a form of policy integration. Lassar and Zinn (1995) suggest that successful relationships aim to integrate channel policy to avoid redundancy and overlap while seeking a level of cooperation that allows participants to be more effective at lower cost levels. Policy integration is possible if there are compatible cultures and management techniques among the chain members.

The implementation of SCM needs the **integration of processes** from sourcing, to manufacturing, and to distribution across the supply chain (Cooper, Lambert, et al., 1997). The integration can be accomplished through cross-functional teams, in-plant supplier personnel, and third-party service providers (e.g., Cooper, Lambert, et al., 1997; Manrodt, Holcomb, & Thompson, 1997).

Stevens (1989) identified four stages of supply chain integration and discussed the planning and operating implications of each stage:

Stage 1 represents the baseline case; the supply chain is a function of fragmented operations within the individual company and is characterized by: staged inventories, independent and incompatible control systems and procedures, and functional segregation.

Stage 2 begins to focus internal integration characterized by an emphasis on cost reduction rather than performance improvement, buffer inventory, initial evaluations of internal trade-offs, and reactive customer service.

Stage 3 reaches toward internal corporate integration and is characterized by full visibility of purchasing through distribution, medium-term planning, tactical rather than strategic focus, emphasis on efficiency, extended use of electronics support for linkages, and continued reactive approach to customers.

Stage 4 achieves supply chain integration by extending scope of integration outside the company to embrace suppliers and customers.

Effective SCM is made up of a series of partnerships and, thus, SCM requires
partners to build and maintain long-term relationships (Cooper, Ellram, et al.,
1997; Ellram & Cooper, 1990). Cooper, Ellram, et al. (1997) argue that the time
horizon of the relationship extends beyond the life of the contract—perhaps
indefinitely—and, at the same time, the number of partners should be small to
facilitate increased cooperation.

Gentry and Vellenga (1996) argue that it is not usual that all the primary
activities in a value chain—inbound and outbound logistics, operations, marketing, sales, and service—are performed by any one firm to maximize customer value. Thus, forming strategic alliances with channel partners such as
suppliers, customers, or intermediaries (e.g., transportation and/or warehousing services) provides competitive advantage through creating customer value
(Langley & Holcomb, 1992).

SCM as a Set of Management Processes

Davenport (1993) defines a process as a structured and measured set of activities designed to produce a specific output for a particular customer or market.
La Londe (1997) proposes that SCM is the process of managing relationships,
information, and materials flow across enterprise borders to deliver enhanced
customer service and economic value through synchronized management of
the flow of physical goods and associated information from sourcing to consumption. Ross (1998) defines supply chain process as the actual physical business functions, institutions, and operations that characterize the way a particular channel system moves goods and services to market through the supply
pipeline. In other words, a process is a specific ordering of work activities
across time and place, with a beginning, an end, clearly identified inputs and
outputs, and a structure for action (Cooper, Lambert, et al., 1997).

Lambert et al. (1998) propose that to successfully implement SCM, all firms
within a supply chain must overcome their own functional silos and adopt a process approach. Thus, all the functions within a supply chain are reorganized as
key processes. The critical differences between the traditional functions and
the process approach are that the focus of every process is on meeting the customer's requirements and that the firm is organized around these processes
(Cooper, Lambert, et al., 1997). Lambert et al. (1998) suggest that the key processes would typically include customer relationship management, customer
service management, demand management, order fulfillment, manufacturing flow management, procurement, and product development and commercialization.

Supply Chain Management Versus Supply Chain Orientation

Although these perspectives of defining supply chain management are helpful, a careful examination indicates that the literature is actually *trying to define two concepts with one term*, that is, supply chain management. The idea of viewing the coordination of a supply chain from an overall system perspective, with each of the tactical activities of distribution flows viewed within a broader strategic context (what has been called SCM as a management philosophy) is more accurately called a **supply chain orientation**. The actual implementation of this orientation, across various companies in the supply chain, is more appropriately called **supply chain management**.

This perspective leads us to the definition of one of these crucial constructs. **Supply chain orientation** is defined as *the recognition by a company of the systemic, strategic implications of the activities and processes involved in managing the various flows in a supply chain.* One of the executives we interviewed summarized it this way:

> You can't have implementation devoid of a philosophy [orientation]. Whoever is leading and setting the direction of the supply chain . . . has a philosophy and a belief about it. . . . It's not just a recognition . . . but embracing . . . critical elements of the supply chain and their impact.

Thus, a company possesses a supply chain orientation (SCO) if its management (in its entirety, not just one or two individuals) can see the implications of managing the upstream and downstream flows of products, services, finances, and information across their suppliers and their customers. From this definition, a company does not have a supply chain orientation if it sees the systemic, strategic implications in only one direction. Thus, in Figure 1.1b, the company in the middle of the basic supply chain may have an SCO, but the two companies on the ends do not (because the supplier is only focused down the channel—a historical "channels" orientation—and the customer is only focused up the channel—a historical "procurement" orientation).

Further, this does not mean the firm with the SCO can implement it—such implementation requires an SCO *across* several companies directly connected in the supply chain. The firm with the SCO may implement individual, disjointed supply chain tactics (such as just-in-time delivery or electronic data interchange with suppliers and customers), but this is *not* supply chain management unless they are coordinated (a strategic orientation) over the supply chain (a systemic orientation).

The implementation of an SCO requires several companies in the supply chain to utilize the processes discussed in the previous section to realize the activities listed in Table 1.1. In other words, **supply chain management** is the *implementation of a supply chain orientation across suppliers and customers.* Companies implementing SCM *must first have a supply chain orientation.* In the extended supply chain in Figure 1.1c, all the companies involved have a supply chain orientation, except the first supplier and the last customer. Because the first supplier is focused only on its customer and because the last customer is focused only on its supplier, neither can be said to have an upstream *and* downstream orientation.

In other words, a supply chain orientation is a management *philosophy*, and supply chain management is *the sum total of all the overt management actions undertaken to realize that philosophy.* This brings us closer to understanding and defining supply chain management. Before we can accomplish this fully, however, we must also examine the antecedents and consequences, and the scope, of supply chain management.

Antecedents and Consequences

Because supply chain relationships are typically long term and require considerable strategic coordination, we can examine the antecedents and the consequences supply chain management at the strategic level (see Figure 1.2).

Antecedents to SCO and SCM

Antecedents to SCM are the factors that enhance or impede the implementation of an SCO philosophy. First, Morgan and Hunt (1994) propose that **cooperation** arises directly from both relationship trust and commitment. Moorman, Deshpande, and Zaltman (1993) define **trust** as a willingness to rely on an exchange partner in whom one has confidence. Although both trust and commitment are essential to make cooperation work, trust is a major determinant of relationship commitment (Achrol, 1991; Morgan & Hunt, 1994). Thus, trust has both direct and indirect relationships with cooperation. Dwyer, Schurr, and Oh (1987) emphasize the role of trust in overcoming difficulties such as power, conflict, and lower profitability. Trust therefore has an effect on the sharing of risks and rewards. Dwyer et al. (1987) define commitment as "an implicit or explicit pledge of relational continuity between exchange partners" (p. 19). **Commitment** is an essential ingredient for the successful long-term relationships that are a component of the implementation of SCM (e.g., Gundlach, Achrol, & Mentzer, 1995). Lambert et al. (1998) also point out that the necessary commitment of resources and empowerment to achieve stated goals is important to implement SCM.

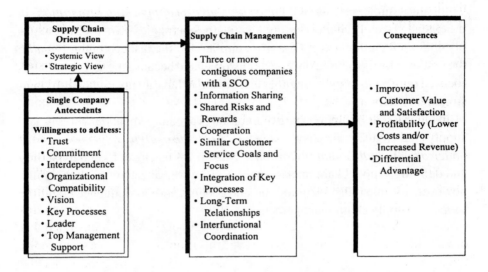

Figure 1.2. Supply Chain Management Antecedents and Consequences

In discussing supply chain relationships, one executive we interviewed said:

> Let's don't get away from that word trust. Contracts are good and fine for
> attorneys, but if you don't have that trust, and if you call a vendor and you
> want a certain special thing that is maybe outside of the contract, and if they
> say well, let me pull the contract and see if that's included, you may be in
> trouble. Over the years, some of the better relationships I've had is people
> that we don't even have contracts with, you call them and they know your
> need and they do it. You know that what they submit to you as the cost of
> their services is gonna be reasonable. I think we've got to keep that word in
> mind—we always have to be reasonable.

Putting together the effects of trust and commitment, Morgan and Hunt
(1994) state, "Commitment and trust are 'key' because they encourage marketers to (1) work at preserving relationship investments by cooperating with
exchange partners, (2) resist attractive short-term alternatives in favor of the
expected long-term benefits of staying with existing partners, and (3) view
potentially high-risk actions as being prudent because of the belief that their
partners will not act opportunistically" (p. 22). As such, trust and commitment
lead directly to cooperative behaviors in the implementation of an SCO across
several companies to achieve SCM.

The mutual dependence of a firm on a partner (**interdependence**) refers to the firm's need to maintain a relationship with the partner to achieve its goals (Frazier, 1983b). Acknowledged dependence is a prime force in the development of supply chain solidarity (Bowersox & Closs, 1996). In addition, this dependence is what motivates willingness to negotiate functional transfer, share key information, and participate in joint operational planning (Bowersox & Closs, 1996). Ganesan (1994) proposed that dependence of a firm on another firm is positively related to the firm's long-term relationship orientation.

Corporate philosophy or culture and management techniques of each firm in a supply chain should be compatible for successful SCM (e.g., Cooper, Ellram, et al., 1997; Cooper, Lambert, & Ellram, 1998; Cooper, Lambert, et al., 1997). **Organizational compatibility** is defined as complementary goals and objectives, as well as similarity in operating philosophies and corporate cultures (Bucklin & Sengupta, 1993). Bucklin and Sengupta (1993) demonstrated that organizational compatibility between the firms in an alliance has a strong positive impact on the effectiveness of the relationship (i.e., the perception that the relationship is productive and worthwhile). Cooper, Lambert, et al. (1997) also argue that the importance of corporate culture and its compatibility across channel members cannot be underestimated. Given our earlier definition of SCO, organizational compatibility in a supply chain means that companies must *all have* an SCO to achieve SCM.

Lambert et al. (1998) suggest that there should be an agreement on SCM **vision and key processes**. Ross (1998) contends that the creation and communication of a market-winning competitive SCM vision shared not just by individual firms but also by the whole supply chain (SCO, by our definition) is essential before any SCM project can begin. Visioning provides firms with specific goals and strategies concerning how they plan to identify and realize the opportunities they expect to find in the marketplace (Ross, 1998). The key processes will be addressed in greater depth in the section on the functional scope of SCM.

In terms of power and leadership structure of a supply chain, there needs to be a firm that assumes the leader role (Lambert, Stock, & Ellram, 1998). By the same token, Bowersox and Closs (1996) argue that supply chains need leaders as much as individual organizations. Ellram and Cooper (1990) propose that a **supply chain leader** is like a channel captain (Stern & El-Ansary, 1988) and plays a key role in coordinating and overseeing the whole supply chain. Bowersox and Closs (1996) suggest that, in many situations, a specific firm may function as a supply chain leader as a result of its size, economic power, customer patronage, comprehensive trade franchise, or initiation of the interfirm relationships.

The success of supply chain management is directly related to the presence of constructive leadership capable of stimulating cooperative behavior between participating firms (Schmitz, Frankel, & Frayer, 1994). Forced participation by a strong supply chain leader, however, will encourage exit behavior if the opportunity exists (Cooper, Lambert, et al., 1997).

Finally, several authors (e.g., Felton, 1959; Hambrick & Mason, 1984; Kotter, 1990; Tosti & Jackson, 1994; Webster, 1988) suggest that **top management** plays a critical role in shaping an organization's values, orientation, and direction. Day and Lord (1988) found that top-level managers have a substantial impact on organizational performance. Cooper, Lambert, and Ellram (1998) suggest that top management support, leadership, and commitment to change are important antecedents to the implementation of SCM. In the same context, Loforte (1993) contends that lack of top management support is a barrier to SCM.

In Figure 1.2, the willingness to address these antecedents by a particular company is represented as an SCO. When contiguous companies in a supply chain each achieve an SCO, they can begin to address these antecedents to realize SCM. In other words, a willingness by one company to address the issues listed in Figure 1.2 from a strategic, systemic perspective is an SCO. Management of the supply chain is accomplished only when several companies in line in the supply chain have that orientation and move toward implementing the management philosophy of SCO. As one of our interviewed executives put it, "It is more than support, it's a commitment. . . . At some point top management has to be actively involved in the process."

An analogy may help at this time. A supply chain is much like a river, with products and services flowing down it instead of water. Whether anyone recognizes the systemic, strategic implications of managing the water basin, the river still exists. Similarly, whether any company recognizes the systemic, strategic implications of the supply chain of which it is a part, it still exists. When one state through which the river flows recognizes the need for states above it in the water basin to conserve and preserve the water supply *and* recognizes its own need to do the same for states below it, the state has taken a systemic strategic orientation—the river equivalent of a supply chain orientation. Without the cooperation of the states above and below it, however, there is little it can do about implementing this orientation. It is only when a number of contiguous states adopt such a similar orientation and actively manage the resources of the river that we can say the water basin is managed. Similarly, supply chain management can result in a managed supply chain only when several companies directly linked in the supply chain have an SCO and actively manage to that orientation.

Consequences of SCM

The motive behind the formation of a supply chain arrangement is to increase channel competitiveness or competitive advantage (e.g., Bowersox &

Closs, 1996; Monczka et al., 1998). Porter (1980) defines two basic types of competitiveness or competitive advantage: cost leadership and differentiation. According to Giunipero and Brand (1996), improving a firm's competitiveness and profitability through SCM can be accomplished by enhancing overall customer satisfaction. By the same token, La Londe (1997) proposed that SCM aims at delivering enhanced customer service and economic value through synchronized management of the flow of physical goods and associated information from sourcing to consumption. According to Porter (1985), competitive advantage grows fundamentally out of the customer value a firm creates, and it aims to establish a profitable and sustainable position against the forces that determine industry competition. Thus, it is proposed that the implementation of SCM enhances customer value and satisfaction, which in turn leads to enhanced competitiveness of the supply chain, as well as of each member firm. This ultimately improves the profitability of the supply chain and its members.

Specific objectives to improve profitability, competitiveness, and customer value/satisfaction of a supply chain, as well as its participants, are suggested by several researchers. For example, a key objective of SCM is to lower the costs required to provide the necessary level of customer service to a specific segment (e.g., Cooper & Ellram, 1993; Houlihan, 1985; Jones & Riley, 1985). The other key objective is to improve customer service through increased stock availability and reduced order cycle time (Cooper & Ellram, 1993). Customer service objectives are also accomplished through a customer-enriching supply system focused on developing innovative solutions and synchronizing the flow of products, services, and information to create unique, individualized sources of customer service value (Ross, 1998). Finally, low cost and differentiated service help build a competitive advantage for the supply chain (Bowersox & Closs, 1996; Cavinato, 1992; Cooper & Ellram, 1993; Lee & Billington, 1992). As such, SCM is concerned with improving both efficiency (i.e., cost reduction) and effectiveness (i.e., customer service) in a strategic context (i.e., creating customer value and satisfaction through integrated channel management) to obtain competitiveness that ultimately brings profitability. As one executive put it,

> The whole reason for (managing) the supply chain is about prosperity. . . . What combinations are the best ones for each company to make the kind of money and grow the kind of business they want to grow?

If we distinguish between the operational function of customer service and the resultant goal of customer value and satisfaction, then this discussion leads us to conclude that the consequences of SCM are **improved customer value and satisfaction** and **profitability** to achieve **differential advantage**.

Scope

The scope of SCM is functional and organizational. The functional scope of SCM, on one hand, refers to which traditional business functions are included or excluded in the implementation and the process of SCM. The organizational scope of SCM, on the other hand, concerns what kinds of interfirm relationships are relevant to the participating firms in the implementation and the process of SCM.

Functional Scope of SCM

Because process refers to the combination of a particular set of functions to get a specific output, all the traditional business functions should be included in the process of SCM. First of all, we have to keep in mind that the supply chain concept originated in the logistics literature (Bowersox, Carter, & Monczka, 1985; Christopher, 1994; Jones & Riley, 1985), and logistics has continued to have a significant impact on the SCM concept (Bechtel & Jayaram, 1997). In this context, Tyndall and colleagues (1998) propose that "SCM logistics" is the art of managing the flow of materials and products from source to user. In other words, SCM—or the logistics system—includes the total flow of materials, from the acquisition of raw materials to delivery of finished products to the ultimate users, as well as the related counterflows of information that both control and record material movement (Tyndall et al., 1998).

According to Lambert et al. (1998), however, there exist important differences between the definition of supply chain management and the Council of Logistics Management's (CLM) 1985 definition of logistics: "Logistics is the process of planning, implementing and controlling the efficient flow and storage of raw materials, in-process inventory, finished goods, services, and related information from point of origin to point of consumption (including inbound, outbound, internal and external movements) for the purpose of conforming to customer requirements." CLM (1998) apparently agrees, because its new definition states, "Logistics is *that part of the supply chain process* that plans, implements, and controls the efficient flow and storage of goods, services, and related information from the point of origin to the point of consumption in order to meet customers' requirements" (emphasis added). Thus, CLM also distinguished between logistics and supply chain management, and it acknowledged that logistics is *one of the functions* contained within supply chain management.

Ross (1998) explains that the role of logistics spans from warehousing and transportation to integrating the logistics operations of the entire supply chain, whereas SCM merges marketing and manufacturing with distribution functions to provide the enterprise with new sources of competitiveness. Logistics puts more emphasis on efficient movement and storage to fulfill customer requirements. Customer value and satisfaction that help a supply chain improve competitiveness and profitability, however, require more than logistics (Giunipero & Brand, 1996).

Thus, Cooper, Lambert, et al. (1997) argue that SCM is more comprehensive than logistics: SCM means the management of multiple business processes, including logistics processes. According to Bowersox (1997), Cavinato (1992), and Mentzer (1993), marketing research, promotion, sales, information gathering, research and development, product design, and total systems/value analysis should also be included. Bechtel and Jayaram (1997) also propose that new product development should be included in the functional integration in SCM.

Thus, we can conclude that the functional scope of SCM encompasses all the traditional intrabusiness functions, and these are addressed more fully in our later discussion of Figures 1.3 and 1.4.

Organizational Scope of SCM

According to Christopher (1992a), leading-edge companies have realized that the real competition is not company against company but, rather, supply chain against supply chain. Cooper, Lambert, et al. (1997) argue that organizational relationships tie firms to one another and may tie their success to the chain as a whole. In this context, a supply chain as a whole may have its own identity and function like an independent firm. To create this ultimate supply chain, however, all companies in the supply chain must have a supply chain orientation. The result is a fully managed supply chain.

Ellram and Cooper (1990) suggest that effective supply chain management is made up of a series of partnerships among firms working together and mutually sharing information, channel risks, and rewards that yield a competitive advantage. In the same article, they also contend that the successful supply chain relies on forming strategic partnerships with long-term orientations. Christopher (1992a) suggests a network of organizations, through upstream and downstream linkages, as the organization for SCM.

According to Webster (1992), networks are the complex, multifaceted organizational structures that result from multiple strategic alliances. Thus, it is proposed that a network is a well-recognized organization for SCM. The basic characteristic of a network organization is a confederation—a loose and flexible coalition guided from a hub where the key functions include development and management of the alliances themselves, coordination of financial resources and technology, definition and management of core competencies and strategies, development of relationships with customers, and management of information resources that bind the network (Webster, 1992).

From this discussion, and given our earlier definition of supply chains, we see the organizational scope of SCM as implementation of the processes of SCM across three or more companies, all of which must have an SCO. This implementation and process must also include the systemic, strategic management of the activities listed in Table 1.1.

Putting It All Together

In this chapter, we have discussed the issues and facets concerning the definitions of supply chain management—as well as supply chain, the antecedents and consequences of SCM, and the boundaries of SCM. The relationships between all of these is illustrated in Figure 1.2.

Although, historically, the term supply chain management has a number of definitions, we believe it is possible to develop a single, encompassing definition of SCM. Reviewing the literature illustrated that supply chain management involves multiple firms, multiple business activities, and the coordination of those activities across functions and across firms in the supply chain. Pulling together these disparate aspects of supply chain management, for the purposes of this book, **supply chain management** is defined as *the systemic, strategic coordination of the traditional business functions within a particular company and across businesses within the supply chain, for the purposes of improving the long-term performance of the individual companies and the supply chain as a whole.*

This definition implies much about the management of a supply chain. To fully examine this definition, we need to first examine the individual business functions involved. We then need to examine how they are coordinated *across functions* and then how they are coordinated *across companies.* Finally, we examine the long-term performance goals of SCM. Although this takes place through the remainder of the book, our purpose in the rest of this chapter is to turn this definition of supply chain management into a model that can be used as the guiding framework for the book.

This framework is illustrated in Figures 1.3 and 1.4. Both figures can be imagined as a picture of a pipeline, with Figure 1.3 as a view from the side, showing directional flows of all SCM activities toward ultimately providing value and satisfying the customer, and Figure 1.4, as a cross section of the pipeline, showing the critical role of customer value and satisfaction to achieve differential advantage at the center of the pipeline, with the functional areas, their coordination, the coordination of the companies in the supply chain, and the global environment all impacting SCM.

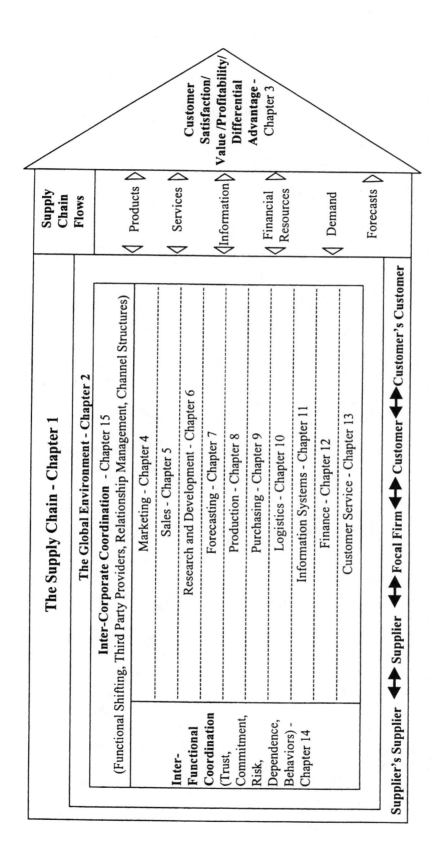

Figure 1.3. A Model of Supply Chain Management

Figure 1.4.   A Model of Supply Chain Management

Conclusions and Organization of This Book

In this chapter, we provided an integrative framework on the phenomenon called SCM that should help practitioners as well as researchers understand what SCM is, as well as what its prerequisites are and its potential effects on business and channel performance. Without a clear understanding of SCM, we cannot expect wide application of SCM in practice or research.

We also highlighted the need for rigor to further develop a framework of SCM. The framework we presented in this chapter not only functions as the core upon which the rest of the book is built but also provides a number of potential future research questions into supply chains and SCM, which we examine in the individual chapters.

Because many, if not most, present-day supply chains function within a global environment, in Chapter 2 we address the global supply chain environment. Similarly, because one of the primary goals of SCM is improved customer value and satisfaction to achieve profitability and differential advantage, we address this issue early in the book, in Chapter 3.

In the next 10 chapters, we examine the traditional business functions from the perspective of SCM. At a minimum, in each of these chapters we discuss the role of each function within a company and how this role changes when expanded to encompass a supply chain. In Chapters 14 and 15, we look more closely at the issues of functional and organizational scope—that is, how functions and companies should be coordinated within the supply chain. The managerial issues surrounding measuring and rewarding performance across the supply chain are examined in Chapter 16, and the research and managerial implications of this book are discussed in Chapter 17. In each of these chapters, our discussion of each topic is guided by the existing literature, our experience in SCM, and our interviews with executives who are in SCM positions today.

As an aid to managerial understanding, we provide an executive summary at the beginning of each of the remaining chapters. Our purpose is to provide busy executives trying to understand SCM with a quick primer on the subject in each chapter. We hope you will take the time to read this book in the order of the chapters presented; however, for those managers who do not have the time to read the chapters in order, we hope this feature provides a quick overview of the intricacies of each chapter's topic and acts as a guide to which chapters should be studied in more depth and in what order based on the needs of that manager's company.

2

Supply Chain Management in the Global Environment

NANCY W. NIX

Executive Summary

This chapter describes the globalization of the world economy, the diversity and environmental factors that influence a firm's global strategies and approach, drivers influencing firms to become increasingly global, and the different approaches to globalization that be adopted by firms. Implications for supply chain structure and processes for the various approaches to globalization pursued by firms are outlined, and issues and objectives of supply chain management important in a global environment are described.

In this chapter, I do the following:

- Examine the drivers for economic globalization
- Describe the diversity inherent in the global environment and the resulting issues of uncertainty, complexity, and asymmetry faced by firms operating globally
- Describe four distinct business models that might be adopted by firms operating beyond national borders as well as the differences in strategic thrust, organizational structure, and management processes of each
- Identify differences in approach and objectives of supply chain management inherent in the four business models

- Draw from research in functional areas of the supply chain to identify unique issues and objectives of supply chain processes in a global environment

From this discussion, I conclude that

- Different approaches to globalization require different degrees of supply chain integration as well as different supply chain strategies and structure
- Whatever approach to globalization and global supply chain management is adopted, firms face the challenges of understanding and managing the greater complexity and risks inherent in the global environment
- Global supply chain strategies must be developed in support of the strategic thrust of a firm's globalization initiatives and must consider opportunities for global efficiency, management of risks, learning to enable innovation and adaptation, and the need to balance global efficiency and local responsiveness
- Global supply chain processes should provide operating flexibility to respond to changes in the macroeconomic environment or government policies that adversely affect supply chain performance
- Design and management of supply chain activities must consider the influence of differences in culture, industry structure, legal requirements, and infrastructure in different countries on customers, suppliers, competitors, and supply chain partners
- The management of financial systems in a global supply chain must address differences in financial accounting systems, comparability of data, management of terms of sale and ownership transfer to minimize risk and optimize profits, optimization of transfer pricing to minimize taxes, the minimization of foreign exchange risks, and the use of countertrade
- A much broader set of skills is required of supply chain professionals to successfully manage on a global basis, including operating knowledge of the global environment, understanding how to manage inherent risks, and the ability to deal with difference in language and culture
- Compatibility of information technologies and standardization of systems and data are critical to a firm's ability to integrate supply chain operations on a global basis
- Decision support tools that incorporate global variables and allow "what if" scenario analysis are important to enable managers to more effectively manage the complexities and uncertainties of the global environment

No matter which approach to globalization is pursued, firms are faced with the challenges of understanding and managing the complexities and risk inherent in the global environment. Global supply chain managers must develop capabilities that allow them to understand the complexities in the global environment, anticipate significant changes, and adapt to those changes as needed. Systems and processes must be designed to address important environmental variables, and organizational skills and capabilities must be developed to deal with different languages, cultures, and business environments. Developing the organizational capability and infrastructure to manage supply chain activities on a global basis and to support the globalization strategies of the firm represents a significant and increasingly important challenge for supply chain managers.

Introduction

The globalization of businesses has received a great deal of press in recent years. The pressure of global competition is frequently cited as a primary driver for greater customer demands for improved products and services. These increased demands have caused businesses to pursue improvement initiatives, such as implementation of just-in-time (JIT) and quick-response (QR) inventory management policies, business reengineering, and supply chain management as tools to enhance their competitiveness (Jones & Riley, 1985). At the same time, firms increasingly look to foreign markets for growth opportunities, or to foreign suppliers for improved sourcing opportunities. This increased interest in foreign business has been reflected in several trends. The value of world exports has grown from $108 billion in 1958 to more than $5 trillion in 1995. Foreign direct investment (FDI), which has been utilized by firms as a means to expand into foreign markets and access foreign supply, has grown faster than world trade (Kreinin, 1998). An estimated 40,000 parent firms had 250,000 foreign affiliates with sales of approximately $5.2 trillion in 1992 (Kreinin, 1998).

As firms increase their participation in a global economy, developing an understanding of supply chain management issues and opportunities in a global context becomes increasingly important. In this chapter, research relevant to global supply chain management is surveyed, issues and opportunities that must be considered when managing in a global context are highlighted, and directions for future research are identified. First, the trends that act as drivers for increasing globalization of the worldwide economy are highlighted. Then, the diversity that makes operating in the global environment different from operating in a domestic environment is discussed. Next, the multiple approaches to globalization adopted by firms are discussed and implications of those approaches for supply chain management highlighted. Relevant literature from supply chain related disciplines (such as strategy, purchasing, logistics, and marketing) that pertains to managing in a global environment is then surveyed, and the implications for supply chain management in a global context are identified.

Finally, observations regarding the current state of and future directions for both research and practice are offered.

Drivers for Economic Globalization

Over the past several decades, a number of factors have led to the increasing globalization of the world economy, and as a result, the competitive environment faced by firms has changed dramatically. These drivers for globalization are (a) decreasing tariffs; (b) improving transportation, communications, and information technology; (c) globalization of products, services, and markets; (d) global competition; and (e) economic regionalism (see Figure 2.1). Trade barriers have been dramatically reduced under GATT (General Agreement on Tariffs and Trade), with average tariff rates for manufactured goods reduced from a range of 10%-25% in many developed countries in the 1950s to approximately 3.9% by the year 2000 (Hill, 1997). Technological improvements in transportation, communications, and information processing have made global production increasingly viable and have also contributed to the development of global markets. These changes have enabled global competitors to make products and services available to consumers worldwide, and the results have been a proliferation of choices for consumers and a need for firms to offer greater product and service quality at lower cost in order to remain competitive. These pressures have led to increased emphasis on reengineering internal business processes and working more collaboratively with customers and suppliers to better integrate planning and operations throughout the supply chain as a means to reduce costs and improve service.

Changes in technology and globalization of products and services have also resulted in increasingly dynamic markets and greater uncertainty in customer demand. Consumers have greater access to more goods and services, and the introduction of new products is occurring at faster rates. Thus, a firm's competitive position depends on its ability to understand changes in consumer demands and respond appropriately with goods and services that will meet those demands. Supply chain management tools and techniques are seen as mechanisms that will allow a firm to respond to these environmental changes. By working more collaboratively with supply chain partners, a firm can better understand changes in customer requirements and respond more quickly to those changes. As firms have searched for ways to enhance their competitive position, supply chain management concepts have emerged as increasingly important. By sharing risks across supply chain partners, firms may be able to improve their own performance in increasingly volatile and competitive global markets.

Supply chain management is seen as a mechanism to maintain competitive position in domestic markets, in light of increasing global competition. At the same time, firms increasingly respond to global competitive pressures by becoming more global themselves—looking to foreign markets for growth opportunities or to foreign suppliers for raw materials. This is evidenced by the growth in world trade, foreign direct investment, and global affiliations seen over the past several decades. As firms respond to global competition by becoming more global themselves, the challenges and benefits associated with supply chain management become increasingly complex. The growing number of trade agreements and economic unions is reconfiguring the boundaries of trade and, in many cases, changing the rules for competing within a region. To take advantage of reduced trade barriers with a region, foreign firms may invest in new facilities to establish a local presence or increase local content of manufactured goods. At the same time, established firms within a region may consolidate facilities as a response to reduced trade barriers. In either case, the trend toward economic regionalism results in the need to reconfigure and manage supply chains on a more global basis.

The Global Business Environment

Most discussions about the differences between doing business on a global versus a domestic basis highlight the increased complexity and uncertainty associated with the global environment. The complexity is a reflection of the fact that political, economic, and cultural factors differ across countries, resulting in a complex set of variables to be considered when operating across multiple countries. This global diversity is reflected in differences in government regulations and legal requirements, different states of economic and infrastructure development, differences in consumer demands, and differences in the social and business processes among different countries (see Figure 2.1). Uncertainty is increased by the fact that, in some countries and regions of the world, economic and political instability may result in dramatic exchange rate shifts, unpredictable inflation rates, and unexpected changes in political climate, government regulations, or legal requirements. This environmental uncertainty is reflected in the following comment from one executive:

> There is a sense that all the participants in that [global] supply chain really have no control over macro conditions . . . but, the things beyond your control within your supply chain are the things within which you have to develop your strategies.

A third factor resulting from this global diversity is the asymmetry to be managed when doing business between countries with very different economic statuses or very different cultures. Recent changes in the global economy have

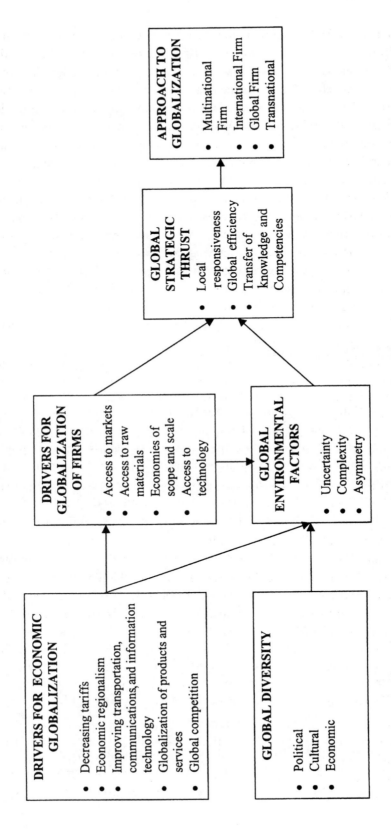

Figure 2.1. Factors Influencing the Globalization of Firms

led to an increase in the economic interface between countries with very dramatic differences. Relatively slow growth in the developed markets of the United States and Europe, coupled with greater openness in developing markets, has led firms to pursue investment strategies in less developed countries (LDCs) over the past several decades. Rapid economic growth and potential access to markets in Asia and Latin America have provided incentives for firms to locate production or assembly operations in those regions. Opening of markets in Russia and Eastern European countries has also provided attractive opportunities for firms pursuing growth strategies. Although the opening of markets in developing and transitional economies offers attractive opportunities, it may also bring about inherent difficulties and added risk. Differences in culture, infrastructure, and economic status are even more pronounced between developed economies and developing or transitional economies; thus, asymmetry between business entities or infrastructure may be great. Additionally, economic crises in the Asia-Pacific region, Russia, and Latin America served as reminders of the potential for volatility and uncertainty in the global economic environment and of the need to develop appropriate strategies and operating flexibility to deal with those uncertainties.

Another factor influencing the global strategies of firms is the increasing trend toward economic regionalism that is reconfiguring the economic boundaries in many regions. Two of the most prominent examples of economic regionalism are the European Union (EU) and the North American Free Trade Agreement (NAFTA). The removal of tariffs and trade barriers between EU member countries has provided incentives for firms to reconfigure networks of production and distribution to achieve greater economies of scale within the region. Firms in non-EU countries are also pursuing new investment strategies in the region to gain access to what has become the world's largest consumer market.

NAFTA, which eliminates tariffs and opens trade between the United States, Canada, and Mexico over a 15-year period, provides the same incentives for consolidation and/or investment in the North American region. Rules of origin and content requirements that products must meet to qualify for reduced tariffs in these economic regions also provide incentives for firms to develop new procurement and production strategies. Such a reconfiguration of sourcing, production, and distribution patterns in response to the formation of regional trading blocs will require strategic management of a firm's global supply chain.

These changes in the global economy offer a number of opportunities and challenges for firms. Differences in industries or between firms will result in different drivers for a firm's globalization efforts (see Figure 2.1). One firm's globalization efforts may be driven by the need to access raw materials with superior quality or at lower cost, or to access superior technology from global sources, whereas another firm's efforts may be driven by the desire to access

Table 2.1 Approaches to Globalization

Unit	Multinational	International	Global	Transnational
Strategic thrust	Local responsiveness	Transfer of knowledge and competencies	Global efficiency	Balance of local responsiveness, global efficiency, and transfer of knowledge and competencies
Configuration of assets and capabilities	Decentralized and nationally self-sufficient	Sources of core competencies centralized, others decentralized	Centralized and globally scaled	Dispersed, interdependent, and specialized
Role of overseas operations	Sensing and exploiting local opportunities	Adapting and leveraging parent company competencies	Implementing parent company strategies	Differentiated contributions by national units to integrated world-wide operations
Development and diffusion of knowledge	Knowledge developed and retained within each unit	Knowledge developed at the center and transferred	Knowledge developed and retained at the center	Knowledge developed jointly and shared worldwide
Supply chain implications	▪ Multiple domestic supply chains operating in different political, economic, and cultural contexts ▪ Decentralized development of SCM capability ▪ Limited sharing of knowledge and resources across borders	▪ Supply chain operations across multiple borders and in multiple countries ▪ Centralized development of SCM capability ▪ Transfer of knowledge and resources from corporate headquarters to other countries	▪ Integrated management of a global network of supply and demand ▪ SCM aimed at efficiency and operating flexibility ▪ Centralized development of SCM capability ▪ SCM processes and policies dictated by corporate headquarters	▪ Supply chain network integrated to achieve economies of scale but locally responsive to different markets ▪ Skills and capabilities developed and shared worldwide ▪ Joint decision making, with appropriate global/local balancing

SOURCE: Adapted from Bartlett and Ghoshal (1998), p. 75.

34

new markets. Still other firms may be driven to expand globally by the desire to take advantage of global economies of scope or scale. Differences in the drivers also leads to differences in strategic thrust and approach to globalization, but in any case, the diversity of the global environment is a consideration for the management of the firm's supply chain activities.

Dealing with complexity and uncertainty in the global environment is not new; however, the degree to which firms are operating on a global basis and the rate of change in the global environment over the past decade have increased. As a result, the ability of firms to manage on a global basis and monitor and respond to changes in the global environment is becoming more critical. In a global context, a firm's supply chain management process needs to provide the tools and techniques to understand and manage existing complexities and uncertainty, as well as to respond to rapid changes in the environment, in support of the globalization strategies of the firm.

Approaches to Globalization

Just as there is a lack of consistency in defining "supply chain management" (as highlighted in Chapter 1), there is also a lack of consistent definition of what global or international management means. Bartlett and Ghoshal (1998) identified four distinct business models that differentiate businesses operating in multiple countries. Each model has different strategic thrusts, organizational structures, and management processes, which would suggest different approaches to supply chain management. These four models are (a) the multinational company, (b) the international company, (c) the global company, and (d) the transnational company (see Figure 2.1). The business model adopted by a firm will be a reflection of the specifics driver and strategic thrusts for the firm's globalization efforts. For example, the ability to access foreign markets may require local responsiveness, whereas the ability to capture global economies of scope or scale may require global efficiency and the desire to access technology may require the transfer of knowledge. Thus, a firm's approach to globalization is influenced by the specific globalization drivers of the firm as well as the global environment within which they operate.

Characteristics of the four approaches to globalization differ in terms of how assets and capabilities are configured, the role of corporate headquarters versus overseas operations, and how knowledge is developed and diffused. Each also has different implications for a firm's approach to supply chain management (see Table 2.1).

In the first model, the *multinational company* typically has operations in multiple countries that operate with a great deal of freedom and autonomy from corporate headquarters or other company operations. This approach allows a firm to focus on building a local presence and responding to national differences in local markets. In this model, a firm manages multiple domestic supply chains in different countries with differing political, economic, and cultural contexts. Skills and capabilities are developed independently within each country, with little sharing of knowledge and resources across borders.

The second model, the *international company*, is one in which the firm is focused primarily on transferring and adapting the parent company's products and ideas to foreign markets. The parent maintains centralized control, and multinational subsidiaries have limited independence and autonomy. This approach allows a firm to exploit the company's knowledge and expertise through global diffusion and adaptation. In this model, a firm may be heavily export oriented or may duplicate corporate systems and processes in other countries. Multiple supply chains may operate both across national boundaries and within multiple foreign countries. Skills and capabilities are developed and maintained centrally, and processes and procedures are dictated to operations in other countries.

The third model, that of the *global company*, treats world markets as an integrated whole and manages their worldwide operations to serve the global marketplace. The firm's focus tends to be on centralized management of global operations to achieve cost advantages through economies of scale and to minimize risk. For firms adopting this approach, supply chain management focuses on managing a global network of supply and demand to achieve global economies of scale and on providing operating flexibility to respond to political or economic changes, thus reducing the risk of operating on a global basis.

These three models have been utilized historically by companies operating on a global scale. Bartlett and Ghoshal (1998) suggest that, in the past, each of these three models could be effective, as long as the firm's approach fit the strategic demands of its business. Now, however, increasing pressures toward global integration, local differentiation, and worldwide innovation require firms to manage toward global efficiency, local responsiveness, and worldwide transfer of knowledge and capability simultaneously. Thus, to compete now and in the future, a firm must manage its global operations with a different model that utilizes a more balanced approach, becoming what Bartlett and Ghoshal (1998) describe as a *transnational company*. The transnational company operates a dispersed, interdependent, and specialized network of assets and capabilities, leveraging globally where it makes sense, yet being responsive to differences in local markets where required. Supply chains, likewise, take advantage of global networks to achieve scale but operate locally when advantageous. Skills and capabilities are developed jointly among worldwide operations and shared across the entire network.

Clearly, there is no single "best" approach to global supply chain management. A firm's corporate supply chain strategy will differ based on the approach to globalization adopted by the firm (see Figure 2.2). The multinational firm may manage independent domestic supply chains in multiple countries, in which case the firm may rely on local managers, suppliers, and transporters, and is not faced with cross-border movements and multiple currencies. On the other hand, international firms may manage imports and exports across national borders, or local supply chains in multiple countries, with supply chain knowledge and expertise maintained in corporate headquarters in the home country. In this case, the firm must work across countries and cultures and must manage the complexities associated with customs, tariffs, currency exchange, and multiple entities in the delivery process. A global company may manage supply chains across multiple national borders, operating in an integrated global environment and managing a global network of supply and demand. In this case, an integrated approach to planning on a global basis is critical, and information technology that gives the firm global supply chain visibility and allows decision making on a global scale is required. Finally, the transnational firm is selective in managing supply chain activities both globally and locally, taking advantage of global scale where appropriate while establishing local management and responsiveness where appropriate. Knowledge and expertise are developed and shared across operations worldwide. In the case of the transnational company, collaborative planning between local and corporate managers and decision support systems that allow the firm to understand and manage trade-offs become critical.

A firm's supply chain management strategy in a global context is dependent on the overall strategy of the firm and on the global business model which the firm adopts. Consequently, the supply chain processes and the globalization issues faced by supply chain managers are influenced by the approach to globalization and the supply chain strategy adopted, as well as by the diversity in the global economic environment (see Figure 2.2). Issues associated with managing supply chain processes on a global basis, which are summarized in Table 2.2, have been identified through a review of the literature relevant to global supply chain management and are discussed in the following sections of the chapter.

Review of Relevant Literature

As highlighted in Chapter 1, the scope of SCM is both functional and organizational. The functional scope encompasses a broad range of traditional business functions, whereas the organizational scope is concerned with relationship issues important to participating firms. To gain an understanding of supply chain management in a global context, a broad range of literature examining global issues with respect to both supply chain functions and organization was included in this review.

Because of the overlap between supply chain management and strategy, global strategy literature has been included. For example, supply chain management has been described as a strategic tool to be incorporated into overall company strategy (Houlihan, 1988). At the same time, discussion of concepts pertaining to the value chain, often used synonymously with supply chain management, is found in the strategy literature. Thus, current research regarding global strategy offers useful insights regarding global supply chain management.

Similarly, because of the growing interest in SCM in the logistics discipline and the fact that the term "supply chain management" is often used as a synonym for logistics, the literature pertaining to global or international logistics was also included. Likewise, literature pertaining to global procurement was reviewed, because the procurement process is clearly a critical link between members of the supply chain and, thus, is an important component of supply chain management (Novack & Simco, 1991). In summary, literature pertaining to global supply chain management, global strategy, global logistics, and global procurement is discussed in this chapter.

From an organizational or relationship perspective, many of the underlying concepts associated with supply chain management can be traced to research in the areas of channel management and systems integration (Cooper, Lambert, & Pagh, 1997). For example, transaction cost analysis (TCA), with its foundation in economics, has been applied to discussions of supply chain management and coordination in vertical markets in both the marketing channels and logistics literature (Ellram, 1991b). Similarly, alliances and strategic partnerships are important concepts in supply chain management. Thus, to examine the organizational implications for supply chain management in a global environment, the literature pertaining to global alliances and global channels is also discussed in this chapter.

Global Supply Chain Management

To date, research specific to global supply chain management has been limited. Four articles were reviewed that specifically addressed the topic of supply chain management in a global context. Of the four, two provided a comparative analysis of supply chain management concepts in non-U.S. countries. Ellram and Cooper (1993) explored the similarities and differences between the Japanese system of *keiretsu* and supply chain management. Although the authors identified many similarities between the two, they also noted differences in the cultural roots and national legal systems which make the interlinkage of companies in Japan more effective than in the United States. Chiappe and Herrero (1997) analyzed the status of supply chain management in Argentina's food industry. They note that the shift from a period of high inflation (which led to a mind-set that high levels of inventory are good) to a more stable economic environment led to an increasing need for "state of the art" supply chain processes.

Comparative analyses of SCM in different countries, although not directly dealing with managing global supply chains, provide useful insights regarding

(text continues on page 42)

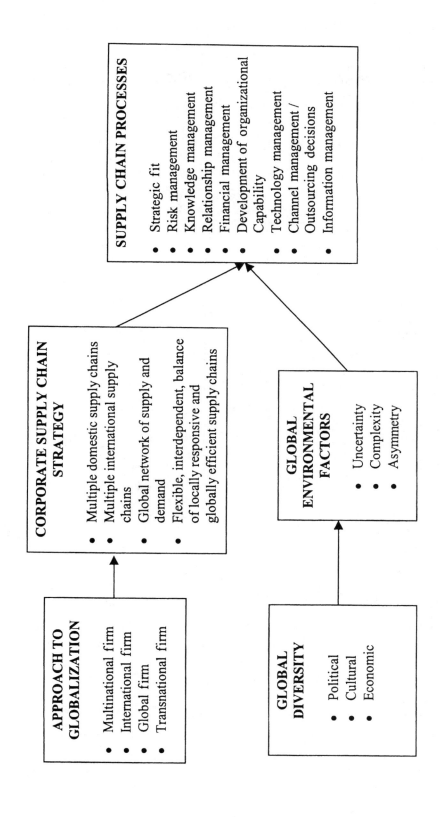

Figure 2.2. Factors Influencing Global Supply Chain Processes

39

Table 2.2 Global Supply Chain Business Processes

Unit	Issues and Objectives
Strategy	▪ Supply chain strategies in support of corporate strategies
	▪ Achieving efficiency in current activities through economies of scope and scale
	▪ Managing risks associated with current activities
	▪ Developing learning capabilities to enable innovation and adaptation to environmental changes
	▪ Balancing local responsiveness/global efficiency
Risk management	▪ Environmental scanning and operating flexibility
	– Monitoring and adapting to changes in the macroeconomic environment (wage and interest rates, exchange rates)
	– Monitoring and adapting to changes in government policy (taxes, duties, legal requirements, technical standards, local content requirements)
	▪ Understanding and planning for behavior of global competitors with differences in industry structure and legal requirements
	▪ Understanding, planning for, and managing resource capability in multiple countries and cultures
Knowledge management	▪ Developing organizational processes that allow for innovation, learning, and adaptation across countries and cultures
	▪ Protecting proprietary technology

Relationship management	• Structuring relationships that enable the firm to meet strategic objectives and manage risk • Understanding the implications of culture in managing relationships with customers and suppliers (e.g., difference in customer requirements, differences in perceptions and responsive behaviors) • Structuring relationships to meet strategic objectives while managing risk and to meet legal requirements in multiple countries • Understanding and managing geographic, social, and cultural asymmetry • Understanding the implications of culture in negotiations
Financial management	• Understanding differences in financial accounting systems and comparability of cost data • Managing terms of sale and ownership exchange to minimize risk and optimize profitability • Optimizing transfer pricing to minimize taxes and duties • Developing systems and processes to manage countertrade and foreign exchange
Organizational capability	• New skill sets required (knowledge of language, customs, exchange rates, opportunities in foreign markets, foreign logistics) • Understanding and managing differences in mind-set resulting from historical business practices (e.g., inventory is good in periods of inflation) • Understanding cultural implications on motivation, developing appropriate reward and recognition systems
Information management and technology	• Developing compatible information technologies on a global basis • Standardization of operating systems • Developing decision support tools that consider global variables, allow "what if" scenario analysis, and enhance decision making • Developing information systems that allow access to and utilization of global data for supply chain strategy and operations • Managing documentation flows associated with cross-border movements • Compatibility of data and information systems

41

the influence of cultural, political, and economic factors on the supply chain process. For a firm operating in multiple countries, whether as a multinational, international, global, or transnational company, an understanding of the influence of these differences on the management of supply chains is important. For example, factors identified as important to SCM, such as organizational compatibility, trust, information sharing, and interfunctional coordination, are likely to be influenced by firms' economic, legal, and cultural histories. Effective SCM requires an understanding of the implications of historical experience and culture on important supply chain processes. Thus, for firms managing supply chains on a global basis, these comparative studies provide important insights about the issues faced; however, additional research, which incorporates cross-border and cross-cultural issues, is also needed.

In a frequently cited article, Houlihan (1988) noted that transfer pricing, divisional or geographic autonomy, local systems and standards, and incompatible operating systems create problems in an international context. Although this article does highlight additional issues important in managing the flow of goods across borders, such as transfer pricing and systems incompatibility, it does not provide additional insights regarding the influence of those variables on supply chain management.

Perhaps the most comprehensive approach to global supply chain management is by Arntzen, Brown, Harrison, and Traffon (1995). Describing the development and application of the Global Supply Chain Model (GSCM), a number of variables unique to global supply chain management were highlighted. The GSCM is an optimization model that minimizes either cost or weighted cumulative production and distribution times, subject to meeting estimated demand, restrictions on local content, offset trade (or countertrade), and joint capacity for multiple products, echelons, and time periods. Cost factors include fixed and variable production charges, inventory costs, and distribution expenses via multiple modes, taxes, duties, and duty drawbacks. This model incorporates a number of variables unique to configuring a supply chain in a global context and has been used for strategic planning purposes to redesign Digital Equipment Corporation's network of production and service facilities based on global demand patterns. An analysis of DEC's manufacturing supply chain using GSCM led to a reduction from 33 to 12 manufacturing facilities while revenues and output continued to increase. The recommended configuration was for three major, relatively self-contained, customer regions (Pacific Rim, Americas, and Europe). Over a 2-year period, manufacturing costs were reduced by $167 million and logistics costs were reduced by more than $200 million. Although a global approach to planning was required to achieve these results, the optimum configuration for DEC's supply chain operations was found to be regional, rather than global. It is important to note that as variables in the global environment change (e.g., demand patterns, exchange rates, tariffs, or transportation costs), the optimal solution may be very different. This suggests that global planning is required on an ongoing basis to ensure that the firm is able to respond to changes in the global environment.

Although these articles provide useful insights regarding SCM in a global context, what is notably lacking is a coherent body of literature that addresses the full complexity of global supply chain management. Although useful insights are gained from comparative studies, they do not address the issues associated with managing supply chains across national borders. Optimization modeling techniques that integrate costs associated with cross-border movement and differences in national policies with typical supply chain cost factors provide a sound basis for strategic decisions regarding network design. Other techniques such as simulation, however, are required to model the uncertainty in the environment, allow "what if" scenario analysis, and enhance understanding of the impact of changes in certain variables on the process. Additionally, although such modeling techniques can be powerful analytical tools to understand and manage the economic trade-offs in a global system, they neglect the behavioral processes associated with effective supply chain management. What is needed, in addition to such modeling techniques, is programmatic research regarding strategy, structure, systems, and processes in a global supply chain context.

Review of Literature From Related Disciplines

A diverse set of perspectives can be found in the literature pertaining to global strategy, global purchasing, global logistics, global channels management, and global alliances. For each set of literature surveyed, a review of content, limitations, and implications for supply chain management is provided.

Global Strategy

The literature on global strategy is relatively rich conceptually, but its relevance to supply chain management is implied rather than overt. At the same time, concepts of supply chain management are frequently linked to strategy in the literature, suggesting commonality between the two. Houlihan (1988) suggests that what were once seen as logistics issues have become significant issues of *strategic management* and that supply chain management becomes a strategic tool to be incorporated in overall company strategy. Others link supply chain to *strategic alliances* (Gentry & Vellenga, 1996), *strategic decision making* (Ellram, La Londe, & Weber, 1989; Houlihan, 1988), *strategic planning* (Bechtel & Jayaram, 1997; M. C. Cooper & Ellram, 1993), *strategic lead time* (Horscroft & Braithwaite, 1990), and *strategic alignment* (Gattorna, Chorn, & Day, 1991). A common theme in the supply chain literature is the idea that effective supply chain management should be related to a firm's strategy; however, the influence of the firm's strategy on supply chain strategy or tactics has not received adequate attention. Stevens (1990) suggests that the focus of traditional approaches to supply chain management is at the operational and planning levels, rather than on strategic needs of the business, yet objectives and policies for the supply chain must be developed in terms of overall business strategies if supply chain management is to be used as a weapon for competitive advantage.

As highlighted earlier, globalization and global competition are often seen as drivers for supply chain management. As firms expand their geographic scope of operations, the firm's globalization strategies become increasingly important in determining appropriate supply chain objectives and strategies. Much conceptual ambiguity also exists concerning what "global" strategy means. Although early work focused on firms whose competitive position in one national market was significantly affected by its competitive position in another market, current research on global strategy is linked to "how the firm structures the flow of tasks within its world-wide value-adding system" (Ghoshal, 1987, p. 426). Prescriptions for global strategies have been different, and often contradictory, suggesting such approaches as product standardization, exploiting economies of scale, exploiting economies of scope, cross-subsidization, and multiple sourcing or production shifting to benefit from advantageous factor costs and exchange rates. Ghoshal suggests that corporate objectives are multidimensional and often mutually contradictory, and that identifying the trade-offs between these objectives is required to understand the potential costs and benefits of different strategic alternatives. He identifies three broad categories of goals of an organization that must be balanced in the strategic actions of a firm: (a) achieving efficiency in current activities, (b) managing risks associated with current activities, and (c) developing internal learning capabilities to enable innovation and adaptation to future changes.

The first strategy highlighted by Ghoshal (1987) is that of achieving efficiency in the current activities of the firm. In a global context, efficiency can be enhanced through three fundamental approaches: exploiting differences in input factors and markets in different countries, exploiting economies of scale, and exploiting economies of scope. The achievement of this objective requires optimizing the configuration of a firm's supply chain to achieve efficiency in the use of resources. Efficiency of current activities is also typically a key objective of supply chain management in a domestic context and is accomplished through streamlining activities and reducing operating costs across firms. The requirement of managing even more complex supply chains in regions with a diversity of cultures, political and social structures, and infrastructure and resource capabilities suggests that strategies and tactics for managing supply chains in such an environment will be very different. The optimization modeling approach used by DEC is an example of an efficiency strategy that considers global operations and manages trade-offs among the complex variables encountered in the global environment (Arntzen et al., 1995).

Differences in customer requirements in different countries may require different strategies or different product designs, brands, and packaging (Carpano, Chrisman, & Roth, 1994). For example, a firm may pursue one strategy in the United States and Europe because of the similarities in economic status and cultures but pursue a different strategy in China or India because of the greater differences in economic status and culture. Changes in trade policies or reconfiguration of trade boundaries such as have taken place in Europe and North America may also bring about a need for reconfiguring sourcing networks. The requirement for managing differences in operating environments or changes in the global economic landscape efficiently may require a greater degree of flexibility in supply chain management than is typical in a domestic environment (Kogut, 1985).

The second objective of managing risk must consider four broad categories (Ghoshal, 1987): (a) macroeconomic risks, (b) policy risks, (c) competitive risks, and (d) resource risks. Macroeconomic risks include cataclysmic events and economic shifts in factors such as wage rates, interest rates, exchange rates, and prices, factors often cited as important in a supply chain context. Policy risks arise from actions of national governments. Changes in legal requirements, technical standards, duty and tax structures, and trade policies have significant implications for a firm. Competitive risks arise from uncertainty about competitor response to a firm's strategy. For example, differences in industry structure, culture, and laws may lead to differences in competitive behavior. Resource risks are the risks that the adopted strategy will require resources beyond the firm's capability. To manage resource risk effectively, differences in capability of resources in multiple countries must be understood and considered as part of strategic planning. Managing these risks in such a complex environment becomes a critical issue for global firms. A key factor in a firm's performance is tailoring organizational structure and control systems appropriately to monitor risk factors, such as exchange rate fluctuations or changes in legal requirements, inherent in the global environment and to allow operating flexibility to respond to changes. Managing operating risks in such an environment becomes a strategic issue for a firm, and structural configuration and operating flexibility of a firm's supply chain are both critical to the process (Ghoshal, 1987; Govindarajan, 1988).

The third objective that must be considered in strategy is that of innovation, learning, and adaptation. Potential drivers for globalization include exploiting existing technology or capability and accessing additional technology or capability. This objective can be accomplished only through appropriate interorganizational processes that allow the diffusion of technology or capability to occur. This implies that this objective also influences the strategic choices a firm makes relative to how a supply chain is managed. For example, the desire to access technology or knowledge in a global venture may cause a firm to configure work flows and operating controls in a way that best facilitates the diffusion of technology and knowledge across national borders (Gupta & Govindarajan, 1991).

Although globalization is recognized as an important factor in a firm's supply chain strategy, limited research has been done as to how to best manage supply chains to deal with the issues of complexity and uncertainty inherent in global operations. Issues faced by managers in determining and executing supply chain strategies are highlighted in Table 2.2. Differences in corporate strategy require different strategies and objectives for supply chain management. The pursuit of global efficiency requires both a global approach to planning and appropriate information technology to allow global coordination and visibility. Global learning and technology transfer to take advantage of innovation worldwide require the structuring of work flows and organizational interfaces to allow the transfer of knowledge across borders. The need to balance local responsiveness and global efficiency requires a great deal of collaboration among organizations in multiple countries. Managers must understand the differences in strategic requirements and must develop supply chain approaches consistent with the firm's overall objectives.

The elements of risk inherent in the global environment require managers to ensure that they are monitoring risk factors and developing flexible supply chains that allow them to adapt to changes in those factors. The management of risk includes recognizing differences in industry structure or historical experience that may influence the behavior of competitors or supply chain partners, and involving the functions affected by these risk factors in developing strategies for coping with the risk.

Firms operating in the global environment will become increasingly dependent on their ability to manage global supply chains effectively. Configuration of supply chain systems and processes may be critical to the capability of a firm to achieve the strategic objectives of globalization. Additionally, the variables introduced in a global context are important components to consider in the development of supply chain strategies and processes. Additional insights about the impact of operating in a global environment are gained from reviewing literature from the functional areas of purchasing and logistics.

Global Purchasing

The primary focus of the articles pertaining to global purchasing is on the purchasing process within a firm. Caddick and Dale (1987) note the complexities of buying from less developed countries (LDCs), resulting from unpredictable inflation rates and exchange rates as well as the problems associated with high levels of government intervention. They also note that although there may be a benefit from reduced cost, there are also disadvantages—such as lower levels of quality, extension of supply lines, and delivery risk—with which firms must cope. The uncertainty and problems associated with sourcing from LDCs requires production, finance, marketing, materials management, and logistics involvement in the purchasing decision to develop strategies to cope with the added risks. Min and Galle (1991) also identify some of the complexities in sourcing internationally, citing greater variety of uncertain and uncontrollable factors, complex documentation requirements, trade regulations, quotas, duty structures, currency exchange rates, cultural differences, unique ethical standards, and complex distribution systems.

Monczka and Trent (1991) suggest that firms typically move through four stages relative to international sourcing. In Phase 1, firms source on a domestic basis only. In Phase 2, a firm begins to buy from foreign sources based only on need. Firms may find that it is necessary to source internationally to ensure access to raw materials or components in order to remain competitive. In Phase 3, international sourcing is viewed as a procurement strategy. International sourcing is no longer viewed as a necessity for survival but rather as a means to access cost, quality, or technological capability that contribute to competitive advantage. In Phase 4, a firm integrates and coordinates global sourcing requirements to maximize leverage, organization, and information systems, and it develops global sourcing measurement and reward systems. In this final phase, a firm's total sourcing requirements are coordinated and managed across a global set of suppliers (Monczka & Trent, 1991). In Phases 3 and 4, where global sourcing becomes an important component of a firm's strategy, a supply chain orientation becomes critical. Achieving competitive advantage through sourcing globally requires an integrated approach to managing that considers both internal supply chain operations and external customers' requirements.

Carter and Narasimhan (1990) note the need for different skills in sourcing professionals, cross-functional support, integration with manufacturing, and appropriate organizational structure to support global sourcing strategies. In a survey of multinational companies (MNCs), respondents cited the following as the most important keys to effective global purchasing: (a) development of international purchasing skills, (b) knowledge of exchange rates, (c) understanding foreign markets and opportunities, (d) knowledge of foreign customs, and (e) development of foreign logistics. Further, because of the longer lead times and uncertainty associated with international sourcing, purchasing also needs to more closely link to other functional areas in the firm, and planning and control systems must be tightly integrated (Carter & Narasimhan, 1990). This need for strong intra- and interfirm integration suggests that a firm's ability to utilize global sourcing as a part of competitive strategy also depends on its supply chain management capability.

Several empirical studies provided descriptive statistics on reasons for sourcing internationally and the obstacles encountered (Birou & Fawcett, 1993; Min & Galle, 1991; Monczka & Giunipero, 1984). The reasons for international sourcing consistently cited across studies are lower price, availability, quality, and access to technology. The most frequently cited obstacles are related to logistics or the supply chain, including problems with JIT programs, inventory, and distance. Other obstacles cited frequently fall into the category of lack of knowledge and capability of dealing with differences and uncertainties in the international environment. These findings generally support the conclusion that global sourcing may be important to a firm's competitive position as a means to access raw materials, improve quality, lower cost, or access technology. Further, pursuing a global procurement strategy successfully requires that a firm possess a supply chain orientation and the skills to deal with the complexities and uncertainties of the global environment.

In an examination of the characteristics of the seller in an international buyer-seller relationship, Dominguez and Zinn (1994) identified factors predicting success in long-term relationships between foreign suppliers and U.S. firms. Based on interviews with five Central American suppliers to U.S. firms, these authors found commitment to exports, heightened perception of the bureaucratic and logistics problems in exporting, the use of formal market research, and a focus on customer service to be positive predictors of export success. The dependent variable, export success, was measured in terms of export volume, export intensity, and profitability.

Although global sourcing is recognized as an important strategy for accessing materials and technology or for achieving strategic leverage, it appears that few firms have developed global sourcing capability. The long lead times and environmental uncertainty associated with global sourcing appear to be significant barriers to implementation. Additionally, purchasing professionals' lack of skills and capabilities required to manage across national borders appears to be a significant impediment. It is important that managers understand the potential benefits, as well as the barriers, associated with pursuing a global sourcing strategy, so that appropriate investments in skills and capabilities of people, as well as in information technology, can be made.

This set of literature provides evidence of the increasing importance of global sourcing. The focus, however, is predominantly on the functional process of buying foreign goods within a U.S. firm and descriptive analysis of firms' buying practices, with only peripheral discussion of the supply chain management implications. Because supply chain issues were frequently cited as major obstacles in the global sourcing process, research regarding the role of supply chain management in support of a firm's global sourcing strategy is warranted. Several authors offer insights regarding the complexity of variables to be considered in a global context, but very little attention is given to how those variables influence the purchasing process. Further research is needed regarding tools and techniques that can be utilized by managers to develop appropriate global sourcing strategies and SCM systems and processes to support those strategies.

Global Logistics

The dominant theme in the logistics literature is the increased complexity of the logistics processes in a global environment. Wood (1990) used a channels framework to categorize types of complexity as a transactions channel, a documentation/communications channel, and a distribution channel. The transactions channel deals with when and where to transfer title and payment of goods, how the process is managed to deal with the uncertainties of exchange rate fluctuations and inflation rates, and the increased risk associated with fraud and piracy. The documentation/communication channel involves the complex and multiple legal requirements involved in cross-border movements as well as the increased difficulty of communicating across spatial and cultural barriers. The distribution channel deals with the physical flow of goods and incorporates the international complexities of packaging and labeling requirements in different countries, as well as mode choice. Taylor (1996) highlighted the implications of differences in infrastructure and logistics services across countries as issues to be considered in determining whether to pursue anticipatory or postponement inventory management strategies.

Rao and Young (1994) examined the role of third-party logistics providers in an international context. Using a case study approach, these researchers conducted interviews with 44 firms (including 15 global shippers, 21 carriers and forwarders, and 8 providers of infrastructure services) to investigate factors influencing a firm's outsourcing behavior and the logistics complexities that drive outsourcing behavior in an international setting. Five factors were seen as critical to the decision to outsource international logistics functions.

1. Centrality of the logistics function; that is, which of the international logistics functions is central to the core competency of the firm? Most of the planning and administrative functions were seen as core functions to be retained in-house; however, decisions about whether other specific supply chain functions are central or critical to a firm's core mission depend on the complexity and structure of the firm's products, processes, and networks. This suggests that a firm's supply chain strategy is a key driver for the outsourcing decision in a global context.

2. Risk liability and control related to a firm's responsibility for safe storage and handling of hazardous materials influences the decision to retain ownership of products and control of operations. Interestingly, risk and liability associated with service failures from poor performance in supply chain operations was not highlighted as a significant issue in the outsourcing decision.

3. Operating costs/service trade-offs; that is, does retaining the activity in-house provide cost-effective service at a quality level that is competitive with what's available in the marketplace? Shippers may look to outsourcing as a way to take advantage of scale economies or specialization that improves the cost/service trade-off.

4. Information and communication systems; that is, does outsourcing allow access to systems capabilities not available in-house to deal with the complexities and global reach required in international supply chains?

5. Market relationships; that is, does a third party offer value to the shipper in relationships with customers? Third-party providers are seen as having the potential to provide market intelligence and information systems services across multiple shippers more effectively than individual shippers can by retaining these functions in-house.

Outsourcing of logistics activities is seen as an important mechanism for helping managers deal with the lack of skills, capabilities, or infrastructure required to manage the complexities of the global environment. It is important for managers to understand the globalization objectives of the firm and ensure that requirements for achieving those objectives are a part of the outsourcing decision. For example, if the firm's objective is to transfer knowledge and technologies or to achieve global efficiency, does the use of a third party allow the organizational interfaces or the global supply chain visibility required to meet these objectives?

As in the literature from other disciplines, these logistics-related articles once again highlight the uncertainties and complexities associated with the global business environment and the importance of managing beyond the firm's boundaries in an international context. Additional insight is needed to understand how to manage those uncertainties, to develop tools and techniques to ensure appropriate supply chain visibility and manage complex trade-offs on a global basis, and to understand the implications of managing across national boundaries and cultures.

Channels in a Global Context

The literature related to global channel management is relatively diverse. The articles reviewed for purposes of this discussion include an examination of the variables influencing choice between independent distributors or captive agents, comparative analysis of distribution channels in different countries, and an analysis of predictors of satisfaction within foreign channel relationships. This literature is based on empirical research, with the majority of the articles building on existing theoretical frameworks such as transaction cost analysis (TCA).

Using TCA as a theoretical framework, two studies examined the variables influencing a firm's choice between independent distributors or captive agents as distribution channels in foreign countries (Anderson & Coughlan, 1987; Bello & Lohtia, 1995). Results of these studies indicated that technological complexity and the need for extensive training of human resources (asset specificity) leads to the use of captive agents. These findings are consistent with previous research findings in domestic channels. In both these studies, environmental uncertainty associated with greater differences in cultural environment in the foreign country was correlated with a choice to use independent distributors. For example, Bennetton made a decision to outsource retail stores because of concerns about the ability to meet the high service levels required in the foreign setting that could result from anticipated problems in managing and motivating employees from very different cultures (Dapiran, 1992).

Anderson and Coughlan (1987) found that firms tend to expand in a market with their existing channels, whether channel members are independent distributors or captive agents, to exploit economies of scale. This suggests that the initial choice of a channel partner may be critical to long-term strategy. However, Bello and Lohtia (1995) found that more experienced firms, or firms with greater export intensity, in terms of both volume and resources engaged in the process, tended to use captive agents to exploit economies of scale. These somewhat contradictory findings suggest that future research in the area of choice regarding channel partners is important, given the potential for the long-term strategic importance of the initial decision.

Comparative studies highlight national and cultural differences that have an influence on channel structure, behavior, and relationships. In a comparative study of quick response in retail channels in the United Kingdom, United States, Europe, and Japan, considerable variation both within and between countries was noted. These differences were attributed to factors such as extent of retail power, degree of supply chain control, geographic spread, relative logistics costs, and relative sophistication of the distribution industry (Fernie, 1994). In a study of Japan's distribution system, Goldman (1991) found that the traditional retail sector structure and process in Japan reduce the opportunities for the expansion of new entrants and, therefore, inhibit new entrants' ability to gain economic efficiencies. It is important that managers understand existing industry structure, business practices, and national policies that might influence their ability to be successful with their existing business practices in a foreign country. Comparative studies highlight the influence of national and cultural differences on channel structure and behavior but offer limited contribution to an improved understanding of managing channels, or supply chains, across national boundaries and cultures.

A prominent theme in channels research is the role of power in influencing the behavior of channel members. One empirical study of Japanese distributors (Johnson, Sakano, Cote, & Onzo, 1993) examined how the distributors perceive the exercise of power on the part of U.S. suppliers. The results suggest that the Japanese do not view power sources along the mediated (reward, coercion, and legal legitimate) and nonmediated (referent, expert, traditional legitimate, and information) dichotomy, as is attributed to Western cultures. Rather, results indicate that they perceive power sources based on an authoritative- nurturing dichotomy. The authors suggest that differences in perception of power sources by the two parties may lead to misinterpretation of actions, and responses may be different than expected. The authors also noted that the Japanese seem more comfortable with the exercise of power by channel partners than do Western firms. Managers must understand such differences in perceptions in order to select appropriate partners and develop successful long-term relationships in a global context.

Global Alliances

The importance of relationships in effective supply chain management is well documented (Gentry & Vellenga, 1996). Factors that play an important role in relationship management include cultural fit, goal congruence, goal compatibility, trust, shared commitment, and information network structure. Appropriate relationship management presents many challenges between firms, even with close geographic proximity, common language, and similar national cultures. Thus, the implications of managing supply chain relationships with wide geographical, cultural, and social asymmetry are significant.

Johansson (1995) suggests that international alliances in distribution and marketing have increased as an efficient response to increasing competitive intensity and degree of globalization of markets. Through strategic alliances, a firm is able to access technology, reach new markets more quickly, or manufacture efficiently without investing time and capital in building a new plant. Drivers in the development of global alliances include opportunities for expanding markets, achieving economies of scale, and accessing new technology or production capacity (Ellram, 1992; Johansson, 1995; Rinehart, 1992). Some 722 international alliances were reported in *The Wall Street Journal* for the period 1983-1988 (Ellram, 1992). Of these, 130 involved logistics, with all but 28 a combination of logistics and marketing, operations, purchasing, technology, or some multiple of these functions. Ellram (1992) suggests the multidisciplinary nature of these alliances indicates a supply chain orientation. Of the 722 alliances analyzed, 65% were joint ventures, 28% contract, 4% supply agreements, and 3% licenses.

Johansson (1995) also examined the question of why the focus on international alliances has become so great now, since historically ownership has been a dominant method of expanding into other countries. He suggests that the alliance did not emerge as a viable organizational form to accomplish these objectives earlier because of the need to protect proprietary know-how. The increasing rate of technology diffusion has decreased the value of proprietary technology, making it a necessary but not sufficient key success factor rather than a differentiating factor. Because protection of technology is no longer such an important issue, firms are increasingly pursuing alliances as a viable alternative to the joint venture or wholly owned subsidiary when expanding into foreign countries.

An international alliance can take several forms. One common form is that of the *shared distribution network*, where, for example, Nissan agrees to sell Volkswagens in Japan. Another is *licensed manufacturing*, where one firm will agree to manufacture for another to utilize excess capacity. A third form is that of *collaborating on research and development*. For example, Sony and Philips joined together to develop the new videodisc. Two drivers for R&D alliances are to share the high cost of R&D and to jointly establish common standards. By working together to create common standards across countries, firms can facilitate the movement of goods across borders to serve global or multiple markets. Different forms of alliances may be appropriate, depending on the strategic objectives of the firm, and each form may have different implications for a firm's supply chain management strategies and objectives.

Utilization of alliances also poses potential drawbacks. By depending on an alliance, a firm may limit its own ability to learn about new markets, to acquire additional capability, or to pursue growth strategies in foreign markets (Johansson, 1995). Thus, the decision to form alliances in configuring a global supply chain has strategic implications for the firm as well as the potential to either enhance or inhibit the firm's ability to achieve its strategic objectives.

Whether a firm pursues its globalization strategies through an alliance or through some other organizational form such as a joint venture, wholly owned subsidiary, licensing arrangement, or merger, environmental factors will influence the negotiation process between parties from two different countries (Rinehart, 1992). Bargaining strategies should consider regulatory and political constraints, competitive and cultural constraints, and capital and financial constraints that are unique to the countries involved. Another consideration in international negotiations is that the cost/benefit relationships may be altered by the environmental constraints, resulting in an increased cost of negotiation and a reduced benefit from the process (Rinehart, 1992).

Although the formation of alliances has become increasingly important in the global business environment, the decision to form an alliance versus some other alternative organizational form depends on the firm's strategic objectives. At the same time, differences in geographic, economic, and cultural differences must be considered in terms of strategy and structure, as well as in the negotiation process. Further understanding of how to develop and manage global alliances to achieve the firm's strategic objectives, in light of environmental variables unique to such cross-cultural and cross-national relationships, is an important area for future research.

Global Supply Chain Management

The diversity of perspectives found in the literature is illustrative of the diversity of approaches to globalization by firms (see Table 2.1). Firms differ in their approach to globalization depending on their historical evolution as well as their strategic objectives (Bartlett & Ghoshal, 1998). Consequently, global supply chain strategies differ among firms. A multinational company, with autonomous operations in multiple countries, is unlikely to have a great deal of integration or sharing of knowledge across national boundaries. For such firms, comparative analyses of supply chain management in different countries can provide useful insights that facilitate the firm's decision-making processes within individual countries. On the other hand, an international company with an objective of leveraging parent company competencies in multiple countries is likely to manage both product and knowledge flows from the corporate center to dispersed operations in various countries. For such firms, understanding how and when to pursue supply chain integration across borders and cultures, or how to facilitate knowledge transfer across cultures, is critical.

For firms pursuing the global model, the joint objectives of achieving economies of scale and minimizing risk drive supply chain strategies. Firms adopting this model configure systems and processes to balance supply and demand on a global basis, and to minimize risk by reconfiguring their utilization of global networks of assets in response to shifts in the global environment. Issues such as network optimization, operating flexibility, and environmental scanning become important to firms adopting this model.

The transnational firm, pursuing a strategy that balances global efficiency, local responsiveness, and global learning, faces the challenge of managing a dispersed, interdependent network of assets to achieve scale economies where appropriate, yet retain local responsiveness where required. The firm must optimize networks, maintain operating flexibility, and access and utilize information about the economic environment; in addition, the ability to understand and respond to the needs of a diverse set of customers is critical. Skills and capabilities can no longer be retained in a central organization but must be developed and shared worldwide so that each organization can contribute based on its own unique capabilities.

Whatever strategy a firm pursues in its globalization efforts, it will be confronted with the added complexity and uncertainty associated with doing business in a global environment, as well as management of the added risk. As the pressures for global integration increase, however, it is likely that firms will shift from multinational or international strategies to global or transnational strategies, and the degree of complexity and uncertainty will also increase. At the same time, the importance of strategic management of that complexity and uncertainty also increases. Supply chain managers need to ensure that the configuration and operation of global supply chain activities is appropriate to the firm's strategic objectives. Critical to success are ongoing monitoring of environmental variables and supply chain flexibility that allows a firm to adapt to changes in economic conditions or legal requirements.

Supply Chain Processes—Issues and Objectives

Although the literature surveyed is relatively fragmented and diverse, useful insights can be gleaned regarding critical supply chain processes and the issues and objectives that must be considered when managing in a global environment (see Table 2.2). Not all these issues and objectives are relevant to every firm, but firms engaged in conducting business beyond domestic borders should consider the implications of each in light of their globalization strategies.

Strategy

The key strategic consideration for supply chain managers is fit with corporate strategy. To contribute to a firm's competitive advantage, supply chain processes and infrastructure must be aligned with and supportive of the firm's globalization strategies. Whether the firm's globalization strategies are aimed at global efficiency through economies of scope and scale, managing risk, transfer of knowledge, or a combination of these three, the ability of supply chain activities to assist in achieving these objectives is critical.

Risk Management

Given the complexity and uncertainty inherent in the global environment, management of risk is an issue that must be addressed by any firm doing business globally. Environmental scanning to monitor changes in the macroeconomic or political environment, along with operating flexibility that allows a firm to respond to those changes, is critical to a firm's ability to manage risk. Changes in a country's economic situation, which may affect currency exchange rates, wage rates, and/or interest rates, may require changes in a firm's operations. Changes in government policy may bring about changes in tax or duty structures, legal or local content requirements, or technical standards that require changes in a firm's products or operations. One executive we interviewed indicated that his firm maintains an entire department focused on customs and taxation, so that "supply chain management policies are married with an understanding and evaluation of international taxation policies to best benefit the supply chain." Having the flexibility to reconfigure sourcing and production flows in response to those changes—and thus to minimize the risk of operating globally—depends on the firm's supply chain management strategies and processes.

Another element of risk is introduced by the asymmetry of political, economic, and cultural environments. For example, in countries with different legal requirements or industry structures, competitors may behave differently or respond in unexpected ways. Likewise, channel members or employees may respond differently, resulting in differences in organizational capability to achieve strategic or operating objectives. To manage the competitive and resource risk effectively, managers must understand and plan for the influence of political, environmental, and cultural differences in competitor responses and resource capabilities.

Knowledge Management

Although the importance of transferring knowledge and capability across countries and cultures is recognized, little attention has been given to the implications for supply chain management. Depending on the approach to globalization adopted by the firm, knowledge and skills may be developed and maintained within each country of operation, held at corporate headquarters and transferred out to other regions, or developed and shared worldwide. Almost certainly, supply chain strategies and process design determine what skills are developed in what location and how those skills are transferred to other countries. Managers need to identify the skills and capabilities throughout global operations and develop processes to identify best practices and ensure that those best practices are shared and utilized across global operations.

Relationship Management

Relationships with customers and suppliers are a critical component of managing the supply chain. Three key questions must be considered in appropriately structuring and managing relationships:

1. How should relationships be structured to enable the firm to achieve its strategic objectives, while maintaining operating flexibility to manage risk in the global environment?
2. How do social and cultural asymmetry influence the relationship (e.g., differences in perceptions of power, behavioral responses, negotiations), and how can those differences be managed effectively?
3. How do differences in the political, legal, and economic environment influence appropriateness or desirability of relationship structures?

Managers need to understand risk factors and cultural differences across countries and ensure that supply chain professionals have the knowledge and capabilities required to select appropriate partners and to develop and maintain appropriate relationships with those partners.

Financial Management

Several financial management issues critical to supply chain management were highlighted throughout the literature (see Table 2.2). Appropriate planning depends on access to comparable cost data for the firm's operations. For firms operating in multiple countries, managers must understand differences in financial accounting systems and take steps to ensure comparability of data to make informed supply chain decisions. Given the significance of the multinational corporation in global trade and the high level of intracompany transfers, the optimization of transfer pricing to minimize taxes and duties is a significant supply chain management issue in a global context. In the case of intercompany transactions, managing the process of ownership exchange to minimize risk becomes an important issue. Managing the selection and execution of terms of sale (which determine responsibilities in the flow of products, documentation, and cash, and determine when the exchange of ownership and assumption of risk takes place) is a significant issue that firms operating globally must address. Finally, developing the systems and processes to manage currency risk and countertrade are important to a firm's success in achieving its global strategies.

Organizational Capability

In addition to the supply chain skills requirement, a new set of skills and capabilities are required for effective global supply chain management. These capabilities include the ability to transfer knowledge and work effectively across cultures and to manage political, economic, and cultural asymmetries. Examples of specific skill sets include language skills as well as knowledge of foreign markets, international and foreign logistics, import/export requirements and customs processes, and foreign exchange issues. Finally, organizational systems and processes need to reflect legal and cultural differences (e.g., cultural implications for employee motivation, appropriate reward and recognition systems).

Information Management and Technology

The importance of information management and technology to supply chain management is beyond the scope of this chapter but is addressed in Chapter 11; however, several issues unique to operating globally should be acknowledged here. Once again, managing the complexity of the environment and asymmetries between countries is a critical challenge. Compatibility of information technologies and standardization of systems and data are critical to a firm's ability to integrate operations on a global basis. Decision support tools that consider global variables and allow "what if" scenarios enable a firm to more effectively manage the complexities and uncertainties of the global environment. Finally, information and documentation requirements associated with cross-border movements are significant.

In summary, global supply chain strategy decisions are influenced by the complexity and uncertainty associated with the global environment, thus requiring systems, processes, and capabilities beyond those required in a domestic environment. Although a firm's choices about how to manage supply chains on a global basis necessarily differ based on the approach to globalization and strategic thrust specific to the firm, the issues and objectives highlighted in this chapter are important considerations in that choice process.

Conclusions

The subject of supply chain management is important to both academics and practitioners. It has long been recognized there are benefits to be gained from focusing beyond the boundaries of the firm and optimizing resource utilization to reduce cost and increase value to improve performance across a supply chain. What is not so clear is what specific objectives, strategies, and tactics are most appropriately adopted by a firm, and what factors are important in making this determination. As firms struggle to manage in an increasingly complex environment, it is increasingly critical that they possess the ability to make appropriate strategic choices and deploy limited resources toward those strategies and tactics that provide the greatest benefit. This ability becomes even more critical for firms operating in a global environment.

Although firms conducting business beyond domestic borders may choose to do so in different ways, the complexity and uncertainty in the global environment are significant factors in every case. The frameworks presented in this chapter should provide useful insights to managers about the environmental variables to consider in global supply chain design. Supply chain managers must understand the firm's globalization objectives and strategies to effectively design supply chain processes in support of those strategies. Supply chain strategies, structure, and processes must address issues of strategic importance to the firm, such as the ability to gain efficiency through economies of scope or scale, to share technology and innovations, to balance local responsiveness and global efficiency, and to manage the risks inherent in the global environment. The environmental risks faced by the firm must be understood, and the appropriate environmental scanning mechanisms and operating flexibility must be developed to anticipate and respond to changes in the global operating environment. A firm's ability to anticipate or sense significant changes in economic, legal, or political conditions, and to reconfigure supply chain operations in response to such changes, can be an important source of competitive advantage.

Managers must also develop appropriate information technology to support global supply chain strategies. Such systems must provide the capability to manage global transactions as well as to access and utilize data and information about global operations. Appropriate decision making is impossible without access to data on a global scale. Organizational systems and processes must take into account cultural asymmetries and foster the development of appropriate capabilities and skill sets. Finally, supply chain processes should address political, economic, and cultural influences on channel structure and behavior.

A review of the literature on supply chain management noted that the majority of articles on supply chain management have been case studies or conceptual, with little attempt to provide a theoretical underpinning. Recommendations for future research include the need to build and test theory, to incorporate a multidisciplinary approach to research, and to address differences in supply chains across industries and the effects of those differences (Bechtel & Jayaram, 1997). Other calls for research include determining differences in level of supply chain integration based on such differences in importance to strategic goals, complexity of products, and corporate cultures (Cooper, Lambert, et al., 1997).

There is no coherent body of literature or research in the area of global supply chain management. Many articles are depicted as supply chain related but only address functional aspects of supply chain management, generally from the perspective of a single firm. Others address the relationships between two firms, with the primary focus on the process of importing purchased goods or exporting finished products. These processes are generally treated as handoffs, with very little integration involved.

The various supply chain related disciplines also reflect notable differences in scope. The focus in the strategy literature is on the management of global supply networks, whereas most of the functional literature addresses either interfirm or intrafirm processes associated with importing or exporting. The one notable exception is the discussion of the Global Supply Chain Model, an optimization used to reconfigure the global supply network for Digital Equipment Corporation (Arntzen et al., 1995).

As is typical in the early stages of study in any discipline, the bulk of the literature reviewed is conceptual or descriptive in nature, with very little theory building or testing. Several issues may contribute to the lack of a systematic body of research aimed at developing and building theory in this area. First, the lack of consensus about definition and terminology makes programmatic research difficult at best and results in many different approaches and perspectives being reflected in the literature. The taxonomy of global supply chain process issues found in Table 2.2 provides a useful guide to the systems and processes that should be studied within the domain. A program of research to build knowledge in a systematic way and with greater clarity for both the academic and practitioner communities is required.

An area that deserves a great deal of attention in discussion of future research issues is research methodology. Although developing a strong knowledge base in research methodology is important in any field of study, the study of global supply chain management is particularly challenging. The complexity of research design increases dramatically when multiple firms and multiple entities within firms are involved in the process studied. Control of extraneous factors, development of appropriate measures, and representative sampling become very difficult challenges in research design in a global context. Similarly, the complexity associated with study of a phenomenon across cultures and countries makes research design very difficult. Even the best measures in one culture may be inappropriate in a different culture. Further, in some countries, availability of data is extremely limited. Research endeavors must include developing tools and techniques to research complex interfirm systems and processes, then to extend research methods appropriately to different cultures and different countries.

3

The Consequences of Supply Chain Management

Creating Value, Satisfaction, and Differential Advantage

NANCY W. NIX

Executive Summary

This chapter describes the overall objectives of supply chain management (SCM) of both creating value for customers and achieving differential advantage and improved profitability for supply chain firms. Dimensions of value that may be important to customers are described, and the mechanisms whereby differential advantage and improved profitability can be achieved for supply chain members are discussed.

This chapter will

- Point out that the supply chain is a complete value system delivering products and services to the end consumer
- Discuss the SCM objectives of customer value, customer satisfaction, and differential advantage, and describe the interrelationships between them
- Define customer value and highlight dimensions of value important to customers
- Discuss the critical steps in implementing a value delivery strategy
- Examine definitions of customer satisfaction and differential advantage

- Describe the role of SCM in creating differential advantage with the ultimate consumer
- Discuss the influence of customer satisfaction on customer behavior and financial performance

These discussions lead to the conclusions that

- The objective of SCM is to increase the differential or competitive advantage of the channel as a whole, rather than to increase the advantage of any single firm
- The means to accomplish differential advantage is through creating value for downstream customers greater than that offered by competitors
- Customer value is created through collaboration and cooperation to improve efficiency (lower cost) or market effectiveness (add benefits) in ways that are most valuable to key customers
- Value is not inherent in products or services but rather is perceived or experienced by the customer
- To compete through creating customer value, a firm must understand and deliver the value *perceived as important by its customers*
- Because the value perceived as important will differ across customer segments, a firm must identify the customer segments important to its long-term success and match the capability of the firm to delivering the value important to those key customers
- Value can be created at many points along the chain by making the customer firm at that point in the chain more effective in serving its markets or more efficient and cost-effective in its operations
- Delivering customer value in dimensions important to customers better than the competition leads to customer satisfaction and differential advantage
- By satisfying customers and achieving differential advantage, firms in a supply chain influence customers to make choices and behave in ways that improve the financial performance of the supply chain and the firms within it

The degree to which value is created for customers and the customer's perception of the value received relative to that offered by the competition both are reflected in the customer's satisfaction with the offering. Customers who are satisfied with value created in areas important to them are expected to behave in ways that are beneficial to a firm's or a supply chain's success. Purchase behavior, customer loyalty, and positive communications about products and services result from customer satisfaction and, at the same time, contribute to a firm's or supply chain's success. To achieve these objectives, supply chain managers must work collaboratively with customers and suppliers to identify and deliver value considered important by critical downstream customers.

Introduction

> Historically, what goes on between companies (in a supply chain) is aimed at how the pie will be divided among them. Nobody is focused on how to make the pie bigger. The purpose of SCM is for companies to work together to increase the size of the pie.
>
> —*Chemical industry executive*

One of the most dominant paradigms of competition concerns power—building sustainable positions of power in an industry among competitors, customers, and suppliers (Porter, 1985): in other words "dividing the pie." Supply chain management, on the other hand, is about competing on value—collaborating with customers and suppliers to create a position of strength in the marketplace based on the value delivered to the end consumer—in other words, working together to "increase the size of the pie."

As highlighted in Chapter 1, the overall objective of SCM is to increase the competitive advantage of the supply chain as a whole, rather than to increase the advantage of any single firm. As one interviewee put it, "The whole reason for managing the supply chain is prosperity, to allow each company to grow the kind of business they want to grow."

The means to accomplish this objective is through creating customer value superior to the competitor's value offering and, thus, to enhance customer satisfaction, either through improving efficiency (lower cost) or effectiveness (added benefits). The degree to which customers are satisfied by the value created in dimensions important to them influences purchase choices and behaviors that improve the financial performance of the supply chain and the firms within it.

Because it is the achievement of this related set of objectives—customer value, customer satisfaction, and differential advantage—that dictate the success of SCM endeavors, understanding the implications of each to SCM strategies and activities is critical. As illustrated in Figure 3.1, SCM management activities that improve efficiency or increase effectiveness for customers create customer value. It is important to note that value is not inherent in products and services, but rather is perceived and experienced by customers. The degree to which the value created is perceived as important to the customer, and is superior to that offered by the competition (or has a differential advantage), influences the customer's satisfaction. The customer's perception of differential

64

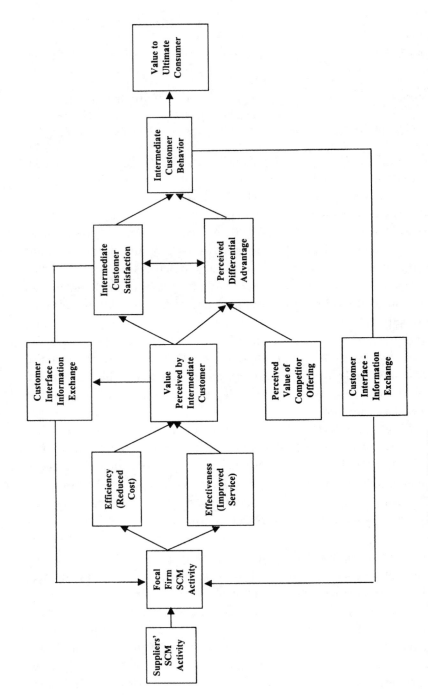

Figure 3.1. Consequences of Supply Chain Management

value and degree of satisfaction influences behavior toward the supplier firm as well as the value delivered to downstream customers.

The supply chain as a whole can be considered a complete value system delivering products and services to the end consumer. Value can be created at many points along the chain by making the customer firm at that point in the chain more effective in serving its markets, or more efficient and cost-effective in its operations (Slater & Narver, 1994b). The ultimate basis for value at each step along a supply chain is the role of the product or service in the value created for the ultimate consumer. It is the value needs of the ultimate consumer that dictate the intermediate customer's needs (Porter, 1985). Thus, an understanding of the entire supply chain is critical in identifying and delivering value that improves the competitiveness of the chain as a whole (Slater & Narver, 1994b; Woodruff, Locander, & Barnaby, 1991).

Although objectives of SCM are routinely described as those of creating value, customer satisfaction, and differential advantage for the supply chain as a whole, clearly this is a case of "easier said than done." Individual firms struggle to identify the value important to key customers and match their own firm's capability to the task at hand. Working across multiple firms to accomplish these same objectives is even more challenging. Little work has been done to guide firms in their endeavors to accomplish these objectives as a supply chain. Many important questions regarding how to apply value-based strategies in an SCM context remain to be addressed; and a first step toward achieving these objectives can be made if supply chain managers begin to ask these questions. For example, what is the process that should be used to identify and target key customers for the supply chain as a whole? How can firms locate and improve the most critical sources of value along the supply chain? What is the role of value creation and customer satisfaction at each intermediate customer in the chain? How can customer learning be shared across members in the supply chain? Only if individual firms begin to adopt a supply chain orientation—that is, to think from a supply chain perspective—can the objectives of SCM be realized.

In this chapter, customer value, is defined, dimensions of customer value important to customers are identified, and a process for developing and implementing value-based strategies is highlighted. The theoretical concepts of customer satisfaction and the influence of customer value on satisfaction are then reviewed, and the concept of differential advantage is defined. The expected influence of customer satisfaction on customer behavior and financial performance is then highlighted. Finally, managerial and research implications of developing and applying value-based strategies from a supply chain management context are discussed.

Creating Customer Value

As the business landscape has become more competitive, the ability of firms to acquire and keep important customers has become increasingly important to long-term success. It is five times as expensive to acquire a new customer than to keep an existing customer (Slater & Narver, 1994b); thus, investing in long-term relationships with customers is a key strategy for long-term success and profitability. Creating customer value is seen as a means of maintaining and enhancing long-term relationships with key customers. As such, it is important to understand what exactly customer value is and how firms can successfully identify and create customer value.

What Is Customer Value?

A key element of customer value is that it is *as perceived or experienced by the customer* (Day, 1994; Goodstein & Butz, 1998; Narver & Slater, 1990; Novack, Langley, & Rinehart, 1995; Woodruff & Gardial, 1996; Zeithaml, 1988). Goodstein and Butz (1998) describe value as the customer's perception of how well his or her needs are met, whereas Narver and Slater (1990) describe value as the difference between what the buyer perceives as expected benefits and expected sacrifice (total acquisition and use costs). Novack et al. (1995) define logistics value as the customer's perceptions of the relationship between the service performed and the service received. Although there are differences in precise definitions of what constitutes value, there is consensus that value is created through the experience and perspective of the customer and is not inherent in the products or services offered by a firm (Woodruff & Gardial, 1996). Thus, understanding customers and their needs and expectations becomes a critical first step toward creating value.

Among the various definitions of customer value found in the literature, there are several distinct approaches. One suggests that value is synonymous with economic utilities, in terms of form, place, time, and possession utilities (Fawcett & Fawcett, 1995). Research has shown, however, that the meaning of value held by the customer may differ at a higher level of abstraction, suggesting that utility models that do not distinguish between product and service attributes and more abstract meanings of value are insufficient (Zeithaml, 1988). Zeithaml (1988) found four different perceptions of value among consumers: (a) Value is low price, (b) value is whatever I want in a product, (c) value is the quality I get for the price I pay, and (d) value is what I get for what I give. For those who equated value with low price, the most significant dimension of value seemed to be what they had to give up. For those customers equating value with "whatever I want in a product," benefits seem to be the critical element in their perception of value. This might equate to a utility approach to value

(Zeithaml, 1988). For consumers who viewed value as the quality received in exchange for the price paid, value was perceived as the trade-off between a single benefit (quality) and a single sacrifice (price). Finally, those consumers who viewed value as "what I get for what I give" seemed to consider all the relevant benefits as well as all the relevant sacrifices or costs (Zeithaml, 1988). Thus, customer value must be defined from the customer's perspective, based on the relative importance *to the customer* of the various elements of perceived price, perceived total cost of acquisition and use, and perceived benefits of owning or using the product or service.

Dimensions of Customer Value

Slater and Narver (1994b) suggest that the two critical dimensions of customer value are efficiency and effectiveness. At any point along a supply chain, value can be created by making the customer firm either more efficient in its operations, thus lowering cost, or more effective in its markets. Efficiency improvements influence the cost side of the value equation either through reducing total cost to the customer or through contributing to the efficiency of the customer's operations, thus reducing cost to downstream customers. Effectiveness, on the other hand, makes the customer more successful by increasing the perceived benefits of owning or using products or services.

Conceptualizing the critical value dimensions as efficiency and effectiveness is consistent with the model of competitive advantage based on cost leadership and/or differentiation through superior value. The conceptual meaning of the word "value" in this chapter is somewhat different, however, from that used by Porter (1985) and requires clarification. Porter (1985) differentiates between a low-cost strategy and a differentiation strategy, describing the differentiation strategy as one in which a firm "seeks to be unique in its industry along . . . dimensions that are widely valued by buyers." (p. 4) Research indicates, however, that customers' perceptions of value are based on relative importance of elements of both benefits received and sacrifices made, with price being an important component of the sacrifice. Thus, for purposes of this discussion, both efficiency and effectiveness are considered important elements of creating value for customers, with cost reduction being one component of efficiency.

Treacy and Wiersema (1993) suggest that companies have differentiated themselves by focusing on superior performance in one of three value disciplines—operational excellence, customer intimacy, or product leadership. Operational excellence provides customers with reliable products or services at competitive prices and minimal inconvenience, thus reducing the customer's perceived costs of purchase and use (efficiency). For example, Dell Computer created a new model of product delivery that allowed customers to acquire state-of-the-art technology more easily and inexpensively. By cutting out the middleman and selling directly to customers, Dell was able to build to order, reduce inventories, and cut costs, achieving an advantage over Compaq and other PC manufacturers that focused on products and continued to sell through the dealer system (Treacy & Wiersema, 1993).

Firms pursuing a strategy of customer intimacy focus on tailoring products and services to fit the needs, or create value, for specific segments of customers (effectiveness). The focus is on building loyalty and long-term relationships among strategic customer segments, trading off the investment required against the customer's lifetime value to the company. For example, Home Depot has built its business strategy around meeting customers' total need for products, information, and service to help them solve their home-repair problems. Thus, the first priority of store personnel is to make sure that the customers get exactly what they need, and they will spend whatever time is required to ensure this. For firms pursuing a customer intimacy strategy, maintaining a system that can differentiate quickly between customers based on both services required and importance is key to their success.

A product leadership strategy is one that strives to produce a "continuous stream of state-of-the-art products and services" (Treacy & Wiersema, 1993, p. 89) and is also aimed at market effectiveness. A product leadership strategy requires creativity in recognizing and embracing new ideas, innovative capability that allows the firm to commercialize new ideas quickly, and relentless pursuit of new solutions to the problems that its latest product or service has solved (i.e., continuous innovation). Such a product leadership strategy is exemplified by Vistakon, Inc., a division of Johnson & Johnson, with its development and introduction of disposable contact lenses. In 1983, a new, inexpensive manufacturing technique developed by an ophthalmologist in Copenhagen was brought to the attention of Vistakon's president by an executive in another subsidiary of J&J in Denmark. These two executives bought rights to the technology, assembled an organization to develop the product, and built a manufacturing facility to produce the disposable lenses in a 4-year period. By 1991, 8 years after learning of this technology, Vistakon's sales had increased more than tenfold, and it had captured a 25% share of the U.S. contact-lens market. The division also continued to investigate new materials to extend the wearability of the lenses as well as technologies that might replace them. By being open-minded to new ideas and creating a culture that allowed it to quickly develop and introduce a new product, Vistakon was able to successfully capture a product leadership position in the marketplace.

The choice of value discipline on which a firm will focus is really based on the segment of customer market it chooses to serve and the definition of value important to that segment. One segment will define value in terms of the price, convenience, and quality matrix, and a primary mechanism for delivering value will be improved efficiency. A second segment will define value in terms of obtaining precisely what they want or need, even though they may need to make some sacrifice in terms of pricing and delivery to obtain it. The third segment will value new and unusual products (Treacy & Wiersema, 1993). The primary mechanism for serving the latter two segments is through improved effectiveness. For intermediate customers in a supply chain, the type of product or service valued depends on the market segments they in turn serve.

To create value for customers, a firm must first understand how the customer defines value, then identify those dimensions of value that are of critical or strategic importance. Those dimensions that have the greatest impact on the customer's satisfaction or purchase decisions are those that are most critical (Woodruff & Gardial, 1996). The ability to identify those strategically critical value dimensions and design and deliver products and services that deliver value along those dimensions is critical to achieving the objectives of differential advantage and long-term profitability. A key issue facing supply chain managers is how to identify and link those complementary or synergistic capabilities among multiple firms to deliver value effectively along the dimensions identified as important to the supply chain's ultimate consumer.

Delivering Customer Value

After a U.S. luxury car manufacturer surveyed its customers about specific product and service features and benefits, it received responses that indicated that customers were "highly satisfied." The company was quite surprised when many of those customers traded in their American car for a luxury import. The surveys it had used to learn about its customers had captured customers' satisfaction with the value dimensions that the manufacturer perceived to be important rather than those perceived to be important by customers (Thompson, 1998). To deliver customer value, a firm must be able to develop a clear understanding of exactly what kind of value a customer really wants or needs.

Market-driven firms develop the capability to gather, interpret, and use market information in a systematic, thoughtful, and anticipatory way (Day, 1994). This is an important first step in the process of delivering value to customers. Woodruff and Gardial (1996) identify a series of critical steps that managers can utilize to develop and implement a value delivery strategy.

1. *Identify the value.* The ability to understand the dimensions of value important to customers is a critical first step in planning a customer value delivery strategy.
2. *Choose the value.* The firm must determine which customer segment it will service. The challenge in this step is to understand the organization's capabilities or core competencies, then match them against the value sought by customers in the various segments.
3. *Provide the value.* The value delivery strategy must be translated into action. All aspects of the firm's offerings must be designed to deliver an integrated product and service offering that meets the needs of target customers. Products or services, support or auxiliary services, distribution or delivery services, and pricing must all be considered in the implementation process.

4. *Communicate the value.* An integrated communications campaign should help customers understand the value that is offered. Advertising, promotional activities, and personal communications need to consistently communicate the value of the firm's offering.

5. *Assess the delivered value.* In this step, the actual delivery process is evaluated to determine whether improvements are needed. Understandings of how customers perceive the actual delivered value, how satisfied they are, and how they perceive the value relative to competitors' offerings are all critical in assessing the delivered value.

Differential advantage can be achieved only when customers are satisfied and perceive the delivered value of the firm's product or service offering as superior to the competition in areas important to them. Each step in the process outlined above offers the potential for a firm to gain an advantage over the competition. Superior capability in understanding customer value, matching organizational capability to customers' desired value, or implementing and continuously improving the delivery process all offer the potential for advantage (Woodruff & Gardial, 1996). The challenge for firms in a supply chain is to collaboratively identify and deliver value important to the ultimate consumer in the supply chain in a manner superior to that of competing supply chains.

Customer Satisfaction

Customer value and customer satisfaction are related but different concepts, as was seen in the case of the luxury car manufacturer whose customers were "highly satisfied" but chose to purchase another manufacturer's product (Goodstein & Butz, 1998; Thompson, 1998; Woodruff & Gardial, 1996). Customer value is the nature of the relationship between the user and the product or service, and customer satisfaction is the customer's reaction to the value received from the purchase or utilization of the offering (Woodruff & Gardial, 1996).

Defining Customer Satisfaction

The dominant theory of customer satisfaction is the expectancy-disconfirmation model (Oliver, 1980; Woodruff, Cadotte, & Jenkins, 1983; Woodruff & Gardial, 1996). In this model, the customer's satisfaction is determined based on the customer's perception of product/service performance compared to some standard that represents the customer's expectation. The satisfaction or dissatisfaction of customers is based on their evaluation or judgment of the difference between what was expected and what was received

(Woodruff & Gardial, 1996). Some of the key factors in the comparison are highlighted below.

> *Expectations* represent what the customer believes about how a product will perform. These expectations may be based on experience with the particular product, with a competitor's brand, or with a substitute product.
>
> *Ideals* represent how the customer would like the product to perform. The value dimensions most important to customers are reflected in the ideal standard.
>
> *Promises* made by market communications (e.g., advertisements, sales communications, or corporate communications) may be used as a standard.
>
> *Industry norms* are accepted standards within an industry or product category that may influence the comparison standard.

Customer satisfaction represents the customer's reaction to his or her perception of the value received as a result of using a particular product or service. That reaction will be influenced by the desired value (ideal standard) as well as by the perceived value of competitive offerings (industry norms, expectations based on use of competitor products) (Woodruff & Gardial, 1996). Thus, customer satisfaction is influenced by the perception of the value delivered as well as by the perception of the value offered by competition, as depicted in Figure 3.1. Although customer value represents what the customer desires (future state), customer satisfaction provides a historical perspective on how well the firm is performing in the value delivery process.

Thus, as highlighted earlier, customer value and customer satisfaction are related, but different. Customer value represents what the customer desires from a product or service independent of a particular offering, whereas customer satisfaction represents a customer's reaction to what he or she has received. Customer value defines the objective of the firm in creating a product or service offering, thus providing the firm with direction about what it should do to create value and enhance customer satisfaction. Customer satisfaction provides the organization with feedback as to how well it is doing in its efforts (Woodruff & Gardial, 1996).

Differential Advantage

The creation of customer value, an objective of SCM, is simply a means to other ends. A primary objective, one achieved through the creation of customer value, is that of differential advantage. Differential advantage, in turn, is expected to enhance customer satisfaction and, ultimately, the profitability and long-term success of the firm. Once again, the terminology in the literature is inconsistent, and the overlap in the utilization of the terms *competitive advantage*, *comparative advantage*, and *differential advantage* can be quite confusing (Day, 1994; Day & Wensley, 1988; Hunt & Morgan, 1995; Thompson, 1998; Woodruff & Gardial, 1996).

The terms *comparative advantage* and *competitive advantage* have been used interchangeably with *distinctive competence* or *distinctive capability*, meaning relative superiority in skills and resources (Day, 1994; Day & Wensley, 1988; Thompson, 1998). On the other hand, *competitive advantage* and *differential advantage* are used interchangeably with *positional superiority*, meaning relative superiority in delivering value or achieving lower cost in the marketplace (Alderson, 1957; Day & Wensley, 1988). In other words, if the customer perceives that the value created with the product or service offering of the firm is more important to him or her than that created by the competitors' product or offering, differential advantage is achieved in the marketplace. In this book, the terms *competitive advantage* and *differential advantage* are used interchangeably and represent relative superiority in delivering value as perceived by customers.

Achieving Differential Advantage Through SCM

Several approaches to achieving a superior competitive position have been identified in the literature. The first is the competitive-forces approach, which emphasizes the intensity of competition in an industry and the ability to achieve and defend a position of low cost or differentiation in an attractive market segment. Strategies are aimed at making preemptive moves that keep competitors off balance and allow the firm to maintain a favorable balance of power (Day, 1994; Porter, 1985).

A second approach is the capabilities approach, which is focused on developing and maintaining distinctive skills and resources that enable the firm to deliver superior customer value or deliver value more cost-effectively (Day, 1994). SCM utilizes a capabilities approach to achieving differential advantage through the creation and delivery of customer value.

Day (1994) describes distinctive capabilities as those superior capabilities that allow a firm to outperform the competition in ways that are important to customers and difficult to match. Tests of distinctiveness include the following:

1. Does it make a disproportionate contribution to providing superior customer value or to delivering value most cost-effectively?
2. Can it be readily matched by rivals? That is, is it difficult to imitate?
3. Is it robust enough that it can be used in different ways to readily adapt to environmental change?

Day (1994) categorizes distinctive capabilities in three ways:

1. Capabilities deployed *inside out* are activities with an internal emphasis that are activated in response to external forces.

2. Conversely, *outside-in* capabilities are aimed at anticipating market requirements, monitoring competitors, and creating long-term relationships with customers, channel members, and suppliers.

3. *Spanning capabilities* are required to integrate the inside-out and outside-in capabilities.

Day (1994) notes that the most distinctive features of market-driven organizations are their market sensing and customer linking capabilities.

The focus of SCM is on creating value for the ultimate consumer and differential advantage for the supply chain as a whole. Thus, the ability of firms in the supply chain to collectively utilize market sensing and customer linking capabilities to serve the end consumer more efficiently and effectively is critical to achieving competitive advantage for the supply chain as a whole. Coordination and collaboration among firms is aimed at building distinctive capability among the firms along the chain, enabling the supply chain to compete based on delivering superior value to consumers.

Influencing Customer Behavior

The ultimate objective of value-creating activities along the supply chain is to improve the financial performance and long-term success of the individual firms in the chain. As noted by one interviewee,

> A key objective of SCM is the upside lift or revenue growth that you can get through customer responsiveness, which can lead to market share improvement and increase in shareholder value. This can only be achieved if the value delivered leads to satisfied customers who, in turn, behave in ways that are beneficial to the firms in the supply chain.

Repeat purchases, customer loyalty, and positive word of mouth communications to other consumers about the product or service offering have all been linked to customer satisfaction and value (Oliver, 1980; Westbrook, 1987; Woodruff et al., 1983; Woodruff & Gardial, 1996). These examples of "customer responsiveness" are expected to result in improved share or profitability for firms (Day & Wensley, 1988).

It is also important to note, however, that intermediate firms along the supply chain are also customers in the process, and to ask how the creation of value for intermediate customers influences the behavior in the channel. For example, as highlighted by a logistics executive interviewed by the research team,

A distributor can influence the efficiency of the personnel in a retail store by the way merchandise is shipped and packaged. If the merchandise is shipped so that the retail personnel can quickly get it on the shelves, more time can be devoted to the customers.

Fawcett and Fawcett (1995) note that in a supply chain context customer success rather than customer satisfaction is the objective of the value-creation process, requiring that a firm understand what is important to its customers' customers and help immediate customers deliver that value downstream. There is some indication that delivering higher levels of service to immediate channel partners can influence those partners to deliver higher levels of service to their downstream customers (Faulds & Mangold, 1995). A question for future research is whether customer satisfaction among intermediate customers along the supply chain leads to greater loyalty toward upstream partners and thus influences the quality of the relationship such that communications, collaboration, and cooperation are improved.

Conclusions

To achieve the objectives of SCM, supply chain managers must first adopt a supply chain orientation and begin to think about the supply chain as a single value system. Firms in a supply chain represent sequential value-adding steps in a process aimed at delivering value to the ultimate consumer. It is important for firms to recognize that, to be successful, they can no longer think about competing based on power positions with customers and suppliers. Rather, they must think about developing distinctive capabilities focused on delivering greater value to the end consumer. Questions must be addressed of how to identify target consumer segments and how to understand the value dimensions important to those consumer segments for the supply chain as a whole. Identifying the capabilities required to deliver value to target segments and effectively utilizing capabilities at the most appropriate point along the chain are also critical tasks. Finally, an important challenge lies in developing measures that can assess performance of the supply chain and pinpoint areas of improvement, based on the actual value delivered to the end consumer.

It is important to note that SCM is not an objective but rather a means to an end. It is an approach aimed at creating value, satisfying customers, and achieving differential advantage as a means of enhancing the profitability and long-term success of supply chain participants. As noted by one interviewee, SCM requires an investment of time and resources, so "there has to be a payback." Like any other investment, decisions should be made on the basis of the potential for return on investment. If resources are focused on SCM initiatives that improve the efficiency or effectiveness of the entire system and provide differential advantage with the end user, the potential for return on investment is great. Otherwise, as suggested by one executive we interviewed, "there is the risk that the resource drain will cause a firm to lose focus and become less competitive individually in its role within the supply chain." Identifying the costs associated with pursuing an SCM strategy and appropriately weighing those costs against potential benefits are critical to making sound decisions about investment in SCM initiatives.

Most of the research pertaining to customer value and customer satisfaction has reflected the perspective of a dyad—examining value as perceived by a single customer, and satisfaction of a direct customer with the product or service offering of the supplier. When viewed from a supply chain perspective, the focus of creating value must take into account multiple customers and their activities aimed at creating value for an end consumer. This difference in approach raises multiple questions that warrant further research.

- How is the value desired by intermediate customers influenced by their perceptions of the value desired by their downstream customers?
- Are there values important to intermediate customers that do not contribute to value created downstream but are still important for suppliers to consider in an SCM context?
- What is the role of value and satisfaction at the intermediate customer?
- How might value and satisfaction influence the intermediate customer's behavior toward upstream suppliers?
- How will it influence behavior toward downstream customers?

A critical component of competing on value is the ability to learn about key customers and disseminate and utilize that knowledge throughout the organization. Research is needed to develop tools and techniques that will enable supply chain partners to target key supply chain consumers, to acquire information about the ultimate consumer's values and needs, and to effectively disseminate and utilize that knowledge throughout the supply chain.

Finally, an objective of SCM is that of creating differential advantage —delivering value to consumers that is superior to the competition's. In a supply chain context, however, the competition no longer can be viewed as individual firms competing for customers at the next level in the channel. In fact, one interviewee suggested that "at any given time, companies could be members of different supply chains which might require them to compete against each other at one point in time and cooperate with each other at another point in time." Tools and techniques to identify competition in a supply chain context, and to understand the distinctive capability and value offered by competitors to the ultimate consumer, are important components of being able to achieve differential advantage.

SCM is an approach that requires firms to work collaboratively to deliver superior value to the ultimate consumer, thereby increasing consumer satisfaction and influencing consumer choice. The belief is that satisfied consumers will be loyal customers who will continue to purchase a firm's or supply chain's goods and services, as well as influence others to purchase those same goods and services. This approach requires firms to identify important consumer segments, understand the value required by those consumers, and develop and deliver products and services that meet those consumers needs. The challenges for firms are to understand the role of each member of the chain in the entire delivery system and to focus beyond the immediate customer at each link in the chain to the ultimate consumer. Only by delivering superior value to the ultimate consumer can the chain as a whole achieve the objective of differential advantage that will enhance the performance of the chain as a whole, as well as that of the individual members of the chain.

4

The Role of Marketing in Supply Chain Management

SOONHONG MIN

Executive Summary

Supply chain management (SCM) is, by nature, a cross-function phenomenon. This chapter proposes that the ideas of the marketing concept, a market orientation, relationship marketing, and supply chain management are not separate; they are inextricably intertwined. The main purpose of this chapter is to highlight the role of marketing in the implementation of supply chain management by suggesting the cause-and-effect relationships among several important concepts in business research and practice: the marketing concept, a market orientation, relationship marketing, and SCM.

This chapter will

- Describe the marketing concept, a market orientation, and their influences on the management of a firm and a supply chain
- Provide an explanation of how relationship marketing affects supply chain management as well as the management of a firm
- Propose an integrated framework that shows the relationships among the marketing concept, a market orientation, relationship marketing, and supply chain management
- Present the implications of this framework

This discussion will lead to the conclusions that

- The objective of marketing is creating exchanges, and the output of it is customer satisfaction
- The marketing concept consists of the three pillars: (a) customer focus, (b) coordinated marketing, and (c) profitability
- The marketing concept is a business philosophy guiding a firm toward customer satisfaction at a profit
- A market orientation is the implementation of that philosophy, forcing the firm to generate, disseminate, and respond to market information
- The marketing concept, as a business philosophy, not only provides the philosophical foundation of a market orientation but also plays an important role in the management of a firm, inter-functional relationships, and the implementation of SCM
- A market orientation also affects the management of a firm, interfirm relationships, and a supply chain. That is, a market orientation leads a firm to focus on market information generation, dissemination, and responsiveness to satisfy customers, coordinate its marketing efforts, redefine the responsibilities of each function, restructure its organizational system, and achieve superior business performance. At the same time, a market orientation provides an environment that encourages a firm in its efforts to develop, maintain, and enhance close relationships with other firms; achieve organizational learning from other firms; and build commitment, trust, and cooperative norms in the relationships with other firms
- A market orientation is achieved both inside and outside a firm to recognize and respond to customers' needs and to obtain experiences, products, skills, technologies, and knowledge from outside the firm that are not available to other competitors
- A market orientation promotes the implementation of SCM
- Relationship marketing aims at establishing, maintaining, and enhancing either dyadic relationships or multiple relationships in a supply chain to create better customer value
- Relationship marketing helps achieve such objectives of SCM as efficiency (i.e., cost reduction) and effectiveness (i.e., customer service) through increased cooperation in close long-term interfirm relationships among the supply chain partners
- With the help of the marketing concept, a market orientation, and relationship marketing, SCM achieves differential advantage for the supply chain and its partners by reducing costs and investments, and by improving customer service

Supply chain management benefits by such concepts as the marketing concept, a market orientation, and relationship marketing. Thus, the role of marketing through the marketing concept, a market orientation, and relationship marketing is essential for the success of supply chain management.

Introduction

The concept of supply chain management originated in the logistics literature (Bowersox, Carter, & Monczka, 1985; Christopher, 1994; Jones & Riley, 1985), and logistics has continued to have a significant impact on the concept (Bechtel & Jayaram, 1997). The strong influence of logistics in the process of conceptualizing SCM seems to be caused by the weight given to inventory reduction and stock availability issues as the objectives of the implementation of SCM. The purpose of this chapter, however, is to highlight the role of marketing in the implementation of SCM. The approach taken is to review several important concepts in the discipline of marketing—the marketing concept, a market orientation, and relationship marketing, as well as the American Marketing Association's (AMA) definition of marketing—to explore the key linkages between marketing management and supply chain management.

First, the AMA's 1985 definition of marketing and its core concepts are reviewed. Second, the marketing concept, a market orientation, and their influences on the management of a firm and a supply chain are described. Third, an explanation of how relationship marketing affects supply chain management, as well as the management of a firm, is provided. Fourth, an integrated framework that shows the relationships among the marketing concept, a market orientation, relationship marketing, and supply chain management is proposed. Fifth, the implications of this framework are presented.

Definition of Marketing

Kotler (1972) proposed that the essence of marketing is the *transaction*, defined as *exchange of values* actually made between parties. Thus, marketing is specifically concerned with how transactions are created, stimulated, facilitated, and valued. Kotler's delineation of marketing is well reflected in the official definition of the AMA. According to the AMA, marketing is "the process of planning and executing the conception, pricing, promotion, and distribution of ideas, goods, and services to *create exchanges that satisfy individual and organizational goals*." In other words, the objective of marketing is creating exchanges, and the output of it is customer satisfaction.

Marketing scholars (Churchill & Peter, 1995; Kotler, 1997) have defined an exchange as a process in which two or more parties voluntarily provide something of value to each other. According to Kotler (1997), a transaction takes place when an agreement is reached, whereas exchange is the process to produce an agreement. Exchange takes place within a *market*, which is defined as a collection of buyers and sellers who interact, resulting in the possibility for exchange (Pindyck & Rubinfeld, 1992). In this context, Churchill and Peter (1995) proposed that various parties are involved in the marketing effort: firms that produce goods or services, resellers of the goods and services (such as stores), and customers or clients.

The Marketing Concept and a Market Orientation

The marketing concept is essentially a business philosophy (cf. Barksdale & Darden, 1971; McNamara, 1972). Specifically, the marketing concept is the philosophical foundation of a market orientation (Jaworski & Kohli, 1993). Jaworski and Kohli (1993) conceptualized a market orientation as the implementation of the marketing concept, in much the same way that in this book we conceptualize SCM as the implementation of an SCO. Since its introduction in the early 1950s, the marketing concept has represented a cornerstone of marketing thought (see Borch, 1957; Kohli & Jaworski, 1990; McKitterick, 1957).

Conceptualization of the Marketing Concept

Felton (1959) defined the marketing concept as "a corporate state of mind that insists on the integration and coordination of all the marketing functions which, in turn, are melted with all other corporate functions, for the basic purpose of producing maximum long-range corporate profits" (p. 55). King (1965) proposed that the marketing concept is concerned with profits and return on investment as well as with consumer orientation. McCarthy and Perreault (1984) suggested that an organization aims all its efforts at satisfying its customers at a profit under the marketing concept. While delineating the marketing concept, Drucker (1954) argued that customer satisfaction lies at the center of the marketing concept and, thus, profit is not the objective but the reward for creating a satisfied customer. Based upon the previous conceptualizations of the market orientation (e.g., Barksdale & Darden, 1971; Drucker, 1954; Felton, 1959; King, 1965; McCarthy & Perreault, 1984; McNamara, 1972), Kohli and Jaworski (1990) argued that the marketing concept consists of three pillars: (a) customer focus, (b) coordinated marketing, and (c) profitability.

Impacts of the Marketing Concept

The marketing concept has strong influences on the management of a firm, an interfirm relationship, and the supply chain (Figure 4.1). The marketing concept, as a business philosophy, guides firms to look for customer satisfaction at a profit in a coordinated manner. Webster (1992) proposed that marketing as a

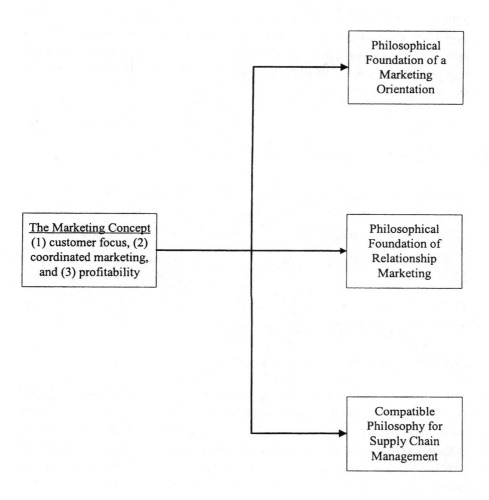

Figure 4.1. The Impacts of the Marketing Concept

culture means a basic set of values and beliefs about the importance of the customer, expressed by the marketing concept, that guide the firm. As such, the marketing concept provides the philosophical foundation for individuals' activities or behaviors (called a market orientation) within a firm.

Cravens (1995) argued that the customer is at the center of the relationship marketing paradigm. In other words, the marketing concept, as a business philosophy, also guides a firm's behaviors (called relationship marketing) to develop, maintain, and enhance interfirm relationships to satisfy customers.

The marketing concept is a necessary component for implementing SCM. Cooper, Ellram, Gardner, and Hanks (1997) suggested that one of the components of the implementation of SCM is a compatible corporate philosophy of partners, at least for key relationships. Nabisco executives also proposed, "Successful SCM begins and ends with the customer. Satisfying customers must always remain the unswerving objectives of (SCM)" (Andraski, Wisdo, & Blasgen, 1996, p. 31). The marketing concept (i.e., the philosophical foundation of a firm's activities) should be one of the compatible philosophies of supply chain partners so that all partners in the supply chain strive to satisfy customers at a profit through inter-functional coordination within and among the supply chain partners. A director with a third-party logistics provider that we interviewed contended that

> sharing is the key item in a model of supply chain management—three or more contiguous companies sharing a common vision and plan for their supply chain, and those other things resulting from it.

Thus, under the marketing philosophy, supply chain partners would become more willing to be efficient (i.e., cost reduction) and more effective (i.e., customer service) toward a common goal (i.e., customer satisfaction at a profit).

Conceptualization of a Market Orientation

Kohli and Jaworski (1990) proposed that a market orientation is the implementation of the marketing concept and that it is composed of three sets of organization-wide activities: (a) *generation* of market intelligence pertaining to current and future customer needs, (b) *dissemination* of the intelligence across departments, and (c) *responsiveness* to market intelligence. As such, the definition of a market orientation focuses on specific behaviors and, therefore, facilitates operationalizing the market orientation construct (Jaworski & Kohli, 1993).

Narver and Slater (1990) defined a market orientation as an organizational culture in which all employees are committed to the continuous creation of superior value for customers through three behavioral components: customer orientation, competitor orientation, and inter-functional coordination. Culture is defined as the pattern of shared values and beliefs that help individuals understand organizational functioning and, thus, provide them with norms for behavior in the organization (Deshpande & Webster, 1989). By the same token, Deshpande, Farley, and Webster (1993) claimed that a market orientation is a set of attitudes or beliefs that should be pervasive throughout the company. Slater and Narver (1994a) argued that their definition of a market orientation is commensurable with that of Kohli and Jaworski (1990; Jaworski & Kohli, 1993) because the measures of market orientation consist of three behavioral components, each of which involves market intelligence generation, dissemination, and managerial action.

Regardless of Slater and Narver's (1994a) commensurability argument, it is proposed that the different conceptualizations of a market orientation as a culture and a set of behaviors are not identical, and the definition of a market orientation as an organizational culture has a critical weakness because it contains circular logic. Deshpande and Webster (1989) defined the marketing concept as referring to a distinct organizational culture, a fundamental shared set of beliefs and values that put the customer in the center of the firm's thinking about strategy and operations. Accepting Deshpande and Webster's (1989) definition of the marketing concept as an organizational culture, Narver and Slater (1990; Slater & Narver, 1994a) and Deshpande et al. (1993) also interpreted a market orientation as an organizational culture. As such, if we take the conceptualization of a market orientation as an organizational culture, we would make a mistake of identifying the marketing concept as a market orientation. Thus, I propose to adopt Kohli and Jaworski's (1990) conceptualization of market orientation as the implementation of the marketing concept (culture).

Impacts of a Market Orientation

A conceptual model of the impacts of a market orientation is presented in Figure 4.2.

Management of a Firm

A market orientation provides a *unifying focus* for the efforts and projects of individuals and departments within a firm (Kohli & Jaworski, 1990). Slater and Narver (1995) also argued that a market orientation is valuable because it focuses the firm on (a) continuously collecting information about target customers' needs and competitors' capabilities and (b) using this information to create continuously superior customer value. A director with a third-party logistics provider we interviewed pointed out that

> in many cases, logistics operations work on operational improvements, not even understanding the financial implications for their company in terms of how they might restructure or change their logistics or supply chain model.

To prevent the suboptimization problem, a firm needs a unifying focus, such as a market orientation.

A market orientation encourages *inter-functional coordination* within a firm. Inter-functional coordination is a firm's coordinated efforts, involving more than the marketing department, to create superior value for the buyers (Narver & Slater, 1990). Customer satisfaction, which is the ultimate goal of a market orientation and the measure of the created customer value by a firm, is affected by many factors that lie both inside and outside the scope of the

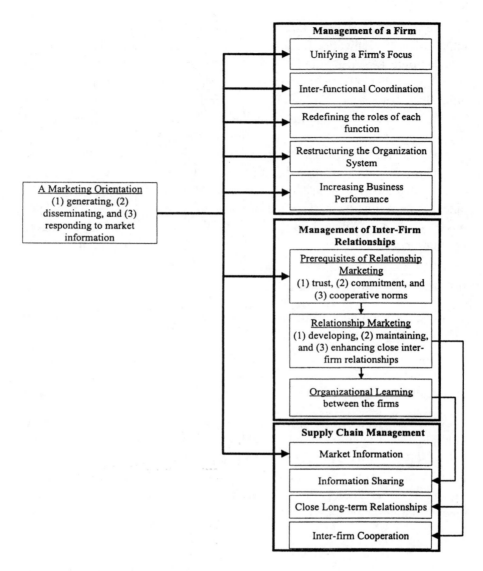

Figure 4.2.   The Impacts of a Marketing Orientation

marketing department (Kotler, 1997). For example, delivery reliability, invoice accuracy, invoice clarity, and personnel are major factors that determine customer satisfaction. By the same token, Day (1994) argued that a market orientation supports the value of thorough market intelligence and the necessity of functionally coordinated actions directed at gaining a competitive advantage that, in turn, brings the firm higher performance.

A market orientation requires a firm to *redefine the roles of each function* within a firm. Narver and Slater (1990) argued that a seller's creation of value for buyers is analogous to a symphony orchestra in which the contribution of each subgroup is tailored and integrated by a conductor. Thus, in addition to traditional marketing activities, marketing should perform a guiding and coordinating role to make sure that the rest of the company delivers on customers' expectations and its own promises (Kotler, 1997). A director with a global beverage producer we interviewed illustrated the coordinating role of marketing in a supply chain context:

> Marketing takes charge of and links the operational execution of channel package strategies that, in turn, coordinate all the activities the company performs in the supply chain all the way back to concentrate suppliers.

In other words, a market orientation becomes instrumental in coordinating the activities of all departments, with the marketing function playing a pivotal role in the success of the firm because everyone is involved in marketing activities.

The responsibilities of functions other than marketing are also broadly redefined so that everyone within the firm becomes a marketer—either on a full-time or part-time basis (Gummensson, 1996)—because any individual in any function in a firm can potentially contribute to the creation of value for customers (Porter, 1985). By the same token, Webster (1988) claimed that marketing could no longer be the sole responsibility of a few specialists; rather, everyone in the firm must be charged with responsibility for understanding customers and contributing to developing and delivering value for them.

A market orientation forces a firm to *restructure its organizational system.* As inter-functionally coordinated actions prevail within a firm and the responsibilities of each function are redefined, the boundaries between each function become blurred. For example, a vice president of customer operations at an office supplies firm we interviewed stated:

> Logistics managers, as a part of the sales teams, report to me and, therefore, salespeople can acquire logistics managers' assistance whenever logistics discussion comes up with their customers. Logistics managers also play a role as customer advocates for logistics issues inside the firm, suggesting breaking cases or shipping partial cases to satisfy customers' needs.

Because the marketing concept is concerned with company-wide efforts (i.e., a market orientation), marketing is not interpreted as a separate management function but rather the whole business as seen from the customer's point of view (Drucker, 1954; Levitt, 1960; McKitterick, 1957). At the extreme, the marketing function could disappear as a distinct management function and specialty (Day, 1992). Thus, Kotler (1997) proposed that a firm should consider managing a set of fundamental business processes, rather than independent functional departments, to create more efficient and effective responses to fulfill customer satisfaction.

Finally, a market orientation should bring superior *business performance* to the firm. Research has found empirical evidence of the positive relationship between a market orientation and a firm's performance (Jaworski & Kohli, 1993; Narver & Slater, 1990; Slater & Narver, 1994a). For example, Kohli and Jaworski (1990) found that a firm's financial performance—return on investment (ROI) and return on assets (ROA)—and employee-related performances of organizational commitment and esprit de corps are positively related to a firm's degree of market orientation. Narver and Slater (1990; Slater & Narver, 1994a) also found a positive relationship between a firm's market orientation and its sales growth and new product success. Deshpande et al. (1993) found a positive relationship between a firm's market orientation and its perceived performance in terms of profitability, firm size, market share, and growth rate relative to competitors. A market orientation thus contributes to a firm's increased business performance.

Management of Interfirm Relationships

The influences of a market orientation do not stop within the boundaries of the firm but extend to interfirm relationships with customers, suppliers, and distributors. Thus, a market orientation provides an environment in which relationship marketing is nurtured.

Nurturing relationship marketing through a market orientation starts with developing commitment, trust, and cooperative norms between the firms. Siguaw, Simpson, and Baker (1998) found that a supplier's market orientation affects its distributor's *commitment* to the relationship and that the distributor's market orientation has a direct effect on its *trust* and perception of *cooperative norms*. Moorman, Deshpande, and Zaltman (1993) defined commitment as an enduring desire to maintain a valued relationship. Because a market orientation requires a supplier to devote considerable resources to satisfying distributors' needs, the distributor commits to maintain the relationship with such a devoted supplier (Siguaw et al., 1998).

Trust is a willingness to rely on an exchange partner in whom one has confidence. Siguaw et al. (1998) argued that a supplier's market orientation contributes to a distributor's trust through (a) voluntary information and advantage sharing with the distributor, (b) favorable motives and intentions passed on to the distributor, and (c) open communications and responsiveness to customer needs.

Cooperative norms reflect the belief that both parties in a relationship must combine their efforts and cooperate to be successful (Cannon & Perreault, 1997). If a supplier is market oriented and working to satisfy a distributor's needs, the distributor is likely to perceive cooperative norms in the dyadic relationship because both parties are working toward the mutual goal of need satisfaction (Siguaw et al., 1998). According to several authors (e.g., Berry, 1995;

Grönroos, 1995; Sheth & Parvatiyar, 1995), the relationship variables such as commitment, trust, and cooperative norms are prerequisites of relationship marketing. Hence, a market orientation influences the implementation of relationship marketing through helping firms to build commitment, trust, and cooperative norms, all of which are prerequisites of relationship marketing.

A market orientation—by its nature—requires close interfirm relationships that are the sources of information outside the firm. Kohli and Jaworski (1990) claim that the market, which is the unit of analysis of a market orientation, includes end users and distributors as well as exogenous forces that affect their needs and preferences. Therefore, a firm should have intimate relationships with its customers to closely monitor their current and future needs and to make sure that customers obtain what they want from the firm. In addition, the firm should have close relationships with distributors, suppliers, and any other participants in the market to identify influences of those market participants on customers' needs and preferences.

Webster (1992) claims that *organizational learning* requires close and extensive relationships with customers, suppliers, and other key constituencies. Other researchers (e.g., Kanter, 1989) also have proposed the strategies of learning from others through benchmarking, forming joint ventures, networking, developing strategic alliances, and working with lead customers to recognize strong needs before the rest of the market, then find solutions to those needs. Organizational learning consists of information acquisition, dissemination, and shared interpretation of information across a firm (Sinkula, 1994). According to Slater and Narver (1995), a market orientation and organizational learning are inseparable.

Like the influences of a marketing orientation, organizational learning does not stop within the boundary of a firm but extends outside the firm. Lei, Slocum, and Pitts (1997) state that all strategic alliances may be thought of as alignments between two or more firms in which the partners seek to learn and to acquire from each other products, skills, technologies, and knowledge that are not available to competitors. As such, organizational learning is practiced within a firm and then extended outside the firm. Thus, organizational learning cannot be separated from close relationships with other firms, and it is posited here that a market orientation directs a firm to move toward relationship marketing to deal with the increasing complexity of building and learning new sources of competitive advantage beyond the firm (Lei et al., 1997).

Supply Chain Management

A market orientation plays a pivotal role in implementing SCM. First of all, a firm's market orientation produces and stores valuable *market information* that is needed in the process of building, maintaining, and enhancing supply chain relationships. For example, because a firm has information about customers, suppliers, competitors, sociopolitical environments, and technological trends, it could answer such questions as which supply chain best serves its customers' needs, with which firms it should work to implement SCM, what should be the objectives to be pursued in SCM, and so on. In addition, Cooper, Ellram, et al. (1997) suggested that one of the components of the implementation of SCM is information sharing through two-way communication between partners within a supply chain. Nabisco executives have contended that "Successful SCM, we discovered, required information systems that all supply chain participants can access and understand" (Andraski et al., 1996, p. 31). A market orientation should indirectly contribute to the information sharing within a supply chain because market information obtained by individual partners could serve as the basis of shared information among the supply chain partners.

Information sharing among the partners in a supply chain may simply be practicing organizational learning within the boundary of a supply chain rather than within the boundaries of individual firms and dyadic interfirm relationships. Brown and Hendry (1997) claimed that (organizational) learning through the supply chain and working better with suppliers are two major changes that occur in firms using SCM practices. A manager at a global courier service firm we interviewed gave an example:

> We had a customer visit, we did not try to sell anything and the customer did not want to buy anything, but both tried to see what kinds of options we [her firm] came up with in helping the customer move its products more quickly.

In the same context, a manager at a multinational chemical company we interviewed argued that

> if supply chain partners know more about each party in the supply chain, the information helps each party understand the other's problems.

When combined, these changes help partners within a supply chain achieve a better two-way relationship with suppliers, with improved information exchange, so that they can better utilize supplier creativity and knowledge, improve processes (particularly for cost savings and performance benefits in the supply chain), and encourage individual learning within an established supply chain context.

Finally, a market orientation facilitates relationship marketing that, in turn, could promote the implementation of SCM indirectly vis-à-vis relationship marketing. Cooper, Ellram, et al. (1997) indicated that building and maintaining *close long-term relationships* among partners beyond the life of a contract that encourage interfirm coordination are needed for the implementation of SCM. Researchers (e.g., Gruen, 1997; Gundlach & Murphy, 1993;

Morgan & Hunt, 1994) have suggested that relationship marketing depends on the notion of interfirm cooperation that focuses on the systematic development of ongoing, collaborative business relationships and, therefore, the implementation of relationship marketing promotes interfirm cooperation in addition to close long-term relationships among the supply chain members. As such, a market orientation has positive, indirect influences on the implementation of SCM.

In summary, the marketing concept is conceptualized as a business philosophy guiding a firm toward customer satisfaction at a profit, and a market orientation is the implementation of that philosophy, forcing the firm to generate, disseminate, and respond to market information. The marketing concept, a business philosophy, not only provides the philosophical foundation of a market orientation but also plays important roles in the management of a firm, inter-functional relationships, and the implementation of SCM. A market orientation also affects the management of a firm, interfirm relationships, and a supply chain. That is, a market orientation leads a firm to focus on market information generation, dissemination, and responsiveness to satisfy customers, coordinate its marketing efforts, redefine the responsibilities of each function, restructure its organizational system, and achieve superior business performance. At the same time, a market orientation provides an environment that encourages a firm in its efforts to develop, maintain, and enhance close relationships with other firms; engage in organizational learning from other firms; and build commitment, trust, and cooperative norms in the relationships with other firms.

A market orientation is used both inside and outside a firm to recognize and respond to customers' needs, and to obtain experiences, products, skills, technologies, and knowledge from outside the firm that are not available to other competitors. Finally, a market orientation promotes the implementation of SCM. For example, the input of market information has indirect, positive effects on the implementation of SCM. In addition, information sharing and organizational learning, both of which are components of SCM, are the broad applications of a market orientation beyond the boundary of an individual firm. A close long-term interfirm relationship and interfirm cooperation, both of which are reinforced by a market orientation, are also components of the implementation of SCM. As such, a market orientation has numerous positive impacts on the implementation of SCM.

Relationship Marketing

According to Gundlach and Murphy (1993), exchange—which is at the center of marketing—takes various forms, depending on its location in the exchange continuum. At one end of the continuum, *transactional exchange* involves single, short-term exchange events encompassing a distinct beginning and ending (Gundlach & Murphy, 1993). Goldberg (1976) described this form as a transaction in which "no duties exist between the parties prior to formation [of the exchange], and in which the duties of the parties are determined completely up-front" (p. 49). At the other end of the continuum, *relational exchange* involves transactions linked together over an extended time frame (Gundlach & Murphy, 1993). Gundlach and Murphy (1993) explain that relational exchanges trace back to previous interactions and reflect an ongoing process. As examples of relational exchanges, Gundlach and Murphy cite the close and long-term relationships established between certain vendors and their industrial customers (e.g., automobile manufacturers and their suppliers), relationship banking, frequent-stay programs at hotels, and priority acceptance for alumni family members at universities.

Marketing strategies differ along the continuum of exchange from relationship-oriented strategies at one end to transaction-oriented strategies at the other (Grönroos, 1995). Gundlach and Murphy (1993) proposed that the characteristics of relational strategy include an emphasis on purposeful cooperation, extended planning, and the establishment of complex webs of operational and social interdependence.

Conceptualization of Relationship Marketing

Berry (1980) defines relationship marketing as attracting, maintaining, and—in multiservice organizations—enhancing customer relationships. Berry and Parasuraman (1991) proposed that relationship marketing consists of attracting, developing, and retaining customers. The unit of analysis is the relationship between a firm and its customers.

With a slightly different perspective, Morgan and Hunt (1994) state, "Relationship marketing refers to all marketing activities directed toward establishing, developing, and maintaining successful relational exchanges" (p. 22). The rationale for this definition is that in many instances of relationship marketing "customers" do not exist, only "partners" exchanging resources (Morgan & Hunt, 1994).

In the same context, Cravens (1995) proposed that marketing relationships involve more than buyer-seller collaboration; they include suppliers, distribution channel members, internal functions, and even competitors. Thus, Morgan and Hunt (1994) and Cravens (1995) expanded the domain of relationship marketing from solely buyer-seller or marketer-customer relationships to all forms of relationship exchanges among the market participants. Grönroos (1990) further expanded the perspective of the domain of relationship marketing and argued, "Marketing is to establish, maintain, and enhance relationships with customers and other parties, at a profit, so that the objectives of the parties involved are met. This is achieved by a mutual exchange and fulfillment of promises" (p. 236). Grönroos's perspective departs from the traditional view of marketing that emphasizes only "exchange" and moves toward the notion of "exchange in relationship." Considering that marketing deals with various forms of exchanges—including discrete and relational ones—and involves more than buyer-seller relationships, Morgan and Hunt's (1994) definition of relationship marketing as all marketing activities directed toward establishing, developing, and maintaining successful relational exchanges is adopted here.

Relationship marketing goes beyond repeat purchase behavior and inducement (Sheth & Parvatiyar, 1995). In the same context, Webster (1992) proposed that repeated transactions are only a precursor of relationships, and customers expect convenience and cost efficiency from repeated transactions. Firms in long-term relationships do not always put relationship marketing into practice. For example, in industrial markets, buyer-seller relationships typically have involved relatively long-term contractual commitments, but even there the relationships have often been at arm's length and adversarial, pitting the customer against the vendor in a battle focused on low price (Webster, 1992). Relationship marketing is beyond purely transactional exchanges, repeated purchases, and even adversarial, long-term relationships. Competitive forces in the global marketplace of the 1980s compelled many firms to move significantly along the continuum from arm's-length relationships with vendors to much stronger partnerships characterized by much greater interdependence (Webster, 1992). As a result, relationship marketing today pursues buyer-seller partnerships, strategic alliances, joint ventures, and networks, all of which assume mutual, total-dependence relationships.

Relationship marketing has some prerequisites. First, Berry (1995) proposed that relationship marketing is built on the foundation of *trust*, which is defined by Moorman et al. (1993) as "a willingness to rely on an exchange partner in whom one has confidence" (p. 82). Berry and Parasuraman (1991) also contend that effective services marketing depends on trust because the customer typically must buy a service before experiencing it.

Second, *mutual benefit* to participating parties is essential for strong relationships (Berry, 1995). In other words, a firm's motivation to engage in relationship marketing to achieve higher business performance is matched by a consumer's motivation to reduce its choice risk in a relationship with the firm.

Third, a firm can earn either financial benefits or competitive advantage only if customers are willing and able to engage in relationship patronage (Sheth & Parvatiyar, 1995). In other words, ongoing and cooperative relationships reflect commitment made by the customer to continue patronizing the particular marketer (Grönroos, 1990; Shani & Chalasani, 1992). Moorman, Zaltman, and Deshpande (1992) state that "Commitment to the relationship is defined as an enduring desire to maintain a valued relationship" (p. 136).

Fourth, Bitner (1995) suggests that service guarantees and two-way communication are vehicles by which promises can be effectively communicated and customers can be informed as to what they can expect and how it will be delivered. This is important because the foundation for maintaining service relationships is the fulfillment of promises made to customers (Grönroos, 1990). Two-way communication is also important because a firm should monitor customer satisfaction through direct communication channels with its customer bases, because ad hoc surveys—which are commonly used in transaction-based marketing—provide only a proxy indication of satisfaction (Grönroos, 1995).

Fifth, relationship marketing requires *cooperation* between marketing and operations (Grönroos, 1995). For example, all the functions interacting with a customer have to reinforce the quality perception by the customer because relationship marketing involves ongoing relationships with customers.

Finally, *internal marketing* is needed to convince other functions to be prepared to assume the role of part-time marketers (Grönroos, 1995). This is important because, for employees and service systems to deliver on the promises made, they must have the skills, abilities, tools, and motivation to deliver (Bitner, 1995).

Impacts of Relationship Marketing

Relationship marketing affects the management of a firm as well as a supply chain, as shown in Figure 4.3. These effects will be discussed below.

Management of a Firm

Seven outputs of relationship marketing are presented as impacts on the management of individual firms. First, *inter-functional coordination* should be reinforced because the decision to either make or break a relationship is contingent on the role of production and delivery processes, as well as marketing (Grönroos, 1995). Webster (1992) also claims that the common focus on customer value and relationship management might result in much stronger coordination of the procurement, sales, and marketing functions in a manner analogous to the merchandising function in retailing firms.

Second, relationship marketing drives a firm to *redefine the responsibilities of each function*. The role of marketing in relationship marketing strategy should be expanded from capturing new customers to getting and keeping customers (Grönroos, 1995). Thus, marketing should not be restricted to the marketing mix activities that are focused on the manipulation of customers but should place increased emphasis on relationship marketing skills. At the same time, the fundamental responsibility of the marketing function of a firm is expertise on the customer and keeping the rest of the network organization informed about the customer (Webster, 1992). Gummensson (1987) uses the phrase "part-time marketer" to stress the critical marketing role performed by

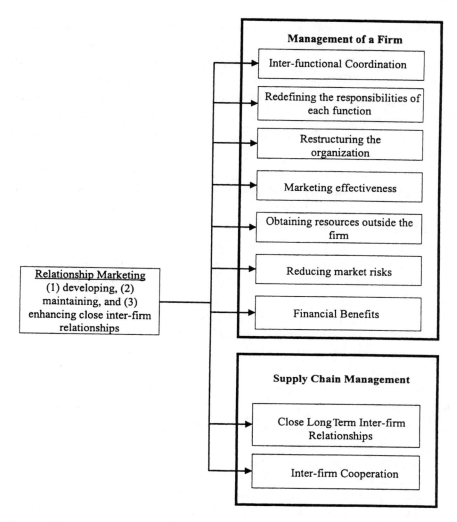

Figure 4.3. The Impacts of Relationship Marketing

customer-contact employees other than the marketing department and argues that part-time marketers are at the heart of relationship marketing.

Third, relationship marketing requires a firm to *restructure the organizational system* into a boundaryless organization. In other words, the results of the reinforced efforts on inter-functional coordination and role shifts in each function should be consistent with the two major trends of elimination of boundaries between management functions within organizations and a blurring of the boundaries between the firm and its market environment (Webster, 1992). In brief, traditional ways of organizing the marketing function and thinking about the purpose of marketing activity must be reexamined, with the focus on long-term customer relationships, partnerships, and strategic alliances (Webster, 1992).

Fourth, relationship marketing improves a firm's *marketing effectiveness* because (a) as a firm is dedicated to customers with long-term commitment, it can appropriately direct marketing resources toward those uses that provide the greatest value for a selective set of customers, and (b) relationship marketing promotes the early involvement of customers so that customers provide valuable information to the firm (Sheth & Parvatiyar, 1995). A good example is Proctor and Gamble's (P&G) inter-functional Customer Business Development Team that works with major customers in identifying mutually beneficial opportunities and ways to add consumer value. The team has succeeded in reducing P&G's inventory and developing a more consumer-responsive product assortment (Drayer, 1999).

Fifth, relationship marketing brings a firm *resources from outside the firm* to satisfy customer needs. In the 1990s, customers became more demanding and competition became more intense (Cravens, 1995). Jockey's president and COO, Edward C. Emma, stated, "we are using our ability, through worldwide sourcing connections . . . to make anything we need, including more fashion products, off shore because we just didn't have the capabilities to make some items domestically" (Abend & Gill, 1999, p. 56).

In this context, Kotler (1997) states, "As firms globalize, they realize that no matter how large they are, they lack the total resources and requisites for success. Viewing the complete supply chain for producing value, they recognize the necessity of partnering with other organizations" (p. xxxiii). A manager at a global courier service firm we interviewed told a story in which

> "a customer approached me and asked for help, explaining the customer firm's technology would be dead in thirty days, and they could not afford to have it sit on a truck or a boat or a railroad car." These trends resulted in relationship marketing—requiring teaming up with other firms—becoming a necessity to satisfy customers in today's market environment.

Sixth, customers are motivated to build and maintain relationships with the suppliers to *reduce risk* (Bauer, 1960; Taylor, 1974). Perceived risk is associated with the uncertainty and magnitude of outcomes (Sheth & Parvatiyar, 1995). In this context, Bitner (1995) argues that having a long-term relationship with a service provider can reduce consumer stress as the relationship becomes predictable, initial problems are solved, special needs are accommodated, and the consumer learns what to expect. This is particularly so when customers need continuous and periodical delivery of services that are important, variable in quality, and/or complex (Berry, 1995; Bitner, 1995). In other words, customers become loyal to the service provider for predictability and comfort as well as service quality itself (Bitner, 1995).

The final impact of relationship marketing on a firm is *financial benefits* such as increased revenue and lower marketing costs (Berry, 1995). For example,

Reichheld and Sasser (1990) found that lowering the customer defection rate from 20% to 10% doubled the longevity of the average customer's relationship from 5 years to 10 years and increased the net present value of the cumulative profit streams for a customer from $135 to $300. In addition, a firm can cut costs by reducing some of the wasteful marketing practices associated with competitive mass marketing and by letting the consumer do such marketer jobs as processing orders, designing products, and managing information directed to the firm (Sheth & Parvatiyar, 1995). For example, EDI ordering and invoicing allows P&G and its customers to automate those processes, thereby improving the delivery system's speed and accuracy (Drayer, 1999).

Supply Chain Management

There are two major impacts of relationship marketing on the implementation of SCM. First, effective supply chain management requires partners to build and maintain *close long-term relationships* (Cooper, Ellram, et al., 1997; Ellram & Cooper, 1990). Ellram and Cooper (1990) contend that a successful supply chain relies on forming strategic partnerships, in which long-term, interfirm relationships with trading partners are expected. In this context, SCM puts more emphasis on a partnership approach or relationship orientation (Morris & Imrie, 1992). In the end, those inter-organizational relationships tie firms to each other and may tie their success to the chain as a whole (Cooper, Lambert, & Pagh, 1997). A partner in a business-consulting firm we interviewed argued that

> sharing risk and sharing information in a supply chain are like linking up the involved parties over the fence like good neighbors. Being good neighbors requires supply chain partners to practice relationship marketing that, in turn, requires commitment and trust . . . it is the people who share risk and cooperate in a supply chain environment, based upon long-term commitment.

In addition, a manager at a multinational chemical company we interviewed stated:

> Contracts don't necessarily build (supply chain) relationships. It's communications and trust between the partners.

Ultimately, Webster (1988) expected the emergence of a network of strategic partnerships among designers, technology providers, manufacturers, distributors, and information specialists that would fit the need of functional integration within a supply chain. Dell's *Virtual Integration* and Chrysler's *Extended Enterprise* concepts involving their parts and components suppliers and distributors are good examples of how firms work together as if they are single entities to create additional value for customers and consumers (cf. Magretta, 1998b; Stallkamp, 1998).

Second, relationship marketing—through close interfirm relationships such as partnerships, strategic alliances, and joint ventures—increases *interfirm cooperation*, including joint inventory and cost reduction as well as joint planning (Cooper, Ellram, et al., 1997). In relationship marketing strategy, buyer-seller partnerships, strategic alliances, joint ventures, and networks are formed, all of which assume mutual, interdependent relationships governed by cooperative norms. The cooperation of the partners involved in these various close inter-organizational forms, in turn, help partners achieve a high level of customer satisfaction in a rapidly changing business environment (Cravens, 1995).

In summary, relationship marketing affects SCM as well as the management of individual firms. Cooper, Ellram, et al. (1997) posit that the implementation of SCM involves reducing channel inventory, increasing channel cost efficiencies, maintaining long-term relationships, encouraging interfirm cooperation, and sharing risks and rewards among the partners. Relationship marketing helps achieve such objectives of SCM as efficiency (i.e., cost reduction) and effectiveness (i.e., customer service) through increased cooperation in close long-term interfirm relationships among the supply chain partners.

An Integrative Framework

Figure 4.4 shows the integrative conceptual framework of this chapter. The marketing concept is implemented in the form of a market orientation that, in turn, promotes the emergence of relationship marketing and the implementation of SCM. A market orientation helps the implementation of SCM by providing valuable market information (e.g., on customers, competitors, potential supply chain partners, market environments), by suggesting a model of information sharing and organizational learning, and by augmenting the practice of relationship marketing that contributes to the success of SCM.

The marketing concept has direct influences on the management of an individual firm, an interfirm relationship, and a supply chain by

1. Providing the philosophical foundation of a market orientation within a firm,
2. Providing the philosophical foundation of relationship marketing between firms to develop, maintain, and enhance interfirm relationships, and
3. Providing a compatible business philosophy for implementing SCM within a supply chain.

A market orientation has direct influences on the management of a firm, on relationship marketing, and, ultimately, on SCM by

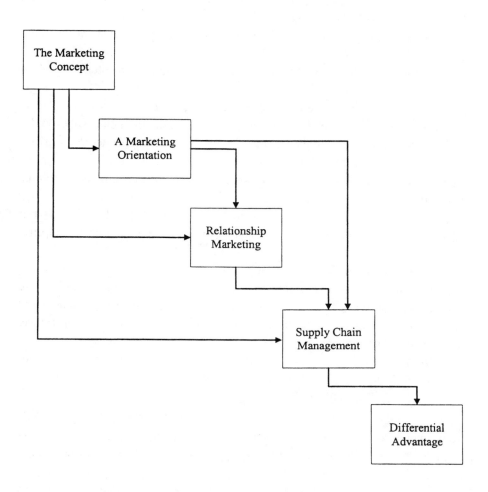

Figure 4.4. An Integrative Model of the Marketing Concept, a Marketing Orientation, Relationship Marketing, and Supply Chain Management

1. Providing managerial focus (i.e., customer satisfaction) to the partner firms,
2. Increasing inter-functional coordination,
3. Redefining the responsibilities of each function,
4. Restructuring the partner firms' organizational system by redefining the responsibilities of each function and promoting inter-functional coordination,
5. Contributing to superior business performance of the partner firms,
6. Increasing trust, commitment, and cooperative norms to the partner firms involved in interfirm relationships that are prerequisites for relationship marketing,

  7. Requiring relationship marketing to build, maintain, and enhance interfirm relationships with the partner firms,
  8. Encouraging organizational learning on the basis of well-implemented relationship marketing,
  9. Supplying valuable market information that could be used before and during the implementation of SCM,
  10. Expanding the application of organizational learning activities to SCM so that partner firms share information and experience within the supply chain, and
  11. Advancing relationship marketing that, in turn, helps implement SCM.

Relationship marketing affects SCM as well as the management of individual firms by

  1. Enhancing inter-functional coordination to satisfy customers with company-wide efforts,
  2. Redefining the responsibilities of each function of a firm,
  3. Restructuring the organizational system,
  4. Improving marketing effectiveness of the partner firms by proper allocation of marketing resources to the other partners and involvement of the partners in marketing process,
  5. Bringing resources outside the firm to satisfy customers who become more demanding in a competitive market,
  6. Reducing risks in the market,
  7. Providing financial benefits such as increased revenue and reduced costs,
  8. Helping build, maintain, and enhance long-term interfirm relationships such as partnerships, strategic alliances, joint ventures, and networks that fit into the goal of SCM, and
  9. Allowing interfirm coordination that is required for the implementation of supply chain management initiatives such as joint inventory and cost reduction as well as joint planning.

Finally, with the help of the marketing concept, a market orientation, and relationship marketing, SCM achieves differential advantage for the supply chain and its partners by reducing costs and investments and by improving customer service.

Conclusions

The concepts of the marketing concept, market orientation, relationship marketing, and supply chain management are not separate; rather, they are inextricably intertwined. At the starting point of the model in Figure 4.3, the marketing concept promotes individual firms' coordinated activities inside and outside the firms to accomplish customer satisfaction at a profit.

A market orientation, which is an implementation of the marketing concept, requires firms to generate, disseminate, and respond to market information. The firm's organizational learning, a major component of a market orientation, goes beyond the boundaries of the firms because there exist a multitude of learning resources and skills to fulfill customers' demands in an efficient and effective way. Thus, a market orientation not only promotes the emergence of relationship marketing but also provides the reasons for it to exist.

Relationship marketing aims at establishing, maintaining, and enhancing either dyadic relationships or multiple relationships in a supply chain to create better customer value. Supply chain management benefits by such concepts as the marketing concept, a market orientation, and relationship marketing. Thus, the role of marketing through the marketing concept, a market orientation, and relationship marketing are essential for the success of supply chain management.

The main purpose of this chapter was to outline of the role of marketing in the implementation of SCM. Specifically, this chapter suggests the cause-and-effect relationships among several important concepts in business research and practice: the marketing concept, a market orientation, relationship marketing, and SCM. Understanding the relationships among the marketing concept, a market orientation, relationship marketing, and supply chain management is critical to managers. First, the marketing concept guides a firm to look to achieve customer satisfaction at a profit in a coordinated manner as if it is a lighthouse for a vessel named SCM, thrown on the heavy seas of global competition. In other words, whenever a firm is lost in the middle of changing its operations as well as its organization toward SCM, management should focus on the ultimate goal of implementing SCM. Second, if a market orientation is found to affect the successful management of a supply chain, managers will learn that a market orientation inside their firms is necessary to manage their supply chain. Third, managers should recognize the fact that a well-managed supply chain in which a market orientation prevails as the norm may enhance the performance of individual firms and the supply chain as a whole. Fourth, given the fact that long-term cooperative interfirm relationships are an essential characteristic of SCM, managers should acknowledge the need of bringing marketing's relationship-building skills into the process of SCM implementation. Finally, managers should be able to utilize the framework of this chapter to diagnose their business performance to find out whether their market orientation, relationship marketing, and supply chain management hinder obtaining higher business performance from their firm.

Mentzer and Kahn (1995b) suggest an iterating process of theory development as moving forward from idea generation through literature review and observation, to substantive justification, to theory formation, to theory testing using hypotheses and constructs, and finally to the analysis of the empirical test. According to Mentzer and Kahn's framework, this chapter takes only the first step in this process and, thus, more work is in order to empirically capture the detailed cause-and-effect relationships among the constructs and any potential moderating and/or mediating constructs in the suggested model (Figure 4.4).

5

The Dynamic Role of the Sales Function in Supply Chain Management

MICHAEL S. GARVER

SOONHONG MIN

Executive Summary

As companies adopt supply chain management, the sales function plays a critical role. The purpose of this chapter is to examine new roles of the sales function in supply chain management. To achieve this purpose, results from the supply chain research group, along with results from an independent qualitative study, will be integrated. The sales function is examined from two different perspectives, those of the sales force and sales management. Specifically, in this chapter we

- Discuss the traditional role of the sales force, along with its limitations in supply chain management
- Discuss the new supply chain management roles for the sales force
- Examine new supply chain management activities for the sales force, along with the necessary expertise to carry out these activities effectively
- Examine the traditional sales management practices, followed by managerial implications and new sales management practices
- Explore overall conclusions and future research in this area

The role of the contemporary salesperson is changing dramatically, and in many situations, the old models of selling are simply outdated, ineffective, and counterproductive to supply chain management goals and objectives. Although most sales organizations focus on prepurchase activities, supply chain partners focus on managing relationships and conducting postpurchase activities to enhance supply chain performance. The sales force is well positioned to implement, facilitate, and coordinate many supply chain management activities. In short, the supply chain sales force should be involved with any supply chain activity that goes beyond organizational boundaries. More specifically, the sales force should be an integral part of

- Implementing cooperative behaviors (i.e., joint planning, evaluating, and forecasting)
- Mutually sharing information
- Nurturing supply chain relationships

To be effective at their new role, the supply chain sales force members must *gain new expertise in logistics and supply chain management.* Salesperson logistics expertise is defined as a customer's perception of a salesperson's knowledge, experience, or skills relevant to logistics issues. Salesperson logistics expertise concerns the seller's and supply chain partners' logistics operations, systems, and processes at both tactical and strategic levels. Thus, salesperson logistics expertise includes the following dimensions:

- Internal (company) logistics expertise
- External (supply chain partner) logistics expertise
- Tactical logistics expertise
- Strategic logistics expertise

Although the logistics manager may be the primary person designing logistics solutions, the salesperson would likely be the primary person representing the supply chain partner's needs and requirements. For effective teamwork and innovative solutions, salespeople and logistics managers need to be able to communicate effectively and work together on supply chain management issues.

To support the sales force in its new supply chain management roles, sales managers need to train, support, and encourage supply chain activities and logistics expertise. To achieve this goal, sales managers must also adopt a new orientation and embrace new management techniques to enhance supply chain performance. Specifically, sales managers must become "change agents" in the sales organization and lead the sales force in a new direction. Traditional training programs, performance objectives, and compensation packages need to be adapted and better aligned with supply chain management.

Introduction

As companies adopt supply chain management, functional areas need to change their traditional ways of conducting business and better align their current management practices to support and enhance supply chain management. The sales function, including both salespeople and sales managers, needs to reexamine their traditional roles. The sales function must examine supply chain management and determine how the sales function adds value to the overall supply chain and various supply chain partners.

Effective supply chain management is complicated and requires management of many interrelated activities between supply chain partners. As discussed in Chapter 1, interrelated supply chain management activities necessitate that

- Supply chain management must develop and maintain multifirm relationships that coordinate product, service, and information (Cooper & Ellram, 1993)
- Supply chain management must synchronize both tactical and strategic plans to maximize value creation in the supply chain (Langley & Holcomb 1992; Ross, 1998)
- Only by understanding customer values and requirements can supply chain partners create unique and innovative solutions that will create value for supply chain partners
- Tactical and strategic information needs to be shared between supply chain partners on a timely basis (Ellram & Cooper, 1990; Novack, Langley, & Rinehart, 1995)
- Supply chain partners must engage in cooperative, integrative behaviors (Bowersox & Closs, 1996; Cooper, Ellram, Gardner, & Hanks, 1997)

When examining key activities of effective supply chain management, the sales function is well positioned to implement, coordinate, and/or facilitate many of these critical activities. For example, the contemporary salesperson today is viewed as a relationship manager (Cravens, 1995; Ingram, 1996). The number one priority of most sales functions is to develop and maintain stronger customer relationships, characterized by delivering value-added services that result in supply chain partner satisfaction, trust, and loyalty (Cravens, 1995; Garver, 1998). As a relationship manager, the salesperson engages in many supply chain activities, including mutually sharing tactical and strategic information; learning about customer requirements; coordinating and facilitating the flow of products, services, and information; engaging in cooperative activities with supply chain partners; and creating unique solutions that create value for supply chain partners (Garver, 1998). Clearly, the sales function plays a critical role in supply chain management and creating value for supply chain partners.

The purpose of this chapter is to examine new roles of the sales function in supply chain management. To achieve this purpose, results from the supply chain research group along with results from an independent qualitative study will be integrated with findings from the literature. The sales function is examined from two different perspectives, those of the sales force and sales management. First, the traditional role of the sales force is discussed along with its limitations in supply chain management. Then, new supply chain management roles for the sales force are discussed. In this discussion, we examine new supply chain management activities for the sales force, along with the necessary expertise to carry out these activities effectively. Then, traditional sales management practices are examined, followed by managerial implications and new sales management practices. Finally, overall conclusions and future research in this area are explored.

The Changing Role of the Sales Function

Across many industries, the role of the contemporary salesperson is changing dramatically. As more and more companies implement supply chain management, which is based on strong relationships among supply chain partners, the role of personal selling and sales management needs to be redesigned and better aligned with this new business strategy. The old models of selling often are simply outdated and ineffective in today's business environment.

Primarily, the traditional role of personal selling has focused on obtaining customer orders and contracts, taking a transactional perspective to selling (Cravens, 1995). Although there are certainly exceptions to this statement, personal selling has primarily engaged and focused on prepurchase activities from a transactional perspective. In many popular press books along with textbooks on personal selling, the main focus is on skills, activities, and techniques to obtain the sale. A great deal of coverage is given to making sales presentations, handling customer objections, and closing sales. The primary objective has been to increase sales, profits, and new business.

Personal selling has also been tactical in nature and *not* strategically oriented (Ingram, 1996). From a tactical perspective, salespeople have been primarily concerned with selling their product and *not* leveraging their company as a strategic resource or partner to the customer (Cravens, 1995). Many salespeople are still mainly detailing product features, benefits, and advantages but *not* exploring how they can help their customers reach their strategic goals and objectives. As the role of the salesperson changes to that of a relationship manager, a salesperson needs to become a strategic resource to his or her customers (Ingram, 1996).

The traditional model of personal selling may often be counterproductive to supply chain management goals and objectives. For example, appropriate inventory management throughout the supply chain is essential to overall supply chain performance (Monczka, Trent, & Handfield, 1998). Traditional selling practices, however, may actually encourage salespeople to stock customers with high inventory levels so that they exceed their monthly sales volume quotas. Although most sales organizations are concerned with prepurchase activities, supply chain partners are clearly more concerned with managing the relationship and the necessary postpurchase activities to enhance supply chain performance.

In many situations, salespeople are simply displaying behaviors that have been encouraged and reinforced through a culture of traditional selling beliefs, sales training programs, and sales management practices. Each of these factors has reinforced a transactional view of selling that is *not* aligned with supply chain management. For example, many sales training programs are focused primarily on product knowledge and selling techniques (Ingram & LaForge, 1992). Although these topics are important, they are not adequate in preparing salespeople to add value through relational development in a supply chain. A recent study noted that product knowledge was recognized as the most common type of sales training and received the most attention in sales training sessions (Honeycutt, Howe, & Ingram, 1993). Managing relationships and supply chain management activities were not even mentioned as categories in which salespeople were trained. Thus, if salespeople develop supply chain management skills, it is likely by chance or in an ad hoc manner.

Traditional sales management practices may encourage behaviors that are counterproductive to developing effective supply chain relationships. As Mentzer and Bienstock (1998) put it, what gets measured gets rewarded, and what gets rewarded gets done. Many sales managers currently evaluate and reward their sales force based on increasing sales volume, profits, and new business. These sales management activities encourage and reward salespeople to focus on short-term financial results. In some situations, these sales management objectives have caused salespeople to take a short-term perspective (i.e., increasing this month's sales volume), sometimes to the detriment of longer-term company objectives (i.e., improving supply chain relationships). Under traditional performance objectives, many salespeople focus on short-term sales to reach their monthly quota and do not necessarily examine whether the transaction is in the best interest of their customer.

With the emergence of supply chain management, the traditional role of personal selling and sales management simply does not fit with this new business paradigm—supply chain management as a systems approach. In short, these traditional roles are even likely to be counterproductive to the goals and objectives of supply chain management. Clearly, a disconnect exists between supply chain management and the traditional roles of the sales function. The time has come for personal selling and sales management philosophies and techniques to become better aligned with supply chain management.

Personal Selling in Supply Chain Management

The sales function plays a critical role in implementing many supply chain management activities and behaviors. For the sales force to add value in the supply chain, the contemporary sales force must adopt a new orientation to personal selling (Cravens, 1995), interface more effectively with logistics, and gain new supply chain management skills and expertise.

A New Orientation Toward Selling

Changing the cultural beliefs and mind-set of a sales force and obtaining its buy-in is extremely difficult. The sales force members must view themselves as relationship managers. In this role, their current prepurchase orientation of increasing sales volume needs to be replaced with a postpurchase orientation of delivering services that create valuable solutions for supply chain partners. A key component of this paradigm shift is changing from a selling orientation to a service orientation (Garver, Gardial, & Woodruff, 2000). The primary function of these services must be to meet the needs of various supply chain partners and improve the overall performance of the supply chain. For example, a manager at a global courier service firm we interviewed told about a customer who approached her, asking for help and solutions to problems, stating "You need to help me, because my technology dies in thirty days, and I can't afford for it to sit on a truck or a boat or a railroad car." In this scenario, the supply chain partner is looking to sales for logistical solutions to solve business problems. Another manager at the same company stated that her firm had a customer visit in which "selling" was not part of the meeting. Both parties met and tried to develop unique and innovative options to help the supply chain partner move its products more quickly. In the era of supply chain management, salespeople should be consultants to supply chain partners and not focus solely on selling, but instead include the effective implementation and day-to-day operations of logistics operations, processes, and systems in the supply chain (Garver & Mentzer, in press). Salespeople who focus on creating value for supply chain partners become valuable resources to the supply chain and help develop and strengthen relationships between supply chain partners (Garver, 1998).

Another component of this new orientation is that salespeople need to work with and develop relationships with various supply chain members, both upstream and downstream of their firm. Webster (1992) suggests that in network organizations (i.e., supply chains), marketing and sales have a unique role that is different from the traditional role in hierarchical structures. This new role is to help design and negotiate strategic partnerships with vendors and technology partners through which the firm deploys its distinctive competence to serve particular market opportunities. As a result, marketing and sales may be involved in relationships with vendors at least as much as, if not more than, relationships with customers as part of the process of delivering superior value to customers (Webster, 1992). Negotiating skills that traditionally are associated with managing major customer accounts must also be used to work with suppliers and distributors in a supply chain management context.

The Sales-Logistics Interface

Bowersox, Mentzer, and Speh (1995) argue that the strategic linkage between marketing, sales, and logistics occurs where logistics capabilities and resources are translated into effective drivers of differentiation, in addition to providing cost leadership obtained by efficient logistics operations. A vice president of customer operations at an office supply company we interviewed stated,

> Customer logistics managers are a part of the sales teams and report to him and, therefore, the salesperson will acquire logistics managers' assistance whenever logistics discussion comes up. Logistics managers also play a role as customer advocates for logistics issues inside the firm, suggesting breaking cases or shipping partial cases to customers.

This comment suggests that salespeople and logistics managers work together to solve supply chain partner's problems. Although the logistics manager may be the primary person designing logistics solutions, the salesperson is likely the primary person representing the supply chain partner's needs and requirements. To achieve effective teamwork and innovative solutions, salespeople and logistics managers need to work together closely. Both need to fully grasp the supply chain partner's needs and requirements and the internal processes to satisfy those requirements. Sales and logistics need to be able to communicate effectively and speak the same language (i.e., supply chain partner's needs and logistics solutions). Although the sales force needs to integrate with numerous departments, supply chain management suggests that integration with logistics is particularly important. In the era of supply chain management, salespeople must possess *logistics expertise* to be effective team members—effective service providers, problem solvers, and relationship managers within the supply chain.

The supply chain management literature stresses cross-functional integration (Cooper, Lambert, & Pagh, 1997; Manrodt, Holcomb, & Thompson, 1997). It is likely in a supply chain management context that salespeople will be part of a multifunctional (inter-functional) team to better consult supply chain partners on supply chain issues and problems. According to Cespedes (1996a), multifunctional teams differ from most traditional account-management programs in two ways: (a) the buyer-seller exchange places a premium on effective supply chain management, and the team's primary responsibilities often involve reducing acquisition, delivery, and possession costs for buyers and sellers; and (b) account management requires the alignment of multiple areas of expertise at both the buyer and seller ends so that consideration be given to include service, finance, and/or logistics functions. Sales must take a leadership role in these to represent the supply chain partner's needs and requirements and facilitate/ensure that internal process development satisfies those needs and requirements. To accomplish this task, salespeople need to broaden their experience base and gain diverse functional expertise, especially logistics expertise.

Sales Force Activities and Behaviors in Supply Chain Management

The sales force is in a natural position to implement, facilitate, and/or coordinate many supply chain management activities. In short, the supply chain sales force should be involved with any supply chain activity that goes beyond organizational boundaries. More specifically, the sales force should be an integral part of (a) implementing cooperative behaviors (i.e., joint planning, evaluating, and forecasting), (b) mutually sharing information, and (c) nurturing supply chain relationships.

Cooperative Behaviors

To maximize supply chain performance, the sales force needs to work cooperatively with supply chain partners on many integrated projects. These integrated projects include joint planning, evaluation, and demand forecasting. To achieve the goals of the supply chain, partners need to work toward common goals and objectives (La Londe & Masters, 1994; Lassar & Zinn, 1995). To achieve supply chain goals and objectives, tactical and strategic plans need to be synchronized so that synergies can be realized between supply chain partners (Ross, 1988). To accomplish this objective, the sales force must be actively involved in *joint planning* sessions with other supply chain partners. For example, large manufacturers of consumer goods (e.g., Procter & Gamble, Johnson & Johnson) often conduct joint planning sessions with major retailers (Walgreens, Wal-Mart, etc.). In these joint planning sessions, sales plays a key role in providing critical sales information as well as coordinating various functional areas from the selling firm. Although these joint planning sessions should also include many other representatives from other functional areas, sales must be represented and actively involved in these planning sessions. Sales can contribute real-time information about the market, competitive supply chains, and performance issues associated with various supply chain partners. In this role, the sales force can play a key part in coordinating activities between supply chain partners.

Cooperative planning should also include *joint evaluation* of the supply chain and supply chain partner performance (Cooper et al., 1997; Novack et al., 1995). Because the sales force is a facilitator of many activities with other supply chain partners, salespeople will likely understand their firm's strengths and weaknesses from the supply chain partner's perspective. With this knowledge, the salesperson can represent the "voice of the supply chain" to drive continuous improvement internally, as well as overall relationship management. Furthermore, the sales force can readily identify roadblocks and barriers to effective interfirm coordination. Once these barriers are identified and overcome, supply chain performance should be enhanced. For example, the sales force is often represented in "joint evaluations" in hospital supply chains. As companies in the supply chain meet to discuss performance, salespeople are critical facilitators of evaluating performance in the supply chain.

To improve performance, one must first understand the current position (i.e., strengths and weaknesses). By understanding weaknesses and barriers to performance, salespeople can help drive continuous improvement in the supply chain. For example, Morgan (1995) illustrates how sales representatives have contributed to driving continuous improvement in a supply chain context:

- A sales manager provided a materials manager information on dual-certified material and the material itself so that the company reduced inventory by half.
- A sales representative at a cabinet manufacturer implemented and maintained a consignment inventory program and, as a result, created operating savings of 15% for the company. He also initiated ideas on carton closure procedures and drawer masking procedures, resulting in thousands of dollars in savings.
- An account executive at a form manufacturer helped its customer save $20,000 by setting up a new, efficient system that resulted in the use of two- and three-part forms instead of five-part forms.

Having salespeople involved in joint evaluations can bring about dramatic performance improvements.

To further enhance joint planning and control, many supply chain partners currently have representatives located directly at the supply chain partner's location (i.e., co-location). In this arrangement, the on-site salesperson is constantly available to share his or her expertise about his or her company, products, and logistics processes. In this capacity, the salesperson can offer real-time solutions to various problems that may arise. This setup allows supply chain partners to share accurate information on a real-time basis. For example, concerning the relationship between SC Johnson and Wal-Mart, SC Johnson has salespeople and logistics support people working in Bentonville, Arkansas, Wal-Mart's corporate headquarters.

Accurate *demand forecasting* is a critical activity necessary for maintaining high levels of customer satisfaction while simultaneously resulting in efficiencies and cost savings (Mentzer & Bienstock, 1998). If forecasts are accurate, then partners in the supply chain maintain the appropriate inventory levels, which allow partners to meet their customer's expectations regarding product availability while simultaneously eliminating redundant inventory investment. When this occurs, supply chain partners are satisfied at the lowest total supply chain cost. When forecasts are inaccurate, supply chain partners will either experience stock-outs or carry excess inventory. Through joint planning, control, and frequent contact, salespeople become aware of supply chain partners' demand requirements, both short- and long-term. Best-practice companies statistically derive forecasts that are then qualitatively adjusted (Mentzer & Bienstock, 1998). The salesperson needs to be responsible for qualitatively adjusting statistically derived forecasts (Moon & Mentzer, 1999). For example, salespeople from Lucent Technology regularly adjust and give additional insight to statistically derived forecasts. Given the nature of Lucent's products, forecasting input and adjustments by sales are critical (Moon, Mentzer, & Thomas, in press). Given their knowledge and insight into supply chain partners, salespeople can offer invaluable insight into the forecasting process.

Mutually Sharing Tactical and Strategic Information

Mutually sharing information between supply chain partners is critical to the overall performance of the supply chain (Cooper, Ellram, et al., 1997; Novack et al., 1995). The Global Logistics Research Team at Michigan State University (1995) defines information sharing as the willingness to share both tactical and strategic information. Because salespeople are boundary spanning agents, the sales force plays a key role in mutually sharing critical information among various supply chain partners, up and down the supply chain. Thus, a critical role for the supply chain sales force should be to share accurate information on a timely basis with the appropriate upstream and downstream supply chain partners. Much of this information sharing in the supply chain occurs at both tactical and strategic levels and revolves around logistical issues, operations, integrated processes, and systems.

The impact of salespeople sharing and capturing information on a timely basis is critical to improving efficiency and effectiveness in a supply chain. For example, Li & Fung, a Hong Kong–based multinational trading company, locks up capacity of its weaving and dying suppliers with the promise that they will get an order of a specific size, although Li & Fung does not know the product specification by a large retailer (Magretta, 1998a). This is made possible by its salespeople, who are working closely with customers to capture the market demand and pass this information on to its suppliers on a real-time basis. At the same time, this open communication between Li & Fung's salespeople and other supply chain partners (customers and suppliers) has led to high levels of trust, a necessary ingredient in managing the supply chain.

Relationship Manager

The number one priority for salespeople across industries is to improve customer relationships (Cravens, 1995). A manager at a multinational chemical company we interviewed stated:

> True partnerships are not based on a contract, but trust between people. Salespersons who have direct personal contacts in the market should assume the important responsibility to build, maintain, and enhance trust among the supply chain members.

A partner at a consulting firm we interviewed stated:

> Sharing risk and information are like linking up the involved parties over the fence like good neighbors. In other words, it is people who make supply chain management happen and salespeople are in the center of making good neighbors in a supply chain.

Although salespeople are still responsible for sales volume and profit, the new role of relationship manager becomes imperative and critically important to supply chain performance. As relationship managers, salespeople are responsible for ensuring that their company meets the needs of various supply chain partners. To develop and maintain strong relationships, the salesperson must focus on the supply chain partner's business needs and requirements. This includes supply chain partners upstream and downstream, including those partners who are once removed from the focal firm. Once needs and requirements are understood, they must be communicated to various internal functional areas so that various internal processes can be improved to meet the supply chain partner's requirement. Webster (1992) argues that in this role, marketing and sales must be the integrator, both internally—synthesizing technological capability with market needs—and externally—bringing the customer into the company as a participant in the development and adaptation of goods and services. In supply chain management, many of the supply chain partners' needs and requirements will be associated with logistical issues. The salesperson may need to implement, facilitate, and/or coordinate logistical services delivered to meet the requirements of various supply chain partners.

In this role, the salesperson is the quarterback who is coordinating many of the internal activities to meet the needs of supply chain partners. Sales managers should be change agents who show the big picture of supply chain management in the market and show other functions (e.g., logistics, finance, and production) what the market outcomes are as a result of supply chain optimization. A director at a large third-party logistics firm we interviewed stated:

> I think it tends to be a logistics operation working on operational improvements, and frankly, not even understanding the financial or market implications for their company in terms of how they might restructure or change their logistics or supply chain model.

Salespeople should be the persuaders, negotiators, and partners who bring distributors and end users into the firm's supply chain process integration.

Is the Traditional Sales Force Ready for the Challenge?

In many cases, the traditional sales force is not currently equipped to effectively perform its new supply chain management roles. Traditional sales training programs have focused on selling techniques and product knowledge (Ingram & LaForge, 1992), yet supply chain management issues are often concerned with logistical issues, operations, processes, and systems. How much experience and expertise do salespeople possess in logistics and supply chain management? How much training have salespeople received in logistics? How much training have salespeople received in cooperative behaviors, information sharing, and relationship management? How strategically oriented are salespeople? This raises an interesting question: Does the traditional sales force possess the *expertise* to effectively implement and enhance supply chain management performance? It is doubtful that most salespeople have expertise in these areas. To be effective in its new role, the supply chain sales force must *gain new expertise in logistics and supply chain management*.

Salesperson Expertise

A salesperson's level of expertise is a key attribute/behavior that leads to improved buyer-seller relationships (Crosby, Evans, & Cowles, 1990; Lagace, Dahlstrom, & Gassenheimer, 1991). Crosby et al. (1990) note that a customer's perception of a salesperson's expertise will be based on perceived relevant competencies associated with the goods or service transaction (e.g., product, market, or logistics knowledge). These competencies most often will be exhibited in the form of information provided by the salesperson. In a similar manner, Lagace et al. (1991) define expertise as the extent to which a person possesses knowledge, experience, or skills relevant to a particular topic.

Both conceptualizations of expertise focus on competencies, skills, knowledge, or experience. These definitions are broad enough to include the topic of logistics and supply chain management; however, the focus of past research on salesperson expertise has been primarily on product expertise. Although different dimensions of salesperson expertise (market, logistics, etc.) are mentioned in passing, research has depicted salesperson expertise as solely product expertise. In the current era of supply chain management, salesperson expertise must go well beyond product expertise to include logistics and supply chain management.

Past conceptualizations of salesperson expertise focus on the seller's offering; however, expertise about the supply chain partner's business is equally important. Without a clear understanding of the supply chain partner's requirements, it is difficult for the sales force to provide unique solutions that create value for the supply chain partner. It is imperative that the salesperson understand the supply chain partner's processes and requirements, and this should be a primary responsibility of the sales force. The personal selling literature has a long history of understanding customer needs (Ingram & LaForge, 1992), yet this concept is not integrated into the salesperson expertise literature. Salesperson expertise needs to include an external perspective—expertise in supply chain partner needs, requirements, processes, and systems.

Finally, supply chain management is both tactical and strategic in nature (Ross, 1998), yet these concepts are not conceptualized as dimensions of salesperson expertise. To create value for supply chain partners, salespeople need to possess tactical and strategic expertise. Thus, tactical and strategic dimensions need to be included in the construct of salesperson expertise.

Salesperson Logistics Expertise

Relationships between buyers and salespeople were examined by Garver (1998), using qualitative research methods (i.e., in-depth interviews) with buyers to understand how they perceive buyer-salesperson relationships. Grounded theory data analysis techniques were used to identify and develop constructs and theoretical models. From this study, the construct of salesperson logistics expertise emerged, a construct that has a strong and direct effect on the relationship between buyers and salespeople. Findings from this study suggest that salesperson logistics expertise includes the following dimensions: (a) internal (company) logistics expertise, (b) external (supply chain partner) logistics expertise, (c) tactical logistics expertise, and (d) strategic logistics expertise.

Internal (Company) Logistics Expertise

Buyers want to interact with salespeople who have logistics expertise in their firm's logistics systems, processes, and capabilities, and who can implement, facilitate, and coordinate these tasks efficiently and effectively. For example, can the salesperson expedite orders in case of an emergency? If the buyer is exploring new logistics tactics and strategies, can the salesperson discuss the selling firm's logistics capabilities (e.g., EDI, stockless delivery programs)? If the buyer needs to reduce inventory levels or order cycle time, can the salesperson present the seller's logistics capabilities to assist the buyer? In short, buyers need salespeople with a level of logistics expertise about their internal logistics systems, processes, and capabilities.

External (Supply Chain Partner) Logistics Expertise

Salespeople must have expertise in acquiring knowledge, as well as in-depth knowledge of the supply chain partner's logistical operations and requirements. For example, how do the supply chain partner's operational processes and systems work? What is the supply chain partner's current ordering process? What is the supply chain partner's current order cycle time? How much inventory does the supply chain partner hold in stock, and what are its inventory goals and objectives? From a logistics perspective, what is the current state of logistics operations, and where does the supply chain partner—as well as the entire supply chain—want to go with logistics processes in the future? Consistent with consultative selling, a salesperson who understands the supply chain partner's logistics needs can better coordinate company resources to meet and exceed those needs.

Consistent with these findings, successful salespeople usually possess numerous, in-depth knowledge structures regarding customer needs. Salesperson expertise research has not addressed salesperson expertise associated with understanding the customer, yet expertise in understanding the customer is key to many personal selling approaches, including adaptive selling, customer-oriented selling, and consultative selling (Ingram & LaForge, 1992). The salesperson must first possess supply chain partner expertise, understanding the supply chain partner's needs, wants, and desires. Once these are understood, the salesperson can tailor the seller's offering to meet those needs.

Strategic Logistics Expertise

The Global Logistics Research Team (1995) observed the importance of sharing *strategic* information with supply chain partners. Many supply chain activities are *strategic* in nature (Ross, 1998). Buyers from a qualitative study (Garver, 1998) also discussed their need for salespeople to possess long-term, strategic expertise. Strategic knowledge requires the salesperson to have knowledge of the supply chain partner's strategic plans and objectives, the supply chain's strategic plans and shared goals, and knowledge of how to help supply chain partners reach those strategic objectives by coordinating supplier resources and capabilities.

Traditionally, salespeople have been implementers of strategy; however, the more contemporary salesperson in the era of partnerships needs to be more strategically oriented (Ingram, 1996). The salesperson needs to become a boundary spanning agent who assists in planning, designing, and implementing both strategies and tactics. In this era, salespeople need to do more than just understand and explain their firm's product lines. Salespeople need to possess skills and knowledge in strategic thinking, which requires the salesperson to understand the strategic direction of the supply chain and that of supply chain partners (Ingram, 1996).

Tactical Logistics Expertise

Buyers also need salespeople to possess tactical logistics expertise. In many situations, the salesperson is called upon to supply information to put out fires that arise on a daily basis. Many of these issues are logistics related. For example, short-term logistics issues may include arranging emergency deliveries, expediting orders, substituting available product, and/or tracking certain invoices.

Although the role of the sales force is becoming more strategic in nature, a primary role of the personal selling function is still to implement tactical plans. The salesperson's daily duties often include putting out fires and taking care of daily operations, both within the selling firm and for supply chain partners.

Salesperson Logistics Expertise Matrix

Integrating findings from the literature and the qualitative study by Garver (1998), a broader and more encompassing definition of salesperson logistics expertise can be developed. Salesperson logistics expertise is defined as *a customer's perception of a salesperson's knowledge, experience, or skills relevant to logistics issues*. Salesperson logistics expertise concerns the seller's and supply chain partners' logistics operations, systems, and processes at both tactical and strategic levels. In addition to existing conceptualizations of salesperson expertise, this definition explicitly adds the logistics technical area and includes both an internal/external dimension and a tactical/strategic dimension.

To help conceptualize the entire domain of salesperson logistics expertise, a matrix is presented in Figure 5.1. At the top of the matrix, the internal/external dimension incorporates the need for the salesperson to possess expertise with his or her organization's logistics systems, processes, and capabilities (internal), and with his or her supply chain partner's logistics needs and requirements (external). The left side of the matrix incorporates the tactical and strategic dimensions. The four cells represent the domains of salesperson logistics expertise and include specific logistics and supply chain activities or areas of expertise that may be required of salespeople.

External/Tactical Dimension of Salesperson Logistics Experience

Does the salesperson understand the short-term, tactical logistics needs and requirements of supply chain partners? Expertise in this dimension is centered

	External (SCM Partners) Expertise	Internal (Company) Expertise
Tactical Expertise	Supply chain partner needs and requirements for ■ On-time delivery ■ Inventory level ■ Order processing ■ Order cycle lead times	Company logistical processes and systems ■ On-time service rates ■ Fill rates ■ Packaging designs ■ Order processing systems ■ Information systems
Strategic Expertise	Supply chain partner strategic goals and objectives ■ Current state of logistics competence? ■ SCM partner's logistics goals and objectives? ■ What do they need from a supplier to reach their logistical goals and objectives? ■ Supply chain strategic goals and objectives?	Company strategic logistical capabilities ■ EDI capabilities ■ JIT capabilities ■ Vendor-managed inventory programs ■ Logistics strategic capabilities and limitations

Figure 5.1. Salesperson Logistics Expertise

around fully understanding the day-to-day intricacies of the supply chain partner's logistics operations. For example, does the salesperson know the supply chain partner's current needs and requirements for on-time delivery, inventory staging, packaging, fill rates, and order cycle times? In case of a stock-out or other emergency, does the salesperson know what supply chain partners expect? In case of a problem, does the salesperson know the supply chain partner's system well enough to intervene in a timely fashion and/or recommend specific courses of action tailored to the supply chain partner's operations? Affirmative answers to these questions give the salesperson's company a clear competitive advantage over companies whose salespeople do not possess such expertise.

Internal/Tactical Dimension of Salesperson Logistics Expertise

In this dimension, the salesperson must have operational knowledge and expertise of his or her company's internal logistics systems and processes. For example, does the salesperson understand the intricacies of the order cycle, order processing, packaging, inventory policies, and delivery of the firm's product lines? Does the salesperson understand how the various components of the internal logistics process work together to deliver value to the customer?

When firms are trying to gain competitive advantage through superior logistics services, the salesperson must have expertise in this area to fully explain how his or her firm is differentiated from competitors. Further, the salesperson needs to understand his or her company's internal logistics systems so that he or she can recommend a plan of action that will meet the supply chain partners' requirements. For example, in the case of a back order, does the salesperson understand the selling firm's logistics processes to recommend the most effective plan of action to deliver product to the supply chain partner in a timely manner?

External/Strategic Dimension of Salesperson Logistics Expertise

This dimension includes the salesperson's knowledge of the supply chain partner's strategic initiatives and those of the entire supply chain. For example, what is the overall logistics system design the supply chain partners wants to realize? Are they considering outsourcing certain logistics activities? Would they be willing to pay to have these activities taken over by a supplier with that logistics expertise? What is the current state of this supply chain partner's logistics systems? What is the best way to bridge this gap between existing logistics systems and desired systems? What type of logistics services does the supply chain partner want to deliver to its supply chain partner? For example, the immediate supply chain partner may want to be able to provide overnight order fulfillment to its supply chain partners without any increase in inventory.

Clearly, this increase in service to supply chain partners without any increase in its own inventory levels would require inventory management and staging, plus cross-docking services, from its supplier. The salesperson could not offer this service (which has little to do with product knowledge) unless he or she was aware of this strategic initiative by the supply chain. Thus, to compete effectively in supply chains, the salesperson must fully understand the supply chain partners' strategic logistics goals and objectives.

Internal/Strategic Expertise Dimension of Salesperson Logistics Expertise

This dimension of expertise requires the salesperson to fully understand the strategic logistics capabilities of his or her firm. Does the salesperson know the potential capabilities and/or limitations of the selling firm? Does the salesperson fully understand his or her company's logistics strategies? For example, does the selling firm have EDI capabilities? Can it effectively and efficiently design and implement "just-in-time" or vendor-managed inventory programs? As noted by Ingram (1996), the salesperson needs to be able to recommend strategic possibilities and recommendations to customers. Only by possessing this internal, strategic logistics expertise can the salesperson truly be a "consultant" to supply chain partners.

New Roles for Sales Management

To support the sales force in its new supply chain management roles, sales managers need to train, support, and encourage supply chain activities and logistics expertise. To achieve this goal, sales managers must also adopt a new orientation and embrace new management techniques to enhance supply chain performance. Specifically, sales managers must become "change agents" in the sales organization and lead the sales force in a new direction. Training programs, performance objectives, and compensation packages need to be adapted and better aligned with a supply chain management. As each of these topics is discussed, managerial implications will be discussed accordingly.

Sales Managers as Change Agents

Sales managers must lead the sales force in a new direction and develop a new sales culture. They must develop a sales culture that enhances supply chain performance. Critical values in this new culture must include the salesperson as a relationship manager with a service orientation who creates value for supply chain partners and enhances overall supply chain performance. Changing company culture is a difficult task, but business success in the supply chain relies on such change. Sales training programs, new performance objectives, and new compensation packages are essential in achieving a cultural transition.

Sales Training

Sales training is a key component in developing a new sales culture and developing the necessary expertise to perform supply chain services effectively. In fact, many sales managers are placing more emphasis on sales training programs to better equip their sales force (Honeycutt et al., 1993). To effectively equip the sales force, what should be included in a supply chain management sales training program?

From a content perspective, the importance of supply chain management as a new business paradigm must first be communicated and understood by the sales force. Once this is accomplished, key concepts of supply chain management in general need to be communicated to and understood by the sales force. For example, the importance of cooperative behaviors, information sharing, and strong relationships need to be communicated. Clearly, the sales force must understand key activities of supply chain management and its relationships to overall business success.

Once a general understanding of supply chain management is accomplished, the specific role of the sales force can be addressed. Training programs about the specific role of the sales force should focus on knowledge and skill development. Skill development should include cooperative behaviors, sharing and capturing information, and relationship management. For example, the sales force role of sharing and capturing information among supply chain partners, and knowledge of how this information can contribute to effective and efficient supply chain management, should be discussed. Furthermore, skill development in sharing and capturing information should be discussed and learned through experiential methods (e.g., role playing). The salesperson as a relational manager and the effect of this role on supply chain management should also be addressed and learned through experiential methods. In short, the supply chain activities discussed earlier should be covered, and skills in these areas need to be developed.

Because supply chain behaviors and activities require the salesperson to possess logistics expertise, the salesperson logistics expertise matrix developed earlier can be used to guide sales training.

Developing Salesperson Logistics Expertise

Salespeople who are experts in their firm's logistics activities most likely obtained this expertise through ad hoc experience, and *not* by design. Instead of salespeople learning logistics expertise entirely through ad hoc experience, sales training programs should address this area and help salespeople develop the appropriate logistics skill sets so that they become valuable assets to supply chain partners. Using the salesperson logistics expertise matrix as a guide, sales managers should incorporate supply chain and logistics management education to develop salesperson logistics expertise at both tactical and strategic levels.

Internal Logistics Expertise

Specifically, salespeople need firsthand experience with their firm's internal logistics processes, systems, and capabilities. A full understanding of the operational processes enhances inter-functional coordination and the salesperson's level of logistics expertise. From a tactical perspective, this expertise helps salespeople manage logistics processes and systems to meet the needs of supply chain partners. From a strategic perspective, salespeople will understand the logistics capabilities needed to meet the strategic goals of various supply chain partners and the overall supply chain.

To accomplish this task, traditional lectures delivered in conjunction with sales trainees obtaining actual knowledge and experience in different logistics positions (e.g., shipping, inventory management, materials handling) will help salespeople fully grasp the firm's internal processes from both a tactical and strategic perspective. Gaining firsthand experience will help salespeople understand the intricacies of logistics processes.

External Logistics Expertise

Although most marketers recognize the importance of salespeople fully understanding customer needs and requirements, research suggests that salespeople may have limited knowledge of their customer's logistics needs and requirements (Lambert, Marmostein, & Sharma, 1990; Sharma & Lambert, 1994). These researchers compared buyers and their salesperson's responses on many logistics issues, including average lead time for stock and custom items, acceptable delays for stock and custom items, minimum acceptable fill rate for stock items, and inventory control policies. Concerning the buyer's logistics needs and requirements, salespeople could *not* accurately predict the buyer's desired performance levels on these issues. The sales force in supply chain management needs to thoroughly understand the supply chain partner's logistics requirements, a competency to be developed in sales training programs.

Salespeople should be trained to better understand their customer's logistics processes and systems. For example, what are the logistics trends within their supply chain and within their industry? What logistics goals might their supply chain partners try to accomplish? What are typical logistics problems, issues, and opportunities that their supply chain partners face on a daily basis? Contracting with logistics experts within the industry or internal logistics managers to conduct training seminars may help accomplish these training goals. Once again, traditional lectures delivered in combination with visiting cutting-edge logistics customers may also give the sales force a more in-depth perspective of its customer's logistics operations.

Sales training programs should continue their work in teaching salespeople how to uncover, identify, and understand the customer's needs and requirements. Sales trainers may take a lesson from qualitative researchers, who are experts in gaining an in-depth understanding of certain phenomenon (e.g., a supply chain partner's logistics processes). For example, qualitative researchers are experts in interviewing participants and probing deeply into participants' experiences. Qualitative interviewing techniques, procedures, and mind-sets may help salespeople gain a better understanding of their customers. Interviewing skills can best be developed in an interactive format that may include role playing conducted with people from the logistics function.

Additionally, teaching salespeople participant observation techniques may be particularly helpful in overcoming the limitations of interviewing customers. If properly trained, salespeople can look beyond the customer's verbal reports to identify potential logistics problems and opportunities. Employing this skill, salespeople may be able to uncover logistics issues about which supply chain partners are not even aware. To teach this skill, sales training programs should be designed to train salespeople how to observe logistics operations and identify potential problems and opportunities. Specifically, training videos or other multimedia tools could be developed that "walk" salespeople through different logistics facilities. Throughout this video, certain logistics opportunities and/or problems could be discovered by the salesperson solely through observation. Once these issues are identified, the trainees must make recommendations to solve logistics problems or seize opportunities based on their newly acquired knowledge of logistics and supply chain management.

Performance Evaluation

Performance evaluations should be designed to reinforce and support sales training. Designing appropriate performance evaluations is critically important to bring about desired sales force expertise, activities, and outcomes. Because performance evaluations can have dramatic impacts on sales force behaviors, it is imperative that traditional performance evaluations be redesigned to motivate and encourage the appropriate supply chain behaviors and activities. Inappropriate performance evaluations may in fact motivate behaviors that are *counterproductive* to supply chain performance.

Traditionally, salespeople have been evaluated and compensated primarily based on their contribution to sales volume, profit, and new business. Although these are valuable measures of traditional sales performance, do these outcome measures indicate whether the salesperson is creating value for supply chain partners and fostering effective supply chain performance? Although business has predominantly used sales volume or profit as *the* performance measure of success, supply chain management philosophies suggest that other measures of performance may be better indicators of selling performance.

Earlier, we discussed the need for salesperson logistics expertise and the salesperson's role in facilitating, coordinating, and implementing supply chain management activities (cooperative behaviors, information sharing, relationship building, etc.). To motivate salespeople to effectively develop this expertise and conduct these activities, performance evaluations need to assess how well the sales force is performing these supply chain management roles.

The Global Logistics Research Team (1995) suggests that both internal and external measures of performance are needed to effectively capture logistics and supply chain performance. This logic holds true for evaluating sales force performance in supply chain management. Both internal and external performance measures should be used to motivate and encourage desired supply chain management activities.

From an internal perspective, sales managers need to design measures to evaluate how well the sales force is performing new supply chain management activities and duties. For example, how well is the salesperson sharing and gathering information with other supply chain partners? How well is the salesperson providing information to adjust and improve supply chain forecasts? How well is the salesperson conducting joint planning and goal setting with supply chain partners? Although the specifics of developing many internal measures of performance are company specific, it is important that these internal measures support and encourage the appropriate supply chain management behaviors.

From an external perspective, sales managers need to devise performance measures that tap into the supply chain partners' perceptions of sales force performance. For example, supply chain management activities suggest that salespeople should be developing strong supply chain relationships through salesperson services, information sharing, integrating behaviors, cooperation, and displaying salesperson logistics expertise. Sales managers need to measure performance of these activities from the supply chain partner's perspective. For example, how well is the sales force fulfilling the supply chain partner's needs, wants, and desires? From the supply chain partner's perspective, how well is the sales force developing and maintaining strong relationships? How well is the salesperson displaying salesperson logistics expertise? To measure the supply chain partners' perception of performance, sales managers need to gather objective, external data from supply chain partners. To this end, IBM and Xerox are collecting customer-driven data about the performance of their sales forces. These data are used to evaluate sales force performance in relationship management.

Many firms implementing total quality management have been collecting customers' perceptions of performance for quite some time. To gather external sales force performance data, customer satisfaction surveys need to be updated to include the sales force and its new role in supply chain management. In short, customer satisfaction surveys need to include questions about sales force performance in a supply chain management environment.

These new measures of sales force performance are meant to supplement traditional measures of sales force performance such as sales volume, profits, and increasing new business. Consistent with the balanced scorecard approach to measuring performance, sales force performance should be measured from a financial perspective (i.e., sales volume), an internal perspective, and an external perspective.

Using Performance Evaluations to Identify Sales Force Training Needs

A key aspect of successful training programs is accurately identifying and assessing the training needs of the sales force (Honeycutt et al., 1993). Currently, most companies use managerial judgment to identify training needs, yet Puri (1993) suggests customer perceptions of performance should be used to identify sales force training needs.

To accomplish this, the sales manager must identify an exhaustive list of the supply chain behaviors, elements of salesperson logistics expertise, and drivers of supply chain relationship development. Although desired supply chain behaviors may be different across various supply chains, the supply chain behaviors discussed earlier and elements of salesperson logistics expertise should be useful guides.

Once the appropriate drivers of performance are identified, performance on these dimensions can be assessed. Comparing actual performance scores to goals or some other standards, supply chain management strengths and weaknesses of the sales force can be determined. Comparing actual performance scores to a standard shows where the sales force needs to improve from the supply chain partner's perspective. Thus, sales force weaknesses are identified as training needs.

This information can help identify training needs of individual salespeople, segments of the sales force, and the overall sales force. For example, each salesperson would realize his or her strengths and weaknesses from the supply chain partner's perspective. Individualized training programs and goals could be developed for individual salespeople. Additionally, salespeople could be segmented according to their common training needs. For example, statistical techniques such as cluster analysis could be used to group salespeople with similar supply chain management strengths and weaknesses. Finally, strengths and weaknesses of the entire sales force could be determined readily.

Once the training needs have been identified in this manner, the sales manager and/or sales trainers can devise a training program to improve sales force performance in prioritized areas. Training programs can be designed for the overall sales force or customized for different segments of the sales force based on training needs. After the training has been implemented, objective customer-driven data can be used to assess the effectiveness of the training program. Assessing the effectiveness of training programs is often difficult (Honeycutt et al., 1993), yet implementing a customer-driven data program makes this task relatively easy and effective to implement.

Reward Systems

Compensation is a priority for most salespeople. Many researchers and practitioners believe that salespeople are competitive and are high achievers, and that they often choose careers in personal selling to earn attractive incomes. This drive and determination is important for salespeople to possess and needs to be focused in the right direction. It is important for sales managers to reward sales force behaviors and activities that achieve long-term goals desired by the organization. The key is to motivate the sales force to engage in the appropriate supply chain behaviors and activities and develop stronger supply chain relationships. Compensation needs to be closely aligned with sales force performance evaluations. Clearly, the sales force will look to compensation packages to assess the importance management places on different activities and outcomes. Compensation tied to supply chain management behaviors clearly sends a message to the sales force regarding the importance placed on these activities. The key point is to reward salespeople for performing effective supply chain management activities and behaviors, and for developing and maintaining strong supply chain relationships.

Conclusions

Examining the role of the sales function in supply chain management means exploring new ground for both researchers and practitioners. The purpose of this chapter is to put forth new roles for the sales function, and more research is needed in this area. Because theory development is scant in this area, early research endeavors focusing on relevant theory development would be helpful to both researchers and practitioners. Qualitative research is an excellent tool to help researchers develop relevant theoretical frameworks. To this end, two different perspectives need to be explored: those of the focus firm and of supply chain partners of the focus firm. Examining the focal firm, case study techniques can be used to explore how leading edge firms are redesigning the sales function to create value in a supply chain management environment. Furthermore, effective sales management techniques that support this effort should also be explored.

From a different perspective, qualitative techniques could be used to explore what supply chain partners value in their interactions with salespeople. From a supply chain partner's perspective, what should the role of the sales force be in a supply chain management environment? How can the sales force create value for the supply chain and supply chain partners? What services and activities should the sales force undertake? How do we train, motivate, and compensate the sales force to deliver these services and activities?

As more and more firms compete through supply chain management, the role of the sales force will continue to evolve. Researchers need to examine this change and build new theoretical frameworks that will assist practitioners in effective supply chain management.

6

Research and Development in Supply Chain Management

ZACH G. ZACHARIA

Executive Summary

This chapter describes the role of research and development (R&D) within the firm, with suppliers and customers, and within the supply chain. In this chapter I do the following:

- Examine R&D within the firm (intrafirm) from a traditional perspective and discuss R&D inputs, outputs, and strengths
- Identify the major role of R&D as new product development and discuss the importance of an effective new product development process in the current business environment
- Discuss some of the important success factors associated with new product development such as cycle time, parallel development, cross-functional development, and integrated product development
- Examine R&D between firms (interfirm) and the impact of interfirm integration on new product development
- Look at the importance of incorporating customer requirements and supplier involvement in the new product development process through interfirm R&D
- Discuss the role of R&D within the supply chain, especially in the role of new product development

- Examine four important factors associated with R&D in a supply chain context—globalization, postponement, speed to market, and flexible new product development

These discussions lead to the conclusions that

- Supply chain activities have a major impact on the capabilities and profitability of the supply chain and its member firms in new product development
- Innovative and effective new product development will be important in the turbulent, highly uncertain business environment of the future
- By collaborating with immediate customers and suppliers, R&D teams can significantly improve the new product development process
- By collaborating with customers' customers and suppliers' suppliers along the supply chain, R&D will improve the new product development process
- Companies that are multinational in scope can benefit through globalization of the R&D process and collaborating with global supply chain partners
- The concept of postponement, delaying final product configuration as close to the end consumer as possible, benefits greatly from collaboration with R&D supply chain partners
- Speed to market or reducing the cycle time to develop new products can be improved significantly through supply chain R&D involvement
- Flexible new product development enables companies to incorporate rapidly changing customer requirements and evolving technologies through supply chain R&D involvement

Broadening the knowledge base involved in a firm's R&D process better enables managers to design and develop effective and efficient new product development systems. This suggests that developing a supply chain orientation for research and development leads to opportunities for lower costs, improved customer value, and competitive advantages for the long term.

Introduction

This chapter looks at the role of research and development (R&D) and new product development (NPD) in the context of supply chain management. The first section examines R&D within the firm (intrafirm) in a traditional context with its responsibility for NPD and the need for integration with other functions in the firm for increased NPD success. The second section looks at how going beyond the boundaries of the firm and collaborating with suppliers and

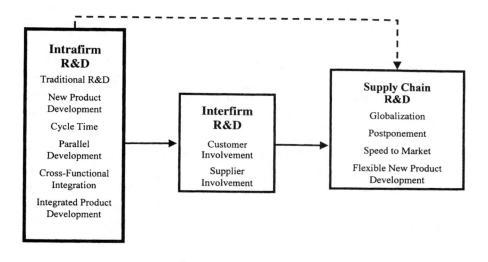

Figure 6.1 R&D Supply Chain Model

customers can facilitate R&D and NPD. The third section considers the advantages of going beyond working with the immediate supplier and immediate customer to consider suppliers' suppliers and customers' customers—in other words, how a supply chain perspective can facilitate R&D.

R&D is an important function in most organizations today. Productive R&D is increasingly necessary for business success and value creation (Menke, 1997). R&D forms the cornerstone of the traditional paradigm for product innovation (Galbraith, 1952; Kamien & Schwartz, 1982; Schumpeter, 1942). In the traditional paradigm, new product outcomes are assumed to depend on the scale of investment in R&D. To fully understand the role of R&D in supply chain management, it is useful to examine intrafirm R&D, interfirm R&D, and supply chain R&D (see Figure 6.1).

Intrafirm R&D

To examine intrafirm R&D fully, we need to look at the traditional role of R&D in the firm, new product development, cycle time, parallel development, cross-functional development, and integrated product development.

Traditional R&D

In a survey of 45 multinational companies, Roger Miller (1995) identified four types of R&D management. The first type is managing R&D at the science frontier (R. Miller, 1995). In these firms, R&D serves two strategic purposes: (a) developing and controlling intellectual property, and (b) interfacing with government R&D support programs in such areas as microelectronics and telecommunications.

The second type is managing R&D in revenue-dependency contexts (R. Miller, 1995). In this type, R&D activities are integrated into the operations of the firm through the introduction of revenue-dependency schemes. Internal clients buy research services from the R&D division to solve their own, or their customers', operational problems.

The third type is managing R&D for total quality management integration (R. Miller, 1995). A number of firms have successfully developed methods to cross-functionally integrate R&D with marketing, engineering, purchasing, and manufacturing. Product development is managed from a life-cycle perspective and involves the merging of functional viewpoints to achieve cost reduction and reduce time to market. In a life-cycle perspective, R&D is involved at all stages of product/process development: advanced research, definition of attributes, design and engineering, transfer to production, and maintenance and services.

The fourth type of R&D management is to incorporate R&D into the strategic arena (R. Miller, 1995). In some firms R&D has moved beyond a preoccupation with processes. The goal is no longer to develop and produce high-quality products at the right time but also to use scientific information to explore new markets. These firms are under pressure to maintain a constant flow of new products, and R&D is a major strategic tool for the firm.

Another methodology, suggested by Hansen, Weiss, and Kwak (1999), to classify R&D is to analyze the allocation of resources for R&D into three types or phases typical of most companies: basic research, applied research, and development. In the pharmaceutical industry, these three types are called discover research, preclinical research, and clinical research. The concept is that different firms choose to allocate resources differently to each of these three phases, according to their particular requirements. Firms that depend on highly innovative products tend to allocate more funds to basic research. In the pharmaceutical industry, for example, 38% of R&D funds are allocated to basic research, whereas in the chemical industry this number drops to 5%, reflecting the large dependence of the pharmaceutical industry on truly new, highly innovative products (Hansen et al., 1999). Basic R&D or technical capability-building generally is seen as solely the responsibility of R&D organizations (Davidson, Clamen, & Karol, 1999).

Another perspective on R&D is provided by Prestwood, Ransley, and Schumann (1995), who suggest that R&D has four goals: (a) to take advantage of the future opportunities in the market (customers, competition, technology) and avoid or minimize the threats, (b) to meet the needs of the firm's stakeholders, (c) to utilize the capabilities of the firm, and (d) to fulfill the desires of the members of the firm. Current capabilities, which include projects, resources, and culture of the organization, should be assessed and evaluated against the future desired state. The difference between the current capabilities and the future desired state necessary to fulfill the firm's vision, mission, and goals may be closed through innovation by R&D (Prestwood et al., 1995).

There has been a reallocation of R&D efforts away from basic longer-range, high-risk research toward products and process development, according to an analysis of changes in the structure of R&D organizations and in management practices from 1988 to 1996 (Whiteley, Bean, & Russo, 1998). This suggests a trend toward more applied research.

Chiesa (1996) suggests that an R&D structure should be designed to assist in three main tasks: constituent technology development, product development, and technical support to other functions. Accordingly, the objectives of R&D are to (a) develop the technical knowledge, skills, and technologies that go into forming the company's own stock of knowledge (its future core competencies); (b) exploit the available stock of knowledge and technologies as well as the innovation process in order to develop new products (Chiesa, 1996); and (c) provide technical service to support the company's other functions, particularly manufacturing and marketing (Chiesa, 1996). This suggests that the traditional role of R&D within most firms is to *develop new products and discover new processes to improve the production process*. This definition of the role of R&D will be used for the remainder of this chapter.

R&D Inputs and Outputs

The inputs to R&D are people, information, ideas, equipment, facilities, specific requests, and funds. As a service department, R&D does much of its work in response to specific requests from marketing, manufacturing, engineering, and other departments (Brown & Svenson, 1998).

The processing system is the R&D lab itself, which turns the inputs into outputs by writing proposals, conducting research, testing hypotheses, and reporting results. Typical outputs include patents, new products, new processes, publications, or simply facts, principles, or knowledge that were unknown before (Brown & Svenson, 1998).

The receiving system comprises the various consumers of R&D outputs: marketing, business planning, manufacturing, engineering, operations, and other departments that make use of R&D's products and services. The receiving system for R&D also includes such external users of its outputs as the academic community (for academic research and publication). For an R&D lab in a profit-making organization, the outcomes are cost reductions, sales improvements, product improvements, new products, market share, and capital avoidance (Brown & Svenson, 1998). R&D outputs are also evaluated by a variety of outside sources (e.g., journal editorial boards, patent offices) as well as internal sources (e.g., R&D management, top management, engineering, manufacturing). Outputs are measured on three dimensions: quality, quantity, and cost. Outputs of R&D include research proposals written, papers published, designs produced, products designed, presentations made, patents received, awards won, projects completed, and books written.

The true product of R&D does not specifically have to be tangible; instead, it can be information that comes from the collective knowledge of scientists, engineers, and technicians (Mills, 1998). This knowledge is embodied in product specifications, prototype formulas, experimental designs and results, process guidelines, and approved production formulas (Mills, 1998).

The need to improve competitive performance has caused companies to search for new and more agile capability, including ways to acquire knowledge rapidly and to manipulate new tools and technology directly (W. L. Miller, 1995). The need to reduce cycle time translates into a need to know sooner about which new capabilities are possible. This has pulled R&D into performing more of the traditional roles of marketing and sales and going beyond simply providing traditional technical support (W. L. Miller, 1995). R&D has a responsibility for identifying latent customer needs that create business opportunities enabled by technology, developing the architecture for new application systems enabled by technology, and performing field tests with customers to target, develop, and validate capabilities that are enabled by technology (W. L. Miller, 1995).

R&D's importance in many firms has grown with increased emphasis on new product development. For many industries, new product development is now the single most important factor driving firm success or failure (Schilling & Hill, 1998). As competitive pressures intensify, manufacturers need to discover new ways to conceive and deliver innovative products more rapidly, while maintaining quality and reducing product costs. In a recent study, 62% of U.S. midsize manufacturers indicated that bringing new products to market rapidly has become increasingly vital (Adrian, 1998). The dramatic increase in emphasis on new product development as a competitive dimension can be traced back to both the globalization of markets and the fragmentation of markets into ever smaller niches (Schilling & Hill, 1998). As new markets develop both internationally and domestically, companies have adapted and modified existing products or developed new products to meet this increased demand.

Successful products and processes that come from R&D translate into improved company performance. The effectiveness of R&D can be improved by broadening the scope of development and discovery to include the discovery of latent customer needs that can be served by new technology-enabled capabilities (W. L. Miller, 1995). R&D develops the means to meet the needs of the customer, typically identified by marketing. R&D also helps to develop new technological levels of performance, which enable new customer benefits to be created (O'Dwyer & O'Toole, 1998). For the purpose of this chapter, the typical output of R&D is taken to be *new products or new processes*.

R&D Strength

Research and development strength refers to a company's resources and capacity for new technology development. In product management studies, R&D strength is expected to be related positively to product advantage, because firms with greater technology development resources are more likely to create products with more innovative features (Hill & Snell, 1989; Szymanski, Bharadwaj, & Varadarajan, 1993). In an investigation of 122 industrial firms, Cooper (1984) observed that R&D strength has a significant effect on a firm's ability to produce "highly innovative and high-technology products—ones that are mechanically and technically complex, affect strongly customer use behavior, and feature several differential advantages" (p. 248). Holak, Parry, and Song (1991) present several scenarios based on the PIMS database that show divergent effects of R&D on outcome measures. In general, they demonstrate that R&D investment exerts a positive impact on performance.

R&D strength is a secondary contributing factor to new product advantage because of its generally recognized role in new product development (Chidamber & Kon, 1994; Freeman, 1994). Day (1994) considers R&D strength a major internal capability and believes that strong R&D provides a technological base indispensable to new product development. Clearly, these authors suggest that R&D has a critical role to play in NPD, which is the focus of the rest of the chapter. This view is especially appropriate considering the trend toward more applied (products and process) research found in most firms today.

New Product Development

New product development (NPD) has been an important concern of business organizations for more than 40 years, and typically it is done within the firm. NPD is still very relevant, especially with the shorter product life cycles and the momentous technological changes going on around us. Booz, Allen, and Hamilton, Inc. (1982) found that over a 5-year period, new products accounted for growth in 28% of the companies surveyed. It also found that the failure rate of new products introduced between 1963 and 1981 was as high as 35%, which was later confirmed by another survey done by Cooper (1990). The importance of NPD has grown dramatically over the last few decades, and NPD is now the dominant driver of competition in many industries (Schilling & Hill, 1998).

Successful firms are those that articulate their strategic intent and map their R&D portfolio to find a fit between their new product development goals and their current resources and competencies (Schilling & Hill, 1998). In industries such as automobiles, biotechnology, consumer and industrial electronics, computer software, and pharmaceuticals, companies often depend on products introduced within the last 5 years for more than 50% of their annual sales (Schilling & Hill, 1998).

Today's climate of new product development is characterized by increased domestic and global competition, continuous development of new technologies that quickly make existing products obsolete, changing customer requirements that truncate product life cycles, rising product development costs, and an increasing dependence on external organizations (Gupta & Wilemon, 1990). The business environment of the 1990s can be characterized as increasingly dynamic in terms of increasing technological complexity, demanding markets, explosion of knowledge, and increasing global competition (Peter, 1996). To continue to survive and grow in this competitive arena, companies have had to look at ways to improve their new product development process.

Successful innovation and new product development are important for the growth and long-term health of the organization (Calantone & di-Benedetto, 1988; Cooper & Kleinschmidt, 1991). A continuous flow of new products is the lifeblood of an organization (Barczak, 1995). Successful new products help companies develop new markets as well as cater to the emerging needs of existing markets (Nakata & Sivakumar, 1996). The successful launch of new products is critical to maintaining market leadership (Rangan, Menzes, & Maier, 1992). Up to one third of the financial growth in companies is a direct result of new products (Dean & Okonkwo, 1989). In the 1970s, new products accounted for 20% of the companies' profits; by the 1980s, profit combinations of new products rose to more than 30% (Takeuchi & Nonaka, 1986), and this was expected to increase in the 1990s. Welter (1989) stated in the 1990s, the average company would generate 40% of its sales from products less than 5 years old.

NPD Defined

New product development is defined as the process of conceiving and creating a new product and the outcomes of that process (Nakata & Sivakumar, 1996; Sheremata, 1998). According to Hall (1991), new products and services can be classified into five categories:

1. The break-through product,
2. The "it's new for us" product,
3. The new improved, next-generation product,
4. The line extension product, and
5. The three Rs (repackaged, repositioned, recycled).

Meyers and Tucker (1989) developed another classification system based on the process of developing and introducing a new product or service:

1. Radical innovation—the market is unfamiliar with the product class and technology,
2. Routine innovation—the market is familiar with the product class but the technology is new,
3. Market modification—the technology is well known but users are unfamiliar with the product, or
4. Product modification—neither the market nor the technoloy is new.

Even though it is possible to categorize new development projects in several ways, such as the five categories used by Hall (1991) or the four categories used by Meyers and Tucker (1989), this chapter focuses on two categories—radical and incremental innovation. Radical products are breakthrough products that are new to the market in terms of product class and technology, for which target customers are unknown, and that rely on unproven production technologies (Lynn, Mazzuca, Morone, & Paulson, 1998, Song & Montoya-Weiss, 1998). Radical NPD is characterized by uncertainty, especially with respect to goals and means. The final shape and form of a marketable product are unclear. Radical new product development is difficult, but consistently developing radical new products provides a dynamic capability that is valuable, rare, inimitable, and nonsubstitutable (Teece, Pisano, & Shuen, 1997). Incremental products, as defined in this chapter, are all other types of innovation, such as products new to the company, line extensions, next-generation products, and repackaged, repositioned, and recycled products.

The traditional innovation system has separated the responsibility for types of knowledge acquisition, with one organization having responsibility for knowledge about customer needs and another for knowledge about technology (W. L. Miller, 1995). Typically, management assigns marketing the responsibility for determining customer needs and assigns R&D the responsibility for supplying the technology (W. L. Miller, 1995). This separation of responsibility for separate knowledge domains works for incremental product development; however, it does not work adequately for "new to the world" product features, products or product platform concepts that are targeting latent customer needs, and attempting to discover new markets or market segments (W. L. Miller, 1995).

Unfortunately, although NPD is so important, many of the NPD processes currently used are not very successful. Only one new product development project in four becomes a winner, and almost 50% of the resources American firms devote to innovation are spent on products that are commercial failures (Cooper, 1990). Many firms continue to neglect the organizational integration required for successful new product development or overlook important activities during their NPD process (Millson, 1993).

In a 1997 survey of U.S. manufacturers, more than 70% indicated that their new product introductions are most often driven by customer demands/requirements; other (less important) new product drivers are competitive pressures

(16%), internal innovation (9%), and new technology (6%) (Adrian, 1998). The time associated with developing new products (NPD cycle time) has become more critical because product life cycles are shrinking and obsolescence is occurring more quickly than in the past, while competition has intensified (Hayes, Wheelwright, & Clark, 1988; Womak, Jones, & Roos, 1990).

Cycle Time

The development cycle time for a new product is the elapsed time from idea generation to product launch (Gupta & Wilemon, 1990). A 1989 study of NPD best practices sponsored by the Product Development and Management Association (PDMA) reported that nearly 41% of the respondents surveyed indicated that overall, their organizations were developing new products more quickly than they had been 5 years previously (Page, 1993). Although product life cycles have compressed, markets have also fragmented into smaller niches (Schilling & Hill, 1998). Product life cycles have been shortening as the innovations of others make existing products obsolete (Schilling & Hill, 1998).

Minimizing time to market—or cycle time—is necessary for a number of reasons (Kessler & Chakrabarti, 1996; Stalk & Hout, 1990). A firm that is slow to market with a particular generation of technology is unlikely to fully amortize the costs of development before that generation becomes obsolete, especially in dynamic industries such as electronics, where life cycles of personal computers and semiconductors can be 12 months. Companies with compressed cycle times are more likely to be the first to introduce products that embody new technologies, and as a result they are better positioned to capture first mover advantages (Schilling & Hill, 1998). Companies with short cycle times can continually upgrade their products, incorporating state-of-the-art technology when it becomes available. This enables them to better serve consumer needs, outrun their slower competitors, and build brand loyalty. It also enables them to offer a wider range of new products to better serve niches (Schilling & Hill, 1998).

Technological development waves are becoming shorter and shorter, which means product life cycles also are becoming shorter (Topfer, 1995). As product life cycles get shorter and technology seems to change at an ever-increasing pace, it becomes especially critical to have an effective, efficient, and successful new product development process. The scope of the NPD process encompasses the delivery of a high-quality, cost-effective product incorporating the latest technology in the shortest time from concept to market (Birou & Fawcett, 1994).

The importance of time-based competition (Stalk, 1988) is also beginning to be recognized as a source of competitive advantage. Firms introducing high-tech products 6 months past the projected release date but within budget realized a 33% decrease in expected profit over the next 5 years. On the other hand, firms introducing products on time but 50% over budget suffered only a 4% reduction in profits (Gupta & Wilemon, 1990). This research was replicated by Gupta and Souder (1998), who were able to demonstrate that companies with short cycle times for new products (a) extensively involve customers and suppliers in their new product R&D processes, (b) adopt a product design philosophy that encourages the development of future innovations at low cost, (c) incorporate manufacturing concerns at the design stage, (d) test new products in user facilities during their development, and (e) have well-developed procedures for transferring learning from one project to another. Short-cycle-time companies were also more profitable than longer-cycle-time companies and exhibited new product success rates above their industry averages, thus demonstrating that short-cycle-time management pays dividends to the bottom line. Time pressures have become more critical, and delay in the delivery of new product innovations can cost firms significant proportions of related profits, but focusing only on speed to market may miss the point. The real challenge is how to create faster, better, and cheaper products, not just to create products faster (Wind & Mahajan, 1997). Despite pressures to introduce products more rapidly, virtually all companies reported that having high-quality products is a vital success factor (Adrian, 1998); however, 88% indicated that the cost of their product is still crucial for their competitive success (Adrian, 1998).

Respondents to a survey conducted by Gupta and Wilemon (1990) identified several contributing factors to the need for accelerated development of new products: (a) increased competition, (b) rapid rate of technological change, (c) consumer demand for new products, (d) shortened length of the product life cycle, and (e) the desire to be first to the market. Reducing cycle time or increasing the speed to market has become more important and critical for companies to increase the chances of new product success.

Parallel Development

In the 1950s and 1960s, and perhaps even today, functions such as marketing, R&D, manufacturing, and logistics worked independently when developing a new product. This has resulted in functional silos working in a linear sequential process. According to Tom Peters (1988), writing on the subject of new product development:

> Rip apart a badly developed project and you will unfailingly find 75 percent of slippage attributable to (1) "siloing" or sending memos up and down vertical organizational "silos" or "stovepipes" for decisions, and (2) sequential problem solving. (p. 211)

NPD traditionally has been viewed as a relay race, with each function passing the baton as the product got developed (Cooper, 1990). In this respect, NPD research could be broadly divided into an integrated (involving more than one function) product development approach or a sequential product development (SPD) approach, where functions such as R&D, marketing, manufacturing, and logistics work independently and in sequence. Typically, firms use a sequential process for new product development, wherein development proceeds sequentially from one functional group to the next. This sequential process includes a number of stages where decisions are made as to whether to proceed to the next stage, send the project back for further work, or kill the project (Schilling & Hill, 1998). R&D tends to take the lead in product design, and manufacturing takes the lead in process design. This can lead to problems when R&D fails to communicate directly with manufacturing, and product design proceeds without manufacturing requirements in mind. A sequential process has no early warning system to indicate that planned features are not manufacturable (Schilling & Hill, 1998). Consequently, cycle time can lengthen as the project iterates between the product design and process design stages (Griffin, 1992).

According to the marketing NPD literature, two models are primarily used in a sequential NPD process. In a technology-driven model, R&D develops a new and innovative product, manufacturing builds it, and marketing sells it (Van de Ven, 1986). Each function works independently. This approach worked well in the 1950s and 1960s, when companies were trying to keep up with demand. Specialization in the assembly line led to lower costs and faster production. Therefore, specializing within each functional group in the NPD process was expected to lead to quicker development. Unfortunately, this did not result in quicker NPD, and it certainly did not translate into more successful new products in the marketplace.

The second sequential NPD model is the customer- or needs-driven model, where marketing comes up with the product idea from customers, the idea is given to R&D to prototype, and finally it passes to manufacturing to produce (Van de Ven, 1986). This approach has increased the rate of successful new products but still results in long development times and an inefficient NPD process.

A solution to this problem is to use a parallel process instead of a sequential process. A parallel process is an integrated approach to new product development that can also lead to compressed cycle time. Process design, for example, starts long before product design is finalized, thereby establishing closer coordination between these different stages and minimizing the chance that R&D will design products that are difficult or costly to manufacture (Schilling & Hill, 1998). Time losses between the product and process design stage typically are reduced or eliminated, which should lead to compressed cycle time.

Kessler and Chakrabarti (1996) argue that integration enables a faster development process. They suggest that faster development is associated with lower development cost. Thus, integration between the functions has been proposed as a key enabler to improve development process performance and NPD project success. Researchers have postulated a relationship between successful NPD and the degree of interorganizational integration that exists during the NPD process between the marketing and R&D functions (Gupta, Raj, & Wilemon, 1985). Other researchers have suggested that all the firm's functional departments need to be integrated during the NPD process (Ruekert & Walker, 1987a). It has also been pointed out that a cooperative organizational climate does not ensure NPD success but that such a climate does appear to be a facilitator (Capon, Farley, Lehmann, & Hulbert, 1992).

Interestingly, project teams with greater representation from different functional groups appear to increase the speed of product development (Kessler & Chakrabarti, 1996). This provides support to the idea of using a cross-functional approach to new product development.

Cross-Functional NPD

Many authors suggest that cross-functional teams should be utilized early in the NPD process (Carmel, 1995; Gupta & Wilemon, 1990; Mabert, Muth, & Schmenner, 1992; Trygg, 1993). In general, this is perceived as the most effective way to reduce product development time. A lack of communication between the marketing, R&D, and manufacturing functions of a company can be extremely detrimental to the NPD process. The use of cross-functional product development teams minimizes miscommunication (S. L. Brown & Eisenhardt, 1995). Cross-functional miscommunication leads to a poor fit between product attributes and customer requirements. R&D cannot design products that fit customer requirements without input from marketing. By working closely with R&D, manufacturing can ensure that R&D designs products that are relatively easy to manufacture. Ease of manufacturing can lower both unit costs and product defects, which translates into a lower final price, higher quality, and shorter cycle times (Schilling & Hill, 1998).

Strong functional/organizational boundaries can be barriers to speed and efficiency (Davidson et al., 1999). This has led to the proliferation of cross-functional/cross-organizational product development teams. The "hand-off" model of moving product development from one function to the next has given way to a team-based approach in which a single team, with support from the respective functions, carries product development from concept through commercialization (Davidson et al., 1999).

Crawford (1994) pointed out in his analysis of new product failure that marketing research (information) is not typically conveyed to the technical product decision makers. Marketing talks to customers, analyzes the needs of the market, and estimates demand, while R&D tries to keep up with the latest in technology to incorporate into new products. Historically in many companies, there was not enough of a difference between the R&D and marketing functions to have an advantage in integrating the two; however, as the R&D and marketing functions have become more and more specialized, there is an increased need to bring them back together.

R&D and Marketing

One of the first articles that explicitly stated the importance of integrating R&D and marketing was by Gupta et al. (1985), who pointed out that R&D and marketing integration may be required in all three phases of the innovation process: (a) the planning phase (establishing priorities and goals, schedules, and budgets), (b) the new product development process (idea generation, idea screening/business analysis, development, testing, and commercialization), and (c) the post-commercialization phase. In a study of more than 200 high-technology firms, they found a clear relationship between new product success and the level of integration achieved between R&D and marketing.

Marketers are primarily concerned with identifying and catering to customer needs and competitor threats, whereas R&D personnel are focused on issues of technical feasibility and functional effectiveness (Ruekert & Walker, 1987a). Ruekert and Walker (1987b) postulated that in a highly uncertain environment or in firms with an aggressive product/market development strategy, the functional departments are more dependent on each other. This leads to using an integrated product development approach.

Working together, marketing and R&D can bring the organization's capabilities to bear on developing products that deliver benefits that meet or exceed customer needs (Beltramini, 1996). The benefits of such functional coordination include the reduction of development cycle time and closer communication to detect potential problems early in the process and reduce costs (Larson, 1988; O'Dwyer & O'Toole, 1998). Marketing identifies and assesses customer needs, while R&D develops the means to meet those needs (O'Dwyer & O'Toole, 1998). R&D also helps develop new technological levels of performance, which enable new customer benefits to be created.

R&D, Marketing, and Manufacturing

Assuming that marketing and R&D work together to develop the final product specifications, the next problem occurs when plans are handed to manufacturing to produce the product. Poor quality and high product cost have always been blamed on inefficient and ineffective manufacturing practices. Recently, the focus has shifted from blaming manufacturing to initial product design as the primary cause of poor quality and, thereby, poor performance in the marketplace. Approximately 40% of all quality problems can be traced back to inferior product design (Raia, 1989). Some of the recent advances in manufacturing, such as lean production, parallel processing, and flexible manufacturing, suggest that manufacturing should be involved earlier in the NPD process and become directly integrated with marketing and R&D in a cross-functional NPD team.

Some of the problems in a linear sequential production model, motivated either by technology or the market, and not having manufacturing involved early in the process of new development were identified by Van de Ven (1986). For example, overlooking a design flaw that showed up only when starting full production, not being able to meet scheduled delivery for a critical subassembly, or extremely tight tolerances in specifications all lead to poor NPD performance.

Additional support for the concept of integrating the three functions (marketing, manufacturing, and R&D) comes from a study conducted by Szakonyi (1994), who suggested that utilizing teams made up of marketing, manufacturing, and R&D during NPD leads to greater commercial success. Many practitioners and researchers feel that new product success rates will increase if firms improve the cross-functional integration among the key functions of marketing, production, and R&D (Clark & Fujimoto, 1991; Hutt, Walker, & Frankwick, 1995). In a broad sense, marketing can provide input on the needs of the marketplace, R&D can provide input on the latest technology advances, and manufacturing can provide input on potential cost savings in the production process. R&D's concern for an elegant solution can be better balanced with marketing's focus on serving the customer's immediate needs and manufacturing's focus on issues of production efficiency and manufacturability (Raffi, 1995). In many instances, significant reductions in production cost can occur if manufacturing is able to interact with R&D and marketing early in the NPD process. It is easier to make production cost trade-off decisions early in the process as to what features need to be kept in the product and what to keep for the next version. The cost incurred during the design stage of the NPD process may be no more than 8% of the total product development cost, but the decisions made in this stage determine as much as 60-80% of total NPD costs (Raia, 1989).

There is a much greater need for integration of all three functions—marketing, manufacturing, and R&D—as product life cycles get shorter and time to market becomes more critical. Unfortunately, these three functions have different objectives—especially in NPD. Manufacturing is rewarded for the achievement of efficiency in production and cost minimization, marketing is rewarded for creating and maintaining markets and satisfied customers, and R&D is rewarded for creating new products (Song, Montoya-Weiss, & Schmidt, 1997).

Dowlatshahi (1992) suggested the following as potential advantages of utilizing an integrated product development approach:

1. Reduction in product development cycle time,
2. Avoidance of costly future redesigns,
3. Reduction in duplication of effort,

4. Better communication and dialogue,

5. More efficient operations and higher productivity,

6. Overall cost savings,

7. Avoidance of product recalls,

8. Lower maintenance costs,

9. More reliable products,

10. Better customer satisfaction, and

11. Improved bottom-line earnings.

Integrated product development can also be aided by reducing the need for a sequential development process. Takeuchi and Nonaka (1986) suggested the use of a "rugby approach" to NPD, characterized by overlapping the distinct phases of the development cycle to move the process from a strictly linear or sequential flow process to a simultaneous sharing of information.

R&D, Marketing, Manufacturing, and Logistics

Assuming that marketing, R&D, and manufacturing together develop a new product, another problem could arise when trying to deliver the new product. Logistics is the function that is responsible for the inbound procurement, warehousing, inventory control, outbound distribution, and spare parts availability, which can all become very important for the success of a new product (Meyers & Tucker, 1989). Logistics also interfaces with marketing, R&D, and manufacturing within the firm. This suggests that logistics, in the same manner as manufacturing, should be integrated earlier in the NPD process together with marketing and R&D.

One of the executives who was interviewed noted the importance of logistics for R&D:

> I can design the best products in the world, but if I can't get it to market, in conjunction with what I need to be competitive, then it's not going to be successful.

Logistics is in a unique interface role with manufacturing, R&D, marketing, and NPD (Morash, Dröge, & Vickery, 1996a). Logistics interfaces with marketing via customer service and manufacturing with regard to product availability, which permits a unique perspective on more effective intrafirm communication and integration (M. C. Cooper & Ellram, 1993). Logistics can also play a vital role in NPD by providing information to reduce the lifetime logistics (distribution and service) costs of the new product and by providing input from both the supplier and the customer. Logistics has a role to play in the development of new products that becomes even more critical in industries where time to market is the distinctive competitive advantage. When individual product life cycle times are short, as in the case of style or fashion goods, logistics processes can make critical contributions to the time it takes a firm to bring a new product to market (La Londe & Powers, 1993). Logistics can also provide customers the nurturing service and warranty support a new product needs to ensure commercial success, especially with radical innovation products (Meyers & Tucker, 1989). Logistics also plays a strategic role in many companies. Many large retail companies, such as Wal-Mart and Benetton, compete based on their highly efficient logistics processes. Their strategic and distinctive competencies are based on their logistics capabilities.

Currently in most companies, logistics is not involved with new products until after they are developed. Logistics is usually just asked to distribute the finished product. Anecdotal stories abound about the horrors of not having logistics input earlier in the new product development process. For example, an automobile manufacturer spent 5 years developing a sports utility vehicle but did not communicate the new vehicle specifications to the logistics group until the vehicles were ready to be delivered. Unfortunately, the changed dimensions of the new sports utility vehicles meant the rail cars typically used could carry only racks of two vehicles whereas in the past they had carried three. This dramatically increased the cost of shipment per vehicle and increased the delivery time— which could have been avoided with early logistics involvement in NPD.

Another example of early logistics involvement with new product development was discussed by one of our interview participants.

> Before we actually go ahead and produce a new model or brand new product and deliver it to any market, there is an advanced purchasing group that gets involved. Typically, some target costing has occurred and we have an idea from engineering what types of materials and volume expectations that we have to try to do a procurement process around. The procurement group sits in on those early meetings and provides feedback to say, "hey, wait a minute, how are we going to deliver that material to our manufacturing and our assembly plant to maximize the transportation capabilities that we have?"

Changes suggested by logistics can translate to marketplace success as they lead to meeting customer needs more effectively. Logistics plays four important roles in NPD, according to Meyers and Tucker (1989):

1. Advisor—provide advice about downstream customer participation and product life-cycle cost control,
2. Liaison—coordinate between NPD teams and external stakeholders, including customers and vendors,
3. Problem troubleshooter—capture data and provide analysis and feedback, and

4. Knowledge library—provide information on past NPD experiences to NPD
teams.

Teams with diverse backgrounds have several advantages over less diverse
teams (Rochford & Rudelius, 1992). Their variety provides a broader knowledge base and increases the "cross-fertilization of ideas," which allows the
project to draw on more information sources. In a survey of 45 multinational
companies' R&D groups, R. Miller (1995) found that a number of firms have
successfully developed methods to cross-functionally integrate R&D with
marketing, engineering, purchasing, and manufacturing. In these firms, product development is managed from a life-cycle perspective and involves the
merging of functional viewpoints to achieve cost reduction and speed in
time-to-market (R. Miller, 1995). From a life-cycle perspective, R&D is
involved at all stages of product/process development: advanced research, definition of attributes, design and engineering, transfer to production, maintenance, and services (R. Miller, 1995).

Many researchers have examined the relationship between NPD success and
the involvement of cross-functional teams in the NPD process (Griffin &
Hauser, 1992; Olson, Walker, & Ruekert, 1995). Having all functions work
together increases knowledge diversity, which leads to increased idea generation (Stringfellow, 1998). One of the factors that R. G. Cooper (1990) identified
as important in NPD was cross-functional team integration. His analysis of 21
companies and more than 103 cases in the chemical industry illustrated that the
team approach really did deliver better results. The key factor to ensure that a
project stayed on schedule and used time efficiently was having a good cross-
functional team approach (Cooper, 1990). Madhavan and Grover (1998) suggested that the major reason a cross-functional team is brought together is
because its members have collective knowledge that cannot be held efficiently
by any of its individual members. This collective knowledge is not present by
definition when the team is assembled; it is only potentially present. A
cross-functional NPD team is a product development vehicle that brings to its
task knowledge that is embedded in its members and their interactions as a team
(Madhavan & Grover, 1998). The potential for new knowledge is embedded in
the team and its interactions. The NPD team possesses embedded knowledge;
the new product is embodied knowledge. The NPD manager's task, therefore,
is to manage the transition from embedded to embodied knowledge (Madhavan
& Grover, 1998).

Companies that considered their NPD process to be successful all adhered to
five simple principles: clarity, ownership, leadership, integration, and flexibility (Davidson et al., 1999). Flexibility is important in NPD because of the need
for balance between establishing elements that are standardized and common
to all users of the process with the flexibility for adjustments for each product or
project team (Davidson et al., 1999). If speed and efficiency are to be achieved,

new product development must be viewed as an enterprise-wide process rather than owned by one function such as marketing or R&D. This view tends to align all parts of the organization with a shared objective, and it instills mutual confidence that each function is working toward this objective (Davidson et al., 1999).

Integrated Product Development Within the Firm

The concept of using integrated product development (IPD) is not new, and according to the literature it has numerous advantages. IPD leads to reduced development lead times with fewer costly redesigns, better communication, reduction in duplication, cost savings from lower maintenance, more reliable products with fewer recalls, and enhanced customer satisfaction (Dowlatshahi, 1992). By using the four functions discussed (R&D, marketing, manufacturing, and logistics) from the onset, there is greater likelihood that the product will have a market, be technologically advanced, be able to be manufactured, and be procured and distributed efficiently, all leading to greater new product commercial success. Analyzing performance results of the furniture manufacturing industry in NPD projects, Morash, Dröge, and Vickery (1996a) found that excellence in one functional area was not likely to be the basis for competitive advantage among better performing firms, but rather that process integration across functional areas led to competitive advantage.

One interview participant discussed how logistics and the entire organization work together with new product development:

> They have an entire process called launch readiness, when they launch a new product to a new market or a new product to an old market or even in some cases an old product to an old market that's had a revision. They look at it as a launch, and they try to meet a specific quantity of units, that they will deliver to a specified date. They build a bunch of processes around the launch from ensuring that in country requirements will be met, the product has been adequately tested by their government for safety measures that might be required, just a whole bevy of different prospects that I think if you have a complicated enough product requires an entire organization.

A number of different approaches have been developed to improve and accelerate the new product development process—integrated product development (Birou & Fawcett, 1994), cross-functional teams, physical co-location (Kahn & McDonough, 1997; Raffi, 1995), concurrent engineering (Swink, Sandvig, & Mabert, 1996), stage gate systems (Cooper, 1990), return map (House & Price, 1991), and quality function deployment (House & Price, 1991). Many of these approaches focused on the specific roles played by the various functions in the firm during new product development.

This section on intrafirm R&D has identified the many advantages that accrue to R&D and the NPD process through involvement of other functions within the firm, such as marketing, manufacturing, and logistics. It should also be noted that collaborating with other functions in the firm can be quite difficult. In fact, many of the executives interviewed for this book indicated that breaking internal functional barriers could be more difficult than overcoming barriers across companies. As one interview participant noted when discussing collaboration:

> Sometimes it's easier collaborating with suppliers and customers than doing it within the four walls of the company, breaking down the functional silos and creating those linkages.

Unfortunately, even with cross-functional teams and an integrated product development approach, there are still several pressing problems with NPD (Cooper & Kleinschmidt, 1986; Millson, Raj, & Wilemon, 1996; Wind & Mahajan, 1997):

1. Many firms lack the resources to develop needed new products,

2. Increased reliance on corporate mergers and acquisitions to obtain growth via new products often creates problems of "fit,"

3. Many firms neglect important NPD activities or perform them poorly, and

4. Even though innovative new products are identified by customers, suppliers, and other outside organizations, such new product information is not heeded.

One possible solution to these NPD problems and to reduce cycle time is to go beyond the boundaries of the firm and develop partnerships with customers and suppliers.

Interfirm R&D

Currently, less than 45% of U.S. manufacturers handle the entire product design process without involvement from major industrial or retail customers (Adrian, 1998). Interfirm R&D partnerships bring several advantages to the participating company. First, research and development over the years has become more and more expensive, and a way to reduce the costs of development is to collaborate with both suppliers and customers. Second, by developing alliances or partnerships with major customers and suppliers, cycle time is reduced. When a firm needs to reposition its competitive posture, partnerships can often be a faster approach to NPD than internal development, and can be less costly, less irreversible, and more feasible than mergers (Porter & Fuller, 1986), which can be particularly effective for firms developing new products in an increasingly turbulent and global environment (Millson et al., 1996).

The new product literature has started to embrace the concepts of integrated product development among the many functions within the firm. R&D, which is typically responsible for new product development, can incorporate marketing's input as the voice of the customer, manufacturing's input on maximizing efficiency of the production process, and logistics input on efficient procurement, inventory, warehousing, and distribution processes. Internally, R&D interfaces with the functions as described in the previous section on intrafirm R&D. Externally, R&D can meet with customers and suppliers to improve the development of new products. This is also an opportunity to incorporate the voices of the supplier and the customer early in the NPD process. Another interview participant noted the importance of customers and suppliers to the firm as a whole:

> If you look at the customer supplier relationship—that's something that we try to make everyone [in the company] aware of.

As can be seen in Figure 6.1, in this section we look at the role of customer involvement and supplier involvement in interfirm R&D.

Customer Involvement

For a new product to achieve significant and rapid market penetration, it must match such customer requirements as new features, superior quality, and attractive pricing (Schilling & Hill, 1998). Despite the obvious importance of this imperative, numerous studies have documented the lack of fit between new product attributes and customer requirements as a major cause of new product failure (Cooper & Kleinschmidt, 1986; Montoya-Weiss & Calantone, 1994). Companies need to ensure that an adequate market and distribution channel exists for their new products. Collaborating with customers and customers' customers further increases the likelihood of developing viable distribution channels.

Many products fail to produce an economic return because they fail to meet customer requirements, especially when financial considerations take precedence over marketing criteria (Schilling & Hill, 1998). One way of improving the fit between a new product and customer requirements is to include customers in the NPD process. By exchanging information effectively with customers, the company helps optimize the product's fit with customer needs. Vendors and customers have always been a valuable source for new product ideas, and it has usually fallen on marketing to provide that input; however, there are benefits of R&D being directly involved with customers.

R&D's definition of customer can be extended to include the concept of stakeholders. Stakeholders exist beyond the boundary of a single organization into a partnership infrastructure, as firms serve a market with multiple distribution channels and with confederations of customers, employees, own-ers, and other partnership organizations such as dealers (W. L. Miller, 1995). According to Miller (1995), R&D should evolve to directly dealing with cus-tomers so that they feel the research is theirs and it becomes an integral part of the customer's search for new capability. Traditional selling involves custom-ers too late in the process to satisfy many latent needs (W. L. Miller, 1995). Direct, peer relationships are formed between people doing R&D for the sup-plier and the customer, without the intermediation of a separate, traditional marketing group (W. L. Miller, 1995).

The essence of quality in R&D, as in other fields, is a market focus. This requires an understanding of who the customer is and what his or her values and expectations are, what the key technologies are and how they can be used to meet customer expectations, and who the competitors are and how they will respond to emerging customer needs (Prestwood et al., 1995). In all likelihood, the best method to understand the customer is to involve the customer directly and early in the NPD process.

To improve the NPD process and reduce cycle time, it is better to incorporate customer and supplier requirements in the product and process design. This early involvement can lead to lower costs and improve the product's chances of meeting customer requirements (Schilling & Hill, 1998). Suppliers are also important in collaborating with R&D, especially in developing new products, processes, and technologies.

Supplier Involvement

By tapping into the knowledge base of its suppliers, a firm expands its infor-mation resources, and suppliers can contribute ideas for product improvement or increased development efficiency. For instance, a supplier may suggest an alternative input (or configuration of inputs) to lower cost. Additionally, by coordinating with suppliers, managers can help ensure that inputs arrive on time and that necessary changes can be made quickly (Asmus & Griffin, 1993; Bonaccorsi & Lipparini, 1994). Consistent with this argument, research has shown that many firms using supplier interaction are able to produce new prod-ucts in less time, at a lower cost, and with higher quality (Birou & Fawcett, 1994).

In the new product process, the literature extols the virtue of supplier involvement early , especially in the automotive industry. A significant portion of the success of Japanese companies can be attributed to the impact of their relationship with their supply base and the early and extensive involvement of their suppliers in NPD (Clark, 1989). Early supplier involvement in new prod-uct development suggests that suppliers should be involved in prelaunch activi-ties such as idea generation, idea screening, and product development. This process of going beyond company boundaries to incorporate customer and supplier input could be used to develop more efficient NPD processes.

In a resource-scarce, dynamic environment, in order to maintain flexibility and benefit from the strengths of suppliers, companies need to build strong, long-term relationships with their suppliers. These relationships will enable them to bring new products quickly into the marketplace (Gupta & Wilemon, 1990). Supplier involvement in new product development is typically referred to as early supplier involvement. The goals of early supplier involvement include a reduction in manufacturing costs, improved manufacturing competitiveness, fewer part numbers, and technology transfer (Birou & Fawcett, 1994).

Research regarding the role of suppliers in NPD has yielded mixed results. Birou (1994) suggests that early supplier involvement (ESI) is negatively correlated with NPD development success. There was a detrimental effect on product cost, quality, performance, and development time (Birou, 1994). Peter (1996) suggests that ESI should be considered only for a small fraction of products because of the large upfront resources needed from both sides. In direct contrast, in an analysis of 122 Japanese automotive component suppliers, Wasti and Liker (1997) found that ESI offered performance benefits for both the supplier and the buyer, especially if there was substantial technological uncertainty. The potential impact of suppliers on the quality and cost of new products is huge: 56% of each sales dollar is spent on procurement of production materials (Burt, 1989).

Ellram and Cooper (1990) discuss an example of a company that had its suppliers involved in new product design. This enabled the company to utilize a technology that the supplier was still developing. If the company had not had the supplier involved early in the NPD process, the company would have had to wait another 3 years until its next model introduction to incorporate the new technology.

Collaborating with carriers who supply transportation to the company can also be important in interfirm R&D. An executive interviewed for this book discussed a firm that collaborates with its carriers in design:

> They partner with some of their carriers in their network by being involved
> in actually designing the equipment or conveyance that would be used to
> deliver and/or to source their products.

Another article that discussed the importance of relationships between buying and selling firms stressed the importance of involving suppliers in joint programs that address key areas of concern to both parties, such as new product development (Monczka, Callahan, & Nichols, 1995). A large percentage of the value added of a new product is the purchased inputs, and these inputs have the potential to influence directly and substantially not only the cost and quality but also the development time of new products (Birou & Fawcett, 1994). To bring quality new products to market as quickly as possible, manufacturers are streamlining processes and collaborating with supply chain partners (Adrian, 1998).

Supply Chain R&D

The focus of R&D in a supply chain management context is beyond the boundaries of the firm, incorporating the focal firm's suppliers' suppliers and customers' customers input early into the new product team. In a study of the auto industry, Clark (1989) found that integration of the capability between upstream and downstream firms is an important determinant of product development success. This suggests that developing relationships with R&D groups from firms along the supply chain leads to increased NPD success.

An interview participant noted that a supply chain orientation can help in new product development:

> When they partner with some of their carriers in their network, they become involved in actually designing the equipment or conveyance that would be used to deliver their products, and/or to source their products, and they also capitalize some of those design and engineering processes for their carriers to go ahead and be able to utilize that conveyance.

The information is shared among the partners in the supply chain so there is a benefit to all these partners.

Four concepts associated with R&D in a supply chain context, as seen in Figure 6.1, are explored in this section: the concept of globalization, postponement, speed to market, and flexible NPD.

Globalization

Increasingly, multinational enterprises face simultaneous pressures for global integration and local responsiveness (Chiesa, 1996). Prahalad and Doz (1987) point out that multinational companies should strike a balance between global integration and the capacity for local response. The recent growth of international competition and the globalization of scientific and technological operations have forced companies to disperse their R&D operations in different countries and to design, put in place, and manage an R&D infrastructure globally, so as to improve their capacity for technological innovation (Chiesa, 1996). Global R&D is seen as a process of locating R&D labs in different countries in order to leverage the technical resources of each facility or country to further the company's overall technological capabilities and increase its global operating profits.

As companies become more supply chain and globally oriented, research and development needs to be managed within a supply chain context. Both management theorists and managers believe that, to respond to this challenge, the international company should be managed as a coordinated network (Chiesa, 1996). Managing in a global context suggests the relevance of an international innovation network, global management of technology, and the capability to leverage the "best" elements of each location to global benefit (Chiesa, 1996). This implies that companies disperse their R&D facilities in different countries to a much larger extent than in the past (Chiesa, 1996).

Integrated global laboratories become important when the sources of market information, the external sources of technology, and the company's technical resources, skills, and capabilities needed to innovate in a particular product line are geographically dispersed (Chiesa, 1996). This geographical dispersion can be the result of the company's international expansion or of developing relationships with firms along the supply chain. In other cases, product requirements vary significantly from country to country, or local facilities develop specific skills, and as a result specialized pockets of skills become dispersed geographically (Chiesa, 1996). Many firms have started the process of collaborating with R&D groups with firms along the supply chain, especially those that are multinational in scope and global in focus.

Postponement

The second benefit of utilizing a supply chain R&D focus is postponement. Postponement is the concept of designing a product such that it is possible to delay differentiation of the product until customer demand for the specific end-product is known (Billington & Amaral, 1999; Feitzinger & Lee, 1997). For example, Hewlett-Packard Company does not insert the power supply (110 volts or 240 volts) in its printers until they reach the customer's country, allowing the company to reduce inventory costs and gain greater flexibility to meet customer demand. Postponement may be more valuable than information sharing in a supply chain, especially under conditions of high demand uncertainty, high cost of a lost sale, and low capacity responsiveness (Billington & Amaral, 1999). Postponement also supports the delivery of mass-customized products quickly and at low cost (Feitzinger & Lee, 1997).

Postponement as a strategy requires R&D to coordinate along the supply chain to develop new product architecture that allows delayed differentiation to be accomplished inexpensively. R&D must redesign the product so that it can be customized at the most efficient point in the supply chain (Feitzinger & Lee, 1997). To practice postponement efficiently requires coordination among several functions along the supply chain, especially the R&D function, to adopt a modular design. Postponing the final product configuration increases the chances that the product closely fits the end consumers' needs.

Speed to Market

The third benefit of utilizing a supply chain R&D focus is speed to market. To be successful at new product development, a firm must simultaneously meet two critical objectives: maximizing the fit with customer needs and minimizing time to market (Schilling & Hill, 1998). As described earlier regarding cycle time, reducing development time or increasing the speed to market allows supply chains to continually upgrade their products, incorporating state-of-the-art technology when it becomes available. This enables them to better serve consumer needs, outrun their slower competitors, and build brand loyalty. It also enables them to offer a wider range of new products to better serve niches (Schilling & Hill, 1998). Firms late to market are likely to incur opportunity costs, such as reduced market share and loss of margin in their pricing (Liker, Collins, & Hull, 1999).

Collaborating with firms along the supply chain reduces cycle time by reducing the need for rework to meet the needs of downstream customers. A firm's ability to respond quickly to changing customer needs through the rapid introduction of new products is a key strategic differentiator (Birou & Fawcett, 1994).

Flexible NPD

The fourth benefit of utilizing a supply chain focus in R&D is flexible NPD. A flexible product development process is one that allows designers to continue to define and shape products even after implementation has begun (Iansiti & MacCormack, 1997). Having a flexible NPD process enables the supply chain to respond quickly to changing customer needs. Incorporating feedback on changing customer requirements from downstream R&D supply chain members into upstream R&D supply chain members increases the likelihood that the new products will meet current and future needs. Flexible new product development enables companies to incorporate rapidly changing customer requirements and evolving technologies into their designs up until the last possible moment before a product is introduced to the market (Iansiti & MacCormack, 1997). Flexible product development also allows upstream R&D designers to sense customer needs, to test alternative technical solutions, and to integrate the acquired knowledge into a coherent product design using an iterative development process.

Conclusions

In the future, it is likely the R&D design teams will also include key suppliers and their suppliers, as well as key customers and their customers, who will work together to develop new products to optimize functioning of the supply chain.

Suppliers will have to hire more design staff, be willing to assume more product liability exposure, and be able to adapt to the design technologies and needs of their customers. Planning of R&D will be more collaborative. R&D functions within the supply chain need to adopt a supply chain-wide perspective. This will become more important and necessary in the future as supply chains continue to compete with each other.

Managerial Recommendations

Managers need to consider ways to improve the new product development process in this era of global competition with short product life cycles. Specific methods that were discussed for R&D and new product development include parallel development, cross-functional new product development, and integrated product development. It should also be clear that managers need to go beyond the boundaries of the firm and start to consider relationships with their suppliers, suppliers' suppliers, their customers, and customers' customers. Research and development should be encouraged to work directly with customers and suppliers early in the new product development process. Managers should also note the benefits of supply chain R&D, such as globalization, postponement, speed to market, and flexible NPD.

Forming partnerships and relationships with other members of the supply chain entails risks that need to be considered. Managers need to determine if the benefits of increased efficiency or increased flexibility warrant the costs associated with developing a supply chain R&D focus.

Researcher Recommendations

Several concepts presented in this chapter need to be further elucidated to determine their applicability in different organizational structures and market environments. The R&D supply chain model offered in Figure 6.1 is just a beginning. The underlying premise of the model is to migrate from traditional R&D to integrated product development, which leads to the need to develop intrafirm R&D, and then interfirm R&D that leads to supply chain R&D. Do companies have to go through the stages as identified, or can they skip interfirm R&D and go directly to supply chain R&D, as implied with the dashed arrow? Further research needs to determine whether the model is applicable only to specific fast-moving industries or instead is a much more general model. Additional constructs may be needed to fully identify other roles of R&D, independent of new product development. There is a further need to refine the factors that are identified to develop theoretical constructs that can be tested. Through the testing and validating of the R&D supply chain model, it is hoped that both the researcher and practitioner communities can benefit from further understanding the valuable role of R&D and new product development in a supply chain.

7

Improving Supply Chain
Sales Forecasting

CARLO D. SMITH

Executive Summary

This chapter describes the increasingly important contribution to
supply chain performance offered through effective sales forecasting
management. A model outlines the evolution of sales forecasting,
starting from an initial focus on forecasting techniques to include
broader considerations for management and behavioral factors that
influence forecasting practices in organizations and across the supply
chain.

This chapter will

- Describe changes in the way forecasting performance has been assessed
  over the past three decades
- Examine the range of factors that can influence forecasting practice
- Recognize an interrelationship between forecasting techniques and systems, on one hand, and the management of the forecasting process as a key
  to improved forecasting performance on the other
- Define forecasting management performance (FMP) and supply chain
  forecasting management performance (SCFMP) as broader measures of
  forecasting effectiveness

- Introduce a framework that describes how forecasting management performance may be improved and how such improvement can affect operations throughout a company and across a supply chain
- Reproduce results from a study of forecasting management best practices and describe how the results may be used in a prescriptive manner to improve forecasting management performance

These discussions lead to the conclusions that

- Supply chain sales forecasting management can significantly influence operating performance within each member, and across members of a supply chain
- To affect supply chain operations in a positive manner, organizations working together in a supply chain must improve FMP (an internally directed measure) as well as SCFMP (a cross-company measure) of forecasting
- The four dimensions of sales forecasting management—functional integration, approach, systems, and performance measurement—can be extended to incorporate a supply chain orientation
- Initiatives such as collaborative planning, forecasting, and replenishment reflect the four forecasting management dimensions and provide for an approach to forecasting that addresses factors that influence FMP and SCFMP

Sales forecasts are an important driver of supply chain operations. To contribute to improved supply chain performance, supply chain managers must go beyond traditional measures of forecast accuracy to understanding and being able to influence the behaviors of individuals and organizations involved in the development and application of sales forecasts.

Introduction

To better synchronize the planning and management of supply chains, companies are sharing greater amounts of information with trading partners. Some of the most critical information exchanged between supply chain participants includes customer demand and the sales forecasts derived from those data. Supply chain initiatives such as quick response (QR); efficient consumer response (ECR); collaborative planning, forecasting, and replenishment (CPFR); and vendor-managed inventory (VMI) each rely on forecasts to help plan and manage operations more effectively. The importance of forecasting in the supply chain was highlighted by Joseph Andraski, Vice President, Customer Development for Nabisco in his contribution to the *Journal of Business Logistics* Strategic Visioning Series.

> If supply chain management begins with a forecast that is substantially in error in terms of timing or quantity, the ramifications will be felt throughout the entire process. The consequences are many: manufacturing will have to adjust and run at less capacity or work overtime to meet customer demand; logistics expenses will be less than optimal; product will be at the wrong place at the wrong time, impacting customer service; the list could go on *ad infinitum*. (1998, p. 10)

To improve forecasting performance, companies have increasingly relied on advances in computer and information system technologies. Point of sale (POS) data collection systems (Smart, 1995), electronic data interchange (EDI) (Mentzer & Kahn, 1997), and more recently, Internet-based applications (Booker, 1999; Verity, 1997) all provide access to near-real-time sales and forecasting information for each supply chain member.

Forecasting systems once housed on mainframe computers and limited to a single forecasting technique for all products and services are now likely to run on desktop computers in client server environments. Rather than using a single forecasting technique, advanced systems evaluate a number of different techniques or employ a combination of techniques to analyze demand and related information (Mentzer & Kahn, 1997; Mentzer & Schroeter, 1993, 1994; Wright, 1988). Despite such advances in technology, sales forecasting accuracy and performance has improved little in the past decade (Andraski, 1998; Mentzer, Bienstock, & Kahn, 1999; Mentzer & Kahn, 1995a).

This chapter investigates the role of forecasting in supply chain management and the factors that influence forecasting performance within, and across, companies in the supply chain. In doing so, it will review the evolution of forecasting research from an early emphasis on technique development, to more recent considerations for behaviors and channel factors that affect forecast creation and application. Contributing to this understanding of forecasting, I merge existing concepts in forecasting management and application to establish a model of supply chain sales forecasting management (SCSFM). The SCSFM model is described within the context of a local supply chain consisting of retailer, manufacturer, and material supplier. The model is used to explain the factors and relationships that influence forecasting performance in companies as well as across supply chains. The final section of this chapter offers suggestions about how managers can benefit from this understanding of forecasting management, as well as the direction researchers should consider to further enhance our knowledge of this important component of supply chain management.

Forecasting in the Supply Chain

Figure 7.1 presents a chronology of issues and advancements that have contributed to our understanding of forecasting and the factors that influence forecasting performance. This understanding has transitioned from an early focus on forecasting techniques to include the individual and organizational behaviors that affect forecasting practice. This expanding scope of forecasting is anchored in two dimensions.

The vertical axis, described as "moving from models to management" (Smith, 1999), acknowledges the human component of forecasting. It recognizes that forecasting entails more than mathematical formulae, operating procedures, and systems. Rather, forecasting involves people, their perceptions and motivations, and their behaviors as they participate in the development and application of forecasts.

The horizontal axis illustrates that forecasting practices more and more frequently consider demand processes and incorporate forecasting techniques that extend beyond corporate boundaries to companies throughout the supply chain. The following sections discuss the content of each quadrant in Figure 7.1 and the contributions that are helping to improve sales forecasting performance in supply chains.

Quadrant I: Evaluating Model Performance

Early efforts to improve forecasting performance sought to identify techniques that produce the most accurate forecasts when considering the varied patterns of product and service demand. Much of this research focused on time series and regression techniques and evaluated those techniques based on traditional measures of forecast accuracy such as percent error (PE) and mean absolute percent error (MAPE).

For reference, PE offers a period by period comparison of actual to forecast sales. The formula for calculating forecast accuracy based on percent error (PE) is

$$\text{Percent Error}_t = \text{PE}_t = [(\text{Forecast}_t - \text{Sales}_t)/\text{Sales}_t] \times 100$$

where t = the time period in which the sales occurred.

PE offers an effective means of assessing individual period (period t) forecast performance and whether forecasts were higher than, or below, demand. When evaluating performance over a number of periods, PE can erroneously reflect a more accurate forecast as positive error from one period is averaged with negative error from a subsequent period. MAPE is a function of PE that eliminates this potential bias in results. MAPE is calculated as

Broadening Scope of Forecasting Research

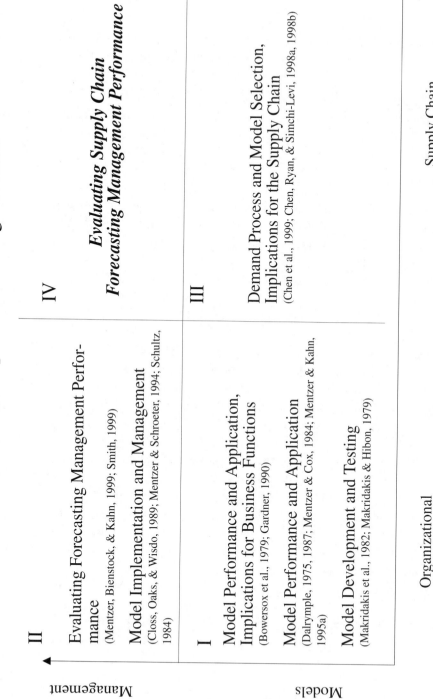

Figure 7.1. Broadening Scope of Forecasting Research

$$\text{MAPE} = \sum |PE|/N$$

where N = the number of periods we have been tracking the percent error
$|PE|$ = the absolute value of the percent error during the periods included.

These and other measures of forecasting performance have been used to assess relative performance among alternative forecasting techniques. Studies designed as forecasting competitions have provided a means to compare results from the application of different forecasting techniques to the same collections of demand data. These competitions have evaluated forecast performance based on accuracy as well as computational efficiency. (For examples of these studies, see Makridakis et al, 1982; Makridakis, Chatfield, Hibon, & Lawrence; 1993; Makridakis & Hibon, 1979; Mentzer & Gomes, 1994.)

Findings from these and similar studies of forecasting performance suggest that more complex or statistically sophisticated techniques do not necessarily lead to more accurate forecasts. Forecasting performance can be affected by a variety of factors including the level of detail and types of demand data used (item by location, all items aggregated to one number, dollars vs. units, etc.) and the length of the forecast interval and horizon (yearly, quarterly, monthly), among other factors. Therefore, rather than focusing on any one technique for sales forecasting, those responsible for forecasting are encouraged to apply a range of techniques individually, and in combination, whenever possible. Furthermore, combining forecasts should extend beyond time series and regression to include judgmental techniques.

This last point can be a rather daunting task for individuals responsible for forecasting if they are expected to understand the intricacies of various forecasting techniques, when they should be used, and how they should be combined. Fortunately, decision models can help guide managers in forecast technique selection. These models have established selection criteria that extend beyond technique evaluation to include factors such as the sophistication of forecast personnel, the number of forecasts to be generated, the level of demand aggregation, the forecast horizon, the forecast budget, and the availability of data related to demand (Mentzer & Gomes, 1990). Such criteria may be employed manually, or in some cases, it may be integrated into a computer-based system to support forecasting.

As computer processing speeds have improved and increased the ability to consider more complex techniques, broader measures of forecasting performance have emerged. Rather than measuring the accuracy posed by alternative techniques, these measures have addressed issues related to forecast application in industry. Surveys of forecasting managers have evaluated their familiarity with alternative techniques as well as their satisfaction with the techniques they employ (Dalrymple, 1975, 1987; Mentzer & Cox, 1984;

Mentzer & Kahn, 1995a). In essence, the performance of any forecasting technique is relevant to business only if the technique is being used, effectively, in practice.

Because they have been repeated over time, these surveys offer some interesting insights about the evolution of forecasting practices in such concerns as changes in techniques, technologies that support forecasting, areas of application, and role of forecasting in business. Results indicate that during the 1980s, despite the growing availability of computer-based forecasting systems, companies continued to rely predominantly on techniques based on subjective input and basic demand extrapolation. In the 1990s, though companies had started to use more computer-based forecasting and forecasters had become familiar with more sophisticated sales forecasting techniques, the level of forecast accuracy reported had not improved. For some, these results indicated a need to look beyond the managerial factors that surround forecasting. As Mentzer and Kahn (1995a) note, "forecasting techniques alone would not necessarily improve accuracy. Rather, managers should consider other issues associated with forecasting including the forecast environment, the data collected, the computer systems used, and how the forecasting process would be administered" (p. 475). Studies that incorporate these aspects of environment and administration will be addressed in greater detail as part of the discussion of quadrant II.

In addition to supporting the application of more sophisticated forecasting techniques, computers have provided a means to evaluate techniques within the context of particular business applications (Bowersox, Closs, Mentzer, & Sims, 1979; Gardner, 1990). Computer-based simulations have been used to investigate relationships between forecasting performance and the performance of functions that use forecasts for decision making. For example, in a study conducted for the United States military, simulation was used to evaluate the impact of alternative forecasting techniques on inventory requirements and customer service on a network of 11 supply centers, each carrying about 50,000 items (Gardner, 1990). Results of the study illustrated that forecasting techniques that produce lower rates of forecast error offer a more efficient trade-off between inventory investment and customer service. The implication for business is that companies can realize substantial savings in inventory investment by applying forecasting techniques that reduce error.

Although this seems a likely conclusion, the ability of the simulation to mimic the relationship between forecasting and operations is playing an increasingly important role in helping managers evaluate forecast performance. Simulations such as the one described above provide managers with a means to assess performance that is more relevant than solely reviewing general measures of forecast accuracy (Gardner, 1990).

Model performance continues to play an important role in efforts to establish new forecasting techniques, to identify the best technique(s) to use under different conditions, to assess the extent that different techniques have been adopted by industry, and to measure the degree that forecast performance affects business operations. It is important to note, however, that forecast performance can be affected by more than model selection. Individuals are responsible for forecast development and application. The next section reviews managerial factors and their influence on forecasting performance.

Quadrant II: Forecasting Implementation and Management

It is apparent from the previous discussion that technique selection can affect forecast performance and that the application of more accurate forecasts can lead to more effective operations in other areas of a company (i.e., inventory management). Forecasting is not, however, solely a quantitative exercise. Qualitative methods also provide a means to forecast future demand for products and services. To benefit from either quantitative or qualitative forecasting techniques, individuals, systems, the forecasting environment, and other related factors must be considered.

Forecasting implementation draws from many of the same factors that affect the implementation of other types of decision support and operations management systems. Key among them is the need to adopt a user's perspective in process and system design (Schultz, 1984). The many individuals who participate in forecasting incorporate different decision styles, educational backgrounds vary, and differences exist in perceptions about forecasting practices and how well they understand those practices. Other factors critical to implementation success include top management support, a recognition of the implications of successful implementation, a commitment of financial and human resources, an attitude of cooperation between users and system designers, and an understanding of the shared goals for the new practices.

To improve the likelihood of success with forecasting process and system implementation, Schultz (1984) recommended the following five steps to guide forecast implementation:

1. Define the current processes and systems supporting forecasting,
2. Measure factors that contribute to implementation success (such as those outlined above),
3. Develop an implementation plan,
4. Build an implementation team, and
5. Establish mechanisms for feedback and control during the implementation process.

Companies following these and similar implementation guidelines have documented significant improvements in forecast accuracy and the operating performance of functions that use forecasts for planning and management (most notably, inventory management) (Closs, Oaks, & Wisdo, 1989; Mentzer & Schroeter, 1993). For example, the implementation of new forecasting practices and systems at Brake Parts, Inc., an automotive parts distributor, yielded an estimated $6 million savings per month due to reduced out-of-stock related lost sales (Mentzer & Schroeter, 1993).

Implementing new forecasting systems and practices can improve forecasting performance; however, such success is not a guarantee of continued forecasting effectiveness or improvement. Over the longer term, forecasting performance relies on management attitude and a company's approach to continuous improvement in forecasting management.

Continuous improvement efforts frequently draw from studies of best practices related to the particular area, or process, of interest. Best practice guidelines offer a means to evaluate existing operations and identify the greatest opportunities for improvement.

Motivated in part by the apparent stagnation in forecasting performance discussed in the introduction to this chapter, Mentzer et al. (1999) conducted a benchmark study of forecasting best practices. Drawing from in-depth analyses of corporate forecasting processes as well as interviews with personnel from functions throughout each of 20 companies participating in the benchmark, they identified four dimensions of forecasting management: (a) functional integration (FI), (b) approach (A), (c) systems (S), and (d) performance measurement (PM).

Functional integration entails the role of communications, coordination, and collaboration in efforts to develop and apply forecasts across business functions. Approach considers the products and services forecast, the forecasting processes followed, and the forecasting techniques applied. Systems addresses the hardware and software used to support forecasting and integrate forecasting with other planning and management systems. Performance measurement is concerned with the metrics used to evaluate forecast effectiveness and its impact on business operations. Within each dimension, Mentzer et al. (1999) identified four stages of sophistication, anchored by Stage 1, which reflects the least sophisticated forecasting practices, and Stage 4, reflecting the most sophisticated practices. The dimensional framework they created provides a useful guide to evaluate forecasting practices and lends itself to prescriptive application (Mentzer et al., 1999).

As a tool for prescription, the characteristics identified along each forecasting management dimension are represented in some form at all stages of sophistication. By comparing forecasting practices to the model, companies can establish their current state of forecasting practices and define a road map leading to improved forecasting management performance.

To illustrate, refer to the benchmarking framework located in the appendix to this chapter (Mentzer et al., 1999). Within the dimension of functional integration, the first bullet in Stage 1 (reflecting the lowest stage of sophistication) is

"Major disconnects between marketing, finance, sales, production, logistics, and forecasting." Review the first bullet at each subsequent stage of the FI dimension and you will see the same theme of communication and coordination. For example, the first bullet in Stage 4 (the highest level of sophistication) is, "Functional integration (collaboration, communication, and coordination) between marketing, finance, sales, production, logistics, and forecasting." In other words, companies that reflect the highest stage of sophistication in functional integration create a structure and environment that facilitates the sharing of information through the organization. This is done in an effort to gain consensus regarding demand and its impact on operations. By using this framework, a company that reflects forecasting characteristics in any stage can begin to improve its performance by establishing practices consistent with companies at a higher stage of sophistication.

The relationship among the four dimensions of forecasting management and their effect on forecasting performance is illustrated in Figure 7.2. In this model, exchange curves are used to explain how forecasting practices can affect forecasting and operating performance. In Figure 7.2, moving to a higher stage of sophistication within any one of the dimensions of forecasting management is expected to have the same effect, on a broader range of factors, as applying a forecasting technique that improves forecasting accuracy. Given this relationship, companies have two options to influence effectiveness and operating investment. Under the first scenario, given the current stage of sophistication along each dimension of forecasting, a company may improve operating effectiveness (customer service) simply by increasing investments in operations (inventories). This option would result in a shift along the exchange curves that represent the current level of sophistication within one or more of the dimensions of forecasting management.

Rather than a direct investment in operations, a company could employ more sophisticated forecasting practices within one or more dimensions of forecasting. This action, as with the application of more accurate forecasting techniques, would shift the exchange curve to a position further from the intersection of the Dimensional Effectiveness (x) and Operating Investment (y) axes and would create the potential for improved dimensional effectiveness (customer service) while maintaining, or reducing, the current operating investment (inventories).

The area designated "current" in Figure 7.2 represents a measure of forecasting performance based on existing practices within each dimension of forecasting management. The area designated "goal" represents forecasting best practices within each dimension. Therefore, the difference between the areas represents the potential for improvement in forecasting management performance (FMP).

Figure 7.3 extends the model of Forecasting management performance by proposing that FMP is positively related to the operating performance of

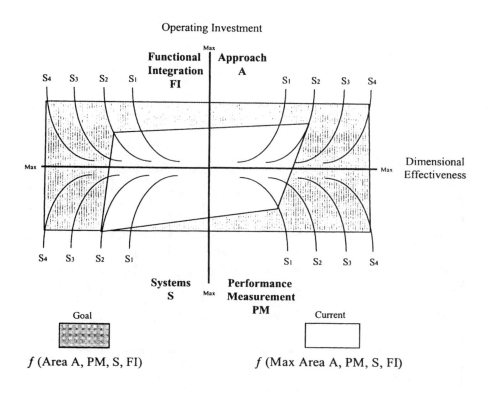

Figure 7.2.   Forecasting Management Performance

functions that utilize forecasts throughout a company. Positive gains in inventory performance achieved through the development and use of more accurate forecasts can be translated into financial gains for the company based on savings from lower inventory carrying costs and operational expenses as well as the potential for higher sales resulting from better in-stock inventory rates. In Figure 7.3, these financial gains represent the value obtained from improved forecasting management performance. By establishing a similar relationship between forecasting management factors and other measures of company operating performance, companies are able to quantify the benefits associated with each dimension of forecasting management and determine where dollars are best invested to improve forecasting and operations.

Quadrant II illustrates that forecasts can influence, and can be influenced by, the perceptions and behaviors of individuals and groups throughout a company. The evaluation of these behavioral factors represents an important shift in

166

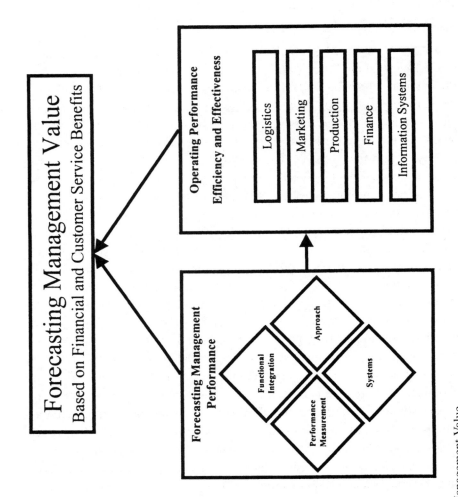

Figure 7.3. Forecasting Management Value

forecasting research, a shift that recognizes the complexities inherent in forecasting practice.

The first two quadrants in Figure 7.1 focus on forecasting and its impact within an individual company. Quadrant III addresses a growing interest in forecasting as a business process that extends beyond the company to other members of a supply chain.

Quadrant III: Model Performance—Implications for the Supply Chain

Forrester's (1958) article on industrial dynamics, introduced in Chapter 1, and subsequent studies of the "bullwhip effect" in the computer industry (Lee, Padmanabhan, & Whang, 1997a, 1997b), have discussed factors that influence demand variability in supply chains. Few other studies, however, have investigated the impact of forecasting techniques when their reach extends outside the company to the supply chain (Chen, Drezner, Ryan, & Simchi-Levi, 1999; Chen, Ryan, & Simchi-Levi, 1998a, 1998b).

Similar to studies included in the first quadrant of Figure 7.1, computer simulation has been employed to document how commonly used forecasting techniques and inventory policies can *systematically* influence the degree of demand variability in the supply chain. For example, moving average techniques help to smooth demand patterns and produce less variability in the supply chain than exponential smoothing techniques. Furthermore, when all companies in a supply chain use the same demand data, the same forecasting technique (i.e., forecasting is centralized), and the same inventory policies, the supply chain experiences reduced demand and inventory fluctuation (the bullwhip effect). On the other hand, when forecasting is not centralized, or when forecasting techniques require estimation of smoothing parameters to address factors such as trend and seasonality, a more substantial bullwhip effect can be experienced in supply chain inventories.

These studies suggest that to minimize demand variability, companies employ forecasting techniques that use greater amounts of history as a means to smooth demand. They also note that centralizing demand information across supply chain companies further reduces variability and the bullwhip effect. Both are viable strategies. In addition, as with forecasting within an organization, management actions and individual behaviors can also influence the development and application of forecasts across companies. This leads us to the role of forecasting management in the supply chain and the fourth quadrant.

Quadrant IV: Forecasting Management Performance in the Supply Chain

Results of studies outlined in the first three quadrants of Figure 7.1 suggest that forecast development and application in supply chains is affected by two dimensions of management. The first is intra-organizational and is concerned with forecasting effectiveness within companies. This dimension draws from insights revealed in the discussion of quadrant II. The second is inter-organizational and is affected by the extent each company in the supply chain has adopted a supply chain orientation (SCO) and activities affiliated with such an orientation.

The inter-organizational dimension extends the concept of forecasting management performance across the supply chain. FMP is defined as the forecast *users'* perception of forecast accuracy and credibility, as well as their application of forecast without modification (Smith, 1999). In the FMP model (Figure 7.2), forecast users include individuals and operations *within* an organization who must satisfy product and service demand, and who use forecasts to plan and execute tasks to accomplish this goal. In the supply chain forecasting management performance (SCFMP) model (Figure 7.4), forecasts' users extend to include other companies in the supply chain that rely on forecasts to plan and execute tasks to satisfy product and service demand.

In a supply chain environment in which companies share forecast information, the effectiveness of the forecasts used by an upstream company for planning and management can be influenced by measurement error (accuracy), a commonly recognized approach to measuring forecast performance. It may also be affected by the extent that forecasts received from a downstream supply chain partner are used to plan and manage operations. In other words, if a forecast shared between companies in a supply chain were devoid of measurement error, performance could still be affected by the extent that each company uses the forecast, ignores the forecast, or modifies the forecasts prior to its use.

Figures 7.5a-c present three alternative supply chain forecasting relationships. Below, each is used to explain how FMP and SCFMP combine to affect supply chain operating performance.

Figure 7.5a illustrates a relationship between retailer, manufacturer, and supplier, where each channel member is focused on its respective internal operations and provides little cross-company demand or forecast information. In this case, orders generated by the downstream channel member are received by the company upstream and used to trigger replenishment as well as feed its own demand forecasting process. For example, the retail organization records consumer demand, perhaps generates statistically based forecasts, and adjusts the forecasts based on qualitative input. The final forecasts are then used in operations such as inventory management to determine inventory requirements and generate orders for manufacturers.

The effectiveness of the retailer forecasts are reflected in retailer FMP (RFMP), which is the extent that forecasts of consumer demand are viewed as accurate and credible, and are used by planning and operations to determine order requirements. Because the manufacturer relies on retail orders as input to its own forecasting process, there is no basis to evaluate SCFMP. The

(text continues on page 173)

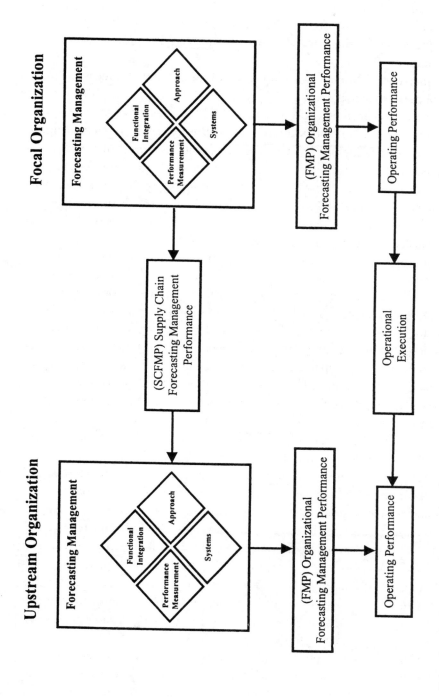

Figure 7.4. Supply Chain Forecasting Management Performance

169

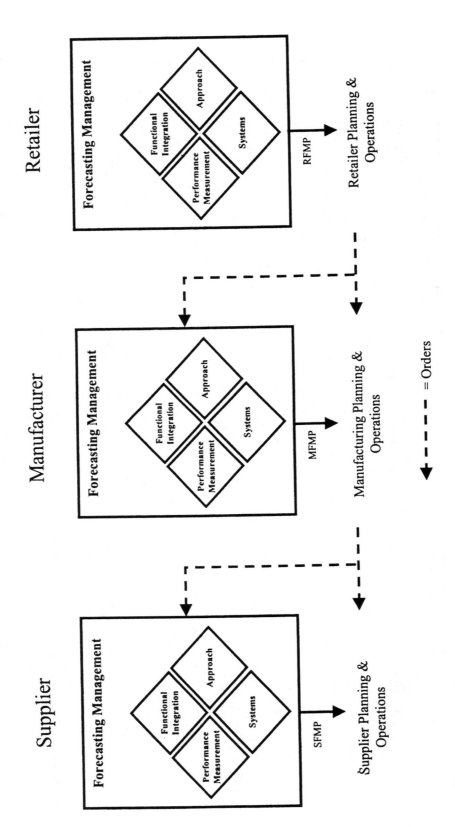

Figure 7.5a. Traditional Channel Relationship

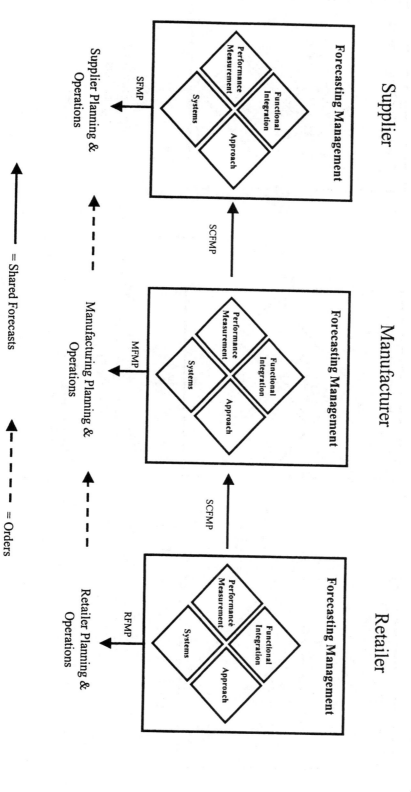

Figure 7.5b. Shared Demand/Forecast Relationship

171

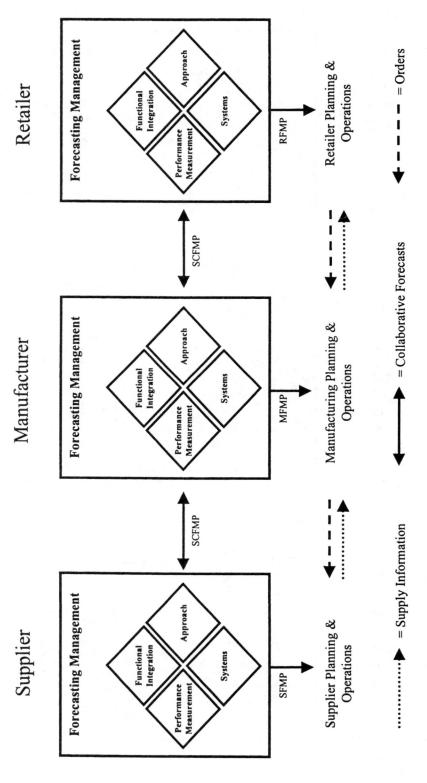

Figure 7.5c. Collaborative Forecasting Relationship

172

manufacturer generates forecasts, as did the retailer, based on the demand for each product from all customers. Capacity planning, scheduling, purchasing, and other related activities at the manufacturer are affected by FMP at the manufacturer level (MFMP). Supplier forecasting and planning would commence in the same fashion.

If each organization used the same forecasting technique with no qualitative adjustment, as well as the same inventory policies, a high level of FMP would result in supply chain inventory performance consistent with that under decentralized forecasting conditions reported by Chen et al. (1999). On the other hand, when each organization generates forecasts independent of one another (decentralized demand information), even if every supply chain member were to use the same forecasting technique and inventory policy, order variance "increases multiplicatively at each stage of the supply chain" (Chen et al., 1999, p. 433). In practice, companies throughout the supply chain are likely to use different approaches to forecasting and inventory management. This suggests the potential for even greater forecast and demand variability, and thus further degradation in supply chain performance.

Figure 7.5b illustrates a channel relationship in which retail forecasts are shared with each member of the supply chain. Chen et al. (1999) describe a similar scenario as a condition under "centralized demand information" (p. 431). Although they relied on sharing demand rather than forecast data originating from the retailer, they assumed that all companies in the supply chain would use the same forecasting approach, thus resulting in the same estimate of mean demand (forecast) for each member of the supply chain.

In a centralized demand environment when each company is applying the same inventory policies, order variability will still increase at each stage in the supply chain (Chen et al. 1999); however, such an increase is an additive function rather than a multiplicative function as in the case of decentralized information and will serve to reduce the bullwhip effect in the supply chain (Chen et al., 1999).

Figure 7.5b is consistent with the centralized demand scenario in its recognition of the value of shared demand/forecast information across channel partners. It differs from that scenario, however, because it incorporates behavioral factors and their influence on the level of FMP exhibited by each company, as well as the level of SCFMP exhibited between the companies.

The interaction between FMP and SCFMP can be realized in a number of ways. For example, if the forecast received from the retailer were considered to be accurate and credible by those responsible for forecasting at the manufacturer (a high level of SCFMP), the forecasts may be used "as is" to feed production planning and distribution. Once part of the forecast at the manufacturer level, however, forecasting management performance within the manufacturer (MFMP) can affect the extent that the original retail forecast is used to manage manufacturing operations. A low level of MFMP, for example, is likely to result in greater supply chain demand variability even though the retailer provided what may have been an accurate demand forecast. If the manufacturer experiences a low level of MFMP, the forecast originating from the retailer may not be reflected effectively in the forecast driving operations. The result is likely to be greater supply chain variability.

In a similar manner, if the relationship between the retailer and manufacturer exhibits a high degree of SCFMP and the manufacturer also maintains a high degree of FMP (MFMP), but the retailer experiences poor RFMP (its orders are not consistent with those based on the forecast and inventory algorithm), the operational execution of the retailer is likely to contain greater variability than reflected in the supply chain forecast shared with the manufacturer. The complexity of these scenarios is magnified when considering that policies driving operations (manufacturing, inventory levels, etc.) are not likely to be the same among supply chain members.

Figure 7.5c is similar to the previous shared forecast scenario. Rather than one-way communication of forecasted demand from retailer to supplier, information now flows in both directions. Information directed upstream from the retailer includes demand forecasts, information about promotions, changes in network structure, significant customer demands, and so forth. From the supplier side, information includes supplier-initiated promotional activities, supply constraints, and so forth. Because information is flowing in both directions, companies receive a better understanding of influences that contribute to forecast development and accuracy. The impacts on supply chain performance are based on the same interactions discussed in Figure 7.5b; however, the nature and extent of the two-way communications between organizations can influence the behaviors of those involved in, and affected by, the relationship. Sharing forecast development and performance information presents an opportunity for a more collaborative approach to forecasting in the supply chain.

In practice, the relationships in Figure 7.5c are reflected in industry initiatives such as collaborative planning, forecasting, and replenishment (CPFR). Organized by the Collaborative Planning, Forecasting and Replenishment Committee, a CPFR future state process model draws on best-in-class vendor-managed inventory practices to outline nine primary process activities:

1. Develop front-end agreement,
2. Create joint business plan,
3. Create sales forecasts,
4. Identify exceptions for sales forecasts,
5. Resolve/collaborate on exception items,
6. Create the order forecast,
7. Identify exceptions to the order forecast,
8. Resolve/collaborate on exception items, and
9. Generate orders.

The process model incorporates four alternative configurations that recognize differences in trading partner competencies in sales forecasting, order forecasting, and order generation.

Incorporating the CPFR process steps into Figure 7.5c, the information sharing relationship is formalized through a front-end agreement between participating companies. As described in the CPFR process model:

> The "front-end agreement" addresses each party's expectations and the actions and resources necessary for success. To accomplish this, the retailer/distributor and manufacturer co-develop a general business agreement that includes the overall understanding and objective of the collaboration, confidentiality agreements, and the empowerment of resources (both actions and commitment) to be employed throughout the CPFR process. (Voluntary Interindustry Commerce Standards [VICS] association, 1998)

Creating a joint business plan establishes the business scenario used to create sales forecasts. In most cases, the CPFR model relies on the retailer to create the initial forecasts, using (POS) data, causal information, and information on planned events. Exception criteria developed jointly by the companies are used to identify forecasts that need further attention. Items flagged based on the exception criteria are reviewed and resolved through e-mail, phone conversations, meetings, and so forth. Changes are reflected in an updated forecast. These actions encourage consensus on final sales forecasts.

Note that there are two forecasts reflected in the CPFR process: the sales forecast based on anticipated demand for products and service, and the order forecast, which incorporates time phasing, inventory levels, and other factors relevant to order generation and release. In an example front-end agreement published by the CPFR committee (VICS, 1998), the order forecast calls for including inventory and logistics personnel in order forecast reconciliation. Reflecting back on Figure 7.5b and Figure 7.5c, participation from these groups supports the notion of higher levels of FMP at each company.

Forecasting practices, and the issues and opportunities that affect them, have evolved from concerns about developing and applying specific techniques to establishing the role of forecasting across companies in a supply chain. The next section addresses the implications of this evolution on current and future forecasting practices.

Conclusions

For forecasting practitioners and researchers, the question is frequently the same: What can we do to improve forecasting performance? The matrix presented in Figure 7.1 suggests four key areas of understanding that can help practitioners improve forecasting performance.

First, develop a better understanding of alternative forecasting techniques, including their benefits and their drawbacks. This does not require the completion of an advanced mathematics degree. Computer-based forecasting systems have done much to eliminate the need to understand specific mathematical formulae. Understanding these techniques does, however, require a good conceptual understanding of how different techniques establish forecasts and the factors that drive those techniques. Furthermore, forecasting techniques are not all quantitative. An understanding of which variables influence demand for products and services frequently can be acquired more effectively through the application of qualitative techniques as a means to adjust quantitative forecasts or establish initial forecasts for products and services.

Along with technique improvement, begin to evaluate the relationship between forecasting and operational performance. The simulations described above offer a means of more explicitly identifying these relationships; however, a similar understanding can be obtained by plotting forecasting performance along with the performance of those operations that use forecasts. Illustrating this type of relationship, whether it is improved production scheduling, transportation utilization, or market planning, offers a means to communicate the importance of improving forecasts throughout the company.

Second, think in terms of forecasting management. As the discussion of quadrant II illustrates, forecasting management incorporates the four dimensions of functional integration, approach, systems, and performance measurement. Mapping current forecasting processes and utilizing the dimensional criteria included in the appendix to this chapter to evaluate the present status of forecasting management reveals those actions that can improve forecasting management performance.

Third, consider the supply chain implications of improved forecasting. Companies that adopt the supply chain orientation (SCO) discussed in Chapter 1 recognize the potential benefits that may be realized through improved synchronization with direct and indirect suppliers and customers. Here again, whether through formal simulation or informed assessment, the impact of improved forecasting can be documented. Documenting and sharing such an assessment with trading partners can establish a collaborative relationship that leads to shared performance benefits across the supply chain.

Finally, evaluate the potential interactions of FMP and SCFMP in any supply chain forecasting relationship. Is there a potential disconnect between FMP and SCFMP driving the planning and operations of trading partners? What factors can help ensure that companies throughout the supply chain are forecasting in a collaborative manner, thus ensuring better synchronization of operations?

As the content addressed in each cell of Figure 7.1 provides direction to forecasting managers, it also suggests a direction for researchers pursuing a supply

chain–oriented approach to forecasting. The collaborative form of sales forecasting outlined by the CPFR committee reflects the need to integrate a greater
degree of supply chain orientation within each of the four dimensions of forecasting identified by Mentzer et al. (1999).

For example, extending functional integration to the supply chain requires
coordination, cooperation, and collaboration across functions in the focal company, as well as for those responsible for forecasting management in other companies in the supply chain. Reconciliation and feedback must extend to the
forecasting and operations planning organizations within each supply chain
participant. Performance measures need to include those responsible for forecast development and reconciliation within and across each company in the
supply chain.

Approach should continue to drive toward a one-number forecast for each
company; however, it also needs to contain a second dimension establishing a
one-number forecast attached to a particular supply chain product. Forecasting
approach needs to address diverging opinions among supply chain partners.
Forecasts need to be developed simultaneously, considering the plans of each
company as well as the supply chain as a whole.

Systems play a critical role in supporting these efforts. EDI is being sup-
planted by Internet-based systems that help synchronize forecasts among supply chain companies. These rules-based systems identify when forecasts
between companies do not meet a predefined tolerance level and facilitate the
review and modification by each company to establish a final consensus forecast for the supply chain. Rather than waiting for demand transactions to be
recorded each day, e-commerce-based systems are making access to POS
information near-real-time for each member of a supply chain.

Finally, multidimensional performance measurement must extend to
include measures of supply chain performance and provide the capability to
better track the sources of forecasting error. Valid and accepted supply chain
forecasting performance metrics are important to help maintain trust among
companies.

Each of these areas has received some anecdotal support. The next step is to
more fully investigate the supply chain sales forecasting management phenomena to understand which factors influence performance and hold the greatest
opportunity to enhance supply chain performance.

Appendix

Sales Forecasting Management Benchmark Dimensions[1]

Exhibit 7.1: Forecasting Benchmark Stages—Functional Integration

Stage 1

- Major disconnects between marketing, finance, sales, production, logistics, and forecasting
- Each area has its own forecasting effort
- No accountability between areas for forecast accuracy

Stage 2

- Coordination (formal meetings) between marketing, finance, sales, production, logistics, and forecasting
- Forecasting located in a certain area—typically operations oriented (located in logistics or production) or marketing oriented (located in marketing or sales)—which dictates forecasts to other areas
- Planned consensus meetings, but with meetings dominated by operations, finance, or marketing—that is, no real consensus
- Performance rewards for forecasting personnel only, based on performance contribution to the department in which forecasting is housed

Stage 3

- Communication and coordination between marketing, finance, sales, production, logistics, and forecasting
- Existence of a forecasting champion
- Recognition that marketing is a capacity unconstrained forecast and operations is a capacity constrained forecast
- Consensus and negotiation process to reconcile marketing and operations forecasts
- Performance rewards for improved forecasting accuracy for all personnel involved in the consensus process

Stage 4

- Functional integration (collaboration, communication, and coordination) among marketing, finance, sales, production, logistics, and forecasting
- Existence of forecasting as a separate functional area
- Needs of all areas recognized and met by reconciled marketing and operations forecast (finance = annual dollar forecasts; sales = quarterly dollar

sales territory-based forecasts; marketing = annual dollar product based-forecasts; production = production cycle unit SKU forecasts; logistics = order cycle unit SKUL forecasts)
- Consensus process recognizes feedback loops (i.e., constrained capacity information is provided to sales, marketing, and advertising; sales, promotions, and advertising can drive demand, etc.)
- Multidimensional performance rewards for all personnel involved in the consensus process

Exhibit 7.2: Forecasting Benchmark Stages—Approach

Stage 1

- Plan-driven, top-down forecasting approach (failure to recognize the interaction between forecasting, marketing, and the business plan)
- Forecast shipments only
- Treat all forecasted products the same
- No defined forecasting hierarchy
- Naive and/or simple statistical approach to forecasting, often with little understanding of the techniques used or the environment ("black box forecasting")
- Failure to see the role of forecasting in developing the business plan (forecasting viewed solely as a tactical function
- No training of forecasting personnel in techniques or understanding of the business environment—no documentation of the forecasting process

Stage 2

- Bottom-up, SKUL-based forecasting approach
- Forecast self-reported demand (demand recognized by the organization) or adjusted demand (invoice-keyed demand)
- Partially defined forecasting hierarchy
- Recognize that marketing/promotion efforts and seasonality can drive demand
- Recognize the relationship between forecasting and the business plan, but the plan still takes precedence over the forecasts
- Limited training in statistics, with no training in understanding the business environment—limited documentation of the forecasting process

Stage 3

- Both top-down and bottom-up forecasting approaches
- Forecast POS demand and back this information up the supply chain and/or utilize key customer demand information ("uncommitted commitments")

- Use ABC analysis or some other categorization for forecasting accuracy importance
- Identification of categories of products that do not need to be forecast (i.e., two-bin items, dependent demand items, make-to-order items)
- Forecast at several levels in the forecasting hierarchy, but no reconciliation of the forecasts
- Use of regression-based models for higher level (corporate to product line) forecasts and time series models for operational (product to SKUL) forecasts
- Recognize the importance of subjective input from marketing, sales, and operations to the forecast
- Forecasting drives the business plan
- Training in quantitative analysis/statistics and an understanding of the business environment—a strong manager/advocate of the forecasting process

Stage 4

- Top-down and bottom-up forecasting approaches with reconciliation
- Vendor-managed inventory factored out of the forecasting process
- Full forecasting segmentation of products (ABC, two-bin, dependent demand, make-to-order, product value, seasonality, customer service sensitivity, promotion driven, life-cycle stage, shelf life, raw material lead time, production lead time)
- Reconciled forecasts at all levels in the forecasting hierarchy
- Understand the "game playing" inherent in the sales force and the distribution channel (motivation for sales to underforecast and for distributors to overforecast)
- Develop forecasts and business plan simultaneously, with periodic reconciliation of both (for instance, consideration of capacity constraints as part of long range plan and forecasts)
- Ongoing training in quantitative analysis/statistics and an understanding of the business environment—top management support of the forecasting process

Exhibit 7.3: Forecasting Benchmark Stages—Systems

Stage 1

- Corporate MIS, forecasting software, and DRP (distribution requirements planning) systems are not linked electronically
- Printed reports, manual transfer of data from one system to another, lack of coordination between information in different systems
- Few people understand the systems and their interaction (all systems knowledge held in MIS)
- "Islands of analysis" exist

- Lack of performance metrics in any of the systems or reports

Stage 2

- Electronic links between marketing, finance, forecasting, manufacturing, logistics, and sales systems
- On-screen reports available
- Measures of performance available in reports
- Reports periodically generated

Stage 3

- Client-server architecture that allows changes to be made easily and communicated to other systems
- Improved system-user interfaces to allow subjective input
- Common ownership of databases and information systems
- Measures of performance available in reports and in the system
- Reports generated on demand and performance measures available on-line

Stage 4

- Open-systems architecture so all affected areas can provide electronic input to the forecasting process
- EDI linkages with major customers and suppliers to allow forecasting by key customer and supply chain staging of forecasts (i.e., real-time POS forecasts to plan key customer demand ahead of supply chain cycle)

Exhibit 7.4: Forecasting Benchmark Stages— Performance Measurement

Stage 1

- Accuracy not measured
- Forecasting performance evaluation not tied to any measure of accuracy (often tied to meeting plan, reconciliation with plan, etc.)

Stage 2

- Accuracy measured, primarily as mean absolute percent error, but sometimes measured inaccurately (e.g., forecast, rather than demand, used in the denominator of the calculation)
- Forecasting performance evaluation based upon accuracy, with no consideration for the implications of accurate forecasts on operations
- Recognition of the impact upon demand of external factors (i.e., economic conditions, competitive actions, etc.)

Stage 3

- Accuracy still measured as mean absolute percent error, but more concern given to the measurement of the supply chain impact of forecast accuracy (i.e., lower acceptable accuracy for low-value noncompetitive products, recognition of capacity constraints in the supply chain and their impact on forecasting and performance, etc.)
- Graphical and collective (throughout product hierarchy) reporting of forecast accuracy
- Forecasting performance evaluation still based upon accuracy, but there is a growing recognition that accuracy has an effect on inventory levels, customer service, and achieving the marketing and financial plans

Stage 4

- Realization that exogenous factors affect forecast accuracy and that unfulfilled demand is partially a function of forecasting error and partially a function of operational error
- Forecasting error treated as an indication of the need for a problem search (for instance, POS demand was forecast accurately, but plant capacity prevented production of the forecast amount)
- Multidimensional metrics of forecasting performance—forecasting performance evaluation tied to the impact of accuracy on achievement of corporate goals (i.e., profitability, supply chain costs, customer service)

Note

1. This appendix is reproduced, with minor changes, from Mentzer, Kahn, and Bienstock (1996).

8

The Evolution and Growth of Production in Supply Chain Management

ZACH G. ZACHARIA

Executive Summary

This chapter describes the role of production within the firm, with suppliers and customers, and within the supply chain.

This chapter will

- Examine production within the firm (intrafirm) using a historical perspective as it evolved from craftsman production, to mass production, to lean production
- Discuss some of the advantages and disadvantages of each of the three types of production
- Examine the reasons why firms change from one production type to another
- Look at the role of production between firms (interfirm) and the need for supplier-customer partnerships
- Discuss two interfirm production methodologies, namely just-in-time (JIT) and tiered production
- Note the trends toward forming partnerships with suppliers and customers who could assist in meeting production goals for the long term

■ Discuss the evolution of partnerships with suppliers that lead to relationships with firms along the supply chain to better manage the production process

■ Evaluate the differences between functional and innovative products that affect the selection of the appropriate supply chain production system

■ Point out the implications of supply chain decisions on production performance of the firm

■ Discuss three supply chain production systems—dispersed production, build-to-order production (mass customization), and postponement

These discussions lead to the conclusions that

■ Supply chain activities have a major impact on the capabilities and profitability of the supply chain and its member firms

■ Functional products in stable markets need a supply chain production system that focuses on reducing volume cost and increasing production efficiency

■ Highly innovative products in uncertain, constantly changing environments need a supply chain production system that focuses on strategic flexibility and speed to market

■ Dispersed production is a supply chain production system of great value in a globally competitive market that focuses on cost efficiency

■ Build-to-order production and postponement are useful supply chain production systems in markets that quickly obsolete existing products, that have rapidly changing customer requirements, and that experience shrinking product life cycles

Understanding the different types of production systems better enables managers to design and develop the production system that is most suitable for the specific market environment. This suggests that developing a supply chain orientation leads to opportunities for lower costs, improved customer value, and long-term competitive advantages.

Introduction

The business environment of the 1990s has been characterized as increasingly dynamic in terms of increasing technological complexity, demanding markets, explosion of knowledge, and increasing global competition (Peter, 1996). In this turbulent environment, flexibility or the ability to adapt as markets change is far more valuable than relying on any one strategy (Hayes & Pisano, 1994). The function at the core of most companies is manufacturing, which has an important role in helping companies become strategically flexible. The goal of strategy becomes strategic flexibility, and the job of manufacturing is to provide that capability (Hayes & Pisano, 1994).

This chapter looks at the role of production from two perspectives. The first is historical, starting in the late 1800s and proceeding to today, covering craft production, mass production, lean production, just-in-time (JIT) production, tiered production, dispersed production, and build-to-order production. The second perspective is a process perspective including intrafirm production, interfirm production, and finally supply chain production.

To understand the role of production in the supply chain, it is useful to first look at the precursors—namely intrafirm and interfirm production. In the early part of the 20th century, the focus was on quality, and the production method that focused on quality was craft production. In the 1930s and 1940s, cost was the overriding factor, and mass production was the dominant production paradigm. In the 1980s, quality combined with low cost was the critical factor, and lean production emphasizing supplier partnerships was the dominant production paradigm. In the 1990s and beyond, the critical factor seems to be flexibility, and the dominant production paradigm is likely to be supply chain production.

Manufacturing (or production) has been one of the key driving forces in the growth of the economy since the early part of the 20th century. Many of the trends and changes in production have had a direct impact on society. The automotive industry is the largest manufacturing industry in the world, and changes in that industry profoundly affect not only other industries but also the way people work, what we buy, how we think, and the way we live (Womack, Jones, & Roos, 1990). To understand how production is affected by the new supply chain focus, it is useful to examine the evolution of manufacturing/production by considering the automotive industry—an industry that is dependent on several thousand suppliers to provide the parts needed to assemble a car.

The first section of this chapter will analyze production within the firm (intrafirm) using a historical perspective as production evolved from craftsman production, to mass production, to lean production. The second section will look at production between firms (interfirm) and the need for supplier-manufacturer partnerships, which leads to tiered production. The third section will look at production as it evolved from partnership to supply chain management and the concept of developing an appropriate supply chain, resulting in the growth of dispersed production and build-to-order production. The three sections, and the corresponding production systems, can be visualized in Figure 8.1, the production supply chain model.

Intrafirm Production

At the beginning of the industrial age, production was simply the manufacturing that occurred within a single structure. Typically, companies would take

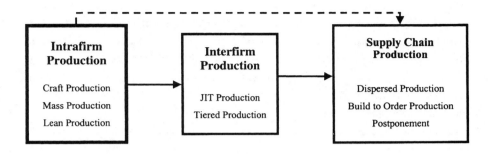

Figure 8.1. Production Supply Chain Model

raw material and manufacture a product entirely within the firm. Craft production was the norm, as each individual craftsman created one product from start to finish. In the early 20th century a new type of production, called mass production, became more common, in which individual workers developed only some part of a final product. In the late 20th century, lean production started to become popular, wherein inventory was minimized and flexible workers assembled parts of a final product.

A wide range of companies involved in intrafirm production today use one of these three different types of production: craft, mass, or lean. For ease of comparison, it is useful to consider a single industry and, for the purposes of this chapter, the auto industry will be used as representative of large-scale production. Many of the concepts developed here are applicable to other industries.

Craft Production

Production at the beginning of the 20th century was primarily craft production. Craftspeople or highly skilled workers using simple and flexible tools made exactly what the customer asked for, one item at a time (Womack et al., 1990). Craft production can handle a high amount of variability in the raw material and can adapt to dynamic markets and to every individual customer instantly. Another term for craft production is "product-focused" production, where craftspeople perform some specialized function and the work moves between them, usually on a build-to-order basis. Bottlenecks occurred often as a result of batching at the different stations. Some craftspeople would have backlogs, and others would have nothing to do. Inventory tended to be very small and primarily finished product. Unfortunately, the cost of having highly skilled adaptable craft workers is also a liability in terms of high variable costs and a very slow rate of production. Another problem is that each product produced can be unique, so that repair cannot be done with standard parts, increasing the cost of maintenance. Examples of this type of production can still be found today with exotic sports cars, custom-made suits, handicraft items, and works of art. In summary, craft production is highly flexible but has a very high cost in terms of labor, material, and time.

Mass Production

Mass production was perfected by Henry Ford and Alfred Sloan in the 1920s and 1930s to reduce the cost of production. In mass production systems, semi-skilled workers use complex inflexible machines to produce large quantities of product at one time. The cost of production is relatively low and products are standardized, reducing the costs of repair and maintenance. Another term for mass production is "functionally focused" production, which is automated and standardized, and where the less skilled worker moves to the work, not vice versa, usually on a build-to-stock (inventory) basis.

Mass production uses narrowly skilled professionals to design products that can be made by unskilled workers tending expensive, single-purpose machines (Womack et al., 1990). Complex manufacturing requiring high levels of skill is handled by reducing the tasks into smaller segments and developing single-skilled specialists. Expensive machines require high utilization rates with long runs of the same part to be profitable. An example in the auto industry is a die machine that is designed to operate at 12 strokes per minute, three shifts a day to make more than a million copies a year of the same part. Changing these dies, which weigh several tons, to make a new part can take more than a day even for a die changing specialist. Machines are also selected for each process stage on the basis of matching capacities as closely as possible, and inventories are used to buffer any variability that might occur between machines (Hayes & Pisano, 1994). Machines and their highly specialized workers cannot handle much variability in terms of their input product or being able to adapt to shifting markets or unique customers.

Managers in automotive mass production companies are evaluated on yield (number of cars produced in relation to schedule) and quality (out-the-door quality, number of vehicles needing defective parts repaired) (Womack et al., 1990). This encourages the mentality that the assembly line must not stop even if defective parts are discovered because defective parts can be fixed at the end of the assembly line. Quality is usually inspected at the end of the process by a specialist instead of at each step along the process. Quality inspection at the end of the process can also mean that many similarly defective products are built before the problem is found. The later the defect is discovered in the production process, the greater the cost associated with fixing the defect. In many automotive mass production companies, more than 20% of the plant area and more than 25% of total hours of effort are spent fixing mistakes (Womack et al., 1990).

In summary, standardized products can be produced at low cost, but the problems with mass production include the inability to handle variability (large, inflexible batch production), inconsistent production quality, and the need for extra inventory, workers, and space to ensure smooth production.

Lean Production

Lean production—developed by Eiji Toyoda and Taiichi Ohno of Toyota in the 1950s and 1960s—uses teams of multiskilled workers with highly flexible machines to produce highly varied products (Womack et al., 1990). Lean production was developed in Japan by Toyota because it was felt that mass production as practiced by Ford and General Motors in the 1950s could not be implemented in Japan. Lean production became more widespread in the 1980s, as the automobile market changed from being somewhat stable and predictable to uncertain and turbulent. Mass production companies—which relied on standardized parts, adversarial market-based supplier relationships, large inventory, and large numbers of suppliers—had trouble adapting to the constantly changing marketplace. Lean production companies that were strategically flexible and able to adapt to a constantly changing environment became more successful.

The fundamental change between mass production and lean production is the increase in flexibility in the workers and the machines. For example, in a lean production automotive company, the dies can be changed in 3 minutes by unspecialized workers as compared to 24 hours in a mass production automotive company. Both the expensive die and the highly specialized worker in lean production tend to be flexible and can adapt to changes as needed.

Lean production companies in the auto industry also evaluate managers based on yield and quality, but quality is the responsibility of each worker instead of a quality specialist at the end of the assembly line. Defective parts or processes are immediately rectified when found by the line worker, dramatically reducing the need for rework areas at the end of the assembly line. Overall, quality of the product improves because no final inspection can detect all the defects that can be assembled into a highly complex part (Womack et al., 1990). The cost of production goes down as lean production companies perform almost no rework and have practically no rework areas (Womack et al., 1990). According to one of the executives interviewed for this book, lean production is the current production method of choice in the automotive industry:

A group called competitive manufacturing is entrusted with the responsibility to implement competitive best practices in the industry which right now in manufacturing for auto makers is Lean Manufacturing processes.

In this lean manufacturing environment, just-in-time methods of production were developed to improve the day-to-day coordination of parts within the company (Womack et al., 1990).

Just-in-Time Production

Just-in-time (JIT) was also first developed at Toyota by Taiichi Ohno as part of the lean production process. JIT is the concept that parts are produced at each step in a process only to supply the immediate demand of the next step (Womack et al., 1990). By using the container used to carry parts to the next step to signal production requirements, it was possible to coordinate the process. As each container was emptied, it was sent back to the previous step, which became the automatic signal to make more parts. Each step in the process made only enough parts to fill the container and waited for the container to be emptied. JIT, however, was extremely difficult to implement because inventories were practically eliminated, so if one small part was not available, the entire production line shut down (Womack et al., 1990). It took more than 20 years to fully implement JIT within the lean production system of Toyota (Womack et al., 1990).

JIT is a process-based, instead of a functionally based, management system. JIT clearly defines the manufacturing process and terminology, along with a clear set of associated metrics (McGrath, 1997). Metrics such as cycle time, rework, inventory waiting to be worked on, setup time, and value added at each step drive new innovative best practices (McGrath, 1997).

In its most basic form, JIT means to produce the required items, at the right quality, and in the exact quantities, precisely as they are needed (Minahan, 1997). The goal of these concepts, contrary to popular belief, is not to reduce inventory, although that is an appealing side benefit. Rather, the goal is to streamline the production process.

In summary, lean production, in contrast to mass production, is adaptable and flexible yet uses less inventory, fewer workers, less factory space, and less specialized tools. The need for high-quality parts produced just in time has prompted firms to look outside the company and to develop interfirm production concepts. As firms continued to focus on reducing costs, they reached the point of diminishing returns within their own boundaries and started to realize that better coordination across corporate boundaries—interfirm production with suppliers and distributors—presented greater opportunities. The next section, on interfirm production, focuses on issues of production outside the firm, primarily dyadic partnership production issues with the supplier or the vendor.

Interfirm Production

As companies expand in size, they have the choice to either vertically integrate and own every step of the process or to rely on other firms to become suppliers. During the 1930s, the Ford Motor Company owned the entire supply chain, from the iron mining company to the dealership where the car was sold. Unfortunately, there were many problems associated with owning the entire supply chain, such as the reduction in overall efficiency when business interactions along the channel are not market based, plus the tremendous amount of capital needed. As companies start to consider production processes outside the firm, the importance of suppliers in the production process increases.

In craft production, suppliers play a much smaller role in providing raw material, as many of the companies pride themselves on being able to produce the entire product within the firm. In mass production, suppliers play a much more important role in providing both raw materials and subcomponents. Suppliers are typically treated as independent businesses, however, and interactions are at arm's length, market based, and short term. The manufacturer develops the detailed design drawings, and suppliers are asked for bids. Suppliers are evaluated on price, quality, delivery reliability, and contract length, but in most cases suppliers provide only the bid price per part, jealously guarding information about their operations. By withholding information on how parts are produced, suppliers believe they are maximizing their ability to hide profits from the manufacturer (Womack et al., 1990). Mass production manufacturers, in turn, focus on costs and price such that competition is constantly encouraged among old and new suppliers, so that there is little incentive to share ideas on improved production techniques. Suppliers are organized in vertical chains and played off against each other in search of the lowest short-term cost. This leads to problems in coordination, lack of flexibility, low quality, and the need for large inventories.

In lean production in the automotive industry, suppliers are selected not only based on bids but also based on past relationships and a proven record of performance. Lean production utilizes approximately one third as many suppliers as mass production because an entire component system of the car is assigned to a single supplier, called a first-tier supplier, who is fully responsible for the design and manufacture of the component system. These suppliers in turn may have a second tier of suppliers who are responsible for manufacturing subcomponents. In lean production, a target price is set for the vehicle, and then the suppliers and the manufacturer work together to determine how the vehicle can be made for that price, while allowing a reasonable profit for both the suppliers and the manufacturer (Womack et al., 1990). Suppliers are assured of a long-term commitment and cooperative relationship with the manufacturer in a lean production system, as compared to the short-term adversarial relationship in a mass production system.

JIT Production

The adversarial relationship that is typical between most buyers and suppliers has to be replaced by one of mutual trust and partnering for JIT to work effectively. JIT production works in a partnering environment because suppliers and buyers are working together to develop cost reduction actions that benefit both firms (Richeson, Lackey, & Starner, 1995). In lean production, suppliers and manufacturers share profits from joint activities but suppliers are allowed to keep the profits from additional activities they undertake (Womack et al., 1990). Mass production supplier relationships are based on the lowest bid price, and both sides are searching for the best deal. JIT production relationships are ideally described as cooperative partnerships in which one of the main goals is to obtain mutually beneficial results (Richeson et al., 1995). Developing strong partnerships with suppliers through JIT actually facilitates better management of supply risk. In the past, supply risk was managed by holding buffer inventories to avoid problems caused by part shortages, defective inputs, and lengthy setup times (Richeson et al., 1995). Partnering arrangements provide the basis for supplier delivery of quality materials as required by JIT (Richeson et al., 1995). This also suggests that for effective interfirm production, a partnering relationship that satisfies the needs of both suppliers and buyers should be developed for the long term.

JIT interfirm production also fosters an emphasis on quality, which is especially critical when dealing with the production of a product, such as an automobile, with multiple parts and multiple suppliers. Many of the essential JIT production techniques such as design standardization, reduced lot sizes, and setup time reduction are very relevant for improved delivered quality, especially with interfirm production. A very important aspect of quality is the need to detect any problems with the product as early as possible, especially when dealing with suppliers and vendors outside the firm. Interfirm production is just like an internal production line in that the cost to fix the error rises dramatically the later the error is detected. With the focus on improving production through total quality management and business process reengineering, many companies have spent the last 10 years or so perfecting their processes inside the plant. This has meant that for companies to further improve and reduce costs, they need to go outside the factory and look at their suppliers (Stein, 1997).

Minahan (1998b) noted that although the JIT concept started in the automotive industry, it has spread to other industries, such as computers, and is now firmly entrenched in the manufacturing psyche of most original equipment manufacturers. Many manufacturers are looking outside their walls for productivity advances by encouraging suppliers to adopt JIT manufacturing practices and possibly help them implement JIT systems.

JIT in lean production has been successful but, unfortunately, there have been many significant failures with JIT as it is practiced in North America.

Researchers have even suggested that JIT can actually drive up costs as suppliers are forced to take on greater amounts of inventory and producers resort to smaller and more frequent shipments to the plant (Bowman, 1996). Many companies try to use JIT in a mass production environment as a way to reduce inventory instead of developing partnerships with their suppliers and perhaps looking beyond their immediate suppliers and vendors to consider the supply chain. An intermediate step between just considering the immediate supplier and vendor to considering the entire supply chain is to utilize another type of production pioneered in the automobile industry called tiered production.

Tiered Production

In tiered production, the buying company deals primarily with the top-tier suppliers, while lower-tier suppliers are managed by those above them in the pyramid (Wilder & Stein, 1997). Figure 8.2 illustrates a simple tiered production system for an automobile manufacturer.

A tiered production system reduces the need for a single company to manage the entire supply chain. Close working relationships are developed between the tiers above and below. For example, Toyota selected a small group of first-tier suppliers to serve it directly. These first-tier suppliers were responsible for everything from design to delivery of a specific component in the automobile. These first-tier suppliers were encouraged to develop partnerships with their suppliers, who in turn may have a third or fourth tier of suppliers. Tighter integration with the suppliers is achieved using the tiered production model found in many automobile companies.

Another advantage of establishing tiers of suppliers is that it permits the focal firm to manage the new product development process more effectively by involving the primary suppliers in the design and development of next-generation products. Using the expertise and knowledge of the primary suppliers can prevent problems at the critical design stage, speed up the product development process, and lead to consideration of alternative designs that help meet target costs (Wilder & Stein, 1997). Suppliers are encouraged to contribute to technological innovation and product design for the next tier in the production channel.

In this fashion, a quasi supply chain is formed with close relationships among the independent suppliers in the chain. Having tiers of one, two, or three suppliers is the beginning of a supply chain that can work together to improve quality and flexibility, as well as reduce costs for the final consumer (Womack et al., 1990).

The tiered supplier model has some weaknesses. First, the model is primarily a set of paired relationships, with independent relationships between the buyer and each of its preferred suppliers (Stuart, Deckert, McCutcheon, &

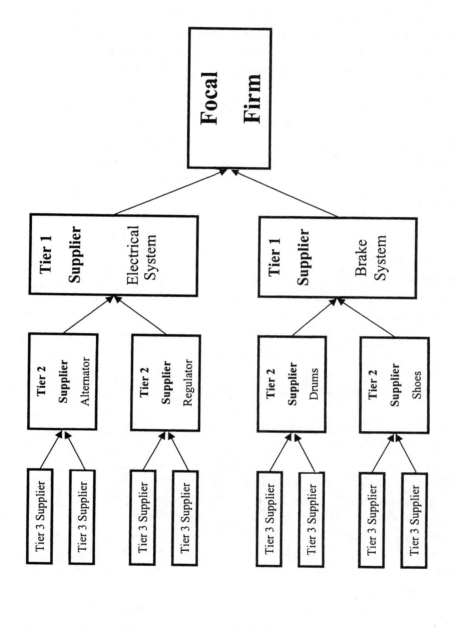

Figure 8.2. Tiered Production

193

Kunst, 1998). This approach can be very limiting for the suppliers as they continue to focus just on the focal firm's specific needs. The tiered supplier model can work in high-volume environments like the electronics and automotive industries, where a few large, powerful buyers strongly influence the scope and direction of the supplier community, but the model might have limited application in other industries. The tiered supplier partnership model clearly focuses on benefiting the buyer (Stuart et al., 1998). Although there are benefits for suppliers in terms of improved information flows, process improvements, increased leverage, and reduced business risk, the direct benefits of marketplace success usually go to the buyer.

In summary, the need for more effective production methods, better quality, and more flexibility led to the development of interfirm production methods such as JIT and tiered production. The drawbacks associated with focussing only on the needs of the focal firm and the need for greater quality and flexibility in an uncertain business environment led to evaluating and improving the entire supply chain. These shifts, in turn, have led to an emphasis on supply chain production, which is discussed in the next section.

Supply Chain Production

The restructuring of global competition has encouraged the development of supply chain management. In the 1980s, the focus was on supplier partnerships to improve cost and quality, but in today's faster-paced markets, the focus has shifted to innovation, flexibility, and speed (Magretta, 1998a). This shift in focus has led to an increasing need for companies to influence what happens outside the company.

According to Hayes and Pisano (1994), competitive strategic flexibility is the ability to switch strategies from low-cost producer to rapid product development relatively quickly and with minimal resources. One essential part of being able to change strategies is to ensure flexible production. The job of production is to provide this capability to switch from low-cost producer to rapid product development (Hayes & Pisano, 1994). In the stable manufacturing environment of the 1960s and 1970s, it was possible to have a single competitive strategy and then have manufacturing focus on improving the efficiency of the production process needed to meet the requirements of that particular strategy. This was ideal in mass production companies where manufacturing looked at reducing the inefficiencies of production. The concept in mass production that there was only one best way to manufacture was challenged by Skinner (1969), who suggested that companies have different strengths and that they should manufacture according to their competitive position and strategy. This has been further expanded to include the concept that companies have to make trade-offs between being a low-cost producer or high-quality producer or focus on speed to market. This paradigm was challenged by Womack et al. (1990), who identified lean production as a process in which companies are able to eliminate the trade-off among productivity, investment, and variety. Lean production companies focus on product variety, continuous efforts to reduce manufacturing costs, cross-functional teams, and delegation of decision making (Hayes & Pisano, 1994). In an uncertain environment, there are greater advantages associated with being flexible and being able to adapt quickly to changing market conditions. Japanese companies using lean production focused on speed and flexibility rather than volume and cost (Hayes & Pisano, 1994). For manufacturing to be flexible and able to respond quickly to an ever-changing environment, it is very useful to develop a supply chain orientation and consider supply chain management.

Supply chain management, as defined in Chapter 1, is *the systemic, strategic coordination of the traditional business functions within a particular company and across businesses within the supply chain, for the purposes of improving the long-term performance of the individual companies and the supply chain as a whole.* A supply chain orientation in very simple terms occurs when the focal firm starts to consider its supplier's supplier and its customer's customer simultaneously. As companies focus on becoming more efficient and flexible in their production methods to handle uncertainty in the business environment, companies need a supply chain orientation.

Before discussing different types of supply chain production, it is useful to identify two different roles played by the supply chain: a physical function and a market mediation function (Fisher, 1997). A supply chain's physical function is to convert raw materials into parts, components, and eventually finished goods, and to transport them from one point in the supply chain to the next (Fisher, 1997). Physical function costs are the costs of production, transportation, and inventory storage.

A supply chain's market mediation function is to ensure that the variety of products reaching the marketplace matches what consumers want to buy (Fisher, 1997). Market mediation costs arise when supply exceeds demand and a product has to be marked down and sold at a loss, or when supply falls short of demand, resulting in lost sales opportunities and dissatisfied customers.

Fisher (1997) divided products into two categories: functional and innovative. Functional products are those products that satisfy basic needs and have a stable, predictable demand with long product life cycles that do not change much over time. Innovative products tend to have high profit margins, volatile demand, and short product life cycles. A flexible supply chain is of value when dealing with innovative products, whereas a constant, continuous replenishment supply chain is of value with functional products (Fisher, 1997).

The predictable demand for functional products makes market mediation easy, so that firms can focus almost exclusively on minimizing physical costs—a crucial goal, given the price sensitivity of most functional products (Fisher, 1997). The entire supply chain focuses on coordinating the ordering, production, and delivery of supplies, thereby minimizing inventory and maximizing production efficiency—a constant, continuous replenishment supply chain.

For innovative products, the uncertain market reaction to innovation increases the risk of shortages or excess supplies, so that market mediation costs are more important than physical costs. As a result, a fast and flexible supply chain is of greater value. The focus in this case is not on minimizing costs but rather on where in the chain to position inventory and available production capacity so as to hedge against uncertain demand (Fisher, 1997). If the product is such that the demand is uncertain, then there are three coordinated strategies that the supply chain can use: (a) reduce uncertainty by developing better supply chain-wide forecasting systems, (b) avoid uncertainty by cutting lead times and increasing the supply chain's flexibility so that it can produce when needed, or (c) hedge against the uncertainty with buffers of inventory or excess capacity.

Developing better forecasting systems is possible with the many new supply chain information systems that are being developed, as discussed in Chapter 11, but forecasting is still a challenge in an uncertain market (see Chapter 7). Supply chains in the 1990s and beyond rarely have the luxury to build buffers of inventory or excess capacity. This suggests that there will likely be a greater emphasis on strategic flexible production. Whether the product is functional or innovative, there are clear advantages to viewing the supply chain as a whole.

In a supply chain, quality has been defined as the exchange of the right quantity of the right goods at the right time between one level in the supply chain and the next (Harrison, 1990). Harrison (1990) also suggests that there are three objectives for quality in a supply chain: (a) delivered goods are fit for their intended purpose, (b) deliveries are on time, and (c) part counts are accurate. Poor quality and late delivery make efficient production, especially JIT production as discussed earlier, impossible for the downstream customer. To ensure quality for interfirm production, it is valuable to consider the supply chain as a whole. One interview participant noted what a supply chain orientation means to an auto manufacturing company:

> Generally we focus on upstream movement, trying to get processes like just-in-time rail delivery and things like that into our lean processes and designing our new manufacturing facilities for lean materials flow and movement throughout the literal manufacturing design itself. And using those definition approaches [supply chain definitions] gives you that foundation from which to start, and then I think it offers an appreciation for the complexity of the different functions that really are involved in a supply chain both internal and external to an organization.

Production systems that utilize a supply chain perspective are difficult to implement and manage. Companies are being forced to adopt a supply chain perspective to compete in the current uncertain business climate. The following sections look at two new types of supply chain production that rely on a supply chain orientation and effective supply chain management—dispersed production and build-to-order production.

Dispersed Production

Dispersed production or manufacturing is the concept of manufacturing in the location that is most appropriate for that specific task. For example, instead of manufacturing an entire garment in one location, yarn is produced in Korea, fabric woven in Taiwan, and zippers manufactured in Japan, and then fabric and zipper are shipped to Thailand for final garment assembly (Magretta, 1998a). Dispersed production means breaking up the supply chain and rationalizing the best location and firm for each activity. Effective management of dispersed production requires not only excellent logistics and transportation but also a supply chain orientation. Companies that utilize dispersed production dissect the manufacturing process and look for the best solution at each step in the manufacturing process (Magretta, 1998a).

Another benefit of managing the supply chain through dispersed production is that production is brought closer to the market. By developing relationships further upstream (closer to the raw material producer), it is possible to reduce the buying cycle that can be critical in consumer-driven, fast-moving markets. Magretta (1998a) discussed a retail supply chain where the buying cycle was shortened from 13 weeks to 5 weeks, a net gain of 8 weeks, to improve the accuracy to anticipate where the market is heading. Good supply chain management strips away time and cost from the product delivery cycles (Magretta, 1998a). Supply chain production is about buying the right things and shortening the delivery cycles. It requires "reaching into the suppliers" to ensure that certain things happen on time and at the right quality level (Magretta, 1998a).

An interview participant noted that a supply chain orientation can help in new product development:

> Caterpillar, when they partner with some of their carriers in their network, becomes involved in actually designing the equipment or conveyance that would be used to deliver their products, and/or to source their products, and they also capitalized some of those design and engineering processes for their carriers to go ahead and be able to utilize that conveyance.

The information is shared among the partners in the supply chain so there is a benefit to all the members of the supply chain.

For supply chain production to work, it is important that companies develop close partnerships using shared information streams to forecast, produce, ship, and assemble in a true just-in-time scheme. The Internet can be used to create a direct link with customers and suppliers, improving communication and enabling the development of a flexible, adaptable organization that can reconfigure itself as needed. Companies can have a supply chain focus by ensuring that engineering change orders are sent not only to their suppliers but to their suppliers' vendors as well (McKeefry, 1998). This is particularly important for those companies that use a JIT system and do not hold inventory in-house.

Becoming more responsive to the customer in a timely fashion means inventory costs will start to fall, but manufacturing costs will start to rise. The objective is to find the optimum total cost. Within a more certain demand environment, the aim is to match production activity more closely with demand, by improving plant responsiveness and focusing on operational performance improvement (Whiteoak, 1993). Once the production environment is stabilized, the use of raw materials can be improved by greater predictability and smoothness of demand, thus liberating upstream JIT opportunities (Whiteoak, 1993).

In an uncertain demand environment, other methods are needed to improve operational performance. The best companies have a supply chain that is twice as fast as that of their competitors to develop and deliver product, which in a fast-moving, competitive market environment is a clear strategic advantage (McGrath, 1997). In a comparison of companies that had a supply chain orientation to those companies without such an orientation, Stein (1997) found that companies without a supply chain orientation needed several months to increase production by 20%, whereas supply chain oriented companies required less than 2 weeks. Supply chain oriented companies met customers' requested delivery dates 96% of the time, compared with 83% for non-supply chain companies (Stein, 1997). A well-coordinated supply chain production system allows companies to be very responsive to changes in the marketplace, perhaps even at the single customer level, which leads to the concept of build-to-order production.

Build-to-Order Production

Build-to-order production or demand-driven manufacturing is a relatively new concept that very few companies have been able to achieve because a well-coordinated supply chain is required. By integrating within a single system such functions as transportation, production, and planning, a supply chain becomes truly demand driven, and build to stock is been replaced by build to order.

One of the companies that has exemplified build-to-order production is Dell Computers. Dell has been able to achieve a phenomenal breakthrough in the production cycle by cutting the total time from a customer order to shipment down to 3.5 days. Dell has expanded its JIT practices from within the company to the entire supply chain as suppliers have been integrated into Dell's operations (Minahan, 1997). The true benefit of JIT is that each supply partner takes ownership of the process and identifies problems as they occur because the next part of the process cannot happen if there is a problem. Dell has also implemented JIT practices on its manufacturing floor, sequencing all production activities in such a way that in-process material continually moves toward the completed product (Minahan, 1997). The goal is to work with suppliers to figure out how to minimize supply chain costs and hold the least amount of inventory.

A trade-off between decreasing costs of inventory and higher transportation costs arises from shipping smaller shipments. Dell has looked for ways to integrate suppliers into its production process and have them understand the business so that variability in demand will not translate into inventory. Suppliers, who own the inventory until it is received by Dell, are responsible for maintaining adequate stock levels and picking parts as needed, which can be on an hourly basis (Minahan, 1997). Trucks make a continuous loop between suppliers and Dell, delivering the sorted parts to the computer maker's plant for final assembly. Dell also encourages suppliers to sell parts stored at the warehouse to other customers, increasing the supplier's efficiency. Dell's parts inventory turnover rate is 12 days (Minahan, 1997).

Dell does not inspect parts for quality, but rather relies on regular on-site audits of suppliers as well as quick, diagnostic tests during the assembly process. For critical parts like circuit boards, Dell directly links to the supplier's manufacturing database to monitor quality on the supplier's assembly line and identify quality glitches before they reach any Dell plant (Minahan, 1997). Dell encourages suppliers and suppliers' suppliers to follow a JIT production process as well. In 1990, Dell's business model was 95% build to stock; by 1995, it was 40% build to order, and it later reached 95% build to order (Vasilash, 1999).

Another company that has embraced the concept of direct production or build to order is Miller SQA, which produces a variety of low-cost, high-quality office furniture on a build-to-order basis. SQA lead times average 7 days, compared to the industry average of 3 to 6 weeks, through integration of JIT production in its supply chain (Minahan, 1997). To improve response time, SQA hired Menlo Logistics to manage a single parts warehouse just 4 miles from the Holland, Michigan, production facility. Currently, suppliers ship more than 1,000 different parts to the Menlo site, where the parts are picked, sorted, and delivered to the SQA plant based on actual production needs within a 4-hour window (Minahan, 1997). At any given time, there is no more than 2 hours' worth of production parts inventory at the SQA plant, a dramatic reduction from previous levels. SQA has been able to reduce total cycle time from 10 hours to 2 hours.

Suppliers are required to keep no more than 10 days' worth of inventory and no less than 2 days' of inventory at the Menlo site, which translates to a 33% inventory reduction in SQA's supply chain (Minahan, 1997). Suppliers have added flexibility in logistics and production processes as they have the opportunity to run lot sizes and stock those lots at Menlo. SQA relies on various information systems to coordinate parts demand, production queues, and delivery schedules in the supply chain and to know when to tap Menlo for more parts and when to place new orders with suppliers (Minahan, 1997). By utilizing supply chain production strategies, SQA has achieved 30% direct production to the customer, which is leading to lower costs, increased sales, and increased market share (Estell, 1999).

Another advantage of build-to-order production is that it gives firms the ability to customize a large volume of products and deliver them at close to mass production prices. In fact, another term for build-to-order production is mass customization. Build-to-order or mass customization (the tailoring of products to different requirements) provides an edge that others less proficient at SCM cannot duplicate (Donlon & Galli, 1998).

Two other companies that have become proficient in build-to-order production are National Bicycle and Lutron Electronics. National Bicycle, a Japanese company that specializes in building custom-tailored bikes, is a good example of the benefits of having a flexible and responsive supply chain (Fisher, 1997). National has little idea what customers will order out of a possible 2 million choices, but its produce-to-order system allows it to match supply with demand as it occurs. Lutron Electronics of Coopersburg, Pennsylvania, became the world leader in dimmer switches and other lighting controls by giving customers an essentially unlimited choice of technical and fashion features that allows customers to configure products as they order. Build to order is usually not as cheap as mass production, yet affluent consumers are willing to pay for high-margin, innovative products. Such products require a different, more expensive, but more responsive production process than mass production products.

Postponement

The third type of production system that benefits greatly from a supply chain orientation is postponement—the concept of designing a product such that it is possible to delay differentiation of the product until customer demand for the specific end-product is known (Billington & Amaral, 1999; Feitzinger & Lee, 1997). For example, Hewlett-Packard Company does not insert the power supply (i.e., 110 volts or 240 volts) until the product reaches the customer's country, allowing it to reduce inventory costs and gain greater flexibility to meet customer demand. Postponement is more valuable than information sharing in a supply chain, especially under conditions of high demand uncertainty, high cost of a lost sale, and low capacity responsiveness (Billington & Amaral, 1999). Postponement supports the delivery of mass-customized products quickly and at low cost (Feitzinger & Lee, 1997).

   Postponement as a strategy requires research and development to coordinate along the supply chain to develop new product architecture that allows delayed differentiation to be accomplished inexpensively. Research and development must redesign the product so that it can be customized at the most efficient point in the supply chain (Feitzinger & Lee, 1997). To be able to practice postponement efficiently requires coordination among several functions, especially production across the supply chain.

Standard Methods of Production

Companies with standard production systems such as craftsman production, mass production, and lean production can all benefit from a supply chain orientation. Most companies have adopted some lean production techniques. JIT and tiered production can be modified easily to become supply chain production systems. Minahan (1998), in discussing the automotive industry, noted the trend of original equipment manufacturers putting pressure on second- and third-tier suppliers to operate more efficiently. This has resulted in more suppliers implementing core JIT principles and adopting a total supply chain perspective (Minahan, 1998). All five of the different types of production—lean production, JIT, tiered production, dispersed production, and build-to-order production—can benefit from developing relationships with both suppliers' suppliers and customers' customers (a supply chain orientation) to better facilitate smooth production, reduce inventory, decrease cost, and develop competitive advantage.

   Supply chain production systems have a significant role to play in many companies because the selection of the appropriate production system can directly affect the strategic capability of the firm. For highly innovative products in an uncertain business environment, a dispersed production, build-to-order, or postponement production systems allow a strategic orientation of speed and flexibility. For functional products in a stable environment, the supply chain production system can focus on volume cost and efficiency to be successful. In summary, developing a supply chain production system and utilizing a supply chain orientation lead to greater opportunities for lower costs, improved customer value, and differential advantage in the future.

Conclusions

This chapter looked at supply chain management from the perspective of production or manufacturing, starting within the firm with craft production, mass production, and lean production. The benefits of looking beyond the firm to interfirm production using JIT production and tiered production were discussed. The importance of suppliers and supplier partnerships in the production process was emphasized. This led to the concept of strategic flexibility, which was shown to be useful in uncertain and changing business environments, leading to the concept of competition between supply chains. This led to the importance of a supply chain orientation and the need to develop a continuous replenishment supply chain for stable markets, versus a strategically flexible supply chain for highly competitive, uncertain markets. Three types of production systems—dispersed, build to order, and postponement—were discussed in the context of supply chain production.

Management Recommendations

The different types of production that still flourish in different markets suggest that no single type of production is appropriate in every market. Managers need to define their product type and the type of market environment to determine the appropriate production type. It should also be clear that managers need to go beyond the boundaries of the firm and consider relationships with their suppliers, suppliers' suppliers, their customers, and customers' customers. Both functional and innovative product types benefit from a supply chain orientation that leads to greater efficiency and effectiveness of a firm's own production system. A company's choice of production strategy is not arbitrary—it must be driven by the company's competitive strategy. Emphasizing the wrong approach can quickly undermine a business. Forming partnerships and relationships with other members of the supply chain entails risks. Managers need to determine if the benefits of increased efficiency or increased flexibility warrant the costs associated with developing supply chain production systems.

Research Recommendations

Several concepts were presented in this chapter that need to be examined further to determine their applicability in different organizational structures and market environments. An effort was made to distinguish between functional products and innovative products. Can firms belong to both a low-cost, high-efficiency supply chain and to a highly flexible, highly innovative supply chain with different products at the same time? Is the distinction really product related, or is it the firm level that determines if some firms need to focus on one type of production or the other?

The production supply chain model offered in Figure 8.1 is just a beginning. It proposes a theory, which needs both refinement and testing by researchers. The underlying premise of the model is the causal relationship between the current business environment and the need to develop intrafirm production systems, then interfirm production systems, that lead to supply chain production systems. Do companies have to go through all the stages as identified, or can they skip a stage, as implied with the dotted arrows? Further research needs to determine whether the model is applicable only to specific industries or instead is it much more general? Additional research may be needed to fully identify all the intermediate steps associated with developing supply chain production systems. There is a further need to refine the factors that are identified to develop theoretical constructs that can be tested. Through the testing and validation of the production supply chain model, it is hoped that both the researcher and practitioner communities can benefit from further understanding the valuable role of production in a supply chain.

9

Purchasing in a
Supply Chain Context

NANCY W. NIX

Executive Summary

In this chapter, the evolution of the role of purchasing is discussed, and the purchasing role in support of a firm's supply chain management (SCM) strategies and objectives is explored. A framework is presented that highlights required shifts in the nature of buyer-seller relationships, as well as in the emphasis, objectives, and role of purchasing in a supply chain management context versus historical approaches. Issues related to organizational structure, communications processes, and information technology are also highlighted.

This chapter will

- Examine the evolution of the purchasing role toward managing in a SCM context in four stages (see Table 9.1)—the traditional role of managing arms-length transactions (Stage 1), managing supplier relationships (Stage 2), the operational supply chain approach of materials logistics management (Stage 3), and the strategic supply chain approach of managing for integrated value added (Stage 4)
- Describe the increased emphasis on supplier relationships resulting from competitive pressures, more demanding consumers, rapid technological change, changes in production processes, and the increased emphasis on outsourcing of noncore activities

■ Point out the influence of environmental situations on the potential benefits of long-term partnerships

■ Highlight the opportunity for benefit from long-term partnerships in dealing with environmental uncertainty or in providing access to resources and technology without incurring the burden of ownership

■ Highlight the opportunities to improve the quality and dependability of critical supply and to reduce total costs through supplier partnerships

■ Examine the effort and costs required to make partnerships successful and point out the fact that the costs may outweigh the benefits in many situations

■ Point out the limitations of managing from a partnership perspective rather than the broader, systemwide supply chain perspective

■ Examine both operational and strategic approaches to SCM and their respective implications for the role of purchasing

■ Review various organizational models for purchasing and highlight advantages and disadvantages of each

■ Examine different approaches to communications in relationships between customers and suppliers

■ Discuss the information technology requirements for managing the purchasing function in a supply chain context

These discussions will lead to the conclusions that

■ Purchasing plays a critical, boundary-spanning role in the supply chain management activities of a firm

■ To achieve the potential benefits of SCM, the role of purchasing must be viewed in a systemwide context and must be focused beyond managing the buyer-seller relationship

■ Managers must understand the potential benefits to be achieved through SCM relationships, based on environmental conditions and specific resource or performance requirements

■ It is important for managers to understand the potential benefits, as well as the costs, of developing such relationships so that appropriate business decisions can be made

■ Success in achieving SCM objectives means that purchasing requirements must be understood within the context of the overall strategy of the firm, supply chain partners must be selected to meet the strategic requirements, and the relationships must be managed appropriately over the long term

■ Cost and quality improvements must be understood and implemented from a systemwide perspective to achieve optimum results

■ To achieve the objectives of improved quality and reliability, reduced inventories, and lower total system cost associated with an operational approach to SCM, an emphasis on the integration of purchasing and logistics is required

- To achieve the objectives of speed, flexibility, and competitive advantage associated with a strategic approach to SCM requires collaboration with strategic supply chain partners focused on redesigning products and business processes to deliver value to customers
- In a strategic context, the role of purchasing is to understand the capability of suppliers and identify ways to match that capability to the needs of strategic customers
- Purchasing can enhance the effectiveness of product and process design by ensuring reliability and quality of supply of materials, components, and services; managing the supplier involvement in the process; and providing insights about the competitive supply environment
- Organizational structure and communications processes must be designed to support the requirements and objectives of the purchasing organization in support of the firm's supply chain management activities
- Information technology is critical to manage the increasing complexity of the purchasing function, to facilitate the integration of processes across firms in a supply chain context, and to provide decision support tools to enable systemwide optimization

To date, researchers and managers alike have primarily focused on supplier partnerships, or building stronger relationships between the buyer and seller firm. Managers and researchers alike must adopt a broader, systemwide approach to understand and achieve the contribution that purchasing can make in an SCM context.

Introduction

> As purchasing becomes an integral part of a firm's ability to achieve organizational goals and strategies, then "like customers, suppliers will be considered to be everyone's business." (Leenders, Nollet, & Ellram, 1993, p. 40)

Just as environmental factors have led to an increased emphasis on supply chain management over the past several decades, they have also been important drivers in the increasing importance and changing role of the purchasing function within organizations. Increased globalization of businesses and the resulting competitive pressures have created a shift from a seller's market to a buyer's market. As a result, the complexity of buying decisions has increased, and the role of the purchasing organization in managing the buyer-seller interface has become more critical. As the rate of technological change has increased, new product introductions have become more frequent, and lead times have short-ened. These changes have resulted in greater demands on suppliers in support of their customers' new product development activities. Competitive pressures have also required firms to improve product quality and to develop more flexi-ble production and inventory management processes to ensure product avail-ability to meet changing customer demands, while continuing to reduce costs and improve profitability (Busch, 1988; Mendez & Pearson, 1994). Each of these, in turn, translates to greater demands on suppliers and changes in the role of the purchasing organization to ensure that these demands are met.

On average, industrial firms' expenditures for purchased goods and services are more than 50% of sales revenues (Cavinato, 1991a; Giunipero & Brand, 1996; Noordewier, John, & Nevin, 1990). Because the contribution of each dol-lar reduction in purchasing costs goes directly to the bottom line, the potential contribution to a firm's profitability is significant. The potential profit contribu-tion from purchasing, however, goes beyond purchase price. In an increasingly volatile environment, with greater emphasis on speed of product innovation, improved product quality, and optimization of the total flow of materials, the focus of purchasing has shifted from purchase price to total cost (Busch, 1988). Thus, increasingly important in the buyer-seller interface are the management of quality, the flexibility and reliability of delivery, the technological capability and responsiveness of the supplier, and the willingness to work in a collabora-tive way toward mutual benefit.

Additional pressures for change in the purchasing role have been brought about as a result of changes in firms' production processes. As a result of the need to focus on rapidly changing demands of customers, many firms have shifted from big production runs of standard products to the manufacturing of individual customer products with many variants. The natural result of these changes is an increase in the complexity of managing materials requirements, with a corresponding increase in cost. Increased complexity and cost have resulted in a much greater emphasis on materials management from a total sys-tems perspective, with the purchasing organization playing a much larger role in the interface between the supplier base and production. This change has led to the necessity for the purchasing role to shift to a larger supply chain context.

A number of factors have also influenced firms to increasingly consider outsourcing of activities traditionally managed within the company. Pressures to improve capital productivity and profitability have led to much greater emphasis on outsourcing as a means to avoid capital investment, to access spe-cialized talent or leading edge technology, or to improve quality, increase flexi-bility, or improve cost performance (Busch, 1988; Graham, Daugherty, & Dudley, 1994; Mendez & Pearson, 1994). To focus on core businesses, organi-zations increasingly turn to outsourcing for noncore activities. This emphasis on outsourcing substantially increases the need to manage the supply of prod-ucts and services to contribute to a firm's competitiveness (Leenders et al.,

Table 9.1 Stages of Development in the Purchasing Role

			Supply Chain Management Context	
	Stage 1 Traditional	Stage 2 Partnership/Relational	Stage 3 Operational Approach (Materials Logistics Management)	Stage 4 Strategic Approach (Integrated Value Added)
Emphasis	Vendor selection and price negotiation	Building closer relations with suppliers, customers, and distributors	Planning, implementing, and controlling information and product flows from point of origin to point of consumption	Redesigning business processes for speed, flexibility, and competitive advantage
Objective	Right goods at right place at right time at right price	Closer relations to reduce total cost and minimize risk	Coordinated activities and streamlined information flow resulting in increased quality and reliability, reduced inventories, and lower total system cost	Collaborative product and process design to reduce cycle time, improve product design and quality, and respond quickly to changing customer requirements
Purchasing role	▪ Service function for business units ▪ Transaction and procedures management ▪ Gatekeeper in buyer-seller relationship	▪ Managing supplier relationships ▪ Qualifying suppliers and reducing supplier base ▪ Make/buy decision making ▪ Managing outsourcing	▪ Managing supply, using considerations of capacity, capability, and location of suppliers as well as scheduling requirements for manufacturing ▪ Managing inbound logistics to achieve system objectives ▪ Facilitating and coordinating linkages between suppliers, manufacturing, and logistics	▪ Environmental scanning to identify opportunities and threats in supply markets ▪ Identify issues and options for supplier contribution to competitive advantage of firm ▪ Incorporate strategic purchasing into organization culture with appropriate objectives, processes, and reward and recognition ▪ Facilitate multidisciplinary coordination and collaboration for product and process design and operation ▪ Assess and facilitate sharing of risks and reward across supply chain firms ▪

Table 9.1 *continued*

		Supply Chain Management Context		
	Stage 1 **Traditional**	Stage 2 **Partnership/Relational**	Stage 3 **Operational Approach** (**Materials Logistics Management**)	Stage 4 **Strategic Approach** (**Integrated Value Added**)
Purchasing objectives	▪ Lowest purchase price ▪ Maintaining alternative sources of supply	▪ Improving quality and reliability ▪ Lowering total cost of purchases ▪ Minimizing risk	▪ Optimizing flow of information and products throughout the system ▪ Reducing systemwide inventories ▪ Reducing systemwide cycle time	▪ Joint product innovation for competitive advantage in meeting customer demand and optimum supply chain performance with shorter lead times ▪ Joint process design that reduces total system cycle time and cost
Nature of relationships	▪ Arm's length ▪ Transactional ▪ Clear differentiation of responsibilities and tasks ▪ Discrete, short-term events	▪ Partnership or alliance ▪ Cooperative and collaborative buyer-seller relationship ▪ Shared responsibilities for tasks ▪ Expectation of continued duration	▪ Multidisciplinary interfirm coordination of operations ▪ Integration of operational planning systems ▪ Elimination of redundant tasks ▪ Joint planning and information sharing to accomplish common objectives ▪ Managing systemwide cost trade-offs and sharing mutual benefits from joint action	▪ Strategic partnerships and alliances ▪ Interactive networks of customers, suppliers, and cross-functional team in the focal firm ▪ Integration of technical and business expertise ▪ Integration of research and development, product and process engineering, and materials management processes

SOURCE: Adapted from Giunipero and Brand (1996).

1993). The purchasing organization may be the logical organization to oversee outsourcing and, as a result, the purchasing role is likely to become more strategic.

As firms increasingly pursue supply chain management (SCM) strategies in response to competitive pressures, the need for purchasing to become integrated into the supply chain, both internally and externally, has increased. As purchasing becomes an integral part of a firm's ability to achieve organizational goals and strategies, then "like customers, suppliers will be considered to be everyone's business" (Leenders et al., 1993, p. 40). Changes in the nature of internal and external relationships and the objectives of the purchasing process, as well as organizational structure, communications processes, and information technology, will be critical to the successful contribution of purchasing activities to SCM.

This chapter explores the changes in the role and objectives of the purchasing function over time as well as the role of purchasing in the context of both operational and strategic approaches to SCM. It examines the evolution of the purchasing role toward managing in a SCM context in four stages, as shown in Table 9.1.

Following the discussion of the four stages in the evolution of the purchasing role, the chapter examines organizational structure, communications processes, and information technology as they relate to the purchasing process. Issues important to the role of purchasing in a supply chain context are highlighted. Finally, implications for purchasing managers and areas for future research are presented. To date, researchers and managers alike have primarily focused on supplier partnerships, or building stronger relationships between the buyer and seller firm. To achieve the potential of SCM and achieve the contribution that purchasing can make in an SCM context, managers and researchers alike must adopt a broader, systemwide approach.

The Changing Role of Purchasing

To understand the changing role of purchasing in a supply chain context, the traditional role of purchasing must first be considered. In the traditional role, the emphasis was on vendor selection and price, relationships were kept at arm's length, and interactions were transactional in nature. In response to the competitive pressures experienced by firms, the purchasing role increasingly became one of managing buyer-seller relationships. In this role, the emphasis shifted to that of building closer relations with suppliers, with the objective of reducing total cost and minimizing risk.

In a supply chain context, the role of purchasing is further expanded to that of a total systems orientation. Two approaches to supply chain management may be taken by firms and must be considered. First, an operational approach to supply chain management may be adopted, with an emphasis on planning, implementing, and controlling information and product flows through the supply chain. Second, a strategic approach to supply chain management may be pursued, with an emphasis on redesigning business processes for speed, flexibility, and competitive advantage. The role of purchasing in a supply chain management context may be different depending on whether a firm pursues a strategic or operational approach to supply chain management.

The basic framework used here to characterize the changing purchasing role is adapted from a framework developed by Giunipero and Brand (1996), which describes the stages of evolution toward supply chain management (Table 9.1). The four stages in the development of the purchasing role are characterized as follows:

> *Stage 1—Traditional Approach:* In the traditional purchasing role, the focus is on selecting and negotiating with suppliers, with the objective of purchasing goods at the lowest price. The purchasing professional plays a gatekeeper role, and relationships are transactional and arm's length in nature.

> *Stage 2—Partnership/Relational Approach:* The partnership or relational approach is focused on linking each element in the production and supply channel through building strong buyer-supplier relationships, aimed at managing the flow of goods from supplier through end user. Based on the conceptual differentiation between partnerships or alliances and supply chain management highlighted in Chapter 1, this stage is not characterized as supply chain management; however, this stage appears to be a critical building block toward supply chain management because of the commonality in factors contributing to successful partnerships and successful SCM relationships.

> *Stage 3—Operational Approach to SCM:* In this stage of development, the emphasis is on managing the flow of goods and information, and an integrative philosophy aimed at optimizing the total system is adopted. In this approach, the relationships involve members of firms throughout the supply chain, as well as multiple functions within each firm. The focus is on planning, implementing, and controlling information and product flows, with the primary objectives being improved efficiency and reduced cost, primarily through reductions in inventory and cycle time. This approach involves the coordination of operational elements of the supply chain.

> *Stage 4—Strategic Approach to SCM:* The "integrative value-added approach" expands the supply chain concept to encompass the entire sourcing process, as well as the value-adding and marketing activities of the firm. In this approach, the emphasis is on redesigning business processes to optimize the performance of the entire system and create competitive advantage for the firm (Giunipero & Brand, 1996).

From the traditional role of acquiring goods at the right price (Stage 1), an expanded role of supply management emerged, with an emphasis on building stronger buyer-seller relationships aimed at working jointly to reduce total cost and uncertainty (Stage 2). Increasing integration of the multiple firms and organizations expanded the role further to one of materials logistics management, or of linking the supply base with the manufacturing and logistics organizations, and ultimately with downstream customers (Stage 3). Stage 3 is characterized as an operational approach toward supply chain management, because the emphasis is on systemwide optimization of operating elements such as product flows, inventory levels, cycle time, and cost. Finally, the strategic approach of managing the purchasing function to enhance the competitive advantage of the firm is reflected in Stage 4, aimed at "integrative value added" (Giunipero & Brand, 1996). In this approach, the purchasing role becomes much broader to include identification of strategic opportunities to enhance the firm's competitiveness through relationships with critical suppliers. This stage is characterized as a strategic approach to supply chain management because the emphasis is on strategic alliances with supply chain partners to reengineer and innovate both products and processes so as to deliver greater value to downstream customers. In the following sections, each of these stages in the role purchasing is discussed in greater detail.

Stage 1: Traditional Approach

The traditional role of the purchasing organization has been alternatively described as one of (a) determining which vendor to select for a purchase based on specific requests for material and quantity from the user organization, (b) negotiating the lowest price, (c) managing adversarial relationships with suppliers, (d) managing paperwork and procedures, and (e) gatekeeping (Busch, 1988; Cavinato, 1991a; Leenders et al., 1993; Graham et al., 1994). Although historically the purchasing emphasis was on vendor selection and price, increasing emphasis on coordinating and controlling the logistics aspects of inbound materials meant a greater involvement of purchasing professionals in decisions about what materials to purchase and when, in what quantity, and how to move those materials (Cavinato, 1991a).

With the objectives of purchasing managers shifting away from negotiating the lowest price toward optimizing total cost, a much greater emphasis is placed on cost of quality, research and design costs, and delivery disturbance costs (Busch, 1988). This broader set of objectives has brought about increasing demands in the management of the buyer-supplier interface, resulting in a trend toward reducing the number of suppliers or even single sourcing. As the number of suppliers is reduced, and as the interface between the customer and the supplier becomes more complex, a supplier can no longer be replaced easily, and the ability to work in a cooperative and collaborative way becomes increasingly important (Busch, 1988).

The traditional expectation of purchasing—aimed at obtaining the right goods and services of the right quality and in the right quantity, at the right time and the right places, and at the right price—reinforced a service role for a purchasing organization. In this service role, the purchasing organization often functioned as a gatekeeper, controlling the buyer-seller interface. The outsourcing of functions and the need to integrate both internally and externally, however, requires more than a service or gatekeeper role (Leenders et al., 1993). The increasing reliance on suppliers for goods and services shifted the purchasing role to one of integrating the firm's internal and external operations, or managing the relationships with suppliers (Leenders et al., 1993).

Stage 2: Partnership/Relational Approach

The recognition of the potential to be gained through collaborative relationships with suppliers has resulted in a move away from an adversarial buyer-seller relationship to a focus on managing long-term relationships to increase supplier contributions to a firm's success (Graham et al., 1994). The nature of buyer-seller relationships may take a variety of forms, however, and the desirability of a given type of relationship may differ in different situations. In the following section, differences in relationship type and context are discussed.

The Influence of Context on Buyer-Seller Relationships

Several authors have drawn on transaction cost analysis (TCA) to develop conceptual frameworks that shed light on the types of buyer-seller relationships, the conditions under which they are formed, and the performance outcomes associated with different types (Graham et al., 1994; Heide & John, 1990; Noordewier et al., 1990). The shift away from the traditional "arm's length" relationship to closer relationships, alternatively characterized as "partnerships" or "alliances," has been described as a shift from a market-based exchange toward bilateral governance (Heide & John, 1990). This shift toward bilateral governance is a way of safeguarding against certain risks without incurring the burden of ownership through vertical integration. For example, risks associated with investing in assets or resources that can be profitable only in a specific relationship (asset specificity) historically have been minimized by owning those assets. Similarly, if raw material quality or production processes were particularly critical to a firm's success or characterized by high levels of uncertainty, it was considered prudent to own and operate production facilities rather than being dependent on the purchase of materials on the open market. If, however, firms can depend on and trust suppliers to act in the best interest of both parties and rely on their long-term commitment to a mutually beneficial relationship, the risk to both parties is reduced.

Heide and John (1990) suggest that as relationships become closer, the nature of the buyer-seller relationship differs along three dimensions—joint action, continuity, and verification of the supplier. In the traditional, arm's-length buyer-seller relationship, the responsibility for a given task, such as product design or inventory management, clearly belongs to one or the other entity. As the relationship moves toward a partnership or alliance, joint action is increased, and firms work collaboratively to reengineer products or manage inventories. Heide and John (1990) define joint action as "the degree of interpenetration of organizational boundaries" (p. 25), with responsibilities for tasks being shared in a cooperative or collaborative way. Continuity is defined as the "perception of the bilateral expectation of future interaction" (p. 25). Although the arm's-length relationship is based on discrete and usually short-term events, alliances or partnerships are built on anticipation of a future relationship. Finally, verification is defined as "the scope of efforts undertaken by the buyer *ex ante* to verify the supplier's ability to perform as expected" (p. 25). Although the arm's-length relationship with a supplier requires little, if any, verification or qualification of suppliers, a closer and longer-term relationship requires much greater scrutiny of a supplier's ability to perform as expected. Thus, as firms have moved toward greater dependence on supplier partners, selection and qualification of appropriate partners, long-term commitment, and collaboration have become increasingly important in the management of the buyer-seller relationship.

As mentioned previously, factors thought to bring about a shift toward closer buyer-seller relationships include asset specificity and uncertainty. Asset specificity refers to investment in specific equipment or other capability aimed at meeting a particular customer's requirements. It has been identified as a key factor influencing a shift toward a closer working relationship (Heide & John, 1990). If such assets are of less value outside the particular relationship, the investing firm may wish to safeguard that investment through developing a stronger, long-term relationship with that customer.

Uncertainty has also been identified as a factor influencing the nature of buyer-seller relationships, linked with both increased and decreased closeness in relationships. The three forms of uncertainty examined by Heide and John (1990) are volume or demand unpredictability, technological unpredictability, and performance ambiguity (internal uncertainty associated with component quality and production processes). It is interesting that in their study, volume unpredictability was not found to be a significant contributor to the continuity of the relationship, suggesting that the flexibility to cope with uncertain demand was not seen as a driver for developing closer partnerships among the purchasing managers surveyed. This is somewhat contrary to the common view that SCM relationships improve a firm's ability to deal with changes in customer demand, and it appears to be an area important to future research. Technology unpredictability was found to reduce the expectations of continuity, suggesting that firms wish to retain flexibility to terminate relationships and develop new ones with suppliers who have new or more appropriate technologies. Uncertainty associated with internal product and process quality, however, was found to increase the efforts to verify that a supplier is a capable and trustworthy partner, which in turn tends to lead to closer, longer-term relationships.

A basic premise of the work by Heide and John (1990) is that the shift from an arm's-length relationship toward establishing closer buyer-supplier ties is not universally desirable. Rather, it is useful only when the risks associated with specificity of assets and uncertainty make it beneficial to invest the time and resources required to develop and maintain a close relationship (Heide & John, 1990). Thus, understanding both the costs and risks associated with developing stronger buyer-seller relationships is important for purchasing managers.

Noordewier et al. (1990) examined performance outcomes associated with various forms of buyer-seller relationships in different environmental contexts. In a study of the purchase of repetitively used industrial supplies among OEM (original equipment manufacturer) purchasers of bearings, closer relationships between buyers and suppliers were found to improve performance when environmental uncertainty is high but to have no effect when environmental uncertainty is low. Environmental uncertainty was assessed with a five-item scale measuring various aspects of market turbulence and vendor-related uncertainties. Purchasing performance measures used in the study included (a) possession costs, in the form of inventory turnover, and (b) acquisition costs, measured as lateness of deliveries and extent of unacceptable items, which would influence the amount of expediting, order follow-up, and rework required by the buying firm. In other words, in the case where environmental uncertainty was high, closer relationships with suppliers led to lower total costs (including both inventory and acquisition costs). When environmental uncertainty was low, closer relationships were not found to have any effect on the performance of the firm. This finding once again raises a question as to the impact of demand uncertainty on the potential benefits associated with closer relationships.

Ellram (1991a) also suggests that partnerships may be more appropriate for certain operating environments. JIT systems, a constrained supplier base, criticality of quality and dependability, uncertainty of consistent quality of supply, and tightly coupled supply and manufacturing systems may all be factors influencing the desirability of building partnerships. Potential advantages of such partnerships include (a) reduced time and effort to manage the relationship, (b) stability and dependability of supply, (c) access to technology or design capability, (d) shared financial risk, and (e) lower total costs.

The development of long-term, close partnerships with suppliers clearly offers a number of potential benefits, but at the same time it is not desirable or beneficial in all buyer-seller relationships. Research indicates that there are certain environmental factors that influence whether partnerships with suppliers are in fact beneficial to a firm. The criticality of supply, the uncertainty and risk inherent in the relationship, and the need for specific assets or resource capabilities to make the relationship successful are factors that must be considered by managers in determining the most appropriate choice.

Creating Successful Partnerships

A decision to pursue a partnership relationship with a supplier is essentially a cost-benefit decision. In certain situations, the benefits associated with a partnership may be substantial, but those benefits must be weighed against the investment in time and resources required to make the partnership work (Ellram, 1991a; Heide & John, 1990). Thus, an understanding of what is required to create and maintain successful partnerships is important.

Graham et al. (1994) identified the following as critical factors in the successful management of buyer-seller partnerships: (a) selective matching, (b) information sharing, (c) role specification, (d) defining ground rules, (e) development of exit provisions, and (f) long-term commitment. When individual partners have compatible corporate values and cultures (selective matching), operating philosophies are more readily blended and there is a greater likelihood of creating a mutually rewarding partnership. Likewise, the sharing of information, both strategic and technical, is necessary to facilitate decision making and joint planning. Role specification is seen as a means of allowing both parties to focus responsibility and accountability, and of maintaining an appropriate balance of power in the relationship. Ground rules developed up front allow partners to handle both routine and unexpected events in predictable and positive ways, and they can also establish how partners share in the risks and rewards associated with the partnership. Establishing exit provisions up front may facilitate the building of trust in the relationship. Finally, long-term commitment is seen as one of the most critical success factors, one that provides buyers some assurance of consistent product quality and availability. In a study among manufacturing firms, the length of time that partnership relationships have been in place was found to be a significant factor in the degree of success a firm experienced in achieving desired purchasing strategies and outcomes (Graham et al., 1994).

Noting that the purchasing firm plays a critical role in developing and maintaining such partnerships, Ellram (1991a) offered a normative model to guide the process of developing and implementing partnerships. Phase 1 is defined as the preliminary phase of establishing the strategic need for a partnership, forming an internal team, and ensuring top management support for developing a partnership. In Phase 2, selection criteria are established and potential partners identified. In Phase 3, potential partners are screened and evaluated, and a candidate is selected. Suggested criteria for evaluating the potential for a partnership include cultural compatibility of the firms, long-term strategies, financial stability, management compatibility, and location of facilities (Ellram, 1991a). In Phase 4, the expectations of the relationship are established, and appropriate monitoring and feedback mechanisms are put in place. In Phase 5, the relationship is continually evaluated and adjusted as appropriate (Ellram, 1991a).

The shift from managing arm's-length, transactional relationships to managing partnership relationships with suppliers introduces greater complexity into the role of the purchasing organization. Requirements must be understood in the context of the firm's strategy, partners must be selected carefully to meet the needs of the partnership, and relationships must be managed appropriately over the long term. Each of these areas requires a much broader perspective, skill base, and organizational involvement than the traditional role of gate-keeping and transactional purchasing based on lowest price.

Objectives of Buyer-Seller Partnerships

As firms have moved to a partnership or relational approach to purchasing, researchers have utilized the transaction cost analysis (TCA) framework to describe buyer-seller relationships. Within this framework, as discussed earlier, the purchasing objectives are to minimize risk and safeguard investment in assets specific to the relationship through building stronger partnerships. Other specific objectives of buyer-seller partnerships include improving the quality, as well as reducing total cost, of purchased goods and services.

A 1993 survey by *Purchasing* magazine (cited in Larson, 1993b) found that quality and costs were the two major concerns of professional buyers. Empirical evidence suggests that a higher level of cooperation between buyers and suppliers leads to higher product quality and lower total costs (Larson, 1993b). Product quality measures for the Larson (1993b) study reflected eight dimensions: (a) conformance to specifications, (b) performance, (c) reliability, (d) durability, (e) serviceability, (f) intangible quality enhancements, (g) delivery as scheduled, and (h) protectiveness of packaging. Measures of total cost included (a) inventory carrying cost, (b) transportation, (c) order processing, (d) back-orders, (e) inspection, (f) rework, (g) scrap, and (h) purchase price. Noting a recent survey finding that only 18% of respondents were using total cost models to evaluate purchases, Larson (1993b) concluded that it is important that buyers and suppliers work together to develop appropriate tools and systems to evaluate and make decisions on a total cost basis.

A cautionary note to managing the quality of supply is provided by Tagaras and Lee (1996), who found that the total cost of quality is influenced not only by the supplier's quality but also by the degree of imperfections in the buyer's manufacturing process. The capability of the internal process, therefore, must be considered in specifying the appropriate level of quality required from the supplier. One implication is that higher-quality materials may not improve internal performance because of the capability limitations of the internal manufacturing process (Tagaras & Lee, 1996). This suggests that a systemwide approach to optimization of product quality, rather than a focus on quality within each firm, may be beneficial to partners in a supply chain.

Building on the economic order quantity (EOQ) or economic lot size (ELS) formula, Banerjee (1986) developed a joint economic lot size model for the case where a vendor produces to order for a purchaser on a lot-for-lot basis under deterministic conditions. Although the assumptions used limit generalizability, this model clearly demonstrates that an optimal or near-optimal policy for one party may not be optimal jointly. The author demonstrated that lack of symmetry in certain parameters (such as a difference in the supplier's setup costs versus the buyer's ordering costs or differences in the carrying costs) can lead to asymmetry in cost impact of order lot size. This suggests that using a jointly optimal ordering policy that considers the characteristics of both firms will reduce total cost. An appropriate price adjustment can ensure that the benefits gained from the joint optimization are shared between the two parties (Banerjee, 1986).

The research associated with buyer-seller partnerships provides evidence of the risk management, cost, and quality benefits that can be gained by working across firm boundaries in a mutually beneficial way. It also points out that systemwide trade-offs must be understood to make appropriate decisions, and that partnerships are not desirable in every buyer-seller relationship. What has not been given adequate attention is the implication of managing in a supply chain context, where three or more firms cooperate to manage systemwide trade-offs at an even higher level.

Stage 3: Operational Approach to SCM

In this stage of development, the role of purchasing becomes an integral part of a firm's SCM operations, with emphasis on planning, implementing, and controlling information and product flows from initial suppliers to ultimate customers in the value-adding chain. The objectives of this approach are the coordination of activities and streamlining of information flow aimed at improving quality and reliability, reducing systemwide inventories, and lowering total system cost. This approach is referred to in Table 9.1 as the "materials logistics management" approach to SCM.

The following definition of materials management was put forth at the first World Congress of the International Federation of Purchasing and Materials Management in 1977 (in Busch, 1988):

> Materials management is a total concept involving organizational structure, unifying in a single responsibility the systematic flow and control of

materials from identification of the need through customer delivery. Included within this concept are the materials functions of planning, scheduling, buying, storing, moving, and distributing. These are logically represented by the disciplines of production and inventory control, purchasing, and physical distribution. The objective of materials management is to contribute to increased profitability by coordinated achievement of least total material cost. This is done through optimizing capital investment, capacity, and personnel consistent with the appropriate customer service level. (p. 28)

The definition of logistics put forth by the Council of Logistics Management (CLM, 1998), states:

Logistics is that part of the supply chain process that plans, implements, and controls the efficient flow and storage of goods, services, and related information from the point of origin to the point of consumption in order to meet customers' requirements.

Although there is clearly a great deal of commonality between these definitions of materials management and logistics, one notable difference is the lack of reference to purchasing in the logistics definition. Generally speaking, materials management refers to the management of functions associated with the flow of materials inbound to and through the production process, and it typically includes the purchasing function. Logistics, which has its roots in the physical distribution function, traditionally has dealt with the flow of outbound materials. In the past several decades, the logistics function has evolved to incorporate both inbound and outbound flows of a firm, and the definition of logistics has been broadened to incorporate flows from initial suppliers to ultimate customers. The traditional purchasing functions, however, typically have not been included in logistics. Because the term *materials logistics management* generally has been used in reference to the flow of materials throughout the entire pipeline and clearly incorporates the purchasing function, this terminology will be used to characterize this stage in the development of the purchasing role.

Bowersox, Carter, and Monczka (1985) characterized the materials logistics management process as incorporating two flows: (a) information from customers to suppliers and (b) the change in form and location of inventory as part of the primary value-adding process. Target objectives include controlled customer service, inventory reduction, minimum variance, minimum total cost (at higher levels of trade-offs), and product quality control. The interfaces between physical distribution, customers, and manufacturing are highlighted as critical to managing demand, scheduling production and distribution, and optimizing inventories, as well as executing postponement and flexibility strategies. Thus, with an operational approach to SCM, there is an emphasis on the integration of purchasing and logistics activities.

Increasingly, the purchasing organization has become an integral part of key logistics needs and decision making for the firm. Examples include (a) managing inbound logistics from suppliers; (b) analyzing make/buy decisions with logistics service providers, the supplier's fleet, or the company fleet; (c) managing inbound materials inventories; (d) coordinating the firm's production schedule with vendors (e.g., managing supplier JIT performance and integrating materials requirements planning systems with the supplier); (e) identifying outsourcing opportunities for logistics activities; and (f) coordinating logistics and other roles in the relationship with the supplier (Cavinato, 1991a).

Even with these key areas of interface between purchasing and logistics, however, there is limited attention given to the purchasing process in the logistics literature. For example, an analysis of *Transportation Journal* from 1978 through 1989 indicated that relatively few articles focused on the purchasing process. Most research has focused on the logistics process and relationships between suppliers of products and manufacturing firms, with very little research on the relationship between purchasing firms and logistics service providers, or the carrier link to a JIT or supply chain system (Novack & Simco, 1991).

Novack and Simco (1991) suggest that the purchasing process begins the quality process of an organization and is an essential component in maximizing the effectiveness of the supply chain. In the operational stage of supply chain management, with a focus on the materials logistics process, the purchasing role is viewed as one of managing supply, considering such variables as capacity, capability, and location of suppliers, as well as scheduling requirements of manufacturing aimed at meeting customer requirements. Key activities include managing inbound logistics and facilitating and coordinating linkages between suppliers, manufacturing, and logistics. Information systems are seen as a critical to managing the data and information to make appropriate purchasing decisions in the materials logistics management context (Bowersox et al., 1985). Although there is an emphasis on the entire pipeline in this approach to supply chain management, much of the literature is focused on the management of activities internal to the firm, rather than on external linkages with customers and suppliers.

Cooper and Ellram (1993) suggest that both purchasing and logistics functions logically provide leadership in establishing and managing supply chain relationships because of the boundary-spanning role outside the firm traditionally played by each. Managing the information flows, monitoring activities, and assessing appropriate sharing of risks and rewards across supply chain partners is a natural extension of these traditional boundary-spanning roles. Both purchasing and logistics have served boundary-spanning roles inside the firm, which provides a base from which to build the emerging role as facilitator and coordinator of a multifaceted, multilevel relationship with supply chain partners (Cooper & Ellram, 1993).

Clearly, both purchasing and logistics play a critical role in a firm's SCM initiatives. In an exploratory study of 52 manufacturing firms, however, Giunipero and Brand (1996) found that supply chain management is a relatively new concept in purchasing organizations, with the emphasis focused fairly narrowly on "good relationships with suppliers." Only a small group of respondents in this study seemed to view supply chain management in a broader, systemwide context. It appears that most purchasing professionals have focused primarily on strengthening relationships with first-tier suppliers and have not extended their focus to integration with second- and third-tier suppliers, or to integration of their suppliers with their customers. To achieve the potential value from adopting SCM, however, purchasing managers must look beyond the immediate buyer-seller relationship to identify those multiple-level linkages that have the greatest opportunity to improve total supply chain performance.

Objectives of SCM Operations

In the study, the small group of purchasing managers who did appear to focus on optimizing the product and information flow through the channel saw the benefits of supply chain management as (a) improved coordination from supplier to customer, (b) reduced lead time, (c) greater productivity in the firm's operations, (d) lower inventories, and (e) increased reliability of delivery (Giunipero & Brand, 1996). Clearly, these respondents associated SCM with improved efficiency and reduced cost. Thus, even those respondents who viewed their role from a supply chain perspective seemed to focus on operational improvements, rather than strategic objectives aimed at improving the effectiveness of the supply chain.

The operational or materials logistics management approach to supply chain management is focused on the objectives of streamlining the flow of information and products and on reducing inventories and total cost throughout the system. By integrating operations planning and coordinating implementation across disciplines and across firms, redundant tasks can be eliminated and systemwide trade-offs can be made to optimize total system cost. This approach requires purchasing to play a role of facilitating communications between other organizations internally and across multiple functions in a supplier organization, a dramatic change from the role of gatekeeper or even from that of buyer-seller relationship management. The emphasis is on cooperation aimed at understanding and optimizing operating plans and activities across firms to improve operating efficiency and reduce total cost by reducing systemwide inventories and cycle times. Consequently, the purchasing role must be broadened to facilitate cross-functional integration within the firm, as well as interfirm integration across multiple firms.

To date, research has focused on the dyad, investigating critical success factors, antecedents, and consequences of buyer-seller partnerships, with little attention given to SCM in a broader context (see Table 9.2). This research can offer useful insights for purchasing managers as to the appropriateness and process for building and maintaining long-term relationships with suppliers; however, SCM requires firms to work beyond the next level in a supply chain (i.e., immediate customers or immediate suppliers) to integrate and improve performance across multiple firms. Research in working collaboratively across firms in a partnership should be extended to examine the issues and outcomes associated with working collaboratively across three or more firms in a supply chain context. Additionally, the materials management or logistics approach, though integrative, tends to focus on operational efficiency and does not overtly address the contribution of the purchasing organization to improving effectiveness to achieve competitive advantage. Only in Stage 4, where an integrated value-added approach is taken, is the potential recognized for strategic contribution by the purchasing organization to the overall effectiveness of the supply chain.

Stage 4: Strategic Approach to SCM

In Stage 4 in the evolution of purchasing toward SCM, a more strategic, or "integrated value-added," approach is taken. In this stage, the emphasis is on an integrated approach to redesigning business processes for speed, flexibility, and competitive advantage. Collaboration is aimed at improvements and innovations that can increase the effectiveness of the supply chain as a whole. New products or services, or improved operations that provide the speed and flexibility to effectively meet changing customer requirements, are the primary focus, rather than cost reductions associated with improved planning and reduced inventories. Although limited research has been done looking across multiple firms in a supply chain, research has been done that emphasizes the strategic role of purchasing. This research can provide useful insights about the issues and objectives associated with a strategic approach to SCM.

With the increasing importance of purchasing in satisfying customer requirements, the management of both intracompany and intercompany relationships toward that end is increasingly recognized as critical to a firm's competitive success (Rajagopal & Bernard, 1993). These authors suggest that an effective purchasing system is one that matches capabilities with the competitive advantages being sought by the firm. A three-phase process for developing a purchasing strategy is suggested. In Phase 1, the purchasing organization is focused on the gathering and appraisal of information. Because the purchasing function is the key interface between the firm and the supply environment, the authors suggest that environmental scanning to identify opportunities and threats as they emerge is a natural role for a purchasing organization to play.

Table 9.2 Categorization of Purchasing/Supply Chain Literature

	Stage 2 Partnership/Relational	Stage 3 Operational Focus	Stage 4 Strategic Focus
Normative	▪ "A Managerial Guideline for the Development and Implementation of Purchasing Partnerships" (Ellram, 1991a)	▪ "The Industrial Procurement Process: A Supply Chain Perspective" (Novack & Simco, 1991)	▪ "Adapting Purchasing to Supply Chain Management" (Leenders, Nollet, & Ellram, 1993) ▪ "Strategic Procurement and Competitive Advantage" (Rajagopal & Bernard, 1993)
Conceptual		▪ "Integrated Materials Management" (Busch, 1988) ▪ "Materials Logistics Management" (Bowersox et al., 1985)	▪ "Purchasing's Role in Supply Chain Management" (Giunipero & Brand, 1996)* ▪ "Purchasing's Role in a Concurrent Engineering Environment" (Dowlatshahi, 1992)
Descriptive	▪ Survey to determine how purchasing executives perceive SCM and their role in managing suppliers* (Giunipero & Brand, 1996)	▪ "Evolving Procurement Organizations: Logistics Implications" (Cavinato, 1991a): Qualitative interviews on internal management of procurement function.	▪ "Purchasing's Role in Product Development: The Case for Time-Based Strategies" (Mendez & Pearson, 1994): Survey to determine changes in team involvement for product development by purchasing function
Theoretical research	▪ "Alliances in Industrial Purchasing: The Determinants of Joint Action in Buyer-Supplier Relationships (Heide & John, 1990) ▪ "Performance Outcomes of Purchasing Arrangements in Industrial Buyer-Vendor Relationships" (Noordewier et al., 1990) ▪ "The Long-Term Strategic Impact of Purchasing Partnership" (Graham et al., 1994) ▪ "Buyer-Supplier Co-operation, Product Quality and Total Costs"(Larson, 1993a) ▪ "Economic Models for Vendor Evaluation With Quality Cost Analysis" (Tagaras & Lee, 1996) ▪ "The Impact of Alternative Vendor/Buyer Communication Structures on the Quality of Purchased Materials" (Carter & Miller, 1989) ▪ "A Joint Economic-Lot-Size Model for Purchaser and Vendor" (Banerjee, 1986)		

NOTE: *Includes empirical study reflected in another cell.

Environmental scanning becomes an important component of the purchasing process, with the objective of identifying and managing risk, as well as of identifying opportunities for suppliers to contribute to the competitive advantage of the firm and the supply chain as a whole.

The second phase of the strategic planning process is one of identification of relevant issues and options to achieve desired objectives. In this phase, objectives of the purchasing function are identified, suppliers and purchased materials are classified in terms of strategic importance to the firm, and decisions about how to manage the purchasing function and the supplier base are made, given the market structure and organizational capabilities. Organizational decision making includes establishing appropriate internal and external relationships to effectively integrate planning and operations management. It is in this stage that the link to overall corporate and SCM strategies must be made.

Finally, strategic purchasing intent must be incorporated into the organizational culture in ways that motivate and reward purchasing behaviors that contribute to the firm's competitive strategies. Employees are provided with appropriate skills and tools to enable them to work effectively toward the strategy (Rajagopal & Bernard, 1993).

Although discussions of various components of a strategic approach to purchasing are found in the literature, there is still a relatively limited focus on strategy. An examination of the *Journal of Purchasing and Materials Management* from 1965 through 1986 (Novack & Simco, 1991) revealed that only a small percentage of articles focused on strategy and planning (4.5% and 8.76%, respectively). The majority of articles focused on implementation and "environmental" factors such as organizational, behavioral, ethical, and legal aspects of purchasing (Novack & Simco, 1991). There is also little indication that firms have developed a strategic approach to purchasing in practice. In the study of 52 manufacturing firms mentioned earlier (Giunipero & Brand, 1996), the more strategic or integrative value-added approach was not found to be a part of current practice. There is strong consensus in the literature, however, that the role of the purchasing organization is evolving to one of greater significance and broader responsibilities than has traditionally been the case, and there is significant potential for purchasing to contribute to a firm's strategy and competitive advantage.

Objectives of the Strategic Approach to SCM

The objectives associated with a strategic approach to purchasing are to innovate products and processes and, ultimately, to reduce cycle time, improve product design and quality, and respond more quickly to changing customer requirements. Literature relevant to this stage is primarily focused on collaborative product and process reengineering, with a major emphasis in the new product development arena. Work in this area has also typically focused on partnership relationships between two members of a supply chain and has not been extended to a true supply chain context. The concepts developed in a partnership context, however, can be important building blocks toward understanding the strategic role of purchasing from a supply chain perspective.

Working collaboratively with suppliers can avoid redundant research work, and the time required to develop new products can be shortened by reducing miscommunications and ensuring clarity up front (Busch, 1988). Concurrent engineering is a concept that focuses on the simultaneous consideration of design attributes influencing downstream performance. Design attributes to be considered in the early stages of product design include manufacturability, procurability, reliability, maintainability, schedulability, and marketability (Dowlatshahi, 1992). The purchasing role as a key contributor to product design, both internally and externally, is significant and is necessary to ensure that supply implications are considered in new product development.

Working with internal product designers, purchasing can provide input on specifications that ensures that suppliers are capable of providing parts and materials at a reasonable cost. Interchangeable parts available from suppliers with better performance or lower cost may be identified. Opportunities for standardization and simplification that improve parts availability or reduce inventory costs may also be identified (Dowlatshahi, 1992). Mendez and Pearson (1994) suggest that purchasing can play a more active and effective role through participating in multidisciplinary design teams. Because of the unique skills, resources, and capabilities found in each functional area, the effectiveness of the design process can be enhanced through such team involvement. The unique role of purchasing on such teams includes (a) ensuring continuous supply of materials, components, and service; (b) certification of suppliers; (c) evaluation of make-buy decisions; (d) development of strategic alliances; (e) determination and timing of supplier involvement; (f) purchasing tooling and equipment; (g) suggesting alternative materials; and (h) providing insights into the competitive supply environment (Mendez & Pearson, 1994). If purchasing is to play such a strategic role—interfacing and contributing effectively to research and development or design activities—it becomes important to have both business and technical expertise on the purchasing team.

Working externally with suppliers on product design, the purchasing organization can ensure that essential features are designed into the product, but nonessential features are not. Purchasing can also provide input regarding requirements for quality, safety, and performance for the buying firm. Working collaboratively to ensure early consideration of such factors can improve the effectiveness of the product design process (Dowlatshahi, 1991; Mendez & Pearson, 1994). Again, the need to work collaboratively with suppliers to reengineer products and processes suggests that technical skills must be integrated into the purchasing environment, in addition to the business skills traditionally required (Busch, 1988).

Monczka, Trent, and Handfield (1998) highlight a number of both tangible and intangible benefits that can result from a strategic, supply chain approach to purchasing. Case studies have provided evidence of price reductions from 5% to 25%; quality, cost, and delivery improvements from 75% to 98%; and a supply base that is better than the competition. Intangible benefits include improvements in corporate decision making through linking technology strategies across the supply base, the integration of strategies across functions, and the ability to influence and develop the supply base to improve competitiveness (Monczka et al., 1998).

This examination of the role of purchasing from a more strategic perspective shows significant differences between an operational and strategic approach to purchasing in an SCM context. Although the focus of an operational approach to SCM is on improving efficiency and reducing the total cost of supply chain operations, the strategic approach is focused on redesigning products and processes to make the supply chain as a whole more effective and to create competitive or differential advantage with the end consumer (Chapter 3). This more strategic approach requires purchasing to play a significantly expanded role.

In one example of such a strategic approach, the company adopted a purchasing strategy of becoming an agent for its preferred suppliers. The objective was to have these suppliers "designed in" to the next generation of products for original equipment manufacturers (OEMs), in exchange for preferential pricing and technology. The purchasing organization was responsible for identifying suppliers with significant technologies and cost capabilities, as well as for developing long-term "value partnerships" with them. To accomplish this, purchasing needed to work with customer-specific supply chain teams to influence supplier selection early in the design stage, and to act as a liaison with suppliers throughout the life of the product, focusing on reducing cost, creating upside flexibility, and managing risk. Up-front involvement with engineering allowed purchasing professionals to identify opportunities for competitive pricing or different supply base options (Center for Advanced Purchasing Strategies [CAPS] Research, 1997).

In a sense, the purchasing role in a strategic SCM context is to understand the capability of suppliers and to identify ways to match that capability to the needs of strategic customers. Environmental scanning to identify opportunities and threats in supply markets and to identify important strategic partners is a key part of the purchasing role. Additionally, an understanding of the firm's strategy and key customer markets is required to match supplier capability with customer needs. This requires strong cross-functional integration within the firm. At the same time, collaboration between firms to design innovative products and processes will require connectivity between multiple functions in both firms. Thus, the purchasing role becomes one of facilitating appropriate cross-functional interaction both between and within firms. Integration of R&D for product and process engineering requires both business and technical expertise in the purchasing process. Finally, the ability to assess and facilitate the sharing of risk and rewards is necessary to create the trust and collaborative sharing that is necessary to achieve the objectives of a strategic approach to SCM.

A significant shift from the traditional purchasing role is required for firms adopting either an operational or a strategic approach to SCM (as highlighted in Table 9.1). Because of this shift in role, it is also likely that a different approach to organizational structure, communication processes, and information technology will be required.

Organization, Communication, and Information Technology

As the role of purchasing evolves from the traditional gatekeeper role toward a strategic supply chain role, organizational structure, communications processes, and information systems also need to change to support the different roles and objectives. As suppliers gain access into firms through links other than the purchasing department, with such initiatives as joint operational planning and concurrent engineering, changes may also be required in the purchasing organization (Cavinato, 1991a). To achieve the objectives associated with supply chain management, the purchasing role must become one of facilitating and coordinating between suppliers and multiple internal disciplines. New organizational structures and processes are required to enable purchasing to play this expanded role.

Organizational Models

Based on qualitative interviews in a number of firms, Cavinato (1991a) described various purchasing organizational models. Although several models focus on centralization versus decentralization, other models focus on the integration of purchasing with other functions. *Centralized purchasing* organizations provide the firm with a single, collective sourcing and buying power. Cavinato (1991a) suggests that this structure provides an advantage in that logistics impacts and decisions relating to procurement practices can be coordinated through a centralized procurement group. A disadvantage is that a centralized organization reinforces the traditional role of gatekeeper and makes the facilitation and coordination across internal disciplines more difficult.

Decentralized organizations place purchasing responsibility in field locations, which may minimize corporate overhead but prevents the ability to achieve managerial or negotiating strength. When purchasing organizations are decentralized, differentiated pricing by suppliers to different divisions of a firm is not uncommon. This approach may, however, facilitate the integration of purchasing with other business activities.

A *centralized coordinator* may reside at corporate headquarters and facilitate coordination on matters or issues important to the entire firm, while the purchasing activities reside at a plant or in a strategic business unit. The centralized coordinator acts in a consulting role and enables the firm to achieve the advantage of decentralized purchasing, but with greater negotiating strength, by dealing with suppliers at the corporate level.

An *area planner approach* maintains a centralized purchasing group to create relationships with suppliers, but field production and logistics planners manage the actual operating flows. This approach streamlines information flow, thus improving the ability to coordinate the flow of products and minimize inventories while retaining the ability to negotiate and manage relationships with suppliers from a corporate perspective (Cavinato, 1991a). This approach appears to offer some advantages over the centralized approach for a firm pursuing an operational approach to supply chain management.

The *logistics pipeline approach* intertwines the supplier and customer organizations to eliminate duplication of logistics functions and improve product flows. Inventories may be managed jointly, one firm is responsible for managing such activities as order entry, and both firms use a single forecast. Thus, in a supply chain context, redundant functions are eliminated and processes are redesigned to enable joint-firm cost reduction or enhanced service. This approach may be most advantageous for a firm managing in a supply chain context with an operational focus.

The *supply manager concept* has a group responsible for materials management for entire product lines of a business. This model puts responsibility for supply, acquisition, materials, and production in one person or organization, which manages product flow from suppliers, through production and delivery to the customer (Cavinato, 1991a). Because this person or organization has total responsibility and authority for product flow, from the firm's suppliers, through operations, to delivery to the customer, systemwide trade-offs are feasible. This approach may also enable a more strategic approach to purchasing if the supply manager functions as a part of the overall business leadership team.

Commodity teams have a full product orientation, which includes attention to engineering, design, materials, manufacturing, costing, distribution, and marketing for a particular product. In this case, logistics becomes a part of the overall product cost and value context managed by the team. Cavinato (1991a) suggests that this approach allows the team to have an integrated view of engineering, design, production, procurement, materials and logistics management, manufacturing, costing, and marketing, as well as a view of the needs related to the product from the perspective of the customer. This approach also allows a view of total cost and total value associated with a particular product. Such an approach enables systemwide trade-offs from both cost and customer value perspectives. Thus, this approach may be most advantageous to a firm with a strategic approach to purchasing in a supply chain management context.

In this study by Cavinato (1991a), in general, purchasing organizations were found to be flattening and adopting a process orientation. Time and integration are becoming increasingly critical to the process. Finally, there appears to be an increased emphasis on the creation of value or competitive advantage through the management of supplier relationships. Cavinato (1991a) suggests that the issue of centralization or decentralization is much less important than in the past; rather, the communications, information systems, and integrative decision-making processes contributing to the goals of the firm are the determinants of organizational structure (Cavinato, 1991a). Likewise, the choice of the most appropriate structure in an SCM context depends on the specific objectives of a firm's SCM strategies.

Communications Processes

Carter and Miller (1989) examined the influence of two types of communications processes (described as serial and parallel) on the quality of purchased materials. A serial communications process represents traditional buyer-seller relationships. Each of the various functions in the customer firm communicates with the buyer, while those in the seller firm communicate with the sales representative. These two representatives act as the sole communication link (as gatekeepers) between the two firms, passing information pertaining to the various disciplines. In addition to the economic efficiency of having a single focal point for communications, serial communications processes allow a firm to better control and leverage its purchasing power and reduce confusion associated with conflicting messages.

Conversely, the parallel communications process is one in which the buyer and the sales representative act as facilitators, with direct communications between appropriate individuals in multiple functions within each organization. For example, the supplier's manufacturing organization communicates directly with the customer's manufacturing organization. The same is true for R&D or design engineering. This form of communication allows greater exchange of technical information and reduces miscommunications to improve joint development processes; however, time and resource requirements for such a process are substantial. Like any other investment decision, the appropriate decision regarding communications with suppliers is based on an understanding of the costs and benefits of each approach. Carter and Miller (1989) found that a shift to a parallel communications process within a firm positively correlated with significantly higher levels of quality.

The communications process utilized in the relationships between suppliers and customers is an important issue in an SCM context. Whether a firm pursues an operational or a strategic approach to SCM, the open exchange of information is critical to the coordination and/or collaboration required to achieve joint objectives. Because of the traditional role played by purchasing in managing relationships between a firm and its suppliers, facilitating the most appropriate communication process is likely to be an important role in the future. Understanding the costs and benefits associated with various communications processes is an important first step.

Information Technology

The characteristics of the "ideal" purchasing information system highlighted by Monczka et al. (1998) are

1. Centralized coordination of information flows;
2. Total logistics management—integrating all transportation, ordering, and manufacturing systems;
3. Order-change notices that trigger a cascading series of modifications to production schedules, logistics plans, and warehouse operations;
4. Shared transportation resources across business units and national boundaries;
5. Global inventory management—the ability to locate and track the movement of every item;
6. Global sourcing—consolidation of the purchasing function across organizational lines, facilitating purchasing leverage and component standardization across business units;
7. Inter-company information access—clarity of production and demand information residing in organizations both upstream and downstream throughout the value chain;
8. Data interchange between affiliates and nonaffiliates through standard telecommunications channels;
9. Data capture—the ability to acquire data about an order at the point of origin and to track products during movements and as their characteristics change;
10. Transformation of the business from within—managers who can see the "big picture" and accept the new forms of business processes; and
11. Improvements in supplier-customer relationships to justify investments in EDI linkages.

This "ideal" system would make a consolidated, real-time set of information available to any party within the supply chain, including customers, suppliers, distributors, assemblers, retailers, manufacturing, and engineering/design organizations. The ability to access information on changes in requirements allows immediate response by all parties involved. Note that the characteristics described here as ideal are primarily focused on managing supply chain operations. Additional shared capability, for example in computer-aided-design (CAD) systems, may be required to pursue strategic opportunities such as joint product design and development.

Transaction systems (enterprise-wide resource planning systems such as SAP, for example) provide the data capture and integration capabilities required for SCM. By themselves, however, these enterprise-wide systems do not enable optimization of the supply chain. Managers in purchasing and other supply chain functions need access to appropriate decision support systems to allow them to make systemwide optimization decisions.

Finally, it is important to note that the use of Internet and intranet capability to enhance supply chain linkages is rapidly growing in importance. The global access possible through the World Wide Web offers great potential for sharing information worldwide. The possibilities for using this medium in the purchasing area are just beginning to be explored by purchasing organizations (Monczka et al., 1998).

The role of information technology (IT) in SCM is significant and will be an important enabler for purchasing to play a more integrative and strategic role. However, as one interviewee indicated, "the investment required for IT is significant, and there must be a sufficient payback." It is important for managers to identify the information technologies available and to understand the potential benefits as well as the costs, so that appropriate investment decisions can be made that support purchasing managers in achieving the objectives of SCM.

Conclusions

There appears to be consensus in the literature that the role of purchasing has changed as a result of the increasingly competitive environment faced by firms today. From the traditional role of gatekeeper in an arm's-length buyer-seller relationship, the role has evolved to one that is more integrative, both internally and externally. As a result, the management of relationships has become a more critical component of the purchasing function. The traditional objective of the purchasing organization focused on purchasing at the lowest cost, but now objectives are becoming more focused on total cost and system performance. What was once viewed as a service role to the business units is increasingly viewed as a critical component of a firm's competitive strategy. The extent to which the purchasing organization can realize its potential for contribution depends on the ability to facilitate the multidisciplinary coordination and collaboration required for improved performance in a supply chain context.

This chapter makes several contributions of importance to managers and researchers regarding the role of purchasing in supply chain management. The framework in Table 9.1 can provide guidance as to the role of purchasing in the various stages of a firm's evolution toward supply chain management. By understanding differences in the role and objectives at various stages of development, managers can more effectively develop organizational capabilities and focus resources to meet those objectives. The framework can also help identify important areas for future research.

Managerial Implications

The role of purchasing in support of a firm's SCM initiatives depends on the strategy of the firm and what approach is taken to SCM. If the firm's SCM objectives are those of improving efficiency and reducing systemwide inventory, cycle time, and costs, the purchasing role will focus on coordinating activities with suppliers and streamlining data and information flows to facilitate the flow of products and information throughout the system (Stage 3). To achieve these objectives, managers should focus resources on integrating operational planning systems with suppliers and on establishing information and communication linkages. These linkages would allow firms to have real-time access to a common database that allows everyone in the supply chain to see changes in demand. It is also important that the purchasing organization facilitate coordination among multiple disciplines across SC member firms so that SC activities can be streamlined to manage systemwide trade-offs and costs. Organizational structure, communications processes, and information technology should be designed to facilitate the operational interfaces between firms and across functions within the focal firm.

If the firm's strategy requires a strategic approach to SCM aimed at creating value for downstream customers through product and process innovation (effectiveness), the challenges facing purchasing managers become more complex. Although the need to facilitate relationships among multiple disciplines of multiple firms is important in both cases, in the more strategic role the emphasis shifts from one of coordination in managing operational activities to collaboration on strategic planning processes and research and development activities. Integration of both technical and business capabilities in the purchasing process becomes important in the latter case. Identifying strategic partners and developing long-term, collaborative relationships with those partners becomes more important, and purchasing managers must ensure appropriate environmental scanning to identify strategic opportunities and threats in critical supply markets.

Whatever the SCM strategy of the firm, purchasing managers need to ensure that the purchasing processes and infrastructure are designed appropriately to achieve SCM objectives. Organizational structure, communications processes, and information technology should be designed to facilitate the coordination or collaboration required among multiple disciplines and across multiple firms, and decision support tools that allow managers to evaluate systemwide trade-offs will be critical to success.

Research Implications

The literature relevant to the role of purchasing in a supply chain context can be characterized using the stages of development framework adapted from

Giunipero and Brand (1996) (see Table 9.2). Because the majority of the literature regarding supply chain management is definitional or conceptual (Giunipero & Brand, 1996), it is not surprising that the literature regarding the role of purchasing in a supply chain context remains primarily in the realm of normative, conceptual, or descriptive work. No theory-based empirical research dealing with the integration of purchasing across functions and multiple firms within a supply chain context was found in the literature.

There is, however, a body of theoretical work that focuses on the nature of the buyer-seller partnership. Empirical studies building on transaction cost analysis (TCA) focus on the dimensions, antecedents, and outcomes of buyer-seller partnerships. Mathematical modeling techniques have also been used to examine such concepts as quality cost analysis and economic lot size when viewed from the joint perspective of the buyer and seller, rather than from the viewpoint of a single firm. Research related to managing across partnerships should be extended to consider supply chain management, or managing across three or more firms.

Previous research has pointed to situational factors influencing the desirability of building closer buyer-supplier relationships. Similarly, an understanding of the circumstances under which it is beneficial for firms to pursue a supply chain management approach should be important for both managers and researchers. Additionally, it is important to understand the investment in time and resources required to manage successfully from a supply chain perspective. Both the costs and the benefits of a supply chain management approach must be understood for firms to make appropriate decisions about when and where to pursue such an approach.

Another important area for future research is the role of the purchasing organization in understanding and responding to environmental forces. Environmental scanning to identify opportunities and threats in supply markets has been identified as a key activity for the purchasing organization pursuing a strategic approach to supply chain management. This points to several questions important for managers and researchers to consider. What are the important factors to be considered in environmental scanning, and what are the implications of those factors to the strategy of the firm? How should such environmental factors influence a firm's decision making about selection of supply chain members for collaboration and the nature of such collaborations?

Information sharing is widely recognized as critical to supply chain management, but research as to the role of information technology and communications processes for purchasing in a supply chain context is limited. Several questions regarding information sharing should be considered by managers and researchers. How can information technology enhance the analysis and decision-making process of the purchasing organization? What information should be shared routinely between supply chain members and functions internal to the firm? What is the most effective mechanism for sharing such information, and how can it be most effectively utilized? These are important considerations for managers and researchers alike.

Other areas identified as important in developing buyer-seller partnerships must also be understood in a supply chain context. For example, as supply chain partners work collaboratively to improve performance and reduce cost, where are tasks most appropriately performed, and how should performance be monitored and evaluated? What are the elements of risk that must be managed, and how can they be shared appropriately across supply chain members? Alternatively, how can the benefits of the relationship be measured and appropriately shared? What are the appropriate tools and methodologies to manage trade-offs on a systemwide basis? How can firms assess the limiting factors in a supply chain (i.e., the location of the limiting factor in optimizing performance or reducing cost), and how and when should such limitations be removed? What organizational structure is most appropriate for the purchasing function in a supply chain management context? Does this differ across industries and firms, or in different situations? Each of these questions suggests important areas for consideration by managers and for future research.

10

The Role of Logistics
in the Supply Chain

SOONHONG MIN

JAMES S. KEEBLER

Executive Summary

This chapter describes logistics in the supply chain, including the major functions constituting logistics, emerging logistics strategies, and logistics competencies that drive competitive advantage for the firm. This chapter will

- Discuss the functions and management of order processing, inventory, warehousing, network design, and transportation
- Examine emergent logistics strategies and the characteristics underlying successful logistics performance
- Describe the capabilities and competencies of the logistics organization and their potential contribution to competitive advantage for the firm

These discussions lead to the conclusions that

- Logistics activities have a major impact on the capabilities and profitability of the supply chain and its member firms
- Logistics functions are key operating components of an organization that require design and management consistent with corporate strategy and changing competitive environments

- Logistics strategies need to be implemented that support corporate strategies and are based on the needs of the marketplace and distinct capabilities of the firm
- Corporate leaders who can understand and shape logistics competencies can dramatically enhance firm competitiveness

Capitalizing on these opportunities requires the ability to build alliances within and between firms, a commitment to planning and integrating information flows, and the ability to measure performance to guide the improved design of the logistics system and supply chain processes. The importance of the supply chain manager's ability to leverage logistics competencies will increase in the future.

Introduction

This chapter covers various operational and strategic issues associated with logistics in the supply chain. It first discusses the functions and management of order processing, inventory, transportation, and warehousing. Emphasis is on the fulfillment process, because sourcing and procurement are covered elsewhere. Next, it discusses variations of logistics strategy. Finally, it discusses the implications of competencies in logistics capabilities for providing competitive advantage in the supply chain.

Order Processing

We begin our discussion of logistics in the supply chain with a look at order acquisition and processing because *demand* drives the logistics system, and this is how demand is captured. Time to complete the activities of order processing is at the very heart of customer service and represents a significant portion of the fulfillment process. More than 20 years ago it was estimated that the activities associated with order preparation, transmittal, entry, picking, and packing represented 50% to 70% of the total order cycle time in many industries (La Londe & Zinszer, 1976). Although reductions in order transmission time made possible by computers and high-speed data lines have reduced the absolute time for order processing, the use of faster delivery means has kept the order processing proportion of total order cycle time high.

Components of Order Processing

Order processing includes order preparation, order transmittal, order entry, order filling, and order status reporting (Ballou, 1992). Order preparation involves the customer or salesperson filling out an order form, voice communication by telephone to a sales clerk, or selection from a computer menu. This activity has greatly benefited from the use of bar coding, scanners, and laptop computers.

Order transmittal involves transferring the order request from its point of origin to the place where the order entry can be handled. Order transmission is accomplished in two fundamental ways: manually and electronically. Manual transmission can include the mailing of orders by the customer or sales representative to the point of order entry. This is a slow but inexpensive method. Electronic transmission has been made very popular with the use of toll-free telephone numbers, data phones, computer modems, facsimile machines, and satellite communications. This almost instantaneous transfer of order information, with its high degree of reliability and accuracy, has nearly replaced manual methods.

Order entry includes (a) checking the accuracy of the order information such as item description and number, quantity, and price; (b) checking the availability of the requested items; (c) preparing back order or order cancellation documentation, if necessary; (d) checking the customer's credit status; (e) transcribing the order information as needed; and (f) billing preparation, which might be adjusted if there are shipment discrepancies. These activities can be completed entirely manually, automatically, or by combinations of the two.

Order filling is represented by the physical activities required to (a) acquire the items through stock retrieval, production, or purchasing; (b) pack the items for shipping; (c) schedule the shipment for delivery; and (d) prepare the shipping documentation. A number of the activities might take place concurrently with those of order entry, thus compressing total processing time.

Order status reporting ensures good customer service by keeping the customer informed of any delays in order processing or delivery. Specifically, this includes (a) tracing and tracking the order throughout the entire order cycle and (b) communicating with the customer as to where the order may be in the order cycle and when it may be delivered. This is a monitoring activity and does not affect the overall order processing time.

Managing Order Processing

The order cycle, and particularly order processing activities, can serve as a framework for logistics control (Novack, 1989). Order processing activities, if properly managed, can improve customer service and simultaneously reduce inventory levels. This is a significant consequence. According to a recent study, Hewlett Packard believes that poor order fulfillment costs it a million dollars a day (Johnson & Davis, 1998). The phenomenon of exaggerated order swings and inventory levels is commonly known as the bullwhip effect. Order batching in order processing activities is one of the major causes of the bullwhip effect

(Lee, Padmanabhan, & Whang, 1997b). The reduction of batch sizes and concurrent processing activities can work together to overcome surge effects resulting in excessive inventory investment and poor customer service.

The details of order processing practices are often invisible to senior management. It has been suggested that managers "staple themselves to an order" to understand all the steps and interfaces involved in order processing (Shapiro, Rangan, & Sviokla, 1992). This horizontal view of the organization's processing of orders can help to identify ways to reengineer and improve its performance. A relatively new, simple, and comprehensive measure of customer service and logistics effectiveness, called the "Perfect Order," measures the percentage of orders that proceed through every step of the order management process without fault, exception, handling, or intervention. Companies measuring the percentage of their customers' orders that meet the Perfect Order criteria are finding on average that less than 10% of their orders are perfect (Copacino, 1993). As a result, these companies are reengineering their order management activities to eliminate unnecessary steps, align functional objectives, and speed up order cycles.

Effective management of order processing is critical to the maintenance of good customer relationships. Both shortening the order cycle time and its improving its consistent predictability are important to customers and result in lower inventory requirements. This critical customer interface should be designed to be convenient, easy, "friendly," and fail-safe in its operation.

Inventory

A primary consideration in many proposed definitions of supply chain management is the "flow of goods," or the "flow of materials" from the source of raw materials to the ultimate end use consumer. Inherent in the flow of materials and goods, whether at the level of the production line, the plant, the company, or the entire supply chain, are the inventories that may be necessary to achieve the operational and strategic objectives of the organization(s) involved in production and distribution. Inventories provide a means to combat uncertainties in component/product supply and demand, take advantage of scale economies in processes used to transform and transport components and products, and target specific levels of component/product availability necessary to meet customer expectations (Ballou, 1999). At the same time, inventories can present a threat to corporate profitability. Inventory assets tie up capital that might be invested more effectively in other areas of the organization. These assets also represent an expense to the organization, the cost of capital necessary for their maintenance.

Literature in logistics, management science, operations, and supply chain management has addressed various aspects of inventory management: the factors that can influence inventory requirements (Closs & Thompson, 1992; Rafuse, 1996; Sandelands, 1994), the policies and procedures that control the movement and storage of inventories (Loar, 1992; Perry, 1988; Song & Zipkin, 1996), and the impact of inventory on corporate and supply chain investment and customer service (Banerjee, 1986; Jones & Riley, 1985; Rosenberg & Campbell, 1985). Research has presented mathematical algorithms that may be applied in an effort to improve inventory management (e.g., Lee, Padmanabhan, & Whang, 1997b; Scott, 1989), normative models that provide guidelines to establish inventory policies under different scenarios (Ravi & Yehuda, 1999), and experiments that have used dynamic simulation as a means to evaluate the impact of various inventory policies (Towill, Naim, & Wikner, 1992).

Factors Influencing Inventory Levels

Several factors influence inventory policy and practice for the firm. These include desired levels of customer service, production economies, purchasing economies, transportation savings, seasonality of demand or supply, and supply source maintenance (Coyle, Bardi, & Langley, 1996). Customer service issues might require positioning inventory close to or within all major markets to reduce delivery times and avoid lost sales from potential stock-outs. This is particularly relevant for products that have high substitutability; where customers have other, immediate choices; and for markets with only a few, large customers, where individual variability in demand cannot be spread over a large customer base. Having products for sale in the assortment, quantity, location, and time that customers want them is fundamental to the logistics mission. The costs of carrying stocks of inventories for sale have to be balanced with the costs of not having them.

Production economies can often be achieved by supporting long, uninterrupted production runs to achieve the lowest cost per unit produced. This strategy usually results in large quantities of finished goods being produced that are not needed until some future time and that must be stored and rehandled. These "avoidable" storage costs should not exceed the production costs avoided. On the inbound side of firm logistics, safety stocks of raw materials and components are calculated and maintained to guard against costly production shutdowns resulting from variations in supplier delivery performance.

Purchasing economies often can be achieved by taking advantage of purchase discounts for large-quantity purchases. As long as the amount saved on the purchase price discount exceeds storage costs, companies might be willing to accumulate raw material inventories or goods purchased for resale. Separately, some goods are purchased on a speculative basis or as a hedge against possible future price increases, strikes, changing political policies, or fluctuations in the availability of critical raw materials. Such speculative purchasing also affects production economies.

Transportation savings can affect the size of shipments and resulting inventory surges. Historically, transportation has been priced cheaper per unit for carload or truckload quantities. The decision is whether to purchase, or ship, larger quantities less often at cheaper transportation costs, or instead to purchase only as required or in smaller quantities with greater frequency, at higher transportation costs. This opportunity is greater for products having lower per unit value, such as coal or canned goods, versus higher valued goods, such as auto parts or consumer electronics.

Seasonality of demand might require the preproduction of inventory to support surges in sales demand associated with various "seasons," such as the traditional calendar seasons or holiday seasons associated with Christmas, Easter, Halloween, and other holidays. Similarity, certain agricultural products, such as canned fruits or vegetables, must be committed to finished goods inventory when the crops are ripe. Production may occur for only 2 months, leaving a 10-month inventory supply to be managed.

Maintaining supply sources is an important consideration for many firms. Large manufacturing firms often use small suppliers to provide subassemblies or semifinished goods. The small firms are more sensitive to variations in demands for their goods, especially if they are "captive" to a few customers. Should the large manufacturer not continue to buy products from the small supplier during sales downturns, the small supplier might go out of business, jeopardizing the large firms' capability in the short run. The cost of inventory accumulated must be compared to the cost of losing the small supplier.

Types of Inventories

Inventories can be categorized into various functional types (Ballou, 1992, Coyle et al., 1996): cycle stock, in-process stock, safety stock, seasonal stock, promotional stock, speculative stock, and dead stock. Cycle stock is that portion of a company's inventory that is depleted through normal sale or use and replenished through the routine ordering process. The cycle stock of a particular inventory item is that amount necessary to meet the average demand during the time between successive replenishments. The amount of cycle stock is highly dependent on production lot sizes, economical shipment quantities, storage space limitations, replenishment lead times, price-quantity discount schedules, and inventory carrying costs.

In-process stock includes raw materials, semi-finished goods actively involved in the manufacturing or conversion process (otherwise known as work in process, or WIP), and goods in transit (that inventory a carrier is transporting to a customer or between warehouses). Goods in transit are normally still owned by the shipper and consequently have financial implications as an asset of the firm until the revenue is recognized as a cash sale or account receivable. For some businesses that use slow forms of transportation, goods in transit represent a significant, and sometimes overlooked, investment in inventory.

Safety stock, or buffer stock, is a calculated minimum quantity of inventory kept on hand to protect against uncertainties in demand rate, lead time length, or both. It is an ongoing investment to avoid the costs of being out of stock, either for production or for sale.

Seasonal stock is that inventory accumulated and held in advance of the period during which the firm will need it to satisfy anticipated demand. Certain industries must commit large investments to seasonal stocks, such as sporting goods, winter goods, toys, and seasonally harvested crop products like tomato paste and tomato juice.

Promotional stock is that inventory held in the distribution pipeline that allows the firm to respond quickly and effectively to a planned marketing promotion. Examples include consumer products such as televisions, tires, personal computers, movies, music CDS, and novelty items featured in fast food restaurants. The success of marketing promotional programs depends on the capability of the logistics system to deliver large amounts of goods promoted into the marketplace on short notice.

Dead stock, or "nonmoving" inventory, represents those goods that no longer have sufficient sales demand to justify keeping them in inventory. The definition of dead stock varies by business. Demand of less than 50,000 cases per year of a particular cake mix item might put it on the dead stock list in a large food manufacturing company, while an expensive oil drilling rig component with sales of only six units a year might not qualify as dead stock in another firm. The importance of dead stock is that it will continue to take space, attention, and investment away from profitable inventory items until it is disposed of. Products continually move through the stages of the product life cycle at different rates. Products in the mature stage must be watched so that as they enter a decline stage, existing inventories can be managed to minimize the consequential dead stock.

Inventory Carrying Cost

The four major components of inventory carrying cost are capital cost, storage costs, inventory service cost, and inventory risk cost (Lambert, 1976). Capital cost is sometimes called interest or opportunity cost. Capital cost is frequently the largest component of inventory carrying cost and focuses on the value of capital tied up in inventory. It is usually expressed as a percentage of the dollar value of the inventory a company holds. For example, a capital cost expressed as 20% of a product value of $100 equals a capital cost of $20 per year. Similarly, if the inventory value were $300, then the capital cost would be $60 per year. Often it is calculated as the firm's "hurdle rate," or the minimum rate of return expected on new investments. This approach allows the firm to compare inventory decisions to alternative investments in advertising, new plants, or computer equipment. The inventory valuation method is a critical part of calculating the cost of capital. According to Lambert and Stock (1993):

> The opportunity cost of capital should be applied only to the out of pocket investment in inventory. . . . This is the direct variable expense incurred up to the point at which inventory is held in storage. (pp. 378-379)

Although it is tempting to use industry averages or percentages found in textbooks (such as 20% or 25%), such a practice might produce highly inaccurate results. It is best to have the finance department recalculate the cost of capital every 6 months or so. Another common way to determine cost of capital is the interest rate at which the company can borrow short-term money.

Storage space cost includes handling costs associated with moving products into and out of inventory as well as storage costs such as rent, heating, and lighting. Storage costs are relevant to the degree that they increase or decrease as inventory levels rise or fall. Firms should include variable rather than fixed expenses. When a firm uses public warehousing, virtually all handling and storage costs vary directly with the amount of inventory stored. When a firm uses private warehousing, many storage space costs, such as depreciation on the facility, are fixed and are not relevant to inventory carrying cost.

Inventory service cost includes insurance and taxes. Depending on the product value and type, the risk of loss and damage might require high insurance premiums. In addition, many states impose a tax on inventory value, sometimes on a monthly basis. These factors affect carrying costs as well as inventory location decisions.

Inventory risk costs include the costs associated with obsolescence, damage, pilferage, theft, and dramatic losses of quality and market value. Particularly vulnerable to this cost are products with short life cycles such as personal computers, semiconductors, and fashion goods.

Inventory Management

The management of inventory historically involved two fundamental questions: how much to reorder and when to reorder. The complexity of inventory management has increased regarding considerations of where inventory should be held and what specific line items should be available at specific locations. These questions challenge the analytical capabilities and creativity of inventory decision makers.

Four major approaches to inventory management often found in the literature are economic order quantity (EOQ), materials requirements planning (MRP), distribution requirements planning (DRP), and just-in-time (JIT). It is beyond the scope of this chapter to treat these approaches in depth; however, it is useful to understand the circumstances best suited to the use of each approach. Those circumstances have to do with the nature of the demand (i.e., dependent versus independent demand), the type of system (i.e., push versus pull), and the level of solution (i.e., systemwide or single facility).

Demand for a given inventory item is termed "independent" when such demand is unrelated to demand for other items, and conversely it is termed "dependent" when it is directly related to or derived from another inventory item or product (Orlicky, 1975). A retailer of bicycles purchases completed bicycles from the manufacturer. To the manufacturer, those orders are independent demand; however, handlebars ordered from its supplier, a component of the bicycle, are "dependent" on the sale of the complete bicycle.

A "pull" system, sometimes called a reactive system, relies on customer demand to pull product through the logistics system. In contrast, a "push" system, sometimes called a proactive system, uses inventory replenishment to anticipate future demand. A fast food restaurant operates basically on a pull system, waiting for individual purchasers to "trigger" more food item production. A food catering business operates on a push system, anticipating what customers need and preparing and delivering items prior to actual demand. Researchers have suggested that ideal conditions for a pull system, which applies more to independent demand, are when order cycle time or demand levels are uncertain, or when market-oriented warehouses or distribution centers have capacity problems (Bowersox, Closs, & Helferich, 1986). The same researchers advocate the push, or planning-based, approach when working with highly profitable segments, dependent demand, scale economies, supply uncertainties, source capacity limitations, or seasonal supply buildups (Bowersox et al., 1986).

A single-facility inventory solution is easier and less expensive than a systemwide approach, which can be very complex. An optimal single-facility solution, however, will likely provide suboptimal systemwide results.

EOQ is an appropriate approach in a pull system involving independent demand items for a single-facility solution. MRP is best applied in a push system of dependent demand items where a systemwide solution is desired. DRP is a preferred approach where a push system of independent demand items exists and a systemwide solution is desired. JIT is most applicable to pull systems for dependent demand items and single-facility solutions.

Regardless of the approach taken to resolve these questions, inventory decisions must consider issues relating to cost and customer service requirements. Conventional wisdom held that increasing levels of inventory produced higher levels of customer service. Although there is some validity to this relationship, a high priority today is on identifying logistics solutions that result in higher levels of customer service along with reduced investments in inventory. Several factors make this an achievable objective (Coyle et al., 1996):

1. More responsive order processing and order management systems;

2. Enhanced ability to strategically manage logistics information;

3. More capable and more reliable transportation resources; and

4. Improvements in the ability to position inventories so they are available when and where needed.

Transportation

Transportation is the spatial linkage for the physical flows of a supply chain. Together with staging, defined here as the temporary holding of commodities, materials, parts, or products for market-timing or value-added processes, transportation creates the time and place utilities that drive the "product" and "place" components of marketing's four Ps (along with price and promotion). This section will review transportation's role under regulation as well as the developments following deregulation as competition and decreasing prices created flexibility and options for supply chain users of transportation. It will examine the relationship of transportation carriers to their customers and offer some thoughts on transportation's future structure and supply chain role.

The Physical Flows of a Supply Chain

As the concept of supply chain is expanding its functional role through the inclusion of behavioral and customer aspects beyond traditional logistics, as well as increasing its global and geographic scope because of world markets, transportation continues to be a core component of the physical flows in a supply chain (see Figure 10.1).

Today supply chains have an opportunity to examine how to time deliveries of goods through effective use of transportation with needed value-added processes accomplished in distribution or staging centers (SCs) with minimal inventory levels. The following discussion focuses on the transportation aspects of the flow of goods in supply chains.

Transportation Definitions

Transportation's definition has its roots in the Latin words *trans* and *portare*, which mean "to carry across." The root meaning of transportation has significance for supply chains because the transportation function provides the physical and figurative linkages, the carrying across, between the components of a supply chain's complex functional structure and extensive global geographical structure. Logistics, according to Allen (1997), is like a beginning-to-end analysis of the ordering, transport, and storage of the product or service being

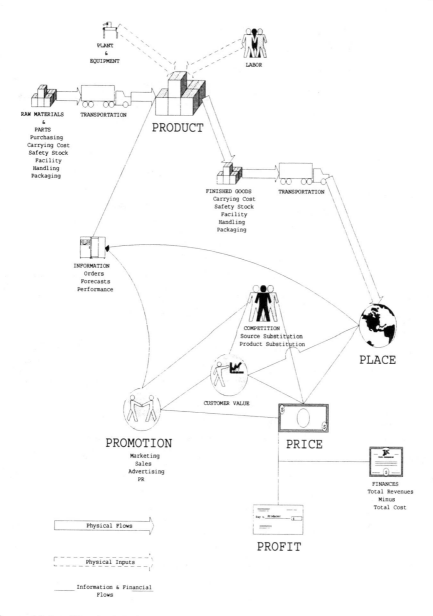

Figure 10.1. Physical, Information, and Cash Flows in the Supply Chain
SOURCE: From an unpublished working paper by William J. DeWitt. Reprinted
with permission.

produced and of the inputs required to produce it, and transportation is only
one—albeit quantitatively the largest—of many functions that make up logistics. As early as 1967, Blaine had described transportation as a part of a larger
communication complex, of which the end product is mobility, which is
three-dimensional, involving movements over space and through time at the

lowest total resource cost. Transportation therefore can be seen not only as part of the logistics function within the supply chain but also, on another level, as the mechanism to deal with three dimensional movements in space and time. This latter perspective addresses the time and place utilities of getting goods to the right place at the right time in response to customer requirements and values while keeping in mind competitive factors and the need for profits.

> Transport functionality provides two major functions: product movement and product storage. . . . Since transportation utilizes temporal, financial and environmental resources, it is important that items be moved only when it truly enhances product value. . . . A less common transportation function is temporary storage and a second method is diversion. (Bowersox & Closs, 1996, pp. 312-313)

This perspective of transportation that addresses the spatial or place utility is a traditional look at transportation's function. The transportation function of temporary storage, addressed as staging in this discussion, also has traditional aspects when used in the context of, for example, holding bulk goods in private rail cars in lieu of storage facilities. There are also some nontraditional perspectives and approaches to transportation in the supply chain. As demand information and forecasting become more available through enterprise-wide systems, and as transportation services execute with high reliability, goods in transit may have the potential to replace some or all of the goods traditionally held in SCs. Thus, transportation may fulfill not only the role of place utility but also the staging role of goods through goods in transit. The drivers for this perspective are inventory levels and time, and "although one element of the performance cycle is transportation, which provides spatial closure, the key factor in inventory economics is time" (Bowersox & Closs, 1996, p. 503). The role of transportation involves place and time, in the traditional sense of market-required timing, and also may now become a focus for the financial impacts of inventory time and cost. The roles of time and place utility are not new for transportation; however, the focus, emphasis, and potential impact of transportation on supply chains is changing. Transportation is no longer just a regulated, unavoidable cost to be minimized. A holistic supply chain perspective may well cast transportation in a new light.

Transportation Prior to Deregulation

Transportation, for much of the development period of the United States, was a significant factor in commerce. Without the infrastructure we have today, markets for goods produced were very localized. For example, during the 19th century, it required 3 days for two yoke of oxen to make a round trip of 35 miles. Corn, even if it could have been grown at no cost, could not have been marketed beyond 25 miles because of the high cost of transportation. To move a ton of iron 10 miles in Pennsylvania was more costly than to move it across the Atlantic Ocean (Blaine, 1967). With the development of the rail system and the telegraph in the last half of the 1800s, markets and goods began to flow with less spatial restriction than Blaine described. The advent of the highway system and large airplanes during the 1900s expanded the alternatives and capabilities available to users of supply chains, limited primarily by economic regulation and the lack of information systems available today.

Allen (1997) explains that when transport was heavily regulated and rates were basically fixed, many managers viewed the transport and logistics function as a necessary evil. They chose not to be involved in this area because of arcane sets of rules that only a small set of people had mastered (and were willing to master). Because all of one's competitors had to play by the same set of rules and faced the same structure of rates, however, management was not overly concerned with transportation: One could predict competitors' rates with great accuracy.

The impact on logistics and supply chain was substantial. As La Londe, Grabner, and Robeson (1993) explain, prior to the decade of the 1960s, except in isolated cases, the total distribution mission of the firm was not conceptualized by management as an integrated task. For example, customer order processing was the responsibility of the accounting function, traffic or transport management fell to manufacturing, warehousing was the job of marketing, and so on. This lack of coordination resulted in suboptimization that led not only to poor distribution performance from the customer's viewpoint but also in some cases to inefficiency, waste, and morale problems from a management point of view. Traffic managers, for example, evaluated on the size of their freight bill, shipped by full car lots and by the most economical transport mode, but this did not necessarily result in the lowest cost for the enterprise as a whole (La Londe et al., 1993, p. 4).

Not only did regulation cause transportation to be viewed as a necessary cost to be minimized, but in addition years of government regulation resulted in transportation market stability at a tremendous efficiency cost (Corsi, 1997). During the period of regulation, transportation was structured into its strict modal and functional components without an effective ability, because of regulation or interest, to utilize or capitalize on alternative transportation roles in place and time utilities, with resulting impact on inventories. That regulatory-style approach is beginning to change as we move several generations from management brought up under the regulatory mind-set.

Transportation After Deregulation

As deregulation took place in the late 1970s and early 1980s, the logistics and supply chain world began to ask a different set of questions about the integrated nature of logistics and the role of transportation. During the 1950s and 1960s there were probably four primary factors that shaped the development of distribution thinking (La Londe et al., 1993):

1. Renewed interest in scientific management of the business enterprise (which we may be seeing again in the form of a renewed interest in modeling due to enterprise-wide data and tools such as Geographic Information Systems),
2. Advent of new technology in data processing (a driver again today as desktop computing far surpasses the mainframe computing of the 1950s and 1960s),
3. Management recognition of the importance of providing customer satisfaction (with delivered customer value as a driver and the recognition of the total market structure for the supply chain, this again has come into focus), and
4. Profit leverage available from reduced logistics costs (today the profit concept should include the other half of the profit equation—revenues).

These factors, which are "new again," are also complemented by La Londe's four factors (La Londe et al., 1993) that in the 1970s were considered key elements that "will shape" the development of distribution:

1. Increased acceptance of the systems approach,
2. Increased customer or user demands,
3. Challenges of multinational distribution, and
4. Increased governmental influence in distribution policy and practice, still somewhat of a factor due to noneconomic issues (environmental, labor, international relations), even though economic deregulation has effectively occurred in the United States).

All this change in the supply chain environment for transportation, along with the advent of data and data processing capability, began to drive logistics and the transportation function in a different direction. As Allen (1997) relates, top management had read about such events as deregulation and improvements in technique such as sophisticated modeling advances. Managers wanted to see results, as they were under pressure to cut costs. In addition, because their competitors were now operating under a new set of regulatory rules—that is, no rules—they worried that they couldn't handle transportation and other logistics concerns in the old way; their opponents could be gaining on or outdistancing them.

The new role for transportation in the initial period after deregulation tended to be price driven. This behavior showed some success, as seen in data showing transportation costs increasing at a substantially lesser rate than GDP growth.

> Before deregulation, the purchase of transportation was a fairly straight-forward corporate decision because of regulated pricing and service

controls. However, after deregulation of the major transportation modes between 1978 and 1984—especially motor carriers and railroads in 1980—transportation became a commodity to be purchased in much the same way as steel, coal, and other basic items.... Firms traditionally have viewed transportation carriers as independent entities that provide a service: that of moving a product from point A to point B. However, in today's environment, many carriers have become part of their customer's logistics networks. (Stock, 1988, pp. 15 and 16)

Bowersox and Closs (1996) echo this perspective, noting that deregulation allowed more pricing flexibility for carriers and significantly reduced restrictions on transportation services and relationships. Increased pricing freedom and availability of new services and relationships, they note, require logisticians to be more proactive in identifying the combination of carrier services and pricing structures that best meets the firm's objectives. Finally, they note the increase in the range of transportation alternatives for product or raw material movement.

Stock (1988) was very optimistic that "transportation has matured into a corporate resource to be mastered and utilized for profitable means, rather than a corporate cost center to be minimized" (p. 15). Today, the idea of transportation as a resource to be mastered and utilized for profitable means by a supply chain is gaining popularity.

Transportation in the Supply Chain of the Future

The changing role of transportation and carriers in the supply chain of the future requires a discussion of the range of options available to carriers. There is a concern expressed for carriers that do not deal proactively with supply chain issues.

Carriers that opt for the "status quo" will find themselves at a competitive disadvantage with only price as an effective means to compete.... Successful carrier firms have recognized that transportation is more than just moving goods from one point to another—it involves the delivery of transportation/logistics services that meet the needs of the customers.... Some carriers have expanded their product offerings to include non-transportation services such as warehousing, customer billing, and logistics consulting. (Stock, 1988, p. 16 and 27)

In 1998, however, John Langley (quoted in Saccomano, 1998) expressed a concern for carriers. Langley asked whether carriers are giving short shrift to logistics at their own expense, stating that the transportation industry as a whole has not demonstrated a significant priority on becoming familiar with the principles of logistics. He stated that some people believed that the emphasis on logistics has taken away the importance of transportation, but he disagreed with that position, arguing that it has magnified transportation's importance. For example, a good just-in-time operation will be effective in part because is has a well-run transportation component. The problem, Langley stated, is that failing to look at the bigger supply-chain picture means missing an opportunity to see how customers are using services. No one buys transportation for its own sake, he said, then asked when the transportation industry is going to commit itself to becoming a leader in the supply-chain process. The alternative, he argued, is that the transportation industry will assume its position as another provider of commodity-based services unable to differentiate itself in anyone's eyes.

Added to the question of carriers' behavior and role is Corsi's perspective on the structure and nature of the transportation industry in the 21st century. Corsi, projecting to the mid-21st century, thinks the surface freight transportation system in the United States will be a fully integrated, multimodal network operating at near maximum efficiency with seamless interfaces between the modes (Corsi, 1997). This perspective would seem to imply that members of the supply chain would want to understand the efficiency of each mode and its optimal application. In addition, in Corsi's vision, the structure of transportation will change with a reduction to two transcontinental national railroads, all truck-load traffic of more than 500 miles will be intermodal, national LTL (less-than-truckload) companies will be merged into a limited number of multimodal or small shipment companies, and regional and specialized carriers will fill the niches. The overall efficiency of this surface transportation system is ensured in the mid-21st century by the almost complete reliance by shippers on third parties for logistics management. Only transportation providers capable of interfacing with the third-party providers in their range of service offerings will survive the competitive marketplace (Corsi, 1997). Corsi thus sees third-party providers as the mainstay of the transportation structure of the next century. This is not too far off the perspective that

> shippers also need to evaluate each of their logistics activities and determine which of them could best be performed by a logistics service company. This logistics application of the concept of "functional shiftability" involves the recognition that carriers can provide non-transportation services and thereby become marketing arms of the company. In essence, they become partners in the firm's strategic plans. . . . Firms with logistics systems that provide high levels of customer service at reasonable cost have found that viewing the carrier firm as a strategic partner can result in a marketing advantage. Logistics has been used in those firms as an offensive marketing weapon that created competitive advantage in the marketplace. (Stock, 1988, p. 25)

Nigel Johnson, CEO of The Eclipse Group, discussed the broader perspective of what supply-chain management is really about (quoted in Saccomano,

1998). He related that supply-chain management is not logistics, which is an offshoot of transportation; it encompasses the entire business and knowledge of all the different functions of an organization—whether it's procurement, sales and marketing, finance or operations. People must have a better appreciation of what others in an organization actually do, from continuous replenishment and efficient consumer response to collaborative planning, forecasting, and replenishment, which has a goal of creating synchronization. Supply-chain management, he concluded, will eventually mirror the structure of a mutual fund. It will be a portfolio of services that will be judged by the proficiency of the fund manager.

Supply Chain Trade-Offs: Transportation's Significance

If logistics becomes an "offensive marketing weapon," as described by Stock (1988), what are the drivers causing this, and what are the issues that will shape this competitive and profit role for transportation? Part of the answer comes from understanding transportation, its roles, and the trade-offs it can create in the supply chain. The idea of trade-offs in the supply chain is not new. Dupuit (1844/1952) discussed the idea of trading one cost for another (transportation costs for inventory costs) in an analysis of the selection between road and water transport. He said that the fact that carriage by road is quicker, more reliable, and less subject to loss and damage poses advantages. It may well be, however, that the lower freight charges for canal shipping induce merchants to use the canal. To offset the slowness and irregularity of canal shipping, mechants can buy warehouses and increase floating capital so as to have a sufficient supply of goods on hand.

Implicit in Dupuit's work is the issue of inventory costs relative to transportation costs. According to Allen (1997), this was reintroduced in modern times in the classic work of Meyer et al. (1959). Prior to Meyer et al. (1959), the typical way to view comparative advantage of one mode over others was to perform a break-even analysis, plotting the transportation bill versus distance for each mode. Meyer et al. argued that the modal comparison should include inventory costs based on the time required by each mode and the shipment size moved by each mode.

Meyer's approach was one of cost minimization, however, and not profit maximization. Allen (1997) countered that trade-offs are a hallmark of logistics analysis. These trade-offs exist on a multidimensional basis, and all should be driven by a standard of profit maximization.

The concept of trade-offs is driven by the idea that transportation is part of a larger system, the supply chain system. As noted by Blaine (1967), transportation has taken on the characteristics of a specialized sector in advanced industrial economies. Much of the carriage is performed by individuals, partnerships, and corporations, as commercial carriers for compensation, who are not connected with the actual production, marketing, or ownership of the goods being transported by them. This has resulted in transportation being considered as a distinct industry rather than as a subsystem of the total economic complex. Blaine (1967) therefore perceives a tendency to think of each mode as independent and without relating it adequately to the total transport system. The greater the subdivision the more difficult it is to achieve coordination of the several segments. If transportation is to be considered in its proper context, Blaine (1967) notes, it should be approached from its macro as well as its micro aspects. The subsystems of the transportation complex should be related to the total system, and these in turn should be related to the larger economic complex.

Blaine sees transportation from its historical and regulated role as the central focal point of the supply chain system. Today we see transportation as critical to the supply chain to enable time and place utilities to be fulfilled, but no longer the central focus. The potential role of transportation to play a more significant role in the delivered value marketplace will be explored, but for now we are looking at the issues around a holistic systems approach. Blaine addresses the strategy for mobility, his three-dimensional communication concept, requiring the coordination of the development of transportation with the development of the other sectors of an economy. This cannot be achieved if it is dealt with as a separate sector (Blaine, 1967). Blaine addresses the shortcomings of trying to deal with transportation only as a subset of a larger system, in our case, the supply chain.

The focus and trade-offs are not only in the transportation-inventory arena. Rangan and Jaikumar (1991) also link transportation and selling costs, a precursor to the supply chain approach that looks at total market issues. Rangan and Jaikumar (1991) found that strategy versus tactical analysis and decisions, for example direct sales versus reps, are closely linked and have transportation and selling costs as major components in the trade-offs and in the outcomes of those trade-offs for service and profitability. This perspective was echoed in Abrahamsson's (1993) case study that looked at different corporate approaches to the marketplace (see Table 10.1).

Transportation is but one of several interdependent cost components in the mix of trade-offs to be considered in managing a logistics system or a supply chain. Inventory policy and distribution alternatives that meet customer service requirements will affect the transportation component in timeliness and cost. Although the focus of many firms will remain on transportation costs, shippers have realized that carrier needs and practices must also be considered.

Carriers and Shippers: The Need for Relationships

To create and enhance the optimal role for transportation in the supply chain, the relationships between shippers and carriers need to be explored. Benefits to shippers of an expanded role of transportation carriers have included higher

Table 10.1 Five Different Structural Changes Taken From Connections Between Centralized Distribution and Inventory/Transportation Costs

	Structural Change	*New Structure*
Phase 1: Production	Reduction of the number of production units	Larger production units Centralization of production with a more specialized production process
Phase 2: Supply	Reduction of the number of suppliers (e.g., single sourcing instead of dual or multiple sourcing)	Supplier structure with first-line and second-line suppliers
Phase 3: Physical distribution	Reduction in the number of warehouses in the distribution system	A structure with a centralized distribution center (DC) making direct deliveries to customers
Phase 4: Administration	Centralization of the transactions and the management control systems in a multinational organization	A structure with only one administrative center (AC) Sales companies transferred to asset free branch offices
Phase 5: Sales	Decentralized sales organization Focus on alternative sales concepts (e.g. direct marketing, key-customer accounts)	A flexible structure with a mobile sales force EDI-connected to the DC and AC

SOURCE: Adapted from Abrahamsson (1993).

levels of productivity, financial payoffs resulting from increased operational and marketing flexibility, and greater control over the supply chain. For example, shippers are not always required to have a capital investment in transportation equipment, data processing capacity, or expensive software and systems, resulting in increased market flexibility that lets someone else take the chances (i.e., financial risk) (Stock, 1988). This perspective of risk shifting may be viable but may not always create a sustainable relationship for the marketplace. Stock (1988) saw it as imperative for shippers and carriers that shippers consider new transportation and logistics options as carriers respond in new ways to the environment. Those new options have included carriers offering a broader array of both transportation and logistics services to shippers. Given an environment where transportation service has become viewed as an undifferentiated commodity by user firms, the only viable alternative has been for the carriers to develop different marketing strategies (Stock, 1988). Stock did go on to state that shippers must work more closely with carriers in developing transportation contracts that contain provisions that benefit both parties (Stock, 1988).

The new relationships between carriers and supply chain members is contained in Gentry's (1996) adaptation of the ideas of Jones and Riley (1985) and Ellram (1990) when stating that the philosophy of supply chain management extends the concept of partnerships into a multifirm effort to manage the total flow of goods inventory from the supplier to the ultimate customer. The chain is viewed as a whole—a single entity—rather than fragmented groups performing their own functions (Gentry, 1996). Within this context, firms need to know their carriers. This is an absolute requirement of a partnership arrangement. Finally, in the same way that shippers must know their carriers, carriers must know their shippers. Carriers need to be aware of the marketing, production, and general business plans/objectives of their present and/or potential customers (Stock, 1988). He carries this even further, noting that shippers should provide more advance notice to carriers about shipping needs and future marketing efforts, so that carriers can develop or modify their efforts in such areas as pricing, equipment, and routing/scheduling. Stock feels that in the future it is certain that carriers and shippers will attempt to develop relationships that are more symbiotic. To a larger degree, carriers can become participating members of the marketing networks of the shipper firms they service (Stock, 1988).

Gentry (1996) explored these concepts through a survey methodology with shippers and receivers, not including carriers, and a case study methodology in the second phase that used three-party alliances—shipper, carrier, and receiver. Gentry found that carriers within partnerships are more likely to embody the following dimensions:

1. Long-term commitments,
2. Open communications and information sharing,
3. Cooperative and continuous improvements on cost reductions and increased quality (profitability was not addressed), and
4. Sharing of risks and rewards of the relationships (focusing on carrier risk and reward, and not addressing the shipper willingness to do the same).

While carriers were perceived as critical or important in meeting overall partnership goals and objectives, they were not included in strategic planning. This limits the carrier's ability to increase overall service and cost objectives (Gentry, 1996). Once again, the focus is on cost and not supply chain profits. The joint shipper-receiver management of carriers and joint problem solving with carriers suggests a solution to the inclusion and increased performance level of the carrier. When only one firm is responsible for managing carriers, either shipper or consignee, it is less likely that all three firms will work together. It was concluded that when carriers are the sole responsibility of either the supplier or the buyer, transportation considerations are not perceived to be as critical in the relationship (Gentry, 1996). When buyers and suppliers extended partnership relations to carriers utilized within the strategic partnerships, this multifirm alliance could be viewed as a segment of the overall supply chain. By further integrating carriers into buyer and supplier operations, the entire supply chain can increase its ability to improve its competitive position in the marketplace. Carriers also were perceived to play an important role in meeting operational objectives. Carriers were perceived to be most critical in the areas that are emphasized the most throughout the supply chain management literature—reducing inventory investment in the supply chain and increasing customer service levels. The integration of carrier operations into the overall buyer-supplier planning and communication processes can better facilitate this transformation (to a successful supply chain) and increase the likelihood of maximizing supply chain efficiency (Gentry, 1996).

Some trade-off areas that the tri-party supply chain relationship of shipper-carrier-receiver could explore can be found in a National Council of Physical Distribution Management's study (Temple, Barker & Sloane, 1982):

- Increasing order quantities to utilize specific transportation modes
- Utilizing a faster transportation mode to improve service
- Utilizing a more reliable (but not necessarily faster) mode of transportation
- Utilizing many transportation modes and carriers to gain flexibility

This study also found that the complexity of the shipper's transportation system—as measured by the number of origins and destinations, link distances, density of traffic volume, and numbers and types of products transported—is an important customer characteristic for transportation strategies (Temple, Barker, & Sloane, 1982). As the multiparty approach to transportation in the supply chain is considered, the shipper response options to transportation strategic issues should be evaluated according to four criteria (Temple, Barker & Sloane, 1982):

- Financial—transportation capital and operating costs, total physical distribution and logistics costs, improved profitability because of better customer service and increased market share
- Nonquantifiable benefits—morale, improved relations
- Risks—of failure in whole or in part, of incorrect strategy, of forgone opportunities
- Implementability—internal/external constraints, time

We have seen that transportation is again considered a significant component of the supply chain because of the time and place utilities of delivered value and also because of the potential to utilize in-transit inventory in lieu of static warehouse-based inventories. In the past, transportation had been considered significant, within the limited focus of the traffic function, only to transportation and warehousing, not considering the other aspects and costs in a supply chain. Today's role for logistics and supply chain management, and the associated transportation, has the potential to be very powerful. Abrahamsson and Brege (1997) state that according to tradition, logistics has been a tool to fine tune individual activities and operations to make them more efficient, but it also coordinates activities and operations to achieve flow-oriented materials management, production, or physical distribution. From the perspective of supply chain management, increased efficiency within individual activities and operations is not enough; managers need to manage a global pipeline and organize logistics and supply chain activities.

Abrahamsson (1993), through case studies already discussed, identified five different phases or structural change processes that could affect supply chains and transportation. A common pattern for all five phases is that it is not traditional cost rationalization within an existing structure but a redesign that has resulted in totally new structures. Abrahamsson and Brege (1997) identified the following prerequisites for structural change:

- Modern information technology and, in some cases, new transportation solutions are very important in order to tie separated functions together.
- The change process in distribution is not dependent on an earlier structural change of the production. However, to reach the full potential of a time-based distribution concept, flexible production is essential.
- Centralization of the sales company's administration to an administrative center concept implies an earlier centralization of the physical distribution to a distribution center concept. If sales companies are still responsible for distribution from local warehouses, the centralization of administrative activities is of less importance.

Abrahamsson and Brege (1997) identified a trend "to a more transparent organization structure, which has been made possible by modern information technology. The transparency makes it possible to achieve continuous control over all activities governing distribution costs, as well as those that affect total lead time" (p. 43). The approach and ability to deal with interactive holistic supply chain structures gives each of the subfunctions of a supply chain the ability to contribute in a way that often is not possible when the subfunction is treated as a stand-alone process. It is time for transportation to be reincorporated into the supply chain perspective and process, and capitalize not only on the traditional transportation roles of place and time as an endpoint but also to address the inventory management potential of in-transit inventory.

Transportation Summary

We have seen that transportation has been discussed as a subject for transportation and inventory trade-offs as early as Dupuit in 1844. In the early development of the United States, transportation became a significant factor in breaking spatial restrictions for producers of goods and services. In these early days, and in fact until the movement toward integrated logistics in the 1960s and the supply chain focus of today, transportation has been considered only as a significant cost to be minimized. Today the

> carrier selection decision is a specialized purchasing process whereby a firm purchases the services of a carrier to provide the necessary link among logistics facilities. The carrier selected directly affects the operation of the logistics facility and other logistics system functions. However, basing transport method selection upon lowest transport costs does not guarantee the least-cost decision for the whole logistics supply chain. (Coyle et al., 1996, p. 319)

The supply chain concept may be starting to look at transportation in the context of its total value and cost/profit trade-offs. In addition, the last few years have seen (La Londe et al., 1993)

- Inventories being "pushed back" in the channel from retailers and/or end users in their attempts to cut inventory holding costs
- Reliability of delivery gaining a new focus coming from the realization of what safety stock is required to cover erratic delivery patterns
- More concern with reliability or consistency than with speed
- International trade and deregulation leading to middlemen with multimodal capability and a wide range of intermediate distribution functions

All these changes in the nature of the global marketplace will continue to drive supply chains and their transportation components. A goal for the future will be to enhance the relationships between carriers and members of the supply chain and explore ways to meet time and place utilities while maximizing profit for all members of the supply chain. This goal may mean a powerful new role for transportation as a partner in the supply chain. The transportation structure in the United States and in the world continues to evolve. Carriers will have to decide what role they want to play, accepting either a "commodity" role arranged by third-party logistics firms as outlined by Corsi (1997) or the challenge to manage their supply chain role themselves as outlined by Langley and Holcomb (1992).

In either case, the design of supply chains and the relationship issues addressed in this discussion need to be addressed for the most effective use of transportation in supply chains. With enterprise-wide information systems, a customer-driven pull system, and international markets driving a global network, inventory in transit may become more significant for supply chains. There may be an opportunity for transportation to become a significant replacement for static or nonmoving inventory in warehouses. Speed and reliability in the transportation component of supply chains may not only reduce overall inventory levels but also permit more profitable supply chain–delivered value to satisfy the customer.

Warehousing and Network Design

A warehouse is a location where a firm stores or holds raw materials, semi-finished goods, or finished goods for varying lengths of time. Holding goods in a warehouse stops or interrupts the flow of goods, adding handling and storage costs to the products involved; however, warehousing can also add value to the products being distributed by the functions it serves.

Functions of Warehousing

The functions of warehousing include stockpiling, stock mixing, transloading, and contingency protection (Ernst & Whinney, 1985). Stockpiling, or holding goods in storage, facilitates economies in purchasing or production. Seasonal goods are also stockpiled to provide an adequate supply when demand is triggered, as well as smoothing out the firm's manufacturing capacity investment (Coyle et al., 1996).

Stock mixing, or sorting out larger shipments into smaller ones and consolidating assortments of smaller shipments into larger ones, is a primary value-added function of warehousing. This product mixing capability reduces the total transportation cost of shipments of finished goods to customers. It also aid in accumulating multiple items for release to production at one time, facilitating the manufacturing process.

Transloading uses the warehouse as a transfer station of shipments that require a change of transportation mode or the splitting of larger shipments into smaller ones. A commonly used term for this function is cross docking. One or more suppliers deliver to one side of the warehouse, and the shipments are divided among multiple-destination delivery vehicles on the other side of the warehouse, avoiding storage and multiple handling costs and delays.

Protection against contingencies, such as national disasters or strikes that could interrupt the flow of goods, can be achieved by locating warehouses apart from plants or not restricting them to key markets.

Warehousing Activities

Warehousing can be viewed as a physical system, involving facility space, labor, and equipment, where inbound products are put away, stored, and protected until the outbound product shipment-related processes occur. The warehousing "system" has controls to manage the physical flow, to ensure the proper care and handling of materials, and to document all activities occurring in the warehouse. The major activities of warehousing are receiving; put-away; storage; order picking; packing, marking, and staging; and shipping (Ernst & Whinney, 1985). Another important activity, considered by some as equally important, is housekeeping (Ackerman, 2000).

Receiving is considered by many to be the key control for the warehouse function. This activity consists of verifying from the manifest or carrier delivery documentation that the goods received are authorized for receipt (usually matching to the purchase order); unloading the truck, railcar, or container; checking the products received for damage; and noting any exceptions on the receiving documentation. The location for storing the goods is identified manually or by computer, and the goods are put away. Uncertainty or inaccuracy in receiving can cause problems when orders are to be filled.

Many warehouses have separate areas for bulk storage of large quantities, for order-pick storage, and for smaller quantities or smaller units of measure (e.g., a bottle of pharmaceuticals instead of a case). Order picking occurs when products are retrieved from storage and inventory records are updated. The order-picking area is replenished from the bulk stock area as quantities are depleted upon filling orders.

After an order is assembled, through either zone picking or batch picking, or a combination of each, it is forwarded to packing and marking, where goods are appropriately packaged, wrapped for protection, and labeled. The products are then staged on the loading dock in a location and order to facilitate shipping. Shipping includes the actually loading of the delivery vehicle and preparation of necessary shipping documentation.

The operation of a stocking point can be considered fairly generic; however, the design of the network of facilities involved in the flow of goods is a very complex issue of strategic significance.

Network Design

The supply chain is a complex network of facilities and organizations with different, conflicting objectives (Ballou, 1999; Simchi-Levi, Kaminsky, & Simchi-Levi, 2000). This is so because the supply chain network consists of suppliers, warehouses, distribution centers, and retail outlets as well as raw materials, work-in-process inventory, and finished products that flow between

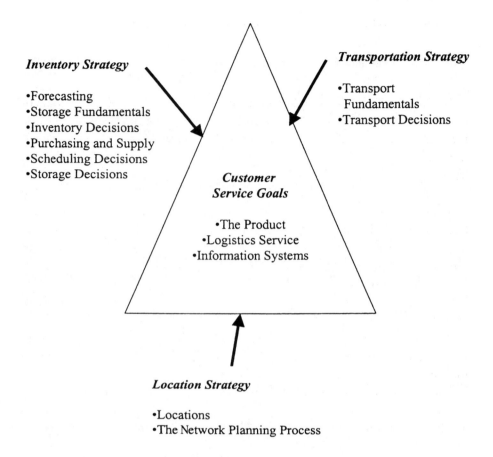

Figure 10.2.   Three Essential Supply Chain Strategies

SOURCE: Adapted from *Business Logistics Management* (4th ed.)., Ballou, © Copyright 1999 by Prentice Hall. Reprinted with permission.

the facilities (Simchi-Levi et al., 2000). According to Ballou (1999), the supply chain network strategy is a part of three important strategies a firm's management should make toward satisfying customer service goals in terms of the product, logistics services, and information systems: inventory strategy, transport strategy, and supply chain network strategy (see Figure 10.2).

The problem of network configuration is one of specifying the structure through which products will flow from their source points to demand points to match supply and demand (Simchi-Levi et al., 2000). Specifically, management of the firm should determine the following (Ballou, 1999; Simchi-Levi et al., 2000):

1. What facilities, if any, are to be used?
2. How many facilities are needed, and where should they be located?

3. Which products and customers should be assigned to each?
4. Which transport services should be used between them?
5. How should the facilities be served?

Network design is of great importance because a firm pursues the goals of minimizing the total production, inventory, and transportation costs and satisfying customer service requirements through selecting a set of warehouse locations and capacities, production levels for each product at each plant, and transportation flows between facilities in its supply chain. At the same time, firms try to get products to market as quickly and efficiently as possible (Simchi-Levi et al., 2000). Supply chain network design is a challenging task because (a) supply chain networks are frequently large and complex, executing the flows of various products, services, and information through a number of physical facilities of supply chain partners; (b) supply chain networks must effectively respond to customer requirements; and (c) supply chain networks must be cost-efficient while effectively meeting market needs (Chapman, 1994).

The network design has five different aspects: strategic, tactical, operational, spatial, and temporal. The strategic decisions deal with decisions that have a long-lasting effect on the firm and can involve the number, location, and capacity of warehouses and manufacturing plants as well as the flow of material through the logistics network (Simchi-Levi et al., 2000). The tactical decisions are made between quarterly and annually and deal with purchasing and production decisions, inventory policies, and transportation strategies such as frequency of customer visit (Simchi-Levi et al., 2000). Operational decisions are about day-to-day operations such as scheduling, lead time quotations, routing, and truck loading (Simchi-Levi et al., 2000). Spatial decisions refer to determining geographic locations; sizes of facilities such as plants, warehouses, and retail outlets; considering customer service requirements; production/ purchase costs; inventory carrying costs; facility costs (storage, handling, and fixed costs); and transportation costs (Ballou, 1999). Finally, temporal decisions are made to maintain the availability of product to meet customer service targets and maximize customer satisfaction through order response time and maintaining inventory close to the customer, while minimizing capital costs, order-processing costs, and transportation costs (Ballou, 1999).

Techniques to Solve Supply Chain Network Design Problems

Hicks (1997) suggests a four-step process to solve the network design problem: identify the problem, model the problem, apply a technique (mathematical, computational, or heuristic) to find a good solution to the model, and then use the solution to the abstract problem to change and improve the real-world problem. In the whole process of solving the network problem, much of the following data are needed (Ballou, 1999; Simchi-Levi et al., 2000):

1. Location of customers, retailers, existing warehouses, distribution centers, manufacturing facilities, and suppliers;
2. All products in the product line, with data on volumes and special transportation modes (e.g., refrigerated);
3. Annual demand for each product by customer location;
4. Transportation rates by mode;
5. Transit times, order transmittal times, and order-fill rates;
6. Warehousing costs, including labor, inventory carrying changes, and fixed operating costs;
7. Purchasing and production costs;
8. Shipping sizes and frequencies for customer delivery;
9. Order processing costs and order timings;
10. Inventory levels by location and by product, and the methods to control them;
11. Capital cost;
12. Available equipment and facilities with capacity limitations;
13. Distribution pattern to meet current sales; and
14. Customer service requirements and goals.

Among the required data illustrated above, those relating to transportation costs, facilities costs (e.g., warehouses, distribution centers, factories, computing center, etc.), geographic conditions, and current and future service level requirements are essential to solve supply chain network problems.

Data are available from such sources as business operating documents, accounting reports, logistics research, marketing research, published information, and judgment by management. Once data are gathered, aggregating data based on distribution patterns (e.g., similar sources and destinations) or product types (e.g., style or packaging) is needed. This can be accomplished using a grid network or other clustering techniques: All customers within a single cell or a cluster are replaced by a single customer located at the zone (Simchi-Levi et al., 2000).

Management should analyze data using various modeling techniques, such as chart, compass, and ruler techniques; simulation techniques; heuristics; optimizations; and expert system models (Ballou, 1999). Chart, compass, and ruler techniques refer to various intuitive techniques that may be used with a relatively low level of mathematical analysis (Ballou, 1999). Simulation techniques provide a mechanism to evaluate specific design alternatives created by replicating the cost structures, constraints, and order factors that represent the network in a reasonable manner (Ballou, 1999; Simchi-Levi et al., 2000). Heuristics techniques find good solutions, but not necessarily optimal solutions, with a rule or a computational procedure based on the analogous human trial-and-error process or reaching acceptable solutions to problems for which optimizing algorithms are not available (Hinkle & Kuehn, 1967; Simchi-Levi et al., 2000). Optimization techniques (i.e., exact algorithms) are guaranteed to find optimal solutions (best alternatives) based on precise mathematical procedures for evaluating alternatives (Ballou, 1999; Simchi-Levi et al., 2000). Finally, an expert system is an artificially intelligent computer program that solves problems at an expert level by utilizing the knowledge and problem solving logic of human experts. With an expert system, the planner is likely to develop insight as to how the problem is solved in a variety of situations (Ballou, 1999; Cook, 1989; Mentzer & Gandhi, 1992, 1993).

Emerging Market Trends and Changing Supply Chain Network Design Issues

Today's business environment can be summarized as fierce time- and quality-based competition and booming e-commerce.

Time- and Quality-Based Competition

Time- and quality-based competition depends on eliminating waste in the form of time, effort, defective units, and inventory in manufacturing-distribution systems (Larson & Lusch, 1990; Schonberger & El-Ansary, 1984; Schultz, 1985). The most popular time- and quality-based concepts that are facilitated by partnering in a competitive market are just in time (JIT), quick response (QR), and vendor-managed inventory (VMI) (Mentzer, 1999).

Time- and quality-based competition requires firms to practice such logistics strategies as just-in-time management, lean logistics, vendor-managed inventory, direct delivery, and outsourcing of logistics services so that they become flexible and fast, to better satisfy customer requirements. Dell is a model of just-in-time manufacturing, applying the same time standards to its supply chain members. To be successful in just-in-time manufacturing, Dell warehouses the bulk of its components within 15 minutes of a Dell factory and requires most of its suppliers to keep components warehoused just minutes from Dell's factories in Austin, Texas; Limerick, Ireland; and Penang, Malaysia (McWilliams, 1997).

Many businesses have dramatically cut the number of inventory holding points in the last few years to reduce costs and increase speed. Wal-Mart's cross-docking practice utilizes its distribution centers as switching stations rather than warehouses so that Wal-Mart saves both inventory carry costs and warehouse and dock spaces (Stalk, Evans, & Shulman, 1992). By the same token, several suppliers of Delphi, one of the world's largest auto parts firms, frequently deliver small lots of parts to a single plant or a distribution center, which acts as a switching point rather than a warehouse, to ensure that inventories are nearly zero at all times (Parker, 1999).

Wal-Mart pushes its suppliers to take over costly warehousing and shipping. For example, SC Johnson Wax studies Wal-Mart's weekly sales figures, forecasts demand for its shaving gels and air fresheners, and places them on the shelves (Gross, 1998). Dell also utilizes a vendor-managed inventory strategy: Suppliers restock the warehouse and manage their own inventories at Dell's warehouses, while Caliber—a third-party supply chain manager for Dell—whisks the parts to Dell as needed (McWilliams, 1997).

CUC International, a telemarketer, sells various products—including cars, book, airline tickets, car rentals, hotel reservations, and even home appliances—with no warehouses, stores, or inventory. Instead, customers dial in to CUC operators to order their merchandise, then the merchandise is shipped directly from the manufacturer (Kuntz, 1995).

Finally, Dell integrates third-party logistics companies as a part of its supply chain management. For example, Airborne Express or UPS serve as Dell's logistics department to pick up computers and monitors from Dell and its parts suppliers at different locations around the world, match up the products with orders, and deliver them to customers (Magretta, 1998b). In the United States, for example, Caliber Logistics manages a warehouse 15 minutes from Dell's Austin, Texas, assembly plant (McWilliams, 1997), so Dell does not need many warehouses or shipping points of its own. Thus, a firm that hires third-party service providers will have relatively less constraints in locating its own facilities thanks to service providers who are willing to be flexible in locating their facilities.

Because of time- and quality-based competition, firms have started to rethink the locations of their physical facilities. In the automotive, electronics, and computer industries, just-in-time management requires firms to locate its warehouses as close as possible to their manufacturing sites for fast delivery of the components for the final product assembly. Dedicated suppliers relocate their warehouses close to their customers to fulfill just-in-time standards and to restock and manage customer inventory. Through cross docking, lean logistics, and direct distribution by manufacturers, firms try to operate fewer holding locations, and existing warehouses function as flow-through or cross-docking facilities. For example, to speed up material flows, Intel reshuffled its globall ogistics and directs a substantial part of its production flow through three warehouses located next to airports in Malaysia, the Philippines, and Costa Rica (Brown, 1998). In summary, logistics network design deals with consolidated, leaner physical facilities and locations beyond a single firm's boundary. This requires a collaborative, well-woven strategy of supply chain facility networks, so the supply chain as a whole gains speed, efficiency, and cost reduction.

E-Commerce

E-commerce allows the creation of virtual companies (e.g., Amazon.com) that distribute only through the Web and, thus, do not need to maintain retail stores and, in many cases, warehouse space. This can result in reduced costs and lower prices (Simchi-Levi et al., 2000). Getting rid of brick and mortar facilities, however, does not automatically bring e-tailers (i.e., on-line retailers) cost reductions and sales increases. One big mistake e-tailers make is not getting their hands on the right goods fast enough. In the age of e-commerce, customers buy their products on-line because of convenience, price, and the speed of delivery, and they switch between on-line e-tailers unless e-tailers deliver products on time (Brooksher, 1999). Successful e-commerce thus requires conventional retailers and manufacturers to become logistics companies with efficient distribution and logistics networks. For example, such companies as Wal-Mart, the largest off-line toy retailer in the country, and Toys R Us realized in 1999 that they could not deliver merchandise before Christmas because of a lack of logistics capabilities (Vogelstein & Holstein, 1999).

Supply chain network design to choose the right location(s), create the appropriate facility design that offers the most flexibility and expansion capabilities, and select the correct logistics optimization services will become critical in the future. Controlling the back-room functions of e-commerce, such as warehousing, shipping, and transportation, could provide the competitive advantage so lacking on the wide-open Web (Hof, 1999b; Vogelstein & Holstein, 1999). Jeffrey Wilke, Amazon's General Manager of Operations, says:

> When you think about distinctive competitive advantage, you can look at lots of other distribution networks or transportation networks, but there's nobody else whose sole purpose is essentially to break down container and truckloads into lot sizes of one and send it directly to a retail customer. If I define the distinct nature of our supply chain, that's it. (quoted in Hof, 1999a).

That is why Amazon spent $300 million to build 5 million square feet of warehouse space. E-tailers should also consider building distribution facilities to secure control and deliver the best possible offerings to customers and, in the end, to gain distinctive competitive advantage.

An emerging solution to solve logistics problems of e-tailers is to partner with a distribution expert who will guide an e-commerce company through the logistics process (Brooksher, 1999). Many e-commerce players hire help to try to catch up to the e-leaders fast, without building their own warehouses (Hof, 1999b). For example, to help e-tailers process orders and ship goods, Fingerhut, a third-party logistics service provider, offers services to fulfill on-line orders for Wal-Mart, e-Toys, Macy's, and Bloomingdale's (Hof, 1999b; Vogelstein & Holstein, 1999). In the rapidly changing climate of on-line retailing, logistics service providers are needed who are proactive in developing strategic distribution networks while demonstrating the ability to react with speed and efficiency to the changes in the e-commerce market (Brooksher, 1999).

Where should the facilities of e-tailers be located? Schriner (1999) suggests several solutions for locating e-tailer warehouses and manufacturing facilities. First, if customers are not as delivery sensitive, build "mega" warehouses of 2 million square feet or more within 200 miles of major population centers. Second, to serve consumers demanding next-day delivery, companies may want to locate warehousing facilities near the hubs of overnight carriers, in places such as Memphis (home of FedEx) and Louisville (United Parcel Service's main U.S. hub). Third, e-commerce is putting added pressure on firms to more quickly configure their product and service delivery, to respond to global markets, to cope with ever increasing inventory turn rates, and to assemble "virtual companies" consisting of design, engineering, finance, marketing, and systems teams from around the world. In terms of data processing and computing, it is possible for firms to consolidate all the vital computing systems—such as financial information, human resources, data processing, systems design, and e-mail—into a smaller number of locations (Moeller, 1999; Schriner, 1999).

New Supply Chain Network Designs for Emerging Market Trends

In summary, in the age of just-in-time logistics and e-commerce, a particular company must decide which strategy it should employ to fulfill customer requirements: a cross-docking strategy, a classical distribution strategy in which inventory is kept at warehouses, or a direct shipping strategy in which items are shipped from suppliers directly to stores. Whichever way companies choose to shape their supply chain, the goals are the same: speed, efficiency, and cost control (Gross, 1998). At the same time, supply chain network design should not be confined to in-house and/or supplier/distributor facility networks, but should consider outsourcing facility networks. In other words, it is not a matter of company locations and facilities but a matter of a supply chain network with suppliers, distributors, end users, and third-party logistics service providers.

Network Design Summary

In this section, we defined the supply chain network and network design, and we briefly introduced techniques to solve network design problems. We also discussed the changing requirements for network design to meet emerging market trends. Performance of the supply chain system cannot be any better than the configuration the network allows (Ballou, 1999). While designing supply chain networks, management should consider such factors as inventory availability, transportation availability, and overall supply chain costs, while maximizing customer satisfaction. As we observe in today's e-commerce environment, customer service is the most important component in designing the supply chain network. Because the real competition in the future is not company against company but supply chain against supply chain, supply chain network design decisions should embrace the location decisions of the entire supply chain.

Logistics Strategy

It has been suggested that a logistics strategy has three objectives: cost reduction, capital reduction, and service improvement (Ballou, 1992). Cost reduction is directed toward minimizing the variable costs associated with the movement and storage of goods. The best strategy is usually formulated by evaluating alternative courses of action, such as choosing among different warehouse locations or selecting among alternative transportation modes or carriers. Service levels typically are held constant while cost minimizing alternatives are analyzed. Profit maximization is the prime goal.

Capital reduction is directed toward minimizing the level of investment in the logistics system. Maximizing the return on investment is the motivation for this strategy. Examples include shipping directly to customers to avoid warehousing, choosing public warehouses over privately owned warehouses, selecting a just-in-time stocking approach rather than stocking to inventory, or using third-party providers of logistics services. This strategy might result in higher variable costs than strategies requiring a higher level of investment, but the return on investment can be increased.

Service improvement strategies usually recognize that revenues are a function of the level of logistics services provided. Although costs increase rapidly with increased levels of logistics customer service, increased revenues may more than offset the higher costs. To be most effective, the service strategy is developed in contrast to that of competitors, providing differentiating services that customers value and that are not provided by competitors.

Logistics Strategy Orientations

Bowersox and Daugherty (1987) investigated linkages between organization structure and logistics strategy. They identified three distinct strategies: process, market, and information. In a later study, information strategy was renamed channel strategy (Bowersox, Daugherty, Dröge, Rogers, & Wardlow, 1989). A processed-based strategy is concerned with managing a broad group of logistics activities as a value-added chain. Emphasis is on achieving efficiency from managing purchasing, manufacturing, scheduling, and physical distribution as an integrated system. A market-based strategy is concerned with managing a limited group of logistics activities for a multidivisional single business unit or across multiple business units. The logistics organization seeks to make joint product shipments to common customers for different product groups and seeks to facilitate sales and logistical coordination by a single order invoice. A channel-based strategy is concerned with managing logistics activities performed jointly with dealers and distributors. The strategic orientation places a great deal of attention on external control. Significant amounts of finished inventories typically are maintained downstream in the distribution channel (Bowersox et al., 1989, p. A13).

These typologies are not mutually exclusive. Firms can exhibit, to varying degrees, aspects of each strategy. The researchers did find similar characteristics, or commonalties, of "advanced" logistics organizations, which suggests that there are a number of underlying factors that contribute to successful formation and execution of logistics strategy. These 10 commonalities of advanced logistics organizations, according to Bowersox and Daugherty (1987), are

1. A well-defined logistics mission fits into corporate strategy,
2. Report to a senior executive,
3. Logistics contribution and potential are ingrained in the corporate culture,
4. Emphasis on planning,
5. Formal performance measurement,
6. Emphasis on managing relationships,
7. Significant users of management information systems (MIS),
8. Premium on flexibility,
9. Seek to coordinate operations, and
10. Frequent organizational change.

What was unclear, and a subject for future research, is how each characteristic is related to the three strategic orientations.

McGinnis and Kohn (1990) conducted a two-phased study to test the Bowersox and Daugherty classifications. Their results provided tentative support for the existence of process and market strategies in logistics. Channel strategy was not supported. Using cluster analysis, McGinnis and Kohn identified three substrategies to both the process and market strategies: intense logistics strategy, balanced logistics strategy, and unfocused logistics strategy. These substrategies suggest that logistics responses are based on environmental and competitive conditions. For example, an intense logistics strategy is identified with an emphasis on customer service and logistics coordination in a very competitive and moderately unpredictable environment.

Contrasting the Logistics Strategy Orientations

A later study utilized exploratory factor analysis to simplify factor interpretation in testing the relationship of the 10 characteristics (commonalties) of advanced logistics organizations mentioned above to the three logistics strategy orientations (Clinton & Closs, 1997). These researchers were able to support 6 of the 10 commonalties (numbered 4, 5, 6, 7, 9, and 10 above). They found that emphasis on managing relationships and significant users of MIS were most important to both process and market strategies. Emphasis on planning and formal performance measurement were more important to channel strategy. Although all three strategies have the common objective of trying to manage the logistics process, each strategy demonstrated a somewhat different emphasis. The process focus emphasized internal integration and efficiency, along with the development and control of relationships. The market strategy focuses on the identification, monitoring, and delivery of products and services to meet the needs of specific customer segments, emphasizing responsiveness and effectiveness. Market strategies seem to demonstrate a stronger sense of relationship as demonstrated by consideration of issues such as employee co-location and reverse logistics. The channel strategy exemplifies a stronger focus on integrated planning and operations, on information-sharing capability, and on a shared view of the channel design's impact on the consumer (Clinton & Closs, 1997).

Logistics Capabilities and Competitive Advantage

Competition is at the core of the success or failure of firms, and competitive advantage aims to establish a profitable and sustainable position against the forces that determine industry competition (Porter, 1985). The marketing concept, a business philosophy, holds that achieving organizational goals depends on determining the needs and wants of target markets and delivering the desired satisfactions more effectively and efficiently than competitors (Kotler & Armstrong, 1994). Thus, competitive advantage over competitors grows fundamentally out of the value a firm is able to create for its buyers that exceeds the firm's costs of creating it (Porter, 1985). As a result, one universal process that all firms must complete successfully is the creation of customer value to gain competitive advantage (Bowersox & Closs, 1996). Day and Wensley (1988) and Varadarajan and Cunningham (1995) have proposed that a firm's distinctive capabilities and unique resources are the sources of its competitive advantage.

Creating customer value may be possible with a wide range of tools and approaches. Among the more prominent and comprehensive are emphasis on logistical customer service, management of the supply chain, and the development of strategic alliances (Langley & Holcomb, 1992). Logistics has become the lead component for making meaningful decisions and is accountable for the boundary-spanning nature of an organization's interfaces (Manrodt, Holcomb, & Thompson, 1997; Morash, Dröge, & Vickery, 1996a). In today's global and ultra-competitive environment, sustainable competitive advantage created through supply chain management must be based on the continuous flow concept (Manrodt et al., 1997). It is proposed in this chapter that logistics and supply chain management have the capability to provide competitive advantage through creating customer value that, in turn, contributes to a firm's profitability in today's highly competitive environment (Figure 10.3).

Competitive Advantage

According to Porter (1985), there are two basic types of competitive advantage: cost leadership and differentiation. Cost leadership entails being able to perform value chain activities at a cost lower than competitors' while offering a parity product (Day & Wensley, 1988; Porter, 1985). Differentiation has two dimensions: differentiation relative to competitors and uniqueness of product or service. The dimension of differentiation relative to competitors entails being able to offer goods or services that customers perceive as consistently different with respect to important attributes relative to competitors' offerings (Porter, 1985). The dimension of uniqueness occurs when a business offers value-adding activities in a way that leads to perceived superiority along dimensions that are valued by customers (Day & Wensley, 1988). Traditionally, differentiation is proposed to be obtained by marketing activities: superior service, a strong brand name, innovative features, and superior product quality (Day & Wensley, 1988).

Prahalad and Hamel (1990) argue that in the short run a company's competitive advantage is generated from the price/performance attributes of current products, and in the long run competitive advantage derives from an ability to build, at lower cost and more speedily than competitors, the core competencies that spawn unanticipated products.

The fundamental basis of above-average performance in the market in the long run is sustainable competitive advantage (SCA). Competitive advantage cannot be sustained automatically (Barney, 1991; Day & Wensley, 1988). Barney (1991) proposes that if the resources available to a firm are valuable, rare, costly to imitate, not substitutable, and efficiently organized, they may lead to sustained competitive advantage. In addition, Day and Wensley (1988)

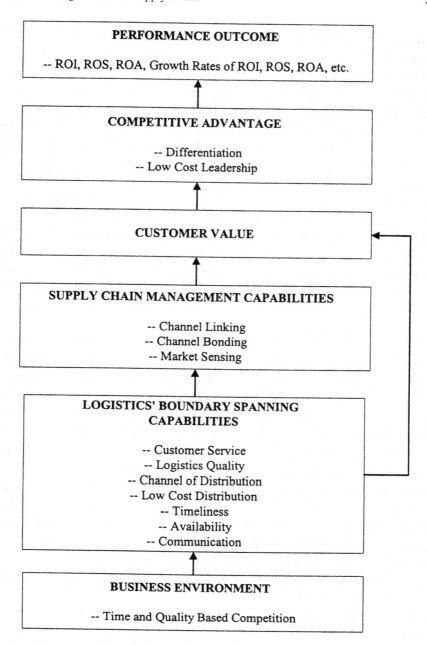

Figure 10.3.   Supply Chain Management Capabilities

suggest that SCA must be unclear as to how it works so that competitors cannot find cause and effect relationships, must be durable, and must not be vulnerable to rapid depreciation or obsolescence. Furthermore, early movers have the power to deter duplication by competitors due to SCA. Hunt and Morgan (1995) suggest that competitive advantage results in superior financial performance.

Thus, competitive advantage is a broad performance measure that includes efficiency (i.e., price/performance) and adaptability (i.e., the core competencies to build unanticipated products), providing improved financial performance.

Two sets of factors are the sources of a firm's competitive advantages: its distinctive skills (or capabilities) and unique resources (or assets) (Day & Wensley, 1988; Varadarajan & Cunningham, 1995). "Superior skills are the distinctive capabilities of personnel that set them apart from the personnel of competing firms and superior resources are more tangible requirements for advantage that enable a firm to exercise its capabilities" (Day & Wensley, 1988, pp. 2-3). Firm capabilities are also defined as those things that a company does especially well that allow it to compete successfully and prosper in the marketplace (Conant, Mokwa, & Varadarajan, 1990). Superior resources are more tangible requirements for advantage that enable a firm to exercise its capabilities (Day & Wensley, 1988). Examples of superior resources or assets include the scale of the manufacturing facility, its location, the breadth of sales force and distribution coverage, the availability of automated assembly lines, or the family brand name (Day & Wensley, 1988). Superior skills and resources, taken together, represent the ability of a business to do more or do better (or both) than its competitors (Day & Wensley, 1988). Stalk et al. (1992) emphasize behavior as the primary object of strategy, arguing that capabilities are rooted in organizational practices and business processes. In this sense, superior capabilities are enhanced based upon superior resources, but possibly not the other way around. Capabilities are therefore further discussed as a source of competitive advantage.

Capabilities

According to Day (1994), "Capabilities are complex bundles of skills and collective learning, exercised through organizational processes, that ensure superior coordination of functional activities" (p. 38). The strategic importance of capabilities lies in their demonstrable contribution to sustainable competitive advantages and superior profitability (Day, 1994). Other authors (Barney, 1991; Prahalad & Hamel, 1990) argue that capabilities allow a firm to achieve superior performance and sustained competitive advantage over competitors. Thus, it is proposed that a firm's capabilities lead into its competitive advantage and, in turn, its superior performance.

To contribute to competitive advantage that earns superior performance, capabilities should be distinctive. Day (1994) suggests evaluation criteria for the distinctiveness of capabilities:

1. Can it make a disproportionate contribution to the provision of superior customer value or permit the business to deliver value to customers in an appreciably more cost-effective way?

2. Can rivals readily match it?
3. Is it robust, and can it be used in different ways to speed the firm's adaptation to environmental changes?

According to Day (1994), capabilities span several functions and several organizational levels and involve extensive communication.

Today's Business Environment

In the 1980s, companies discovered time as a new source of competitive advantage (Stalk et al., 1992). Concurrent with the pressure to reduce lead times, there was and is a significant trend to emphasize quality not only in the production of products or services but also throughout all areas in a company. The logistics pipeline has become a major focal point of total quality management programs because in the final analysis, it is the customer's perceived receipt of quality that is most important (Coyle et al., 1996). Logistics capabilities therefore have become critical as firms compete in the market based on time and quality.

Time- and quality-based competition focuses on eliminating waste in the form of time, effort, defective units, and inventory in manufacturing-distribution systems (Larson & Lusch, 1990; Schonberger & El-Ansary, 1984; Schultz, 1985). Specifically, the increased preoccupation of firms with quick response systems (QR), efficient consumer response initiatives (ECR), and just-in-time supply chain programs (JIT) is evidence that logistical distinctive capabilities are emerging as valuable factors in the development of customer-oriented corporate strategies aimed at developing sustainable competitive advantage to enhance performance (Olavarrieta & Ellinger, 1997). According to Bowersox, Mentzer, and Speh (1995), JIT deals with inbound materials and results in significant marketing benefits such as higher customer satisfaction resulting from better products with zero defects, more consistent availability, and faster product delivery. QR, on the contrary, deals with outbound finished products. It influences total customer service with increased inventory velocity and total cost reduction (Bowersox et al., 1995). Service responsive logistics aims at achieving customer satisfaction through inventory availability, timely delivery, fewer product failures, and, thus, fewer lost sales or returns/complaints (Stalk et al., 1992). In fact, many successful organizations—particularly those operating in commodity or convenience goods markets—succeed as a result of their logistics systems rather than their marketing strategies (Christopher, 1994). As distinctions between products themselves diminish, service capabilities—such as logistics capabilities—are rapidly becoming the premier means of differentiation available to firms (Olavarrieta & Ellinger, 1997).

Logistics Capabilities

The Council of Logistics Management (CLM) (1998) defines logistics as that part of the supply chain process that plans, implements, and controls the efficient flow and storage of goods, services, and related information from the point of origin to the point of consumption in order to meet customers' requirements. Novack, Rinehart, and Wells (1992) propose that logistics involves the creation of time, place, quantity, form, and possessing utilities within and among firms and individuals through strategic management, infrastructure management, and resource management, with the goal of creating products/ services that satisfy customers through the attainment of value. Langley and Holcomb (1992) suggest that logistics is one of the strategic supra-systems that are responsible for creating customer value. Day and Wensley (1988) also implicitly suggest that a perception of superior service, which ultimately leads to customer satisfaction, might be gained by various logistics activities such as faster delivery of orders, choice of technology, shipping methods, or order handling activities.

Bowersox and Closs (1996) define logistics capability or competency as a relative assessment of a firm's capabilities to provide competitively superior customer service at the lowest possible total cost. Thus, it is proposed that the distinctive capability of logistics is instrumental for creating customer value. Bowersox et al., (1989) found that competitive pressures in the 1990s led many organizations to structure logistics as a core competency (or capability) area to lead the firm internally. In other words, either cost savings in logistics or a stronger marketing position resulting from an improved logistics system can cause improved bottom line performance of a firm (Lambert & Stock, 1993). As a result, a well-designed and -operated logistics system may have a high customer response capability while controlling operational variance and minimizing inventory commitment to achieve competitive advantage (Bowersox & Closs, 1996).

Logistics capabilities become distinctive when the development and maintenance of logistics capabilities are complex owing to a combination of such factors as physical assets, organizational routines, people skills, and knowledge. In addition, logistics capabilities may require the formation of relationships with logistics suppliers or providers, which are demanding and complex undertakings. As a result, there is a growing consensus in the literature that a logistics distinctive capability represents a powerful strategic source of sustainable competitive advantage (Olavarrieta & Ellinger, 1997). Lambert and Stock (1993) also argue that logistics can differentiate product or service offerings because distribution can be used as the primary reason why a target market will purchase, and distribution can be designed as a unique offering not duplicated by competition. In summary, a firm's logistics capabilities can be valuable, scarce, and difficult to imitate, and consequently can become a strategic resource capable of explaining differences in performance among firms in the same industry (Olavarrieta & Ellinger, 1997).

Dimensions of Logistics Capabilities

Morash, Dröge, and Vickery (1996a, 1996b) categorize a firm's logistics capabilities into demand-management interface capabilities and supply-management interface capabilities. Demand-management interface capabilities of logistics are for product or service differentiation and service enhancement. They include customer service and logistics quality (Morash et al., 1996a) and timeliness (Morash et al., 1996b). Customer service is defined and measured as the capability to be flexible and responsive in satisfying changing customer requirements and demands (Christopher, 1994; Christopher, Schary, & Skjott-Larson, 1979; Schary, 1979). Customer service is also measured as the ability to provide "core" services and facilitating or extra services that promote, differentiate, and facilitate the basic "core" product/service offering of the firm (La Londe, Cooper, & Noordewier, 1988; La Londe & Zinszer, 1976; Ozment & Morash, 1994). Specifically, customer service of logistics capabilities might include such things as presale customer service, postsale customer service, and responsiveness to target market(s) (Morash et al., 1996b).

Logistics quality is defined by Morash et al. (1996a) in terms of performance "gaps" and is measured as the ability to distribute a product or materials in conformance with customer requirements and standards. According to Morash et al. (1996a), logistics quality is also measured as the ability to deliver products, materials, and services without errors, defects, mistakes, or other gaps from customers' expectations. Although Morash et al. (1996b) do not explicitly define delivery speed and delivery reliability as a part of the timeliness dimension of logistics's demand-management interface capabilities, these two measures belong to the timeliness dimension in other studies (e.g., Emerson & Grimm, 1996; Mentzer, Gomes, & Krapfel, 1989).

Delivery quality (Emerson & Grimm, 1996) and physical distribution quality (Bienstock, Mentzer, & Bird, 1998; Mentzer et al., 1989) are identical except in name and are consistent with the definition of logistics quality proposed by Morash et al. (1996b). As a result, the terms physical distribution quality, delivery quality, and logistics quality can be used interchangeably. According to Mentzer et al. (1989), logistics quality consists of three different dimensions: timeliness, availability, and quality. Bienstock et al. (1998) refined the three distinct dimensions of logistics quality and proposed that logistics researchers should combine the outcomes dimensions of timeliness, availability, and condition with service quality process, as well as attributes such as price and product quality, to better explain industrial customers' purchasing patterns. Availability refers to orders available in inventory close to the customer facility when ordered in a consistent manner; timeliness refers to delivery speed, short lead time, and consistent delivery time; and quality refers to the condition of the products delivered, order accuracy (i.e., items ordered arrive, not unordered items), and convenient packaging. In addition to the three dimensions of logistics quality proposed by Mentzer et al. (1989) and Bienstock et al. (1998), Emerson and Grimm (1996) added a communication dimension, which includes inventory availability information given during order placement, advance information on cancellations/delays, and projected delivery date information given at order placement.

Mentzer, Flint, and Kent (1999) expanded Bienstock et al.'s (1998) customer-based approach to further develop logistics service quality with an organization that serves multiple market segments to see if logistics service quality serves to achieve logistics leverage. In a study with customers of the Defense Logistics Agency, Mentzer et al. (1999) identified nine dimensions of logistics service quality, including information quality, ordering procedures, ordering release quantities, timeliness, order accuracy, order quality, order condition, order discrepancy handling, and personnel contact quality. Several of these dimensions are not new, but fall into the four dimensions proposed by previous authors (Bienstock et al., 1998; Emerson & Grimm, 1996; Mentzer et al., 1989): timeliness, ordering release quantities (i.e., availability), order accuracy and order condition (i.e., order condition), and information quality (i.e., communication). Information quality, ordering procedures, order quality, order discrepancy handling, and personnel contact quality emerged as new dimensions beyond the operationally based approach and embrace communication, personnel, and product quality aspects of logistics service quality. As such, logistics service quality dimensions should be customer focused and multidimensional and should take key roles in demand management interface capabilities toward achieving logistics leverage.

Supply-management interface capabilities are operational capabilities and include channels of distribution, total cost minimization, or lowest total cost distribution. Specifically, channels of distribution capability is measured as the ability to intensively distribute materials and products to selected target markets (Morash et al., 1996a) as well as the ability to extensively distribute to wide geographical areas (Lynagh & Poist, 1984). Total cost minimization or low cost distribution is measured as the ability to minimize total system costs so that cross-functional cost trade-offs are explicitly considered (Morash et al., 1996a). According to Morash et al. (1996a), total cost minimization or low cost distribution is also measured as total process optimization, rather than suboptimization. Among the measures of logistics capabilities, Morash et al. (1996a) found that delivery speed, reliability, responsiveness, and lowest total cost distribution have strong relationships with any of the firm's performance measures relative to competitors in terms of ROI, ROS, and growth in ROI or ROS.

While presenting a new conception of corporate strategy called capabilities-based competition, Stalk et al. (1992) cited logistics capabilities as the source of competitive advantage. Examples of logistics capabilities included customer service, product availability, time advantage, and low-cost distribution. Wal-Mart's competitive advantage, for example, was made possible by cross docking and a fast and responsive transportation system that generated benefits such as fast delivery of goods customers wanted; low costs of purchasing, inventory, and handling; and everyday low prices for customers. Cross docking depends on Wal-Mart being in continuous contact among its distribution centers, suppliers, and point of sale data in every store. This ensures that orders are processed, consolidated, and delivered within a matter of hours. Wal-Mart built close relationships with its suppliers. Through its logistics capabilities, Wal-Mart achieves multiple goals: providing customers access to quality goods, making these goods available when and where customers want them, developing a cost structure that enables competitive pricing, and building and maintaining a reputation for absolute trustworthiness (Stalk et al., 1992).

Mentzer et al. (1989) suggest that customer benefits from logistics-unique service, as opposed to marketing customer services, have three major dimensions: customer perceptions of performance with respect to availability, timeliness, and physical distribution quality. Each dimension can be represented by different indicators: (a) the availability dimension by in-stock rate and percentage of orders, units, and lines filled out completely; (b) the timeliness dimension by consistent delivery, lead time, average delivery time, order cycle time reliability, and minimum order cycle time; and (c) the physical distribution quality dimension by minimum damage in transit and order-filling accuracy (Mentzer et al., 1989).

Emerson and Grimm (1996) modified and tested the three dimensions of logistics capabilities proposed by Mentzer et al. (1989) and found strong support for availability and logistics quality dimensions, but not for the timeliness dimension. The availability dimension included such measures as order or line fill rate (percentage of orders or lines completely filled), minimum back orders, and accuracy of orders shipped. Delivery quality included physical condition of goods on receipt, correct product received, dependability of freight carriers, and driver cooperation at delivery. The timeliness dimension—including order cycle time consistency, average order cycle time, and on-time delivery—was dropped from the analysis because of lack of discriminant validity (Emerson & Grimm, 1996).

Delivery quality (Emerson & Grimm, 1996) and physical distribution quality (Mentzer et al., 1989) are identical except in name and are consistent with the definition of logistics quality proposed by Morash et al. (1996b). As a result, the terms physical distribution quality, delivery quality, and logistics quality can be used interchangeably. In addition to the three dimensions of logistics capability in the Mentzer et al. model, Emerson and Grimm (1996) added and confirmed a communication dimension, which includes inventory availability information given during order placement, advance information on cancellations/delays, and projected delivery date information given at order placement.

In summary, six different logistics capabilities have been proposed as sources of competitive advantage: customer service, logistics quality, channel of distribution, low-cost distribution, availability, timeliness, and communication. Those logistics capabilities are boundary spanning both inside and outside the firm, coordinating and integrating interdependent activities, functions, and even members in a supply chain.

The Boundary-Spanning Nature of Logistics Capabilities

According to Morash et al. (1996a), logistics capabilities (i.e., the capabilities of demand and supply chain management) are boundary-spanning interfaces of logistics with other functional areas, so that logistics must work closely together with production and marketing to plan, coordinate, and integrate their cross-functional activities. Morash et al. (1996a) argued that in the process of interfacing different functions, logistics can be used as a vehicle for cross-functional integration, as a nexus for communication and coordination, and for better system performance, so that logistics's boundary-spanning role works as a major and unique source of competitive advantage. Langley and Holcomb (1992) also argue that strategic logistics distinguishes itself from the traditional perspective through its ability to coordinate and integrate a number of interdependent activities simultaneously across major functional areas, thereby providing various additional dimensions and ways of creating incremental customer value. They further argued that adopting a total channel perspective of the logistics function such as supply chain management enhances customer value.

To be fully effective in today's competitive environment, firms must expand their integrated behavior to incorporate customers and suppliers (Bowersox & Closs, 1996). By expanding logistics beyond the existing company structure to involve suppliers and vendors, parties involved in the logistics process obtain benefits such as asset productivity, operational effectiveness, and cost efficiencies in addition to logistical capabilities (Langley & Holcomb, 1992). Although logistics cannot claim full credit for conceptualizing supply chain management, it has had a dramatic impact in developing and implementing the enabling practices of the supply chain management concept. For this reason, much can be learned about supply chain opportunities and hurdles by studying logistics and transportation. Essentially, those who adopt a supply chain perspective see logistics as one of the company's most important strategic initiatives (Manrodt et al., 1997). As a result, logistics contributes to the benefits of supply chain management. In the end, both logistics and supply chain management play important roles in delivering enhanced customer service and economic value that, in turn, provide competitive advantage.

Capabilities of Supply Chain Management

La Londe (1997) proposes that the goal of SCM is the delivery of enhanced customer service and economic value, to be achieved through synchronized management of the flow of physical goods and associated information, from sourcing to consumption. Langley and Holcomb (1992) suggest that the real objective of SCM should be the synchronization of all channel activities in a manner that will create the greatest net comparative value for the customer. Stevens (1989) also argues that synchronizing the requirements of the customer with the flow of materials from suppliers is one of the objectives of SCM. Houlihan (1985) and Jones and Riley (1985) argue that the objective of SCM is to lower the total amount of resources required in providing the necessary level of customer service to a specific segment. Similarly, Cooper and Ellram (1993) suggest three major objectives of supply chains: reduce inventory investment in the chain, increase customer service through increased stock availability and reduced order cycle time, and help build a competitive advantage for the supply chain. Other scholars seem to agree (Bowersox & Closs, 1996; Cavinato, 1991b; Lee & Billington, 1992). As such, SCM is concerned with improving both efficiency (i.e., cost reduction) and effectiveness (i.e., customer service) in a strategic context (i.e., creating customer value through integrated channel management).

According to Ellram and Cooper (1990), supply chain management is a systems approach to viewing the channel as a whole rather than as a set of fragmented parts. In detail, supply chain management has the following characteristics (Cooper, Ellram, Gardner, & Hanks, 1997):

1. Partners jointly reduce channel inventories;
2. Partners pursue channel-wide cost efficiencies;
3. Partners build and maintain long-term relationships;
4. The time horizon of the relationship extends beyond the life of the contract, perhaps indefinitely;
5. Information sharing is required for planning and monitoring processes, and information flows are bidirectional;
6. Interfirm coordination is not limited to the needs of the current transaction and happens at several management levels (e.g., top management and operational managers), involving cross-functional coordination across the channel members;
7. There is an ongoing process of planning, evaluation, and implementation over multiple years;

8. Corporate philosophies of partners are compatible, at least for key relationships;

9. The number of partners is small to facilitate increased coordination;

10. Channel leadership is needed for coordination focus;

11. Risks and rewards are shared over the long term;

12. Distribution center orientation emphasizes inventory velocity and interconnecting flows (EDI, JIT, and quick response across the channel); and

13. Information systems are compatible and are a key to communications.

In addition, supply chain management places a premium on the adoption of a cross-functional, externally focused view of logistics (Manrodt et al., 1997).

Effective supply chain management is made up of a series of partnerships among firms working together and mutually sharing information, channel risks, and rewards that yield a competitive advantage (Ellram & Cooper, 1990). In other words, the development of strategic alliances or partnerships is a form of implementing supply chain management, providing participating firms' capabilities. Gentry and Vellenga (1996) argue that it is highly unlikely that all the primary activities in a value chain—inbound and outbound logistics, operations, marketing and sales, and service—will be performed by any one firm to maximize customer value. Forming strategic alliances with channel partners such as suppliers, customers, or intermediaries (e.g., transportation and/or warehousing services) is a way of leveraging a "win-win" relationship into strategic alignment of the capabilities of both firms to create customer value (Langley & Holcomb, 1992). As such, supply chain management, a systems perspective to include both the supply and demand sides of the channel, has the capabilities to create competitive advantage and customer value. In addition, it is emphasized here that logistics and supply chain management together, through the development of strategic alliances, provide competitive advantage through creating customer value (Langley & Holcomb, 1992).

Channel Linking and Channel Bonding Capability

Day (1994) argues that a close buyer-seller relationship that is beyond arm's length, called customer linking, becomes a distinctive capability. As buyer-seller relationships continue their transformation, a customer-linking capability—creating and managing close customer relationships—is becoming increasingly important. In a close relationship, the seller has an incentive to be open with buyers to develop superior or dedicated capabilities. In this manner, the relationship can create durable linkages with customers, channel members, and suppliers and, thus, become channel bonding, a distinctive capability.

Cooperative relationships based on joint programs and close communication links seek advantages through total quality improvement and reduced time to market (Day, 1994). Porter (1985) argues that coordinating and jointly optimizing with channels (outbound) and suppliers (inbound) can lower cost or enhance differentiation, and he refers to the capabilities of buyer-seller relationships as vertical linkages. Vertical linkages reflect interdependencies between a firm's activities and the value chains of suppliers and channels (Porter, 1985, p. 76). Typical examples of supplier linkages important to cost reduction include the linkages important to deliveries and the level of a firm's raw material inventory, the linkage between supplier application engineering and a firm's technology development cost, and the linkage between a supplier's packaging and a firm's materials handling cost. According to Porter (1985), uniqueness in meeting buyer needs may also be the result of coordination with suppliers. Close coordination with suppliers can shorten new model development time if a supplier is ready to produce parts when the focal firm is ready to produce the new model (Porter, 1985).

By the same token, Gentry and Vellenga (1996) suggest that logistics alliances provide capabilities to each firm to gain competitive advantage in various ways. First, a logistics alliance is an extension of superior skills of each partner to do value-added activities within the supply chain. For example, McDonald's has outsourced its entire logistics function, allowing it to concentrate on its core business (Ellram & Cooper, 1991a). Bowersox et al. (1995) also suggest that a vendor's logistics competence has an impact on the buyer's costs and operations, so that the vendor's logistics system may be the most effective way to create and support a sole-source relationship. Second, a logistics alliance between a shipper and a logistics provider is a method for jointly reducing operating costs and minimizing risks. For example, because each company is specializing in a function through a dedicated resource base, there exist economies of scale. Strategic alliances with carriers also allow shippers to contract long-term rate and service agreements to reduce administrative costs and carrier switching costs (Allen, 1990). Third, the alliance can also lead to innovative new products and processes that become valuable resources. For example, Robin Transport designed trailers in which auto parts could be loaded and unloaded in places where standard trailers could not go, thus allowing General Motors to set up its production assembly to benefit from more efficient materials handling (Bowersox, 1990). Fourth, because a delivery system can become a part of the product offering, a logistics alliance can increase carrier performance and identify potential service problems early. Finally, service reliability is increased through long-term shipper-carrier alliances because, with fewer carriers, shippers can effectively manage the information exchange and work out system problems. Shippers and carriers both benefit from the learning experience.

The pooling of resources and skills in a supply chain can lead to a competitive advantage by enabling the partners to perform various value chain activities at a lower cost and/or in a way that leads to differentiation (Varadarajan & Cunningham, 1995). This way of doing business suits their better suppliers, who confront potential intense competition with their product and service advantage, commanding, controlling, and denying competitors' access to the market (Day, 1994).

For the channel linking capabilities, Day (1994) suggests the required collaboration between buyers and suppliers as the following two items.

1. Close and joint problem solving: Suppliers must be prepared to develop team-based mechanisms for continuously exchanging information about needs, problems, and emerging requirements, and then taking action. Communication must occur at many levels and across many functions of the customer and supplier organizations.
2. Coordinating activities: Customers and suppliers should jointly plan and schedule production, manage information system links, and mutually commit to the improvement of quality and reliability. Customers and suppliers should also have integrated strategies.

Supply chain management has the characteristics to fulfill the requirements for channel linking as a distinctive capability (Cooper, Ellram, et al., 1997).

Market Sensing Capability

The marketing concept is a managerial philosophy concerned with total corporate efforts toward satisfying customers at a profit (Felton, 1959; King, 1965; McCarthy & Perreault, 1984; McNamara, 1972). A market orientation is an operational component of the marketing concept (Kohli & Jaworski, 1990; Narver & Slater, 1990) that focuses on creating superior customer value while pursuing profits (Day, 1994; Deshpande, Farley, & Webster, 1993; Kohli & Jaworski, 1990; Narver & Slater, 1990; Shapiro, 1988). As scholars have agreed (Kohli & Jaworski, 1990; Slater & Narver, 1994a), a market orientation includes key behavioral components—generation and dissemination of market intelligence and responsiveness to it through shared interpretation. According to Slater and Narver (1994), those key behavioral components lead to customer satisfaction and new product success. Some scholars have found a positive relationship between market orientation and business performance of a firm (Deshpande et al., 1993; Jaworski & Kohli, 1993; Narver & Slater, 1990; Slater & Narver, 1994a). Day (1994) sees market orientation as a distinctive capability called market sensing, involving learning about customers, competitors, and channel members. Other authors (Jaworski & Kohli, 1993; Kohli & Jaworski, 1990; 1993; Narver & Slater, 1990; Slater & Narver, 1994; Webster, 1988), however, do not consider a market orientation in the relationship with other firms but limit their studies to the inter-functional relationships inside the firms. In other words, market information is gathered by multiple functions including marketing, logistics, production, sales, market research, and new product development, which is shared among the different functions and responded to collectively by the firm.

Market sensing capability may expand beyond the boundary of management of a firm into a supply chain. The important role of supply chain management in building market sensing capability is abundant in the literature. First, supply chain members are major targets of understanding. Kotler and Armstrong (1991) define marketing intelligence as everyday information about developments in the market environment that helps managers prepare and adjust marketing plans. According to Kotler and Armstrong (1991), a company's marketing environment includes forces close to the company that affect its ability to serve its consumers, such as other departments in the company, channel members, suppliers, competitors, and the public. It also includes broader demographic and economic forces, political and legal forces, technological and economic forces, and social and cultural forces.

By the same token, Zaltman, Duncan, and Holbek (1973) argue that the external environment of an organization includes a customer component, a supplier component, a competitor component, a sociopolitical component, and a technological component. In other words, a market is not merely composed of a firm, its customers, and its competitors but embraces other components. Porter (1980) also suggests that five competitive forces of a market (suppliers, potential entrants, substitutes, buyers, and rivalry among existing firms) jointly determine the intensity of industry competition and profitability. As such, it is clear that a firm should understand not only customers and competitors, but also suppliers and distributors, to effectively deliver customer value. Porter (1985) introduces the "value chain," which desegregates a firm into its strategically relevant activities—support and primary activities. Support activities include firm infrastructure, human resource management, technology development, and procurement, whereas primary activities include inbound logistics, operations, outbound logistics, marketing and sales, and service. In this way, a firm is linked with other firms. Day and Wensley (1988), who suggest that a market orientation requires that a seller understand a buyer's entire value chain, may best highlight the importance of supply chain management in the nature of market sensing.

Supply chain members are also major sources of market orientation activities or market sensing—gathering and sharing of market intelligence and responding to it. Kotler and Armstrong (1991) suggest that market intelligence can be gathered from many sources including suppliers, resellers, and customers. Other scholars also emphasize the importance of potential sources of market information, other than competitors and customers, such as suppliers and others that possess knowledge valuable to the firm in the process of a market orientation (Achrol, 1991; Dickson, 1992; Kanter, 1989; Slater & Narver, 1995; Webster, 1992).

In the supply chain management literature, sharing of information and joint planning based on the information shared are the major characteristics of supply chain management (Cooper & Ellram, 1993; Cooper, Lambert, & Pagh, 1997; Ellram & Cooper, 1990; Houlihan, 1985). The Global Logistics Research Team (1995) defined information sharing as the willingness to make strategic and tactical data available to other members of the supply chain. It was proposed that shared information varies from strategic to tactical in nature and from information about logistics activities to general market and customer information. In a supply chain, suppliers, customers, and third-party providers share information and plans necessary to make the channel more efficient and competitive. If we take a view of supply chain management as an integrative managerial philosophy (Christopher, 1992; Cooper & Ellram, 1993; Cooper, Ellram, et al., 1997; Ellram & Cooper, 1990), market sensing may be accomplished even outside the firm, in relationships with supply chain members.

Conclusions

In this chapter, we addressed the capabilities of both logistics and supply chain management to gain competitive advantage through creating customer value, which in turn contributes to improved firm performance. The contribution of logistics to competitive advantage is significant in both cost leadership and differentiation. Logistics capabilities for competitive advantage include customer service, logistics quality, channels of distribution, low-cost distribution, availability, timeliness, and communication. Logistics capabilities also play an important role in boundary-spanning interfaces with other functional areas and even other firms. For example, when integrated with marketing, logistics can be a strong tool to differentiate product or service offerings. Logistics also links suppliers and distributors with the focal firm to deliver customer value and to give benefits to participating parties in a supply chain. Supply chain management provides channel linking, channel bonding, and market sensing capabilities for competitive advantage through cost reduction and differentiation that provides benefits for all the parties involved in supply chain management.

This chapter provides benefits for both researchers and practitioners. First, we present a comprehensive view of logistics capabilities described in the literature. Second, we suggest the potential capabilities of supply chain management in terms of effectiveness—such as channel linking, channel bonding, and market sensing—beyond the benefits of efficient management of a supply chain such as reduced inventory level and lowest total costs. Practitioners are presented with a strategic view of how logistics and supply chain management can produce a competitive advantage, beyond the traditional view of cost reduction and better inventory management. Second, we also point out ways of utilizing the capabilities of logistics and supply chain management as sources of competitive advantage.

Although this chapter provides a framework to reconsider logistics and supply chain management in a strategic context, it is lacking in the development of the constructs of the dimensions of both logistics and supply chain management. Further research is needed to develop and refine appropriate constructs of the capabilities of logistics and supply chain management. In addition, empirical studies are required to test the value of those capabilities in terms of providing competitive advantage through creating customer value and contributing to a firm's performance.

11

The Evolution and Growth of Information Systems in Supply Chain Management

ZACH G. ZACHARIA

Executive Summary

This chapter describes the role of information systems within the firm, the role of information systems with suppliers and customers, and the role of information systems within the supply chain. It notes how information systems are inextricably intertwined with the growing importance and success of the Internet and e-commerce.

This chapter will

- Look at the evolution and growth of information systems in supply chain management
- Examine several trends such as functional integration, time- and quality-based competition, and increasing computing power in the business environment that suggest that information systems are a critical enabler in facilitating the functioning of the supply chain, the Internet, and e-commerce
- Develop a model that traces the evolution of information systems from within the firm (intrafirm), between firms (interfirm), and within a supply chain

- Discuss six different representative intrafirm information systems—namely decision support systems, expert systems, warehouse management systems, transportation management systems, intranet, and enterprise resource planning
- Discuss two intrafirm applications—material resource planning and distribution resource planning—that are facilitated greatly through the use of intrafirm information systems
- Consider interfirm information systems that go beyond the boundaries of the firm to partner with either the supplier or the customer
- Examine two representative interfirm information systems—electronic data interchange and the Internet—that improve the efficiency of information flow between firms
- Discuss two applications—JIT and cross docking—that are facilitated through the use of intrafirm information systems
- Examine two representative supply chain information systems that benefit from a supply chain orientation, namely forecasting software and extranets
- Discuss four applications of supply chain information systems—quick response, efficient consumer response, vendor-managed inventory, and automatic replenishment technology

These discussions will lead to the conclusions that

- As the business environment continues to emphasize more variety and quicker response to a dynamic, customer-driven marketplace, better and more effective information systems need to be developed
- One of the best ways to serve a demanding marketplace is to develop effective intrafirm information systems
- Intrafirm information systems such as enterprise resource planning systems are an important precursor to improve the flow of information between firms
- Managers need to determine if the benefits of effective and efficient information flow mitigate the risks associated with developing partnerships with either the supplier or the customer
- By developing relationships with members of their supply chains, firms can develop more efficient and effective information systems that facilitate better supply chain integration utilizing the enabling capabilities of the Internet
- In the future, the Internet will allow true supply chain management through transparent, real-time connections of all supply chain links

It appears that managers have little choice but to embark on the path to developing information systems that enhance and integrate the supply chain. This in turn augments the competitiveness of firms in terms of lower costs, improved customer value, and maintaining long-term competitive advantages in the rapidly changing, customer-driven, Internet enabled, e-commerce business environment.

Introduction

A key aspect of supply chain management (SCM) is the ability to make strategic decisions quickly, based on accurate data, and this requires an efficient and effective information system. Every supply chain has an information chain that parallels the flow of product (Andel, 1997). Information is vital for a supply chain to function. Without information relayed at the right time to the right place, there are no purchase orders, no shipment messages, and no payments, and the supply chain shuts down (Zuckerman, 1998). Technology forms the backbone of most corporate supply chains (Cooke, 1999a). Managing the flow of information in the supply chain may be as important as managing the flow of products (Factor, 1998). Inherently, SCM should be based on the exchange of substantial quantities of information among the buyer, supplier, and carrier to increase the efficiency and effectiveness of the supply chain (Carter, Ferrin, & Carter, 1995).

Information sharing is important when integrating the supply chain. At the ultimate level of integration, all member links in the supply chain are continuously supplied with information in real time (Balsmeier & Voisin, 1996). Information is such a vital part of a supply chain that the Council of Logistics Management (1998) incorporates information in its definition of logistics as "the part of the supply chain process that plans, implements, and controls the efficient flow and storage of goods, services, and related *information* from the point of origin to the point of consumption in order to meet customers' requirements" (emphasis added). Effective supply chain management is not possible without information systems designed to provide readily accessible and accurate information to all supply chain participants (Balsmeier & Voisin, 1996). With the Internet bringing customers closer both to the firm and to its competitors, supply chain management has become more and more vital to survival. The Internet has been identified as the perfect communication channel for information that will be used to interconnect supply chain partners, through which the essential process of managing and synchronizing supply chains are carried out (Bauknight, 2000). The "e" in e-value is about propagating information of value across the supply chain in real time (Salcedo & Grackin, 2000).

Before examining the role of information systems in supply chains, it is useful to define the specific terms that will be used in this chapter. Even though information is the underlying concept in an information system, this chapter focuses on the systems and technology that are used to facilitate the transfer of information. Information systems or information technology (considered synonymous in this chapter) is viewed as the enabler of information flow within the firm, between firms, and across the entire supply chain. This chapter does not focus on the many different technologies that exist to improve functional specialization, such as bar coding, scanners, and radio frequency technology, but rather looks at systems and technologies that are being used to capture, store, and transmit information.

Clearly, information systems have a vital and critical role in an effective and efficient supply chain. To understand the role of information systems within supply chain management, this chapter begins by examining business environmental factors that influence the development of information systems. The second section examines intrafirm information systems, and the third section considers interfirm information systems. The fourth and final section analyzes supply chain information systems—systems that consider supply chain issues as a whole.

An information systems supply chain model can be seen in Figure 11.1. The solid arrows in Figure 11.1 suggest an evolution or progression from one stage to the next, while the dotted arrows suggest that it is possible to bypass stages. For example, it is possible to focus on building a supply chain information system, directly responding to the business environment, but in this chapter it is suggested that a more effective and efficient supply chain information system can be built by following the stages outlined. First, develop an information system within the firm (an intrafirm system), then expand the capabilities of the information system by connecting to suppliers or customers (an interfirm system), and then add capabilities to connect to the supplier's supplier and customer's customer (a supply chain information system).

The Business Environment

Information technology is at the center of virtually every aspect of business, especially in today's dynamic, uncertain, and highly competitive environment. The competitive environment is undergoing major change: Markets are becoming more international, dynamic, and customer driven; customers are demanding more variety, better quality, and greater service in terms of reliability and response time; product life cycles are shortening; and product proliferation is expanding (Fliedner & Vokurka, 1997). In discussing today's customer, one interview participant said:

> Customers, even though they know where we are located is not going to change, don't care about our location—all they are looking for is their product on a timely basis, when they want it, and at the lowest cost—we

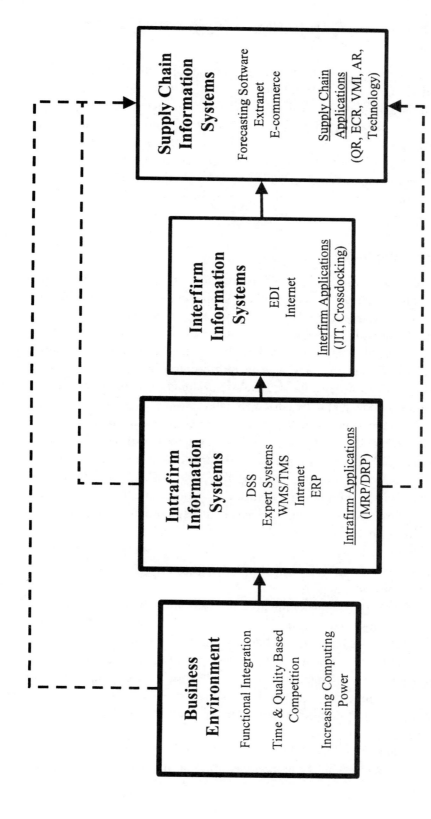

Figure 11.1. Information System Supply Chain Model

need to focus on turnaround time, transit time, and reducing costs all at the same time.

E-commerce applications and e-enabled capabilities that rely on efficient information transfer have the potential to completely revolutionize the existing business environment. Businesses are directly affected by the need for increased customer service, shortening product life cycles, and the increasingly turbulent business environment (Sheombar, 1992). The business environment—as illustrated in the information systems supply chain model (Figure 11.1)—has become increasingly turbulent through three major trends. These trends have led to a greater emphasis on developing sophisticated information systems.

Functional Integration

The pressure for functional integration directly influenced the information systems that were developed to facilitate supply chain management. A good example of functional integration is logistics integration (Ellram & Cooper, 1990), noting the suboptimization that occurs if each individual logistics function attempts to optimize its own results rather than integrate its goals and activities with other functions to optimize the results of the firm. Logistics has been evolving steadily from being viewed as a clerical function involving adversarial relationships among suppliers, customers, and transportation providers to becoming a strategic function that is essential for competitive advantage and is forcing the formation of inter-organizational systems (Lewis & Talalayevsky, 1997). Quinn (1998) identified the need to integrate logistics-related functions such as inbound and outbound transportation, distribution, warehousing, and fleet management within the organization before integration can occur throughout the entire supply chain. Supply management activities such as sourcing, vendor selection, and purchasing, as well as manufacturing-related activities such as production planning, scheduling, and packaging, must be part of the integration effort as well (Quinn, 1998). A key enabler of the integration of functions is information technology.

One of the major benefits of integrating functional activities through information technology is reducing the associated costs. Integration helps minimize inventory that builds up at critical business interfaces while improving transport and warehouse asset utilization and eliminating duplication of efforts (Gustin, Daugherty, & Stank, 1995). In some firms, functional integration includes controlling the financial and human resources committed to manufacturing support and purchasing operations as well as physical distribution (Bowersox, Daugherty, Dröge, Germain, & Rogers, 1992). The trend toward functional integration has encouraged the growth of information systems to facilitate information sharing among the different functions.

Time- and Quality-Based Competition

The second major trend in the business environment influencing the development of information systems is the emphasis on speed to market with high-quality products. Time- and quality-based competition can be defined as the elimination of waste in the form of time, effort, defective units, and inventory in manufacturing distribution systems (Mentzer, 1999). Time-based competition (Stalk, 1988) is also beginning to be recognized as an important source of competitive advantage. Product life cycles are shortening, and product choices are proliferating (Fliedner & Vokurka, 1997). In this rapidly changing environment, firms are forced to compete based on quality products, consistent product availability, and faster product delivery to meet customer demand. Information systems have evolved to meet these requirements of time- and quality-based competition.

Two capabilities that are useful in a time- and quality-based competitive environment are agility and flexibility. With faster product innovations, decreased product life cycles, and rapid imitative competition, only firms that are agile and flexible will survive. Agility is the ability to respond quickly to changes in the marketing environment (Fliedner & Vokurka, 1997). Agile firms are able to successfully market low-cost, high-quality products with short lead times in varying volumes that provide enhanced value to customers through customization. Flexibility is defined as the capability of changing from one task to another rapidly when changing conditions are defined ahead of time (Fliedner & Vokurka, 1997).

Information systems provide firms with the agility and flexibility necessary to survive. The need for a flexible, responsive information system to support a widely dispersed customer base is critical to logistics strategy (Perry, 1991). To be efficient, logistics managers need information systems that enable them to be more flexible and responsive (Perry, 1991). Marketing managers can better respond to the needs of actual and potential customers through gathering, sharing, and responding to market information. Market orientation, a fundamental concept in marketing, has been conceptualized as pursuing customer value creation through capturing, sharing, and responding to market information in a strategic context (Kohli & Jaworski, 1990). In turbulent environmental settings, firms with superior market information exhibit superior responsiveness, typically through organizational innovativeness (Han, Kim, & Srivastava, 1998). Organizational structures must be revamped to implement time-based strategies and affect closer linkages with trading partners (Bowersox & Daugherty, 1995). Information systems have evolved to enable firms to be agile and flexible in the current business environment.

Increasing Computing Power

The third major trend in the business environment that has helped increase the growth of information systems is the tremendous increase in computing power at very low costs. Calculators that are available today for under $100 have more processing power than mainframe computers that were used in the Apollo space program in the 1960s. It is now possible to put sophisticated information systems on desktops at all levels of the organization.

There has also been a movement away from centralized mainframe computing to decentralized peer-to-peer distributed computing. Advances in information technology and low-cost, high-power communication systems are affecting the distinction between centralized versus decentralized decision making. Information technology offers structural alternatives that facilitate centralized strategic planning and day-to-day execution on a decentralized basis (Bowersox & Daugherty, 1995). The evolution of information technology and diminishing transaction costs will lead to a fundamental restructuring of industry practices for distributing and supporting products (Lawis & Talalayevsky, 1997).

According to Bowersox and Daugherty (1995), advances in information systems will likely cause four changes:

1. More transparent organizational structures,
2. More strategic alliances,
3. Increased emphasis on performance measurement, and
4. Greater reliance on time-based strategies.

The increase in processing power at a decreasing cost has enabled the growth of sophisticated intrafirm, interfirm, and supply chain information systems.

Intrafirm Information Systems

The large number of changes in the business environment has encouraged the development of information systems that have specific applications within the firm. These information systems can be used to encourage collaboration by different functions within the firm. The next level of coordination from functional integration within the firm is collaboration outside the firm with its direct customers and suppliers (Bauknight, 2000). Many of the executives interviewed for this book indicated that breaking internal functional barriers could be more difficult than crossing barriers across companies. In fact, as an interview participant noted when discussing change initiatives:

> The people in the organization is obviously the toughest change management issue that we face, which is not a surprise, and it's harder typically within the company, within the four walls, because of all of the politics and

the metrics, and the incentives that have been established over the years. Sometimes it's easier collaborating with suppliers and customers than doing it within the four walls of the company, breaking down the functional silos and creating those linkages.

Another executive participant stated:

I can manage a supply chain okay and I can even optimize it within the logistics realm, but I can't optimize it [the supply chain] overall logistically, financially, and from the marketing perspective for the company unless I collaborate with the forecasting people, and the marketing people [within the firm].

This suggests that firms could develop more effective supply chain information systems if they first developed effective intrafirm information systems. This section begins with a background discussion of information systems, followed by specific applications—starting with functional information systems such as warehouse management systems (WMS) and transportation management systems (TMS), and inter-functional systems like the intranet and enterprise resource planning (ERP). This is followed by intrafirm applications, such as material resource planning (MRP) and distribution requirements planning (DRP) systems.

Information Systems Background

Before examining specific information systems, it is useful to consider the role of information within the firm. An interview participant explained:

I think we have seen an explosion with information technology—there has been a lot more integration through information technology than we have ever seen. CFOs have said, "I need to know how much I am spending and how fast it's getting there," and the marketing people want to know, okay it got there fast, is that improving customer satisfaction—everybody wants to know about it and they want to know about it now—so we have seen a huge surge in that kind of integration.

Managers have identified information substitution (the intensive use of information to achieve better control and visibility, resulting in lower costs and higher customer service) as a major trend (Perry, 1991). Information systems now provide better visibility of physical goods as they move within the firm (Lewis & Talalayevsky, 1997). Accurate, timely information facilitates better decision making. Substituting information for inventory influences strategic decisions and enables significant cost reductions (Rogers, Dawe, & Guerra, 1992). High levels of information enable firms to develop unique capabilities to achieve competitive advantages (Gustin et al., 1995). According to Dröge and Germain (1991), information on customer service levels—such as fill rate and on-time delivery—and service quality levels—such as a number of credit claims and number of damaged shipments—is most valuable for logistics.

A survey conducted by Gustin et al. (1995) found that the successful implementation of the integrated logistics concept was related to high levels of information availability. More information provides greater decision-making capabilities at the strategic, tactical, and operational level. Gustin et al. (1995) also found that firms with integrated logistics functions exhibited enhanced information systems performance compared to nonintegrated firms. The difference between mediocre and excellent logistics is often the firm's information technology capabilities (Rogers et al., 1991).

Market orientation—a fundamental concept in marketing—is dependent on three organization-wide coordinated behaviors: generating, disseminating, and responding to market information (Kohli & Jaworski, 1990; Slater & Narver, 1994b). Information systems are also valuable in promoting learning within the firm, which consists of information acquisition, dissemination, and shared interpretation of information across the functions within a firm (Sinkula, 1994). Information systems that permit freely flowing information are of great benefit to all functions of the firm, such as marketing, sales, R&D, logistics, production, purchasing, and finance. Not having an effective information system or allowing free information flows within the firm can be very detrimental, as it can lead to distrust and antagonism that result in ineffective group processes (Argyris, 1966).

Information systems within specific functions have been developed to be ideally suited to meet the needs of those functions. To manage the logistics component of their supply chains, most companies have purchased single-point solutions, that is, applications designed to oversee specific tasks such as warehousing, transportation, order management, or inventory control (Cooke, 1999a). The next section provides a brief overview of a few of these major intrafirm information systems, such as decision support systems (DSS), warehouse management systems (WMS), and transportation management systems (TMS). Applications that benefit from intrafirm information systems such as MRP and DRP are then discussed.

Decision Support Systems

Decision support systems (DSS) are integration subsystems that provide information to aid a decision maker in making better choices than would otherwise be possible (Lambert & Stock, 1993). DSS are interactive, computer-based systems that provide data and analytic models to help decision makers solve unstructured problems—those with many difficult-to-define variables (Helferich, 1983). General decision support systems include artificial intelligence (AI) and expert systems (ES). Expert systems are computer programs that mimic human logic to solve problems (Newquist, 1986). They use the experience of one or more experts in some problem domain, codify it, and apply that problem-solving expertise to make useful inferences for the user of the system (Waterman & Hayes-Roth, 1986). Expert systems are useful in ensuring consistency of decision making in an environment of well-defined problems. Once an expert system is developed, knowledge becomes part of the knowledge base for use in future problem solving (Mentzer & Gandhi, 1992). Marketing provides many opportunities for expert system development where problems in specific domains cannot be solved in a limited time with common sense (Mentzer & Gandhi, 1992). Decision support systems tend to be developed on a functional basis using considerations of the type of information managers need to make informed decisions. Warehouse management systems and transportation management systems are examples of systems developed to meet the needs of particular functions.

Warehouse Management Systems

Warehouse management systems (WMS) are software packages concerned with meeting the two objectives of warehousing: maximize the use of space, equipment, and labor; and exceed customer expectations (Peters, 1996). WMS accomplish these goals by directing labor, providing inventory and location control, and managing the flow of orders and processes in the warehouse. In essence, WMS are concerned with managing the opportunities within the four walls of the warehouse. One benefit of WMS technology is that it is real-time and, as a result, a WMS can support a reduction in lead times in order processing and inventory management (Peters, 1996). Amer, Chase, and Brumett (1999) note that a WMS can deliver accuracy improvements, labor savings, and better space utilization. These benefits can support better customer service and quicker turn on inventory, both of which provide financial savings in warehousing operations. Warehouse software vendors are also developing partnerships with enterprise resource planning (ERP) vendors because buyers are looking for systems that are compatible with their existing brand of ERP software and database (Trunk, 1998).

Transportation Management Systems

Another functionally focused type of system is transportation management systems (TMS). According to Peters (1996), TMS provide monitoring of five basic items:

1. Freight payment auditing,
2. Transportation planning,

3. Carrier performance,

4. Trailer loading, and

5. Highway mileage.

The transportation function spends the vast majority of its time answering questions, performing administrative tasks, reviewing freight bills, and managing the carrier relationships. Unfortunately, these tasks leave very little time for the actual planning of the transportation process. TMS allow many of these tasks to be automated. Automation of these functions provides significant opportunities for improvement, allowing the transportation division to manage instead of reacting to transportation events and opportunities (Peters, 1996).

Once WMS and TMS have been implemented successfully within their respective functions, further benefits can be realized by communicating relevant output data within the organization through an intranet.

Intranet

The intranet is a type of information system that facilitates communication within the firm, among widely dispersed departments, divisions, and regional locations. An intranet is a network that utilizes the Internet as the communication platform but limits access to members within the firm. Intranet technologies can be used to share shipping status, inventory, and order status information within the firm (Witt, 1998). By utilizing the intranet, a firm does not have to build a separate network but can use the existing worldwide Internet to communicate.

Enterprise Resource Planning Systems

One of the newest types of intrafirm information systems that facilitate information sharing within the firm is enterprise resource planning (ERP). ERP systems allow companies to replace their existing information systems, which are often incompatible with one another, with a single, integrated system, thereby streamlining data flows throughout an organization and promising dramatic gains in a company's efficiency and bottom line (Davenport, 1998). ERP systems have helped companies reduce inventories, shorten cycle times, and lower costs, which in turn have helped improve overall supply chain management practices (Minahan, 1998a). On the most basic level, ERP is a complex software system that ties together and automates the basic processes of business, from taking customers' orders to monitoring inventory levels to balancing the books. As the name implies, ERP systems utilize a company-wide framework, tying all the smaller process-driven information systems together into one system.

As described earlier, because of the high price of computers, important data historically have been stored in large mainframe systems that rely on the centralized computing paradigm. As more powerful, lower-cost computers became available, local area networks and client server technologies became the norm, and data tended to be stored in desktop computers. Unfortunately, the many different systems that were developed independently within a company usually were incompatible, which led to problems when attempting to share information. This, in turn, led to a focus on enterprise-wide data and the emphasis on ERP systems. The major impact of ERP systems is the development of common hardware, common resource planning software, and common database systems throughout the enterprise (Gould, 1998). In addition, ERP systems are excellent as transaction systems that are valuable for capturing, storing, and sorting enterprise-wide information. Popular ERP packages include SAP, Oracle, BAAN, and PeopleSoft. Each of these forces firms to adopt common standards for data. ERP systems can also utilize information that comes from functional information systems, such as WMS and TMS.

Intrafirm Applications

Intrafirm applications are those concepts and techniques that have benefited greatly through the many advances in information systems and computer technology. Two specific applications that are primarily used within the firm to schedule production and minimize inventory are material resource planning (MRP) and distribution resource planning (DRP).

MRP is used to manage the supply side of a firm by computing net requirements for each inventory item, time phasing them, and determining their proper coverage (Orlicky, 1975). DRP is used to manage the distribution side of a firm by applying MRP principles to the flow and storage of finished products. Together, MRP and DRP can be used to manage the total logistics pipeline, from transportation costs and warehousing requirements to inventory quantities and positions within the firm. In fact, DRP causes a closer integration of the complete logistics network and, as a result, drives savings through the total network (Peters, 1996). A benefit of both MRP and DRP is that companies can centralize the buying and planning processes, giving companies greater control over their inventory. DRP also provides the capability to model distribution bills and translate time-phased demand into supply requirements (Sengupta & Turnbull, 1996). By themselves, MRP and DRP do not solve the supply and distribution planning problems; however, they do enhance the capabilities of the logistics network of an organization (Sengupta & Turnbull, 1996). A properly implemented DRP system, according to Peters, will

- Allow for increased inventory turns
- Permit quicker responses to market changes

- Support just-in-time replenishment
- Shrink the percent of obsolescence
- Anticipate and minimize future inventory problems

The concept of centralized data has become a reality with the advent of ERP systems and MRP/DRP systems that utilize information data from the enterprise. ERP systems provide the information foundation that is necessary for any supply chain information systems to be used effectively (Gould, 1998). These enterprise-wide data have resulted in new opportunities for software vendors to develop the supply chain decision making and planning systems discussed later in this chapter.

The future of supply chain management has become intimately tied to the emerging ERP wave that has captured the attention of corporations around the globe (Sengupta & Turnbull, 1996). The next step in the evolution of supply chain information systems is information systems that go beyond the focal firm, discussed in the following section.

Interfirm Information Systems

Interfirm information systems and technologies are those systems that facilitate information flow between the focal firm and a supplier or customer associated with the flow of the physical goods, services, and finances—such as purchase orders, waybills, and payments. These systems typically deal with a single supplier or single customer, where an alliance or partnership is developed instead of a supply chain focus. Successful interfirm information systems lead to more effective and efficient supply chain information systems.

One of the reasons there has been such growth in interfirm information systems is the increase in uncertainty in the business environment. Firms become interdependent when each organization has access to a resource needed by the other and when environmental uncertainty can affect the supply of such resources (Keep, Hollander, & Dickinson, 1998). Industry uncertainty is another reason why companies choose to form alliances (Lambe & Spekman, 1997). Environmental uncertainty can affect the supply of resources, which can alter the value of working with one firm (Pfeffer & Salancik, 1978). Research conducted by Ellram and Krause (1994) found that the top reason for entering supplier partnerships was to secure a reliable source of supply (important in dealing with a turbulent, uncertain market).

Simply linking information systems between the firm and its customers and suppliers in the area of product flow, service flow, and financial flow has benefits. Andel (1998) suggests that interconnecting information systems leads to improvements in the manufacturing scheduling processes, reduces finished product inventories, improves efficiency of loading and distribution operations, reduces requirements for paperwork and rework, lowers prices, and provides better value to the consumer. Partnerships with cooperative efforts to develop shared information systems have the potential benefits of eliminating redundant pools of inventory and duplicate service operations and, therefore, reducing costs (Narus & Anderson, 1996). The promise of intercompany integration over the Internet suggests unlimited potential to gain productivity through information technology (Parker, 2000).

The use of information technology and interfirm information systems grew out of two trends: increasing product variety and back-to-core business (Sheombar, 1992). Increasing product variety has resulted from increased customer service requirements and a shift from a seller to buyer markets (Sheombar, 1992). Companies are increasingly focusing on their core businesses and subcontracting parts of their business, which is leading to the development of close relationships with their subcontractors (Sheombar, 1992).

The interfirm information systems examined in this section are electronic data interchange (EDI) and the Internet.

Electronic Data Interchange

Electronic data interchange (EDI) is one of the more significant changes in interfirm information systems in recent years (Kahn & Mentzer, 1996). It has been suggested that EDI can improve the way a firm does business and that it will become an essential technology for the firm (Sriram & Banerjee, 1994). Researchers have characterized EDI as one of the most important changes to affect logistics in recent history, second only to deregulation" (La Londe & Cooper, 1989). Long-term strategic relationships are replacing the short-term transactional relationships of the past, and EDI is often the glue that binds long-term relationships (Bowersox, 1988). EDI plays an important coordinating role in managing the interfaces between firms as business processes go beyond the boundaries of the firm.

Definitions of EDI include the transmission of standard business documents in a standard format between industrial trading partners from computer application to computer application (Walton & Marucheck, 1997) and the interorganizational exchange of business documentation in a structured, machine-processable form (Emmelhainz, 1990). EDI is intrinsically different from other types of message exchange such as postal, fax, and telex because of the speed of message exchange and the ease of data capture with high reliability (Sheombar, 1992). EDI provides a means to respond in a timely manner to customers who demand reliable, efficient, and top-quality services quickly (Rogers, Daugherty, & Stank, 1992).

The purpose of EDI is to act as an external information accuracy enabler. EDI takes externally produced and transmitted information and allows it to be electronically received into the host system while also allowing the host system to electronically send information to another external computer system (Peters, 1996). EDI and information technology systems are assuming an increasingly significant role in purchasing by eliminating many of the time-consuming steps involved in traditional information flows (Pagell, Das, Curkovic, & Easton, 1996).

EDI allows the incorporation of more timely and accurate information into internal planning and scheduling systems such as JIT and inventory systems (Emmelhainz, 1988). EDI is also used to communicate and track sales; it can increase sales because buyers can make more frequent and smaller orders, keep less inventory, and react quickly to changes in demand (Emmelhainz, 1988). As computer and telecommunication technologies have become more powerful and cost efficient, EDI has started to directly affect business practice (Walton & Marucheck, 1997). Implementing EDI does not have to be cost driven or technology driven; it can be driven by the desire to obtain a competitive advantage (Emmelhainz, 1988). EDI has the potential for efficiency improvements resulting from the availability of complete, timely, and accurate information (Rogers et al., 1992). EDI is viewed not only as a tool for improving transaction efficiency but also as a tool for improving customer service (Emmelhainz, 1988).

The adoption of EDI in the early 1990s grew rapidly because of its alleged strategic potential, especially in the area of logistics (Sheombar, 1992), but recent improvements in the Internet have reduced the drive to convert to EDI. Firms with EDI capability, however, still have the potential to gain strategic advantage (Rogers et al., 1992). To analyze the value of EDI for strategic advantage, it is useful to first consider why organizations adopt EDI.

Williams (1994) analyzed the adoption of EDI in two types of channels—a transactional or marketing channel that focuses on negotiating long-term relationships between buyers and sellers and a logistical channel that coordinates and manages the actual flow of products. The marketing channel was analyzed by surveying suppliers and customers, and the logistics channel was analyzed by surveying shippers and carriers. The results suggest that in the marketing channel EDI was adopted by customers and suppliers who perceive high levels of demand uncertainty and suppliers who are large organizations (Williams, 1994). In addition, in the marketing channel, demand uncertainty in the environment may force suppliers and buyers to adopt EDI because the channel now becomes electronically linked (Williams, 1994). Each member is able to look into its partner's production schedule, inventory levels, and freight tracking systems (Williams, 1994). This immediate access to information reduces time and uncertainty while bringing the channel closer together.

In the logistics channel, EDI was adopted by shippers who have unilateral power or who act as the channel captains, and by carriers who have little power and high levels of demand uncertainty (Williams, 1994). Channel power becomes important when dealing with EDI because it is interorganizational in nature and needs to be adapted from a single organization to the channel (Williams, 1994). Power is defined as the influence one channel member has over another channel member, and this can be important in forcing channel members to accept EDI. In the logistics channel, shippers had unilateral power and could force carriers to adopt EDI or risk losing their business (Williams, 1994).

EDI utilization can position a firm to be more responsive and flexible, as well as facilitate closer ties and communication exchange with trading partners (Rogers et al., 1992). Providing the supplier with information on the focal firm's customer demand far in advance of when the product is needed results in a lower cost of providing the product and a lower incidence of customer service failures due to stock-outs (Mentzer, 1999). EDI linkages speed up information flow and, thus, decision making (Rogers et al., 1992). As a result, flexibility is enhanced. EDI linkage provides a connection, which creates closeness between the service supplier and its customers. This linkage can create a "seamless" operating environment for the service supplier and its customers in which the EDI capability is merely an extension of the buying firm (Rogers et al., 1992). An example of integrated EDI transactions can be found with many of the large retailers such as Wal-Mart, where inventory is set up on bar-code scanners and every time an item is sold, it is scanned and the information goes to the supplier, who will replenish the item as needed.

The major benefits that users of EDI technology cited by Balsmeier & Voisin, (1996) are:

- Quick access to information
- Better customer service
- Reduced paperwork
- Better communications
- Increased productivity
- Improved tracing and expediting
- Cost efficiency
- Competitive advantage
- Accuracy and improved billing

EDI initially grew out of the need to automate order entries and invoices in the early 1970s as a transaction-based process, but it has become far more valuable in gaining strategic advantage. FedEx and United Parcel Service (UPS) use EDI as the sole means of billing their largest corporate customers and provide individual package tracking to their customers through EDI (Johnson, Wood, Wardlow, & Murphy, 1999).

For EDI to be effective, it must be an integral part of a procurement strategy that includes managing supplier relationships and information sharing (Walton & Marucheck, 1997). It has been suggested that EDI has a positive impact on relationships between trading partners (Emmelhainz, 1988), suggesting that the growth of EDI may enhance the current movement from adversarial, arm's-length relationships to more cooperative relationships between trading partners. Long-term strategic relationships are replacing the short-term transactional type relationships of the past (Williams, 1994).

Much of the growth in outsourcing and external alliances results from advances in communications capabilities, including EDI (Bowersox & Daugherty, 1995). Companies that wish to improve their logistics operations should consider the benefits associated with EDI technologies. Research by Walton and Marucheck (1997) has shown that EDI can be used to achieve improved supplier reliability by providing both trading partners with better information as EDI technology becomes more routine in the company. One of the interview respondents noted, in describing its use of EDI, "We've used EDI a lot, and yes, that's a vital link of what we do."

Firms are migrating to other information systems because there are several drawbacks associated with the use of EDI technology. Although EDI has provided cross-enterprise business links for years, it is batch oriented, rigidly formatted, and prohibitively expensive for the small companies that are increasingly becoming trading partners with larger enterprises (Wilder & Stein, 1997). For companies seeking real-time updates of inventory or factory-floor data, EDI is a 1970s solution (Wilder & Stein, 1997). EDI can also be very expensive, and with the increasing focus and ease of access to the Internet, there has been a shift from utilizing proprietary EDI hardware and software to utilizing the Internet.

The Internet

The Internet (including e-mail) is rapidly becoming a business communication system of choice. The Internet is a low-cost method for sharing information both internally (intranets) and externally (Internet and extranet) (Salcedo & Grackin, 2000). The focus of this section is on utilizing the Internet for interfirm communications. Supply chain communication via the Internet is dealt with in the supply chain section.

More companies are looking at the Internet as the most useful system to communicate with shippers and suppliers, as it provides virtually instant communication. Security issues still exist concerning the use of the Internet, but it may become a key channel to communicate with supply chain partners as well as with consumers. A survey of more than 200 North American manufacturers and distributors revealed that the Internet would replace traditional EDI channels within 3 years (Factor, 1998).

The Internet, in some ways, has the potential to change the structure of supply chains through facilitating electronic commerce (e-commerce), e-business, and e-applications. The Internet represents a new way of developing enhanced relationships with trading partners and customers (Salcedo & Grackin, 2000). Supply chains exist as a result of the separation between producers and consumers. The gap between production and consumption is narrowing, and as this gap narrows, the very existence of the marketing channel becomes tenuous (English, 1985). The Internet, by facilitating electronic (e) applications, may change the relationship between different members of a channel (i.e., supplier, manufacturer, wholesaler, retailer, and consumer). As consumers have taken over many of the retailer functions and much of the retailer initiative, retailers have been forced back to the wholesaler level, and wholesalers and manufacturers have retreated to the subcontractor or component supplier level (English, 1985). The Internet will fundamentally change customers' expectations about convenience, speed, comparability, price, and service (Hamel & Sampler, 1998). There has been a shifting of initiative as consumers use Internet technology to purchase their own goods directly from wholesalers and bypass the retailer. Amazon.com, for example, bypasses the retail distribution store, offers a much larger selection of titles than is possible in a single retail store, and gives its customers a range of delivery options from next-day air to surface mail. The Internet is an enabler providing radical improvements to the performance of many supply chain activities (Bauknight, 2000).

Internet technology and information systems such as EDI enable value-adding partnerships where the coordination of boundary-crossing logistical processes is the key to good logistical performance (Sheombar, 1992). Information systems can help reduce the cost of supplier coordination and enhance buyer-supplier relationships. This suggests that information systems play an important role in supplier reliability and supplier partnerships.

Interfirm Applications

Two specific applications that benefit greatly from information systems technology that goes beyond the firm are just-in-time (JIT) manufacturing and cross docking. Both these technologies have existed for some time, but applying JIT and cross docking beyond the firm requires coordination between firms that is highly dependent on the free flow of information and effective and efficient information systems.

Just-in-Time Manufacturing

Just-in-time (JIT) manufacturing was first developed at Toyota in the early 1960s by Taiichi Ohno as part of Toyota's lean production process (Womack, Jones, & Roos, 1990). JIT is the concept that parts are produced at each step in quantities sufficient only to supply the immediate demand of the next step. This concept was extremely difficult to implement because inventories between the different production steps were practically eliminated, so if one small part was not available the entire production system failed (Womack et al., 1990). The logistics function became directly involved when JIT was further expanded outside the factory to include suppliers in the Toyota production system. The success of JIT manufacturing within the firm led to the development of JIT beyond the firm through information systems technology.

Business processes such as just-in-time delivery require effective information technology support (Lewis & Talalayevsky, 1997). JIT systems require fast and accurate communications between the buyer and supplier that can be improved using information technologies such as EDI (Emmelhainz, 1988). To achieve the gains in productivity that are possible from JIT, real-time information sharing is needed between suppliers and buyers (Lewis & Talalayevsky, 1997). Among the many impediments to implementing JIT is the need for direct access to one's suppliers through information technology to enhance communication and coordination. Richeson, Lackey, and Starner (1995) found evidence that establishing communication links that allow information flow between manufacturers and suppliers is important to the synchronization of production operations of both partners.

Traditional supplier relationships are based on the lowest bid price and both parties searching for the best deal. JIT relationships are cooperative partnerships in which one of the main goals is to obtain mutually beneficial results (Richeson et al., 1995). For JIT to work successfully, suppliers need to be viewed as partners in a cooperative relationship. Partnering arrangements provide the basis for supplier delivery of quality materials as required by JIT (Richeson et al., 1995).

One of the foundations of JIT is effective and open communication between the focal firm and the supplier through information systems. Open communication channels foster the development of trust between a buyer and supplier (Richeson et al., 1995). The adversarial relationship typical between most buyers and suppliers is replaced by one of mutual trust and partnering if JIT is to work effectively across firms. Richeson et al. (1995) found that effective communication with suppliers makes a difference in performance of JIT manufacturers. The greatest impact of improved communication between JIT manufacturers and suppliers is improving delivery performance; less of an impact comes from improving quality and cost performance (Richeson et al., 1995). For JIT to work effectively, good supplier relationships are needed. This is even more important for an effective supply chain with JIT (Bowman, 1996).

Cross Docking

Cross docking is a system where the incoming shipment is transferred into an outgoing shipment without entering the warehouse. The goal of cross docking is to reduce materials handling by moving goods directly to the end user, eliminating the need for storage (Witt, 1998). Because it requires considerable supply and demand synchronization, an effective information and planning system must be in place for cross docking to work. Cross docking also requires close interfirm collaboration.

According to Witt (1998), the key to getting the most out of cross docking is to identify the needs of the information system, as well as the needs of the physical system. Information technology allows managers to have faith in inventory accuracy and delivery time accuracy—both key components of a successful cross-docking system. In today's cross-docking applications, materials handling has been enhanced by information that is transmitted rapidly via computers (Witt, 1998). Cross docking literally allows a company to receive and ship at the same time through an effective information system. Cross docking is likely to increase as more firms invest in effective communication and information systems. It allows firms to flow goods instead of store goods so that there is a movement from the buy-and-store mentality to a sort-and-ship mentality. Pic 'n' Pay's distribution center near Charlotte, North Carolina, for example, operates its warehouse with more than 70% of the incoming goods placed directly for assignment before they arrive to be loaded onto outgoing trucks without going into storage (Anonymous, 1989).

Partnerships

One of the reasons interfirm information technology applications can be difficult to implement and take a long time to become effective is the need to develop long-term partnerships. Developing strong partnerships through information technology actually facilitates better management of supply risk. In the past, supply risk was managed by holding buffer inventories to avoid problems caused by part shortages, defective inputs, and lengthy setup times (Richeson et al., 1995).

There is a trade-off between the costs associated with holding inventory and the risk associated with irregular supply. Developing good partnerships has a direct cost that can be offset by the reduction in inventory cost. Externally focused strategies such as partnerships and strategic alliances are dependent on the adoption of appropriate information systems that eventually can lead to a supply chain focus. Relationships such as partnerships or alliances are highly dependent on information support (Gustin et al., 1995).

Forming supplier partnerships requires investments in assets (usually technology based) by the supplier and/or focal organizations that are specific to the partnership. Many of these technology-based assets are idiosyncratic (little value in other partnerships) and nonfungible (cannot be sold at any appreciable price) (Mentzer, 1997). The major risk carried by the company investing in asset-specific technology is the need to recoup its investment. This might lead to opportunistic behavior that is ultimately a threat to the partnership

(Gundlach, Achrol, & Mentzer, 1995). Interfirm information systems are one of the foundation tools for successful trading partnerships, especially if the two companies are to become closely integrated and aligned, with the same logistics goals (Peters, 1996). The many issues associated with partnerships such as trust and commitment are discussed in detail in Chapter 14, which examines inter-functional coordination, and Chapter 15, on inter-corporate coordination.

Partnerships and strategic alliances can lead to the concept of looking beyond the boundaries of one's own supplier and customer to considering the supplier's supplier and the customer's customer, which eventually can lead to looking at the entire supply chain. The next step in achieving greater logistics efficiencies is to consider ways to better integrate the supply chain. Improvements in information technology have reduced transaction costs and promoted better communication between firms—initial steps in the development of a supply chain.

Supply Chain Information Systems

The focus of this section is on information systems that go across multiple organizations and facilitate the flow of information from a source to a customer. Information systems are essential to managing a supply chain. Collaboration between supply chain partners leads to the idea of synchronization of all supply chain participants, both within and outside the firm, to the demands of the end consumer through the Internet (Bauknight, 2000). The Internet provides the communication channel for information that is necessary for the tight coordination found in superb supply chains (Bauknight, 2000). The supply chain information systems that are discussed in this section rely on either EDI or the Internet to transmit information within the supply chain. The explosion of the Internet and the World Wide Web, coupled with low access costs and emerging standards such as XML (extensible markup language), will force older technologies like EDI to reinvent themselves (Salcedo & Grackin, 2000).

According to one interview participant asked to comment on why companies would commit to joining a supply chain:

> Looking across the supply chain is a win-win for all players in the system. Typically, there is a lot of non-value added, a lot redundancy, a lot of costs that don't necessarily need to be there, so when we focused on the right things, we reduced costs for pretty well everyone in the supply chain.

A valuable initial element in managing a supply chain is developing supply chain information systems. It is especially critical that supply chain partners have access to information on activities they do not control (Gustin et al., 1995). The concept of supply chain management is built on functional integration, which is supported and often catalyzed by information technology (Larson, 1994). Accurate information is critical for a supply chain to function effectively (Gustin et al., 1995).

Mutually sharing information among the members of a supply chain is required, especially for planning and monitoring processes (Ellram & Cooper, 1990; Novack, Langley, & Rinehart, 1995). Rapid response is a key to creating value in the supply chain that requires real-time communication as demand changes along the supply chain (Salcedo & Grackin, 2000). Cooper, Lambert, and Pagh (1997) emphasize frequent information updating among the supply chain members for effective supply chain management. The Global Logistics Research Team at Michigan State University (1995) defines information sharing as the willingness to make strategic and tactical data available to other members of the supply chain. It also proposed that the open sharing of information such as inventory levels, forecasts, sales promotion strategies, and marketing strategies reduces the uncertainty between supply partners and results in enhanced performance. A new, complex, and more committed form of collaboration, "collaborative business communities," requires companies to share proprietary information such as inventory levels, pricing, and manufacturing capacity with firms along the supply chain (Taylor & Terhune, 2000).

The importance of being able to communicate within the supply chain was identified by another interview participant:

> Communication is so important, from ordering day all the way to delivery day—so you know more about each part of the chain, each mode, who's going to deliver the product, who's going to clear it through customs, what carrier you're gonna use. It helps each other understand the other's perspective.

This participant explained the benefit of information systems this way:

> Our company is in the process of making major investments in information systems to get retail point of sale data back up the supply chain to improve the information flow. We do not expect our supply chain members to purchase SAP or our ERP system, but we do expect them to be able to communicate. As long as information is conveyed, we are not necessarily as concerned about the software that is used.

As businesses embrace supply chain management, they must maintain instant communication between computers in different corporate departments as well as with partners outside the company walls. According to Cooke (1998), computer communication makes it possible to marshal the flow of goods from the distribution center to the customer quickly and efficiently. Companies can use SCM to develop close partnerships in which each partner collaborates using shared information streams to forecast, produce, ship, and assemble in a true just-in-time scheme (Donlon & Galli, 1998). Supply chain information systems are needed to communicate and convey information through the supply chain. Ellram and Cooper (1990) suggest that effective supply chain management is a series of partnerships among firms working together and mutually sharing information, channel risks, and rewards that yield a competitive advantage. Lusch and Brown (1996) note that the more channel firms exchange information with each other, the better they are able to anticipate and respond to each other's needs, which leads directly to better performance of the channel as a whole.

To achieve functional integration within the supply chain, it is necessary to develop information systems that manage product flow, information flow, and cash flow from end to end. Electronic methods of sharing information can facilitate collaborative/iterative planning (Salcedo & Grackin, 2000). Such supply chain information systems allow companies to coordinate production with demand, slash inventory and cycle times, better manage logistics, improve customer satisfaction, and reduce overall costs. In a supply chain, suppliers, customers, and third-party providers share information and plans necessary to make the channel more efficient, effective, and competitive (Cooper & Ellram, 1993). Effective sharing of information across organizational boundaries in a synchronized manner can overcome existing organization barriers within the supply chain (Salcedo & Grackin, 2000); however, information systems, in the final analysis, are best used as tools to support an overall supply chain or business strategy (Minahan, 1998a).

Information systems technology allows the physical network to be separate from the information network. Supply chain processes consist of three separate processes: physical flow of goods, flow of finances, and flow of information related to those goods and finances. Traditionally, the same structure was used for all these flows, but information technology allows them to be separately optimized (Lewis & Talalayevsky, 1997). Physical goods cannot flow efficiently in a single-level hierarchy from origin to destination, whereas information and finances can. For example, passengers are routed in a hierarchical manner (from large aircraft to smaller aircraft) through hubs to reach their final destination. Information on the passengers travels on a network different from the physical network, with no hierarchical distinction between various parts of the network (Lewis & Talalayevsky, 1997).

Information systems are shrinking the logistics and marketing channels that separate suppliers from end consumers. Through information technology, suppliers are able to drastically cut response times, intermediaries such as distributors are eliminated, and distribution is recognized as an inter-organizational process requiring the cooperation of all parties (Lewis & Talalayevsky, 1997). Information technology allows suppliers real-time access to point of sale information. Where exactly a company's products are and how long it takes to get them from Point A to Point B is essential for retailers and manufacturers to know as they strive to find profit by cutting inefficiencies out of the supply chain. Improvements in information technology reduce transaction costs and promote better communications between firms (Lewis & Talalayevsky, 1997).

One of the components of the implementation of supply chain management is information sharing through two-way communication between partners within a supply chain (Cooper, Ellram, Gardner, & Hanks, 1997). Information gathered by individual firms serves as the basis of shared information among supply chain partners, thereby encouraging a supply chain orientation and facilitating supply chain management. The activities of information generation, storage, and utilization in individual firms in a supply chain are essential to implement supply chain management. Members of a supply chain need real-time visibility of performance data across the entire supply chain (Salcedo & Grackin, 2000). For example, Dell Computer's direct relationships with its customers create valuable information that, in turn, allow the company to coordinate its entire supply chain back through manufacturing to product design (with other firms) (Magretta, 1998b).

Sharing retail customer-demand information throughout the supply chain fosters better inventory and production planning (Johnson, 1998). Helping buyers better manage their inventories in turn reduces wide swings in demand caused by inefficient retailer buying policies. The sharing of detailed retail sales information helps ensure product availability on retailer shelves while enabling the manufacturer to reduce its own inventories (Johnson, 1998). Brunell (1999), in discussing a multicompany supply chain, noted that seamless information flow was the backbone of developing an integrated supply chain. Supply chain information systems typically rise out of existing interfirm applications that work in a dyadic framework with a supplier and retailer or a manufacturer and distributor. These systems, such as JIT in manufacturing and ECR in retailing, are more effective when utilizing a supply chain focus.

Forecasting Systems

Supply chain information systems use past sales history to create forecasts of future demand. In the search for greater efficiency and quicker response within the supply chain, accurate forecasting systems are needed. By incorporating timely information about downstream demand into their supply chain planning, suppliers can deliver products when needed at a lower cost (Andel, 1997).

In discussing forecasting and the supply chain, one interview participant explained:

> Forecasting is the area where I have seen the greatest cooperation between different people in different places in the supply chain—maybe because that's an easy one as everyone gets their own benefits out of forecasting and

there is no argument about whether you should be giving me some money for this.

The benefits of fewer stock-outs and lower costs become available when final customer forecasts are transmitted electronically up the supply chain (Kahn & Mentzer, 1996). A key part of ensuring quality in the supply chain is to use forecasting systems and information systems to speed the transfer of data up the supply chain from customer to supplier to reduce duplication and error, notifying of schedule changes as they occur.

Extranets

An emerging network is an extranet, which utilizes the Internet to communicate, but with access limited to some subset of members. Firms that are vertically related, such as a manufacturer, carrier, distributor, and retailer, are linked via an extranet and are able to communicate shipping information in real time (Witt, 1998). According to Bruce (1998), information systems are the glue behind business strategies of mass customization, as in Levi's custom-fit jeans and Gateway's mass customization of PCs. Extranets enable rapid reconfiguration of product specifications to meet each customer's needs and also increase speed to market by allowing direct connection to the manufacturing and production processes (Bruce, 1998). Extranets allow collaborative business applications and transactions to occur between firms and along the supply chain.

Supply Chain Technology

Technology forms the backbone of most supply chains (Cooke, 1999a). Automatic identification (auto ID) equipment and logistics software become more important as firms look to gain market share or cut manufacturing and logistics costs by synchronizing product flow with customer demand. Auto ID equipment marking of products, parts, and components for tracking through a distribution channel is expected to grow from $11.3 billion in 1998 to more than $19 billion by the year 2002. This includes bar code scanners, 2-D symbology, and radio frequency identification.

Supply Chain Applications

Several systems have become more popular recently through advances in information systems technology that use accurate point of sale (POS) information and eliminate substantial variability in the performance cycle (Bowersox & Closs, 1996). Quick response (QR), efficient consumer response (ECR), vendor-managed inventory (VMI), and automatic replenishment (AR) all focus on rapidly replenishing inventory based on real-time sales data. QR is implemented by monitoring retail sales using POS data and sharing that information across the supply chain. Continuous information exchange reduces uncertainty in the total supply chain and creates the opportunity for reduced inventory and improved availability. ECR originated in the grocery industry, where the focus is on a consumer-driven system in which members of a supply chain work together. It depends on timely, accurate, paperless information flow. One ECR study, sponsored by the Food Marketing Institute, estimated that 42 days could be removed from the typical grocery supply chain, freeing up $30 billion in current costs and reducing inventories by 41% (Sengupta & Turnbull, 1996).

VMI is a modification of QR in that the vendor does not have to wait for the replenishment order, but instead assumes responsibility for directly replenishing the retail inventory. The goal of VMI again focuses on having a flexible supply chain that is updated continuously with real-time sales information. Automatic replenishment (AR) extends QR and VMI by giving suppliers the right to anticipate future requirements and replenish accordingly (Bowersox & Closs, 1996). Suppliers accept responsibility for inventory in return for access to retail stores, and retailers reduce the cost of holding and managing inventory.

QR, ECR, VMI, and AR can work only with effective information flow throughout the supply chain. Better information systems improve coordination between all members of the supply chain and increase the opportunity to improve operational efficiency of the entire supply chain. An important point often ignored in discussions of these systems, however, is the supply chain implications of this information for marketing. The ability to see real-time POS reactions of customers to various product, promotion, and pricing strategies can have profound impacts on marketing strategy and implementation but has not, to date, been fully appreciated.

EDI can also be used as part of an overall supplier management strategy to improve supplier performance and reduce the costs associated with materials acquisition (Walton & Marucheck, 1997). EDI plays an important role in integrating the supply chain, especially with international trading partners that require a great deal of documentation on frequent shipments.

EDI can allow partnership sales forecasting, which allows suppliers to receive the retailer forecast and point of sale (POS) demand as it occurs (Kahn & Mentzer, 1996; Mentzer, 1997). An EDI alliance can benefit all channel members by eliminating much of the need to do product forecasts by everyone except the retailer, which should lead to a reduction in overstocks and stock-outs and minimize uncertainty in the channel (Kahn & Mentzer, 1996).

Increasing sophistication of Internet technologies has led to the development of the electronic marketplace. Supply chain information systems that facilitate electronic commerce (e-commerce) and e-business applications will become more important as the electronic marketplace gains in popularity, security, and efficiency. Members of the supply chain need access to key business data at any time anywhere in the world, so supply chains will become more and more reliant on information storage that resides in networks rather than on the premises of a particular company (Andel, 1999).

Another type of software that benefits from a supply chain focus is enterprise resource planning (ERP). The major ERP vendors are all adding supply chain capabilities and functionality. ERP SCM systems are designed to help stream-line production schedules, slash inventories, find bottlenecks, respond quickly to orders, and provide final market information. Used properly, the software removes supply chain barriers by creating a seamless flow of supplies and fin-ished products (Willis, Klimek, & Hardcastle, 1998). To date, however, few companies have taken full advantage of the technology because the software assumes that information and decision making flow freely throughout the sup-ply chain, whereas in reality divisional, departmental, and company barriers are formidable (Willis et al., 1998).

These supply chain planning applications take in the data from ERP orders or past sales history and create forecasts to aid in planning (Minahan, 1998). ERP supply chain systems have helped large companies reduce inventories, shorten cycle times, lower costs, and improve overall supply chain manage-ment practices (Minahan, 1998). Although SCM requires companies to link with customers and suppliers via an information system, most ERP users have not finished connecting their own organizations, bringing into serious question the effectiveness of a supply chain ERP system. Only through true supply chain management can the full potential of these ERP systems be realized.

A consolidation is also occurring with logistics-related software. Ware-house software vendors are allying with ERP software vendors because buyers are shopping for a WMS that is already partnered with the buyer's brand of ERP software and existing database (Trunk, 1998). The advent of enterprise infor-mation systems and technology is providing global information better, faster, and with greater impact (Tyndall, 2000). There is no doubt these new supply chain planning offerings will make ERP systems more useful, better manage operations, improve customer satisfaction, and reduce overall costs. ERP sys-tems, however, cannot be used directly for supply chain management or to plan effectively across enterprises (Gould, 1998). They typically have been built with an internal perspective and rarely incorporate an external perspective. ERP systems are primarily transaction based and not constraint based, so they do not take into consideration whether all the resources needed to execute the plan are in place. Supply chain applications, on the other hand, tend to look for bottlenecks and allow users to adjust due dates or resources until they find a sat-isfactory schedule (Stein, 1997).

Barriers to Supply Chain Management Information Systems

Supply chain management systems require companies to link with custom-ers and suppliers through the use of information systems. Unfortunately, most companies have not been able to completely develop their own company-wide and unified information systems. Very few companies have been able to link financial management information systems with manufacturing automation systems, a critical link in developing a central system for supply chain management (Mullin, 1998). Further, these companies have not linked these systems to their marketing information systems.

One consequence of developing supply chain information systems is identifying the need to shift supply chain costs to another part of the supply chain. Forcing other members of the supply chain to incur expenses can sabotage efforts to become better partners. Shifting costs within a supply chain requires cooperation with other members of the supply chain to minimize their additional expenses and increase their willingness to share any reasonable additional costs (Witt, 1998).

Although information systems are critical for SCM, Gold, Dranove, Shanley, Shiber, and Hogan (1998) found that a gap exists between the strategic requirements of technology solutions and current abilities to meet them. Information technology remains an area of considerable visibility and dissatisfaction for the vast majority of companies. Although 87% of the companies view information systems as strategically important to supply chain management, systems that truly integrate and manage information across multiple enterprises and disparate systems are not yet commonplace (Gold et al., 1998).

Competing Supply Chains

In the future, extended supply chain communities will form open-ended, information system-enabled supply chains that will compete against one another (Donlon & Galli, 1998). Using many of the information systems discussed in this chapter could lead to the development of such supply chains. Donlon and Galli (1998) also focused on the ability of information systems to enable supply chains to become rapidly reconfigurable organizations, linked by Internet commerce software, that can come together at will. Quinn (1998) summarizes the long-term goal of an ideal supply chain through the use of information systems as

> one that embraces all of the partners in an overlapping manner, free from the rigid gaps that traditionally have separated parties in the business transaction, goods move seamlessly from sources to consumers, information flows immediately and openly up and down the chain, [and] activity in the funds conduit is triggered when the consumer actually purchases the product. (p. 39)

Supply chain information systems have become more essential with the rising importance of business-to-business commerce on the Internet, especially for firms in highly fragmented industries with complex products or services. The rate of change in the marketplace is increasing as the Internet becomes more ubiquitous as part of the business marketplace. E-commerce, e-procurement, e-fulfillment, and other Internet-enabled business processes benefit greatly from supply chain information systems.

Supply chain information systems are at the onset of becoming more prevalent in the business environment. Clearly, there is a trend for greater integration and information sharing within a supply chain that depends on the development of an effective and efficient supply chain information system.

Conclusions

Recent technology developments and trends in the current business environment suggest that the information systems discussed in this chapter are critical for a supply chain to function. Several issues of interest that have a direct and practical relevance have also emerged from this chapter. First, the business environment continues to emphasize more variety, better quality, greater reliability, and quicker response to a dynamic, customer-driven marketplace. Second, one of the best ways to serve this demanding market is to develop effective intrafirm information systems such as ERP, Intranet, WMS, TMS, MRP, and DRP. Third, interfirm information systems that go beyond the boundaries of the firm to the supplier/vendor, like EDI and the Internet, improve the efficiency of information flow.

Managers need to determine if the benefits of effective and efficient information flow mitigate the risks associated with developing partnerships with suppliers/vendors. This perspective can be further broadened to include those members of the supply chain who are willing to partner. It appears that managers have little choice but to embark on the path to developing information systems that enhance and integrate the supply chain if they are to continue to be competitive in the current rapidly changing, customer-driven business environment.

The information systems supply chain model offered in Figure 11.1 is just a beginning. It proposes a theory that needs both refinement and testing. The underlying premise of the model is the causal relationship between the current business environment and the need to develop intrafirm information systems, then interfirm information systems, that lead to supply chain information systems. Do companies have to go through all the stages as identified, or can they skip stages, as implied by the dotted arrows? Further research is needed to determine whether the model is applicable only to specific industries or is a more general model. Additional constructs may be needed to fully identify all the relevant software that is associated with supply chain information systems. There is further need to refine the factors that are identified to develop theoretical constructs that can be tested. Testing and validation of the information systems supply chain model, it is hoped, will benefit both the researcher and practitioner communities by further explicating the critical, valuable, and necessary role of information systems in a supply chain.

12

Financial Issues in
Supply Chain Management

JAMES S. KEEBLER

Executive Summary

This chapter describes the financial implications of supply chain decisions, trends in supply chain costs, a financial model for evaluating
investments, and issues of concern for financial and supply chain
management.

This chapter will

- Examine the issues of supply chain constituencies
- Look at the significance and trends of logistics costs relative to the U.S.
  economy
- Describe the general structure of business accounting models, known as
  the profit and loss statement and the balance sheet
- Point out the implications of supply chain decisions for the financial performance of the firm
- Review historical approaches to logistics financial analysis and related
  measurement issues
- Discuss new technologies that enable improvements, if not in measurement then in data capture
- Examine key industry initiatives that are driving improved financial performance within and across companies

These discussions lead to the conclusions that

- Supply chain activities have a major impact on the capabilities and profitability of the supply chain and its member firms
- Supply chain activities affect the profit and loss statements, balance sheets, and costs of capital
- Significant opportunities exist for the competent supply chain manager to reduce expenses, generate better returns on invested capital, and improve cash flows
- Controlling supply chain expenses can improve profit margins
- Reducing the level of assets (both current and fixed) can improve returns on assets
- Continuing to shorten cycle times can enhance cash flows
- Superior supply chain performance can also produce the leverage and competitive advantage to increase revenues and the supply chain's share of market
- Traditional accounting techniques do not provide accurate and timely information that informs the financial aspects of supply chain trade-off decisions
- Activity-based costing is not widely employed
- The potential benefits of improved supply chain management are stymied by the absence of activity-based financial data and the inability to link performance measurement with cost
- The expanded use of activity-based costing seems to offer the mechanism to remedy this deficiency
- Improved collaboration between the finance and the other business and supply chain functions is necessary to facilitate the process to develop activity-based costing
- This collaboration should help to overcome the seemingly widespread inability of supply chain managers to articulate the costs and benefits of supply chain activities

Capitalizing on these opportunities requires the ability to plan for and measure supply chain performance and to effectively communicate performance implications in financial terms. The supply chain manager's ability to articulate the financial implications of exchanges between firms will become more important in the future.

Introduction

Customer value and satisfaction are important ingredients in the business formula for success. No one business function alone can create superior value for customers. All departments must work together in this important task. Each company department can be thought of as a link in the company's value chain (Porter, 1985). That is, each department carries out value-creating activities to design, produce, market, deliver, and support the firm's products. Marketing managers pay attention to understanding customer needs, understanding the company's ability to satisfy them, and creating revenues to sustain future growth and profitability. Logistics managers historically have focused their time and attention on three core functions of business operations: inventory policy and practice, facility location and design, and transportation of materials and products (Ballou, 1993). Financial managers strive to obtain borrowed funds at the lowest cost, to select projects that offer the best returns, to balance the financial risks taken with investor expectations of returns, and to keep the business liquid. The firm's success depends not only on how well each department performs its work but also on how well the activities of various departments are coordinated.

Today, the successful supply chain organization is shifting from a *single-firm cost focus* on inventories, facilities, and transportation to a *multi-enterprise focus* on cycle time compression, systemwide cost reduction, and improved value for end customers (Langley & Holcomb, 1992). Having satisfactory or even excellent products and services no longer guarantees a competitive advantage in today's marketplace. Successful companies find that they must also establish supply chain partnerships to reduce costs and complement their product portfolios with value-adding relationships (Battaglia, 1994).

This chapter deals with the financial issues and opportunities confronting executives in supply chain environments. It will first briefly examine the issues of supply chain constituencies, then look at the significance and trends of logistics costs relative to the U.S. economy. It will describe the general structure of business accounting models, known as the profit and loss statement and the balance sheet, and illustrate the financial impact of supply chain decisions using the du Pont model. A brief review of the historical approaches to logistics financial analysis and related measurement issues will be presented. The chapter will then discuss new technologies that enable improvements in data capture, as well as key industry initiatives that are driving improved financial performance within and across companies.

Financial Issues of Supply Chain Constituencies

The management of every business wrestles with a common problem: How do we allocate the resources required to effectively and efficiently meet the expectations of our various constituencies? Those needs and expectations vary by constituent. Owners and investors desire reasonable rates of return given the level of risk they assume compared with alternative opportunities. Employees need and expect to be adequately compensated and rewarded for their contributions to the success of the firm. Customers require multiple values from the products and services they purchase. Resellers of the firm's products expect help in marketing and managing their activities. Suppliers expect timely payment for goods and services provided. The community expects socially responsible behavior, whatever the costs to the firm. Of course, government expects its share of the economic profits, as well as regulatory compliance. Ultimately, every enterprise must satisfy and manage these expectations of multiple constituents. The challenge for supply chain managers is to seek out ever-improving ways to satisfy all these constituencies.

Manufacturing, wholesaling, and merchandising firms commit a significant amount of their spending to getting their products to market, or satisfying the "place" utility of their marketing mix. Several studies have found that order processing, transportation, warehousing, and inventory carrying costs of manufacturing and merchandising companies total about 25% of their value-added expenses (Ballou, 1992). The end consumer of a product often pays a multiple of the manufacturer's cost to make the product because of the added costs of middlemen in the supply chain. This works only if the end consumers appreciate the value added by these intermediaries. Management and control of the accumulated supply chain costs are essential to the competitiveness of each supply chain participant. In other words, supply chain managers must be mindful that added costs should produce added value for the supply chain's consumer. Otherwise, costs must be reduced within the supply chain. Because logistics costs, and especially transportation and inventory costs, are a large component of supply chain expense, it is helpful to understand how the U.S. economy has been performing in this area.

Trends in Logistics Costs: The Macro View

Expenditures of the U.S. business logistics system include several costs: the carrying costs of inventory (i.e. interest, taxes, depreciation, obsolescence, and insurance), warehousing costs, transportation costs, and logistics administration costs. Cass Information Systems has maintained a database of U.S. logistics costs since 1977. In the last 20 years, the Gross Domestic Product (GDP) has increased from $2.03 trillion to $8.51 trillion, unadjusted for inflation (see Table 12.1). At the same time, total business logistics systems costs have risen from $277 billion to $898 billion. Between 1977 and 1993, as a percentage of GDP, logistics costs declined from 13.7% to 10.2%, reflecting productivity gains in the reduction of relative inventory levels and lower relative transportation costs (see Table 12.1).

Table 12.1 The Cost of the Business Logistics System in Relation to Gross Domestic Product[a]

Year	GDP ($ Trillions)	Values of All Business Inventory	Inventory Carrying Rate (%)	Inventory Carrying Costs	Transpor- tation Costs	Adminis- trative Costs	Total U.S. Logistics Costs	Logistics as % of GDP
1977	2.03	473	24.4	115	151	11	277	13.7
1978	2.29	549	26.8	147	173	13	333	14.5
1979	2.56	649	29.9	194	193	16	403	15.7
1980	2.78	717	31.8	228	241	18	460	16.5
1981	3.12	769	34.7	267	228	20	515	16.5
1982	3.24	776	30.8	239	222	18	479	14.8
1983	3.51	776	27.9	217	243	18	478	13.6
1984	3.90	841	29.0	244	268	20	532	13.6
1985	4.18	865	26.9	233	274	20	527	12.6
1986	4.42	866	25.6	222	281	20	523	11.8
1987	4.69	900	25.7	231	294	21	546	11.6
1988	5.05	969	26.6	257	313	23	593	11.7
1989	5.44	1,030	28.1	289	329	25	643	11.8
1990	5.75	1,071	27.2	291	351	26	668	11.6
1991	5.92	1,060	24.9	264	355	25	644	10.9
1992	6.24	1,072	22.7	243	375	25	643	10.3
1993	6.56	1,106	22.2	245	396	26	667	10.2
1994	6.95	1,163	23.4	272	420	28	720	10.4
1995	7.27	1,249	24.9	311	445	30	786	10.8
1996	7.66	1,285	24.4	314	467	31	812	10.6
1997	8.11	1,330	24.5	326	503	33	862	10.6
1998	8.51	1,368	24.5	334	529	35	898	10.6

SOURCE: Adapted from *A look back in anger at logistics productivity* (10th annual State of Logistics Report), p. 6, Delaney, Copyright 1999 by Robert V. Delaney/Cass Logistics. Reprinted with permission.

a. Dollar amounts are in billions of dollars, except for GDP

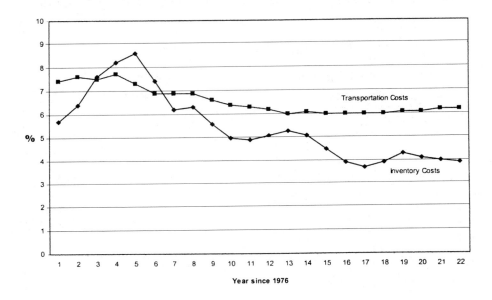

Figure 12.1. Changes in Inventory and Transportation Costs as a Percentage
of GDP

Although continuous improvement in the cost of logistics as a percentage of
GDP has occurred for many years since 1977, logistics cost productivity veered
off in the wrong direction in 1994. Higher interest rates, freight costs, and
inventory levels were to blame (Bradley, 1995). Since the 1992 low of 10.2% of
GDP, logistics costs have ranged upward to 10.8% and flattened out at 10.6%
for 1996, 1997, and 1998. The difference between the 10.2% rate and succeed-
ing higher rates represents a cumulative loss of more than $16 billion in logis-
tics productivity per year since 1992 (Delaney, 1999).

Major reductions in inventory relative to GDP have occurred since 1981,
when the prime interest rate was at an all-time high. When we look at the
changes in total transportation and inventory costs graphically, it appears that
productivity improvements have bottomed out (see Figure 12.1).

Are further cost reductions possible? A concern could be raised that the economic value of logistics to the macro supply chain is not increasing. How does
the individual firm plan for and evaluate the reductions in its logistics costs?
How does the *individual firm* meet the economic claims of its various constituencies, reduce its logistics costs, and achieve acceptable profitability and
returns on investment?

The Income Statement is the Basis for the Profit Margin Model

Net Sales

- Cost of Goods Sold

= Gross Margin (Profit)

- Operating Expenses

= Net Profit

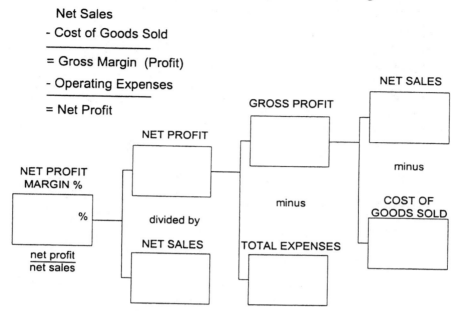

Figure 12.2.   Margin Management

Three Paths to Economic Success: The Micro View

There are basically three paths that an enterprise can take to manage its profitability and rate of return: margin management, asset management, and financial management.

Margin management is concerned with the revenue streams generated from sales, less the cost of goods and services provided by suppliers, and less the firm's selling and other operating expenses. The result is net profit. The marketing and R&D functions are concerned with supplying the right products and services for present and future customers. Their actions primarily influence company revenues and incoming cash flows. Although top management is concerned with the absolute amount of revenue dollars, margin management focuses on net profit divided by sales, which equals net profit margin. The income statement is the financial document that brings these data together (see Figure 12.2).

Asset management is concerned with the investments made to produce the revenues of the company. These include cash, accounts receivable, inventory, and other current and fixed assets (fixed assets include facilities, equipment,

The Balance Sheet is the Basis for the Asset Turnover Model

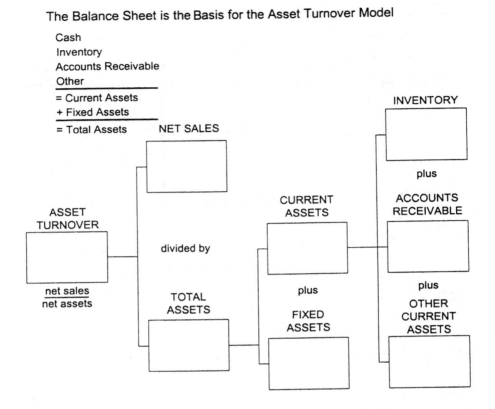

Figure 12.3.   Asset Management

and hardware) that are used in the business to generate its income. The productivity of these assets is an important managerial concern. As an important measure of enterprise productivity, the asset turnover measure is computed by dividing the value of sales generated for the period by end of period total assets (see Figure 12.3). The balance sheet is the financial statement that captures these data.

Financial management is concerned with the source of funds used to conduct the business (i.e., debt, equity, or retained earnings) and the capital structure relationship of debt to equity employed. Because the cost of capital and associated risks vary by source of funding, financial management is focused on achieving balance between debt and equity to provide an acceptable amount of financial risk and leverage to achieve targeted returns on equity. The proportion of equity and debt on the balance sheet (see Figure 12.4) determines the risk/leverage strategy of the firm. The greater the use of debt, the greater the financial leverage and the greater the risk to stockholders, who take a back seat to lenders in claims on assets should the company liquidate.

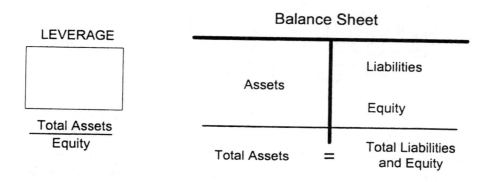

Figure 12.4. Financial Management

The du Pont Model

F. Donaldson Brown created a useful tool for today's supply chain executive,
known as the du Pont model, or the strategic profit model, while he was working for E. I. du Pont de Nemours & Co.'s Treasurer's Department in 1914
(Chandler, 1962). The financial analysis technique Brown used involved tying
together the profit and loss statement and the balance sheet so that changes in
working capital could be associated with changes in sales (see Figure 12.5).
Brown's creation provided du Pont executives with a consistent methodology
with which to evaluate each operating unit's performance, locate sources of
deficiencies, and prepare and adjust budgets and forecasts.

The du Pont model is a reliable tool to aid supply chain managers in determining the outcome of project ideas (Cavinato, 1989). Using this model, financial simulations are easy to construct that reveal the impact of possible supply
chain decisions on the firm's financial performance.

Supply chain executives often have responsibility for a significant portion of
the costs of goods sold and operating expenses, and, therefore, have a major
impact on margin management. Decisions and expenditures associated with
procurement, inbound transportation, production planning, and materials management are directly related to the net profits of the firm. Supply chain executives have responsibility for a sizable array of assets—inventories, facilities,
handling equipment, transportation equipment, and computer and communications systems—used in the operation of the business. Their decisions on asset

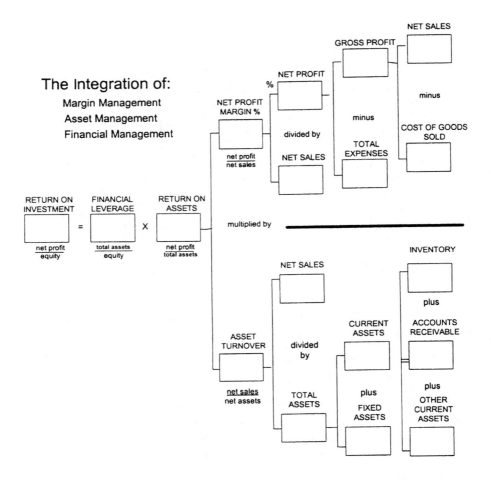

Figure 12.5.   The du Pont Model

acquisition, utilization, replacement, and disposal affect the rate of asset turnover.

The ability of the supply chain executive to perform financial analysis affecting supply chain decisions is critical in competing for funds and adding value to the firm and the supply chain. The supply chain executive must be able to implement the often-competing strategies of cost minimization, value-added maximization, and control/adaptability enhancement (Speh & Novack, 1995). This requires the use of financial tools.

An Illustration of the du Pont Model

An example using the du Pont model can easily illustrate the impact of supply chain management decisions on the profitability and market value of the

Base Case

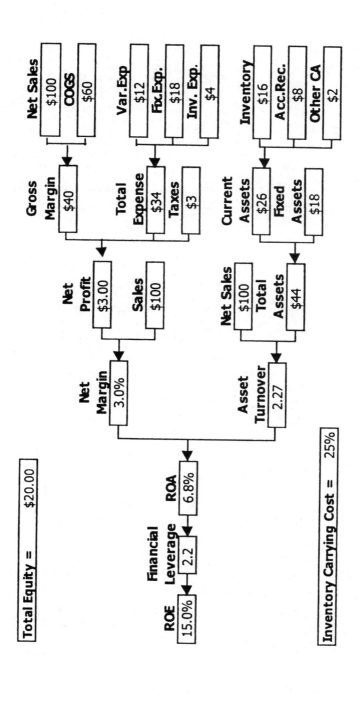

Figure 12.6.   Illustration of the du Pont Model

Reduce Inventory and Receivables and Maintain Debt

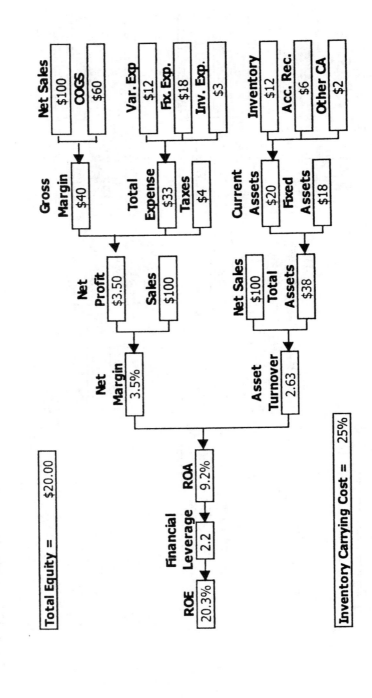

Figure 12.7.   Illustration of the du Pont Model

Reduce Inventory and Receivables and Lower Debt

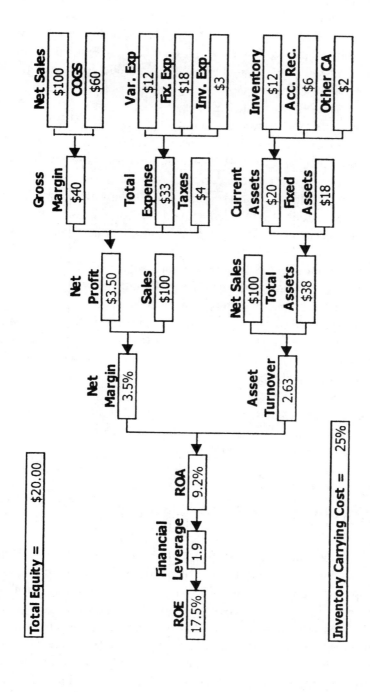

Figure 12.8. Illustration of the du Pont Model

firm (see Figure 12.6). A hypothetical company has net sales of $100 million and a gross margin of $40 million. We can identify the costs of carrying inventory to be $4 million within the total fixed and variable expenses of the business. The firm produces a net profit margin of 3%. This company held an inventory worth $16 million and carried accounts receivable averaging $8 million. Net current and fixed assets totaled $44 million, producing an asset turnover ratio of 2.27. Because return on assets was only 6.8%, the company chose to risk a high amount of debt financing relative to equity so it could generate a stockholder-required 15% return on equity.

The firm reduced average inventory levels by 25% and improved billing practices, which resulted in a 25% reduction in accounts receivable. These actions eliminated $6 million in current assets on the balance sheet and improved the asset turnover ratio to 2.63. Because inventory carrying costs were 25%, these actions also reduced inventory expense by $1 million on the income statement. At a 50% tax rate, an additional $500,000 net profit was realized, improving the net profit margin to 3.5%. Taken together, these supply chain decisions improved the firm's return on assets from 6.8% to 9.2%. The firm's return on equity jumped to 20.3% (see Figure 12.7).

The chief financial officer recognized the opportunity to restructure the balance sheet and reduce the level of risk to stockholders. Applying the $6 million in cash freed up by the supply chain decisions to debt reduction reduced the leverage factor from 2.2 to 1.9. The return on equity jumped from 15% to 17.5%. Risk to the stockholders went down, and return on investment went up (see Figure 12.8).

Supply chain decisions affect the firm's capital structure, risk level, cost structure, profitability and, ultimately, market value. Supply chain management should receive boardroom attention.

Financial Focus of the Supply Chain Executive

It was not long ago that operations performance was measured in strictly negative terms, such as costs over budget, damaged goods and shortages, late or missed shipments, and stock-outs (Barks, 1989). Increasingly, firms have begun to appreciate how improved supply chain performance produces increases in sales, productivity, and profits. No longer is supply chain management focused only on internal operational activities and measures. Economic measures, *both internal and external*, are increasingly used to justify, judge, and reward the supply chain organization (Koota & Takala, 1998). There are three areas of financial focus in which the supply chain executive must demonstrate competency: expense control, capital budgeting, and cash flow generation.

Expense Control

Expense control goes beyond merely managing expenses to the constraints of the budget. Expense control requires a deliberate and continuous search for more efficient ways of getting value-added work performed while eliminating non-value-added activities. Some companies naively install computers and other technologies to automate and speed up outdated business practices. The power of computers and technology should be used to "reengineer" the work, to abandon inferior yet institutionalized ways of working, and to create better practices and processes that better align with customer needs (Hammer, 1990).

Capital Budgeting

Supply chain executives must understand capital budgeting techniques, including their advantages and disadvantages, to contribute effectively to investment decision making. They must speak the language of finance. They must know which acceptable methods of investment evaluation will best sell their proposals. Several capital budgeting techniques can be used simultaneously on a single investment proposal (Byrne, 1992). Decision makers must consider the amount and timing of cash outflows and cash inflows, as well as the cost of capital or some internal hurdle rate of return. Some firms use the simple payback method of evaluation or the benefit-cost ratio (Pegels, 1991). More sophisticated techniques, such as the internal rate of return method or net present value method, consider the time value of money in the analysis. These discounted cash flow methods are more accurate and practical than payback or benefit-cost techniques, and they should be used for supply chain investment decisions (Cavinato, 1990b). Evidence indicates that the financial community prefers the net present value method (Brealey & Meyers, 1991). It should be the preferred method of investment valuation for the supply chain manager.

An extensive survey of logistics professionals revealed several focus areas that are central to successful logistics performance (Perry, 1991). The number one focus area was found to be asset productivity, which requires good capital budgeting. Supply chain managers should remember that only cash flows are relevant in capital budgeting, not accounts payable or receivable. Using the net present value formula can become routine, but forecasting cash flows can be a hazardous occupation. Perhaps this is why capital budgeting has been left to the financial managers, and also why supply chain managers must understand cash flow issues.

Cash Flow Generation

Cash flows of the firm can be improved as a result of many business practices. Historically, accounting departments attempted to improve working capital by aggressively collecting accounts receivable from customers while simultaneously delaying payments to suppliers. Such behavior rarely produces any net benefit across the supply chain (Rafuse, 1996).

Today, companies are evaluating managers on their ability to turn products into cash faster (i.e., "turbo cash flow") (Cavinato, 1990a). Tying up cash in the supply chain in the form of inventories is in competition with a chief financial officer's opportunity to invest that money elsewhere. A key to the notion of a cash cycle is to view the entire logistics, manufacturing, and sales process across the supply chain with regard to what it means for cash flow. Upper management wants to speed up the cash flow cycle in the areas of purchasing, materials management, production, distribution, and sales. More attention is paid to inventories, processing times, transportation costs, terms of sale, and credit terms.

An effective cash flow strategy reduces the level of inventory and frees up the cash committed to those assets throughout the supply chain. A significant generator of positive cash flow has been the systemwide reduction in inventory levels caused by compression in cycle times. An asset, like inventory, is a use of funds. A "permanent" reduction in the level of inventory frees up cash and improves asset productivity.

Care must be taken in how that inventory reduction is accomplished. Just-in-time (JIT) manufacturing techniques have become a "best practice" of manufacturers in most industries, but savings in inventory investments associated with JIT practices can be more imagined than real. The basis for this argument has been that a downstream manufacturer merely displaces its inventory holding requirements to upstream suppliers, thereby decreasing its own costs while increasing supplier costs. Even with coordination throughout the supply chain, the benefits of JIT might not be realized unless financing and operational decisions are addressed. When costs are fixed and cash flow changes do not accompany changes in production scheduling, savings from inventory reductions are often overestimated (Chikara & Weiss, 1995).

There is evidence that cash flows are being improved by the use of electronic data interchange (EDI). Also referred to as electronic commerce (e-commerce), this paperless form of computer-to-computer exchange, much of which is transacted via the Internet, can be used in conjunction with buyers' and sellers' banks to transfer funds. Edibank was formed in 1994 to accomplish this (Orr, 1996). Automated freight payment software is available to preaudit, summarize, batch, and pay carriers by electronic check on a scheduled basis (Cooke, 1996). To offset the faster cash outflow, shippers receive discounts from carriers in exchange for fast payment. This practice reinforces the "partnering" relationship between the parties in the supply chain.

A study of distributors on the allocation of credit extended along industrial supply chains and its consequences for supply chain performance found that only 1% of distributors charged interest for credit given to customers and only 5% were charged interest for credit taken (Neal, 1994). Only 12% of the respondents offered more generous price discounts when customers did not take credit. Only 5% received bigger discounts when they did not take credit from suppliers. These results suggest that, in these supply chains, credit provisions are a key factor in supplier choice among distributors and their customers, and that suppliers often finance their customers' transactions through the extension of "free" credit. Other supply chains and industries might have more restrictive credit terms to reduce their "product-to-cash" cycle, thereby improving cash flows.

Cash flow is affected by terms of sale. Time and place of payment are factored into FOB negotiations. Trading firms agree who should arrange inland freight, ports, ocean/air, duties and clearances, and final deliveries. As with the cost of inventory, dollars tied up in a shipment represent either a lost opportunity for those funds or an interest cost. Buying and selling companies often have different capital costs, which raises the possibility of improving supply chain performance by having the company with the lowest cost of capital own the goods for as long a period as possible.

Cash forwarding is a program that allows firms to fund expansion by improving cash flow and quickly turning shipments into cash. A financial organization acts as a factor, financing both domestic and export shipments by purchasing those receivables, at a discount, eliminating the seller's extension of credit terms and their incurring payment delays from letters of credit (Davis, 1998).

Lead time reductions affect cash flows. Many firms systematically work on controlling and reducing lead times and have achieved impressive results. An economic evaluation of lead time reduction should examine the impact on future cash flows across all business functions, or at the organizational level, not just the product level (Wouters, 1991).

So far, we have seen that supply chain costs are a significant factor in the economic performance of the business enterprise and the supply chain. We have reviewed financial statements and a financial model that easily describes the economic implications of supply chain plans and actions. We have acknowledged a business-wide and supply chain-wide reduction and containment of logistics costs relative to the GDP. Would it be logical to think that a large part of the potential savings in supply chain costs already has been achieved? On the contrary, studies show that tremendous opportunity remains, yet even leading edge companies have not begun to prospect for the gold.

A Gold Mine of Opportunity Left Unmined

Inefficiencies in the supply chain can waste as much as 25% of operating costs. Companies considered to be best practice organizations in moving product to market enjoy a 45% supply chain cost advantage over their median competitors. Their order-cycle time is half that of their competition, their inventory days of supply are 50% less, and they meet their promised delivery dates 17% more often than the competition (Quinn, 1998).

Key Performance Areas Are Not Being Measured

The capability to do functional and process assessments and to benchmark best practices is an essential business competency, according to a report by the Global Logistics Research Team (1995). This same report claims that measurement information has become more available in firms between 1989 and 1995. The authors reported that as recently as 1995, however, many key performance areas were not being measured universally. Half of the asset management measures, specifically ROA, ROI, and ABC inventory classification, were not available in 12-19% of the firms. The seventeen "supply chain cost" measures used were

1. Total cost,
2. Cost per unit,
3. Cost as a percentage of sales,
4. Inbound freight,
5. Outbound freight,
6. Administrative,
7. Warehouse order cost,
8. Direct labor,
9. Comparison of actual versus budget,
10. Cost trend analysis,
11. Direct product profitability,
12. Customer or customer segment profitability,
13. Inventory carrying,
14. Cost of returned goods,
15. Cost of damage,
16. Cost of service failures, and
17. Cost of backorders.

Only five of these measures were found to be available in at least 90% of the firms. Availability of key "cost" measures—like "inbound freight" at 75.8% availability, "inventory carrying" at 81.8%, cost of "returned goods" at 70.6%, and "cost of a backorder" at 33.3% availability—indicates that these measures are absent in 20% or more of the firms. These findings demonstrate a continuing challenge and opportunity for firms to install adequate performance measurement within the enterprise (Global Logistics Research Team, 1995). The study failed to inquire about cash flow measures.

Another study (Novack, Langley, & Rinehart, 1995) surveyed 396 logistics managers and concluded the following:

> Most of these executives indicated that they measure the costs of traditional logistics activities as well as measure the logistics service, such as product availability. They also indicated that a strong relationship exists between logistics service levels and their firms' revenues. Although not as strong, a relationship also exists between logistics costs and firm profits. Even though these relationships were identified to exist, the logistics executive respondents were really not able to quantify these relationships. Even though they believe logistics adds value to their firms' output, these logistics executives said they were not able to quantify this value. (p. 84)

These studies indicate four significant findings:

- There is great opportunity for supply chain cost reduction.
- There is an insufficiency of information and measurement.
- There is widespread inability to articulate the cost-benefit of supply chain management.
- Many of the savings cross supply chain corporate boundaries.

Tools Are Not Being Used, and Financial Interfaces Are Weak

A study conducted to examine overall business performance prescribed quantitative methods in two categories: financial measurement methods and engineered physical measures. The study concluded that the weakness of modern measuring systems often lies in a measurement gap between an economist's and an engineer's approach (Andersson & Storhagen, 1989).

Another study fully detailed operational and financial measures of productivity, utilization, and performance for all the functional logistics activities (Byrne & Markham, 1991). It is remarkable that, given the tools available, more progress has not been achieved in integrating supply chain and financial measures of performance. We have not seen the increased use of financial measures of supply chain performance that would have been expected, given the level of normative literature published in the last few years (Keebler, Mandrodt, Durtsche, & Ledyard, 1999).

A study exploring strategic planning issues reported an interesting finding regarding cross-functional interfaces during the planning process. The greatest amount of interface by the marketing department was found to be with the finance department during the planning process. The same condition was found for the manufacturing function—its greatest amount of interface was also with the finance function. Logistics *staffs*, however, were found to interface, in order, with marketing, MIS, manufacturing, and then finance during the planning process. Logistics *operational units* reported most interfaces with marketing, MIS, finance, and then manufacturing (Cooper, Innis, & Dickson, 1992). These findings suggest inadequate integration directly between the logistics and financial functions for strategic planning purposes.

Interest in Finance Has Waned

For many years, the annual survey of Council of Logistics Management (CLM) members conducted by The Ohio State University reported that logistics managers, if given the opportunity to return to college for 90 days, would select a curriculum topic in finance. In recent years, the survey shows that the preference for additional knowledge of finance slipped out of first position. In 1997 only 14% of the respondents selected finance as their preference (La Londe & Masters, 1997). This suggests that managers of the supply chain process are not as interested as they used to be, and perhaps should be, in developing financial skills.

Implications for Supply Chain Partners

Meanwhile, it is necessary that the supply chain executive understand the impact of capital structure and sources of funds on the firm *and the supply chain* in order to sell appropriate investment proposals. These investment decisions can help facilitate the quality of exchange between the firm and its supply chain partners. One obvious outcome of a change in cost structure for the firm is a change in the price it charges for its outputs. Financing a capital investment in supply chain productivity through the use of low-cost money might allow the firm to pass along savings in the form of lower prices. Previous research has shown, however, that executives do not believe that external customers react to improvements in operations productivity or operations cost decreases (Speh & Novack, 1995). The rationale for this might be that operations cost reductions are not passed on in the form of price reductions to external customers but used, instead, to satisfy the needs of internal customers.

A counterargument to the view that profits generated by operations improvements are typically contained within the firm can be found in the growth of "gainsharing" between companies and third-party logistics providers to which they outsource their logistics operations (Richardson, 1997). Under gainsharing, as the business partners implement improvements that result in lower costs, both share the savings in an equitable manner. This changes the behaviors between the partners, from a customer trying to bargain down price and a supplier focused on cost reductions to avoid or defer price increases, to collaborative, supply chain behaviors where gains from productivity and cost improvements are shared. An accurate understanding of activity and process costs is a requisite for implementing gainsharing programs. It is not clear what benefits pass to the customer from the shipper and third-party provider's gainsharing. A case could be made to include the customer in these gainsharing agreements between the supplier and third-party provider, especially because they affect the nature of services provided.

Technologies Enabling Financial Improvements

Technology improvements in computers and telecommunications provide firms with increased capability for standardization and automation of data capture, storage, and transmission. Accessibility to data within a company, particularly in those environments where systems are integrated or operate on a single enterprise-wide resource planning system (ERP), is a critical requirement of decision makers. The implementation of electronic data interchange (EDI) between companies over the last 15 years has greatly reduced cycle times and allowed the acceleration of cash flows.

A study reporting supply chain savings potential in the North American automobile industry through the use of EDI concluded that the savings could be $1 billion annually (Anonymous, 1996). The Automotive Industry Action Group based this estimate on an 18-month project with Ford, General Motors, and Chrysler and their second- and third-tier suppliers. Order error rates were cut 72%. Lead times were reduced 58%. Inventory turns improved 20%. Cycle time compression is one of the major emerging logistics strategies that have significant financial impact on supply chain performance (La Londe & Masters, 1994).

Decision support systems provide a capability to model present and alternative business practices to evaluate their financial implications. They include simple input-output models (van der Meulen & Spiverman, 1985), fourth-generation language simulation models (Harrington, Lambert, & Sterling, 1992), data development analysis models (Kleinsorge, Schary, & Tanner, 1989), and total cost/value models (Cavinato, 1992). One of the major issues highlighted in almost every financially oriented logistics model is the reliance on standard costing techniques and the deficiencies of the traditional accounting systems.

Outdated cost accounting and management control systems are a major obstacle in the collection and relevance of logistics financial measures. They can distort measures of performance and fail to give complete and accurate information for decision making (Kaplan, 1984).

The Evolution of Supply Chain Costing

Limitations of traditional accounting systems have spawned efforts to develop supplementary approaches. The evolution of costing approaches can be traced beginning with direct product profitability (DPP) through activity-based costing (ABC), total cost of ownership (TCO), efficient consumer response (ECR), and supply chain costing (La Londe & Pohlen, 1996). These efforts at creating accurate and integrated cost measures were undertaken to increase the visibility of costs within the supply chain so that cost reduction opportunities could be identified and pursued. By making use of standard and engineered times and existing rate information, the supply chain costing approach considers activities across the firms in the supply chain.

There are two significant constraints. First, those firms that have not implemented activity-based costing cannot provide supply chain-related costs at the activity level. Second, the detailed level of information about process steps and costs of activities that must be shared by the enterprises requires a highly coordinated or integrated partner relationship between them. Such interfirm relationships are difficult and slow to develop. Ultimately, restructuring the supply chain to exploit efficiencies also requires a mechanism capable of identifying and equitably allocating costs and benefits between the partners as changes are implemented.

Direct product profitability (DPP) was an accounting system developed specifically for the grocery industry in the 1970s (Joint Industry Project on Efficient Consumer Response, 1994). Its objective was to calculate fully loaded product profitability. An improvement on gross margin costing, DPP determined profitability by not only subtracting the cost of goods from sales but also adding direct revenue and subtracting direct product costs. One major weakness of DPP was that it failed to recognize overhead and administrative expenses and, therefore, could not be used for total company costing purposes. DPP also required a great deal of supporting data about the physical characteristics of products that continually required updating.

Activity-based costing (ABC), which emerged in the 1980s, improved on DPP by recognizing both direct and overhead costs. ABC goes a step further by tracing the activity costs to objects consuming those activity costs. ABC analysis allows managers to pinpoint the activities, products, services, or customers consuming overhead resources. Examination of current business activities at this level allows for actual costs to be discovered, inefficient practices to be reengineered, and resources to be freed up for additional output or eliminated to effect cost savings. One suggestion for how to start the process to reduce costs and create value for the customer using ABC is to "staple yourself to an order" (Shapiro, Rangan, & Sviokla, 1992). Such a perspective on the order management system, experiencing the total sequence of handlings and internal interfaces of a customer transaction, provides great opportunity for identifying improvement opportunities. Knowing how much it costs just to process an order can be very enlightening.

Product and customer profitability analysis performed by firms using ABC has significantly altered management perceptions. One such study found that 20% of customers generated 225% of the profits, while 70% of the customers hovered around the break-even point. The remaining 10% of customers generated a 125% loss (Cooper & Slagmulder, 1991). Profitability analysis using ABC can focus management effort. High-cost products and customers can be targeted for corrective action. Applied broadly to supply chain management, ABC is helping companies finally understand their total costs (Barr, 1996).

A study involving 100 firms produced some interesting findings (Pohlen & La Londe, 1994). At that time, 38% of the firms reported implementing ABC, 14% decided against, and 19% had not considered ABC. The proposal to implement ABC was originated by finance in 48% of the companies and by logistics in only 4%. A later study reported that most firms have not implemented ABC and cannot provide logistics or supply chain related costs at the activity level (La Londe & Pohlen, 1996). The most recent study published by the Council of Logistics Management reports slow progress in the adoption of activity-based costing (Keebler et al., 1999). The research found that only 11% of those surveyed had implemented ABC for some aspect of their operations. Another 9% had an implementation underway. Twenty-four percent said they were considering the use of ABC. A disappointing 56% indicated they had no plans at all for ABC. The potential benefits of improved supply chain management are stymied by the absence of activity-based financial data and the inability to link performance measurement with cost.

Initiatives persist to advance the development of improved cost measurement practices. In the marketing literature, transaction cost analysis (TCA) has received considerable attention in the past decade (Rindfleisch & Heide, 1997). The "balanced scorecard" performance measurement system includes both financial and operational measures and allows executives to track progress toward multiple goals (Kaplan & Norton, 1993). This balanced scorecard language is appearing frequently in the business press. ABC repackaged is emerging now as a "cost and effect" initiative (Kaplan & Cooper, 1997). Cost and effect is based on the principles of ABC and examines how these principles and practices can be fully integrated with enterprise-wide systems, using "knowledge-age" tools to make real-time decisions.

Economic value added (EVA) is another initiative that allows companies to measure whether or not supply chain activities boost the bottom line (Cooke, 1995). EVA provides a broader perspective on the company's use and return on capital. A growing number of financial executives are using EVA and two other approaches—cash flow return on investment (CFROI) and total shareholder return (TSR)—to get a clear picture of the business unit's capital efficiency (Birchard, 1994).

Research and Managerial Implications

This investigation of financial issues in supply chain management has evoked many questions for further research. Why are financial measures not more widely used? Why has activity-based costing not become more widely adopted? To what degree is the supply chain manager involved in financial decisions of the firm? To what degree are financial evaluations used to measure supply chain activities, to justify new investments, and to identify and prioritize value-adding opportunities? How competent and confident are supply chain managers in their financial skills? What would their bosses say about that? What training is called for, and how should it be implemented? What is the appropriate interface between the financial function and the supply chain function? What conditions facilitate the exchange of cost and investment information between trading partners with the expectation that improvements will be made and shared? Are there industry differences in the financial competency of supply chain managers? Are there differences based on the company's position in the supply chain (i.e., steps removed from the consumer)? Does the choice of corporate strategy influence the financial competency of supply chain managers? Under what conditions does asset reduction via outsourcing improve the financial performance and market value of the firm? The research agenda is rich with opportunities.

The competency of supply chain managers in utilizing financial tools and techniques to plan, evaluate, decide, implement, and control activities within and between companies in the value chain is a critical antecedent for business success. What requirements should the firm place on its supply chain managers in this area? What benefits and success stories can be claimed through the use of activity-based costing? How do multiple firms collaborate in the financial analysis of the larger supply chain and evaluate what work gets done where, and how incremental costs and savings are shared? How is such an incentive established and maintained? How does a company ensure its successful participation in current supply chains and simultaneously position itself to influence future supply chains? What are the financial implications to partnering, strategic alliances, and outsourcing? Successful supply chain managers will have to address all these questions.

Conclusions

Supply chain activities have a major impact on the capabilities and profitability of the supply chain and its member firms. Supply chain activities affect the profit and loss statements, balance sheets, and the costs of capital. Significant opportunities exist for the competent supply chain manager to reduce expenses, generate better returns on invested capital, and improve cash flows. Controlling supply chain expenses improves profit margins. Reducing the level of assets (both current and fixed) improves returns on assets. Continuing to shorten cycle times can enhance cash flows. Superior supply chain performance can also produce the leverage and competitive advantage to increase revenues and the supply chain's share of market.

Traditional accounting techniques do not provide accurate and timely information that informs the financial aspects of supply chain trade-off decisions. Activity-based costing is not widely employed. The potential benefits of improved supply chain management are stymied by the absence of activity-based financial data and the inability to link performance measurement with cost. The expanded use of activity-based costing seems to offer the mechanism to remedy this deficiency. Improved collaboration between the finance and the other business and supply chain functions is necessary to facilitate the process to develop ABC. This collaboration should help overcome the seemingly widespread inability of supply chain managers to articulate the costs and benefits of supply chain activities.

The du Pont model provides a simple tool to facilitate the improved interfacing of the supply chain management and financial management functions. Its usage is recommended.

Asset reductions through outsourcing tactics should be aggressively pursued. Traditional control-through-ownership strategies are being displaced by control-through-relationship-management strategies. This suggests that future supply chain managers will have different roles than do traditional internal operations managers. Less emphasis on asset management will be required by the focal firm, displaced by more emphasis on the overall performance of local and extended supply chains. Even while there is a current, strong need for improving the financial skills of the supply chain manager, future needs for competencies beyond single-firm "accounting and control" will emerge. The ability of the supply chain manager to articulate the financial implications of transactions between firms will certainly increase in importance.

13

Customer Service in a Supply Chain Management Context

NANCY W. NIX

Executive Summary

This chapter describes elements of customer service management important to supply chain management (SCM), performance outcomes associated with customer service activities and their contribution to supply chain objectives, and customer responses to the outcomes of a firm's customer service activities. This chapter will

- Emphasize the importance of customer service as a means of delivering customer value through improved efficiency and effectiveness, and in turn contributing to increased customer satisfaction for both immediate and downstream customers in a supply chain
- Examine the role of customer service in SCM from three perspectives—as a management activity, as a set of performance outcomes, and in terms of customer responses to service outcomes
- Highlight the evolution in customer service research from an internal focus on management activity to an external focus on creating customer value
- Point out the importance of developing appropriate customer service strategies and highlight various approaches to strategy development, emphasizing key elements of strategy important in a supply chain management context
- Discuss the importance of customer segmentation to identify and deliver elements of customer service that are important to strategic customers

- Point out the importance of managing the customer service interface to enhance the quality of the relationship and facilitate information exchange with customers that can contribute to improved supply chain performance
- Differentiate between customer service performance outcomes as perceived and measured by the supplier and as perceived by the customer
- Highlight the contribution of perceived customer service outcomes to the creation of customer value and satisfaction

These discussions lead to the conclusions that

- To achieve supply chain objectives, customer service activities must be strategic in nature and must be designed based on an understanding of the service levels important to critical customers
- Important customer segments must be identified, and the requirements of those segments understood, for both immediate and downstream customers
- The impact of service levels on customers should be understood, and internal capabilities should be designed to deliver service levels that optimize the overall performance of the supply chain
- The quality of the customer interface is likely to influence the level of trust and openness of information exchange between firms, which can contribute to a better understanding of the customer's needs and improved performance of supply chain management activities
- It is important to measure customer service outcomes *as perceived by the customer* and to understand which performance outcomes are most valued by customers at various levels of the supply chain
- Customer service requirements and performance, as well as the influence of customer service levels on customer behavior, should be understood and monitored for both immediate and downstream customers in a supply chain
- Customer service is not the ultimate objective of supply chain management but rather an outcome of supply chain management that can create value for customers through improved efficiency or effectiveness
- Creating value for customers superior to that created by competition is expected to result in greater customer satisfaction and differential advantage, and to influence customers to behave in ways that improve the performance of the supply chain as a whole

Customer service is often cited as a key objective of supply chain management; however, only if service offerings create value for customers will they lead to behaviors that improve supply chain performance. To achieve this objective, it is important for supply chain managers to manage customer service strategically and develop supply chain capabilities to deliver services viewed as important by critical downstream customers.

Introduction

Customer service is frequently cited as an important objective of supply chain management (SCM). Ellram (1990) describes SCM as a means of maximizing "efficient use of resources in achieving the supply chain's customer service goals" (p. 13), while Stevens (1990) describes the aim of SCM as that of achieving "a balance between the goals of high customer-service and low inventory-investment/low unit-cost goals" (p. 25). Cooper and Ellram (1993) suggest that SCM can "help create a competitive advantage and greater profitability for the channel through coordinated attention to costs, better customer service, and lower inventories" (p. 14). There seems to be a consensus that SCM objectives include those of lower cost at specific levels of customer service or improved customer service. As described in Chapter 1, "SCM is concerned with improving both efficiency (i.e., cost reduction) and effectiveness (i.e., customer service) in a strategic context (i.e., creating customer value and satisfaction through integrated channel management) to obtain competitiveness that ultimately brings profitability."

Although the term "customer service" is used consistently to describe the objectives of SCM, little attention has been given to exactly what the role of customer service is in a supply chain context. To better understand this, it is first necessary to examine more broadly what is meant by customer service. Customer service has alternatively been described as (a) a process, a set of activities, or a function to be managed within the firm (i.e., order processing, invoicing, or handling customer complaints); (b) a performance outcome or measure (i.e., order fill rates, cycle time, percent on-time delivery); (c) a customer-related objective or outcome (i.e., customer perception of availability, quality, and timeliness) leading to customer value and satisfaction; or (d) a management philosophy (Ellram, La Londe, & Weber, 1989; Lambert & Stock, 1993; Langley & Holcomb, 1992; Mentzer, Gomes, & Krapfel, 1989). It is important to note that customer service is an operational function or outcome that contributes to the ultimate goal of customer value and satisfaction; thus, customer service is not the ultimate goal or objective. Only if the service provided is perceived as delivering value important to the customer is the ultimate goal of customer satisfaction and differential advantage achieved (Chapter 3).

Customer service has also been described as encompassing all points of contact between the customer and supplier (including delivery, pre- and post-sales service, technical support, and financial packages) (Stevens, 1990). In a supply chain context, the customer service interface plays a significant role. SCM requires the management of key processes such as customer relationship management, customer service management, demand management, and order fulfillment, which are focused on understanding and meeting the customer's requirements (Cooper, Lambert, & Pagh, 1997; Lambert, Stock, & Ellram,

1998). The customer focus associated with SCM has significant implications for the management of customer service activities and outcomes. In fact, one executive interviewed suggested that the impact of supply chain (management) is all related to customer service. This emphasizes the importance of customer service in successful implementation of SCM.

This chapter is not intended to provide a complete overview of customer service. Rather, the intent is to examine various approaches to customer service and the implications of these approaches for SCM. Because the implementation of SCM is focused on building long-term relationships with customers and suppliers aimed at creating customer value for the ultimate consumer (Chapters 1 and 3), a managerial philosophy oriented toward customer service is considered to be an element of a supply chain orientation. Thus, customer service as a management philosophy will not be addressed further in this chapter.

The issues considered in this chapter are reflected in two key questions: What are the key elements of customer service that are important in a supply chain management context? How do these elements differ from the traditional view of customer service when considered from a SCM perspective? To address these questions, customer service is examined from three different perspectives, which are highlighted in Figure 13.1. First, customer service as a *management activity* is examined and the trend away from an internal focus on customer service management toward a more strategic, customer-focused approach is highlighted. Second, customer service as a *performance outcome* and the potential contribution to SCM objectives of increased efficiency and effectiveness are discussed. Also highlighted here is the importance of differentiating between performance outcomes as perceived or measured by the supplier and performance outcomes as perceived by the customer. Third, the role of customer service in *managing the customer interface* to facilitate information exchange and enhance the quality of the relationship is highlighted. In this area, insights are drawn from services marketing literature in the areas of service quality and relationship marketing, and the influence of the customer service interface on customer satisfaction and behavior is highlighted. Each of these three areas is examined in terms of how it contributes to expected or desired *customer responses* (i.e., how do they contribute to creating customer value, satisfaction, and differential advantage that benefit the supply chain). Finally, managerial and research implications of considering customer service from a supply chain perspective are highlighted.

Defining Customer Service

The term "customer service" typically has been used to describe both marketing and logistics (or physical distribution) activities aimed at enhancing the

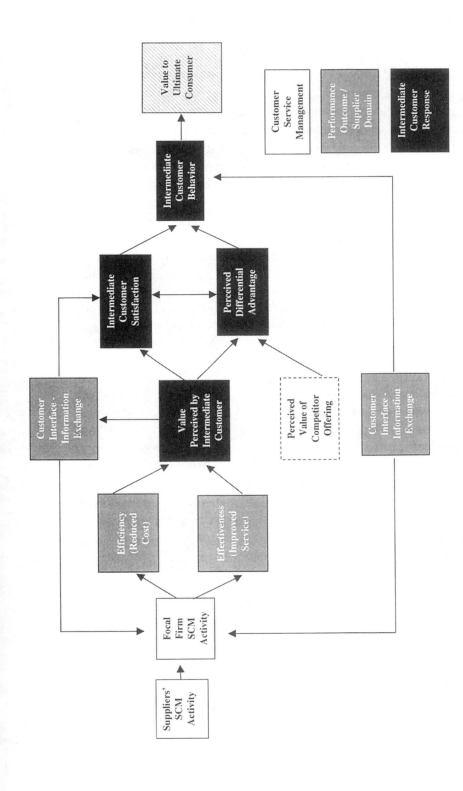

Figure 13.1. Customer Service in a Supply Chain Management Context

351

product offering or facilitating the exchange process between a supplier and the customer. From a marketing perspective, customer service is seen to include the elements of product design and maintenance, training, salesperson attitude and responsiveness, ease of customer interface with the company, guarantees, and price, in addition to the elements of logistics service. Logistics service, as a subset of overall customer service, includes elements associated with the delivery of products to meet customer requests or needs. Delivery reliability, product availability, timeliness or responsiveness, accuracy, and freedom from damage are important dimensions of logistics service (Mentzer et al., 1989; Rinehart, Cooper, & Wagenheim, 1989). Rinehart et al. (1989) note that customer service is the unifying factor for integrating marketing and logistics, and that the performance of both marketing and logistics activities creates the customer service output of the firm. Thus, customer service can be thought of as an integrative activity both within the firm and between firms within the channel.

The International Customer Service Association (ICSA) defines customer service as

> those functions within a business that have customer satisfaction as their responsibility and provide that satisfaction through the fulfillment of sales order demand and/or information needs. (Rinehart et al., p. 64)

Other definitions have focused more explicitly on the logistics or supply chain aspects of customer service. Langley and Holcomb (1992) cite a Council of Logistics Management study definition of customer service as "a process of providing significant value-added benefits to the supply chain in a cost-effective way" (p. 11). This study identified representative measures of logistical customer service as product availability, order cycle time, distribution system flexibility, distribution system information, distribution system malfunction, and post-sale product support. La Londe and Zinszer (1976) define customer service as

> those activities that occur at the interface between the customer and the corporation which enhance or facilitate the sales and use of the corporation's products or service. Therefore customer service is all of the things that a manufacturer does for a customer in moving a product from the end of the production line to the customer. (Manrodt & Davis, 1993, p. 58)

In these definitions, customer service is described as an *organizational process* or set of activities *within the firm*, focused primarily on facilitating the customer interface—delivering product, fulfilling customer orders, and providing information to customers—to enhance customer satisfaction. It is from this perspective that customer service management will be discussed and issues relevant to supply chain management will be highlighted.

Customer Service Management

Consistent with the organizational approach in the above definitions, much of the early work in customer service focused on the internal management and measures of customer service. From the 1960s to the late 1980s, physical distribution service (PDS) research was focused on (a) identification of the elements of PDS, (b) determination of cost effects of PDS, (c) normative discussions of the management and measurement of PDS, and (d) investigation of the impact of PDS on demand (Mentzer et al., 1989). Manrodt and Davis (1993) describe early work in customer service as very supplier oriented, with the focus predominantly on internal management and measurement, with very little emphasis on identifying and meeting the needs of the customer. Only in the 1980s and 1990s did researchers begin to focus on the creation of customer value or competitive advantage through customer service and customer satisfaction (Manrodt & Davis, 1993).

Langley and Holcomb (1992) note several trends in customer service related to this shift toward the creation of customer value. First, firms are becoming more proactive in their approach to providing value-creating services prior to, during, and after the product itself is delivered. Second, the emphasis on customer service is increasing in response to more demanding customers. Third, managing information is seen as the key to increasing levels of customer service. Fourth, there is a trend away from transactional relationships and toward long-term relationships with fewer suppliers. They suggest that with pressures to improve customer service increasing, those firms that are successful in doing so will achieve sustainable competitive advantage. With an increased focus on customer service as a means for creating value for customers and thus of acquiring competitive advantage, the development of an appropriate customer service strategy has become a much more significant aspect of customer service management within the firm.

Customer Service Strategy

Lambert and Stock (1993) note that a firm's marketing efforts can be derailed by inappropriate customer service policies or strategies. As these authors note, "what is the advantage of having a well-researched and needed product, priced to sell and promoted well, if customers cannot find it on the shelf at the retail level?" (p. 119). At the same time, providing services that customers do not need or want reduces corporate profits. Therefore, it is important to develop appropriate customer service strategies that enhance the firm's profitability. In the following discussion, five approaches to strategy development that help firms establish appropriate customer service policies are reviewed: (a) understanding customer reactions to product or service failures (i.e., consumer response to stock-outs), (b) analyzing cost/revenue trade-offs, (c) activity-based costing (ABC) analysis looking at the most profitable customers, (d) internal and external customer service audits, and (e) a competitive position matrix (Lambert & Stock, 1993).

An important element in determining appropriate customer service offerings is the customer's reaction to a product or service failure. For example, in the situation where a part or raw material is a critical component of a downstream customer's production process, a supplier firm's responsiveness to product failures may be critical to the customer's ability to meet the needs of the downstream consumer. In this case, the customer service strategy needs to include very responsive product maintenance and support. In a case where the product is not critical to the customer's process, a warranty that ensures that the product can be returned or repaired with no charge may be more appropriate. Likewise, appropriate levels of logistics service may be dependent on the consumer's reaction to the product not being available. Will the consumer go to another outlet to purchase the product, or wait until the product is available and come back? Or will the consumer simply purchase the competitor's product? If the consumer should purchase the competitor's product, would he or she continue to buy the competitor's product in the future, or would there only be a one-time loss of sales?

These types of questions about consumer responses to service failures have often been the basis for determining the most cost-effective customer service strategies. The idea behind this approach is to determine the optimum service levels based on both the cost of providing service and the cost of sales lost as a result of service failures. In a supply chain context, service costs and customer responses (i.e., cost of service failures) must be assessed across multiple firms, as well as at the level of the end consumer, to determine appropriate customer service strategies for the supply chain as a whole.

A second approach to customer service strategy has been to focus on cost/revenue trade-offs. Using this approach, the firm determines the cost to provide additional services to customers or consumers, then weighs that additional cost against the revenue increases expected as a result of that additional service. This approach requires an understanding of the customer or consumer's reaction to a particular service level or service offering to assess the potential impact on revenue. Additionally, the cost associated with providing the service and the profit contribution associated with the increased sales must be well understood to appropriately weigh the costs and benefits of a particular service offering. Utilizing this approach in a supply chain requires understanding both the costs and profitability across multiple firms that are associated with various levels of customer service provided to the end consumer.

ABC analysis is used to determine the most profitable product/customer segments and to target those segments for higher levels of customer service. This method is designed to provide the most profitable customers with service levels that ensure repeat business. In a supply chain context, this method might be used to determine the most strategic supply chain partners, and ABC analysis might be done jointly with those partners to determine the most profitable target consumer segments. Joint activities would be aimed at providing higher levels of service to those strategic target segments of end consumers that make the supply chain as a whole more profitable.

The customer service audit approach incorporates an external focus (customer segmentation and customer perceptions of services offered) with an internal focus (internal objectives, measures, integration, communication, and control). This approach, somewhat akin to the capabilities approach to competitive strategy (Day, 1994), is designed to identify the elements of service important to customers, examine the adequacy of the current offering in meeting the customers' needs, and implement policies that more effectively meet those needs. An important element of this approach is an assessment of customer satisfaction (i.e., determining how customers perceive current levels of service and whether they are satisfied with those services). In a supply chain context, the external audit would be focused on the end consumer and the internal audit would include an assessment of the capabilities of multiple firms in the supply chain engaged in delivering products and service to that ultimate consumer.

Finally, the competitive position matrix highlights the match between a firm's performance relative to competition and the importance customers attach to a given service. As in the customer service audit approach, an assessment is done to determine the services considered important by customers. An additional element in this approach is the assessment of the strength of the firm's service offering relative to that of the competition. For those services important to customers, a high relative performance rating indicates a major strength or competitive advantage and a low relative performance rating indicates a major weakness or competitive disadvantage. Thus, strategic opportunities can be identified and resources focused on improving relative performance in areas of high importance to customers. Given the overall objective of SCM of creating customer value to achieve both customer satisfaction and differential advantage, the competitive position matrix is particularly appropriate for developing strategies to direct SCM activities.

The traditional objectives of customer service strategy, such as ensuring optimum service levels to enhance the profitability of the firm, matching internal capability to external customer needs, and focusing on service offerings that provide competitive or differential advantage, are important in a supply chain context. It is important, however, to recognize that customer service strategy in a supply chain context must focus beyond the immediate customer-supplier relationship. In addition to the implications of customer satisfaction and customer response in the traditional customer-supplier relationship, the implications of customer service in facilitating the customers' ability to serve their downstream customers must also be considered. For example, a firm should optimize service levels to the intermediate customer firm based on implications for the downstream service provided to the ultimate consumer. Higher levels of responsiveness, while more costly at the level of the focal firm, may enable downstream customers to respond to changes in consumer markets more effectively, thus increasing market share or revenue for the supply chain as a whole. To be more effective, total supply chain capability (including upstream suppliers) must be matched to the needs of downstream customers. To achieve the SCM objectives of improved service to the ultimate consumer, customer service strategies must be developed for the supply chain as a whole. Research is needed to develop tools and techniques for developing, implementing, and evaluating such integrative strategies across firms within the supply chain.

Customer Segmentation

The ABC approach to strategy requires that differing levels of service be offered to different customer segments, based on their profitability to the firm. Another element to consider in segmenting customers is that the dimensions of customer service important to customers differ by situation. Rinehart et al. (1989) note that customer service is viewed differently by different members of a marketing channel. Customer service at the retail level may be viewed as a bundle of services beyond the core product, such as gift wrapping or home delivery, while distributors may focus on such physical elements of product delivery as availability and lead time. Even in a distributor setting, different combinations of technical or outcome versus functional or process aspects of service quality are important in different environments (Bienstock, Mentzer, & Bird, 1997). For example, in the case where demand is stable and additional information is not required about the product, the availability or reliable delivery of the product may be the most critical element. In another situation where demand is highly variable or products are particularly complex, the information exchange at the customer interface may be more important. Because the components of service that are important to customers differ in different situations, the ability of firms to segment customers and offer different bundles of services to different customers in response to their specific needs is important. In a supply chain context, the levels of service required and the importance of service interactions with strategic supply chain partners will also likely be greater than with less strategic channel members. Segmentation of consumers and tailoring of service interfaces and offerings to specific segments allows supply chain partners to more effectively focus resources to achieve specific SCM objectives.

Recognizing the importance of different elements of the customer service process, Manrodt and Davis (1993; Davis & Manrodt, 1991) differentiate between logistics service management (managing product flows) and service response logistics (managing the interaction between the customer and the organization). They suggest that firms must increasingly focus on the service process rather than just product design or delivery. The concept of service response logistics suggests that the delivery process itself must be designed and managed to be responsive to specific customer needs and deliver the desired benefits. Increasingly, the profitability of organizations will be determined by their ability to customize and coordinate the interactions between the firm and its customers to deliver those benefits desired by specific customer segments. The process of service delivery is an increasingly important component of customer satisfaction relative to the technical or core aspects of a product or service offering. Given the increased emphasis on customer relationships and customized solutions to unique problems, service response logistics or the design and management of the service delivery process is likely to become an increasingly important component of customer service management.

Gattorna, Chorn, and Day (1991) note that problems occur when different customers require different levels of service. For example, purchasers of high-volume, undifferentiated products may require quick delivery and low prices, whereas purchasers of highly differentiated, value-added, custom-made products may require higher levels of service. Because of these differences in requirements, there may be an incompatibility between the internal capability of the supplier and the service requirements of the customer, or the delivery requirements for different customers may require conflicting capabilities on the part of the supplier. In such cases, outsourcing to a third party that can act as an "adapter" and interface with the different systems in a compatible way may be a viable option. This third-party organization can tailor management of the service delivery process to meet the specific needs of customers (Gattorna et al., 1991). This also suggests that an important component of customer service strategy in a supply chain context may be the appropriate location of customer service activities with the supply chain partner most capable of effectively delivering the services required by specific customer segments.

The Customer Service Interface

The importance of long-term relationships, cooperation, information sharing, and trust in implementing SCM is widely recognized (Chapter 1). Because customer service activity is a critical interface between supplier and customer, the customer service interface has significant implications for relationship quality and exchange of information between two firms. At the interface, both the customer service management of the focal firm and the customer response to the service provided are important in determining the nature of the interaction (see Figure 13.1). Research in the area of services marketing, specifically in the areas of service quality and relationship marketing, offers useful insights toward understanding the role of customer service in enhancing customer relationships and influencing customer behavior, both particularly relevant in a supply chain context.

Service Quality

Research in service quality has focused predominantly on the process of service delivery in consumer-oriented service applications, such as retail banking, dry cleaning, and credit card companies. For service firms, delivering higher levels of service quality is seen as a strategy for achieving a stronger position in the marketplace. Service quality is conceptualized as a global judgment or attitude, similar to satisfaction, that stems from a consumer's comparison of what service firms should offer (expectations) and their perceptions of the actual performance of the firm.

The dimensions of service quality seen as important to customers include both tangible and intangible aspects. Tangible components include the appearance of customer service personnel and facilities. Intangible components include the process components of the service encounter, such as (a) ability to perform promised services accurately and dependably, (b) willingness to help customers and provide prompt service, (c) knowledge and courtesy of employees, and (d) attentiveness to customers (Parasuraman, Zeithaml, & Berry, 1988). The difference between expectations and perceptions of the service provided by a firm is a measure of service quality (Parasuraman et al., 1988).

Research has shown a significant correlation between service quality and such variables as consumers' willingness to recommend the service provider to a friend (positive word of mouth communications), purchase intentions, and increased market share and profit contribution (Boulding, Kalra, Staelin, & Zeithaml, 1993; Cronin & Taylor, 1992; Parasuraman, Berry, & Zeithaml, 1991). Most of the service quality research, however, has focused on the consumer, with limited investigation of the applicability of service quality concepts in a supply chain or channels context.

Some work has extended the concept of service quality into the arena of logistics service quality (Bienstock et al., 1997; Mentzer et al., 1989; Mentzer, Flint, & Kent, 1999). Logistics service quality differs from the consumer approach in that logistics service is composed of both technical or outcome dimensions and process dimensions, such as those emphasized by the service quality literature (Bienstock et al., 1997). Technical or outcome quality is defined as whether the service delivers the core benefit (i.e., on-time delivery and product availability), whereas the functional or process quality addresses the process of service delivery (i.e., interface with customer service personnel).

There is recognition that customers' expectations and perceptions regarding the service process measures (i.e., convenience, flexibility, personalized attention, and information) are important to a customer's satisfaction, along with the traditional objective logistics service measures such as speed, availability, accuracy, and consistency (Mentzer et al., 1989). Satisfaction-based loyalty has been noted as an important variable in linking logistics service activity to customer intentions. This suggests that the service process associated with the customer-supplier interface may play an important role in enhancing customer satisfaction and influencing customer behavior in a supply chain context.

This raises a number of important questions for both managers and researchers. For example, how does the quality of the service interface influence the behavior of customers toward both upstream supply chain partners and downstream customers? What influence does service quality have on the quality of the relationship or the level of trust between partners? Does service quality facilitate greater willingness to cooperate and freely exchange information between firms? Do higher levels of service quality influence intermediate customers to deliver higher levels of service quality to downstream customers?

Relationship Marketing

Similar questions are raised by the literature in the relationship marketing arena. As highlighted in Chapter 1, SCM as a management process is focused on managing relationships, information, and materials flow to deliver enhanced customer service. Berry (1995) describes relationship marketing as "attracting, maintaining, and—in multi-service organizations—enhancing customer relationships" (p. 236), with the objective of securing loyalty to retain existing customers. Although customer service traditionally is viewed as having the goal of attracting and keeping customers (Lambert & Stock, 1993), an expanded view encompassing a goal of enhancing customer relationships seems warranted in a supply chain context. Because supply chain relationships are built on a foundation of long-term partnerships, the focus on securing loyalty is important. At the same time, the objectives of enhancing customer relationships and securing loyalty to ensure repeat purchases is not likely to be sufficient in a supply chain management context. Rather, the focus needs to be on enhancing the interaction in the relationship with the objective of improving overall supply chain performance. Once again, this raises the question of how the customer service interface influences the satisfaction and loyalty of the intermediate customer and, as a result, the degree of cooperation and information exchange between firms. Will improved customer service and customer satisfaction improve the trust between supply chain partners, facilitating more open sharing of information and the sharing of risks and rewards associated with supply chain improvements?

Key strategy elements in relationship marketing include those of customizing relationships to the individual customer, augmenting core service with extra benefits, pricing services to encourage customer loyalty, and marketing to employees so that they, in turn, perform well for customers (Berry, 1995). Internal activities aimed at establishing, developing, and maintaining successful relational exchanges are mutually beneficial. At advanced levels of relationship marketing, structural solutions to important customer problems are the critical element of the service offering. Similarly, SCM is a philosophy that synchronizes internal and external capabilities to create market value and focuses supply chain members on finding new ways to create unique and innovative solutions that provide value to customers on an individualized basis (Ross, 1998). This suggests that the relationship marketing approach of customizing customer service offerings to strategically important customers and internal marketing to employees to enhance customer-focused performance are important elements of managing the customer service interface in a supply chain context.

Customer Learning and Information Exchange

Another area important to customer service management in a supply chain context is that of learning about customer needs. Grönroos (1995) notes differences in the behavior of firms in the area of customer learning along a continuum from transaction marketing to relationship marketing. Firms pursuing a transaction marketing strategy have limited customer contact and rely on ad hoc customer satisfaction surveys and market share statistics to acquire information about the behavior and satisfaction of their customers. Conversely, firms pursuing a relationship marketing strategy have frequent contact with their customers, and they develop ways to monitor satisfaction and manage the customer interface based on customer communications. Customer service researchers describe the interaction with the customer as a focal point for establishing customer service requirements and influencing customer service performance (Bowersox & Closs, 1996; Rinehart et al., 1989).

Clearly, an important component of developing and implementing successful customer service strategies is the capability of a firm to appropriately access and utilize information about the customer (Stevens, 1990). Because customer service involves the interface between the customer and the supplier, customer service personnel often have access to important information about the customer's problems, the degree to which the customer is satisfied, or even how the customer views the competition. All too often, however, there are no mechanisms for disseminating such information to appropriate internal resources or for utilizing the information to improve customer service strategies or operations. The role of customer service personnel in acquiring information about customers and diffusing information internally is likely to become even more important in a supply chain context.

Stevens (1990) highlights two critical components of customer service in SCM as identification of customer needs and identification of internal activities that meet those needs (i.e., matching organizational capability and customer requirements). Bechtel and Jayaram (1997) note the role of the customer as an information source for other members of the supply chain, suggesting that the customer plays an expanded role of sharing information to enable the supply chain to focus on the end customer. Likewise, the focal firm plays an expanded role in sharing information and focusing activities of upstream suppliers to improve supply chain performance in delivering service to the end customer. In the light of the need for a much broader base of information sharing, supply chain managers should ensure that internal systems and procedures encourage customer learning and allow the dissemination and utilization of such learnings both within the focal firm and across other supply chain firms. The customer service interface should play a key role in the exchange of information between the firm and its customer to coordinate and direct supply chain activities.

As part of the information exchange process, service personnel also play a significant role in communicating to customers the services to be provided (i.e., making promises and establishing customer expectations). Bitner (1995) notes that service relationships are achieved by mutual exchange and fulfillment of promises. The ability of a firm to keep promises to customers depends on (a) making realistic promises and (b) building appropriate service systems and processes, and recruiting, training, and motivating service personnel to ensure organizational capability to deliver against promises. The customer service interface is key to making realistic promises to customers and to adequately communicating internally such that those promises can be fulfilled. Thus, the role of customer interface personnel is critical in the communication and information exchange process in a supply chain. Note that in Figure 13.1, the customer interface and information exchange process is shaded to reflect a dual role of customer service management (to ensure appropriate systems, procedures, and training of customer service personnel) and customer response (to facilitate information exchange and coordination between firms).

Summary

In this section, the discussion has focused on elements important to customer service viewed as a management activity or an organizational process. To achieve the supply chain objective of improving customer service as a means to creating value, satisfying customers, and achieving differential advantage, firms must focus on developing appropriate strategies based on understanding consumer needs and developing supply chain capabilities to meet those needs in a cost-effective way. Differences in service requirements across different customer segments must be understood, and organizational processes must be designed to allow firms (and supply chains) to respond to the different requirements of strategic customer segments. To accomplish these objectives, the customer service interface must be managed in a way that enhances the quality of the relationship and encourages open exchange of information between firms. Important information about customers must be disseminated and utilized to focus the activities of the supply chain to those services that create the greatest value for customers. Thus, a critical element of customer service management is an understanding of the performance outcomes of the customer service process that are perceived as important by customers.

Customer Service as a Performance Outcome

Although much of the literature on customer service is focused on the process or activities associated with providing service to customers, there is also repeated reference to customer service as a performance outcome or as an objective function in the customer/supplier relationship. For example, Stevens (1990) describes customer service as the output from the supply systems. According to Ellram et al. (1989), customer service includes such factors as order completeness, cycle time, consistency of performance, responses to errors and requests for information, special requests, and services.

As highlighted in Chapter 3, the performance outcome objectives of supply chain management are improved efficiency (cost reduction) or effectiveness (improved service). It is important to note that the objective of SCM is to improve efficiency and effectiveness through the supply chain, with a goal of delivering greater value to downstream customers, not simply to improve performance within the focal firm. As one executive noted, supply chain managers should ask themselves the question "Are we doing the right thing for our customers, or are we just trying to accommodate ourselves?" Customer service activities, as an important component of supply chain management, should be aimed at the delivery of the same level of service at a lower cost (efficiency) or improved levels of service at the same or reasonable costs (effectiveness) to deliver value to downstream customers (see Figure 13.1).

Bowersox and Closs (1996) suggest that there are four levels of customer service outcomes, all of which are required to create differential advantage across firms within an SCM context. Different levels of service produce different outcomes in terms of efficiency and effectiveness. These four levels are highlighted below.

1. Efficiency—delivery of basic services at reasonable cost and consistent quality
2. Market access (effectiveness)—customers and suppliers working together sharing basic information to smooth joint operations
3. Market extension (effectiveness)—selectively improving and introducing new services to strengthen and expand the relationship
4. Market creation (effectiveness)—researching and developing new and innovative ways to make customers more successful and more competitive

Efficiency involves providing basic customer service requirements with consistent quality and in a cost-effective manner. Dimensions of basic service important in a supply chain context include product availability, operational performance, and reliability. Each of these has the potential to create value for downstream customers.

Product availability is a critical element of efficient supply chain operations. If product is available to the customer when needed, customer costs associated with not having raw materials or spare parts available when needed can be reduced or minimized.

Operational performance, which includes the dimensions of order cycle time, consistency in performance, flexibility to handle unusual requests, and ability to respond and recover from service errors, is also important to efficient supply chain operations. Reduced cycle time and flexibility to respond to changing customer needs can reduce inventory requirements and improve efficiency in the customer's operation, resulting in lower cost to the ultimate consumer. In addition to improving efficiency and reducing cost, flexibility and reduced cycle time can also enable a firm to respond more rapidly to changes in market demand, thus contributing to greater market effectiveness. This points to the distinction between the customer's perception of performance outcomes and value created and the internal perception or measures of performance outcomes. This distinction will be discussed later in the chapter.

Finally, reliability is an important service outcome for efficient supply chain operations. For example, does the customer know what to expect from the supply chain partner and can the customer depend on product being delivered as promised? If service is reliable, a customer firm can plan its operations and utilize resources more efficiently, as well as minimize the inventory required to buffer against uncertainty, thus reducing overall cost. At the same time, when supply chain partners make commitments to the end consumer and reliably deliver against those commitments, the overall effectiveness of the supply chain is improved.

Although providing the basic service levels in a cost-effective manner contributes to both efficiency and effectiveness in a supply chain, different service offerings may be required to achieve higher levels of effectiveness that contribute to greater value for the customer and competitive or differential value. The market access service level described by Bowersox and Closs (1996) consists of delivering higher levels of service to customers who cooperate with the supplier firm to achieve joint objectives and share information to smooth joint operations. Examples of this might include the sharing of point of sale (POS) data or collaborative forecasting, planning, and replenishment (CFPR). With the market extension service level, higher levels of service and the introduction of additional services are designed to strengthen and expand the business relationship. For example, in exchange for guarantees of certain levels of service, or willingness to perform certain services (such as vendor management of inventories), a customer firm may be willing to designate a supplier as a sole-source supplier. The willingness to perform additional services for key customers is particularly relevant in achieving supply chain integration, as it allows firms to locate services most appropriately. As one executive noted, if a service can be performed more cost-effectively by a supplier than by the customer, even though costs are increased for the supplier, the cost performance of the local supply chain is improved by relocating the service to the supplier organization.

Finally, in the market creation level, the supplier firm becomes committed to the customer's success. Innovative services are designed to make the downstream partner more successful with its customers. At this stage, firms within the supply chain work jointly to enhance the success (and effectiveness) of the supply chain as a whole. This level of sophistication in customer service is the most consistent with the objectives of SCM.

As noted earlier, customer service performance outcomes exist in two domains, the supplier's activity domain and the customer's response domain (Mentzer et al., 1989). Activities and performance measures related to product availability, timeliness, and quality that are internal to the firm are of no consequence to the customer. It is the *customer's perception* of the availability, timeliness, and quality performance outcomes that is important to customers (Mentzer et al., 1989). Thus, as illustrated in Figure 13.1, performance outcomes can be related to the supplier's activity domain (e.g., order cycle time and completeness) or the customer's response domain (e.g., customer's perception of responsiveness and accuracy) (Mentzer et al., 1989).

Although these two domains of performance outcomes may be strongly correlated, it is important to recognize that they are two distinct domains. Measuring performance outcomes in the supplier activity domain is important for the supplier to maintain or improve its customer service performance. It is the customer's perceptions of performance outcomes, however, rather than any internal managerial activities or performance measures, that influence whether the service provided is valued by the customer. If a supplier improves performance in activities that are not important to the customer, it is unlikely that the customer's perception of value or satisfaction will be enhanced. For example, historically, firms have measured on-time performance in terms of whether the product was shipped from a distribution center as scheduled. This was done for several reasons. First, it was very difficult to get information about exactly when a shipment arrived at the customer's dock. Second, managers used this measure to improve performance at the distribution center, so they did not want to measure something over which the distribution center manager had no control. The attitude was that if the carrier did not reach the customer on time, it was not the fault of the supplier—and therefore, the important measure was what the supplier firm actually did (i.e., whether the order was shipped on time). With this approach, it was possible for a supplier firm to achieve high levels of on-time shipments while the customer firm perceived extremely poor performance in on-time delivery. In this case, improved performance on the part of the supplier firm would not result in increased customer satisfaction.

The contribution of customer service to increased efficiency or effectiveness can be significant; however, the contribution must be assessed in terms of both objective measures of performance as viewed by the supplier and perceived measures of performance as viewed by the customer, so that customer service enhancements are based on what is important to the customer. Further, it is important to note that customer service is not the objective; rather, it is a means for improving efficiency and effectiveness in ways that create value important to the customer. The creation of value can, in turn, lead to greater customer satisfaction and differential advantage, influencing customers to behave in ways that are beneficial to the supply chain as a whole.

Customer Responses to Customer Service Performance

Frequent reference is made in the literature to customer service as a means for creating value, satisfying customers, and creating competitive advantage. For example, Gattorna et al. (1991) note that increasing globalization and competitive pressures have made customer service a major differentiating competitive weapon. Similarly, Langley and Holcomb (1992) note increased pressures on firms to enhance customer service. They suggest that firms that are successful in doing so can achieve sustainable competitive advantage. These authors describe customer service as a concept that is closely related to customer value.

A more complete discussion of the concepts of customer value, customer satisfaction, and competitive advantage or differential advantage can be found in Chapter 3. The relatedness of customer service and customer value, customer satisfaction, and differential advantage is noted here and highlighted in Figure 13.1. Customer value has been defined as the benefits that are realized by the customer relative to the sacrifice made to acquire, use, and dispose of a product/service, in comparison to available alternatives (Manrodt & Davis, 1993). Customer service activities are one component of a set of supply chain activities that are aimed at improving efficiency and effectiveness (customer service outcomes) to deliver value to downstream customers. By providing the same level of service at lower cost, or improved service that allows the customer firm to improve its effectiveness, the balance between the benefits and sacrifices can be enhanced and additional value delivered to the customer. It is this value relative to the value delivered by the competition that translates to customer satisfaction and influences customers to behave in ways that benefit the firm or the supply chain as a whole. Likewise, improved efficiency or effectiveness on the part of the intermediate customer can translate to additional value delivered to the ultimate consumer (Figure 13.1).

Conclusions

Although there is frequent reference in the supply chain literature to the importance of customer service as a means to create value and influence customer satisfaction, limited work has directly related customer service and supply chain management. In this chapter, customer service was considered from three distinct perspectives: (a) customer service management, (b) performance outcomes as viewed by both the supplier and customer, and (c) customer responses to customer service outcomes.

Customer Service Management

In Chapter 1, the objectives of SCM were described in terms of both efficiency (cost reduction) and effectiveness (customer service) in a strategic context (creating customer value and satisfaction) to obtain competitiveness that brings profitability. This suggests that, when considered in a supply chain management context, customer service activities must be strategic in nature and must be specifically designed and implemented to enhance the competitive or differential advantage of the firm and the supply chain. To accomplish this objective, several elements of customer service management are important. Customer service strategies should be developed to direct SCM activities to deliver optimum levels of customer service. These strategies should be based on understanding the levels of service important to strategic customers and on developing the organizational capability to provide appropriate levels of service for different customer segments.

Traditional approaches to developing customer service strategies provide useful insights into the elements of strategy that are important in a supply chain context. First, and perhaps foremost, an understanding of the customer impact of various service offerings is critical. To develop such an understanding, important customer segments must be identified, because the requirements of different segments will be different or the strategic importance of particular segments may warrant different levels of service. In an SCM context, it is also important to understand the customer impact at the various levels of the supply chain. Service levels at any given level in the supply chain will affect both the immediate customers and downstream customers. Customer service strategies in support of SCM initiatives therefore must be developed based on the impact of service at multiple levels in the supply chain.

Another important step in developing customer service strategies is to understand the impact of service failures (customer responses, costs, and resulting sales losses) as well as the impact of higher levels of service (expected increase in revenues, increased customer satisfaction, and ability to respond to market changes) on downstream customers. Internal capabilities should be assessed to determine where improvements are needed, and capabilities should be enhanced where necessary to deliver levels of service important to strategic customer segments. From a supply chain perspective, the capabilities of the supply chain as a whole should be assessed and improved to deliver appropriate levels of service to the end consumer. Finally, the firm's (or supply chain's) performance relative to competition in areas considered important by customers should be assessed to identify the most strategic opportunities and to guide SCM activities.

Because of the importance of long-term relationships, trust, cooperation, and information sharing to SCM, the management of the customer interface is also important. The quality of the interface can affect customer satisfaction and loyalty and, as a result, is likely to influence the levels of trust and openness of information exchange between firms. Customer interface personnel may also have access to important information about customers, such as what problems they are trying to solve, how satisfied they are with current levels of service, and how they view competitive offerings. This is important information about customers that can help firms direct their supply chain activities to create greater customer value.

A number of questions for future research are raised when examining customer service management in a supply chain context. For example, what are the trade-offs to be managed in determining optimum service levels at both intermediate levels in the supply chain and for the ultimate consumer? What tools and techniques can be utilized to jointly develop appropriate customer service strategies for the supply chain as a whole? What systems and processes are required to direct and manage both intrafirm and interfirm resources to implement those strategies? How can supply chain firms best manage the service delivery process to provide customized solutions to meet different requirements of different customer segments? What is the role of outsourcing in achieving the appropriate customer service mix? How does the quality of the customer service interface influence the behavior of firms toward both upstream and downstream supply chain members?

Customer Service Performance Outcomes

Historical measures of customer service have been predominantly supplier-oriented measures aimed at improving the internal management of customer service activities (e.g., order fill rates, cycle time, percent on-time delivery, and stock-out levels). Although these measures are valuable tools for the internal management of customer service, there is a recognition that the more important outcome variables are those perceived by the customer (e.g., customer perceptions of availability, timeliness, and quality) (Mentzer et al., 1989). A critical strategic issue that managers must address is understanding the performance outcomes that are most valued by customers at various levels in the supply chain. They must then monitor and measure customers' perceptions of those performance outcomes.

As highlighted earlier, the outcomes most important to customers differ in different situations and contexts. Whereas in one supply chain improved efficiency may be the most important outcome, in another improved effectiveness may be more important. An important area for future investigation is how the importance of customer service outcomes varies in a supply chain context. Managers should take steps to understand not only how current levels of service are perceived by customers but also what services will be most valuable to customers in the future.

In the case where a supplier and customer firm are planning jointly and are coordinating activities to improve downstream customer service, the customer service performance outcomes become much more complex. Performance outcomes at both intermediate and downstream customer levels are important. Supply chain managers must work across firms to jointly identify those service outcomes that create the greatest value for end consumers, and to monitor and measure those performance outcomes to improve total supply chain performance.

Customer Responses to Service Outcomes

Customer service has frequently been linked in the SCM literature to the creation of customer value and satisfaction. The customer's perception of the value created by a service is directly linked to satisfaction and perceived differential advantage of the firm's offering. It is these customer response variables that influence the customer's subsequent behaviors both toward the supplier firm and perhaps toward its downstream customers. In consumer service industries, customer satisfaction resulting from service quality has been linked to greater customer loyalty, repeat purchases, and positive word of mouth communications about the service provider. Customer satisfaction resulting from higher levels of customer service is also expected to have a positive influence on customer behavior in a supply chain setting. Research is needed, however, to determine what influence customer satisfaction has on the supply chain-related behavior of intermediate customers. For example, does improved service to immediate customers lead to higher service levels provided to downstream customers? Does improved service lead to an enhanced relationship quality, and consequently to behaviors that facilitate trust, information exchange, coordination, and joint action between the firms?

Customer service has become increasingly strategic in nature and focused on the customer over the past several decades. Although such a strategic, customer-focused approach is consistent with an SCM philosophy, it may not be sufficient to accomplish the objectives of SCM. The key question to be addressed in an SCM context is how customer service can deliver value that benefits the end consumer and how it can provide a differential advantage not only to the focal firm but also to the supply chain as a whole. With such an expanded set of objectives, customer service management and desired performance and customer outcomes must all be examined from the perspective of the supply chain as a whole, rather than simply at the buyer-seller interface.

14

Inter-Functional Coordination in Supply Chain Management

SOONHONG MIN

Executive Summary

The demand for flexibility in today's turbulent business environment requires supply chain management that extends the concept of functional integration beyond a firm to all the firms in the supply chain (Ellram & Cooper, 1990). In other words, implementing SCM inherently requires coordination across the traditional business functions within a firm, as well as interfirm cooperation across the firms in close relationship within a supply chain, to accomplish a common set of goals. This chapter highlights the importance of inter-functional coordination within individual supply chain members to successfully implement supply chain management. This chapter will

- Discuss concurrent management, an essential part of systemic and strategic coordination of successful supply chain management and a driving force of inter-functional coordination; it requires the balance between specialization through division of labor and cross-functional coordination
- Define inter-functional coordination within a particular firm as coordinated efforts across functions to accomplish common goals, such as

creating customer value and responsiveness to market changes, under close relationships among the functions and tight management control

- Explain the various ways of implementing inter-functional coordination, including cooperative arrangements through which personnel from different functional areas perform interaction and collaboration; managerial control, especially integrating managers who are essentially liaison personnel with formal authority over something important across functions (such as budgets); standardization to guide the processes of coordination so that the coordinated work is ensured; providing functional expertise necessary to participation in cooperative arrangements; and providing an organizational structure that integrates the flows of products, services, finance, and information within an organization
- Argue that no organization can rely on a single mechanism and/or organizational structure presented in this chapter and, as a result, organizations must be flexible to utilize a proper combination of these mechanisms to achieve a high level of coordination
- Suggest common goals, trust and commitment among personnel from different functional areas, and top management support as the factors that promote cooperative efforts within a firm
- Propose that well-executed inter-functional coordination brings competitive advantage, in the major forms of reduced cycle time and new product success, and finally profitability

In conclusion, this chapter suggests that individual firms within a supply chain should have functional expertise in key functional areas and, at the same time, achieve functional integration.

Introduction

In a special research forum of the *Academy of Management Journal* on intra- and inter-organizational cooperation, Smith, Carroll, and Ashford (1995) quoted an interesting story from McNeill (1963):

> When the 200 ships of the Greeks defeated the Persian navy at Salamis in 480 B.C., the victory depended upon both intra- and inter-unit cooperation. Inside the individual ships, the Greeks had to row in virtually complete unison and be almost perfectly coordinated to outstrip and outmaneuver their opponents. Inside the fleet, there existed accurate coordination of the 200 ships into effective fleet attack formations. Otherwise the Greek ships could have interfered with each other, and chaos would have occurred. (p. 7)

This event, which occurred more than two thousand years ago, illustrates a good management lesson in how to thrive in a highly competitive business environment through successful supply chain management. Supply chain management (SCM) is defined in Chapter 1 as the systemic, strategic coordination of the traditional business functions and the tactics across business functions within a particular company and across businesses within the supply chain, for the purposes of improving the long-term performance of the individual companies and the supply chain as a whole. Similarly, Ellram and Cooper (1990) posit that SCM borrows from and extends organizational effectiveness concepts in terms of integrating activities between firms, rather than just within firms. In other words, successful SCM presumes interfirm cooperation across the firms, as well as inter-functional coordination within a particular firm. A director with a leading drug store chain whom we interviewed said:

> When you're a company and you absorb ten other companies and you want to present one face to your customer, you have to take steps internally to organize your enterprise to do that, and by and large we have pretty much done it. This is the model that came out of that and now that is kind of spreading out, it's spread out to the big guns, Wal-Mart and K-Mart, and a lot of the big supermarket folks, and now it's getting around to other forms of retailing, chain drug, and specialty. So in most merchandisers, it's becoming a way of life.

In practice within a firm, supply chain managers are often given joint responsibilities for engineering, purchasing, marketing, manufacturing, and logistics (Mentzer, 1993). SCM thus requires not only interfirm cooperation but also coordination across the traditional business functions and tactics within an individual supply chain firm. Therefore, inter-functional coordination and interfirm cooperation are necessary conditions, but neither of them is a sufficient condition by itself to manage a supply chain successfully.

Given that both inter-functional coordination and interfirm cooperation are essential elements of supply chain management, those two important issues are discussed in two chapters of this book—this chapter, "Inter-Functional Coordination in Supply Chain Management," and Chapter 15, "Inter-Corporate Cooperation in Supply Chain Management." The present chapter introduces various definitions and mechanisms to reveal the nature of inter-functional coordination. It then suggests an integrative framework to define inter-functional coordination in a supply chain context and explains how inter-functional coordination affects successful SCM in today's highly competitive business environment. The following section presents the antecedents that promote inter-functional coordination, along with the consequences of integration. Finally, conclusions are presented, along with future research and managerial implications of the ideas presented in this chapter.

Concurrent Management

Concurrent engineering involves faster product development, flexible manufacturing, tailored logistics, and time-based strategies to respond to changing markets (Cespedes, 1996a). Cespedes (1996a) added that, in industrial markets, just-in-time inventory systems and broader supply chain management policies alter how customers buy and, thus, these external market forces require internal coordination within a firm. For example, an automobile manufacturer must ensure that assembly workers carefully coordinate their actions so that their assembly efforts result in the efficient and effective production of a car (Hodge, Anthony, & Gales, 1996).

Just as concurrent engineering improves manufacturing responsiveness, companies wrestling with rapid change in today's markets adopt concurrent marketing (Cespedes, 1996a), where firms better integrate their otherwise isolated product management, sales management, and field service operations. These marketing groups must interact more often, more quickly, and in more depth across more products, markets, and accounts. Coordination beyond and among the marketing groups is also essential in day-to-day operations. Some operations within organizations may require precise timing or scheduling so that actions of different workers or departments fit together. For example, Thrifty Hardware Company found that the timing of ordering was critical so that merchandise arrived before the busy periods of customer traffic. Otherwise, important merchandise was not on display and employees had to divert their attention from customers to stocking tasks (Hodge et al., 1996).

Concurrent management—concurrent engineering and concurrent marketing—is the ability to be more responsive to changing market conditions. It is an essential part of systemic and strategic coordination of successful supply chain management. In turn, it requires balance between the need for specialization and cross-functional cooperation (Cespedes, 1996a). The activities of different functions thus depend on each other's expertise. According to Pfeffer and Salancik (1978), organizations are coalitions of interests that alter their purposes and direction as changes take place in the coalitional structure where departments and functional areas exist. Pfeffer and Salancik (1978) state that "coalitions providing behaviors, resources and capabilities that are most needed or desired by other organizational participants come to have more influence and control over the organization" (p. 27).

In summary, inter-functional coordination needs to be discussed in the context of responding to a rapidly changing market environment. The form of this response is concurrent management, in which different functions are interdependent yet systemically and strategically coordinated toward successful implementation of supply chain management within a firm. As a senior vice

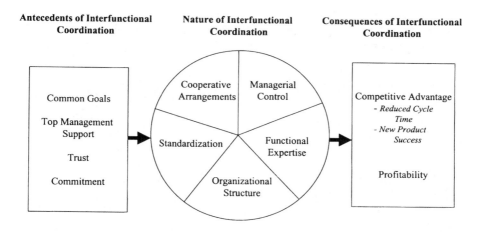

Antecedents of Interfunctional Coordination   Nature of Interfunctional Coordination   Consequences of Interfunctional Coordination

Common Goals

Top Management Support

Trust

Commitment

Cooperative Arrangements | Managerial Control

Standardization | Functional Expertise

Organizational Structure

Competitive Advantage
- *Reduced Cycle Time*
- *New Product Success*

Profitability

Figure 14.1.   An Integrated Model of Inter-Functional Coordination

president with a leading drug store chain whom we interviewed put it, "You should not overlook the internal supply chain, because symbiotic internal relationships may be needed to enhance the flow of goods and services."

The Nature of Inter-Functional Coordination

As a firm begins to divide labor and seek specialization among organizational members, it is necessary to make certain that everyone continues to work toward the common goals of the organization. Thus, coordination and control of actions among firm members become imperative (Hodge et al., 1996; Mintzberg, 1996). Dwyer and Tanner (1999) refer to the common goal as the supragoal, that is, a goal against which other goals are aligned. Inter-functional coordination (hereafter referred to as coordination) is important because the overall tasks and goals of the organization are rarely functional (Hodge et al., 1996). For example, the creation of value for customers is a common goal that any individual in any function in a firm can potentially contribute to (Porter, 1985; Webster, 1988). As such, coordination within a firm is a must in supply chain management where there are common goals of improving the long-term performance of the individual companies and the supply chain as a whole. This section will define the phenomenon called "inter-functional coordination" and explore how the phenomenon is characterized in the literature (Figure 14.1).

Defining Inter-Functional Coordination

Working together across functions or departments is called either "coordination" (Day & Klein, 1987; Hodge et al., 1996; Narver & Slater, 1990; Olson, Walker, & Ruekert, 1995) or "integration" (Kahn & Mentzer, 1998; Lawrence & Lorsch, 1967). Narver and Slater (1990) argue that a seller's creation of value for buyers is analogous to a symphony orchestra in which the contribution of each subgroup is tailored and integrated by a conductor. In other words, coordination is a firm's coordinated efforts, involving more than the marketing department to create superior value for the buyers (Narver & Slater, 1990). Lawrence and Lorsch (1967) define the concept of integration as "the quality of the state of collaboration that exists among departments that are required to achieve unity of effort by the demands of the environment" (p. 67). Both concepts—coordination and integration—are conceptualized as (a) coordinated efforts, (b) inter-functional, and (c) essential to achieve a firm's goals such as customer value creation and responsiveness to environmental changes. As such, both terms are similar in conceptualization.

Beyond these similarities, Hodge et al. (1996) define integration as "the necessary *coordination* among these various tasks to ensure that the overall goals of the organization are achieved" (p. 33; emphasis added) and, therefore, these authors see integration as identical to coordination. Adapting the Hodge et al. (1996) conceptualization of integration, this chapter uses coordination and integration interchangeably, and it defines inter-functional coordination within a particular firm as the coordinated efforts across functions to accomplish common goals, such as creating customer value and responsiveness to market changes, under close relationships among the functions.

Implementation of Inter-Functional Coordination

Coordination can be accomplished through tight controls or cooperative arrangements (Day & Klein, 1987). Without cooperative arrangements and control, some workers may intentionally or unintentionally engage in activities that do not contribute to, or even interfere with, the organization's goals (Hodge et al., 1996). At the same time, the firm must nurture cross-functional collaboration in its marketing activities (Cespedes, 1996a). Combining these dimensions, Mintzberg (1996) proposed six basic coordinating mechanisms:

1. Mutual adjustment: the process of informal communication in which people interact with one another to coordinate.
2. Direct supervision: one person coordinates by giving orders to others.

3. Standardization of work processes: direct specification of the content of work. and the procedures to be followed in order to tightly control different people.

4. Standardization of outputs: specification of what is to be done (i.e., the results of the coordination) so that interfaces between jobs are predetermined.

5. Standardization of skills: loose coordination of people through education on a common body of knowledge and a set of skills that are subsequently applied to the work.

6. Standardization of norms: coordination of people through a common set of beliefs.

If we recategorize Mintzberg's (1996) suggested mechanisms, three different dimensions of coordination exist: cooperative arrangements (mutual adjustment), management controls (direct supervision), and standardization (standardization of work processes, outputs, skills, and norms). In addition to these mechanisms, Cespedes (1996a) found, in interviews with more than 200 managers in the computing, telecommunication services, consumer packaged goods, and medical products industries, that implementing "concurrent marketing" requires functional expertise and lines of authority rather than downsizing specialists out of the organization in a bid for more generalist team players. Finally, to exercise coordination, members of the organization need a formal structure that specifies roles, responsibilities, and relationships among organizational members. Based upon this literature, I propose that the implementation of inter-functional coordination has five different dimensions: cooperative arrangements, management control, standardization, functional expertise, and organizational structure.

Cooperative Arrangements

Mintzberg (1996) proposed mutual adjustment as one of the mechanisms of coordination. He conceptualized mutual adjustment as the process of informal communication in which people interact with one another to coordinate, much as two canoeists in white-water rapids adjust to one another's actions. Situational bargaining (negotiations) to resolve issues between functions and establishing joint committees to identify and discuss matters of interest to the functions are examples of cooperative arrangements (Murphy & Poist, 1992). Kahn and Mentzer (1998), however, argue that coordination is not well defined because what characterizes "coordinated efforts" is not clear. Based upon the literature, Kahn and Mentzer (1998) suggest a composite view of inter-functional coordination that consists of interaction and collaboration, with each a distinct dimension that has unique, significant contributions to defining cooperative arrangements. Kahn and Mentzer (1998) found that both interaction and collaboration positively influence a firm's performance. For the purposes of this chapter, I adopt Kahn and Mentzer's (1998) perspective that the cooperative arrangement dimension of coordination consists of interaction and collaboration.

Interaction: According to Kahn and Mentzer (1998), certain literature characterizes integration as an interactive process, where communication activities such as "meetings" and "documented information exchange" predicate the relationships between departments (e.g., Griffin & Hauser, 1992; Lim & Reid, 1992; Moenaert, Souder, DeMeyer, & Deschoolmeester, 1994; Ruekert & Walker, 1987b; Woodward, 1965). Similarly, Kohli and Jaworski (1990) limit the domain of coordination to inter-functional communication. In other words, the focus of this view is on communication—formal and informal forms of meetings and/or exchange of documented information—among personnel from different functions within a particular firm. Specific examples of interaction activities include committee meetings, teleconferencing, conference calls, hall talk, memoranda, and the exchange of standard documents (Galbraith, 1977; Jaworski & Kohli, 1993; Van de Ven & Ferry, 1980). In this way, managers in particular departments rely on activities to structure relationships between the department and other departments through the diffusion of market information (cf. Kahn & Mentzer, 1998). In the same context, authors have proposed that information flows/updates within a firm and across the firms within a supply chain are essential elements of supply chain management (Cooper & Ellram, 1993; Cooper, Ellram, Gardner, & Hanks, 1997).

Based on the view of coordination as interaction, marketing literature (e.g., Carlsson, 1991; Griffin & Hauser, 1992; Moenaert et al., 1994; Urban & Hauser, 1993) highlights that "effective" coordination is predicated on interaction and, thus, prescribes marketing's increased contact with other departments through information flows (Kahn & Mentzer, 1998). Interaction for information sharing requires establishing information systems or procedures that involve sharing of information between the two functions. The system supports the use of a common database and the sharing of information across functions and divisions. It supports more effective (cross-functional) team performance and is likely to lead to the elimination of gaps (Cohen, Eliashberg, & Ho, 1997).

Collaboration: Kahn and Mentzer (1998) posit that a second stream of literature (e.g., Clark & Fujimoto, 1991; Lawrence & Lorsch, 1986; Schrage, 1990) describes coordination as a collaborative process, where "teams" and "resource sharing" typify interdepartmental relationships. This perspective assumes that functional areas do exist within a firm and, thus, the focus is how to cross through the silo structure to work together with other functions toward common goals. The role of cross-functional teams for product development has long been recognized as an important factor of best practice (Cohen et al., 1997). Dwyer and Tanner (1999) propose internal partnering among such functions as marketing, purchasing, manufacturing, engineering (R&D), and finance. Similarly, Lambert, Stock, and Ellram (1998) suggest key supply chain processes that should be integrated: selling, customer order fulfillment, manufacturing flow, procurement, and product management.

The importance of cross-functional team seems to have increased. For example, in the 1993 report on cross-functional sourcing teams by The Center for Advanced Purchasing Studies (CAPS), 80% of U.S. companies surveyed said they planned to emphasize the use of such groups over the next 3 years to support procurement and sourcing decisions (Hyman, 1996). A simple form of cross-functional team may be the functional specialist within a particular department who is designated to other functional activities (cf. Murphy & Poist, 1992). The cross-functional team concept is easily found in such areas as logistics (e.g., Murphy & Poist, 1992) and purchasing (Hyman, 1996). A vice president with a large office supply company we interviewed contended:

> I have a logistics person assigned to all of our team accounts whom we call customer logistics managers. They are part of the sales team and they report to Customer Operations. Our sales person never gets into logistics discussions or if they do they quickly get on the phone and bring in the customer logistics managers. The role of customer logistics managers is the customer advocate in our organization.

Another example is Procter & Gamble's (P&G) Multifunctional Account Teams that bring product and sales managers together. P&G staffs teams with salespeople from different divisions and brand people assigned to a large account. Team members spend 1 to 2 years at customer sites and acknowledge what is involved in executing brand programs through the distribution channel (Cespedes, 1996a). Finally, customer-focused teams (CFT), which consist of people from sales, manufacturing, shipping, finance, purchasing, and engineering, ensure inter-functional communication by removing formal communication barriers and require communication at the point of need (Dwyer & Tanner, 1999).

Management Controls

In a traditional functional silo structure with a narrow functional view, decision making that involves several different functional areas is pushed up the organizational hierarchy to top management (Hodge et al., 1996). Slow decision making by overloaded top management, however, is not appropriate for successful supply chain management that requires coordination of expertise of different functions and time- and quality-based competition. Instead, integrating managers—essentially liaison personnel with formal authority—provide stronger coordination (Mintzberg, 1996). Mintzberg (1996) suggests that these managers are given authority not over the units they link, but over something important to those units, like budgets. A senior vice president with a leading drug store chain we interviewed insisted:

> Without understanding the impact on the rest of the system it is a part of so there is no recognition of some of the interdependencies in activities ... the overall best managed supply chain might require some people incurring costs that they might not normally incur if they were just managing their own part.

Integrating managers are the champions who manage the team, using input from all stakeholders (Cooper, 1993; Wind & Mahajan, 1988, 1997). An example is marketing managers who ascribe to a collaborative view of integration that promotes efforts to instill collective goals, mutual respect, and teamwork between departments (Kahn & Mentzer, 1998).

The processes by which strategic decisions are made (i.e., the way in which team leaders elicit, receive, and respond to team members' input) have a significant impact on team members' coordination (Korsgaard, Schweiger, & Sapienza, 1995). This is true especially when team leaders show strong consideration of members' input and when team members see the decision-making process as fair and, consequently, have greater commitment to the decision, attachment to the team, and trust in the leader. Korsgaard et al.'s (1995) empirical findings are applicable to better managing cross-functional teams within individual members of a supply chain to improve the chances of gaining cooperation and commitment to decisions without sacrificing the quality of decisions in the process.

Standardization

Mintzberg (1996) argued that coordination can be achieved through standardization because standards predetermine what people do and, thus, ensure that their work is coordinated. The standardization of work processes is accomplished by behavioral formalization that imposes operating instructions, job descriptions, rules, and regulations (Mintzberg, 1996). Unlike functional silo structure, people involved in supply chain processes should be given job descriptions, operating instructions, and behavioral norms for seamless, efficient flows of products, services, information, and finances in addition to those within a particular functional area. Standardization thus becomes a useful mechanism of coordination toward supply chain management.

Standardization of Output: Planning systems, which specify the results of specific actions before they are taken, and performance control systems, which specify the desired results of a whole range of actions after the fact, are used to standardize output (Mintzberg, 1996). In addition, a market orientation, which is the operationalization of the marketing concept, is a way of standardizing output, especially the creation of superior customer value. The creation of superior customer value entails an organization-wide commitment to continuous information gathering and coordination of customers' needs, competitors' capabilities, and the provisions of other significant market agents and authorities as well as different functional areas within a firm (cf. Kohli & Jaworski, 1990; Slater & Narver, 1994a). What should be done (i.e., the output) rules what to do (i.e., coordination toward supply chain management) in the standardization of output.

Standardization of Skills: Training is the use of formal instructional programs to establish and standardize the requisite skills and knowledge in people to do particular jobs in organizations (Mintzberg, 1996). People from sales, marketing, manufacturing, engineering, procurement, and finance should understand the importance, characteristics, and output of a supply chain orientation and supply chain management through well-structured training programs. At the same time, most organizations train employees to function as a contributing group or team member in supply chain management (Lambert et al., 1998). In this way, specific roles of each functional area in supply chain management, knowledge, and skills should be developed accordingly. A senior vice president with a leading drug store chain whom we interviewed said, "I think in the last 20 years we saw many more undergraduate and graduate people running warehouses with a whole total set of skills than we ever did before."

Training may also include topics such as appreciating diversity, individual differences, team interaction, and team accountability (Harrington, 1993). As a result, people need to clearly understand such key activities as interaction and collaboration to coordinate the activities of supply chain management, as well as team dynamics within a firm.

Standardization of Norms: Cooper, Lambert, and Pagh (1997) suggest that a unified policy governing the activities of supply chain members is essential for the success of supply chain management. A unified policy should be first indoctrinated in each supply chain partner. First, the marketing concept as a corporate norm also drives a firm to practice inter-functional cooperation. Kohli and Jaworski (1990) posit that the marketing concept consists of three pillars: customer focus, coordinated marketing, and profitability. Second, the philosophy of coordination refers to providing or instilling in logistics personnel a spirit or philosophy of cooperation toward marketing (Murphy & Poist, 1992). In a survey study of members of the Council of Logistics Management, Murphy and Poist (1992) found cooperative culture as the most important factor for the success of inter-functional coordination. Finally, a supply chain orientation is a coordinating philosophy with which people within a company see the implications of managing the upstream and downstream flows of products, services, finances, and information across their suppliers and their customers. As such, inter-functional coordination within a firm, which is encouraged by the marketing concept and the coordination philosophy, is essential to create customer value that, in turn, helps the firm obtain competitive advantage and, ultimately, satisfy customers.

Functional Expertise

Although cross-functional coordination is a must, the need for functional in-depth expertise should not be ignored. Each management discipline has seen increasing sophistication in its concepts and methods, and each requires mastery of this knowledge (Cespedes, 1996a; Wind & Mahajan, 1997). To form a cross-functional team, firms should look for people who work effectively with other multidisciplinary team members in addition to mastering their functional expertise (cf. Deschamps & Nayak, 1995; Katzenbach & Smith, 1993; Wind & Mahajan, 1997).

Organizational Structure

An ideal organizational structure for coordination within a firm is an integrated supply chain process for seamless flows of information, products, services, and finances. In supply chain management literature, authors highlight the needs of process integration from sourcing, to manufacturing, to distribution within a firm and across the firms in a supply chain (e.g., Cooper, Ellram, et al., 1997; Cooper, Lambert, et al., 1997; Manrodt, Holcomb, & Thompson, 1997). Similarly, Stevens (1989) posits that an internally integrated process has full systems visibility from distribution through to purchasing. Hewitt (1992) argues that supply chain integration is not simply realignment of existing functional organizations but a natural result of redesigned business processes. A director with a leading drug store chain whom we interviewed argued:

> If you are a process organized enterprise you are probably one of the people that is working on an ultimate supply chain or working more toward that end of the spectrum because the process is what you're interested in, and the process touches all of those different things. If you are a functionally organized enterprise, then you tend to focus on getting the product from point A to point B efficiently.

In other words, supply chain management requires a structure beyond a functional silo structure in which people are not able to go between the functions.

Unfortunately, it is not clear what forms of organization are ideal for effective inter-functional coordination. Concerning organizational communications, Hall (1999) suggests such possible solutions as ubiquitous meetings, matrix-like systems, project groups or task forces, and proper documentation. Considering the fact that coordination requires appropriate information sharing (cf. Kahn & Mentzer, 1998), committee meetings, matrix-like systems, project groups, or task forces are suitable organizational structures for coordination. Mintzberg (1996) also suggests that liaison devices such as liaison positions, task forces, standing committees, and a matrix structure based upon *interdependent relationships* among different functional areas are organizational structures used to encourage mutual adjustment.

According to Hall (1999), meetings have the potential to yield common meanings among participants. Committees are formed to resolve a certain, focused issue either within a specified time (i.e., ad hoc committees) or within an indefinite time frame (i.e., standing committees) (Lambert et al., 1998). Except for standing committees, meetings and ad hoc committees are temporary organizational structures for particular needs.

The essence of the matrix-like system or matrix organization is the joint existence of functional (vertical or column) groupings and output (horizontal or row) groupings (products, projects, or programs) that overlap (Hodge et al., 1996). Thus, the matrix organization requires coordination of activities across organizational units (Lambert et al., 1998). Matrix organizations are unique in responding to the need for responsiveness to environmental conditions and high levels of scarce functional expertise.

Project groups or task forces typically are composed of personnel from a variety of organizational units to develop a new product or service for the organization (Hall, 1999). These groups (or teams) are useful to combine complementary skills and expertise to achieve a common goal (Lambert et al., 1998).

Recently, virtual organizations have gained ground as an alternative organizational structure. Virtual organizations are a collaborative network of employees, linked by integrated computer and information technologies that allow organizations to create more flexible structures designed to maximize the experience and expertise of their employees and make it available wherever needed (Anderson & Vincze, 2000). Because supply chain management requires systemic and strategic coordination and is, thus, interactive and complex in nature, virtual organizations may be the best organizational structure for supply chain management. A virtual organization can reach outside the organization. Thus, a core organization can carry out critical functions to which the organization is particularly well suited, and functions outside this core competence may be performed by organizations with which the core organization has formed alliances or affiliations (Hodge et al., 1996). In this way, a virtual organization may help a firm expand its supply chain activities into the supply chain to which it belongs.

Regardless of the formal structure chosen, inter-functional relationships remain a key component and, thus, organizations are not limited to the use of one type of temporary team or committees or any other formal and indefinite organizational structures, including the matrix organization and the virtual organization. I propose, however, that firms should build a virtual organization-like structure that is flexible in configuration and reconfiguration of functional experts and is expandable outside the single firm to cooperate with other firms within a supply chain.

Putting It All Together

In summary, Mintzberg (1996) argues that no organization can rely on a single mechanism, and that as organizational work becomes more complicated, the preferred means of coordination shifts from mutual adjustment to direct supervision, then to standardization, finally reverting back to mutual adjustment. Similarly, supply chain management requires that a firm coordinate its traditional business functions in various ways such as mutual adjustment (i.e., information sharing), direct supervision (supply chain managers), standardization of outputs (i.e., inventory control and customer service), and standardization of norms (i.e., a supply chain orientation and the marketing concept).

Antecedents of Coordination

For the coordinating mechanisms to work, an organization should have common goals that it tries to accomplish through coordinating efforts, trust, and commitment among the personnel from different functional areas, and top management support to achieve an optimal level of coordination.

Common Goals

Common or integrated goals refer to establishing joint or mutual goals and performance measures between two different functions (Murphy & Poist, 1992). Achievement of the company's goals requires extensive cross-functional coordination, which may be difficult when functional departments think narrowly in terms of their own functional goals (Hodge et al., 1996). A director with a leading drug store chain we interviewed said:

> Even though it is very expensive to move multiple small quantities of product, that is the right thing to do at the enterprise level for our vision of customer service. . . . If you separate logistics and inventory and marketing into three separate pieces of a supply chain, they will tend to optimize themselves rather than the supply chain.

In this context, common goals affect the relationship between functional areas and sub-units within organizations (Fisher, Maltz, & Jaworski, 1997). In an empirical study of members of the Council of Logistics Management (CLM), Murphy and Poist (1992) found that lack of perceived benefits is a key obstacle to inter-functional coordination between marketing and logistics. In other words, without pre-established goals that fulfill common interests of different functions, inter-functional coordination will not succeed.

A way of establishing common goals is incentive systems that involve the sharing of benefits and risks between different functions for any cooperative efforts as well as incorporate greater goal integration (Coombs & Gomez-Mejia, 1991; Hauser, Simester, & Wernerfelt, 1994; Murphy & Poist, 1992). McCann and Galbraith (1981) argue that rewarding employees who contribute to organizational profits rather than individual or departmental benefits encourages inter-functional interaction because functional areas are interdependent in goal attainment. In addition, goal integration should reduce the incidence of coercive influence attempts by increasing functional interdependence and, therefore, the need to cooperate (Fisher et al., 1997).

Trust and Commitment

McAllister (1995) proposes that informal relations are central to the real work of organizations. Dwyer and Tanner (1999) argue that internal partnering among personnel from different functional areas requires trust and commitment. According to McAllister (1995), the beliefs of managers about the *trustworthiness* of peers can be measured along two dimensions, the extent of affect-based trust and the extent of cognition-based trust, and some level of cognition-based trust is necessary for affect-based trust to develop. McAllister (1995) defines cognition-based trust as grounded in individual beliefs about peer reliability and dependability, and affect-based trust as grounded in reciprocated interpersonal care and concern. His study results further indicate that affective foundations are essential for interpersonal trust, and affect-based trust facilitates effective coordinated action in organizations.

In the context of interaction, Moorman, Zaltman, and Deshpande (1992) found a correlation between interaction quality and an information receiver's trust in the information sender. Maltz and Kohli (1996) also found that a receiver's trust in a sender of intelligence increases frequency of information dissemination and the receiver's perceived intelligence quality, and thereby affects interactions through market intelligence use. Because inter-functional coordination is built on interactions between two different parties in an organization, interpersonal trust in informal relations precedes inter-functional coordination.

Commitment is a condition in which members of a group give their efforts, abilities, and loyalties to the organization and its pursuit of its goals in return for satisfaction (Hodge et al., 1996). Commitment makes people dedicate resources to maintain the relationship and also enables the relationship to survive either party's mistakes and environmental disturbances that are neither party's fault (Dwyer & Tanner, 1999). Maltz and Kohli (1996) argue that people who are committed to their organization have the desire to further their organization's goals and thus are motivated to seek inter-functional interactions to find ways of attaining those goals. Accordingly, Maltz and Kohli (1996) found that the greater the organizational commitment of personnel, the greater the frequency of information dissemination. Thus, commitment is a key antecedent of coordination.

Top Management Support

Murphy and Poist (1992) report that top management support is one of the most important and most frequently used techniques to encourage inter-functional coordination. Similarly, Hodge et al. (1996) argue that integrating the activities, tasks, and sets of tasks performed throughout the organization into a coordinated whole is the primary responsibility of management. Leaders differentiate tasks, group employees together, and integrate work so that the organization can conduct itself in a smooth and seamless manner (Hodge et al., 1996).

Consequences of Coordination

Many of the benefits of cooperation, at least to an organization, can be defined in such non-economic benefits as faster cycle time of product to market, improved quality, high-quality decision making, improved competitiveness, and so on. These dimensions can be seen as the intervening variables that help to explain why coordination might enhance performance of and customer satisfaction with an organization. Nevertheless, researchers would benefit from examining a broader set of outcome variables (Smith et al., 1995). I suggest, therefore, that well-executed inter-functional coordination brings a firm competitive advantage through reduced cycle time, new product success, and finally profitability.

Competitive Advantage

Gareth Jones (1998) argues that although many functional and organizational resources are not unique and can be imitated, an organization's ability to coordinate and motivate its functions and departments is difficult to imitate. Similarly, Porter (1980) argues that the ability to coordinate linkages of such activities as operations, outbound logistics, and service (e.g., installation) often reduces cost or enhances differentiation. According to Jones (1998), it might be possible to buy the functional experts or technical knowledge of 3M or Microsoft, but the purchase would not include access to the practices and methods that either firm uses to coordinate its resources because these intangible practices are embedded in the way people interact in a firm. In this way, coordination ability becomes a source of core competence with which an organization coordinates its functional and organizational resources to create maximal value (Jones, 1998). Effective coordination of resources therefore leads to competitive advantage (Hill & Jones, 1988). I propose that there are two important means of providing competitive advantage through coordination: reducing cycles time and new product success.

Reducing Cycle Time: Most executives today recognize that cross-functional teams offer the benefits of different perspectives and skill sets, and that a functionally diverse team can improve the quality of products developed and reduce the cycle time necessary to launch new products or services (McDougal & Smith, 1999). Researchers (Carmel, 1995; Griffin, 1997; Gupta & Wilemon, 1990; Mabert, Muth, & Schmenner, 1992; Trygg, 1993) also have suggested that a cross-functional team reduces product development cycle time. This is especially true when a cross-functional team approach is used for developing newer products (as opposed to incremental products) because cross-functional teams produce a greater variety of inputs to decisions, which may lead to higher problem-solving creativity and thus reduce cycle time (Griffin, 1997). Thus, it is suggested that a cross-functional team, if used in a more complex problem-solving situation, reduces cycle time.

Reduced cycle time, in turn, contributes to a firm's higher business performance either directly or indirectly. Ittner and Larcker (1997) examined the performance implications of product development cycle time using data from a 1991 consulting company survey covering two industries (automobiles and computers) in four countries (Canada, Germany, Japan, and the United States). Although faster cycle time alone may not increases a firm's performance, faster product development cycles when combined with certain organizational practices, such as cross-functional teams and the use of advanced design tools, are associated with a firm's perceived overall performance.

New Product Success: Inter-functional coordination has also been identified as an important determinant of new product success (e.g., Griffin & Hauser, 1992, 1993; Song & Parry, 1996, 1997). For example, in an empirical study of 404 Japanese firms, Song and Parry (1997) suggest that inter-functional coordination has the largest total effect on relative new product success. They found that coordination is a key driver in diffusing market and customer knowledge among all members of the project team in Japanese firms and, thus, coordination ensures that an understanding of market needs, desires, and behavior in the early stage of development constitutes the foundation for technological applications valued by customers (Song & Parry, 1997).

Profitability

Ruekert and Walker (1987b) propose that inter-functional coordination activities favorably affect the performance of marketing managers. In an empirical study with hospitals, McDermott, Franzak, and Little (1993) confirmed that higher levels of inter-functional coordination activities are related to higher profitability. This inter-functional coordination entailed (a) involving other department heads in the marketing planning process, (b) sharing competitor information with other departments, (c) involving board members in the marketing planning process, and (d) organizing inter-departmental teams to call on potential customers.

Conclusions

Copacino (1998) suggests that supply chain leaders have developed depth of skills in key functional areas such as procurement, manufacturing, transportation and distribution, and customer care and also have managed these functions in an integrated way (i.e., inter-functional coordination). Inter-functional coordination thus appears key to successful supply chain management. This chapter provided a definition of inter-functional coordination and proposed the nature of the coordination, including the mechanisms of mutual adjustment, management control, standardization, functional expertise, and the management of emerging structural forms to encourage coordination in a supply chain context. I have attempted to provide managers with insights into how inter-functional coordination can be fostered, maintained, and enhanced within a firm that is deeply involved in supply chain management and to provide insight into expected outcomes of the coordination. This chapter also attempted to integrate existing theories of inter-functional coordination into one model relevant to the study of supply chain management.

Although the contribution of this chapter is important, much work remains to be done in the development of theory regarding inter-functional coordination in supply chain management. Empirical research is called for to confirm or disconfirm the theory developed in this chapter. Especially, a more systematic examination is needed of the theoretical mechanisms that govern inter-functional coordination within a firm toward supply chain management within a supply chain that consists of multiple firms. The coordinating mechanisms illustrated in this chapter are extensively borrowed from organizational theories; supply chain management-specific mechanisms are needed that can be verified by broad empirical tests. There have been only a few theory tests performed in the study of supply chain management (e.g., Ellram & Cooper, 1990; Spekman, Kamauff, & Myhr, 1998), and the focus of the existing studies was on interfirm relationships in a supply chain. It is time for researchers to turn their attention to intrafirm mechanisms for successful implementation of supply chain management. At the same time, advancement is needed in the study of ideal organizational structures in the age of supply chain management. Authors (e.g., Christopher, 1992a; Cooper & Ellram, 1993) have suggested organizational structures of a supply chain that consists of multiple firms, but not those of individual supply chain partners. Future research thus is called for in the areas of effective coordinating mechanisms and organizational structure in a firm context.

15

Inter-Corporate Cooperation in Supply Chain Management

SOONHONG MIN

Executive Summary

This chapter describes the importance of interfirm cooperation in supply chain management, illustrates examples of how industry leaders work together with their supply chain members, and suggests a model of interfirm cooperation from drivers, to prerequisites, to the outcomes of successful cooperative relationships in a supply chain context.

Specifically, this chapter will

- Discuss today's business environment, which puts stresses on cooperative relationships with other firms, including power shifts from corporate buyers to end users, the requirements for mass customization, globalization, time- and quality-based competition, advances in technology, increasing knowledge intensity, and changing government policies
- Define interfirm cooperation in a supply chain context
- Describe the characteristics of interfirm cooperative relationships, all of which are illustrated with the examples in a supply chain context, such as limited set of partners, reward sharing, joint improvement driven by mutual interdependence, existence of conflict-resolution mechanisms,

open and complete exchange of information, working together to adapt to a changing marketplace, and active involvement of partners in supply chain activities

- Examine the following antecedents of interfirm cooperative relationships that may either hinder or promote cooperative behaviors among supply chain members: trust, commitment, cooperative norms, interdependence, compatibility, managers' perceptions of environmental uncertainty, and extendedness of the relationship
- Discuss the expected results of interfirm cooperation, such as reducing risks, obtaining resources, and gaining competitive advantage
- Illustrate how today's market environment, interfirm cooperative behaviors, and the antecedents and consequences of cooperation are linked in an integrative framework

From this, it is concluded that

- The demand for flexibility in today's turbulent business environment requires supply chain management, rather than the vertical integration or arm's-length relationships of the past
- Supply chain management (SCM) extends the concept of functional integration beyond a firm to all the firms in the supply chain and, therefore, each member of a supply chain needs to help each other to improve the competitiveness of the supply chain
- Implementing SCM inherently requires cooperation, which is defined as a set of joint actions of firms in a close relationship to accomplish a common set of goals that bring mutual benefits
- The supply chain manager's ability to build, maintain, and enhance cooperative interfirm relationships is essential in the future when competition will not be company against company, but supply chain against supply chain

Introduction

A transaction orientation has been a major influence in business research and practice throughout the industrial era (Gruen, 1997). Goldberg (1976) explains that in a transaction exchange, no duties exist between the participating parties prior to formation of the exchange, and duties of the parties are determined completely up front. According to Gruen (1997), a transaction orientation is based on two fundamental economic axioms: (a) competition and self-interest are drivers of value creation, and (b) maintaining an arm's-length relationship is considered vital for marketing efficiency. As a result, even though cooperation has been known for decades to be essential in such areas as channels of distribution, the marketing literature on relationships has focused disproportionately on power and conflict as focal constructs (Morgan & Hunt, 1994). Morgan and Hunt (1994) argue that marketers have long noted the absence of a theory that explains cooperation.

Recently, the powerful forces of globalization of industries, the total quality management (TQM) movement, rapid advances in technology, and a shift in the balance of power toward customers have fundamentally changed the rules for business success (Gruen, 1997). Gruen (1997) suggests that, as a result of these changes, there has been a shift in relationships from adversarial to cooperative and a shift in goals from market share to share of customers. He further suggests that the key to obtaining a higher share of each customer's lifetime business is the systematic development and management of cooperative and collaborative partnerships. The results of cooperative strategies are positive: A survey by Coopers and Lybrand found that firms involved in alliances increased their revenues faster by generating 23% more goods and services than those not involved in them (Gruner, 1996). Cooperative strategies have become increasingly popular since the mid-1980s (Hitt, Ireland, & Hoskisson, 1999).

SCM is defined in Chapter 1 as the systemic, strategic coordination of the traditional business functions and the tactics across these business functions within a particular company and across businesses within the supply chain, for the purposes of improving the long-term performance of the individual companies and the supply chain as a whole. SCM extends the concept of functional integration beyond a firm to all the firms in the supply chain and, therefore, each member of a supply chain helps each other improve the competitiveness of the chain (Ellram & Cooper, 1990). Thus, Cooper, Ellram, Gardner, and Hanks (1997) propose that long-term, functional cooperation across channel members at several management levels is required for successful implementation of SCM. In this context, Anderson and Lee (1999) consider cooperation among supply chain partners the cornerstone of changes in how companies manage supply chain operations—not because it enhances value, but because it has become a requirement for survival. There is thus a call for taking a close look at what cooperation is, how it works, and what are the benefits of it.

The purpose of this chapter is to outline what is known about cooperation. Based on a critical literature review, I suggest an integrative framework to understand the nature and the working mechanisms of the concept of cooperation in a supply chain context. The next section of this chapter discusses the market forces that drive firms to adopt cooperative strategies. Next, this chapter discusses the nature of cooperation—its definition and components. The following section presents the antecedents that either hinder or promote cooperation, as well as the consequences of cooperation. Finally, it presents an integrative framework of cooperative strategies in a supply chain context.

Changing Markets and Supply Chain Management

The fierce competition in today's markets is led by advances in industrial technology, increased globalization, tremendous improvements in information availability, plentiful venture capital, and creative business designs (Bovet & Sheffi, 1998). In highly competitive markets, the simple pursuit of market share is no longer sufficient to ensure profitability and, thus, companies focus on redefining their competitive space or profit zone (Bovet & Sheffi, 1998). For example, companies pursue cooperative relationships to capture lifetime customer share rather than mass market share through systematic development and management of cooperative and collaborative partnerships (Gruen, 1997). Markets have been changed by such factors as power shifts from corporate buyers to end users, the requirement for mass customization, globalization, time- and quality-based competition, advances in technology, increasing knowledge intensity, and changing government policies.

Power in a broad spectrum of channels has shifted downstream toward the customer or (end) user (La Londe, 1997); as a result, customer satisfaction becomes the ultimate goal of a firm. As the customer increasingly is in charge in the marketplace, interfirm cooperation is critical to satisfy customers. Manufacturers and their intermediaries must be nimble and quick or face the prospect of losing market share; thus, relationships and predictable performance become very important in a supply chain (La Londe, 1997).

Mass customization is a new way of viewing competition for both manufacturing and service industries, and mass customization at its core provides a tremendous increase in variety and customization without sacrificing efficiency, effectiveness, or low costs (Pine, 1993). As Pine (1993) states, "At its limit, it is the mass production of individually customized goods and services. At its best, it provides strategic advantage and economic value" (p. 13). In other words, customers want it all: low cost with high levels of service, and customization with availability (Bovet & Sheffi, 1998). Pine (1993), therefore, argues that mass customization can be achieved only through the committed involvement of employees, suppliers, distributors, retailers, and end customers.

Firms are competing in a global economy and, thus, the unit of business analysis is now the world, not just a country or region. The communications revolution and globalization of consumer culture will not tolerate hand-me-down automobile designs or excessive delivery times (Bovet & Sheffi, 1998). In this context, Kotler (1997) states, "As firms globalize, they realize that no matter how large they are, they lack the total resources and requisites for success. Viewing the complete supply chain for producing value, they recognize the necessity of partnering with other organizations" (p. xxxiii).

Time- and quality-based competition focus on eliminating waste in the form of time, effort, defective units, and inventory in manufacturing-distribution systems (Larson & Lusch, 1990; Schonberger & El-Ansary, 1984; Schultz,

1985). In addition, there has been a significant trend to emphasize quality, not only in the production of products or services but also throughout all areas in a company (Coyle, Bardi, & Langley, 1996).

La Londe and Powers (1993) suggest that the most profound and influential changes that directly influence companies are information technology and communications. With the advent of modern computers and communications, monolithic companies, which had become highly bureaucratic, started eroding. Fast communication that links all the members of a company decreased the need for multiple layers of people who were once the information channel and control mechanism. The decreased cost and ready availability of information resources allow easy linkages and eliminate time delays in the network (La Londe & Powers, 1993).

In the new competitive landscape, knowledge (information, intelligence, and expertise) is a critical organizational resource and is increasingly a valuable source of competitive advantage (Hitt et al., 1999). Similarly, La Londe and Powers (1993) characterized the 1990s as the era of reassembly or reintegration after that of disintegration. Current reintegration is based not on position or pre-scribed roles in a hierarchy but on knowledge and competence (La Londe & Powers, 1993). Bringing together the knowledge and skills to serve the market effectively requires coordination (Malone & Rockart, 1991).

Finally, government policy may encourage cooperative strategies among firms. The 1996 Telecommunications Act and subsequent court battles have created significant uncertainty for the firms involved, and consequently a significant number of alliances have emerged (Hitt et al., 1999). The enactment of the National Cooperative Research Act of 1984, as amended in 1993, eased the U.S. government's antitrust policy to encourage firms to cooperate with each other to foster increased competitiveness of American industries (Barlow, 1994; Bowersox & Closs, 1996).

As discussed above, today's business environment puts stress on both relations with customers and the service provided to such customers (Hitt et al., 1999). Kotler (1997) argues that "Customers are scarce; without them, the company ceases to exist. Plans must be laid to acquire and keep customers" (p. xxxii). The level of competition to capture customers in both domestic and international markets demands that organizations be quick, agile, and flexible to compete effectively (Fliedner & Vokurka, 1997; La Londe, 1997).

The Nature of Cooperation

Surprisingly, cooperation seldom has been studied explicitly as a construct (Anderson, Håkansson, & Johanson, 1994). Axelrod (1984) argues that the word "cooperation" is frequently used in a general sense with no specific definition. Although there have been many studies identifying the prerequisites and the benefits of cooperative strategies, there has been limited research on the nature of cooperation.

Defining Interfirm Cooperation

Cooperation, from the Latin *co*, meaning "together," and *operari*, meaning "to work," refers to situations in which parties work together to achieve mutual goals (Anderson & Narus, 1990). Cooperation has been defined as joint striving toward a common object or goal (Day & Klein, 1987; Stern, 1971). In other words, cooperation is the process of coalescing with others for a good, goal, or value of mutual benefit (Stern & Reve, 1980). According to Stern and Reve (1980), cooperation is an activity in which the potential collaborators are viewed as providing the means by which a divisible goal or object desired by the parties may be obtained and shared. As such, cooperation is conceptualized as a set of joint behaviors of involved parties toward a common set of goals. Heide and John (1990) propose the construct of joint action, in which two firms in a close relationship carry out "focal activities in a cooperative or coordinated way" (p. 25).

Day and Klein (1987) see cooperation and coordination as different concepts. According to them, coordination can be accomplished through tight controls or cooperative arrangements. They argue that it is possible that tight coordinating mechanisms can operate without a spirit of cooperation as a result of goodwill and mutual necessity. They further suggest that in the long run, however, such a situation may transition to one of both cooperation and coordination in vertically integrated equity arrangements. On the other hand, they suggest that the meaning of cooperation parallels Salmond and Spekman's (1986) definition of collaboration, which emphasizes the extent to which a constructive problem-solving approach is taken to the resolution of conflict. Contrary to Day and Klein's (1987) suggestion of a gradual congruence of cooperation and coordination, Anderson and Narus (1990) propose that cooperation can be defined as similar or complementary coordinated activities performed by firms in a business relationship to produce superior mutual outcomes or singular outcomes with expected reciprocity over time. As such, the terms "cooperation," "coordination," and "collaboration" are not clearly differentiated in the literature.

Based on the literature, I propose that cooperation occurs between firms to accomplish a common set of goals, whereas coordination takes place between the functions within a firm, in which tight control is involved under the same leadership. **Cooperation** is defined as *a set of joint actions of firms in close relationship to accomplish a common set of goals that bring mutual benefits.*

Alliances give shape to cooperative behaviors in an interfirm context. Lambe and Spekman (1997) define an alliance as a collaborative relationship among firms to achieve a common goal that each firm could not easily accomplish alone. Gulati (1995) also suggests that alliances encompass a variety of agreements whereby two or more firms agree to pool their resources to pursue specific market opportunities. Gulati (1995) argues that perhaps the most significant manifestation of the rise in interfirm cooperation has been the dramatic increase in interfirm strategic alliances. Gentry (1996) proposes that a strategic partnership between any two firms, whether it is between buyer and seller or manufacturer and carrier, could be a segment of an extended supply chain. This is so because each partner in a strategic alliance, which is a primary cooperative strategy, brings knowledge and/or resources to the partnership (Lyles & Salk, 1996). In other words, a "supply chain" is a set of firms among which cooperation may take place.

Characteristics of Cooperation in Supply Chain Management

Grandori and Soda (1995) propose that to maintain long-term cooperation, repeated sequential communications, decisions, and negotiations must take place. Monczka, Trent, and Handfield (1998) add reward sharing, joint improvement efforts, working together to adapt to market changes, and quality control by suppliers rather than quality inspection by buyers as attributes of cooperation. Managers also recognize important aspects of interfirm cooperation in a supply chain context. For example, one of the executives we interviewed indicated that "sharing risks and sharing information are like linking up the involved parties over the fence like good neighbors." The characteristics of cooperative interfirm relationships are presented in Table 15.1.

A powerful means of enhancing the likelihood of achieving cooperative action among firms is the selection of partners based on some good predictors of relevant cooperative behaviors (Grandori & Soda, 1995). It is impossible for a buyer to develop and maintain close relationships with thousands of suppliers; as a result, each purchased item or family of items has only a limited

Table 15.1 Characteristics of Cooperative Interfirm Relationships

1. One of a few partners for each major item
2. Reward sharing
3. Joint improvement driven by mutual interdependence
4. Existence of conflict-resolution mechanisms
5. Open and complete exchange of information
6. Working together of firms to adapt to a changing marketplace
7. Active involvement of the firms in supply chain activities

SOURCE: Adapted from Monczka, Trent, and Handfield (1998, pp. 143-144).

number of suppliers (Monczka et al., 1998). For example, Siemens Telecom Networks (STN) reduced its number of suppliers and now tightly works together with that limited set of suppliers to achieve its quality and cost-reduction targets. In return, the remaining suppliers benefit by getting more business volume (Schwalbe, 1998).

In a complex relationship in which performance is difficult to measure, profit or income sharing based on incentive schemes is an important cooperation mechanism (Grandori & Soda, 1995). By the same token, Monczka et al. (1998) propose that a win-win approach to share the rewards of the business between both parties is required. Proctor and Gamble (P&G), for example, rewarded customers who adopted highly efficient logistics practices such as 2-hour carrier turnaround, on-time customer pickup, electronic purchase orders and invoicing, use of a pallet pool, and ordering in unit-load quantities, all of which brought P&G significant economic benefits (Drayer, 1999). Chrysler also expected its suppliers to submit cost-reduction suggestions that resulted in savings equal to 5% of their annual sales to Chrysler. Chrysler, in turn, rewarded them for continually improving Chrysler (Stallkamp, 1998).

A joint effort is driven by a desire to improve supplier performance in all critical performance areas, including cost reduction, quality improvement, delivery improvement, and supplier design and production capabilities (Monczka et al., 1998). For example, Toyota, with its Toyota Production System (TPS) that assumes the development of close cooperative relationships between Toyota and its supplier network, performs objective and accurate assessments of each supplier's performance and provides direct assistance to improve each supplier's quality and reliability (Langfield-Smith & Greenwood, 1998). Similarly, STN sends a team to a supplier's facility for about 3 days to work with the supplier's team to identify where waste could be eliminated (Schwalbe, 1998).

Participating firms work together to resolve disputes through mechanisms that support joint problem solving (Monczka et al., 1998; Salmond & Spekman, 1986). Dant and Schul (1992) found that, in a franchise context, if the relational properties of solidarity, mutuality, or role integrity are high, franchisers are likely to use mechanisms such as problem solving and persuasion. Useful mechanisms include inter-functional teams working across firms and co-location, both of which allow exchange of personnel. For example, both Chrysler employees and supplier employees co-locate at the Chrysler Technology Center to develop new Chrysler cars and trucks (Stallkamp, 1998). Presumably, the participants grow to appreciate the other's point of view and carry more understanding when returning to their original positions (Kotler, 1997).

Participating firms practice an open exchange of information (Monczka et al., 1998). For example, to minimize inventory in the supply chain, information systems must be able to track and communicate production and customer requirements at different levels in the chain (Cooper, Lambert, & Pagh, 1997). In addition, information about new products, supplier cost data, and production schedules and forecasts for purchased items should be shared among supply chain members (Monczka et al., 1998). Information sharing is found to be an essential enabler of synchronization of the supply chain through cooperative design (Anderson & Lee, 1999). Wal-Mart is very open and willing to work with its vendors, shares point of sale data with suppliers, and has employees communicate with suppliers' employees on a regular basis (Gill & Abend, 1996). Shared information between supply chain partners can be fully leveraged only through process integration, collaboration between buyers and suppliers, joint product development, and common systems (Christopher, 1999).

Participating firms maintain a credible commitment to work together during difficult times (Monczka et al., 1998). For example, a buyer does not eliminate a supplier who experiences short-term production problems. Cooperative relationships require joint action to resolve concerns about the market environment affecting both parties. When Chrysler expected future cost hikes in purchasing headliners used inside Dodge Intrepid and Chrysler Concorde sedans, Chrysler and its key suppliers worked together to realize cost savings that far exceeded those expected from traditional competitive bidding (Stallkamp, 1998).

Finally, participating firms are deeply involved in supply chain activities. For example, in the upstream flows in a supply chain, Chrysler invited suppliers to a "teardown" program, in which it took competitors' products apart, piece by piece, to learn how they build them, and actively asked the suppliers to submit proposals to improve the Chrysler minivan (Stallkamp, 1998). STN also looked for suppliers' improvement ideas in such areas as purchasing efficiency, make/buy decisions, design, specification, packaging, lead time, and quality via the Internet, fax, or file transfer (Schwalbe, 1998). In the downstream flows in a supply chain, P&G let its customers participate in its project to simplify pricing, standardize ordering, and reduce invoices and system errors (Drayer, 1999). In addition, helping distributors set quotas for customers, studying the market potential for distributors, forecasting a member's sales volume, and inventory planning and protection are all examples of involvement of a firm in the downstream flows in a supply chain (Mallen, 1963). Anderson and Lee (1999) also propose cooperative demand planning, order fulfillment, and capacity planning among supply chain partners to send a more accurate demand signal throughout the supply chain, which minimizes waste and maximizes responsiveness.

Antecedents and Consequences of Cooperation

As discussed in the previous section, cooperation is a set of joint actions of firms in a close relationship to accomplish a common set of goals that bring mutual benefits. This section discusses the antecedents and consequences of cooperation.

Antecedents

The antecedents of cooperative behavior can be categorized as (a) trust and commitment, (b) cooperative norms, (c) interdependence, (d) compatibility, (e) managers' perceptions of environmental uncertainty, and (f) extendedness of a relationship.

Trust and Commitment

Morgan and Hunt (1994) propose that cooperation arises directly from both relationship trust and commitment. Kumar, Scheer, and Steenkamp (1995) propose that trust is a concept with two dimensions: "honesty" and "benevolence." First, the partner's honesty is a firm's belief that a partner stands by its word (Anderson & Narus, 1990; Schurr & Ozanne, 1985), fulfills promised role obligations, and is sincere (Dwyer & Oh, 1987; Scheer & Stern, 1992). Second, the partner's "benevolence" is the party's belief that its partner is interested in the firm's welfare (Deutsch, 1958; Larzelere & Huston, 1980; Rempel, Holmes, & Zanna, 1985), is willing to accept short-term dislocations (Anderson, Lodish, & Weitz, 1987), and will not take unexpected actions that have a negative impact on the firm (Anderson & Narus, 1990). Moorman, Deshpande, and Zaltman (1993) define trust as a willingness to rely on an exchange partner in whom one has confidence. Thus, it is proposed that trust represents the partner's honesty, benevolence, and willingness.

Dwyer, Schurr, and Oh (1987) define commitment as an implicit or explicit pledge of relational continuity between exchange partners. Committed partners are willing to invest in valuable assets specific to an exchange, demonstrating that they can be relied upon to perform essential functions in the future (Anderson & Weitz, 1992). Gundlach, Achrol, and Mentzer (1995) conceptualize commitment as (a) an input dimension of the credibility and proportionality of resources committed to the relationship, (b) an attitudinal dimension of long-term commitment intentions, and (c) a temporal dimension of the consistency of inputs and attitudes brought to the relationship over time. Kumar et al. (1995) see commitment as a two-dimensional construct: (a) affective commitment that is the desire to stay in the relationship because of the positive affect toward the other party (Meyer, Allen, & Smith, 1991), and (b) incorporating continuity expectations and willingness to invest (e.g., Anderson & Weitz, 1992). Thus, commitment is proposed as a multidimensional construct consisting of the partner's (a) inputs of credible and proportional resources, (b) attitudes (e.g., intentions and desires) toward commitment, (c) continuity expectations and willingness to invest, and (d) consistent inputs and attitudes toward commitment over time.

Trust and commitment influence cooperation in several ways. Dwyer et al. (1987) argue that trust works to overcome mutual difficulties such as power conflict and lower profitability. Schurr and Ozanne (1985) argue that trust significantly stimulates favorable attitudes and behaviors, including communication and bargaining with respect for the current supplier. According to Granovetter (1985), mutual trust in a relationship reduces the development of opportunistic intentions and thus may eliminate the need for structural mechanisms of control. Thus, as Pruitt (1981) proposes, trust and a desire to coordinate with another party are closely related. Finally, commitment is an essential ingredient for successful long-term relationships that are required for cooperation (cf. Gundlach et al., 1995). In summary, Morgan and Hunt (1994) state that

> Commitment and trust are "key" because they encourage marketers to (1) work at preserving relationship investments by cooperating with exchange partners, (2) resist attractive short-term alternatives in favor of the expected long-term benefits of staying with existing partners, and (3) view potentially high-risk actions as being prudent because of the belief that their partners will not act opportunistically. (p. 22)

Cooperative Norms

Cooperative norms reflect the belief that both parties in a relationship must combine their efforts and cooperate to be successful (Cannon & Perreault, 1997). In this context, Siguaw, Simpson, and Baker (1998) defined cooperative norms as "the perception of the joint efforts of both the supplier and distributor to achieve mutual and individual goals successfully . . . while refraining from opportunistic actions" (p. 102). Cannon (1992) suggests measures of cooperative norms that should be developed inside firms: (a) no matter who is at fault, problems are joint responsibilities; (b) both sides are concerned about the other's profitability; (c) one party will not take advantage of a strong bargaining position; (d) both sides are willing to make cooperative changes; and (e) we do not mind owing each other favors.

Interdependence

Interdependence or mutual dependence has a positive impact on cooperation (Aiken & Hage, 1968; Heide & Miner, 1992; Pfeffer & Salancik, 1978; Rogers & Whetten, 1982; Williamson, 1985). Dependence of a firm on its partner refers to the firm's need to maintain a relationship with the partner to achieve its goals (Frazier, 1983a). Heide and John (1988) indicate that dependence of a firm on its partner is increased when (a) outcomes obtained by the focal firm from the partner are important and highly valued and when the magnitude of the exchange is high, (b) outcomes obtained by the focal firm exceed outcomes available to the focal firm from the best alternative partner, and (c) the focal firm has few alternative sources or potential sources of exchange.

Interdependence is related to cooperation in several ways. First, Lusch and Brown (1996) found that high bilateral dependence between a supplier and a wholesale-distributor increases relational behavior. Buchanan (1992) argues that when mutual dependence between a wholesale-distributor and its supplier is high, both parties have a high stake in ensuring the relationship's success. In such cases, both parties have invested time, effort, and money in the relationship and are committed to the relationship (Anderson & Weitz, 1992). On the contrary, in channels with low levels of mutual dependency, neither party has much of a stake in the relationship and, therefore, relational behavior will not develop to a significant degree.

Second, acknowledged dependence is a prime force in the development of supply chain solidarity (Bowersox & Closs, 1996). In addition, this dependence is what motivates willingness to negotiate functional transfer, sharing key information, and participating in joint operational planning (Bowersox & Closs, 1996). Finally, Ganesan (1994) proposes that dependence of a firm on another firm is positively related to the firm's long-term relationship orientation.

Compatibility

Organizational compatibility is defined as having complementary goals and objectives, as well as similarity in operating philosophies and corporate cultures (Bucklin & Sengupta, 1993). Bucklin and Sengupta (1993) tested and confirmed that organizational compatibility between firms in an alliance, a form of cooperation, has a strong positive impact on the effectiveness of the relationship (i.e., the perception that the relationship is productive and worthwhile). By the same token, Stern and Reve (1980) propose that cooperation involves a combination of object- and collaborator-centered activities that are based on compatibility of goals, aims, or values. Similarly, Cooper, Lambert, and Pagh (1997) suggest that although meshing cultures and individuals' attitudes is time-consuming, it is necessary at some level for the channel to perform as a chain.

Managers' Perceptions of Environmental Uncertainty

The development of alliances, which are many forms of interfirm cooperation (Nooteboom, Berger, & Noorderhaven, 1997), is positively associated with key managers' perceptions of environmental uncertainty (Dickson & Weaver, 1997). Managers' perceived environmental uncertainty is posited as a multidimensional construct that includes (a) high general uncertainty, (b) high technological volatility and demand, (c) low predictability of customer demands and competitor actions, and (d) demands for internationalization (Dickson & Weaver, 1997).

Dickson and Weaver (1997) also found a significant three-way interaction among perceived uncertainty, entrepreneurial/conservative orientation, and individualism/collectivism. For example, the probability of the increasing use of alliances with greater perceived general uncertainty is higher for collectivist managers than for individualistic managers, and the probability is the greatest for collectivist managers with low entrepreneurial orientations and lowest for individualistic managers with high entrepreneurial orientations (Dickson & Weaver, 1997). Dickson and Weaver's findings may be explained by the facts that managers with an entrepreneurial orientation are more likely to take risks in the face of uncertainty (e.g., Covin & Slevin, 1991; Palich & Bagby, 1995) and that managers with collectivist orientations emphasize the importance of belonging to a stable, select in-group, value cooperation with the in-group, and expect the group to help provide for the welfare of group members (cf. Hofstede, 1980, 1984; Hui, 1988; Hui & Triandis, 1986; Hui & Villareal, 1989). As such, alliance formation may be contingent upon taken-for-granted orientations and cultural norms of the management team members (e.g., perceived uncertainty, entrepreneurial orientation, and individual culture) who want to hedge against risk and uncertainty.

Extendedness of a Relationship

Heide and Miner (1992) define the extendedness of a relationship as the degree to which the parties anticipate that the relationship will continue into the future with an indeterminate end point. Based on their observations of the Prisoner's Dilemma game, Heide and Miner (1992) argue that, although anticipated open-ended interaction does not require cooperation, it does make it possible—even when neither party has altruism or concern about the other party's well-being. The first implication of the iterated game framework of Heide and Miner (1992) is that, in a Prisoner's Dilemma situation, extendedness in a relationship should increase the probability of a pattern of cooperation. Thus, Heide and Miner (1992) hypothesized and confirmed that extendedness in a relationship, or open-ended interaction, has a positive effect on the level of cooperation between two interacting firms.

Consequences

Several authors (Ansari & Modarress, 1990; Day, 1994; Frazier, Spekman, & O'Neal, 1988; Lamming, 1993; Lei & Slocum, 1991) have suggested that cooperative relationships bring both buyer and supplier improved product quality and productivity, reduced lead time, quick market entry, and cost reductions, all of which lead to competitive advantages. In other words, cooperation enhances the competitive position of a firm. A good example is Toyota's cooperation with its suppliers, which enhances its competitive position in the global automobile industry (Hill, 1995).

In addition to competitiveness, cooperative interfirm relationships help firms reduce risks in uncertain business environments (Nooteboom et al., 1997), enhance their own core competencies (Nooteboom et al., 1997), and acquire access to complementary competencies (Porter & Fuller, 1986). These benefits sought from strategic alliances, a form of interfirm cooperation, can be categorized as (a) risk reduction, (b) access to resources, and (c) competitive advantage.

Reducing Risks

Traditionally, risk has been defined only as either unanticipated variation or negative variation (Miller, 1992; Miller & Leiblein, 1996). Thompson (1967) argues that control of uncertainty and risk in the environment is the essence of management. Thus, risk sharing or risk controlling has been proposed as an important justification for joining strategic alliances (Das & Teng, 1998; Kogut, 1988). Das and Teng (1998) propose that cost and risk in research and development (R&D), marketing, and production can be inordinately high for a single firm, whereas strategic alliances allow multiple firms to share the total cost and risk.

Many researchers have identified risk control and risk reduction in R&D as a key rationale for R&D-related alliances (Gulati, 1995; Osborn & Baughn, 1990; Teece, 1992), and others have referred to risk reduction in investments as a stimulus for strategic alliances (Hagedoorn, 1993). Lambe and Spekman (1997) also argue that it is industry uncertainty that truly drives firms to use alliances to acquire technology, which is an outside resource, in the face of rapid innovation because uncertainty can elevate the potential costs of a merger/acquisition to an unacceptable level. Clearly, firms look to minimize the cost of selecting the wrong technology. In this respect, alliances, typical forms of cooperative relationships are far more attractive because they typically require a much lower overall investment, pose considerably less risk than potentially failed mergers/acquisitions, and provide added flexibility to shift to new technologies as necessary (Harrigan, 1983).

Obtaining Resources

A firm or a set of firms can benefit from cooperation by obtaining competitive advantage (e.g., cost leadership and differentiation) directly, or by acquiring resources—financial, technological, physical, and managerial (Das & Teng, 1998)—that are the sources of competitive advantage. In this sense, capabilities are a form of resources and are defined as complex bundles of skills and collective learning, exercised through organizational processes that ensure superior coordination of functional activities (Day, 1994).

According to Day (1994), as buyer-seller relationships continue their transformation, a customer-linking capability—creating and managing close customer relationships—is increasingly important. In a close relationship, the seller has an incentive to be open with buyers to develop superior or dedicated resources. In this manner, the relationship creates durable linkages with customers, channel members, and suppliers, and thus creates channel bonds, a distinctive capability. In essence, strategic alliances are about accessing resources that a particular firm does not already possess but are critical for improving its competitive advantage (Das & Teng, 1998; Porter & Fuller, 1986). In this context, Badaracco (1991) observed that embedded knowledge of the firm, a firm-specific resource, drives firms to develop strategic alliances. The brief description of resources includes

1. Financial resources: the availability of capital (Das & Teng, 1998);
2. Technological resources: "secret know-how or superior R&D capability," including patents (Chi, 1994, p. 271);
3. Physical resources: raw materials, production capacity, and distribution channels provided by the firm (Grant, 1995); and
4. Managerial resources: upper-level people and the skills necessary for running a business organization effectively (Das & Teng, 1998).

Resource-based theory assumes that resource portfolios are heterogeneous across firms (cf. Barney, 1991). Prahalad and Hamel (1990) suggest that, in the light of the increasing importance of fixed costs, rapid technological development, and rising complexity of market inputs and outputs, firms must concentrate on core competencies to succeed. For example, the need for rapid new product development often precludes internal development of critical technologies, elevating the attractiveness of an external technology acquisition method, such as an alliance (Lambe & Spekman, 1997).

Christopher (1999) also proposes that cooperation based on shared information leveraged by joint actions and process information in a supply chain is prevalent as companies focus on managing their core competencies and outsource all other activities. The heterogeneity of resources of each firm thus deepens. The greater the degree of heterogeneity among firms in the market, the higher the likelihood of forming alliances that would create rents—defined as a return in excess of the firm's opportunity cost (Tsang, 1998). Alliances combine the heterogeneous resources of partners to the benefit of all parties involved (Devlin & Bleackley, 1988; Pisano & Teece, 1989). Robert J. Schwalbe (1998), Vice President of Purchasing and Materials for STN, stated, "Managing your entire supply chain is a simple process *if* you are super human and have unlimited resources at your disposal. In the real world, . . . successful SCM requires a targeted strategy that embraces both the external and internal elements of the supply chain" (p. 69). Firms should obtain resources through interfirm cooperation as well as inter-functional coordination to successfully implement SCM, which in turn brings them competitive advantage.

Gaining Competitive Advantage

Porter (1985) argues that coordinating and jointly optimizing with channels (downstream) and suppliers (upstream) lowers cost and/or enhances differentiation. He refers to the capabilities of buyer-seller relationships as vertical linkages that reflect interdependencies between a firm's activities and the value chains of suppliers and channels. In the same context, Stern and Reve (1980) suggest that cooperative behavior facilitates coordination and programming of activities within the channel that, in turn, provide potential cost advantages and improve competitive strength. Given this, there is a positive relationship between the level of cooperation within the channel and the joint profits obtained by it.

According to Porter (1985), there are two basic types of competitive advantage: cost leadership and differentiation. Cost leadership entails being able to perform value chain activities at a cost lower than competitors' while offering a parity product (Porter, 1985; Day & Wensley, 1988). Linkages, whether inside or outside a firm, create the opportunity to lower the total cost of the linked activities (Porter, 1985). One retail executive we interviewed stated:

> Even though from a counterintuitive standpoint it may cost more in the cost of goods for manufacturers to perform a service for us, their ability to do that may be less expensive than our own ability to do that. It may actually raise the cost of goods but lower the overall cost of goods into the store.

In such a way, supply chain partners lower the total cost of the flows from suppliers to customers. In addition, relational contracting with affiliated companies may save on the cost of negotiating and drawing separate contracts with different partners, as well as on the cost of monitoring everything from the quality of supplies to the soundness of an investment project (Aoki, 1988). Kalwani and Narayandas (1995) found that supplier firms in long-term relationships with select customers are able to retain or even improve their profitability levels more than firms that employ a transactional approach to servicing customers. This means that supplier firms are able to achieve greater profitability because of such factors as lower customer turnover, higher customer satisfaction that leads to lower service costs, and higher effectiveness of selling expenditures (Kalwani & Narayandas, 1995).

Cost saving through cooperation is also possible, even in fast-moving technology-based industries. Generally speaking, technology is more expensive when acquired through a merger/acquisition rather than through an alliance. Although a firm has more control of technology gained through merger/acquisition, it must pay for that control. An alliance, on the other hand, allows a firm to avoid acquiring superfluous technology and assets (Hamel & Prahalad, 1994).

Many times, the locus of innovation is other than the manufacturer (i.e., with suppliers and members of the supply chain) (Urban & Hauser, 1993). For example, DuPont invented Teflon cookware, which benefited cookware manufacturers as well as DuPont, and ALCOA pioneered the idea of aluminum truck trailers for heavy-duty hauling (Urban & Hauser, 1993). Thus, supplier linkages mean that the relationship with suppliers is not a zero sum game in which one gains only at the expense of the other, but a relationship in which both gain (Porter, 1985). As such, uniqueness in meeting buyer needs may be the result of cooperation with suppliers. This is also the case in channel linkages with customers. For example, discussions with the butchers in grocery stores led Mrs. Budd's Foods to develop a fresh meat pie that would increase the margins for the fresh meat section of the store (Urban & Hauser, 1993).

Close coordination with suppliers also provides differentiation by shortening new model development time. For example, suppliers may tool up for producing new parts at the same time that a firm is completing the design of equipment to manufacture the new model. A carefully selected and managed (single-source) supplier offers the greatest guarantee of consistently high quality, namely, commitment to the product because suppliers feel part of the family and permits manufacturers to subject them to rigorous inspection, certification, and education (Burt, 1989). Burt (1989) also argues that allowing suppliers to review the design of the entire subassembly before committing to it not only teases out new ideas but also helps the supplier understand what its customer really needs—or may need in the future.

An Integrative Framework

Based on the discussion above, an integrative framework that shows the nature of cooperation, its antecedents and consequences, and the market environment that forces firms to cooperate with each other is presented in Figure 15.1. Companies are forced to engage in inter-organizational cooperation because of changing market environments. There are seven major forces that drive firms to adopt cooperative behaviors: a power shift from corporate buyers to end users, requirements for mass customization, globalization, time- and quality-based

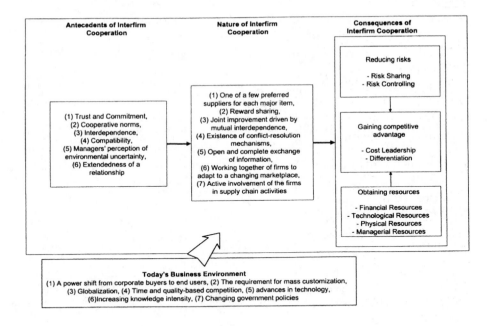

Figure 15.1 The Nature, Antecedents, and Consequences of Interfirm Cooperation

competition, advances in technology, increasing knowledge intensity, and changing government policies.

Cooperation is conceptualized as a set of joint actions of the firms in close interfirm relationships to accomplish a common set of goals that bring mutual benefits. Interfirm cooperation requires a wide range of behaviors (e.g., behaviors associated with planning, control, and execution) that are jointly performed by participating parties to accomplish common goals. Cooperation can be defined with such characteristics as (a) one of a few preferred suppliers for each major item, (b) reward sharing, (c) joint improvement driven by mutual interdependence, (d) existence of conflict-resolution mechanisms, (e) open and complete exchange of information, (f) working together of firms to adapt to a changing marketplace, and (g) active involvement of the firms in supply chain activities.

Antecedents of cooperative behaviors include (a) trust and commitment, (b) cooperative norms, (c) interdependence, (d) compatibility, (e) managers' perception of environmental uncertainty, and (f) extendedness of a relationship.

Finally, the consequences or benefits of interfirm cooperation are (a) reducing risks, (b) obtaining resources, and (c) gaining competitive advantage.

Conclusions

The demand for flexibility in today's turbulent business environment requires supply chain management, rather than the vertical integration or arm's-length relationships of the past. Supply chain management requires open communication lines that allow everyone in the entire chain to focus on the next customer, and most of all on the end customer, combined with activities that process concurrently rather than sequentially (Pine, 1993). As such, supply chain management provides solutions to firms competing in today's volatile business environment, because SCM is a systems approach to viewing the channel as a whole, a single entity, rather than as a set of fragmented parts, each performing its own function (Ellram & Cooper, 1990; Houlihan, 1985).

Managers should realize that cooperation in SCM is not another buzzword but a requirement that enables firms to realize efficient operations and effective services to achieve customer satisfaction. Thomas T. Stallkamp (1998), then-president of Chrysler, stated, "We want to work with only the best performers to create stronger, more efficient relationships while improving communication and performance throughout the [supply] chain" (p. 20). Similarly, the principal reason firms fail to achieve dramatic supply chain improvements is lack of sufficient synchronization of their work with partners. Synchronization is the only way to realize the benefits of scale between partners (Westbrook, 1999). As such, cooperation is a core component of successful SCM. This chapter contributes to practicing SCM by describing the details of cooperative actions.

16

Measuring Performance in the Supply Chain

JAMES S. KEEBLER

Executive Summary

This chapter describes performance measurement in the supply chain. Specifically, it will

- Examine the issues of supply chain measurement
- Review the key literature on supply chain measurement
- Identify the problems associated with measurement
- Describe approaches to deal with the problems of measurement
- Provide directions and priorities for future research to improve supply chain performance measurement

These discussions lead to the conclusions that

- Supply chain activities are *not* adequately defined, measured, or improved
- Supply chain measurement research is largely focused on the single firm
- Research has emphasized internal efficiency over external effectiveness
- There is an absence of multifirm performance measurement, or measures across the supply chain
- Interdependent planning and governance structures do not appear to exist across firms

- Supply chain members still appear to act largely as independent channel members, focused on self-interest
- Vertical conflicts exist within supply chains that could be resolved with joint planning and measurement
- Activity-based costing, a critical performance measurement capability, is not widely employed
- Potential benefits of improved supply chain management are stymied by the absence of activity-based financial data and the inability to link performance measurement with cost

Capitalizing on these opportunities to plan and measure key supply chain processes will improve both single-firm performance and supply chain outcomes. Supply chain measurement is in its infancy but will become more important in the future.

Introduction

A supply chain consists of three or more firms directly linked by one or more of the upstream and downstream flows of products, services, finances, and information from a source to a customer (see Chapter 1). Channels of distribution and vertical marketing systems are other terms used to describe supply chains; the former are characterized as loose collections of independent companies showing little concern for overall channel performance, and the latter are characterizing as having channel members acting in a unified manner (Armstrong & Kotler, 1999). The marketing and logistics functions of channel members are largely responsible for supply chain activities. Although logistics includes both supply sourcing and demand fulfillment activities, it had its roots in transportation and warehousing, which together were known as distribution.

Although the earliest text to address distribution issues (those relating to farm products) appeared in 1901, most of what we know today about logistics can be traced to articles and textbooks on distribution published in the 1950s and 1960s (Kent & Flint, 1997). The corporate concern for linking the inbound and outbound flows of goods produced the more integrative perspective of logistics. Today, the business logistics function includes the activities of forecasting, procurement, production planning, inventory control, warehousing, transportation, customer service, and post-sales support. For many companies, the sum of logistics costs can exceed half of the value added by the firm. For other companies, the firm's competitive advantage in the marketplace is generated by its logistics capabilities. The performance of logistics has a significant impact on the success of the enterprise. One would expect, then, that the measurement and control of logistics activities, both within a firm and between firms, would be highly refined. This is not the case. Current research finds that measurement of logistics and supply chain activities is not occurring to the degree desirable and necessary to effect superior performance of the supply chain.

The purpose of this chapter is to present a model of performance measurement in the supply chain. It will provide a review of the relevant literature, share the contributions of various researchers, identify gaps in the literature, and discuss directions and priorities for future research and managerial implications.

Literature Review

The literature related to supply chain performance measurement can be grouped under several topics and orientations:

A. Conceptual articles
   1. Performance definition
   2. Theoretical evaluation criteria
   3. Models
   4. Issues with measures themselves
B. Empirical articles and books
   1. Descriptive studies
   2. Methods
   3. Taxonomies
   4. Benchmarking
   5. Prescriptive performance improvement activities

The conceptual works tend to focus on measurement constructs and prescriptive methodologies. The empirical works tend to focus more on performance *content* than on measurement *process*. Little research has been conducted on multifirm performance or measures across a supply chain. The research focus has been on single-firm activity measurement, emphasizing efficiency over effectiveness.

Conceptual Articles

Logistics efficiency and effectiveness are two major concerns for logistics scholars. Armitage (1987) presented a management accounting technique for measuring and improving efficiency and effectiveness in distribution operations. Rhea and Shrock (1987a, 1987b) defined physical distribution effectiveness and presented a framework for the development of measures for distribution customer service programs. They made an important distinction between effectiveness determinants (i.e., customer satisfaction) and effectiveness dimensions, such as timeliness and accuracy. Harrington, Lambert, and Christopher (1991) provided a formal vendor performance measurement model that used defined criteria and weighted scores to assess the performance of suppliers. The model was tested and successfully implemented.

Mentzer and Konrad (1991) reviewed the construction and use of performance measures from an efficiency and effectiveness perspective, provided an understanding of how performance measures should be constructed, and described the strengths and weaknesses of their use. They also reviewed existing practices in logistics performance measurement and suggested methods of improvement. Problems they cited in establishing performance measures included lack of resources, incomplete information, comparability, measurement error, evaluation and reward systems that encourage dysfunctional behavior, and underdetermination.

The variables used in a measure might not *entirely* measure (i.e., they underdetermine) all the aspects of actual inputs and outputs. For example, delaying a truck departure until it is filled with multiple shipments may improve the value of the transportation cost measure, but it does not reflect the customer service damage done as a consequence of late delivery. Neither the transportation cost measure nor the on-time delivery measure reveals the ill will of the customer or captures the value of a subsequent lost order. Logistics measures are fragmented, and they only partially account for the full performance picture. The underdetermination problem produces an inherently flawed measure, especially when the view of performance is a cross-functional one. Thus, it is important to select performance measurement criteria and establish performance measures carefully. The authors stated that good measurements should

1. Cover all aspects of the process being measured,
2. Be appropriate for each situation,
3. Minimize measurement error, and
4. Be consistent with the management reward system.

Chow, Heaver, and Henriksson (1994) provided a summary of logistics performance literature published in five leading logistics journals between 1982 and 1992. Some publications reviewed focused on accounting techniques, some on customer service, some on the supplier interface, and some on the variety of operational aspects of logistics performance. Practically all the literature provided "soft" measures of performance based on using mail surveys as the data collection method. Only a few references presented "hard" measures, such as net income or accounting measures based on research of archival data. A wide variation existed in the definition of logistics performance. Generally, the literature found that firms tend to focus on their own, internal performance, and are especially concerned with efficiency measures. Discussions of supply chain measures were noticeably absent. The variety of performance dimensions suggested by the literature include efficiency, effectiveness, quality, productivity, quality of work life, innovation, profitability, and budgetability. It was generally concluded that defining and measuring performance in logistics is a difficult task for both researchers and practitioners. The authors offered five suggestions:

1. Researchers need to be more specific about the definitions and limitations of performance measures.
2. More innovative research designs are needed to complement the "rate-your-own-company" studies.
3. Contingency models of logistics performance need to be developed to stimulate research on the primacy of various performance dimensions, depending on the nature of the industry, company, and products involved.
4. Consideration should be given to assessing the performance of the supply chain, not just that of individual participants.
5. More bridge-building between theory and practice is needed.

Their review of the logistics literature revealed a variety of constraints that make it difficult to draw broad inferences about the relationship between a given logistics strategy and performance. With the exception of the mathematical/economic studies, nearly all the empirical studies utilized soft measures for the outcome variable. Nevertheless, both soft and hard measures are associated with strengths and weaknesses, which limits a researcher's ability to infer the existence of relationships between logistics performance and its antecedents. Conceptually, logistics performance may be viewed as a subset of the larger notion of firm or organizational performance. The latter has attracted a large volume of diverse research over the years. Increased attention to the development of valid measures is warranted. Researchers might do well to explore contingency models of logistics and supply chain performance.

Caplice and Sheffi (1995) addressed the need for a method with which to evaluate existing logistics metrics. These authors addressed this need by suggesting a set of evaluation criteria for individual logistics performance metrics and identifying the inherent trade-offs. A classification of logistics performance metrics, organized by process rather than by function, was presented, and the metrics were evaluated using the established criteria. A performance measurement system that is well designed at the strategic level can be flawed at the individual metric level. The authors advocated reevaluation of the existing individual metrics rather than developing novel metrics. The "goodness" of a metric can be evaluated along many criteria. The authors presented a synthesis of the prior research to establish eight such criteria: validity, robustness, usefulness, integration, economy, compatibility, level of detail, and behavioral soundness.

The discussion of the trade-offs between criteria, specifically the first four, is enlightening for those converting from functional to cross-functional and process views of performance. The trade-off between validity and robustness implies that as more situation-specific aspects of a process are included in the metric, the less comparable (widely acceptable) it becomes. The trade-off between integration and usefulness suggests that the more a metric promotes coordination across different functions (or firms), the less guidance it will provide for the particular function (or firm) manager. The most useful metric for an internal manager is one that focuses on his or her function without any additional exogenous factors. These two major trade-offs for metrics, between valid and robust, and between integrative and useful, are a major dilemma for the design of benchmarkable supply chain metrics.

Empirical Articles and Books

The Council of Logistics Management (CLM) has done much to advance the contribution to knowledge about measurement in logistics. Research contracted to A. T. Kearney resulted in a publication in 1978 that gave a perspective to the size of productivity improvement and cost reduction opportunities in the U.S. economy related to distribution (Kearney, 1978). A second study published 6 years later described measurement and improvement opportunities, presented criteria for success in improving productivity, and highlighted case studies of successful companies (Kearney, 1984). In 1991, a third study was published that described quality and productivity improvement opportunities through logistics measurement (Byrne & Markham, 1991). This third publication provided a solid foundation for understanding, developing, and applying appropriate logistics measures *within* the firm. It presents specific measures of productivity, utilization, and performance for activities within the various functions of transportation, warehousing, purchasing, materials planning and control, customer service, and logistics management. It also presents lists of potential performance improvement actions for each of these functions. This landmark CLM publication provides a detailed taxonomy and suggested improvement actions that should be useful to every logistics manager. It focuses the manager on the elements of the task and activities within functions. Companies that seek stability and control would employ the measures described to have command of their internal logistics process. It fails to address, however, measurement between firms and across supply chains.

Meanwhile, other Council of Logistics Management research studies (Bowersox et al., 1989; Global Logistics Research Team at Michigan State University, 1995) highlighted the benefits for logistics measurement experienced by both leading edge and world class companies. The Global Logistics Research Team (1995, chap. 6) reported that the capability to do functional and process assessments and to benchmark best practices is an essential business competency. It also reported that better measurement information availability occurred in the firms surveyed between 1989 and 1995. The study reported a significant gap in such information availability between the upper third and lower third of firms surveyed. It is notable that the 1995 study found that many key performance areas were not being widely measured. Half the asset management measures, specifically return on assets (ROA), return on investment (ROI), and activity-based costing (ABC) inventory classification, were not available in 12-19% of the firms. Of the 17 "cost" measures, only 5 were found to be available in at least 90% of the firms. Availability of key "cost" measures such as "inbound freight" at 75.8% availability, "inventory carrying" at 81.8%, cost of "returned goods" at 70.6%, and cost of a "backorder" at 33.3%, indicates that these measures were absent in 20% or more of the firms. Customer service measures such as "fill rate" (79.4% availability), "cycle time" (85.3%), "response time to inquiries" (41.9%), "customer complaints" (69.7%), "sales force complaints" (40.6%), and "overall satisfaction" (67.7%) indicated some management blindness in this area. Information availability was found to be in a range of 50-80% for 10 productivity measures. Quality information was not available for accuracy measures—picking, order, and document accuracy—in more than 25% of the firms. These findings demonstrate a continuing challenge and opportunity for firms to install adequate performance measurement *within* the enterprise.

These last two studies create a compelling call to action for business managers. They demonstrate that measurement in even these best companies has much room for improvement.

The most recent CLM-sponsored study provided a definition of key logistics processes extending *between* trading partners and a methodology and case for action to measure and improve logistics performance (Keebler, Manrodt, Durtsche, & Ledyard, 1999). This study also reported that measurement of key logistics activities and processes is not being widely conducted. This study reported that the percentage of survey respondents not capturing key measures was remarkably high. Examples include the following:

Measure	*Percentage Not Capturing*
Outbound freight cost	13
Order fill rate	19
On-time delivery	21
Customer complaints	23
Inbound freight cost	31
Order cycle time	38
Forecast accuracy	46
Invoice accuracy	48
Equipment downtime	54

The measures for logistics activities directly affecting a customer frequently are not defined. Less than 60% of the measures were either defined *by* the customer or jointly defined *with* the customer. The failure to achieve agreed-upon definitions of performance and the measures that report that performance is a critical obstacle to logistics competency in the supply chain.

An important contribution of the last study mentioned was the identification of the three key logistics processes in supply chain management: order fulfillment, sourcing/procurement, and planning, forecasting, and scheduling. This study also determined the level of measurement *between firms* on these key logistics processes to be very low (Keebler et al., 1999). Only 59% of the firms were measuring the fulfillment process. Only 22% were actually taking action to coordinate or integrate activities to improve performance based on the fulfillment measurement. Nearly 60% of the firms were *not* measuring the other two key logistics processes. This research reconfirms the conclusions of earlier studies: Key supply chain activities and processes are not being measured adequately.

Popular Topics

The most popular subjects of articles written on measurement in logistics include the four major topics of activity-based costing, quality, benchmarking, and reengineering. Pohlen and La Londe (1994) traced the evolution of costing approaches beginning from direct product profitability (DPP) through activity-based costing (ABC), through total cost of ownership (TCO), through efficient consumer response (ECR), to supply chain costing. These efforts at creating accurate and integrated cost measures were undertaken to increase the visibility of logistics costs within the supply chain so that cost reduction opportunities could be identified and pursued. By making use of standard and engineered times and existing rate information, the supply chain costing approach considers activities across the firms in the supply chain (La Londe & Pohlen, 1996).

There are two significant constraints. First, those firms that have not implemented ABC cannot provide logistics or supply chain-related costs at the activity level. Second, the detailed level of information about process steps and costs of activities that must be shared by the enterprises requires a highly coordinated or integrated partner relationship between them. Such interfirm relationships are difficult and slow to develop. Ultimately, restructuring the supply chain to exploit efficiencies also requires a mechanism capable of identifying and equitably allocating cost benefits between the partners as changes are implemented.

Activity-based costing can take many forms. ABC systems span a continuum from the traditional cost model with a single cost driver to a very elaborate cost system with activities for every conceivable type of work and corresponding activity drivers. The level of ABC sophistication varies by the proportion of overhead costs and the amount of diversity experienced within the firm. Other articles covering activity-based costing (Koota & Takala, 1998; Pirttilä & Hautaniemi, 1995; Walton, 1996) emphasized its importance in affecting supply chain performance improvements. Nevertheless, implementation of ABC lags. Of the 330 firms surveyed by the recent CLM study (Keebler et al., 1999), 56% indicated they were not planning implementation of activity-based costing, 24% were planning implementation, 9% had ABC implementation under way, and 11% had completed an ABC implementation.

Additional articles treat other aspects of financial measures of logistics (Eccles & Pyburn, 1992; Pegels, 1991; Speh & Novack, 1995), problems with accounting measures (Kaplan, 1984), cost and effect (Kaplan & Cooper, 1997), balanced scorecards (Kaplan & Norton, 1992, 1993), economic value added and shareholder value (Glassman and Stern & Stewart Co., 1997), the total cost/value model (Cavinato, 1992), linkages to financial statements (Cavinato, 1989), the stakeholder approach (Atkinson, Waterhouse, & Wells, 1997), transaction cost analysis (Rindfleisch & Heide, 1997), and the economics of lead-time reduction (Wouters, 1991).

Quality measures in logistics are a second major area covered by the literature. Topics include continuous improvement measures (Fortuin, 1988), quality control systems (Hillman, Mathews, & Huston, 1990), process controls (Novack, 1989), and quality programs in logistics (Read & Miller, 1991). Related topics of research include logistics measurement for strategic planning (Fawcett & Clinton, 1996), strategic performance (Chakravarthy, 1986), outsourcing (Aertsen, 1993; Foster, 1998), design (Perry, 1991; Stevens, 1989), and flow analysis (Farris, 1996; Scott & Westbrook, 1991).

Customer service has become a crucial measure of competitiveness in markets throughout the world. As competition has become more intense, service quality has become a primary determinant of overall customer satisfaction. The necessity to achieve service excellence in markets characterized by shrinking margins and tight budgets has created a powerful challenge for supply chain management. The challenge is to balance these operational realities with the need for quality customer service. Service quality can be managed effectively, even when market conditions are difficult and resources are limited, if the organization can focus on a limited number of high-priority logistics service features (La Londe & Cooper, 1988). One study presents a technique for the evaluation and management of customer service quality (Harding, 1998). Another study presents a customer's perspective on product and information flows (Rhea & Shrock, 1987b). Customer satisfaction has been shown to depend directly on measurement of effective order fulfillment (Davis, 1998).

Benchmarking topics abound, especially in the trade press. Most logistics managers want to have a guide to what *to* measure, and to compare their own operational performance to that of their competitors, or to a "best-in-class" model. Most benchmarking articles are concerned with the *values* of measures and not the numerators and denominators of them, leaving the comparability and validity of the values at question. One notable exception to the emphasis on content rather than process benchmarking is found in the efforts of the Supply Chain Council (Pittiglio, Rabin, Todd, & McGrath, 1994). Started in 1994 by a consulting firm that formed a consortium of many major manufacturers, the emphasis was on developing a standard process model, called the Supply Chain Operations Reference Model, or SCOR (Cohen, 1996). It identified four top-level processes—plan, source, make, and deliver—and decomposed these into multiple levels of categories and elements. Participating companies must further decompose the model into the activities and tasks particular to their operations. There has been no published evidence of the value of this approach to generating good measurement, and the approach has been faulted on the basis that there is no *one* set of governing standards that define a business model, especially because differentiation is implicit in competitiveness (Mesher, 1997).

Finally, the reengineering movement beset the logistics infrastructure in 1990 with an article that focused attention on process mapping, process improvement, process owners, and process customers (Hammer, 1990). Unfortunately, the same need for an orientation toward *measures* having owners and customers has not been well represented in the literature. One way to challenge the need for the mountains of measures found in many companies, and the time and expense to produce and communicate them, is to systematically challenge and eliminate all measures that cannot claim an interested customer and owner. This orientation is necessary for internally focused measures. It is even more difficult to adopt measures *across* firms in the supply chain unless customers and owners are formally established.

Conceptual Model of Measurement

There is a need to improve our understanding of the antecedents of measurements and the relationships of the basic types of measurements to the key logistics processes in the supply chain. Such a model could help inform the academic and practitioner of the interrelationships of processes and performance.

Start With Strategy

Environment is important to strategy formation. Some scholars believe that strategies must be constrained by, and must react to, ever-changing environmental conditions (Ackhoff, 1981). Other scholars maintain that strategy can enact the environment, and that the deliberate selection from available strategic choices shapes the emergent environment (Miles & Snow, 1978). In either case, there is universal agreement that strategy selection and articulation are fundamental to setting direction and objectives for the firm (see Figure 16.1).

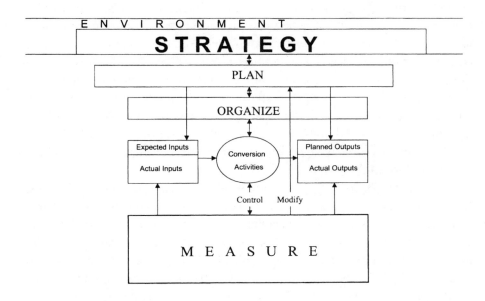

Figure 16.1. Measurement Within the Firm: Strategy Comes First

Porter (1980) presented an approach to strategy, combined with a tool-kit for practitioners. He described five forces that drive industry competition: potential entrants, suppliers, buyers, industry competitors, and substitutes. He reported entry barriers to be scale, differentiation, capacity requirements, switching costs, distribution channel access, raw material access, government policy, and retaliations. He described exit barriers as being economic, strategic, and emotional. All these factors should be considered in evaluating strategic choices. He imparted three generic strategies for competition: low-cost, differentiation, and focus. He warned firms about getting "stuck in the middle" with a halfhearted mix of options, not emphasizing one of the three strategies. He stated that the strategic choices cannot be pursued simultaneously, but they can be pursued sequentially, as opportunities dictate. Porter described four diagnostic components to developing strategy: future goals that drive it, current strategy (or what the firm is doing and can do), assumptions about itself and the industry, and capabilities. Porter recommended a strategy to seek the most favorable buyer, build up buyer switching costs, and reduce costs to switch from suppliers. This last recommended strategy is no longer consistent with the orientation of strategic sourcing and procurement relationships necessary to sustain integrated supply chains.

A modernized version of Porter's strategic competitive choices uses slightly different terms: operational excellence, product leadership, and customer intimacy (Treacy & Wiersema, 1991). The choice of strategy should drive the measurement emphasis placed on its various activities. A firm deciding to be operationally excellent will focus on cost reduction. A firm deciding to be a product leader will emphasize speed to market of its new product offerings. A firm emphasizing a customer-intimate strategy will value flexibility and responsiveness in its logistics activities, especially customer service. The key logistics measures for these organizations might be the same, but emphasis on them will vary with the choice of strategy.

Hamel and Prahalad (1994) provide a handbook on how to think strategically, focusing on leadership, strategy, and the changing market environment. Hamel and Prahalad state that strategy is both a process of understanding and shaping competitive forces, and a process of open-ended discovery and purposeful incrementalism. Firms need to exercise leadership and create their futures, to enact them by being better and, especially, different. Change the rules of the game. Reduce boundaries. Blur the lines. Create new industries. Lead and influence. Control the firm's destiny by influencing change in the industry. Path breaking is more important than benchmarking. The authors' view of strategy is to unlearn the past, have foresight, and leverage core competencies. Stable value chains do not exist. Companies need to build new profit engines, forge alliances, experiment, and learn. Strategy is now more about competing for position in tomorrow's industry than competing within today's industry. An important implication for logistics is that business strategies are evolving and changing, making it important to constantly monitor and adjust logistics strategies, plans, *and measurements* to ensure alignment to evolving corporate strategies. Segmentation and differentiation often require companies to support multiple strategies, which can be confusing and confounding to logistics managers. Logisticians must pay increased attention to being effective, not just efficient.

Conduct Iterative Planning

Planning follows the articulation of strategy. Planning has been defined as a deliberate process to produce systematically a preconceived outcome based on an integrated system of decisions (Mintzberg, 1994). Planning helps us prepare for the inevitable, preempt the undesirable, and manage uncontrollable events. Planning involves objective setting, that is, predetermination of the intended outcomes. It also includes extensive and ongoing audits of the external and internal environments. Planning involves analyses and decision making, including changing decisions previously made based on newly acquired knowledge. Planning contemplates the implications of current decisions and future possible decisions. Planning involves forecasting and scheduling. It contemplates and directs measurement of actual performance and emergent outcomes to allow for their comparison to planned performance and intended outcomes. Planning is an essential antecedent to measurement. Unless the supply chain manager predetermines what performance is intended or expected, it makes no sense to measure it. The value of a measure can inform a decision only if it can be compared to a stated goal; otherwise, it is non-actionable, and not worth calculating (see Figure 16.2).

Planning the design of the logistical system historically focused on inventory policy, facility location, and transport selection/routing (Ballou, 1993). Today, supply chain planners are also concerned with sourcing, outsourcing, and integrated information systems that extend beyond the direct, or unilateral, control of the firm. These planning activities include tasks *and* relationships. Segmentation and mass customization strategies have added complexity. Cycle time compression and customer-mandated quality in execution have created a need for urgency and precision in planning. Several major initiatives confront planners: asset productivity, horizontal management, information substitution, integrated planning, and system flexibility (Perry, 1991). With increasing integration of business activities within and between businesses, supply chain success calls for connectivity, collaboration, interdependency, and influence, not unilateral command and control.

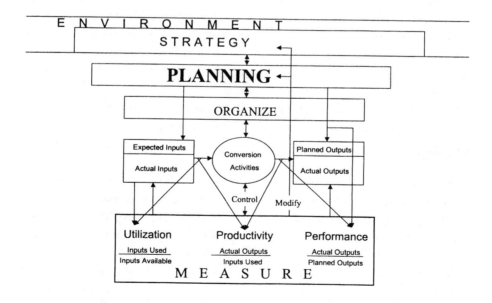

Figure 16.2 Planning Precedes Measurement, Here Internally Focused

Organize Resources and Inputs, and Direct Action

No literature was found that suggested an ideal organizational form for logistics or supply chain organizational structure. There have been empirical studies, however, inquiring into the spans of control for logistics units. Generally, a company pursuing a strategy of low cost opts for a centralized, wide span of control logistics organization, while a more customer-intimate firm prefers smaller, more focused, and flexible logistics organizations. There is no research to support the implication that the wider the span, the greater the control and integration. Perhaps increasing complexity associated with larger logistics organizations gets in the way of coordinating and integrating its activities. This is an area for future research.

Identification of the three key logistics processes in the supply chain requires the inclusion of supplier and customer interfaces in the planning and organizing of logistics activities. Understanding specifically what customers want and their resulting input expectations is fundamental to achieving customer satisfaction. Similarly, as a customer of its supplier, the firm must articulate its specific needs and expectations to the supplier. Only then can a measure of supplier performance be gauged (see Figure 16.3).

Measurement and Control

In controlling the work of people and technologies, only two phenomena can be observed, counted, and monitored: behavior and the outputs that result from the behavior (Ouchi, 1977). Control can be conceptualized as an evaluation process that is based on the monitoring and evaluation of behavior or outputs. It is a process of monitoring something, comparing it to some standard, and then providing some selective rewards or adjustments.

Ouchi (1977) reported that an antecedent condition was necessary to apply either form of control. To apply behavior control, the organization must have at least agreement, if not true knowledge, about means-ends relationships.

> The process by which inputs are transformed into outputs must be felt to be known before supervisors can rationally achieve control by watching and guiding the behavior of their subordinates. Except at the extremes, the dean of a school of business cannot control his faculty research by observing the behavior of faculty members. At best, he can control the quantity of output, but certainly not the quality through these means. On the other hand, the manager of a tin can plant (with engineered, standardized production processes) can observe the behavior of his employees, and if they behave as he knows they should, he can be certain that the expected tin cans are being produced. (p. 97)

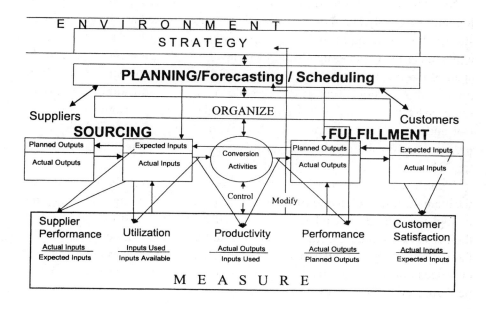

Figure 16.3 Three Key Logistics Processes in Extending the Internal Horizon

In the case of output control, the transformation process does not need to be known. The requisite antecedent to apply output control is a reliable, valid, agreed-upon measure of the desired outputs. The manager of the tin can plant can merely sample the output of his organization and ignore the behavior of his employees. The supply chain manager can count the number of deliveries made on time, if he and the customers have agreed on how to measure on-time delivery, without regard to the behavior of the drivers.

These two parts of the control process—the antecedent conditions and the forms of control (i.e., behavior or output)—can be combined into a matrix (see Figure 16.4).

Accordingly, either behavioral control or output control (Cell 1) can be applied when the supervisor has a high degree of knowledge about the value-added transformation process and the output measures are predetermined, available, and precise (Ouchi, 1979). Where there is low task programmability and low understanding or the absence of output measures (Cell 4), neither control form is appropriate. The organization must then exercise a form of ritual

Level of Knowledge of the Input-Output Transformation Process (Task Programmability)

	High (Perfect)	**Low (Imperfect)**
High	1 Behavior Control Or Output Control	3 Output Control
Low	2 Behavior Control	4 Ritual Control (Aka Clan Control or Cultural Control)

Availability and Precision of Predetermined Output Measures

Figure 16.4 Three Key Logistics Processes in Extending the Internal Horizon

SOURCE: This model is adapted from Ouchi (1979) and Govindarajan and Fisher (1990).

control, also known as cultural or clan control (Govindarajan & Fisher, 1990). Correct behaviors and outputs cannot be identified ahead of time. The selection process might be the only means of controlling in these cases.

As Porter pointed out (1980, p. 35), the primary focus of a strategic business unit (SBU) with a low-cost strategy is cost control. Businesses pursuing low-cost strategies have similar characteristics. They

- Vigorously pursue cost reduction,
- Have employees with high levels of experience,
- Practice all possible economies of scale,
- Acquire process engineering skills,
- Routinize the task environment, and
- Produce standard, undifferentiated products.

A standard product with a routine task environment implies that the knowledge of ends and means is relatively high, which indicates high task programmability. Businesses employing a low-cost strategy can apply control forms of Cells 1 and 3 in Figure 16.4. Only in the case of first-line supervisors, who can constantly observe behavior of employees in this context, can the conditions of Cell 1 apply. Middle and top managers removed from the transformation process must rely on output measures (Cell 3) to control their functions. The primary form of control for low-cost producers is output control.

Firms pursuing a differentiation strategy attempt to produce a product that is unique. The task of producing, marketing, and distributing a unique product implies low task programmability (Cell 4). Creative flair, strong basic research, product engineering, and long-term relationship building defy the short-term output measurement associated with monthly, quarterly, and annual periods, limiting the use of output controls. Consequently, differentiators are left with Cells 2 and 4 as control forms, that is, behavior or ritual control. Both forms are subjective.

Output control is not appropriate if the goals of an organization are not understood or agreed upon, and if outputs are unobservable or unreliable, and thus not good predictors of behavior. The selection of measures of the management control system depend on the strategy chosen, the knowledge of the transformation process, the level of precision in determining goals and measures of outputs, and trained, observable behaviors of employees.

Differences in Accounting and Operational Measures

The capability to measure actual performance relative to plan is critical to effective management and control. In the accounting and control system, the plan (budget) can be rolled down and up the organization. It is highly integrated.

Top- and low-level managers understand the plan and the implications for measured deviations from it. They share a common language. Each has a specific
goal. There is alignment.

The operational measurement and control system, where physical measurement takes place, does not share this alignment characteristic with the financial
control system. It is not possible for the warehouse manager's measure of cases
picked per labor hour, or the fleet manager's measure of deliveries per hour, to
be integrated into a CEO's interest in revenue dollars billed today. This poses a
dilemma. What should be measured, and how? How can the physical measure
be integrated with others to provide insight, value, and direction to different levels of management? This is an area for future research.

An interim solution could be pursued in the form of activity-based costing
(ABC) and activity-based management (ABM). Many articles have demonstrated the technique and value of analyzing physical measures in economic
terms. Unfortunately, this methodology is difficult and time-consuming to
install. Once engaged in ABC, practitioners are made aware of opportunities to
reengineer processes and design improved performance into the operational
activities. These managers are then confronted with several questions: Who are
the customers and who are the owners of these processes and measures? What
do these customers require? How well are the processes performing against
those requirements? What must the owners do, based upon the values of the
measures and the goals of the firm, to meet or reset those customer
expectations?

The Problems With Measures

The literature suggests many problems with measurements dealing with
capability, timeliness, adequacy, actionability, and integration. From a managerial perspective, the best measure accomplishes four things:

1. Captures specific aspects of the activity measures,
2. Provides actionable guidance for management intervention,
3. Allows comparability between it and other measures, and
4. Promotes coordination between managers of interdependent upstream and
   downstream flows of activities.

Unfortunately, these four measurement criteria cannot be satisfied *simultaneously*. At the operational level, where measures can both capture specific
aspects of the activity and provide actionable guidance, the degree of validity
and usefulness of the measure is highest. As measures are consolidated into
higher or more strategic levels of reporting, their validity and usefulness

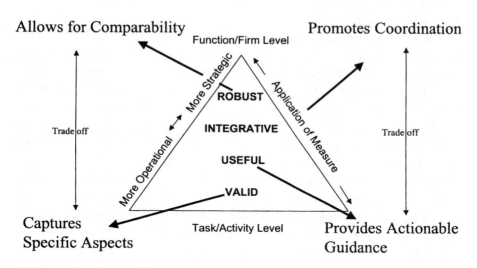

Figure 16.5. Measurement Criteria and Trade-Offs
SOURCE: Adapted from Caplice and Sheffi (1995)

diminish. The reverse is true for the criteria of comparability and coordination. The degree of robustness (generalizability) and integrativeness is greatest at the consolidated or strategic level and lowest at the operational level (see Figure 16.5).

The following is a summary list of problems associated with measures and the implementation of a measurement program (Caplice & Sheffi, 1995; Keebler et al., 1999; Mentzer & Konrad, 1991):

- Unavailable information
- Lack of resources to collect data
- Incomplete/inaccurate information
- Comparability
- Measurement error
- Lack of a customer of the measure
- Lack of an owner of the measure
- May not be jointly defined or similarly interpreted
- Might not facilitate trust
- Conflicting goals/conflicting measures
- Misdirected evaluation and reward systems
- Might not encourage appropriate behaviors

- Underdetermination
- May not be quantitative—soft versus hard
- May be accurate but not useful
- Strategic-level measures may not be actionable
- Operational level measures may not roll up
- Trade-off between validity and robustness
- Trade-off between integration and usefulness
- Benchmark measures may not be comparable
- May not be easy to understand
- Might not be collected economically
- Too many versus not enough measures
- Efficiency versus effectiveness measures
- Measures are always backward looking
- Measurement takes time and is hard work

These are some of the issues practitioners must deal with when designing measurement systems for their own departments, functions, and firms. A supply chain orientation is necessary to construct supply chain goals, strategies, planning, and governance structures; within this orientation, multifirm dimensionality adds greater complexity and challenge to performance measurement.

Accomplishments and Gaps in the Literature

Excellent conceptual work has been offered on the definition of a good measure. Several books published by the Council of Logistics Management have described the need for, benefits of, and barriers to implementation of logistics measurement programs. The publications have created awareness of activity-based costing and reported on the success of firms that have employed it. The focus of measurement has been restricted, however, largely to single-firm performance. The focus has been on measurement of inputs, outputs, and firm performance. Measurement research has been confined to antecedents and behaviors. It has not extended to evaluate consequences or outcomes (as illustrated in Figure 16.6).

Outcomes are results that fall outside the domain of a single company manager. A full measure of firm effectiveness should include an evaluation of the *consequences* of firm performance or outcomes as well as the impact of those outcomes on the *various members* of the distribution channel, or supply chain.

Gaps in the literature also exist in several areas important to logistics measurement. The literature has not adequately addressed the need to designate or identify both *owners* of measures and *customers* of measures, the importance being that customers of measures should be involved in predetermining the

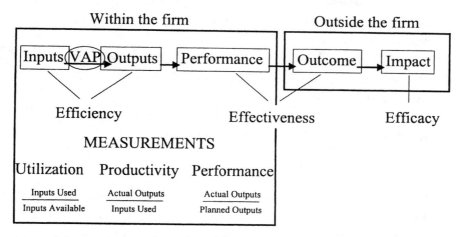

Figure 16.6.   Various Measurement Focuses

expected or required performance. Joint determination between owners and customers of measures is crucial to producing the right outcome.

The issue of evaluating marketing and logistics accountability for process performance cannot be resolved until key processes are identified and ownership is established. This step will create better balance between efficiency and effectiveness efforts of supply chain managers. Firms, separately and in combination, could expand their focus beyond just input and output measures toward more important outcome and impact measures.

Another gap in the literature is the near absence of a process orientation to measurement. Historically, physical measurement discussions have been at the task, activity, and functional levels within the firm. The requisite supply chain orientation calls for a process view of performance spanning multiple firms. Combined with this need to address interfirm process measures is the need to expand research into measures of *relationships*. Economic, physical, *and* psychological measures are equally important in planning and controlling the utilization, productivity, and performance of logistics resources across the supply chain.

Directions and Priorities for Future Research

Future research should continue to study and demonstrate successful implementations of activity-based costing. Cost-to-serve measures and value-of-service measures need to be developed. Emphasis should be placed on continued evaluation of the alignment of corporate and logistics goals and strategies. Key processes in the supply chain should be identified, as well as appropriate measurement methodologies. A study is needed of the concept of integration of activities into processes to understand the implications of the choices of what and how to measure when studying the combination of activities that constitute these key processes. We should study whether it is better to "get one's measurement house in order" before integrating with trading partners, or to understand and improve the interfaces externally before measuring and reengineering the internal operations. Under what circumstances does inside-out, or outside-in, integration and supply chain performance improvement happen best? What organizational structures are best suited for logistics organizations, given the different corporate strategies? How does a supply chain orientation affect organizational forms and governance structures for both interfirm and intrafirm logistics?

Additional research should be conducted on technology enablers of real-time visibility and connectivity that permit ad hoc performance measurement. What is the impact of data warehouses on measurement collection and reporting? Empirical research is needed to investigate the possibility of eliminating measurement reporting. With on-line, interactive databases, should not managers be able to inquire into the supply chain data warehouse, on an ad hoc basis, and find whatever combinations of numerators and denominators constitute measures of interest?

Measurement has been associated with physical and economic inputs and outputs. In terms of the human component, measurement has been confined to labor hours, person-days, or some form of "paid time." Is research into measurement of knowledge workers possible? This dimension has been overlooked because it involves elements of intuition, prior experience, training, skills, and creativity, each of which is an important aspect of logistics performance. Can the capacity and productivity of marketing and logistics knowledge workers be captured in measures that inform supply chain management?

We need to look beyond suboptimization, whether it is at the functional level within firms or at the process level among firms, and understand supply chain outcomes and impacts on the consumer, on the environments in which supply chains compete, and on the individual supply chain members (see Figure 16.7).

Managerial Implications

Companies still have much ground to cover to design and install measurement systems that will drive improved business performance. The impression is that firms are moderately to grossly underperforming, compared with their

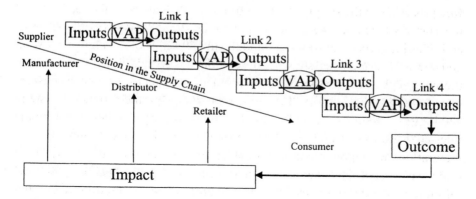

How do we plan and *measure* the Outcome at the Consumer Level
and the resulting Impact on this and competing Supply Chains?

Figure 16.7. Supply Chain Performance Measurement: An Outcome- and
Impact-Based View

SOURCE: Adapted from Caplice and Sheffi (1995).

potential. Various *barriers* to performance measurement have been identified
for those firms not making much progress. These include the following
(Keebler et al., 1999):

- Upper management support/leadership
- Clarity of business strategy
- Resource availability to do the work
- Degree of resistance/acceptance of change
- Skill set of employees
- Organizational culture
- Budget or project approval
- Trust
- Reward/recognition systems

It is amazing that the same study found these same factors cited as *enablers*
for firms making progress in performance measurement. Something must have
happened in the successful firms to coordinate and align the multiple forces that
motivate and reinforce the work required in creating relevant and meaningful

measurement systems. Why do the majority of firms seem to be reactive rather than proactive in measuring performance? What were the catalysts that engaged the more progressive firms? The operational question always seems to be "Who wants to do this anyway?" Lacking a compelling event and a champion for change, the status quo is expected to continue.

Corporate managers should be aware of two recent trends in performance measurement. First, the government has, through the Government Performance and Results Act of 1993 (GPRA), set guidelines for strategic planning and performance measurement across the federal government. Congress has mandated that the Department of Defense respond with a plan and strategy demonstrating top management commitment to implement the GPRA, with priorities for performance measures and management controls, and with migrations of systems, data standards, and process improvements (National Academy of Public Administration for the Department of Defense, 1996). This activity will have an impact on the private, supplier sector.

Second, a new measure, called return on management (ROM), has been suggested to account for management's time and energy (Simons & Antonio, 1998). Designed specifically to reflect how well a company implements its strategy, this new measure is based on five questions:

1. Do employees know which opportunities do not contribute to the organization's strategic mission?
2. Do managers know what it would take for the organization to fail?
3. Can managers recall their key diagnostic measures with relative ease?
4. Is the organization free from drowning in a sea of paperwork and processes?
5. Do all employees watch the same performance measures that their bosses watch?

It appears that clarity, alignment, and focus on and conformance to strategy and related performance measures are growing in importance.

Summary

If performance is important, then measurement ought to be, just as is the planning that goes into creating business results. Organizations, to a great degree, are not measuring key logistics activities, supply chain processes, or outcomes that they recognize as important. Linking measures to evolving corporate strategies and supporting plans is necessary to ensure alignment and focus. Performance measurement systems should be formally evaluated and managed; otherwise, the result is a performance measurement "system" in which the interrelations between the measures are not known, duplication is frequent, and omission is undetectable. Measurement is a key competency of successful enterprises. Processes, as well as their measures of performance, need customers and owners working together to jointly determine the ever-changing standards and measures of success.

Perhaps it remains for the "early adopters" to show the way and accrue the benefits of performance improvement through measurement of activities under the control of the single firm. Measurement *across* multiple firms, with interdependent planning and governance structures, does not exist in the context of supply chains as they have been defined. The potential outcomes of such integration pose threats to weak, inefficient, or outdated channel structure members. Their future could rest on their attitude toward performance measurement.

17

Managing the Supply Chain

Managerial and Research Implications

JOHN T. MENTZER

Executive Summary

This chapter summarizes the managerial conclusions from the rest of the book and uses this base to draw additional managerial conclusions and delineate future research directions. From this discussion, it can be concluded that

- To effectively and efficiently manage supply chains, managers must recognize that the company has a multitude of customers, including downstream and upstream companies. Furthermore, the value delivered to any of these customers may be the key to differential advantage.
- Not all customers are equally important to the company or the supply chain.
- Treating customers differently based on their importance to the supply chain leads ineluctably to serving different customers in different ways. By viewing the supply chain and all its members as a whole, supply chain management teaches us to look for the most effective way to reach each customer.
- True differential advantage comes from providing customers with something they value, something they cannot get from the competition, and something they recognize as coming from the provider. This combination requires an understanding of the customers' values, delivering those

values, and marketing that value delivery to the customers. Various aspects of supply chain management are all required, and must be coordinated, to achieve this differential advantage.

- Just as all customers are not created equal, neither are all products.
- Inventory is not the answer. One overriding managerial conclusion from this book is that supply chain management should drive inventory out of the supply chain, while finding coordinated solutions to provide increased value to the customer.
- Supply chain management invariably substitutes information for inventory.
- Information is a key source of differential advantage for and within the supply chain.
- Just as it is a maxim of business, it is also true in supply chains that "What gets measured gets rewarded, and what gets rewarded gets done."
- Little research was found that truly addressed complete supply chains.
- Although much of traditional supply chain management research has looked at the operational and financial aspects of supply chains, it is apparent from this book that much of what must be managed in supply chains falls within the realm of behavioral research.
- Many of the managerial conclusions discussed relate to the development and use of information. As supply chains evolve, the role of an "information broker" within the supply chain could become a powerful one.
- Finally, many of the executives we interviewed felt that much is being said about supply chain management, but few companies are achieving true supply chain management.

Research to determine the true extent of supply chain management, as defined in Chapter 1 of this book, would be a worthwhile benchmark. From this base, additional research to explore the stages of supply chain management sophistication, how companies can identify in which stage they are located, and how to move to higher stages would all be valuable.

Introduction

In this book, we have tried to cover the mosaic of all that is involved in supply chain management (SCM). To do this, we first defined and explored the myriad different definitions of supply chain management, and its related concepts, to settle on a definition of each. We also interviewed top supply chain management executives in 20 leading companies. This led us to the model of supply chain management presented in Chapter 1 as Figure 1.3 and reproduced here as Figure 17.1.

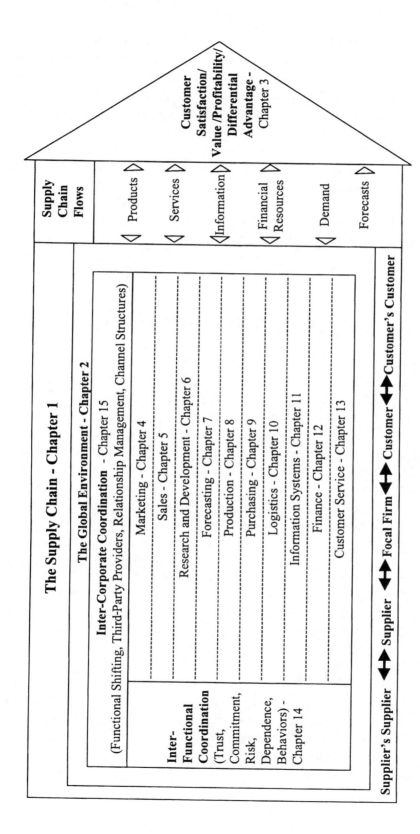

Figure 17.1 The Supply Chain

439

Our definition encompassed a focal firm, its suppliers and suppliers' suppliers, its customers and customers' customers, and all the typical business functions to create the supply chain flows of products, services, information, financial resources, demand, and forecasts. Several chapters focused on how these functions, suppliers, customers, and flows are coordinated to produce customer satisfaction, value added, profitability, and differential advantage for individual supply chain members and the supply chain as a whole.

The purpose of this chapter is to build upon this base to draw some conclusions about what all this means for managing the supply chain and about where future research into supply chain management should be headed. To do this, it will first briefly review the findings of the chapters up to this point. It will then present some supply chain managerial guidelines. Finally, it will discuss future research needs.

What We Have Learned About Supply Chain Management

In reviewing the many discussions and definitions of supply chains, supply chain management, and related concepts, we found many points of disagreement but also many points of commonality. This review, and our executive interviews, led us to four definitions related to supply chains:

A **supply chain** is a set of three or more companies directly linked by one or more of the upstream and downstream flows of products, services, finances, and information from a source to a customer.

A **basic supply chain** consists of a company, an immediate supplier, and an immediate customer directly linked by one or more of the upstream and downstream flows of products, services, finances, and information.

An **extended supply chain** includes suppliers of the immediate supplier and customers of the immediate customer, all linked by one or more of the upstream and downstream flows of products, services, finances, and information.

An **ultimate supply chain** includes all the companies involved in all the upstream and downstream flows of products, services, finances, and information from the initial supplier to the ultimate customer.

From these definitions, we realized that supply chains exist whether they are managed or not. Realization of the scope and interactions that supply chains encompass, along with attempts to manage the components under one company's direct control, precedes any overt attempt to actually manage the supply chain as a whole. We defined this initial recognition by one company of the potential in managing the supply chain as a supply chain orientation.

A **supply chain orientation** is the recognition by a company of the systemic, strategic implications of the activities and processes involved in managing the various flows in a supply chain.

Supply chain management is the implementation of a supply chain orientation across suppliers and customers. This led to the definition of supply chain management that we have used throughout this book.

Supply Chain Management is the systemic, strategic coordination of the traditional business functions within a particular company and across businesses within the supply chain, for the purposes of improving the long-term performance of the individual companies and the supply chain as a whole.

Such a definition required us to examine the traditional business functions, both individually and in relation to how they fit within supply chain management, and how functions and corporations are coordinated. First, however, we examined the global environment in which supply chains exist today, along with the desired output from managing the supply chain. A quick look at Figure 17.1 illustrates this overall conceptualization of supply chain management and how it was treated in various chapters of this book. We will now briefly review each of these findings.

The Global Supply Chain Management Environment

Chapter 2 described the globalization of the world economy, the diversity and environmental factors that influence a firm's global strategies and approach, drivers influencing firms to become increasingly global, and the different approaches to globalization that might be adopted by firms. From these discussions, we concluded that

- Different approaches to globalization require different degrees of supply chain integration as well as different supply chain strategies and structures
- Whatever approach to globalization and global supply chain management is adopted, firms face the challenges of understanding and managing the greater complexity and risks inherent in the global environment
- Global supply chain strategies must be developed in support of the strategic thrust of a firm's globalization initiatives and must consider opportunities for global efficiency, management of risks, learning to enable innovation and adaptation, and the need to balance global efficiency and local responsiveness
- Global supply chain processes should provide operating flexibility to respond to changes in the macroeconomic environment or government policies that adversely affect supply chain performance

- Design and management of supply chain activities must consider the influence of differences in culture, industry structure, legal requirements, and infrastructure in different countries on customers, suppliers, competitors, and supply chain partners
- The management of financial systems in a global supply chain must address differences in financial accounting systems, comparability of data, management of terms of sale, and ownership transfer to minimize risk, optimize profits, optimize transfer pricing to minimize taxes, minimize foreign exchange risks, and use countertrade effectively
- A much broader set of skills is required of supply chain professionals to manage successfully on a global basis, including operating knowledge of the global environment, understanding how to manage inherent risks, and the ability to deal with differences in language and culture
- Compatibility of information technologies and standardization of systems and data are critical to a firm's ability to integrate supply chain operations on a global basis
- Decision support tools that incorporate global variables and allow "what if" scenario analysis are important to enable managers to more effectively manage the complexities and uncertainties of the global environment

Managerial Conclusion: No matter which approach to globalization is pursued, firms are faced with the challenges of understanding and managing the complexities and risk inherent in the global environment. Global supply chain managers must develop capabilities that allow them to understand the complexities in the global environment, anticipate significant changes, and adapt to those changes as needed. Systems and processes must be designed to address important environmental variables, and organizational skills and capabilities must be developed to deal with different languages, cultures, and business environments.

SCM Outputs

Chapter 3 described the overall objectives of supply chain management of creating both value for customers and differential advantage and improved profitability for supply chain firms. The dimensions of value that may be important to customers were described, and the mechanisms whereby differential advantage and improved profitability can be achieved for supply chain members were discussed. From these discussions, we concluded that

- The objective of SCM is to increase the differential or competitive advantage of the channel as a whole, rather than to increase the advantage of any single firm
- The means to accomplish differential advantage is through creating value for downstream customers greater than that offered by competitors

- Customer value is created through collaboration and cooperation to improve efficiency (lower cost) or market effectiveness (added benefits) in ways that are most valuable to key customers

- Value is not inherent in products or services, but rather is perceived or experienced by the customer

- To compete through creating customer value, a firm must understand and deliver the value perceived as important by its customers

- Because the value perceived as important will differ across customer segments, a firm must identify the customer segments important to its long-term success and match the capability of the firm to delivering the value important to those key customers

- Value can be created at many points along the chain by making the customer firm at that point in the chain more effective in serving its markets, or more efficient and cost effective in its operations

- Delivering customer value in dimensions important to customers in ways that are better than those of the competition leads to customer satisfaction and differential advantage

- By satisfying customers and achieving differential advantage, firms in a supply chain influence customers to make choices and behave in ways that improve the financial performance of the supply chain and the firms within it

Managerial Conclusion: The degree to which value is created for customers, and the customer's perception of the value received relative to that offered by the competition, are reflected in the customer's satisfaction with the offering. Customers who are satisfied with value created in areas important to them are expected to behave in ways that are beneficial to a firm's or a supply chain's success. Purchase behavior, customer loyalty, and positive communications about products and services result from customer satisfaction and, at the same time, contribute to a firm's or supply chain's success. To achieve these objectives, supply chain managers must work collaboratively with customers and suppliers to identify and deliver value considered important by critical downstream customers.

The Role of Marketing in SCM

Chapter 4 highlighted the role of marketing in the implementation of supply chain management by suggesting cause-and-effect relationships among the marketing concept, a market orientation, relationship marketing, and SCM. Based on these discussions, we concluded that

- The objective of marketing is creating exchanges, and the output of it is customer satisfaction

- The marketing concept consists of three pillars: customer focus, coordinated marketing, and profitability

- The marketing concept is a business philosophy that guides a firm toward customer satisfaction at a profit
- A market orientation is the implementation of that philosophy, forcing the firm to generate, disseminate, and respond to market information
- The marketing concept not only provides the philosophical foundation of a market orientation but also plays an important role in the management of a firm, inter-functional relationships, and the implementation of SCM
- A market orientation also influences the management of a firm, interfirm relationships, and a supply chain; that is, a market orientation leads a firm to focus on market information generation, dissemination, and responsiveness as means to satisfy customers, coordinate its marketing efforts, redefine the responsibilities of each function, restructure its organizational system, and achieve superior business performance
- At the same time, a market orientation provides an environment that encourages a firm in its efforts to develop, maintain, and enhance close relationships with other firms, organizational learning from other firms, and building commitment, trust, and cooperative norms in the relationships with other firms
- A market orientation appears both inside and outside a firm to recognize and respond to customers' needs as well as to obtain experiences, products, skills, technologies, and knowledge from outside the firm that are not available to competitors
- A market orientation promotes the implementation of SCM
- Relationship marketing aims at establishing, maintaining, and enhancing either dyadic relationships or multiple relationships in a supply chain to create better customer value
- Relationship marketing helps achieve such objectives of SCM as efficiency (i.e., cost reduction) and effectiveness (i.e., customer service) through increased cooperation in close, long-term interfirm relationships among the supply chain partners
- With the help of the marketing concept, a market orientation, and relationship marketing, SCM achieves differential advantage for the supply chain and its partners by reducing costs and investments and by improving customer service

Managerial Conclusion: The role of marketing through the marketing concept, a market orientation, and relationship marketing is essential for the success of supply chain management.

The Role of Sales in SCM

The purpose of Chapter 5 was to examine the new roles of the sales function in supply chain management. To achieve this purpose, results from the Supply Chain Research Group interviews, along with results from an independent qualitative study, were integrated.

The role of the contemporary salesperson is changing dramatically, and in many situations, the old models of selling are simply outdated, ineffective, and counterproductive to supply chain management goals and objectives. Although most sales organizations focus on prepurchase activities, supply chain partners focus on managing relationships and conducting postpurchase activities to enhance supply chain performance. The sales force is well positioned to implement, facilitate, and coordinate many supply chain management activities. In short, the supply chain sales force should be involved with any supply chain activity that goes beyond organizational boundaries. More specifically, the sales force should be an integral part of implementing cooperative behaviors (i.e., joint planning, evaluating, and forecasting), mutually sharing information, and nurturing supply chain relationships.

To be effective in its new role, the supply chain sales force must gain new expertise in logistics and supply chain management. Salesperson logistics expertise was defined as a customer's perception of a salesperson's knowledge, experience, or skills relevant to logistics issues. Salesperson logistics expertise concerns the seller's and supply chain partners' logistics operations, systems, and processes at both tactical and strategic levels. Thus, salesperson logistics expertise includes internal (company) logistics expertise, external (supply chain partner) logistics expertise, tactical logistics expertise, and strategic logistics expertise.

Although the logistics manager may be the primary person designing logistics solutions, the salesperson is likely to be the primary person representing the supply chain partner's needs and requirements. For effective teamwork and innovative solutions, salespeople and logistics managers need to be able to communicate effectively and work together on supply chain management issues.

Managerial Conclusion: To support the sales force in its new supply chain management roles, sales managers need to train, support, and encourage supply chain activities and logistics expertise. To achieve this goal, sales managers must also adopt a new orientation and embrace new management techniques to enhance supply chain performance. Specifically, sales managers must become "change agents" in the sales organization and lead the sales force in a new direction. Traditional training programs, performance objectives, and compensation packages need to be adapted and better aligned with supply chain management.

The Role of Research and Development in SCM

Chapter 6 described the role of research and development (R&D) within the firm, with suppliers and customers, and within the supply chain. From these discussions, we concluded that

- Supply chain activities have a major impact on the capabilities and profitability of the supply chain and its member firms in new product development
- Innovative and effective new product development will be important in the turbulent, highly uncertain business environment of the future
- By collaborating with immediate customers and suppliers, R&D can significantly improve the new product development process
- By collaborating with customers' customers and suppliers' suppliers along the supply chain, R&D improves the new product development process
- Companies that are multinational in scope can benefit through globalization of the R&D process and collaborating with global supply chain partners
- The concept of postponement, or delaying final product configuration as close to the end consumer as possible, benefits greatly from collaborating R&D with supply chain partners
- Improving speed to market, or reducing the cycle time to develop new products, can be achieved through supply chain R&D involvement
- Flexible new product development enables companies to incorporate rapidly changing customer requirements and evolving technologies through supply chain R&D involvement

Managerial Conclusion: Broadening the knowledge base involved in a firm's R&D process better enables managers to design and develop effective and efficient new product development systems. This suggests that developing a supply chain orientation for R&D leads to opportunities for lower costs, improved customer value, and competitive advantages for the long term.

The Role of Forecasting in SCM

Chapter 7 described the increasingly important contribution to supply chain performance offered through effective sales forecasting management. A model outlined the evolution of sales forecasting, starting from an initial focus on forecasting techniques to include broader considerations for management and behavioral factors that influence forecasting practices in organizations and across the supply chain. From these discussions, we concluded that

- Supply chain sales forecasting management can significantly influence operating performance within each member and across members of a supply chain
- To affect supply chain operations in a positive manner, organizations working together in a supply chain must improve forecasting management performance (an internally directed measure) as well as supply chain forecasting management performance (a cross-company measure)
- The four dimensions of sales forecasting management—functional integration, approach, systems, and performance measurement—can be extended to incorporate a supply chain orientation

- Initiatives such as collaborative planning, forecasting, and replenishment reflect the four forecasting management dimensions and provide an approach to forecasting that addresses factors that influence forecasting management performance and supply chain forecasting management performance

Managerial Conclusion: To contribute to improved supply chain performance, supply chain managers must go beyond traditional measures of forecast accuracy to understanding the overall supply chain demand planning process, and they must be able to influence the behaviors of individuals and organizations involved in the development and application of sales forecasts.

The Role of Production in SCM

Chapter 8 described the role of production within the firm, with suppliers and customers, and within the supply chain. From these discussions, we concluded that

- Functional products in stable markets need a supply chain production system that focuses on reducing volume cost and increasing production efficiency
- Highly innovative products in uncertain, constantly changing environments need a supply chain production system that focuses on strategic flexibility and speed to market
- Dispersed production is a supply chain production system of great value in a globally competitive market that focuses on cost efficiency
- Build-to-order production and postponement are useful supply chain production systems in markets with quickly obsolete existing products, rapidly changing customer requirements, and shrinking product life cycles

Managerial Conclusion: Understanding the different types of production systems better enables managers to design and develop the production system that is most suitable for the specific supply chain market environment.

The Role of Purchasing in SCM

Chapter 9 discussed the evolution of the role of purchasing and explored the purchasing role in support of a firm's SCM strategies and objectives. A framework was presented that highlighted required shifts in the nature of buyer-seller relationships as well as the objectives and role of purchasing in a supply chain management context versus historical approaches. Issues related to organizational structure, communications processes, and information technology were also highlighted. From these discussions, we concluded that

- Purchasing plays a critical, boundary-spanning role in the supply chain management activities of a firm

- To achieve the potential benefits of SCM, the role of purchasing must be viewed in a systemwide context and must be focused beyond managing the buyer-seller relationship

- Managers must understand the potential benefits to be achieved through SCM relationships, based on environmental conditions and specific resource or performance requirements

- It is important for managers to understand the potential benefits, as well as the costs, of developing such relationships so that appropriate business decisions can be made

- To be successful in achieving SCM objectives, purchasing requirements must be understood within the context of the overall strategy of the firm, supply chain partners must be selected to meet the strategic requirements, and the relationships must be managed appropriately over the long term

- Cost and quality improvements must be understood and implemented from a systemwide perspective to achieve optimum results

- To achieve the objectives of improved quality and reliability, reduced inventories, and lower total system cost associated with an operational approach to SCM, an emphasis on the integration of purchasing and logistics is required

- To achieve the objectives of speed, flexibility, and competitive advantage associated with a strategic approach to SCM, collaboration with strategic supply chain partners focused on redesigning products and business processes to deliver value to customers is required

- In a strategic context, the role of purchasing is to understand the capability of suppliers and identify ways to match that capability to the needs of strategic customers

- Purchasing can enhance the effectiveness of product and process design by ensuring reliability and quality of supply of materials, components, and services; managing supplier involvement in the process; and providing insights about the competitive supply environment

- Organizational structure and communications processes must be designed to support the requirements and objectives of the purchasing organization in support of the firm's supply chain management activities

- Information technology is critical in managing the increasing complexity of the purchasing function, facilitating the integration of processes across firms in a supply chain context, and providing decision support tools to enable systemwide optimization

Managerial Conclusion: To date, researchers and managers alike have focused primarily on supplier partnerships, or building stronger relationships between the buyer and seller firms. To achieve the potential of SCM, managers and researchers alike must adopt a broader, systemwide approach that will aid them in understanding and achieving the contribution that purchasing can make in an SCM context.

The Role of Logistics in SCM

Chapter 10 described logistics in the supply chain, including the major functions constituting logistics, emerging logistics strategies, and logistics competencies that drive competitive advantage for the firm. From these discussions, we concluded that

- Logistics activities have a major impact on the capabilities and profitability of the supply chain and its member firms
- Logistics functions are key operating components of an organization that require design and management consistent with corporate strategy and changing competitive environments
- Logistics strategies need to be implemented that support corporate strategies and are based on the needs of the marketplace and distinct capabilities of the firm
- Corporate leaders who can understand and shape logistics competencies can dramatically enhance firm competitiveness

Managerial Conclusion: Capitalizing on these opportunities requires the ability to build alliances within and between firms, a commitment to planning and integrating information flows, and the ability to measure performance to guide the improved design of the logistics system and supply chain processes. The importance of the supply chain manager's ability to leverage logistics competencies will increase in the future.

The Role of Information Systems in SCM

Chapter 11 described the role of information systems within the firm, the role of information systems with suppliers and customers, and the role of information systems within the supply chain. From these discussions, we concluded that

- As the business environment continues to emphasize more variety and quicker response to a dynamic customer-driven marketplace, better and more effective information systems need to be developed
- One of the best ways to serve a demanding marketplace is to develop effective intrafirm information systems
- Intrafirm information systems such as enterprise resource planning systems are an important precursor to improving the flow of information between firms
- Managers need to determine if the benefits of effective and efficient information flow mitigate the risks associated with developing partnerships with either suppliers or customers

- By developing relationships with members of their supply chains, firms can develop more efficient and effective information systems that facilitate better supply chain integration utilizing the enabling capabilities of the Internet
- In the future, the Internet will allow true supply chain management through the transparent, real-time connection of all supply chain links

Managerial Conclusion: Managers have little choice but to embark on the path to developing information systems that enhance and integrate the supply chain. This will augment the competitiveness of firms in terms of lower costs, improved customer value, and maintaining long-term competitive advantages in the rapidly changing, customer-driven, Internet-enabled e-commerce business environment.

The Role of Finance in SCM

Chapter 12 described the financial implications of supply chain decisions, trends in supply chain costs, a financial model for evaluating investments, and issues of concern for financial and supply chain management. From these discussions, we concluded that

- Supply chain activities affect profit and loss statements, balance sheets, and the costs of capital
- Significant opportunities exist for the competent supply chain manager to reduce expenses, generate better returns on invested capital, and improve cash flows
- Controlling supply chain expenses can improve profit margins
- Continuing to shorten cycle times can enhance cash flows
- Superior supply chain performance can produce the leverage and competitive advantage to increase revenues and the supply chain's share of market
- Traditional accounting techniques do not provide accurate and timely information that informs the financial aspects of supply chain trade-off decisions
- Activity-based costing is not widely employed
- The potential benefits of improved supply chain management are stymied by the absence of activity-based financial data and the inability to link performance measurement with cost
- Improved collaboration between finance and other business and supply chain functions is necessary to facilitate the process of developing activity-based costing
- This collaboration should help to overcome the seemingly widespread inability of supply chain managers to articulate the costs and benefits of supply chain activities

Managerial Conclusion: Capitalizing on these opportunities requires the ability to plan for and measure supply chain performance and to effectively communicate performance implications in financial terms. The supply chain manager's ability to articulate the financial implications of exchanges between firms will become more important in the future.

The Role of Customer Service in SCM

Chapter 13 described elements of customer service management important to supply chain management, performance outcomes associated with customer service activities and their contribution to supply chain objectives, and customer responses to the outcomes of a firm's customer service activities. From these discussions, we concluded that

- To achieve supply chain objectives, customer service activities must be strategic in nature and must be designed based on an understanding of the service levels important to critical customers

- Important customer segments must be identified, and the requirements of those segments understood, for both immediate and downstream customers

- The impact of service levels on customers should be understood, and internal capabilities should be designed to deliver service levels that optimize the overall performance of the supply chain

- The quality of the customer interface is likely to influence the level of trust and openness of information exchange between firms, which can contribute to a better understanding of the customer's needs and improved performance of supply chain management activities

- It is important to measure customer service outcomes as perceived by the customer and to understand which performance outcomes are most valued by customers at various levels of the supply chain

- Customer service requirements and performance, as well as the influence of customer service levels on customer behavior, should be understood and monitored for both immediate and downstream customers in a supply chain

- Customer service is not the ultimate objective of supply chain management but rather an outcome of supply chain management that can create value for customers through improved efficiency or effectiveness

- Creating value for customers superior to that created by the competition is expected to result in greater customer satisfaction and differential advantage, as well as to influence customers to behave in ways that improve the performance of the supply chain as a whole

Managerial Conclusion: Customer service is often cited as a key objective of supply chain management; however, only if service offerings create value for customers will they lead to behaviors that improve supply chain performance. To achieve this objective, it is important for supply chain managers to manage customer service strategically and develop supply chain capabilities to deliver services viewed as important by critical downstream customers.

Inter-Functional Coordination in SCM

The demand for flexibility in today's turbulent business environment requires supply chain management that extends the concept of functional integration beyond a firm to all the firms in the supply chain. In other words, implementing SCM inherently requires coordination across the traditional business functions within a firm, as well as interfirm cooperation across the firms in close relationship within a supply chain, to accomplish a common set of goals. Chapter 14 highlighted the importance of inter-functional coordination within individual supply chain members to successfully implement supply chain management. From these discussions, we concluded that

- Concurrent management in supply chain management requires a balance between specialization through division of labor and cross-functional coordination

- Inter-functional coordination within a particular firm consists of the coordinated efforts across functions to accomplish common goals, such as creating customer value and responsiveness to market changes, under close relationships among the functions and tight management control

- The various ways of implementing inter-functional coordination include cooperative arrangements through which personnel from different functional areas perform interaction and collaboration; managerial control, especially integrating managers who are essentially liaison personnel with formal authority over something important across functions (such as budgets); standardization to guide the processes of coordination; functional expertise necessary for participation in cooperative arrangements; and organizational structure that integrates the flows of products, services, finance, and information within an organization

- No organization can rely on a single mechanism and/or organizational structure; as a result, organizations must be flexible to utilize a proper combination of these mechanisms to achieve a high level of coordination

- Common goals, trust and commitment among personnel from different functional areas, and top management support are the factors that promote cooperative efforts within a firm

- Well-executed inter-functional coordination brings competitive advantage in terms of reduced cycle time, new product success, and finally profitability

Managerial Conclusion: Individual firms within a supply chain should have expertise in key functional areas and, at the same time, achieve functional integration as a precursor to supply chain management.

Inter-Corporate Coordination in SCM

Chapter 15 described the importance of interfirm cooperation in supply chain management, provided examples of how industry leaders work together with their supply chain members, and suggested a model of interfirm cooperation from drivers, to prerequisites, to the outcomes of successful cooperative relationships in a supply chain context. From these discussions, we concluded that

- The demand for flexibility in today's turbulent business environment requires supply chain management rather than the vertical integration or arm's-length relationships of the past
- Supply chain management extends the concept of functional integration beyond a firm to all the firms in the supply chain and, therefore, each member of a supply chain needs to help each other member to improve the competitiveness of the supply chain
- Implementing SCM inherently requires cooperation, which is defined as a set of joint actions of firms in a close relationship to accomplish a common set of goals that bring mutual benefits

Managerial Conclusion: The supply chain manager's ability to build, maintain, and enhance cooperative interfirm relationships will be essential in the future when competition will not be company against company but instead supply chain against supply chain.

Performance Measurement in SCM

Chapter 16 discussed performance measurement in the supply chain. From these discussions, we concluded that

- Supply chain activities are not adequately defined, measured, or improved
- Supply chain measurement research is largely focused on the single firm
- Research has emphasized internal efficiency over external effectiveness
- There is an absence of multifirm performance measurement, or measures across the supply chain
- Interdependent planning and governance structures do not appear to exist across firms
- Supply chain members still appear to act largely as independent channel members, focused on self-interest
- Within supply chains, vertical conflicts exist that could be resolved with joint planning and measurement
- Activity-based costing, a critical performance measurement capability, is not widely employed

■ Potential benefits of improved supply chain management are stymied by the absence of activity-based financial data and the inability to link performance measurement with cost

Managerial Conclusion: Capitalizing on these opportunities to plan and measure key supply chain processes will improve both single-firm performance and supply chain outcomes. Supply chain performance measurement is in its infancy but will become more important in the future.

Additional Managerial Conclusions

In addition to the preceding managerial conclusions that are tied to particular chapters, the Supply Chain Research Group uncovered a number of overall managerial conclusions. These were a result of the executive interviews, the literature review, and many integrative discussions among the research team.

Who Is Your Customer?

The first managerial conclusion is embodied in the question, Who is your customer? Traditional corporate management has viewed the immediate buyer as the customer. If management is particularly far-sighted, perhaps the buyer's buyer is also considered. To manage supply chains effectively and efficiently, managers must recognize that the company has a multitude of customers, including downstream and upstream companies. Furthermore, the value delivered to any of these customers may be the key to differential advantage.

Take, for example, a company in the auto aftermarket, a supply chain that provides replacement parts to auto repair shops through a network of distributors called warehouse distributors or WDs. This company held approximately 30% market share in this channel, about the same as its two major competitors, with the remaining 10% divided among minor competitors. The product in this supply chain is eventually installed by a mechanic as part of an auto repair. As a result, there is virtually no brand recognition in this process—the owner of the car simply wants the car repaired and seldom asks for a specific brand. In fact, market research revealed that car owners valued only three things in this process: (a) They wanted their car back the same day in which they took it in for repair, (b) they wanted the problem fixed (i.e., they did not want the replacement part to fail as long as they owned the car), and (c) they were sensitive to the price of the parts. This led the auto mechanics to value the same three things.

This situation led one company executive to describe the industry as a "commodity business"—there is no difference between the competitors in the market with respect to promotional programs, or product quality or features, so the only basis on which to compete is price. Because the major competitors had identical types of manufacturing plants, identical suppliers, and identical supply chains (the same supplier delivery systems to the plants and the same WDs to distribute the products to the same auto mechanics), their cost structures were very similar and any reduction in price was matched immediately by the competition.

The road to logistics leverage began when the new CEO of the company formed a task force to implement his personal vision of the company—to change the corporate vision from the company as a "manufacturer of products in the auto aftermarket" to "a marketer and distributor of products in the auto aftermarket." In other words, the CEO wanted to focus the attention of the company not on the product itself but on how it got to the customer.

This profound shift in focus of the company from competitor focused to customer centered led to the realization that the company did, in fact, make a commodity product. The company's customers saw no difference in product quality or features, and the promotional programs were largely ignored by all members of the supply chain. This did not mean, however, that the company could not come up with marketing and/or logistics services that would differentiate it from the competition. In other words, the CEO realized that having a commodity product does not mean you have a commodity business: There are always services that can be offered with a product that can differentiate it in the minds of the customers.

The important aspect of this point is that services offered with the product often hold the key to differentiating a commodity product from its competition for some customer in the supply chain. Because all the competitors in this industry used the same suppliers and had the same manufacturing processes, the upstream supply chain was deemed to not hold any sources of logistics leverage. Similarly, the market research focused at the car owners and the auto mechanics revealed little regarding how to differentiate the company from the competition. The WDs were the customers most important in this company's supply chain.

At the time of this example, there were 2,000 warehouse distributors in the United States, which meant that virtually every county with an auto repair shop had at least one WD. Their function in the supply chain is to provide ready access to inventory for the auto mechanic, who carries little or no inventory. When a customer would call to schedule an auto repair, the mechanic would assess the parts likely needed to make the repair, call the local WD to ascertain whether the parts were in stock, and, if parts were available, send someone over to pick them up.

The WD operation usually consisted of a reception area with a counter for waiting on pickup customers and a huge warehouse to hold in inventory all the parts any auto mechanic could conceivably order. As a result, WDs were small operations with huge inventory levels. In fact, the average inventory turn ratio for a WD was less than 1.0, resulting in huge inventory carrying costs compared to sales levels. Not surprising, most WDs were only marginally profitable.

The company embarked on a 3-year plan to develop a wide area network for inventory planning and accompanied this with a plan to stage fast-moving inventory at various locations in North America and pull slow movers back to a central distribution center. When these plans were implemented, the company made the following offer to all WDs: The company guaranteed that any order placed with it that was not *completely filled* within 24 hours would be free. In other words, if an order for 160 different parts was placed and only 1 of those parts was not delivered in 24 hours, there was no charge for the entire order. Further, each WD was given 1 year to try out the program and, when it was convinced that the company never missed a 24-hour delivery, the company would buy back from the WD its excess inventory. This was an offer hard to resist because the WD would be turning a business liability (the cost of carrying excess inventory) into an asset (cash).

The differential advantage for the company came from the fact that once a WD sold its excess inventory to the company, the WD no longer had the ability to buy from the competition. WDs literally were faced with the choice of placing an order with the company and being guaranteed 24-hour delivery, or ordering from the competition and having the order arrive in 7 to 14 days—all when the WD was now carrying, at most, only several days of inventory. Over a 2-year period, the company raised its price 15% above the competition (an act that would have been unthinkable before the new program) and doubled its market share.

What we learn about supply chain management from this example is to look beyond the traditional definition of a customer to all entities in the supply chain. Any of these "customers," and their value needs, may hold the key to differential advantage for the firm and the supply chain as a whole. Successful supply chain management often involves asking the question, Who is our customer? The company in this example conducted considerable market research to identify what the members of its downstream supply chain—WDs, auto mechanics, and car owners—wanted. It eventually focused on the WDs because therein lay a source for differential advantage. Auto mechanics and car owners were still important as customers but did not provide a means by which the company could differentiate itself from the competition.

Not All Customers Are Created Equal

Related to the previous managerial conclusion is the fact that not all customers are as important to the company or the supply chain. One executive with a consumer products company we interviewed pointed out that although the company has thousands of retail customers and millions of ultimate consumers, the top ten retailers through which it sells its products constitute 90% of the total revenue of the company. Similarly, an executive from a large industrial company told us, "Never forget, we are a $30 billion company and we only have 109 customers."

For both of these companies, a very small number of customers hold the key to success or failure for the company and its supply chain. Supply chain research for both these companies revealed that many of these customers actually cost the company money to serve them. The result was a supply chain management plan where certain customers receive differential treatment, others receive minimal service, and still other customers were "fired" because they were costing the company and the supply chain money.

How Do You Reach Your Customers?

Treating customers differently based on their importance to the supply chain leads ineluctably to serving different customers in different ways. By viewing the supply chain and all its members as a whole, supply chain management teaches us to look for the most effective way to reach each customer. One retailer executive we interviewed said:

> Our traditional supply chain was to bring product to the store and get customers in there to shop and buy. However, our national brand recognition is larger than the market area for our stores. So we turned to e-commerce to extend our reach to potential customers who knew our name, but could not reasonably reach our stores. This strategy extends our market reach, satisfies a larger market of customers, and does not cannibalize our store sales.

Supply chain management allows numerous extended supply chains with a multitude of supply chain partners to create many innovative ways to reach customers and provide them with the values they seek.

How Do You Achieve Differential Advantage With Your Customers?

In Chapters 3 and 13, we examined in depth the concepts of customer service, customer satisfaction, and value, and how these lead to differential advantage. As the auto aftermarket example illustrated, true differential advantage comes from providing customers with something they value, something they cannot get from the competition, and something they recognize as coming from the provider. This combination requires an understanding of the customers' values, delivering those values, and marketing that value delivery to the customers. Various aspects of supply chain management are all required, and must be coordinated, to accomplish this differential advantage.

Not All Products Are Created Equal

Just as all customers are not created equal, neither are all products. Some products are large profit-makers for a company, some are marginally profitable, and some actually lose money for the company but are, supposedly, carried for their tie-in sales to profitable products. Similarly, some products may be crucial to maintaining relationships with key supply chain partners, and some may be inconsequential to that relationship. The key in supply chain management is to realize which products fit into each category and manage them accordingly. Products that are marginally or negatively profitable can be turned into profitable products if alternative supply chains can be found for their delivery. For instance, many companies provide direct customer delivery of key products to key customers but use e-commerce sites backed up by third-party delivery partners for delivery of marginal products to marginal customers. This combination allows the company to profitably serve a broader range of products and customers.

Inventory Is Not the Answer

This managerial conclusion requires all participants in the supply chain to answer dual questions: What is the cost of having inventory? and What is the cost of not having inventory? The traditional solution to any supply chain customer service problem was to "throw inventory at the problem." It is safe to say that this is the easiest, and always the wrong, decision. As the auto aftermarket example illustrated, inventory costs more than virtually any supply chain truly realizes. The company in that example could simply have said, "We will guarantee 24 hours delivery by having inventory in staging points all over the country." The cost of capital, however, would have made this solution infeasible in the long run. The answer was improved supply chain communication, coordinated management across functions within the company and across companies in the supply chain, and flexible operations to meet unexpected demand variations. Nowhere in this answer was adding inventory part of the solution. If there is one overriding managerial conclusion to be reached from this book, it is that supply chain management should drive inventory out of the supply chain while finding coordinated solutions to provide increased value to the customer.

Substitute Information for Inventory

The previous point leads to the managerial conclusion that supply chain management invariably substitutes information for inventory. More rapid demand planning information, combined with more accurate sales forecasts, combined with transparent information on the supply chain's operations to meet that demand, lowers the need for excess inventory in the supply chain. It also provides the added benefit of reducing redundant and unnecessary operations, which also drives costs out of the supply chain.

Who Has the Information Needed?

Given these previous conclusions, information becomes a key source of differential advantage for and within the supply chain. Having information, or alternatively identifying who in the supply chain has the information and forming partnerships with them, increasingly will be the source of long-term business success in the supply chains of the future.

E-Commerce Is Part of the Supply Chain

Supply chain management becomes even more essential with the rising importance of business-to-business commerce on the Internet, especially for firms in highly fragmented industries with complex products or services. The rate of change in the marketplace is increasing as the Internet becomes a more ubiquitous part of the business marketplace. Supply chain management is greatly augmented by e-commerce, e-procurement, e-fulfillment, and other Internet-enabled business processes. By the same token, these e-commerce activities greatly benefit from supply chain relationships and, more important, from supply chain execution.

Are Supply Chain Strategies and Reward Structures Aligned?

Just as it is a maxim of business, it is also true in supply chains that *What gets measured gets rewarded, and what gets rewarded gets done.* Developing elaborate supply chain plans that call for coordinated efforts across numerous supply chain partners will not succeed unless the financial benefits are shared by all partners. As one retailer executive we interviewed said:

> The key to growing this company is supply chain partnerships with our suppliers, and these partnerships will not work unless we share the benefits with these suppliers. We cannot share if we cannot measure the impact suppliers have on overall supply chain costs.

For supply chain management to work, all parties involved have to agree on what financial and customer value benefits are to be sought, how to measure whether these benefits are achieved and who is responsible for achieving them, and how to share the financial benefits that accrue. Without this simple recognition of human behavior—people, companies, and supply chains do what they are rewarded for doing—supply chain management cannot succeed.

Research Implications

The research implications of the findings in this book are considerable. Many of these have been addressed in the individual chapters and will not be repeated here. Several research implications can be drawn from the book as a whole.

First, little research was found that truly addressed complete supply chains. Research has been restricted, for the most part, to asking one company to look across its supply chain (i.e., draw conclusions for its partners), or dyadic (i.e., buyer-seller) research. To truly understand the challenges, dynamics, processes, and benefits of supply chain management, future research will need to take as its unit of measure the entire supply chain. Studies that cut across three or more companies in the supply chain should bring us insights into supply chain management that have not been reported previously. By the nature of this challenge, such research probably will be within the realm of case study research. Additionally, longitudinal research is needed to explore the evolution of supply chains over time and the myriad cause-and-effect relationships in supply chains.

Although much of traditional supply chain management research has looked at the operational and financial aspects of supply chains, it is apparent from this book that much of what must be managed in supply chains falls within the realm of behavioral research. How functions within a company can be integrated, how companies can coordinate their activities, and the chain of customer service to customer satisfaction to customer value all represent opportunities to bring the insights of behavioral research to what we know about supply chains.

Many of the managerial conclusions discussed related to the development and use of information. As supply chains evolve, the role of an "information broker" within the supply chain could become a powerful one. How information is developed into differential advantage, what types of information are the most needed in different supply chain scenarios, where this information is obtained, and how it can be utilized are all viable future research questions.

Finally, many of the executives we interviewed felt that much is being said about supply chain management, but few companies are achieving true supply chain management. Research to determine the true extent of supply chain management, as defined in Chapter 1 of this book, would be worthwhile. From this base, additional research to explore the stages of supply chain management sophistication, how companies can identify in which stage they are located, and how to move to higher stages would all be valuable.

Book Summary

In this book, we have tried to provide a uniform set of definitions of supply chain management and its related concepts so future supply chain managers and researchers can all work with a common understanding of the terms. From this base, we explored in depth the many activities involved in supply chain management, addressing the managerial and research issues each activity raised. Finally, we tried to bring some coalescence to this important area of business management in this final chapter, again concentrating on the managerial and research implications. In each chapter, we have tried to provide cogent executive summaries for executives to obtain a quick overview of the conclusions contained within, with the hope that each will lead to a more in-depth reading and understanding of each chapter.

We are indebted to the many scholars who have gone before us and have written extensively on this subject, and for the time and insight provided by the executives who were gracious enough to be interviewed for this book. We could not have written this book without them, and we are grateful for their insights.

Finally, we hope this book will help in future understanding, management, and research in the area of supply chain management. Supply chains have always been with us. The ongoing challenge is for us to continue to learn how to better manage them.

Glossary

Activity—a collection of tasks that have a common purpose, produce a common output, or address a common theme.

Alliances (Partnerships)—cooperative relationships between two companies; distinct from supply chains because this type of relationship does not involve any one company in simultaneous upstream and downstream relationships.

Area planner purchasing approach—an approach utilizing a centralized purchasing group, responsible for relationships with suppliers, while field production and logistics planners manage the actual operating flows between firms.

Automatic replenishment (AR)—systems used to replenish inventory automatically by giving suppliers the right to anticipate future requirements, thereby reducing inventory and increasing availability.

Availability—a logistics capability in terms of in-stock rate and percent orders, units, and lines filled out completely.

Basic supply chain—consists of a company, an immediate supplier, and an immediate customer directly linked by one or more of the upstream and downstream flows of products, services, finances, and information.

Bilateral governance—relational governance mechanisms, such as long-term commitment and trust, that safeguard against risks associated with those relationships (e.g., investment in assets that can be profitable only within the relationship or a great degree of dependence on a firm's raw material quality or production processes).

Build-to-order production—building a product only after it has been ordered. Similar terms include direct production or demand-driven manufacturing.

Capabilities—complex bundles of skills and collective learning, exercised through organizational processes, that ensure superior coordination of functional activities.

Centralized purchasing—a single purchasing organization within a firm that serves as a collective sourcing and buying focus.

Centralized purchasing coordinator—a purchasing professional responsible for coordinating dispersed purchasing activities in the field to achieve greater negotiating strength by dealing with suppliers at a corporate level.

Channel-bonding capability—ability to maintain durable linkages with customers, channel members, and suppliers.

Channel-linking capability—ability to create and manage close customer relationships.

Channel of distribution—a set of companies with the collective ability to intensively distribute materials and products to selected target markets and/or extensively distribute to wide geographical areas and/or market segments.

Collaboration—orientation toward common goal setting and working together between individuals and departments.

Co-location—inside the firm, employees from different functions (e.g., purchasing and engineering) are located in one area or at a physical location to encourage open dialogue and/or collaboration. Across firms, personnel from multiple companies in the supply chain work side by side in one area or at a physical location to work together toward common goals.

Commitment—an enduring desire to maintain a valued relationship that consists of the partner's (a) inputs of credible and proportional resources, (b) attitudes (e.g., intentions and desires) toward commitment, (c) continuity of expectations and willingness to invest, and (d) consistent inputs and attitudes toward commitment over time.

Commodity teams—teams with a full product orientation, including attention to engineering, design, materials, manufacturing, costing, distribution, and marketing for a particular product, allowing an integrated view of engineering, design, production, procurement, materials and logistics management, manufacturing, costing, and marketing.

Communication—extent of information sharing via written, verbal, electronic, and other means.

Competitive advantage—occurs when a firm implements a value-creating strategy in which other firms are unable to duplicate the benefits or find it too costly to imitate. Competitive advantage consists of cost leadership and differentiation.

Concurrent engineering—a part of concurrent management in which a firm integrates product development, flexible manufacturing, tailored logistics, and time-based strategies to respond to changing markets.

Concurrent management—the ability to be more responsive to changing market conditions through concurrent engineering and concurrent marketing practices.

Concurrent marketing—a part of concurrent management in which a firm integrates its otherwise isolated product management, sales management, and field service operations to respond to rapid change in markets.

Cooperative norms—the perception of the joint efforts of both the supplier and distributor to achieve mutual and individual goals successfully while refraining from opportunistic actions.

Coordination—formal structure and required meetings between two or more functional areas.

Cost leadership—the ability to perform value chain activities at a cost lower than competitors' while offering a parity product.

Craft production—craftsmen or highly skilled workers using simple and flexible tools to make exactly what the customer asked for, one item at a time.

Cross-docking—a process where incoming shipments are transferred into an outgoing shipment without entering the warehouse. The goal is to reduce costs by moving goods directly to the end user, eliminating the need for storage.

Cross-functional development—involvement of two or more functions working together concurrently on product development.

Customer intimacy—tailoring products and services to fit the needs of, or to create value for, specific segments of customers and focusing on building loyalty and long-term customer relationships.

Customer learning—accessing and utilizing information about the customer to successfully develop and implement customer service strategies.

Customer responsiveness—positive behaviors by customers as a result of satisfaction with the value created by products and services; these can contribute to the greater market share or improved profitability of the firm. Examples are repeat purchases, customer loyalty, and positive word of mouth communications about the product or service.

Customer satisfaction—the customer's reaction to the product or service, based on a comparison between the perception of the product or service and some standard that represents the customer's expectations of that product or service.

Customer segmentation—identifying different customer groups that require different levels of service, and offering different levels of service to strategic customer groups to achieve customer satisfaction and responsiveness, thus enhancing the business performance of the firm.

Customer service—both an *organizational process* and a *performance outcome*. The organizational process of customer service includes the activities and functions that occur at the interface between a firm and its customers that are responsible for providing customer satisfaction through fulfillment of sales order demand and customer information needs. The performance outcomes of customer service are those outputs of the customer service process that lead to customer value and satisfaction (i.e., availability, quality, and reliability of products or services).

Customer service strategy—a firm's approach to customer service policies and activities which is aimed at focusing service offerings that provide competitive advantage, matching internal customer service capability to external customer needs, and ensuring optimum levels of service to enhance the firm's profitability.

Customer value—the trade-off between perceived benefits of owning and using a product or service and the perceived costs of owning or using the product or service, based on the relative importance of each to the customer.

Decentralized purchasing—dispersement of the purchasing responsibility within a firm to field locations, with each organization responsible for all purchasing activities required to support its individual business or facility.

Decision support systems (DSS)—interactive, computer-based systems that provide data and analytic models to help decision makers solve unstructured problems—those with many difficult to define variables. Information systems that provide information to aid a decision maker in making better choices than would otherwise be possible.

Differential advantage—relative superiority in the marketplace, based on the customer's perception that the value created by a firm's products or services is more important or larger to him or her than the value created by the competition's products or services.

Differentiation—uniqueness of the product or service offering, relative to competitors.

Dispersed production/manufacturing—manufacturing a single product in different locations or manufacturing in a location that is most appropriate for that specific task.

Distribution resource planning (DRP)—managing the distribution side of a firm by determining the flow and storage of finished products to minimize inventory, transportation costs, and warehousing requirements.

E-business—business that relies on the Internet to facilitate information exchange and commercial transactions.

E-commerce—electronic commerce that typically utilizes the Internet to facilitate commercial transactions and the transfer of information.

Economic globalization—interconnectivity of economic activity on a global scale, as exemplified by global competitors making products and services available to consumers worldwide, and rapid growth in world exports and foreign direct investment.

Economic regionalism—the reconfiguration of economic boundaries through trade agreements among countries, aimed at reducing or eliminating tariffs and removing nontariff barriers to trade.

Effectiveness—contributing to a customer's success by increasing the perceived benefits of owning or using products or services.

Efficiency—improvements in the cost side of the value equation, either through reducing total cost to the customer or contributing to the efficiency of the customer's operations, thus reducing cost to downstream customers.

Efficient consumer response (ECR)—originated in the grocery industry and similar to quick response; the goal is to replenish inventory based on real-time sales data obtained from point of sale information that is transmitted back through the supply chain.

Electronic data interchange (EDI)—the transmission of standard business documents in a standard format between industrial trading partners from computer application to computer application. The interorganizational exchange of business documentation in a structured, machine-processable form.

Enterprise resource planning (ERP)—a complex software system that ties together and automates the basic processes of a business, from taking customers' orders to monitoring inventory levels to balancing the books. ERP systems utilize a companywide framework, tying all the smaller process-driven information systems together into one system.

E-tailers—on-line retailers.

Expert systems—computer programs that mimic human logic to solve problems, using the experience of one or more experts in some problem domain and applying their problem-solving expertise to make useful inferences for the user of the system.

Extended supply chain—includes suppliers of the immediate supplier and customers of the immediate customer, all linked by one or more of the upstream and downstream flows of products, services, finances, and information.

Extranet—a network that utilizes the Internet to communicate, but access is limited to some subset of members external to the firm. Typically includes other firms that are vertically related, such as a manufacturer, carrier, distributor, and retailer.

Forecasting approach—consists of four dimensions: approach access, approach design, approach quality, and approach utilization; includes the products and services to be forecast and how they are forecast.

Forecasting functional integration—the degree and level of interaction between individuals involved in forecast development and those involved in forecast application. Forecasting functional integration consists of three dimensions: collaboration, cooperation, and coordination.

Forecasting management performance—the extent to which forecast users within the company believe that forecasts are accurate and use those forecasts to guide behavior and make decisions.

Forecasting management value—the contribution to organizational performance derived from changes in forecasting management performance.

Forecasting performance measurement—the availability and application of forecasting performance measures. Forecasting performance measurement consists of four dimensions: measurement challenge, measurement clarity, measurement criteria, and measurement feedback.

Forecasting systems—the computer and electronic communications hardware and software used to develop, analyze, and distribute forecasts. Forecasting systems consist of four dimensions: system access, system capability, system quality, and systems utilization.

Functional integration—integrating the goals and activities across functions to optimize the results of the firm.

Functional products—products that satisfy basic needs and have a stable, predictable demand with long product life cycles that change little over time.

Global company—a company that treats world markets as an integrated whole and manages worldwide operations to serve the global marketplace. The managerial focus in global companies is on centralized management of global operations.

Global efficiency—efficiency in current activities that can be achieved through exploiting differences in cost and quality of inputs sourced from foreign markets, taking advantage of economies of scale by leveraging volumes on a global basis, and taking advantage of global scope to maximize utilization of resources and capabilities.

Global risk—four categories of risk that are inherently greater in the global environment than in the domestic U.S. environment and that must be considered in a firm's global strategies: (a) macroeconomic risks associated with significant economic shifts in wage rates, interest rates, exchange rates, and prices; (b) policy risks associated with unexpected actions of national governments; (c) competitive risks associated with uncertainty about competitor activities in foreign markets; and (d) resource risks associated with unanticipated differences in resource requirements in foreign markets.

Incremental products—products new to the company, line extensions, next generation products, and repackaged, repositioned, and recycled products.

Information sharing—the willingness to make strategic and tactical data available to other supply chain partners.

Innovative products—products that satisfy nonbasic needs; have volatile, unpredictable demand with short product life cycles; and tend to have high profit margins.

Integrated product development—involvement of two or more functions working together concurrently on product development.

Integration—*see* Interfunctional coordination.

Interaction—the communication activities (either formal or informal) among different functions, such as meetings and documented information exchange.

Interdependence (Mutual dependence)—consists of (a) each channel member's dependence, (b) the magnitude of the firms' total interdependence that is the sum of both firms' dependence, and (c) the degree of relative dependence between the firms that is the difference between the firm's dependence on its partner and the partner's dependence on the firm.

Interfirm cooperation—a set of joint actions of the firms in a close relationship to accomplish a common set of goals and create mutual benefits.

Interfirm production—production that occurs between different firms.

Interfunctional coordination (Integration)—the coordinated efforts (i.e., interaction and collaboration) across functions within a particular firm to accomplish common goals, such as creating customer value and responsiveness to market changes, under close relationships.

International company—a company with strong, central control by the parent, focused on transferring and adapting the parent company's ideas and products to foreign markets. An international company may be heavily export oriented or may duplicate corporate activities in multiple countries but maintain control at corporate headquarters.

Internet—a global network of networks connecting millions of computer users worldwide using a simple standard common addressing system. The connections between the different networks are called "gateways." These gateways serve to transfer electronic data worldwide.

Intrafirm production—production that occurs within the firm.

Intranet—a network that utilizes the Internet as the communication platform but limits access to members within the firm so that it facilitates communication within the firm, among widely dispersed departments, divisions, and regional locations.

Inventory carrying cost—the cost to hold inventories, including safety stock, in-process stock, cycle stock, promotional stock, and dead stock. These costs include capital cost, storage cost, inventory service cost, and damage, loss, and obsolescence costs.

JIT (Just-In-Time)—parts are produced at each step in a process to supply the immediate demand of the next step. Parts are not produced ahead of time or stored in inventory.

JIT production—extends the JIT concept outside the firm, requiring a cooperative partnering environment between suppliers and buyers to develop cost reduction actions that benefit both firms.

Lean production—teams of multiskilled workers with highly flexible machines producing small quantities of highly varied products.

Logistics—that part of the supply chain process that plans, implements, and controls the efficient flow and storage of goods, services, and related information from the point of origin to the point of consumption in order to meet customers' requirements (Council of Logistics Management, 1998).

Logistics capability—a firm's capabilities to provide competitively superior customer service through cost savings in logistics and/or a stronger marketing position due to an improved logistics system. It has seven different dimensions: customer service, logistics quality, channel of distribution, low-cost distribution, availability, timeliness, and communication.

Logistics communication—providing inventory availability information during order placement, advance information on cancellations/delays, and projected delivery date information at order placement.

Logistics pipeline purchasing approach—an interconnection of supplier and customer organizations to eliminate duplication of logistics functions and improve product flows (e.g., inventories managed jointly, one firm manages order entry, and both firms use a single forecast).

Logistics quality—a logistics capability in terms of minimum damage in transit and order-filling accuracy.

Market orientation—implementation of the marketing concept, composed of three sets of organization-wide activities: (a) generation of market intelligence pertaining to current and future customer needs, (b) dissemination of the intelligence across departments, and (c) responsiveness to market intelligence.

Marketing—the process of planning and executing the conception, pricing, promotion, and distribution of ideas, goods, and services to create exchanges that satisfy individual and organizational goals.

Marketing concept—a business philosophy that consists of three pillars: (a) customer focus, (b) coordinated marketing, and (c) profitability.

Market-sensing capability—ability to learn about customers, competitors, and channel members.

Mass production—semiskilled workers using complex, inflexible machines to produce large quantities of one type of product at one time.

Material resource planning—managing the supply side of a firm by computing net requirements for each inventory item to schedule production and determine when they should be purchased and delivered to the plant to minimize inventory, transportation costs, and warehousing requirements.

Measurement feedback—extent of information provided to individuals concerning the outcome of their performance.

Multifunctional (cross-functional, interfunctional) team—a management team that consists of personnel from different functions, and possibly even supply chain partners, to achieve specific tasks.

Multinational company—a company with operations in multiple countries that operate with a great deal of freedom and autonomy from corporate headquarters or other company operations. The managerial focus in multinational companies is allowing each country or regional business to operate independently to concentrate on local markets.

Mutual dependence—*see* Interdependence.

New product development—the process of conceiving and creating a new product or service and the outcomes of that process.

Operational excellence—providing customers with more reliable products or services at competitive prices and minimal inconvenience, thus reducing the customer's perceived costs of purchase and use.

Operational SCM purchasing approach—purchasing in the role of coordinating interfirm relationships to manage the flow of goods and information between firms, with the objective of optimizing the total supply chain system.

Organizational compatibility—complementary goals and objectives, as well as similarity in operating philosophies and corporate cultures.

Parallel communications process—a buyer and a sales representative act as facilitators, with direct communications between appropriate individuals in multiple functions within the supplier and customer organizations.

Parallel development—developing new products in parallel instead of sequentially; for example, starting the process design to manufacture the product before the final product design is finalized, thereby establishing closer coordination between different stages of development and minimizing the chance that R&D will design products that are difficult or costly to manufacture.

Partnerships—*see* Alliances.

Postponement—designing a product such that it is possible to delay differentiation of the product until customer demand for the specific end-product is known. A good example is paint shipped as a standard white color, with color added only when a customer chooses a specific tint.

Process—a series of linked, continuous, and managed tasks and activities that contribute to an overall desired result or outcome. Processes have a specific starting point and ending point as well as cross-functional and, often, business boundaries.

Product leadership—continuous innovation in products and services, introducing state-of-the-art products and services aimed at delivering customer value through increasing the benefits of owning or using a product or service.

Quick response (QR)—a system used to replenish inventory based on real-time sales data obtained from point of sale information that is transmitted to the supplier. The goal is to reduce inventory and increase availability.

Radical products—products that are new to the market in terms of product class and technology, where target customers are unknown; may rely on unproven production technologies.

Relational purchasing approach—purchasing in the role of building strong buyer-supplier relationships, with the objective of managing the flow of goods from the supplier to the customer.

Relationship marketing—all marketing activities directed toward establishing, developing, and maintaining successful relational exchanges, with the objective of securing loyalty to retain existing customers.

Salesperson external (supply chain partner) logistics expertise—the salesperson's expertise in acquiring knowledge of the supply chain partner's logistical operations and requirements.

Salesperson internal (company) logistics expertise—the salesperson's expertise in his or her firm's logistics systems, processes, and capabilities, along with the ability to implement, facilitate, and coordinate these tasks efficiently and effectively.

Salesperson logistics expertise—the salesperson's competencies, skills, knowledge, or experience in (a) internal (company) logistics capabilities, (b) external (supply chain partner) logistics capabilities, (c) tactical logistics capabilities, and (d) strategic logistics capabilities.

Salesperson strategic logistics expertise—the salesperson's expertise in acquiring knowledge of the supply chain partner's strategic plans and objectives, the supply chain's strategic plans and shared goals, and how to help supply chain partners reach those strategic objectives by coordinating supplier resources and capabilities.

Salesperson tactical logistics expertise—the salesperson's expertise in acquiring knowledge of logistics related to operational issues.

Sequential product development (SPD)—functions such as R&D, marketing, manufacturing, and logistics work independently and in sequence.

Serial communications process—a buyer and a sales representative act as the sole communication link between a customer and supplier. All communications from the customer firm flow to the buyer, and all communications within the supplier firm flow to the sales representative, with these two acting as gatekeepers to maintain control.

Service quality—the judgment or attitude of a customer (similar to satisfaction) toward both the tangible and the intangible dimensions of the service offered by a firm. These tangible and intangible dimensions include the dependability, reliability, and accuracy of the service; the appearance of service personnel and facilities; willingness of service personnel to help customers; and courtesy and attentiveness of service personnel.

Strategic SCM purchasing approach—purchasing in the role of facilitating interfirm relationships with the objective of redesigning business processes to optimize the performance of the entire supply chain system and creating competitive advantage for the firm and the supply chain.

Supply chain—a set of three or more companies directly linked by one or more of the upstream and downstream flows of products, services, finances, and information from a source to a customer.

Supply chain management (SCM)—the implementation of a supply chain orientation across suppliers and customers; the systemic, strategic coordination of the traditional business functions within a particular company and across businesses within the supply chain, for the purposes of improving the long-term performance of the individual companies and the supply chain as a whole.

Supply chain network—consists of suppliers, warehouses, production facilities, distribution centers, and retail outlets involved in moving goods and services from producers to consumers.

Supply chain orientation (SCO)—the recognition by a company of the systemic, strategic implications of the activities and processes involved in managing the various flows in a supply chain.

Supply chain production—production that occurs across a supply chain as a whole, requiring understanding from a supplier's supplier through to a customer's customer.

Supply manager purchasing approach—a single organization is responsible for materials management for entire product lines of a business, which includes supply, acquisition, and materials responsibility and product flow from suppliers, through production, to the customer.

Task—a coherent piece of work that can be assigned to an individual or team and completed in a reasonably short period of time as part of a larger activity.

Tiered production—a concept pioneered in the automotive industry in which a group of suppliers directly supplies the main automotive manufacturer, called the first tier. Suppliers who supply the first tier are second-tier suppliers; suppliers who supply second-tier suppliers are third-tier suppliers, and so on.

Time- and quality-based competition—the elimination of waste in the form of time, effort, defective units, and inventory in manufacturing distribution systems.

Traditional purchasing approach—purchasing in the role of selecting and negotiating with suppliers, with the objective of purchasing at the lowest price.

Transnational company—a company that operates a dispersed, interdependent, and specialized network of assets and capabilities, leveraging globally where it makes sense and managing locally where responsiveness to different markets is required. The managerial focus in transnational companies is to develop skills and capabilities jointly among regions and to share them throughout the worldwide network.

Transportation management systems—software packages that typically automate five basic functions: freight payment auditing, transportation planning, carrier performance, trailer loading, and highway mileage.

Trust—the belief that one partner will act in the best interests of the other; consists of the partner's honesty, benevolence, and willingness to rely on an exchange partner.

Ultimate supply chain—includes all the companies involved in all the upstream and downstream flows of products, services, finances, and information from the initial supplier to the ultimate customer.

Vendor managed inventory (VMI)—a modification of quick response in that the vendor does not have to wait for the replenishment order but assumes responsibility for directly replenishing the retail inventory.

Warehouse management systems (WMS)—software packages concerned with meeting the two objectives of warehousing: optimizing use of space, equipment, and labor; and exceeding customer expectations. WMS accomplish these goals by directing labor, providing inventory and location control, and managing the flow of orders and processes in the warehouse.

References

Abend, Jules, & Gill, Penny. (1999). Supply chain success stories: Jockey & VF Corporation. *Supply Chain Management Review, 3*(Summer), 52-58.

Abrahamsson, M. (1993). Time-based distribution. *The International Journal of Logistics Management, 4*(2), 75-83.

Abrahamsson, M., & Brege, S. (1997). Structural changes in the supply chain. *The International Journal of Logistics Management, 8*(1), 35-44.

Achrol, Ravi S. (1991). Evolution of the marketing organization: New forms for dynamic environments. *Journal of Marketing, 55*(October), 77-93.

Ackerman, Ken. (2000). *Warehousing profitably.* Columbus, OH: Ackerman Publications.

Ackhoff, Russell. (1981). *Creating the corporate future: Plan or be planned for.* New York: Wiley.

Adrian, Peter. (1998). Manufacturers gain from streamlining and integrating product development. *Manufacturing Automation, 8*(2), 3.

Aertsen, Freek. (1993). Contracting out the physical distribution function: A trade-off between asset specificity and performance measurement. *International Journal of Physical Distribution and Logistics Management, 23*(1), 23-29.

Aiken, Michael, & Hage, Jerald. (1968). Organizational interdependence and interorganizational structure. *American Sociological Review, 33*, 912-930.

Alderson, Wroe. (1957). Competition for differential advantage. In *Marketing behavior and executive action.* Homewood, IL: Irwin.

Allen, W. Bruce. (1990). Deregulation and information costs. *Transportation Journal, 30*(2), 58-67.

Allen, W. Bruce. (1997). The logistics revolution and transportation. *The Annals of the American Academy of Political and Social Science, 553*, 106-116.

Amer, Mohamed Y., Chase, Ronald D., & Brumett, Chris L. (1999). WMS software selection—all you're betting is the business. *Supply Chain Management Review, 3*(2), 68-76.

American Marketing Association. (1985). Chicago, IL.

Andel, Tom. (1997). Information supply chain: Set and get your goals. *Transportation and Distribution, 38*(2), 33.

Andel, Tom. (1998). Get in shape for the millenium: Logistics and materials handling management. *Material Handling Engineering, 53*(2). Retrieved August 22, 2000, from the World Wide Web: nrstg1s.djnr.com/

Andel, Tom. (1999). Sharpen your supply chain survival skills. *Material Handling Engineering, 54*(4), S4-S8.

Anderson, Carol H., & Vincze, Julian W. (2000). *Strategic marketing management: Meeting the global marketing challenge.* Boston: Houghton Mifflin.

Anderson, David, & Lee, Hau. (1999). Synchronized supply chains: The new frontier. In David Anderson (Ed.), *Achieving supply chain excellence through technology* (pp. 12-21). San Francisco: Montgomery Research.

Anderson, Erin, & Coughlan, Anne T. (1987). International market entry and expansion via independent or integrated channels of distribution. *Journal of Marketing, 51*(1), 71-82.

Anderson, Erin, Lodish, Leonard M., & Weitz, Barton A. (1987). Resource allocation behavior in conventional channels. *Journal of Marketing Research*, *24*(February), 85-97.

Anderson, Erin, & Weitz, Barton. (1992). The use of pledges to build and sustain commitment in distribution channels. *Journal of Marketing Research*, *29*(February), 18-34.

Anderson, James C., Håkansson, Håkan, & Johanson, Jan. (1994). Dyadic business relationships within a business network context. *Journal of Marketing*, *58*(October), 1-15.

Anderson, James C., & Narus, James A. (1990). A model of distributor firm and manufacturer firm working partnerships. *Journal of Marketing*, *54*(January), 42-58.

Andersson, Par Halen, & Storhagen, Nils G. (1989). Measuring logistics performance. *Engineering Costs and Production Economics*, *17*, 253-262.

Andraski, Joseph C. (1998). Leadership and the realization of supply chain collaboration. *Journal of Business Logistics*, *19*(2), 9-11.

Andraski, Joseph C., Wisdo, Joseph P., & Blasgen, Rick D. (1996, Summer). Dispatches from the front: The Nabisco story. *Supply Chain Management Review*, pp. 30-38.

Anonymous. (1989). Integrating the flow of materials and information. *Modern Materials Handling*, *44*(4), 81-85.

Anonymous. (1996). Supply chain savings in EDI. *Purchasing*, *121*(5), 56.

Ansari, A., & Modarress, B. (1990). *Just-in-time purchasing*. New York: Free Press.

Aoki, M. (1988). *Information, incentives, and bargaining in the Japanese economy*. Cambridge, UK: Cambridge University Press.

Argyris, Chris. (1966). *Organization and innovation*. Homewood, IL: Richard D. Irwin.

Armitage, Howard M. (1987). The use of management accounting techniques to improve productivity analysis in distribution operations. *International Journal of Physical Distribution and Materials Management*, *17*(2), 40-50.

Armstrong, Gary, & Kotler, Philip. (1999). *Marketing: An introduction* (5th ed.). Upper Saddle River, NJ: Prentice Hall.

Arntzen, Bruce C., Brown, Gerald G., Harrison, Terry P., & Traffon, Linda L. (1995). Global supply chain management at Digital Equipment Corporation. *Interfaces*, *25*(January/February), 69-93.

Asmus, D., & Griffin, A. (1993). Harnessing the power of your suppliers. *McKinsey Quarterly*, *3*(Summer), 63-79.

Atkinson, Anthony J., Waterhouse, John H., & Wells, Robert B. (1997). A stakeholder approach to strategic performance measurement. *Sloan Management Review*, *38*(3), 25-37.

Axelrod, Robert. (1984). *The evolution of cooperation*. New York: Basic Books.

Badaracco, J. L., Jr. (1991). *The knowledge link: How firms compete through strategic alliances*. Boston: Harvard Business School Press.

Ballou, Ronald H. (1992). *Business logistics management* (3rd ed.). Englewood Cliffs, NJ: Prentice Hall.

Ballou, Ronald H. (1993). Reformulating a logistics strategy: A concern for the past, present and future. *International Journal of Physical Distribution and Logistics Management*, *23*(5), 30-38.

Ballou, Ronald H. (1999). *Business logistics management* (4th ed.). Upper Saddle River, NJ: Prentice Hall.

Balsmeier, P. W., & Voisin, W. J. (1996). Supply chain management: A time-based strategy. *Industrial Management*, *38*(5), 24-27.

Banerjee, Avijit. (1986). A joint economic-lot-size model for purchaser and vendor. *Decision Sciences*, *17*(3), 292-311.

Barczak, Gloria. (1995). New product strategy, process and performance in the telecommunications industry. *Journal of Product Innovation Management*, *12*(3), 224-234.

Barks, Joseph V. (1989). Priceless work?: Survey of financial impact of logistics management. *Distribution*, *88*(12), 50-54.

Barksdale, Hiram C., & Darden, Bill. (1971). Marketer's attitude toward the marketing concept. *Journal of Marketing*, *35*(October), 29-36.

Barlow, Jim. (1994, September 25). What sparks cooperation? *The Houston Chronicle*, Business Section, p. 1.

Barney, Jay B. (1991). Firm resources and sustained competitive advantage. *Journal of Management*, *17*(1), 99-120.

Barr, Stephen. (1996). The big picture. *CFO: The Magazine for Senior Financial Executives*, *12*(7), 37-42.

Bartlett, Christopher A., & Ghoshal, Sumantra. (1998). *Managing across borders: The transnational solution*. Boston: Harvard Business School Press.

Battaglia, Alfred J. (1994, November/December). Beyond logistics: Supply chain management. *Chief Executive*, pp. 48-49.

Bauer, Raymond A. (1960). Consumer behavior as risk taking. In Robert S. Hancock (Ed.), *Dynamic marketing for a changing world* (pp. 389-398). Chicago: American Marketing Association.

Bauknight, Dow N. (2000). The supply chain's future in the e-economy . . . and why many may never see it. *Supply Chain Management Review, 4*(1), 28-35.

Bechtel, Christian, & Jayaram, Jayanth. (1997). Supply chain management: A strategic perspective. *The International Journal of Logistics Management, 8*(1), 15-34.

Bello, Daniel C., & Lohtia, Ritu. (1995). Export channel design: The use of foreign distributors and agents. *Journal of the Academy of Marketing Science, 23*(2), 83-93.

Beltramini, Richard. (1996). Concurrent engineering: Information acquisition between high technology marketeers and R&D engineers in new product development. *International Journal of Technology Management, 1*(1/2), 58-69.

Berry, Leonard L. (1980). Services marketing is different. *Business, 30*(May/June), 33-40.

Berry, Leonard L. (1995). Relationship marketing of services—Growing interest, emerging perspectives. *Journal of the Academy of Marketing Science, 23*(Fall), 236-245.

Berry, Leonard L., & Parasuraman, A. (1991). *Marketing services.* New York: Free Press.

Bienstock, Carol C., Mentzer, John T., & Bird, Monroe Murphy. (1997). Measuring physical distribution service quality. *Journal of the Academy of Marketing Science, 25*(1), 31-44.

Billington, Corey, & Amaral, Jason. (1999). Investing in product design to maximize profitability through postponement. In David L. Anderson (Ed.), *Achieving supply chain excellence through technology* (pp. 64-68). San Francisco: Montgomery Research.

Birchard, Bill. (1994). Mastering the new metrics. *CFO: The Magazine for Senior Financial Executives, 10*(10), 30-38.

Birou, Laura M. (1994). *The role of the buyer-supplier linkage in an integrated product development environment.* Unpublished doctoral dissertation, Department of Management, Michigan State University.

Birou, Laura M., & Fawcett, Stanley. (1993). International purchasing: Benefits, requirements, and challenges. *International Journal of Purchasing and Materials Management, 29*(2), 28-37.

Birou, Laura M., & Fawcett, Stanley E. (1994). Supplier involvement in integrated product development: A comparison of US and European practices. *International Journal of Physical Distribution and Logistics Management, 24*(5), 4-14.

Bitner, Mary Jo. (1995). Building service relationships: It's all about promises. *Journal of the Academy of Marketing Science, 23*(Fall), 246-251.

Blaine, J.C.D. (1967). The dynamics of transportation. *Transportation Journal, 7*(Summer), 19-27.

Bonaccorsi, Andrea, & Lipparini, Andrea. (1994). Strategic partnerships in new product development: An Italian case study. *Journal of Product Innovation Management, 11*(2), 134-145.

Booker, Ellis. (1999, August 20). XML greases supply chain. *Internetweek,* pp. 1, 55.

Booz, Allen and Hamilton, Inc. (1982). *New product management for the 1980's.* New York: Author.

Borch, Fred J. (1957). The marketing philosophy as a way of business life. In Elizabeth Marting & Albert Newgarden (Eds.), *The marketing concept: Its meaning to management* (pp. 3-16). New York: American Management Association.

Boulding, William, Kalra, Ajay, Staelin, Richard, & Zeithaml, Valarie. (1993). A dynamic process model of service quality: From expectations to behavioral intentions. *Journal of Marketing Research, 30* (February), 7-27.

Bovet, David, & Sheffi, Yossi. (1998). The brave new world of supply chain management. *Supply Chain Management Review, 2*(Spring), 14-22.

Bowersox, Donald J. (1988). Logistical partnerships. In Joseph E. McKeon (Ed.), *Partnerships: A natural evolution in logistics.* Cleveland, OH: Logistics Resource Forum.

Bowersox, Donald J. (1990). The strategic benefits of logistics alliances. *Harvard Business Review, 68*(4), 36-45.

Bowersox, Donald J. (1997). Lessons learned from the world class leaders. *Supply Chain Management Review, 1*(1), 61-67.

Bowersox, Donald J., Carter, Philip L., & Monczka, Robert M. (1985). Materials logistics management. *International Journal of Physical Distribution and Materials Management, 15*(5), 27-35.

Bowersox, Donald J., & Closs, David J. (1996). *Logistical management: The integrated supply chain process.* New York: McGraw-Hill.

Bowersox, Donald J., Closs, David J., & Helferich, Omar K. (1986). *Logistical management* (3rd ed.). New York: Macmillan.

Bowersox, Donald J., Closs, David J., Mentzer, John T., & Sims, Jeffrey R. (1979). *Simulated product sales forecasting.* East Lansing, MI: Michigan State University Press.

Bowersox, Donald J., & Daugherty, Patricia J. (1987). Emerging patterns of logistical organization. *Journal of Business Logistics, 8*(Winter), 46-60.

Bowersox, Donald J., & Daugherty, Patricia J. (1995). Logistics paradigms: The impact of information technology. *Journal of Business Logistics, 16*(1), 65-80.

Bowersox, Donald J., Daugherty, Patricia J., Dröge, Cornelia L., Germain, Richard N., & Rogers, Dale S. (1992). *Logistical excellence: It's not business as usual.* Burlington, MA: Digital Press.

Bowersox, Donald J., Daugherty, Patricia J., Dröge, Cornelia L., Rogers, Dale S., & Wardlow, Daniel L. (1989). *Leading edge logistics: Competitive positioning for the 1990's.* Oak Brook, IL: Council of Logistics Management.

Bowersox, Donald J., Mentzer, John T., & Speh, Thomas W. (1995). Logistics leverage. *Journal of Business Strategies, 12*(2), 36-49.

Bowman, Robert J. (1996). Has JIT flopped? *Distribution, 95*(7), 28-32.

Bradley, Peter. (1995). US logistics productivity took a header in 1994. *Purchasing, 119*(1), 101.

Brealey, Richard A., & Meyers, Stewart C. (1991). *Principles of corporate finance* (4th ed.). New York: McGraw-Hill.

Brooksher, K. Dane. (1999). E-commerce and logistics. *Traffic World, 260*(7), 31.

Brown, James E., & Hendry, Chris. (1997). Industrial districts and supply chains as vehicles for managerial and organizational learning: The construction, forms, and consequences of industry networks. *International Studies of Management and Organization, 27*(4), 127-157.

Brown, Mark G., & Svenson, Raynold A. (1998). Measuring R&D productivity. *Research Technology Management, 41*(6), 30-35.

Brown, Shona L., & Eisenhardt, Kathleen M. (1995). Product development: Past research, present finding and future directions. *Academy of Management Review, 20*(2), 343-378.

Brown, Stuart F. (1998). Wrestling new wealth from supply chain. *Fortune, 138*(9), 204C-204Z.

Bruce, Karin. (1998). Can you align IT with business strategy? *Strategy & Leadership, 26*(5), 16-21.

Brunell, Tom. (1999). Managing a multicompany supply chain. *Supply Chain Management Review, 3*(1), 45-52.

Buchanan, Lauranne. (1992). Vertical trade relationships: The role of dependence and symmetry in attaining organizational goals. *Journal of Marketing Research, 29*(February), 65-75.

Bucklin, Louis P., & Sengupta, Sanjit. (1993). Organizing successful co-marketing alliances. *Journal of Marketing, 57*(April), 32-46.

Burt, D. (1989). Managing suppliers up to speed. *Harvard Business Review, 67*(July/August), 127-135.

Busch, Hans F. (1988). Integrated materials management. *International Journal of Physical Distribution and Logistics Management, 18*(7), 28-39.

Byrne, Patrick M. (1992). Target projects that add value. *Transportation and Distribution, 33*, 39-42.

Byrne, Patrick, & Markham, William. (1991). *Improving quality and productivity in the logistics process: Achieving customer satisfaction breakthroughs.* Oak Brook, IL: Council of Logistics Management.

Caddick, J. R., & Dale, B. G. (1987). The determination of purchasing objectives and strategies: Some key influences. *International Journal of Physical Distribution and Materials Management, 17*(3), 5-16.

Calantone, Roger J., & di-Benedetto, C. Anthony. (1988). An integration model of the new product development process: An empirical validation. *Journal of Product Innovation Management, 5*(3), 201-215.

Cannon, Joseph P. (1992). *A taxonomy of buyer-seller relationships in business markets.* Doctoral dissertation, Department of Marketing, University of North Carolina at Chapel Hill.

Cannon, Joseph P., & Perreault, William D., Jr. (1997). *The nature of business relationships.* Working paper, Department of Marketing, Colorado State University.

Caplice, Chris, & Sheffi, Yossi. (1995). A review and evaluation of logistics performance measurement systems. *The International Journal of Logistics Management, 6*(1), 61-74.

Capon, Noel, Farley, John U., Lehmann, Donald R., & Hubert, James M. (1992). Profiles of product innovators among large U.S. manufacturers. *Management Science, 38*(2), 157-170.

Carlsson, Matts. (1991). Aspects of the integration of technical functions for efficient product development. *R&D Management, 21*(January), 55-66.

Carmel, Erran. (1995). Cycle time in packaged software firms. *Journal of Product Innovation Management, 12*(1), 1-14.

Carpano, Claudio, Chrisman, James J., & Roth, Kendall. (1994). International strategy and environment: An assessment of the performance relationship. *Journal of International Business Studies, 25*(3), 639-656.

Carter, J. R., Ferrin, B. G., & Carter, C. R. (1995). The effect of less-than-truckload rates on the purchase order lot size decision. *Transportation Journal, 34*(3), 35-44.

Carter, J. R., & Narasimhan, R. (1990). Purchasing in the international marketplace: Implications for operations. *Journal of Purchasing and Materials Management, 26*(Summer), 2-11.

Carter, Joseph R., & Miller, Jeffrey G. (1989). The impact of alternative vendor/buyer communication structures on the quality of purchased materials. *Decision Sciences, 20*(4), 759-776.

Cavinato, Joseph L. (1989). How to link logistics to financial results. *Distribution, 88*(3), 103-104.

Cavinato, Joseph L. (1990a). Accelerating your product-to-cash cycle. *Distribution, 89*(3), 74-76.

Cavinato, Joseph L. (1990b). How to calculate the rate of return. *Distribution, 89*(6), 68-70.

Cavinato, Joseph L. (1991a). Evolving procurement organizations: Logistics implications. *Journal of Business Logistics, 13*(1), 27-45.

Cavinato, Joseph L. (1991b). Identifying interfirm total cost advantage for supply chain competitiveness. *International Journal of Purchasing and Materials Management, 27*(4), 10-15.

Cavinato, Joseph L. (1992). A total cost/value model for supply chain competitiveness. *Journal of Business Logistics, 13*(2), 285-301.

Center for Advanced Purchasing Strategies (CAPS) Research (1997). Supply chain management. *Best Practices, 1*(4). Retrieved March 26, 2000, from the World Wide Web: www.capsresearch.org/research/best-practices

Cespedes, Frank V. (1996a). Beyond teamwork: How the wise can synchronize; concurrent marketing creates the seamless integration your organization is supposed to enjoy. *Marketing Management, 5*(1), 24-31.

Cespedes, Frank V. (1996b). *Managing marketing linkages.* Upper Saddle River, NJ: Prentice Hall.

Chakravarthy, Balaji S. (1986). Measuring strategic performance. *Strategic Management Journal, 7*(5), 437-458.

Chandler, Alfred D. (1962). *Strategy and structure—Chapters in the history of the industrial enterprise.* Cambridge, MA: The MIT Press.

Chapman, Paul T. (1994). Logistics network modeling. *The logistics handbook.* New York: Free Press.

Chen, Frank, Drezner, Zvi, Ryan, Jennifer K., & Simchi-Levi, David. (1999). The bullwhip effect: Managerial insights on the impact of forecasting and information on variability in a supply chain. In Tayur Sridhar, Ram Ganeshan, & Michael Magazine (Eds.), *Quantitative models for supply chain management* (pp. 419-439). Boston: Kluwer Academic Publishers.

Chen, F., Ryan, J. K., & Simchi-Levi, D. (1998a). *The impact of exponential smoothing forecasts on the bullwhip effect.* Working Paper, Northwestern University.

Chen, F., Ryan, J. K., & Simchi-Levi, D. (1998b). *Quantifying the bullwhip effect in a simple supply chain: The impact of forecasting, lead times and information.* Working Paper, Northwestern University.

Chi, Tailan. (1994). Trading in strategic resources: Necessary conditions, transaction cost problems, and choice of exchange structure. *Strategic Management Journal, 15*(4), 271-290.

Chiappe, Ignacio Sanchez, & Herrero, Victor Angel. (1997). The status of supply chain management in Argentina's food industry. *The International Journal of Logistics Management, 8*(1), 87-96.

Chidamber, Shyam R., & Kon, Henry B. (1994). A research retrospective of innovation inception and success: The technology-push, demand-pull question. *International Journal of Technology Management, 9*(1), 94-112.

Chiesa, Vittorio. (1996). Strategies for global R&D. *Research Technology Management, 39*(5), 19-25.

Chikara, Jitendra, & Weiss, Elliott N. (1995). JIT savings—Myth or reality? *Business Horizons, 38*(3), 73-78.

Chow, Garland, Heaver, Trevor D., & Henriksson, Lennart E. (1994). Logistics performance: Definition and measurement. *International Journal of Physical Distribution and Logistics Management, 24*(1), 17-28.

Christopher, Martin L. (1992a). *Logistics and Supply Chain Management.* London: Pitman.

Christopher, Martin L. (1992b). *Logistics, the strategic issues.* London: Chapman and Hall.

Christopher, Martin L. (1994). *Logistics and supply chain management.* Burr Ridge, IL: Irwin Professional.

Christopher, Martin L. (1999). Creating the agile supply chain. In David Anderson (Ed.), *Achieving supply chain excellence through technology* (pp. 28-32). San Francisco: Montgomery Research.

Christopher, Martin, Schary, P., & Skjott-Larsen, T. (1979). *Customer service and distribution strategy.* New York: John Wiley & Sons.

Churchill, Gilbert A., Jr., & Peter, J. Paul. (1995). *Marketing: Creating value for customers.* Burr Ridge, IL: Richard D. Irwin.

Clark, Kim B. (1989). Project scope and project performance: The effect of parts strategy and supplier involvement on product development. *Management Science, 35*(10), 1247-1263.

Clark, Kim B., & Fujimoto, Takahiro. (1991). *Product development performance: Strategy, organization, and management in the world auto industry.* Cambridge, MA: Harvard Business School Press.

Clinton, Stephen R., & Closs, David J. (1997). Logistics strategy: Does it exist? *Journal of Business Logistics, 18*(1), 19-44.

Closs, David J., Oaks, Susan L., & Wisdo, Joseph P. (1989). Design requirements to develop integrated inventory management and forecasting systems. *Council of Logistics Management Annual Conference Proceedings: Volume II* (pp. 233-259). Oak Brook, IL: Council of Logistics Management.

Closs, David J., & Thompson, Craig K. (1992). Logistics physical resource management. *Journal of Business Logistics, 13*(2), 269-283.

Cohen, Morris A., Eliashberg, Jehoshua, & Ho, Teck H. (1997). An anatomy of a decision-support system for developing and launching line extensions. *Journal of Marketing Research, 34*(Winter), 117-129.

Cohen, Shoshanah. (1996). Supply-chain council introduces the supply chain operations reference-model. *PRTM Insight*, *8*(3). Retrieved March 26, 2000, from the World Wide Web: www.prtm.com/insight/

Conant, Jeffrey S., Mokwa, Michael P., & Varadarajan, P. Rajan. (1990). Strategic types, distinctive marketing competencies and organizational performance: A multiple measures-based study. *Strategic Management Journal*, *11*(5), 365-383.

Cook, Robert L. (1989). Expert system use in logistics education: An example and guidelines for logistics educators. *Journal of Business Logistics*, *10*(1), 68-87.

Cooke, James A. (1995). Does your logistics operation add value? *Traffic Management*, *34*(12), 49-52.

Cooke, James A. (1996). The check's in the computer. *Logistics Management*, *35*(12), 55S.

Cooke, James A. (1998). Crossing the great software divide: Creating logistics software interfaces. *Logistics Management Distribution Report*, *37*(6), 72-74.

Cooke, James A. (1999a). Auto ID, software drive the supply chain. *Logistics Management Distribution Report*, *38*(7), 101-102.

Cooke, James A. (1999b). Web browser brings product demand into focus: Eastman Chemical now disseminates real-time monthly sales forecasts over its corporate intranet, giving users worldwide a clearer picture of product demand. *Logistics Management and Distribution Report*, *38*(5), 67-70.

Coombs, Gary, & Gomez-Mejia, Luis R. (1991). Cross-functional pay strategies in high-technology firms. *Compensation and Benefits Review*, *23*(September/October), 40-48.

Cooper, Martha C., & Ellram, Lisa M. (1993). Characteristics of supply chain management and the implications for purchasing and logistics strategy. *The International Journal of Logistics Management*, *4*(2), 13-24.

Cooper, Martha C., Ellram, Lisa M., Gardner, John T., & Hanks, Albert M. (1997). Meshing multiple alliances. *Journal of Business Logistics*, *18*(1), 67-89.

Cooper, Martha C., Innis, Daniel E., & Dickson, Peter R. (1992). *Strategic planning for logistics*. Oak Brook, IL: Council of Logistics Management.

Cooper, M. C., Lambert, Douglas M., & Pagh, Janus D. (1997). Supply chain management: More than a new name for logistics. *The International Journal of Logistics Management*, *8*(1), 1-14.

Cooper, Robert G. (1984). The impact of new product strategies. *Industrial Marketing Management*, *12*, 243-256.

Cooper, Robert G. (1990). Stage-gate systems: A new tool for managing new products. *Business Horizons*, *33*(3), 44-54.

Cooper, Robert G. (1993). *Winning at new products*. Reading, MA: Addison-Wesley.

Cooper, Robert G., & Kleinschmidt, E. J. (1986). An investigation into the new product process: Steps, deficiencies, and impact. *Journal of Product Innovation Management*, *3*(2), 71-85.

Cooper, Robert G., & Kleinschmidt, E. J. (1991). New product processes at leading industrial firms. *Industrial Marketing Management*, *3*(2), 71-86.

Cooper, Robin, & Slagmulder, Regine. (1991). Profit priorities from activity-based costing. *Harvard Business Review*, *69*(May/June), 130-135.

Copacino, William C. (1993). Creating the perfect order. *Traffic Management*, *32*(2), 27.

Copacino, William C. (1998). Masters of the supply chain. *Logistics Management and Distribution Report*, *37*(12), 23.

Corsi, T. M. (1997). The logistics revolution and transportation. *The Annals of the American Academy of Political and Social Science*, *553*(September), 186-191.

Council of Logistics Management. (1985). Oak Brook, IL.

Council of Logistics Management. (1998). Retrieved from the World Wide Web: www.clm1.org

Covin, J. G., & Slevin, D. P. (1991). A conceptual model of entrepreneurship as firm behavior. *Entrepreneurship Theory and Practice*, *16*(1), 7-25.

Coyle, John J., Bardi, Edward J., & Langley, C. John, Jr. (1996). *The management of business logistics* (6th ed.). St. Paul, MN: West.

Cravens, David W. (1995). Introduction to the Special Issue. *Journal of the Academy of Marketing Science*, *23*(4), 235.

Crawford, C. M. (1994). Significant issues for the future of product innovation. *Journal of Product Innovation Management*, *11*(3), 253-258.

Cronin, J. Joseph, Jr., & Taylor, Steven A. (1992). Measuring service quality: A reexamination and extension. *Journal of Marketing*, *56*(July), 55-68.

Crosby, Lawrence, Evans, Kenneth, & Cowles, Deborah (1990). Relationship quality in services selling: An interpersonal influence perspective. *Journal of Marketing*, *54*(July), 68-81.

Dalrymple, Douglas J. (1975). Sales forecasting methods and accuracy. *Business Horizons*, *18*, 69-73.

Dalrymple, Douglas J. (1987). Sales forecasting practices: Results from a United States survey. *International Journal of Forecasting*, *3*(3/4), 379-391.

Dant, Rajiv P., & Schul, Patrick L. (1992). Conflict resolution processes in contractual channels of distribution. *Journal of Marketing, 56*(Winter), 38-54.

Dapiran, Peter. (1992). Benetton—Global logistics in action. *The International Journal of Physical Distribution and Logistics Management, 22*(6), 7-11.

Das, T. K., & Teng, Bing-Sheng. (1998). Resource and risk management in the strategic alliance making process. *Journal of Management, 24*(1), 21-42.

Davenport, Thomas H. (1993). *Process innovation, reengineering work through information technology* (1st ed.). Boston: Harvard Business School Press.

Davenport, Thomas H. (1998). Putting the enterprise into the enterprise system. *Harvard Business Review, 76*(July/August), 121-131.

Davidson, Jeffrey M., Clamen, Allen, & Karol, Robin A. (1999). Learning from the best new product developers. *Research and Technology Management, 42*(4), 12-18.

Davis, Frank W., Jr., & Manrodt, Karl B. (1991). Service logistics: An introduction. *International Journal of Physical Distribution and Logistics Management, 21*(7), 4-13.

Davis, Karron T. (1998). Cash forwarding expands business for University Medical Products. *Business Credit, 100*(2), 10-12.

Day, D. V., & Lord, R. G. (1988). Executive leadership and organizational performance: Suggestions for a new theory and methodology. *Journal of Management, 14*(3), 453-464.

Day, George S. (1992). Marketing's contribution to the strategy dialogue. *Journal of the Academy of Marketing Science, 20*(Fall), 323-329.

Day, George S. (1994). The capabilities of market-driven organizations. *Journal of Marketing, 58* (October), 37-52.

Day, George S., & Klein, Saul. (1987). Cooperative behavior in vertical markets: The influence of transaction costs and competitive strategies. In Michael J. Houston (Ed.), *Review of marketing* (pp. 39-66). Chicago: American Marketing Association.

Day, George S., & Wensley, Robin. (1988). Assessing advantage: A framework for diagnosing competitive superiority. *Journal of Marketing, 52*(April), 1-20.

Dean, Kortge G., & Okonkwo, Patrick A. (1989). Simultaneous new product development: Reducing the new product failure rate. *Industrial Marketing Management, 18*(4), 301-306.

Delaney, Robert V. (1999, June 5). *A look back in anger at logistics productivity* (10th annual State of Logistics Report). Washington, DC: National Press Club. Retrieved March 26, 2000, from the World Wide Web: www.cassinfo.com/bob_press_conf_1999.html

Deschamps, Jean-Philippe, & Nayak, P. Ranganah. (1995). *Product juggernauts.* Boston: Harvard Business Press.

Deshpande, Rohit, Farley, John U., & Webster, Frederick E., Jr. (1993). Corporate culture, customer orientation, and innovativeness in Japanese firms: A quadrad analysis. *Journal of Marketing, 57*(January), 23-27.

Deshpande, Rohit, & Webster, Frederick E., Jr. (1989). Organizational culture and marketing: Defining the research agenda. *Journal of Marketing, 53*(January), 3-15.

Deutsch, Morton. (1958). Trust and suspicion. *Journal of Conflict Resolution, 2*(4), 265-279.

Devlin, G., & Bleackley, M. (1988). Strategic alliances—Guidelines for success. *Long Range Planning, 21*(5), 18-23.

Dickson, Pat H., & Weaver, Mark K. (1997). Environmental determinants and individual-level moderators of alliance use: Special research forum on alliances and networks. *Academy of Management Journal, 40*(2), 404.

Dickson, Peter Reid. (1992). Toward a general theory of competitive rationality. *Journal of Marketing, 56*(January), 69-83.

Dominguez, Luis V., & Zinn, Walter. (1994). International supplier characteristics associated with successful long-term buyer/seller relationships. *Journal of Business Logistics, 15*(2), 63-87.

Donlon, J. P., & Galli, J. (1998, January 11). Working on the chain gang [Includes related articles and panel discussion]. *Chief Executive,* p. 54.

Dowlatshahi, Shad. (1992). Purchasing's role in a concurrent engineering environment. *International Journal of Purchasing and Materials Management, 28*(Winter), 21-25.

Dowst, Somerby. (1988, January 28). Quality suppliers: The search goes on. *Purchasing,* pp. 94A4-12.

Drayer, Ralph W. (1999). Synchronize for success. *Supply Chain Management Review, 3*(Summer), 60-66.

Dröge, Cornelia L., & Germain, Richard N. (1991). Evaluating logistics management information systems. *International Journal of Physical Distribution and Logistics Management, 21*(7), 22-27.

Drozdowski, Ted E. (1986, March 13). At BOC they start with the product. *Purchasing,* pp. 62B5-11.

Drucker, Peter F. (1954). *The practice of management.* New York: Harper & Row.

Dupuit, Jules. (1952). On the measurement of the utility of public works [R. H. Barback, Trans.]. Reprinted in *International Economic Papers*, *2*, 63-110. (Original work published 1844)

Dwyer, F. Robert, & Oh, Sejo. (1987). Output sector munificence effects on the internal political economy of marketing channels. *Journal of Marketing Research*, *25*(November), 347-358.

Dwyer, F. Robert, Schurr, Paul H., & Oh, Sejo. (1987). Developing buyer-seller relationships. *Journal of Marketing*, *51*(April), 11-27.

Dwyer, F. Robert, & Tanner, John F., Jr. (1999). *Business marketing: Connecting strategy, relationships, and learning.* Boston: Irwin McGraw-Hill.

Eccles, Robert G., & Pyburn, Philip J. (1992). Creating a comprehensive system to measure performance. *Management Accounting*, *74*(4), 41-50.

Ellram, Lisa M. (1990). The supplier selection decision in strategic partnerships. *Journal of Purchasing and Materials Management*, *26*(4), 8-14.

Ellram, Lisa M. (1991a). A managerial guideline for the development and implementation of purchasing partnerships. *International Journal of Purchasing and Materials Management*, *27*(3), 2-8.

Ellram, Lisa M. (1991b). Supply chain management: The industrial organization perspective. *International Journal of Physical Distribution and Logistics Management*, *21*(1), 13-22.

Ellram, Lisa, M. (1992). Patterns in international alliances. *Journal of Business Logistics*, *13*(1), 1-25.

Ellram, Lisa M., & Cooper, Martha C. (1990). Supply chain management partnerships, and the shipper-third party relationship. *International Journal of Logistics Management*, *1*(2), 1-10.

Ellram, Lisa M., & Cooper, Martha C. (1993). The relationship between supply chain management and keiretsu. *The International Journal of Logistics Management*, *4*(1), 1-12.

Ellram, Lisa M., & Krause, Daniel R. (1994). Supplier partnerships in manufacturing versus non-manufacturing firms. *The International Journal of Logistics Management*, *5*(1), 45-53.

Ellram, Lisa M., La Londe, Bernard J., & Weber, Mary Margaret. (1989). Retail logistics. *International Journal of Physical Distribution and Materials Management*, *19*(12), 29-39.

Emerson, Carol J., & Grimm, Curtis M. (1996). Logistics and marketing components of customer service: An empirical test of the Mentzer, Gomes, and Krapfel model. *International Journal of Physical Distribution and Logistics Management*, *26*(8), 29-42.

Emmelhainz, Margaret. (1988). Strategic issues of EDI implementation. *Journal of Business Logistics*, *9*(2), 55-70.

Emmelhainz, Margaret. (1990). *Electronic data interchange: A total management guide.* New York: Van Nostrand Reinhold.

English, W. D. (1985). The impact of electronic technology upon the marketing channel. *Journal of the Academy of Marketing Science*, *13*(3), 57-71.

Ernst and Whinney. (1985). *Warehouse accounting and control: Guidelines for distribution and financial managers.* Oak Brook, IL: National Council of Physical Distribution Management.

Estell, Libby. (1999). Unchained profits: Technology to aid in satisfying customer needs. *Sales and Marketing Management*, *2*(151), 62-67.

Factor, R. (1998). Survey spotlights need to improve capabilities. *Modern Materials Handling*, *53*(April), 17.

Farris, M. Theodore, Jr. (1996). Utilizing inventory flow models with suppliers. *Journal of Business Logistics*, *1*(1), 35-61.

Faulds, David, & Mangold, W. Glynn. (1995). Service quality in the distributor-retailer dyad: Empirical results. *Journal of Marketing Channels*, *4*(3), 95-112.

Fawcett, Stanley E., & Clinton, Steven R. (1996). Enhancing logistics performance to improve the competitiveness of manufacturing organizations. *Production and Inventory Management Journal*, *37*(1), 40-46.

Fawcett, Stanley E., & Fawcett, Stanley A. (1995). The firm as a value-added system: Integrating logistics, operations and purchasing. *International Journal of Physical Distribution & Logistics Management*, *25*(5), 24-42.

Feitzinger, Edward, & Lee, Hau L. (1997). Mass customization at Hewlett Packard: The power of postponement. *Harvard Business Review*, *75*(January/February), 116-121.

Felton, Arthur P. (1959). Making the marketing concept work. *Harvard Business Review*, *37*(July/August), 55-65.

Fernie, John. (1994). Quick response: An international perspective. *International Journal of Physical Distribution and Logistics Management*, *24*(6), 38-46.

Fisher, M. L. (1997). What is the right supply chain for your product? *Harvard Business Review*, *75*(March/April), 105-116.

Fisher, Robert J., Maltz, Elliot, & Jaworski, Bernard J. (1997). Enhancing communication between marketing and engineering: The moderating role of relative functional identification. *Journal of Marketing*, *61*(Summer), 54-70.

Fliedner, G., & Vokurka, R. J. (1997). Agility: Competitive weapon of the 1990's and beyond. *Production and Inventory Management Journal, 38*(3), 19-24.

Forrester, Jay W. (1958). Industrial dynamics: A major breakthrough for decision makers. *Harvard Business Review, 38*(July/August), 37-66.

Fortuin, Leonard. (1988). Performance indicators—Why, where, and how? *European Journal of Operational Research, 34*(1), 1-9.

Foster, Tom. (1998). You can't manage what you don't measure. *Distribution, 37*(5), 63-68.

Frazier, Gary L. (1983a). Interorganizational exchange behavior in marketing channels: A broadened perspective. *Journal of Marketing, 47*(Fall), 68-78.

Frazier, Gary L. (1983b). On the measurement of interfirm power in channels of distribution. *Journal of Marketing, 53*(January), 50-69.

Frazier, Gary L., Spekman, Robert E., & O'Neal, Charles R. (1988). Just-in-time exchange relationships in industrial markets. *Journal of Marketing, 52*(October), 52-67.

Freeman, Chris. (1994). The economics of technical change. *Cambridge Journal of Economics, 18*(5), 463-514.

Galbraith, J. K. (1952). *American capitalism.* Boston: Houghton Mifflin.

Galbraith, J. K. (1977). *Organizational design.* Reading, MA: Addison-Wesley.

Ganesan, Shankar. (1994). Determinants of long-term orientation in buyer-seller relationships. *Journal of Marketing, 58*(April), 1-19.

Gardner, Everette S., Jr. (1990). Evaluating forecasting performance in an inventory control system. *Management Science, 36*(4), 490-499.

Garver, Michael S. (1998). *Buyer-salesperson relationships: Customer value created and delivered by the salesperson and its effect on customer satisfaction, personal trust, and personal loyalty.* Unpublished doctoral dissertation, University of Tennessee.

Garver, Michael S., Gardial, Sarah F., & Woodruff, Robert B. (2000). *Buyer relationships with salespersons: Customer value and its effect on personal loyalty and revenge.* Working paper, Central Michigan University.

Garver, Michael S., & Mentzer, John T. (In press). Salesperson logistics expertise: A contingency framework. *Journal of Business Logistics.*

Gattorna, John L., Chorn, Norman H., & Day, Abby. (1991). Pathway to customers: Reducing complexity in the logistics pipeline. *International Journal of Physical Distribution and Logistics Management, 21*(8), 5-11.

Gentry, Julie J. (1996). The role of carriers in buyer-supplier strategic partnerships: A supply chain management approach. *Journal of Business Logistics, 17*(2), 35-55.

Gentry, Julie J., & Vellenga, David B. (1996). Using logistics alliances to gain a strategic advantage in the marketplace. *Journal of Marketing Theory and Practice, 4*(Spring), 37-44.

Ghoshal, Sumantra. (1987). Global strategy: An organizing framework. *Strategic Management Journal, 8*(5), 425-440.

Gill, Penny, & Abend, Jules. (1996). Wal-Mart: The supply chain heavyweight champ. *Supply Chain Management Review, 1*(Summer), 8-16.

Giunipero, Larry C., Brand, Richard R. (1996). Purchasing's role in supply chain management. *The International Journal of Logistics Management, 7*(1), 29-38.

Glassman, David M., & Stern & Stewart Co. (1997). Contracting for value: EVA and the economics of organizations. *The Bank of America Journal of Applied Corporate Finance, 10*(Summer), 110-123.

Global Logistics Research Team at Michigan State University. (1995). *World class logistics: The challenge of managing continuous change.* Oak Brook, IL: Council of Logistics Management.

Gold, Steven, Dranove, David, Shanley, Mark, Shiber, Nancy, & Hogan, Dylan. (1998). IT poses stumbling block for supply chain management. *Purchasing, 124*(6), 33-34.

Goldberg, Victor P. (1976). Toward an expanded economic theory of contract. *Journal of Economic Issues, 10*(March), 45-61.

Goldman, Arieh. (1991). Japan's distribution systems: Institutional structure, internal political economy, and modernization. *Journal of Retailing, 67*(2), 154-183.

Goodstein, Leonard D., & Butz, Howard E. (1998). Customer value: The linchpin of organizational change. *Organizational Dynamics, 27*(1), 21-33.

Gould, L. S. (1998). SCM: Another acronym to help broaden enterprise management; supply chain management. *Automotive Manufacturing and Production, 110*(3), 64.

Govindarajan, Vijay. (1988). A contingency approach to strategy implementation at the business unit level: Integrating administrative mechanisms with strategy. *Academy of Management Journal, 31*(4), 828-853.

Govindarajan, Vijay, & Fisher, Joseph. (1990). Strategy, control systems, and resource-sharing: Effects on business-unit performance. *Academy of Management Journal, 33*(2), 259-285.

Graham, T. Scott, Daugherty, Patricia J., & Dudley, William N. (1994). The long-term strategic impact of purchasing partnerships. *International Journal of Purchasing and Materials Management, 30*(4), 12-18.

Grandori, Anna, & Soda, Giuseppe. (1995). Inter-firm networks: Antecedents, mechanisms and forms. *Organization Studies, 16*(2), 183.

Granovetter, Mark. (1985). Economic action and social structure: The problems of embeddedness. *American Journal of Sociology, 91*(November), 481-510.

Grant, R. M. (1995). *Contemporary strategy analysis: Concepts, techniques, applications* (2nd ed.). Cambridge, MA: Blackwell.

Greenberg, J., & Folger, R. (1983). Procedural justice, participation, and the fair process effect in groups and organizations. In P. B. Paulus (Ed.), *Basic group processes* (pp. 235-256). New York: Springer-Verlag.

Greene, Alice H. (1991). Supply chain of customer satisfaction. *Production and Inventory Management Review and APICS News, 11*(4), 24-25.

Griffin, Abbie. (1992). Evaluating QFD's use in US firms as a process for developing products. *Journal of Product Innovation Management, 9*(3), 171-187.

Griffin, Abbie. (1997). The effect of project and process characteristics on product development cycle time. *Journal of Marketing Research, 34*(Winter), 24.

Griffin, Abbie, & Hauser, John R. (1992). Patterns of communication among marketing, engineering and manufacturing—A comparison between two new product teams. *Management Science, 38*(March), 360-373.

Griffin, Abbie, & Hauser, John R. (1993). The voice of the customer. *Marketing Science, 12*(Winter), 1-27.

Griffin, Abbie, & Hauser, John R. (1996). Integrating R&D and marketing: A review and analysis of the literature. *Journal of Product Innovation Management, 13*(May), 191-215.

Grönroos, Christian. (1990). *Service management and marketing.* Lexington, MA: Lexington Books.

Grönroos, Christian (1995). Relationship marketing: The strategy continuum. *Journal of the Academy of Marketing Science, 23*(Fall), 252-254.

Gross, Neil. (1998, June 22). The supply chain: Leapfrogging a few links. *Business Week*, pp. 140-142.

Gruen, Thomas W. (1997). Relationship marketing: The route to marketing efficiency and effectiveness. *Business Horizons, 6*(40), 32.

Gruner, S. (1996, February). Benchmark: Partnering for products. *INC* (on-line). Retrieved March 26, 2000, from the World Wide Web: www.inc.com

Gulati, R. (1995). Does familiarity breed trust? The implication of repeated ties for contractual choice in alliances. *Academy of Management Journal, 38*(1), 85-112.

Gummensson, Evert. (1987). The new marketing—Developing long-term interactive relationships. *Long Range Planning, 20*(4), 10-20.

Gummensson, Evert. (1996). Relationship marketing: The emperor's new clothes or a paradigm shift? In *Research methodologies for the new marketing* (pp. 3-19). Latimer, UK: ESOMAR/EMAC.

Gundlach, Gregory T., Achrol, Ravi S., & Mentzer, John T. (1995). The structure of commitment in exchange. *Journal of Marketing, 59*(January), 78-92.

Gundlach, Gregory T., & Murphy, Patrick E. (1993). Ethical and legal foundations of relational marketing exchanges. *Journal of Marketing, 57*(Fall), 35.

Gupta, Anil K., & Govindarajan, Vijay. (1991). Knowledge flows and the structure of control within multinational corporations. *Academy of Management Review, 16*(4), 768-792.

Gupta, Ashok K., Raj, S. P., & Wilemon, David L. (1985). R&D and marketing dialogue in high-tech firms. *Industrial Marketing Management, 14*(4), 289-300.

Gupta, Ashok K., & Souder, William E. (1998). Key drivers of reduced cycle time. *Research Technology Management, 41*(4), 38-43.

Gupta, Ashok K., & Wilemon, David L. (1990). Accelerating the development of technology-based new products. *California Management Review, 32*(Winter), 24-44.

Gustin, C. M., Daugherty, P. J., & Stank, T. P. (1995). The effects of information availability on logistics integration. *Journal of Business Logistics, 16*(1), 1-21.

Hagedoorn, J. (1993). Understanding the rationale of strategic technology partnering: Interorganizational modes of cooperation and sectoral differences. *Strategic Management Journal, 14*(5), 371-385.

Hall, John A. (1991). *Bringing new products to market: The art & science of creating winners.* New York: American Management Association.

Hall, Richard H. (1999). *Organizations: Structures, processes, and outcomes* (7th ed.). Upper Saddle River, NJ: Prentice Hall.

Hambrick, Donald C., & Mason, Phyllis A. (1984). Upper echelons: The organization as a reflection of its top managers. *Academy of Management Review, 9*(2), 193-206.

Hamel, G., & Sampler, J. (1998). The E-corporation. *Fortune, 138*(11), 80-94.

Hamel, Gary, & Prahalad, C. K. (1994). *Competing for the future.* Boston: Harvard Business School Press.

Hammer, Michael I. (1990). Reengineering work: Don't automate, obliterate. *Harvard Business Review*, *68*(4), 104-112.

Han, Jin K., Kim, Namwoon, & Srivastava, Rajendra K. (1998). Market orientation and organizational performance: Is innovation a missing link? *Journal of Marketing*, *62*(October), 30-45.

Hansen, Kent F., Weiss, Malcolm A., & Kwak, Sangman. (1999). Allocating R&D resources: A quantitative aid to management insight. *Research Technology Management*, *42*(4), 44-50.

Harding, Forrest E. (1998). Logistics service provider quality: Private measurement, evaluation, and improvement. *Journal of Business Logistics*, *19*(1), 103-120.

Harrigan, K. R. (1983). *Strategies for vertical integration*. Lexington, MA: Lexington Books.

Harrington, Lisa. (1993). Why managing diversity is so important? *Distribution*, *92*(11), 88-92.

Harrington, Thomas C., Lambert, Douglas M., & Christopher, Martin. (1991). A methodology for measuring vendor performance. *Journal of Business Logistics*, *12*(1), 83-104.

Harrington, Thomas C., Lambert, Douglas M., & Sterling, Jay U. (1992). Simulating the financial impact of marketing and logistics decisions. *International Journal of Physical Distribution and Logistics Management*, *22*(7), 3-12.

Harrison, A. (1990). Co-makership as an extension of quality care. *International Journal of Quality and Reliability Management*, *7*(2), 15-22.

Hauser, John R., Simester, Duncan, & Wernerfelt, Birger. (1994). Customer satisfaction incentives. *Marketing Science*, *13*(Fall), 327-350.

Hayes, Robert H., & Pisano, Gary P. (1994). Beyond world class: The new manufacturing strategy. *Harvard Business Review*, *72*(January/February), 77-87.

Hayes, Robert H., Wheelwright, Steven C., & Clark, Kim B. (1988). *Dynamic manufacturing*. New York: Free Press.

Heide, Jan B., & John, George. (1988). The role of dependence balancing in safeguarding transaction-specific assets in conventional channel. *Journal of Marketing*, *52*(January), 20-35.

Heide, Jan B., & John, George. (1990). Alliances in industrial purchasing: The determinants of joint action in buyer-supplier relationships. *Journal of Marketing Research*, *27*(February), 24-36.

Heide, Jan B., & Miner, Anne S. (1992). The shadow of the future: Effects of anticipated interaction and frequency of contact on buyer-seller cooperation. *Academy of Management Journal*, *35*(2), 265-291.

Helferich, Keith O. (1983). Logistics decision support systems. In *Computers in manufacturing: Distribution management*. Pennsauken, NJ: Auerbach.

Hewitt, Fred. (1994). Supply chain redesign. *The International Journal of Logistics Management*, *5*(2), 1-9.

Hewitt, Frederick. (1992). Supply chain integration. In *1992 Annual Conference Proceedings* (pp. 334-341). Oak Brook, IL: Council of Logistics Management.

Hicks, Donald A. (1997). The manager's guide to supply chain and logistics problem-solving tools and techniques. *IIE Solutions*, *29*(10), 24-29.

Hill, Charles W. L. (1995). The Toyota corporation in 1994. In Charles W. L. Hill & Gareth R. Jones (Eds.), *Strategic management: An integrated approach* (pp. C249-C263). Boston: Houghton Mifflin.

Hill, Charles W. L. (1997). *International business: Competing in the global marketplace*. Chicago: Richard D. Irwin.

Hill, Charles W. L., & Jones, G. R. (1988). *Strategic management: An integrated approach* (4th ed.). Boston: Houghton Mifflin.

Hill, Charles W. L., & Snell, S. A. (1989). Effects of ownership structure and control on corporate productivity. *Academy of Management Journal*, *32*(1), 25-46.

Hillman, Willis T., Mathews, Mike, & Huston, Richard C. (1990). Assessing buyer/planner performance in the supply network. *International Journal of Physical Distribution and Logistics Management*, *20*(2), 16-21.

Hinkle, Charles, & Kuehn, Alfred A. (1967). Heuristics models: Mapping the maze for management. *California Management Review*, *10*(Fall), 61.

Hitt, Michael A., Ireland, Duane R., & Hoskisson, Robert E. (1999). *Strategic management*. Cincinnati, OH: Southwestern College Publishing.

Hodge, B. J., Anthony, William P., & Gales, Lawrence M. (1996). *Organizational theory: A strategic approach* (5th ed.). Upper Saddle River, NJ: Prentice Hall.

Hof, Robert D. (1999a, October 21). Guiding Amazon's foray into bricks and mortar: Q&A with Jeffrey Wilke. *Business Week E.Biz*. Retrieved April 21, 2000, from the World Wide Web: www.businessweek.com/ebiz/index.html

Hof, Robert D. (1999b, November 1). What's with all the warehouses? *Business Week E.Biz*, p. EB 88.

Hofstede, G. (1980). Motivation, leadership, and organization: Do American theories apply abroad? *Organizational Dynamics*, *9*(1), 42-63.

Hofstede, G. (1984). The cultural relativity of the quality of life concept. *Academy of Management Review, 9,* 389-398.

Holak, Susan L., Parry, Mark E., & Song, Michael. (1991). The relationship of R & D/Sales to firm performance: An investigation of marketing contingencies. *Journal of Product Innovation Management, 8*(4), 267-282.

Honeycutt, Earl, Home, Vincent, & Ingram, Thomas. (1993). Shortcomings of sales training programs. *Industrial Marketing Management, 22*(2), 117-123.

Horscroft, Peter, & Braithwaite, Alan. (1990). Enhancing supply chain efficiency—The strategic lead time approach. *The International Journal of Logistics Management, 1*(2), 47-52.

Houlihan, John B. (1985). International supply chain management. *International Journal of Physical Distribution and Materials Management, 15*(1), 22-38.

Houlihan, John B. (1988). International supply chains: A new approach. *Management Decision, 26*(3), 13-19.

House, Charles H., & Price, Raymond L. (1991). The return map: Tracking product teams. *Harvard Business Review, 69*(January/February), 92-100.

Hui, C. Harry. (1988). Measurement of individualism/collectivism. *Journal of Research in Personality, 23,* 17-36.

Hui, C. Harry, & Triandis, Harry C. (1986). Individualism/collectivism and psychological needs: Their relationships in two cultures. *Journal of Cross-Cultural Psychology, 17*(2), 225-248.

Hui, C. Harry, & Villareal, Marcelo J. (1989). Individualism/collectivism and psychological needs. *Journal of Cross-Cultural Psychology, 20*(3), 310-323.

Hunt, Shelby D., & Morgan, Robert M. (1995). The comparative advantage theory of competition. *Journal of Marketing, 59*(April), 1-15.

Hutt, Michael D., Walker, Beth A., & Frankwick, Gary L. (1995). Hurdle the cross-functional barriers to strategic change. *Sloan Management Review, 36*(3), 22-30.

Hyman, Paul. (1996, April 8). Maximizing the cross-functional experience. *Electronic Buyers' News.* Retrieved March 26, 2000, from the World Wide Web: www.techweb.com/se/directlink.cgi ?EBN19960408S0002

Iansiti, Marco, & MacCormack, Alan. (1997). Developing products on Internet time. *Harvard Business Review, 75*(September/October), 108-117.

Ingram, Thomas N. (1996). Relationship selling: Moving from rhetoric to reality. *Mid-American Journal of Business, 11*(Spring), 5-12.

Ingram, Thomas N., & LaForge, Raymond W. (1992). *Sales management: Analysis and decision making.* New York: Dryden.

Ittner, Christopher D., & Larcker, David F. (1997). Product development cycle time and organizational performance. *Journal of Marketing Research, 34*(Winter), 13-23.

Jaworski, Bernard J., & Kohli, Ajay K. (1993). Market orientation: Antecedents and consequences. *Journal of Marketing, 57*(July), 53-70.

Johansson, Johny K. (1995). International alliances: Why now? *Journal of the Academy of Marketing Science, 23*(4), 301-304.

Johnson, James C., Wood, Donald F., Wardlow, Daniel L., & Murphy, Paul R., Jr. (1999). *Contemporary logistics* (7th ed.). Upper Saddle River, NJ: Prentice Hall.

Johnson, Jean L., Sakano, Tomoaki, Cote, Joseph A., & Onzo, Naoto. (1993). The exercise of interfirm power and its repercussions in U.S.–Japanese channel relationships. *Journal of Marketing, 57*(April), 1-10.

Johnson, M. Eric (1998). Giving 'em what they want. *Management Review, 87*(1), 62-67.

Johnson, M. Eric, & Davis, Tom. (1998). Improving supply chain performance by using order fulfillment metrics. *National Productivity Review, 17*(3), 3-16.

Joint Industry Project on Efficient Consumer Response. (1994). *Activity based costing for food wholesalers and retailers.* Washington, DC: Grocery Manufacturers of America.

Jones, Gareth R. (1998). *Organizational theory: Text and cases* (2nd ed.). Reading, MA: Addison-Wesley Longman.

Jones, Thomas C., & Riley, Daniel W. (1985). Using inventory for competitive advantage through supply chain management. *International Journal of Physical Distribution and Materials Management, 15*(5), 16-26.

Kahn, Kenneth B., & McDonough, Edward F., III (1997). An empirical study of the relationships among co-location, integration, performance and satisfaction. *Journal of Product Innovation Management, 14*(3), 161-178.

Kahn, Kenneth B., & Mentzer, J. T. (1996). EDI and EDI alliances: Implications for the sales forecasting function. *Journal of Marketing Theory and Practice, 4*(2), 72-78.

Kahn, Kenneth B., & Mentzer, John T. (1998). Marketing's integration with other departments. *Journal of Business Research, 42*(1), 53-62.

Kalwani, Manohar U., & Narayandas, Narakesari. (1995). Long-term manufacturer-supplier relationships: Do they pay off for supplier firms? *Journal of Marketing, 59*(January), 1-16.

Kamien, Morton I., & Schwartz, Nancy L. (1982). *Market structure and innovation.* Cambridge, UK: Cambridge University Press.

Kanter, R. M. (1989). *When giants learn to dance.* New York: Touchstone.

Kaplan, Robert S. (1984). Yesterday's accounting undermines production. *Harvard Business Review, 62*(4), 95-101.

Kaplan, Robert S., & Cooper, Robin. (1997). *Cost and effect: Using integrated cost systems to drive profitability and performance.* Boston: Harvard Business School Press.

Kaplan, Robert S., & Norton, David P. (1992). The balanced scorecard—Measures that drive performance. *Harvard Business Review, 70*(January/February), 71-79.

Kaplan, Robert S., & Norton, David P. (1993). Putting the balanced scorecard to work. *Harvard Business Review, 71*(September/October), 134-142.

Katzenbach, Jon R., & Smith, Douglas K. (1993). *The wisdom of teams: Creating high performance organizations.* Boston: Harvard Business Press.

Kearney, A. T., Inc. (1978). *Measuring productivity in physical distribution: A $40 million goldmine.* Oak Brook, IL: National Council of Physical Distribution Management.

Kearney, A. T., Inc. (1984). *Measuring and improving productivity in physical distribution: The successful companies.* Oak Brook, IL: National Council of Physical Distribution Management.

Keebler, James S., Manrodt, Karl B., Durtsche, David A., & Ledyard, D. Michael. (1999). *Keeping score: Measuring the business value of logistics in the supply chain.* Oak Brook, IL: Council of Logistics Management.

Keep, W. W., Hollander, S. C., & Dickinson, R. (1998). Forces impinging on long-term business to business relationships in the United States: An historical perspective. *Journal of Marketing, 62*(April), 31-45.

Kent, John L., Jr., & Flint, Daniel J. (1997). Perspectives on the evolution of logistics thought. *Journal of Business Logistics, 18*(2), 15-29.

Kessler, E. H., & Chakrabarti, A. K. (1996). Innovation speed: A conceptual model of context, antecedents and outcomes. *Academy of Management Review, 21*(4), 1143-1191.

King, Robert L. (1965). The marketing concept. In George Schwartz (Ed.), *Science in marketing* (pp. 70-97). New York: John Wiley & Sons.

Kleinsorge, Ilene K., Schary, Philip B., & Tanner, Ray. (1989). Evaluating logistics decisions. *International Journal of Physical Distribution and Logistics Management, 19*(12), 3-14.

Kogut, B. (1985). Designing global strategies: Comparative and competitive value-added chains. *Sloan Management Review, 28*(Summer), 15-28.

Kogut, B. (1988). Joint ventures: Theoretical and empirical perspectives. *Strategic Management Journal, 9*(4), 319-332.

Kohli, Ajay K., & Jaworski, Bernard J. (1990). Market orientation: The construct, research propositions, and managerial implications. *Journal of Marketing, 54*(April), 1-18.

Koota, Pasi, & Takala, Josu. (1998). Developing a performance measurement system for world-class distribution logistics by using activity-based costing and management: Case: Basic metal industries. *International Journal of Technology Management, 16*(1), 267-280.

Korsgaard, M. Audrey, Schweiger, David M., & Sapienza, Harry J. (1995). Building commitment, attachment, and trust in strategic decision-making teams: The role of procedural justice. *Academy of Management Journal, 38*(1), 60-84.

Kotler, Philip. (1972). A generic concept of marketing. *Journal of Marketing, 36*(April), 46-54.

Kotler, Philip. (1997). *Marketing management* (9th ed.). Englewood Cliffs, NJ: Prentice Hall.

Kotler, Philip, & Armstrong, Gary. (1991). *Principles of marketing* (5th ed.). Englewood Cliffs, NJ: Prentice Hall.

Kotler, Philip, & Armstrong, Gary. (1994). *Principles of marketing—Annotated instructor's edition* (6th ed.). Englewood Cliffs, NJ: Prentice Hall.

Kotter, J. P. (1990). *A force for change: How leadership differs from management.* New York: Free Press.

Kreinin, Mordechai E. (1998). *International economics: A policy approach.* Orlando, FL: Harcourt Brace College Publishers.

Kumar, Nirmalya, Scheer, Lisa K., & Steenkamp, Jan-Nenedict E. M. (1995). The effects of supplier fairness on vulnerable resellers. *Journal of Marketing Research, 32*(February), 54-65.

Kuntz, Mary. (1995, November 27). Reinventing the store. *Business Week,* pp. 84-96.

Lagace, Rosemary R., Dahlstrom, Robert, & Gassenheimer, Jule B. (1991). The relevance of ethical sales-person behavior on relationship quality: The pharmaceutical industry. *Journal of Personal Selling & Sales Management, 11*(Fall), 39-47.

La Londe, Bernard J. (1997). Supply chain management: Myth or reality? *Supply Chain Management Review, 1*(Spring), 6-7.

La Londe, Bernard J., & Cooper, Martha C. (1988). *Customer service: A management perspective.* Oak Brook, IL: Council of Logistics Management.

La Londe, Bernard J., & Cooper, Martha C. (1989). *Partnerships in providing customer service: A third party perspective*, Oak Brook, IL: Council of Logistics Management.

La Londe, Bernard J., Cooper, Martha C., & Noordewier, Thomas G. (1988). *Customer service: A management perspective.* Oak Brook, IL: Council of Logistics Management.

La Londe, Bernard J., Grabner, John R., & Robeson, James F. (1993). Integrated distribution systems: A management perspective. *International Journal of Physical Distribution and Logistics Management, 23*(5), 4-12.

La Londe, Bernard J., & Masters, James M. (1994). Emerging logistics strategies: Blueprints for the next century. *International Journal of Physical Distribution and Logistics Management, 24*(7), 35-47.

La Londe, Bernard J., & Masters, James M. (1997). *The 1997 Ohio State survey of career patterns in logistics.* Chicago: Council of Logistics Management.

La Londe, Bernard J., & Pohlen, Terrance L. (1996). Issues in supply chain costing. *The International Journal of Logistics Management, 7*(1), 1-12.

La Londe, Bernard J., & Powers, Richard F. (1993). Disintegration and re-integration: Logistics of the twenty-first century. *International Journal of Logistics Management, 4*(2), 1-12.

La Londe, Bernard J., & Zinszer, Paul H. (1976). *Customer service: Meaning and measurement.* Chicago: National Council of Physical Distribution Management.

Lambe, C. Jay, & Spekman, Robert E. (1997). Alliances and technological change. *Journal of Product Innovation Management, 14*(2), 102-116.

Lambert, Douglas M. (1976). *The development of an inventory costing methodology: A study of the costs associated with holding inventory.* Chicago: National Council of Physical Distribution Management.

Lambert, Douglas M., Marmorstein, Howard, & Sharma, Arun. (1990). Industrial salespeople as a source of market information. *Industrial Marketing Management, 19*, 141-148.

Lambert, Douglas M., & Stock, James R. (1993). *Strategic logistics management* (3rd ed.). Homewood, IL: Richard D. Irwin.

Lambert, Douglas M., Stock, James R., & Ellram, Lisa M. (1998). *Fundamentals of logistics management.* Boston: Irwin/McGraw-Hill.

Lamming, R. (1993). *Beyond partnership strategies for innovation and lean supply.* London: Prentice Hall.

Langfield-Smith, Kim, & Greenwood, Michelle R. (1998). Developing co-operative buyer-seller relationships: A case study of Toyota. *Journal of Management Studies, 35*(3), 331-353.

Langley, C. John, Jr., & Holcomb, Mary C. (1992). Creating logistics customer value. *Journal of Business Logistics, 13*(2), 1-27.

Larson, Paul D. (1993a). Buyer-supplier co-operation, product quality and total costs. *International Journal of Physical Distribution and Logistics Management, 24*(6), 4-10.

Larson, Paul D. (1993b). Quality is still number 1. *Purchasing, 114*(5), 20.

Larson, Paul D. (1994). An empirical study of inter-organizational functional integration and total costs. *Journal of Business Logistics, 15*(1), 153-169.

Larson, Clint. (1988). Team tactics can cut development costs. *Journal of Business Strategy, 9*(5), 22-25.

Larson, Paul D., & Lusch, Robert F. (1990). Quick response retail technology: Integration and performance measurement. *The International Review of Retail, Distribution and Consumer Research, 30*, 111-118.

Larzelere, Robert E., & Huston, Ted L. (1980). The dyadic trust scale: Toward understanding interpersonal trust in close relationships. *Journal of Marriage and the Family, 42*(August), 595-604.

Lassar, Walfried, & Zinn, Walter. (1995). Informal channel relationships in logistics. *Journal of Business Logistics, 16*(1), 81-106.

Lawrence, Paul R., & Lorsch, Jay W. (1967). *Organization and environment.* Cambridge, MA: Harvard University Press.

Lawrence, Paul R., & Lorsch, Jay W. (1986). *Organization and environment: Managing differentiation and integration.* Cambridge, MA: Harvard University Press.

Lee, Hau L., & Billington, Corey. (1992). Managing supply chain inventory: Pitfalls and opportunities. *Sloan Management Review, 33*(Spring), 65-73.

Lee, Hau L., Padmanabhan, V., & Whang, Seungjin. (1997a). The bullwhip effect in supply chains. *Sloan Management Review, 38*(Spring), 93-102.

Lee, Hau L., Padmanabhan, V., & Whang, Seungjin. (1997b). Information distortion in supply chains: The bullwhip effect. *Management Science, 43*(4), 546-558.

Leenders, Michiel R., Nollet, Jean, & Ellram, Lisa M. (1993). Adapting purchasing to supply chain management. *International Journal of Physical Distribution and Logistics Management, 24*(1), 40-42.

Lei, David, & Slocum, John W., Jr. (1991). Global strategic alliances: Payoffs and pitfalls. *Organizational Dynamics, 19*(3), 44-62.

Lei, David, Slocum, John W., Jr., & Pitts, Robert A. (1997). Building cooperative advantage: Managing strategic alliances to promote organizational learning. *Journal of World Business, 32*(3), 203-223.

Levitt, Theodore. (1960). Marketing myopia. *Harvard Business Review, 38*(July/August), 24-27.

Lewis, I., & Talalayevsky, A. (1997). Logistics and information technology: A coordination perspective. *Journal of Business Logistics, 18*(1), 141-157.

Liker, Jeffrey K., Collins, Paul D., & Hull, Frank M. (1999). Flexibility and standardization: Test of a contingency model of product design-manufacturing integration. *Journal of Product Innovation Management, 16*, 248-267.

Lim, Jeen-Su, & Reid, David A. (1992). Vital cross functional linkages with marketing. *Industrial Marketing Management, 21*(2), 159-165.

Loar, Tim. (1992). Patterns of inventory management and policy: A study of four industries. *Journal of Business Logistics, 13*(2), 69-96.

Loforte, Anthony J. (1993). The implications of multicultural relationships in a transnational supply chain. *Annual Conference Proceedings* (pp. 69-77). Tempe, AZ: National Association of Purchasing Management.

Lusch, Robert F., & Brown, James. (1996). Interdependency, contracting, and relational behavior in marketing channels. *Journal of Marketing, 60*(October), 19-38.

Lyles, M. A., & Salk, J. E. (1996). Knowledge acquisition from foreign parents in international joint ventures: An empirical examination in Hungarian context. *Journal of International Business Studies, 27*(Special issue), 877-903.

Lynagh, Peter M., & Poist, Richard F. (1984). Assigning organizational responsibility for interface activities: An analysis of PD and marketing manager preferences. *International Journal of Physical Distribution and Materials Management, 14*(6), 34-46.

Lynn, Gary S., Mazzuca, Mario, Morone, Joseph G., & Paulson, Albert S. (1998). Learning is the critical success factor in developing truly new products [Part 1 of 2]. *Research Technology Management, 41*(3), 45-47.

Mabert, Vincent A., Muth, John F., & Schmenner, Roger W. (1992). Collapsing new product development times: Six case studies. *Journal of Product Innovation Management, 9*(September), 200-212.

Madhavan, Ravindranath, & Grover, Rajiv. (1998). From embedded knowledge to embodied knowledge: New product development as knowledge management. *Journal Of Marketing, 62*(4), 1-12.

Magretta, Joan. (1998a). Fast, global, and entrepreneurial: Supply chain management, Hong Kong Style: An interview with Victor Fung. *Harvard Business Review, 76*(September/October), 103-114.

Magretta, Joan. (1998b). The power of virtual integration: An interview with Dell Computer's Michael Dell. *Harvard Business Review, 76*(March/April), 73-84.

Makridakis, S., Andersen, A., Carbone, R., Fildes, R., Hibon, M., Lewandowski, R., Newton, J., Parzen, E., & Winkler, R. (1982). The accuracy of extrapolation (time series) methods: Results of a forecasting competition. *Journal of Forecasting, 1*, 111-153.

Makridakis, S., & Hibon, M. (1979). Accuracy of forecasting: An empirical investigation. *Journal of the Royal Statistical Society, Series A, 142*(Part 2), 79-145.

Makridakis, Spyros, Chatfield, Chris, Hibon, Michele, & Lawrence, Michael. (1993). The M2-competition: A real-time judgmentally based forecasting study. *International Journal of Forecasting, 9*(April), 5-22.

Mallen, Bruce. (1963). A theory of retailer-supplier conflict, control, and cooperation. *Journal of Retailing, 39*(Summer), 24-32.

Malone, Thomas W., & Rockart, John F. (1991). Computers, networks and the corporation. *Scientific American, 265*(3), 128.

Maltz, Elliot, & Kohli, Ajay K. (1996). Market intelligence dissemination across functional boundaries. *Journal of Marketing Research, 33*(February), 47-61.

Manrodt, Karl B., & Davis, Frank W., Jr. (1993). The evolution to service response logistics. *International Journal of Physical Distribution and Logistics Management, 23*(5), 56-64.

Manrodt, Karl B., Holcomb, Mary C., & Thompson, Richard H. (1997). What's missing in supply chain management? *Supply Chain Management Review, 1*(3), 80-86.

McAllister, Daniel J. (1995). Affect- and cognition-based trust as foundations for interpersonal cooperation in organizations [Special research forum: Intra- and interorganizational cooperation]. *Academy of Management Journal, 38*(1), 24-59.

McCann, Joseph, & Galbraith, Jay R. (1981). Interdepartmental relations. In C. Nystrom & W. H. Starbuck (Eds.), *Handbook of organizational design* (Vol. 2, pp. 60-84). New York: Oxford University Press.

McCarthy, E. Jerome, & Perreault, William D., Jr. (1984). *Basic marketing* (8th ed.). Homewood, IL: Irwin.

McDermott, Dennis R., Franzak, Frank J., & Little, Michael W. (1993). Does marketing relate to hospital profitability? *Journal of Health Care Marketing, 13*(Summer), 18-25.

McDougal, Steve, & Smith, Jeff. (1999). Wake up your product development: Bringing sales into the new product process may improve success rates. *Marketing Management, 8*(2), 24-30.

McGinnis, Michael A., & Kohn, Jonathan W. (1990). A factor analytic study of logistics strategy. *Journal of Business Logistics, 11*(2), 41-63.

McGrath, Michael E. (1997). Improving supply-chain management; the first cross-industry operations reference-model can change the way business is done by all; management philosophies. *Transportation and Distribution, 38*(2), 78-80.

McKeefry, Hailey Lynne. (1998, May 18). The networked S.C.—Software systems help manufacturers extend their enterprise. *Electronic Buyers' News*. Retrieved March 26, 2000, from the World Wide Web: www.techweb.com/se/directlink.cgi?EBN19980518S0080

McKitterick, John B. (1957). What is the marketing management concept? In Frank M. Bass (Ed.), *The frontiers of marketing thought* (pp. 71-82). Chicago: American Marketing Association.

McNamara, Carlton P. (1972). The present status of the marketing concept. *Journal of Marketing, 36* (January), 50-57.

McNeill, W. H. (1963). *The rise of the West.* Chicago: University of Chicago Press.

McWilliams, Gary. (1997, April 7). Michael Dell: Whirlwind on the Web. *Business Week*, pp. 132-136.

Mendez, Eduardo G., & Pearson, John N. (1994). Purchasing's role in product development: The case for time-based strategies. *International Journal of Purchasing and Materials Management, 30*(1), 2-12.

Menke, Michael M. (1997). Essentials of R&D strategic excellence. *Research Technology Management, 40*(5), 40-41.

Mentzer, John T. (1993). Managing channel relations in the 21st century. *Journal of Business Logistics, 14*(1), 27-42.

Mentzer, John T. (1999). Supplier partnering. In Jagdish N. Sheth & Atul Parvatiyar (Eds.), *Handbook of relationship marketing* (pp. 457-477). Thousand Oaks, CA: Sage.

Mentzer, John T., & Bienstock, Carol C. (1998). *Sales forecasting management.* Thousand Oaks, CA: Sage.

Mentzer, John T., Bienstock, Carol C., & Kahn, Kenneth B. (1999). Benchmarking sales forecasting management. *Business Horizons, 42*(May/June), 48-56.

Mentzer, John T., & Cox, James E. (1984). Familiarity, application, and performance of sales forecasting techniques. *Journal of Forecasting, 3*, 27-36.

Mentzer, John T., Flint, Daniel J., & Kent, John L. (1999). Developing a logistics quality scale. *Journal of Business Logistics, 20*(1), 9-32.

Mentzer, John T., & Gandhi, Nimish. (1992). Expert systems in marketing: Guidelines for development. *Journal of the Academy of Marketing Science, 20*(Winter), 73-80.

Mentzer, John T., & Gandhi, Nimish. (1993). Expert systems in industrial marketing. *Industrial Marketing Management, 22*(2), 109-115.

Mentzer, John T., & Gomes, Roger. (1990). Logistics forecasting challenges in the 1990's: Factors affecting technique selection. *1990 Council of Logistics Management Educators Conference Proceedings* (pp. 161-170). Oak Brook, IL: Council of Logistics Management.

Mentzer, John T., & Gomes, Roger. (1994). Further extensions of adaptive extended exponential smoothing and comparison with the M-competition. *Journal of the Academy of Marketing Science, 22*(4), 372-382.

Mentzer, John T., Gomes, Roger, & Krapfel, Robert E., Jr. (1989). Physical distribution service: A fundamental marketing concept? *Journal of the Academy of Marketing Science, 17*(1), 53-62.

Mentzer, John T., & Kahn, Kenneth B. (1995a). Forecasting technique familiarity, satisfaction, usage, and application. *Journal of Forecasting, 14*(5), 465-476.

Mentzer, John T., & Kahn, Kenneth B. (1995b). A framework of logistics research. *Journal of Business Logistics, 16*(1), 231-250.

Mentzer, John T., & Kahn, Kenneth B. (1997). State of sales forecasting systems in corporate America. *Journal of Business Forecasting, 16*(1), 6-13.

Mentzer, John T., Kahn, Kenneth B., & Bienstock, Carol C. (1996). *Sales forecasting benchmark study: Executive summary.* Unpublished manuscript, University of Tennessee.

Mentzer, John T., & Konrad, Brenda P. (1991). An efficiency/effectiveness approach to logistics performance analysis. *Journal of Business Logistics, 12*(1), 33-62.

Mentzer, John T., & Schroeter, Jon. (1993). Multiple forecasting system at Brake Parts, Inc. *The Journal of Business Forecasting, 12*(3), 5-9.

Mentzer, John T., & Schroeter, Jon. (1994). Integrating logistics forecasting techniques, systems, and administration: The multiple forecasting system. *Journal of Business Logistics, 15*(2), 205-225.

Mesher, A. (1997, December 3). Danger: Common reference models for supply chain. *Integrated Logistics Strategies. TopVIEW.*

Meyer, J. R., et al. (1959). *The economics of competition in the transportation industries.* Cambridge, MA: Harvard University Press.

Meyer, John P., Allen, Natalie J., Smith, Catherine A. (1993). Commitment to organizations and occupations: Extension and test of a three-component conceptualization. *Journal of Applied Psychology, 78*(4), 528-551.

Meyers, Patricia W., & Tucker, Frances G. (1989). Defining roles for logistics during routine and radical technological innovation. *Journal of the Academy of Marketing Science, 17*(1), 73-82.

Miles, Raymond, & Snow, Charles. (1978). *Organizational strategy, structure, and process.* New York: McGraw-Hill.

Miller, K. D. (1992). A framework for integrated risk management in international business. *Journal of International Business Studies, 23*(2), 311-331.

Miller, K. D., & Leiblein, M. J. (1996). Corporate risk-return relations: Returns variability versus downside risk. *Academy of Management Journal, 39*(1), 91-122.

Miller, Roger. (1995). Applying quality practices to R&D. *Research Technology Management, 38*(2), 47-54.

Miller, William L. (1995). A broader mission for R&D: Part one. *Research Technology Management, 38*(6), 24-36.

Mills, Wyatt J. (1998). Enterprise formula management. *Business News Publishing Co.: Paint & Coatings Industry, 14*(11), 68-74.

Millson, Murray R. (1993). *A study of internal and external organizational integration, new product development proficiency and success.* Unpublished doctoral dissertation, School of Business Administration, Syracuse University.

Millson, Murray R., Raj, S. P., & Wilemon, David. (1996). Strategic partnering for developing new products: Part 1 of 2. *Research Technology Management, 39*(3), 41-49.

Min, Hokey, & Galle, William P. (1991). International purchasing strategies of multinational U.S. firms. *International Journal of Purchasing and Materials Management, 27*(3), 9-18.

Minahan, Tim. (1997). JIT: A process with many faces. *Purchasing, 123*(3), 42-49.

Minahan, Tim. (1998a). Enterprise resource planning: Strategies not included. *Purchasing, 125*(1), 112-113.

Minahan, Tim. (1998b). JIT moves up the supply chain. *Purchasing, 125*(3), 46-54.

Mintzberg, Henry. (1994). *The rise and fall of strategic planning.* New York: Free Press.

Mintzberg, Henry. (1996). Reading 6.2: The structuring of organizations. In Henry Mintzberg & James Brian Quinn (Eds.), *The strategic process: Concepts, contexts, cases* (3rd ed.). Upper Saddle River, NJ: Prentice Hall.

Moeller, Michael. (1999, August 16). Oracle: Practicing what it preaches. *Business Week,* pp. 74-76.

Moenaert, Rudy K., Souder, William E., De Meyer, Arnoud, & Deschoolmeester, Dirk. (1994). R&D-marketing integration mechanisms, communication flows, and innovation success. *Journal of Product Innovation Management, 11*(1), 31-45.

Monczka, Robert M., Callahan, T. J., & Nichols, E. L. (1995). Predictors of relationships among buying and supplying firms. *International Journal of Logistics Management, 25*(10), 45-49.

Monczka, Robert M., & Giunipero, Larry C. (1984). International purchasing: Characteristics of implementation. *Journal of Purchasing and Materials Management, 20*(Fall), 2-9.

Monczka, Robert M., & Trent, Robert J. (1991). Global sourcing: A development approach. *International Journal of Purchasing and Materials Management, 27*(2), 2-8.

Monczka, Robert M., Trent, Robert, & Handfield, Robert. (1998). *Purchasing and supply chain management.* Cincinnati, OH: South-Western College Publishing.

Montoya-Weiss, Mitzi M., & Calantone, Roger. (1994). Determinants of new product performance: A review and meta-analysis. *Journal of Product Innovation Management, 11*(5), 397-417.

Moon, Mark A., & Mentzer, John T. (1999). Improving salesforce forecasting. *Journal of Business Forecasting, 18*(2), 7-12.

Moon, Mark A., Mentzer, John T., & Thomas, Dwight E., Jr. (In press). Customer demand planning at Lucent Technologies: A case study in continuous improvement through sales forecast auditing. *Industrial Marketing Management.*

Moorman, Christine, Deshpande, Rohit, & Zaltman, Gerald. (1993). Factors affecting trust in market research relationships. *Journal of Marketing, 57*(January), 81-101.

Moorman, Christine, Zaltman, Gerald, & Deshpande, Rohit. (1992). Relationships between providers and users of market research: The dynamics of trust within and between organizations. *Journal of Marketing Research, 29*(August), 314-328.

Morash, Edward A., Dröge, Cornelia L., & Vickery, Shawnee K. (1996a). Boundary spanning interfaces between logistics, production, marketing and new product development. *International Journal of Physical Distribution and Logistics Management, 26*(8), 43-62.

Morash, Edward A., Dröge, Cornelia L., & Vickery, Shawnee K. (1996b). Strategic logistics capabilities for competitive advantage and firm success. *Journal of Business Logistics, 17*(1), 1-21.

Morgan, James. (1995). Best sales reps have ideas and a desire to succeed. *Purchasing, 119*(7), 45-49.

Morgan, Robert, & Hunt, Shelby. (1994). The commitment-trust theory of relationship marketing. *Journal of Marketing, 58*(Summer), 20-38.

Morris, J., & Imrie, R. (1992). *Transforming buyer-supplier relations: Japanese-style industrial practices in a Western context.* London: Macmillan.

Mullin, R. (1998, August 19). Bad time for good news. *Chemical Week*, pp. 33-39.

Murphy, Paul R., & Poist, Richard F. (1992). The logistics-marketing interface: Techniques for enhancing cooperation. *Transportation Journal, 32*(2), 14-23.

Nakata, Cheryl, & Sivakumar, K. (1996). National culture and new product development: An integrative review. *Journal of Marketing, 60*(1), 61-72.

Narus, James A., & Anderson, James C. (1996). Rethinking distribution: Adaptive channels. *Harvard Business Review, 74*(July/August), 112-120.

Narver, John C., & Slater, Stanley F. (1990). The effect of a market orientation on business profitability. *Journal of Marketing, 54*(October), 20-35.

National Academy of Public Administration for the Department of Defense. (1996). *Report, 16*(6). Washington, DC: Author.

Neal, Bill (1994, December). Springing the distribution credit trap. *Credit Management*, 31-35.

Newquist, Harvey P., III (1986). Expert systems: The promise of a smart machine. *Computerworld, 20* (January), 43-60.

Noordewier, Thomas G., John, George, & Nevin, John R. (1990). Performance outcomes of purchasing arrangements in industrial buyer-vendor relationships. *Journal of Marketing, 54*(4), 80-93.

Nooteboom, Bart, Berger, Hans, & Noorderhaven, Niels G. (1997). Effects of trust and governance on relational risk. *Academy of Management Journal, 40*(2), 308-338.

Novack, Robert A. (1989). Quality and control in logistics: A process model. *International Journal of Physical Distribution and Materials Management, 19*(11), 1-44.

Novack, Robert A., Langley, C. John, Jr., & Rinehart, Lloyd M. (1995). *Creating logistics value: Themes for the future.* Oak Brook, IL: Council of Logistics Management.

Novack, Robert A., Rinehart, Lloyd M., & Wells, Michael V. (1992). Rethinking concept foundations in logistics management. *Journal of Business Logistics, 13*(2), 233-267.

Novack, Robert A., & Simco, Stephen W. (1991). The industrial procurement process: A supply chain perspective. *Journal of Business Logistics, 12*(1), 145-167.

O'Dwyer, Marie, & O'Toole, Tom. (1998). Marketing-R&D interface contexts in new product development. *Irish Marketing Review, 11*(1), 59-68.

Olavarrieta, Sergio, & Ellinger, Alexander E. (1997). Resource-based theory and strategic logistics research. *International Journal of Physical Distribution and Logistics Management, 27*(9/10). 559-587.

Oliver, Richard L. (1980). A cognitive model of the antecedents and consequences of satisfaction decisions. *Journal of Marketing Research, 17*(November), 460-469.

Olson, Eric M., Walker, Orville C., Jr., & Ruekert, Robert W. (1995). Organizing for effective new product development: The moderating role of product innovativeness. *Journal of Marketing, 59*(January), 48-62.

Orlicky, Joseph. (1975). *Materials requirements planning.* New York: McGraw-Hill.

Orr, Bill. (1996). EDI: Banker's ticket to electronic commerce. *ABA Banking Journal, 88*(5), 64-70.

Osborn, Richard N., & Baughn, C. Christopher (1990). Forms of interorganizational governance for multinational alliances. *Academy of Management Journal, 33*(3), 503-519.

Ouchi, William G. (1977). The relationship between organizational structure and organizational control. *Administrative Science Quarterly, 22*, 95-113.

Ouchi, William G. (1979). A conceptual framework for the design of organizational control mechanisms. *Management Science, 25*, 833-848.

Ozment, J., & Morash, Edward A. (1994). The augmented service offering for perceived and actual service quality. *Journal of the Academy of Marketing Science, 22*(4), 352-363.

Page, Albert L. (1993). Assessing new product development practices and performance: Establishing crucial norms. *Journal of Product Innovation Management, 10*(September), 273-290.

Pagell, Mark, Das, Ajay Das, Curkovic, Sime, & Easton, Liane. (1996). Motivating the purchasing professional. *International Journal of Purchasing and Materials Management, 32*(3), 27-34.

Palich, Leslie E., & Bagby, D. Ray. (1995). Using cognitive theory to explain entrepreneurial risk-taking: Challenging conventional wisdom. *Journal of Business Venturing, 10*(6), 425-438.

Parasuraman, A., Berry, Leonard L., & Zeithaml, Valarie A. (1991). Refinement and reassessment of the SERVQUAL scale. *Journal of Retailing, 67*(4), 420-450.

Parasuraman, A., Zeithaml, Valarie A., & Berry, Leonard L. (1988). SERVQUAL: A multiple-item scale for measuring consumer perceptions of service quality. *Journal of Retailing, 64*(1), 12-37.

Parker, John G. (1999, November 29). Time to get lean. *Traffic World*, 20-21.

Parker, Kevin. (2000). Surviving in a Web-based world. *Supply Chain Management Review, 4*(1), 93-94.

Pegels, C. Carl. (1991). Alternative methods of evaluating capital investments in logistics. *International Journal of Physical Distribution and Logistics Management 21*(2), 19-25.

Perry, James H. (1988). Firm behavior and operating performance in just-in-time logistics channels. *Journal of Business Logistics, 9*(1), 19-33.

Perry, James H. (1991). Emerging economic and technological futures: Implications for design and management of logistics systems in the 1990s. *Journal of Business Logistics, 12*(2), 1-16.

Peter, M. (1996). *Early supplier involvement (ESI) in product development*. Unpublished doctoral dissertation, University of St. Gallen, Bamberg.

Peters, J. E. (1996). For logistics success, command three fronts. *U.S. Distribution Journal, 223*(7), 14. Retrieved April 21, 2000, from the World Wide Web: *Dow Jones Interactive Publications Library*, nrstg2p.djnr.com/

Peters, Tom. (1988). *Thriving on chaos*. New York: Harper & Row.

Pfeffer, Jeffrey, & Salancik, Gerald R. (1978). *The external control of organizations: A resource dependence perspective*. New York: Harper & Row.

Pindyck, Robert S., & Rubinfeld, Daniel L. (1992). *Microeconomics* (2nd ed.). New York: Macmillan.

Pine, B. Joseph, Jr. (1993). *Mass customization: The new frontier in business competition*. Boston: Harvard Business School Press.

Pirttilä, Timo, & Hautaniemi, Petri. (1995). Activity-based costing and distribution logistics management. *International Journal of Production Economics, 41*(1-3), 131-137.

Pisano, G. P., & Teece, D. J. (1989). Collaborative arrangements and global technology strategy: Some evidence from the telecommunications equipment industry. *Research on Technological Innovation, Management and Policy, 4*, 227-256.

Pittiglio, Rabin, Todd, & McGrath. (1994, October). Integrated supply chain performance measurement: A multi-industry consortium recommendation. *Consortium Report*, 1-16. (Paper presented at the 1994 Council of Logistics Management Conference)

Pohlen, Terrance L., & La Londe, Bernard J. (1994). Implementing activity-based costing (ABC) in logistics. *Journal of Business Logistics, 15*(2), 1-23.

Porter, M., & Fuller, M. B. (1986). Coalitions and global strategy. In Michael E. Porter (Ed.), *Competition in global industries* (pp. 315-344). Boston: Harvard Business School Press.

Porter, Michael E. (1980). *Competitive strategy: Techniques for analyzing industries and competitors*. New York: Free Press.

Porter, Michael E. (1985). *Competitive advantage: Creating and sustaining superior performance*. New York: Free Press.

Prahalad, C. K., & Doz, Yves L. (1987). *The multinational mission: Balancing local demand and global vision*. New York: Free Press.

Prahalad, C. K., & Hamel, Gary. (1990). The core competence of the corporation. *Harvard Business Review, 68*(May/June), 79-91.

Prestwood, Donna C., Ransley, Derek L., & Schumann, Paul A., Jr. (1995). Measuring R&D performance: Part 1 of 2. *Research Technology Management, 38*(3), 45-54.

Pruitt, Dean G. (1981). *Negotiation behavior*. New York: Academic Press.

Puri, Joe S. (1993). Where industrial sales training is weak. *Industrial Marketing Management, 22*, 101-108.

Quinn, Francis J. (1998). Building a world-class supply chain; includes Polaroid's supply chain. *Logistics Management Distribution Report, 37*(6), 37-41.

Raffi, Farshad. (1995). How important is physical collocation to product development success? *Business Horizons, 38*(1), 78-84.

Rafuse, Maynard E. (1996). Working capital management: An urgent need to refocus. *Management Decision, 34*(2), 59-63.

Raia, E. (1989). Quality in design. *Purchasing, 106*(6), 58-65.

Rajagopal, Shan, & Bernard, Kenneth N. (1993). Strategic procurement and competitive advantage. *International Journal of Purchasing and Materials Management, 29*(4), 12-20.

Rangan, V. Kasturi, & Jaikumar, Ramchandran. (1991). Integrating distribution strategy and tactics: A model and an application. *Management Science, 37*(11), 1377-1389.

Rangan, V. Kasturi, Menzes, Melvyn A. J., & Maier, E. P. (1992). Channel selection for new industrial products: A framework, method and application. *Journal of Marketing, 56*(July), 69-82.

Rao, Kant, & Young, Richard R. (1994). Global supply chains: Factors influencing outsourcing of logistics functions. *International Journal of Physical Distribution and Logistics Management, 24*(6), 11-19.

Ravi, Anupindi, & Yehuda, Bassok. (1999). Centralization of stocks: Retailers vs. manufacturer. *Management Science, 45*(2), 178-191.

Read, William F., & Miller, Mark S. (1991). The state of quality in logistics. *International Journal of Physical Distribution and Logistics Management, 21*(6), 32-47.

Reichheld, Frederick F., & Sasser, W. Earl. (1990). Zero defections: Quality comes to services. *Harvard Business Review, 68*(September/October), 105-111.

Rempel, John K., Holmes, John G., & Zanna, Mark P. (1985). Trust in close relationships. *Journal of Personality and Social Psychology, 49*(1), 95-112.

Rhea, Marti J., & Shrock, David L. (1987a). Measuring the effectiveness of physical distribution customer service programs. *Journal of Business Logistics, 8*(1), 31-45.

Rhea, Marti J., & Shrock, David. L. (1987b). Physical distribution implementation effectiveness: The customer perspective. *Transportation Journal, 27*(1), 36-42.

Richardson, Helen L. (1997, January). Get your piece of the profit pie. *Transportation and Distribution*, pp. 2-6.

Richeson, Leslie, Lackey, Charles W., & Starner, John W., Jr. (1995). The effect of communication on the linkage between manufacturers and suppliers in a just-in-time environment. *International Journal of Purchasing and Materials Management, 31*(1), 21-28.

Rindfleisch, Aric, & Heide, Jan B. (1997). Transaction cost analysis: Past, present, and future applications. *Journal of Marketing, 61*(4), 30-54.

Rinehart, Lloyd M. (1992). Global logistics partnership negotiation. *International Journal of Physical Distribution and Logistics Management, 22*(1), 27-34.

Rinehart, Lloyd M., Cooper, M. Bixby, & Wagenheim, George D. (1989). Furthering the integration of marketing and logistics through customer service in the channel. *Journal of the Academy of Marketing Science, 17*(1), 63-71.

Rochford, Linda, & Rudelius, William. (1992). How involving more functional areas within a firm affects the new product process. *Journal of Product Innovation Management, 9*(4), 287-299.

Rogers, D. L., & Whetten, D. A. (1982). *Interorganizational coordination: Theory, research, and implementation.* Des Moines, IA: Iowa University Press.

Rogers, D. S., Daugherty, Patricia J., & Stank, T. P. (1992). Enhancing service responsiveness: The strategic potential of EDI. *International Journal of Physical Distribution and Logistics Management, 22*(8), 15-20.

Rogers, D. S., Dawe, R. L., & Guerra, P. (1991). Information technology: Logistics innovations for the 1990's. *1991 Council of Logistics Management Annual Conference Proceedings* (pp. 245-261). Oak Brook, IL: Council of Logistics Management.

Rosenberg, L. Joseph, & Campbell, David P. (1985). Just-in-time inventory control: A subset of channel management. *Journal of the Academy of Marketing Science, 13*(3), 124-133.

Ross, David Frederick. (1998). *Competing through supply chain management.* New York: Chapman & Hall.

Ruekert, Robert W., & Walker, Orville C., Jr. (1987a). Interactions between marketing and R&D departments in implementing different business strategies. *Strategic Management Journal, 8*(3), 223-248.

Ruekert, Robert W., & Walker, Orville C., Jr. (1987b). Marketing's interaction with other functional units: A conceptual framework and empirical evidence. *Journal of Marketing, 51*(January), 1-19.

Saccomano, Ann. (1998). Shape of supply chain: Geographic information systems potential for logistics. *Traffic World, 254*(10), 34-36.

Salcedo, Simon, & Grackin, Ann. (2000). The e-value chain. *Supply Chain Management Review, 3*(4), 63-70.

Salmond, Deborah, & Spekman, Robert. (1986). Collaboration as a mode of managing long-term buyer-seller relationships. In Terence Shimp (Ed.), *AMA Educator's Proceedings* (pp. 162-166). Chicago: American Marketing Association.

Sandelands, Eric. (1994). Replenishment logistics give food for thought. *International Journal of Physical Distribution and Logistics Management, 24*(3), 17-18.

Schary, Philip B. (1979). Customer service as a system process. In Robert F. Lusch & P. H. Zinger (Eds.), *Contemporary issues in marketing channels* (pp. 165-176). Norman: University of Oklahoma Distribution Research Program.

Scheer, Lisa K., & Stern, Louis W. (1992). The effect of influence type and performance outcomes on attitude toward the influencer. *Journal of Marketing Research, 29*(February), 128-142.

Schilling, Melissa A., & Hill, Charles W. L. (1998). Managing the new product development process: Strategic imperatives. *Academy of Management Executive, 12*(3), 67-81.

Schmitz, Judith M., Frankel, Robb, & Frayer, David J. (1994). Vertical integration without ownership: The alliance alternative. *The Association of Marketing Theory and Practice Annual Conference Proceedings* (pp. 392-396). Statesboro, GA: The Association of Marketing Theory and Practice.

Schneider, Lewis M. (1985). New era in transportation strategy. *Harvard Business Review, 63*(2), 118-127.

Schonberger, Richard J., & El-Ansary, Adel. (1984). Just-in-time purchasing can improve quality. *Journal of Purchasing and Materials Management, 20*(Spring), 1-7.

Schrage, Michael. (1990). *Shared minds: The new technologies of collaboration.* New York: Random House.

Schriner, James A. (1999). E-commerce: Prepare for location decisions. *Industry Week, 248*(22), 20.

Schultz, David P. (1985). Just-in-time systems. *Stores, 67*(April), 28-31.

Schultz, Randall. (1984). The implication of forecasting models. *Journal of Forecasting, 3*, 43-55.

Schumpeter, J. A. (1942). *Capitalism, socialism, and democracy.* New York: Harper.

Schurr, Paul H., & Ozanne, Julie L. (1985). Influences on exchange processes: Buyer's perceptions of a seller's trustworthiness and bargaining toughness. *Journal of Consumer Research, 11*(March), 939-953.

Schwalbe, Robert J. (1998). SMART 2001: Supply chain management, Siemens style. *Supply Chain Management Review, 2*(Fall), 69-75.

Scott, Charles, & Westbrook, Roy. (1991). New strategic tools for supply chain management. *International Journal of Physical Distribution and Logistics Management, 21*(1), 23-33.

Scott, Don. (1989). Marketing, logistics and inventory. *International Journal of Physical Distribution and Materials Management, 19*(5), 26-30.

Sengupta, S., & Turnbull, J. (1996). Seamless optimization of the entire supply chain. *IIE Solutions, 28*(10), 28-33.

Shani, David, & Chalasani, Sujana. (1992). Exploiting niches using relationship marketing. *Journal of Consumer Marketing, 9*(3), 33-42.

Shapiro, Benson P. (1988). What the hell is market oriented? *Harvard Business Review, 66*(November/December), 119-125.

Shapiro, Benson P., Rangan, V. Kasturi, & Sviokla, John J. (1992). Staple yourself to an order. *Harvard Business Review, 70*(4), 113-122.

Sharma, Arun, & Lambert, Douglas M. (1994). How accurate are salespersons' perceptions of their customers? *Industrial Marketing Management, 23*, 357-365.

Sheombar, H. S. (1992). EDI-induced redesign of co-ordination in logistics. *International Journal of Physical Distribution and Logistics Management, 22*(8), 4-14.

Sheremata, Willow Ann. (1998). *Implementing strategies of radical new product development under time pressure in software industries.* Unpublished doctoral dissertation, Stern School of Business at New York University.

Sheth, Jagdish N., & Parvatiyar, Atul. (1995). Relationship marketing in consumer markets: Antecedents and consequences. *Journal of the Academy of Marketing Science, 23*(Fall), 255-271.

Siguaw, Judy A., Simpson, Penny M., & Baker, Thomas L. (1998). Effects of supplier market orientation on distributor market orientation and the channel relationship: The distributor perspective. *Journal of Marketing, 62*(Summer), 99-111.

Simchi-Levi, David, Kaminsky, Philip, & Simchi-Levi, Edith. (2000). *Designing and managing the supply chain management.* Boston: McGraw-Hill.

Simons, Robert, & Antonio, Davila. (1998). How high is your return on management? *Harvard Business Review, 76*(January/February), 70-81.

Sinkula, James M. (1994). Market information processing and organizational learning. *Journal of Marketing, 58*(January), 35-45.

Skinner, W. (1969). Manufacturing—Missing link in corporate strategy. *Harvard Business Review, 47*(May/June), 136-145.

Slater, Stanley F., & Narver, John C. (1994a). Does competitive environment moderate the market orientation- performance relationship? *Journal of Marketing, 58*(January), 46-55.

Slater, Stanley F., & Narver, John C. (1994b). Market orientation, customer value, and superior performance. *Business Horizons, 37*(March/April), 22-28.

Slater, Stanley F., & Narver, John C. (1995). Market orientation and the leading organization. *Journal of Marketing, 59*(July), 63-74.

Smart, Rosemary. (1995). Forecasting—A vision of the future driving the supply-chain of today. *Logistics Focus, 3*(8), 15-16.

Smith, Carlo D. (1999). *Assessing the value of improved forecasting management.* Working paper, the University of Tennessee.

Smith, Ken G., Carroll, Stephen J., & Ashford, Susan J. (1995). Intra- and interorganizational cooperation: Toward a research agenda. *Academy of Management Journal, 38*(1), 7-23.

Song, Jing Sheng, & Zipkin, Paul H. (1996). Inventory control with information about supply conditions. *Management Science, 42*(10), 1409-1419.

Song, X. Michael, & Montoya-Weiss, Mitzi M. (1998). Critical development activities for really new versus incremental products. *Journal of Product Innovation Management, 15*(2), 124-135.

Song, X. Michael, Montoya-Weiss, Mitzi M., & Schmidt, Jeffery B. (1997). Antecedents and consequences of cross-functional cooperation: A comparison of R&D, manufacturing and marketing perspectives. *The Journal of Product Innovation Management, 14*(1), 35-47.

Song, X. Michael, & Parry, Mark E. (1996). What separates Japanese new product winners from losers. *Journal of Product Innovation Management, 13*(September), 1-14.

Song, X. Michael, & Parry, Mark E. (1997). The determinants of Japanese new product successes. *Journal of Marketing Research, 34*(Winter), 64.

Speh, Thomas W., & Novack, Robert A. (1995). The management of financial resources in logistics. *Journal of Business Logistics, 16*(2), 23-42.

Spekman, Robert E. (1988). Strategic supplier selection: Understanding long-term buyer relationships. *Business Horizons, 31*(July/August), 75-81.

Spekman, Robert E., Kamauff, John W., Jr., & Myhr, Niklas. (1998). An empirical investigation into supply chain management: A perspective on partnerships. *International Journal of Physical Distribution and Logistics Management, 28*(2), 630-650.

Sriram, V., & Banerjee, S. (1994). Electronic data interchange: Does its adoption change purchasing policies and procedures? *International Journal of Purchasing and Materials Management, 1*(Winter), 31-34.

Stalk, George. (1988). Time—The next source of competitive advantage. *Harvard Business Review, 66*(July/August), 41-51.

Stalk, George, Evans, Philip, & Shulman, Lawrence E. (1992). Competing on capabilities: The new rules of corporate strategy. *Harvard Business Review, 70*(March/April), 57-69.

Stalk, George, & Hout, T. M. (1990). *Competing against time.* New York: Free Press.

Stallkamp, Thomas. (1998, Summer). Chrysler's leap of faith: Redefining the supplier relationship. *Supply Chain Management Review,* 16-23.

Stein, Tom. (1997, June 23). Manufacturing systems orders from chaos. *Information Week,* 44-52.

Stern, Louis W. (1971). Antitrust implications of a sociological interpretation of competition, conflict, and cooperation in the market place. *The Antitrust Bulletin, 16*(Fall), 509-530.

Stern, Louis W., & El-Ansary, Adel I. (1988). *Marketing channels* (3rd ed.). Englewood Cliffs, NJ: Prentice Hall.

Stern, Louis W., & Reve, Torger. (1980). Distribution channels as political economies: A framework for comparative analysis. *Journal of Marketing, 44*(Summer), 52-64.

Stevens, Graham C. (1989). Integrating the supply chain. *International Journal of Physical Distribution and Materials Management, 19*(8), 3-8.

Stevens, Graham C. (1990). Successful supply chain management. *Management Decision, 28*(8), 25-30.

Stock, James R. (1988). The maturing of transportation: An expanded role for freight carriers. *Journal of Business Logistics, 9*(2), 15-31.

Stringfellow, Anne. (1998). *Managing diversity to achieve knowledge integration, the effective use of cross-functional teams in new product development.* Unpublished doctoral dissertation, University of Florida.

Stuart, Ian, Deckert, Paul, McCutcheon, David, & Kunst, Richard. (1998). A leveraged learning network; Allen Bradley Canada teams up with suppliers. *Sloan Management Review, 39*(4), 81-89.

Swink, Morgan L., Sandvig, Christopher, & Mabert, Vincent A. (1996). Adding zip to product development: Concurrent engineering methods and tools. *Business Horizons, 39*(March/April), 41-49.

Szakonyi, Robert. (1994). Measuring R&D effectiveness—I. *Research Technology Management, 37*(2), 27-32.

Szymanski, David M., Bharadwaj, Sundar G., & Varadarajan, P. Rajan. (1993). An analysis of the market share profitability relationship. *Journal of Marketing, 57*(July), 1-18.

Tagaras, George, & Lee, Hau L. (1996). Economic models for vendor evaluation with quality cost analysis. *Management Science, 42*(11), 1531-1543.

Takeuchi, Hirotaka, & Nonaka, Ikujiro. (1986). The new product development game. *Harvard Business Review, 64*(January/February), 137-146.

Taylor David L., & Terhune, Alyse D. (2000). Collaborative business communities: The next advantage. *Supply Chain Management Review, 4*(1), 36-42.

Taylor, James W. (1974). The role of risk in consumer behavior. *Journal of Marketing, 39*(April), 54-60.

Taylor, John C. (1996). International marketing and the role of logistics. *Advances in International Marketing, 7,* 83-98.

Teece, David J. (1992). Competition, cooperation, and innovation: Organizational arrangements for regimes of rapid technological progress. *Journal of Economic Behavior and Organization, 18*(1), 1-25.

Teece, David J., Pisano, Gary, & Shuen, Amy. (1997). Dynamic capabilities and strategic management. *Strategic Management Journal, 18*(7), 509-533.

Temple, Barker & Sloane, Inc. (1982). *Transportation strategies for the eighties.* Oak Brook, IL: National Council of Logistics Management.

Thompson, Harvey. (1998). What do your customers really want? *Journal of Business Strategy, 19*(July/August), 17-21.

Thompson, J. D. (1967). *Organizations in action.* New York: McGraw-Hill.

Topfer, Armin. (1995). New products—Cutting the time to market. *Long Range Planning, 28*(2), 61-78.

Tosti, D., & Jackson, S. (1994). Alignment: How it works and why it matters. *Training, 31*(April), 58-64.

Towill, D. R., Naim, M. M., & Wikner, J. (1992). Industrial dynamics simulation models in the design of supply chains. *International Journal of Physical Distribution and Logistics Management, 22*(5), 3-13.

Treacy, Michael, & Wiersema, Fred. (1991). *The discipline of market leaders.* Reading, MA: Addison-Wesley.

Treacy, Michael, & Wiersema, Fred. (1993). Customer intimacy and other value disciplines. *Harvard Business Review, 71*(January/February), 84-93.

Treleven, Mark. (1987). Single sourcing: A management tool for the quality supplier. *Journal of Purchasing and Materials Management, 23*(Spring), 19-24.

Trunk, C. (1998). WMS vendors partner for supply chain strength; warehouse management software. *Material Handling Engineering, 53*(7), 13-14.

Trygg, Lars. (1993). Concurrent engineering practices in selected Swedish companies: A movement or an activity of the few? *Journal of Product Innovation Management, 10*(5), 403-415.

Tsang, Eric W. K. (1998). Motives for strategic alliance: A resource-based perspective. *Scandinavian Journal of Management, 14*(3), 207-221.

Tyndall, Gene. (2000). The global supply chain challenge. *Supply Chain Management Review, 3*(4), 13-15.

Tyndall, Gene, Gopal, Christopher, Partsch, Wolfgang, & Kamauff, John. (1998). *Supercharging supply chains: New ways to increase value through global operational excellence.* New York: John Wiley & Sons.

Urban, Glen L., & Hauser, John R. (1993). *Design and marketing of new products* (2nd ed.). Englewood Cliffs, NJ: Prentice Hall.

Van de Ven, Andrew H. (1986). Central problems in the management of innovation. *Management Science, 32*(5), 590-607.

Van de Ven, Andrew H., & Ferry, Diane L. (1980). *Measuring and assessing organizations.* New York: John Wiley & Sons.

van der Meulen, P.R.H., & Spriverman, G. (1985). The logistics input-output model and its application. *International Journal of Physical Distribution and Materials Management, 15*(3), 17-25.

Varadarajan, P. Rajan, & Cunningham, Margaret H. (1995). Strategic alliances: A synthesis of conceptual foundation. *Journal of the Academy of Marketing Science, 23*(4), 282-296.

Vasilash, Gary S. (1999). Getting lean and smart. *Automotive Manufacturing & Production, 111*(4), 58-61.

Verity, John. (1997, November 10). Collaborative forecasting: Vision quest. *Computerworld,* pp. S12-S14.

Vogelstein, Fred, & Holstein, William J. (1999, December 27). Adventures in e-shopping. *U.S. News & World Report,* pp. 34-35.

Voluntary Interindustry Commerce Standards (VICS) association. (1998). Retrieved August 6, 2000, from the World Wide Web: www.cpfr.org/

Walton, Lisa Williams. (1996). The ABC's of EDI: The role of activity-based costing (ABC) in determining EDI feasibility in logistics organizations. *Transportation Journal, 36*(1), 43-50.

Walton, S. V., & Marucheck, A. S. (1997). The relationship between EDI and supplier reliability. *International Journal of Purchasing and Materials Management, 33*(Summer), 30-35.

Wasti, Nazli S., & Liker, Jeffery K. (1997). Risky business or competitive power? Supplier involvement in Japanese product design. *Journal of Product Innovation Management, 14,* 337-355.

Waterman, Donald A., & Hayes-Roth, Frederick. (1986). *An investigation of tools for building expert systems.* Santa Monica, CA: RAND.

Webster, Frederick E., Jr. (1988). Rediscovering the marketing concept. *Business Horizons, 31*(May/June), 29-39.

Webster, Frederick E., Jr. (1992). The changing role of marketing in the corporation. *Journal of Marketing, 56*(October), 1-17.

Welter, T. R. (1989). Product development: Design inspiration. *Industry Week, 238*(4), 54-57.

Westbrook, Bruce. (1999). Synchronize for success. *Supply Chain Management Review, 3*(Summer), 60-66.

Westbrook, Robert A. (1987). Product/consumption-based affective responses and postpurchase processes. *Journal of Marketing Research, 24*(August), 258-270.

Whiteley, Roger L., Bean, Alden S., & Russo, M. Jean (1998). Using the IRI/CIMS R&D database. *Research Technology Management, 41*(6), 16-18.

Whiteoak, Phil. (1993). The realities of quick response in the grocery sector: A supplier viewpoint. *International Journal of Retail and Distribution Management, 21*(8), 3-10.

Wilder, Clinton, & Stein, Tom. (1997, October 6). App integration—Companies are linking enterprise systems to the apps of their suppliers and customers. The payoff: shorter manufacturing cycles. *InformationWeek*, pp. 18-20.

Williams, L. R. (1994). Understanding distribution channels: An interorganizational study of EDI adoption. *Journal of Business Logistics, 15*(2), 173-203.

Williamson, Oliver E. (1985). *The economic institutions of capitalism.* New York: Free Press.

Willis, Clint, Klimek, Mark, & Hardcastle, Nate. (1998, August 24). How winners do it. *Forbes.* Retrieved March 26, 2000, from the World Wide Web: www.forbes.com/asap/98/0824/088.htm

Wind, Yoram, & Mahajan, Vijay. (1988). New product development process: A perspective for reexamination. *Journal of Product Innovation Management, 5*(4), 304-310.

Wind, Yoram, & Mahajan, Vijay. (1997). Issues and opportunities in new product development: An introduction to a special issue. *Journal of Marketing Research, 34*(February), 1-12.

Witt, Clyde E. (1998). Crossdocking: Concepts demand choice. *Material Handling Engineering, 53*(7), 449.

Womack, James P., Jones, Daniel T., & Roos, Daniel. (1990). *The machine that changed the world: Based on the Massachusetts Institute of Technology 5-million dollar 5-year study on the future of the automobile.* New York: Rawson Associates.

Wood, Donald F. (1990). International logistics channels. *International Journal of Physical Distribution and Logistics Management, 20*(9), 3-9.

Woodruff, Robert B., Cadotte, Ernest R., & Jenkins, Roger L. (1983). Modeling consumer satisfaction processes using experience-based norms. *Journal of Marketing Research, 20*(August), 296-304.

Woodruff, Robert B., & Gardial, Sarah F. (1996). *Know your customer.* Cambridge, MA: Blackwell.

Woodruff, Robert B., Locander, William B., & Barnaby, David J. (1991). Marketing in a value-oriented organization. In Michael J. Stahl & M. Gregory (Eds.), *Competing globally through customer value: The management of strategic suprasystems.* Westport, CT: Quorum.

Woodward, Joan. (1965). *Industrial organization: Theory and practice.* London: Oxford University Press.

Wouters, Marc J. F. (1991). Economic evaluation of leadtime reduction. *International Journal of Production Economics, 22*(2), 111-120.

Wright, David J. (1988). Decision support oriented sales forecasting methods. *Journal of the Academy of Marketing Science, 16*(3 & 4), 71-78.

Zaltman, Gerald, Duncan, Robert, & Holbek, Jonny. (1973). *Innovations and organizations.* New York: John Wiley & Sons.

Zeithaml, Valarie A. (1988). Consumer perceptions of price, quality and value: A means-end model and synthesis of evidence. *Journal of Marketing, 52*(July), 2-22.

Zuckerman, A. (1998). The human side of information technology. *Supply Chain Management Review, 2*(1), 80-86.

Index

About the Contributors

William DeWitt completed his doctorate in business administration at the University of Tennessee and joined the faculty at the University of Maryland in 1999. After earning an MBA at the University of Tennessee in 1972, he worked for Burlington Northern Railroad from 1972 until 1995 in operations, strategic planning, and marketing, with his most recent assignment as vice president of marketing and sales for the $500 million forest products business unit. He has published articles in *Transportation Journal*, *Logistics Technology International*, the *Defense Transportation Journal*, *The Council of Logistics Management Conference Proceedings*, and the *American Society of Traffic and Transportation Proceedings*. He coauthored the Transportation Research Board's (TRB) committee reports *Policy Options for Intermodal Freight Transportation* and *Landside Access to U.S. Ports*. He has lectured and presented at various conferences, including the Council of Logistics Management annual conferences (serving as Track Chair for GIS and Logistics), a Northwestern University Transportation Center executive education conference, the Association of American Geographers' annual meeting, the Business Geographics conference, and the Canadian Industrial Transportation League and Intermodal Association of North America conferences (serving as panel moderator). He serves on two TRB committees, the Transportation Education and Training Committee and the Intermodal Freight Transport Committee. He is a certified member of the American Society of Transportation and Logistics and a member of the Council of Logistics Management, the Transportation Research Forum, the Association of American Geographers, and the Lexington Transportation History Group. He served for 3 years on the board of directors of Burlington Northern Motor Carriers and is chairman of the Geography Department Advisory Board.

Michael S. Garver is Assistant Professor of Marketing and Logistics at Central Michigan University. He received his Ph.D. from the University of Tennessee. He was a key account sales representative for more than 6 years after working in logistics for both Kimberly-Clark and General Motors. He has published in the *Journal of Business Logistics*, *Supply Chain Management Review*, *Business Horizons*, and the *Journal of Consumer Satisfaction, Dissatisfaction, and Complaining Behavior* and has presented at numerous conferences. His research interests include buyer-seller relationships, the logistics-sales interface, logistics research methods, and customer value and satisfaction measurement and management.

James S. Keebler has more than 25 years of logistics management experience across several industries—food, pharmaceuticals, health care, electronics, and consumer products. He has also served as a senior consultant for an international logistics consulting firm. He has built and reengineered logistics systems for The Pillsbury Company, Bergen Brunswig Corporation, Digital Equipment Corporation, and Colgate-Palmolive. He has lectured at Ohio State University, Penn State, and MIT. He has taught logistics, transportation, finance, management, and marketing courses at three universities and has been a frequent speaker at various conferences, including the Council of Logistics Management (CLM), the Deutscher Logistics Kongress, and The Planning Forum. He has been actively involved in research conducted by CLM in the areas of quality and productivity improvement, expert systems applications, and performance measurement. He recently coauthored *Keeping Score: Measuring the Business Value of Logistics in the Supply Chain*. He holds master's degrees in finance and management and earned his Ph.D. in logistics and transportation from the University of Tennessee. He is Assistant Professor of Marketing in the G. R. Herberger College of Business at St. Cloud State University (Minnesota).

John T. (Tom) Mentzer is the Harry J. and Vivienne R. Bruce Chair of Excellence in Business Policy in the Department of Marketing, Logistics and Transportation at the University of Tennessee. He has written more than 130 papers and articles for leading publications in marketing research and logistics as well as numerous conference proceedings. He has coauthored five books: *Supply Chain Management*, *Sales Forecasting Management*, *Simulated Product Sales Forecasting*, *Marketing Today*, and *Readings in Marketing Today*; he also edited the monograph *Marketing Education Software*. He was recognized in 1996 as one of the five most prolific authors in the *Journal of the Academy of Marketing Science* and in 1999 as the most prolific author in the *Journal of Business Logistics*. His research has focused on the contribution of marketing and logistics to customer satisfaction and strategic advantage; the application of computer decision models to marketing, logistics, and forecasting; and the management of the sales forecasting function. He serves on the editorial review boards of several publications in the field. He previously served as editor of the Systems Section of the *Journal of Business Logistics*. He serves on the executive committee and is first vice president of the Council of Logistics Management, is president of the board of directors of the Sheth Foundation, and serves on the board of directors of the American Marketing Association Foundation. He was formerly president of the Academy of Marketing Science and is a Distinguished Fellow of the Academy of Marketing Science—a distinction granted to less than 20 scholars worldwide. He has conducted numerous programs and workshops for various segments of the business and government communities, has served as a consultant for more than 70 corporations and government agencies, is on the boards of directors of several corporations, and previously worked for General Motors Corporation.

Soonhong (Hong) Min is Assistant Professor of Logistics and Marketing at Georgia Southern University. He majored in both marketing and logistics at The University of Tennessee before joining the faculty of Georgia Southern. His research interests include issues in the marketing concept and a market orientation in a channel setting, the theory and practice of supply chain management, the marketing and logistics strategic interface, buyer-seller relationships (strategic level issues of alliances and organizational working relationships), and business to business marketing. His work has been published in the *International Journal of Physical Distribution and Logistics Management* and is in the review process at several other journals. He also has presented at numerous conferences and served as a reviewer for the Relationship Marketing Conference and the Society for Marketing Advances annual conference. He represented the University of Tennessee at the Doctoral Consortium of the Council of Logistics Management in 1997 and 1999, the Doctoral Consortium of the Society of Marketing Advances in 1998, and the 1999 Doctoral Consortium of the American Marketing Association. He has had several marketing and outsourcing positions at the University of Michigan and IBM Korea, Inc., and has served as a consultant for a multinational company and a famine relief organization.

Nancy W. Nix is a doctoral candidate in the Department of Marketing, Logistics and Transportation at the University of Tennessee, with a focus on global supply chain management. She has extensive experience in supply chain management, having managed multiple facets of the supply chain (including manufacturing, logistics, purchasing, and customer service) with a *Fortune* 100 company. She also served as an in-house logistics consultant to the executive leadership of the largest and fastest growing private company in India. Her research activities have focused on global supply chain management, management of the sales forecasting function, and distribution service quality. She has taught international logistics, has conducted numerous logistics and supply chain executive education programs, and has served as a logistics and supply chain consultant for numerous companies on a global basis.

Carlo D. Smith is Associate Professor of Logistics Management at the University of San Diego. His primary area of research involves forecasting management performance and its impact on supply chain operating performance. His articles have appeared in the *Journal of Business Logistics*, *Journal of Business Forecasting*, *Business Horizons*, and *Journal of Consumer Satisfaction, Dissatisfaction, and Complaining Behavior.* He completed his dissertation at the University of Tennessee. He has more than 12 years of industry experience as a logistics consultant and executive educator. In addition to forecasting management, his research interests include supply chain management, inventory management, and performance measurement.

Zach G. Zacharia is Associate Director at the Center for Transportation Research at the University of Tennessee and director of the Tennessee Transportation Assistance Program. In addition, he is the principal investigator in the following research projects: Tennessee Department of Transportation (TDOT) Sign Grant Program, National Highway Institute (NHI) Design of Workzone Traffic Control Program, TDOT Circuit Rider Program, TDOT Rural Traffic Count Program, NHI-Railroad Highway Grade Crossing Program, NHI-Mobile Workzone program, TDOT Transportation Training Program, and International Truck and Bus Safety Symposium. He is currently enrolled in the Ph.D. program in logistics and transportation, University of Tennessee; he holds an MBA from the University of Alberta and a B.S. in mechanical engineering from the University of Calgary. He has published in the *Transportation Research Record* and *Materials Performance.* He has more than 15 years of industry experience ranging from GPS and GIS to expert system development and designing modifications on such heavy equipment as hopper sanders, crane dollies, and large trucks.